SOUTHERN
POLITICS
IN THE
1990s

Edited by
ALEXANDER P. LAMIS

SOUTHERN
POLITICS
IN THE
1990s

LOUISIANA STATE UNIVERSITY PRESS
Baton Rouge

Copyright © 1999 by Louisiana State University Press
All rights reserved
Manufactured in the United States of America
First printing
08   07   06   05   04   03   02   01   00   99   5   4   3   2   1

Designer: Amanda McDonald Scallan
Typeface: Bembo
Typesetter: Coghill Composition
Printer and binder: Edward Brothers, Inc.

Library of Congress Cataloging-in-Publication Data

Southern politics in the 1990s / edited by Alexander P. Lamis.
      p.   cm.
   Includes bibliographical references and index.
   ISBN 0-8071-2374-9 (alk. paper)
     1. Republican Party (U.S. : 1854–   )   2. Southern States—Politics
and government—1951–   I. Lamis, Alexander P.
JK2356.S72   1999
324.275′04′09049—dc21   98-50424
                                                               CIP

The paper in this book meets the guidelines for permanence and durability of
the Committee on Production Guidelines for Book Longevity of the Council on
Library Resources ⊗

CONTENTS

Contents

TABLES

FIGURES

PREFACE

In the fall of 1995, I began contacting political scientists and political journalists throughout the South with the idea of joining together to comprehensively analyze the amazing Republican advance that had occurred in the region so far in the 1990s. Over the next three years, as the events of the decade continued to unfold, we investigated, scrutinized, and analyzed all aspects of Dixie's on-going partisan development in order to craft this book.

We had much to cover. Since the mid-1960s, southern politics had undergone a major transformation. The solidly Democratic one-party South had collapsed, giving way to a complicated and uneven two-party system. When the decade of the 1980s came to an end, the challenging Republicans were still in minority status in all major categories of elections in the region. Just a few years later—by the mid-1990s—all that had changed, as is related in detail in Chapter 1.

Recognizing that the first two decades of the emerging two-party South had received extensive treatment, we set our sights directly on the most recent developments. Our goal was to thoroughly explain how and why the GOP reached majority status in southern politics in the 1990s. In the process we aimed to shed light on all aspects of the region's partisan politics in the mature years of the two-party South.

Although there are regional commonalities, which is a continuing legacy of the one-party era, the differences among the eleven states of the former Confederacy are so great that separate state chapters are a necessity. Over fifty years ago, when V. O. Key, Jr., began the research for his classic *Southern Politics in State and Nation*, he reached the same conclusion concerning this approach to the study of regional politics. As his associate in that famous project, Alexander Heard, chancellor emeritus of Vanderbilt University, related the decision years later in a 1984 interview:

> V. O. had originally conceived of the entire book being made up of what I will call functional chapters, treating the South as a unit. He tried to do that and concluded fairly early and very decisively that the variations within each state that made each state different from the other states made it impossible to treat the electoral process in the South . . . as a

process across the entire region without explicit recognition of the individuality of each state. And that conclusion by Key led to the later decision that we would have to have a chapter on each state in the book in addition to having chapters that cross-cut all eleven of the states we were dealing with and that sought to see the uniformities in the processes of Southern politics.[1]

To write each of the state chapters, I was fortunate to be able to recruit a leading journalist and political scientist who both had extensive experience with their state's politics; for a few chapters a third or fourth writer was added. Please turn to the notes on contributors at the back of the book for the impressive credentials these writers brought to their assignments.

Since the contributors came from different backgrounds—newspaper reporting and academia—the hope was that they would bring the best instincts and methods of their respective worlds to bear on the topic, and they did. Each team conducted a series of interviews with major political players, scoured the available political science literature, mined extensive files of newspaper articles, analyzed a variety of survey data, and amassed an array of statistics relevant to electoral politics.

The goal for the state chapters, as expressed in my first guidance letter to the contributors, on December 22, 1995, was "to capture the current partisan dynamics at work in each state." Or, as I put it in my second guidance letter on March 1, 1996, the plan "is for your state chapter to be the place a reader can turn to find out exactly what happened in your state's partisan politics from 1990 through the 1996 elections and why." Throughout the process, we were mindful of Key's injunction on the conduct of this type of research: "In work relating to the electoral behavior of geographical units . . . one needs to bring into the analysis every scrap of evidence to be had."[2]

With the signing of a contract with Louisiana State University Press in late spring 1996, the planning phase gave way to the research and writing stage, which continued throughout 1996 and into the early part of 1997. We then began an extensive revision and rewriting process at my direction that ended in late summer 1997 when the bulk of the manuscript went to the Press's anonymous reviewer. Encouraged by the reviewer's positive comments, we began an intense three-month revision to improve the manuscript in the many helpful ways the reviewer had suggested. I am very appreciative of the highly professional guidance and advice this reviewer gave us.

When the reviewer's consideration of our revisions was completed, I was able to write the contributors on May 4, 1998: "Breakthrough at last! We just cleared the big hurdle—the reader's second report is in, and it's completely positive." During the summer of 1998, we made our last changes to prepare the manuscript for publication. At this time we were able to add a few updates to take account of the events leading up to the 1998 elections, but since we went into the production stage in August 1998, none of the writers was able to comment on the fall general election campaign or the November 1998 results.

The 1998 elections have been over for several weeks as I write this preface, and a quick survey of the results reveals no patterns startlingly different from those depicted in this book's coverage of the years leading up to the 1998 contests. Southern Democrats in 1998 made their best showing since 1990, recapturing the governorship in South Carolina and Alabama and picking up a Republican-held U.S. Senate seat in North Carolina. Despite the Republican gain of the Florida governorship, Democrats were still able in 1998 to cut back on the astonishingly high percentage of the South's top elected offices—69.7 percent—occupied by the Republican party after the 1996 elections. With a net Democratic gain of two, the Republicans controlled 63.6 percent of the thirty-three highest-profile elected positions—governor and U.S. senator—after the 1998 balloting. The battle for the 125 U.S. House seats apportioned to the region ended in a stalemate in 1998; Republicans continued to occupy 71 seats, or 56.8 percent, as they had in 1996. The steady GOP growth at the state legislative level stopped in 1998. Republicans gained 10 seats in southern lower houses but lost nearly an equal number in upper houses to remain at 41.5 percent of the region's 1,782 state legislative seats, a high point the GOP had reached in mid-1998 primarily as a result of dozens of Democratic legislators switching parties after the 1996 elections.

Overall, the 1998 outcome revealed substantial state-by-state variation that can only be covered by probing each state's results in the manner done in this book's state chapters, a task that must await another day. Still, I am confident the reader will find the analysis here fully consistent with the most recent electoral developments. For example, drawing on the pre-1998 coverage in the state chapters, I reached the following conclusion in Chapter 13 concerning Dixie's Democrats: "The [Democratic] biracial alliance is clearly under considerable pressure and undergoing change in the face of the rapid Republican rise of the 1990s, but, taking the region as a whole, the biracial Democratic coalition is very much alive today." That vitality was demonstrated forcefully this November, revealing a rich and complex southern political reality that requires careful study to fully appreciate its dynamic elements.

★   ★   ★

Over the three years it took to prepare this book, I have received assistance from many people. First and foremost, I am most appreciative of the hard work the contributors put into their state chapters. In the initial stages, for example, it was not uncommon for many of us to have long-distance phone conversations running well over an hour at a time. These give-and-take strategy sessions were always cordial and highly informative. I never ceased to marvel at the depth of knowledge these political scientists and journalists have of politics in their respective states. Throughout the project, they exhibited steadfast professionalism and never hesitated to make the unexpected extra effort required from time to time during the editorial process.

Apart from the contributors, the next most important person in the preparation of this book was Andrew M. Lucker, a newly minted Case Western Reserve University Ph.D. in political science and my former advisee. Andrew prepared all the figures in the book, most of which involved use of Paul David's index of Democratic party strength at the state and regional levels. Among other things, this entailed making the necessary index calculations for several recent elections. In addition, he worked with William Claggett of Florida State University to secure the computer-readable updates of David's index that Claggett had prepared for the Inter-university Consortium for Political and Social Research. Andrew also spent hours constructing the fine county-level map of the 1996 presidential vote in the South, which appears in Chapter 1. Further, he provided me with the latest computer technology and instruction on how to use it. He also worked directly with the contributors to prepare polished versions of their various tables, and on more than a few occasions redid the tables himself to facilitate the publication process. In all these tasks, he was an unpaid volunteer, and I owe him a huge debt of gratitude. Incidentally, Andrew's 1998 doctoral dissertation will be of interest to students of southern politics since he wrote a biography of the most prominent southern politics researcher of this century—V. O. Key, Jr.

Elsie Finley, the pleasant and indefatigable reference librarian who handles political science at Case Western Reserve University, went out of her way to make sure that all the latest books on southern politics were quickly available for my use. It is a pleasure to have such congenial and efficient support, and I am most thankful for her help. Dean John Bassett of the College of Arts and Sciences at my university provided me with two small grants that assisted with editorial expenses, for which I am appreciative. My chairman, Vince McHale, was supportive throughout, especially in making sure I was provided with the latest computer equipment.

John Easterly, executive editor of Louisiana State University Press, embraced the project at the outset and enthusiastically supported it throughout, offering invaluable editorial guidance at key points. I am most appreciative to have had his wise and courteous counsel. Sara Anderson, the book's copy editor, labored long and hard to significantly improve each chapter. Our many E-mail exchanges this fall over items large and small were both pleasant and productive; the contributors and I were fortunate to have had such a competent copy editor and are thankful for her assistance. Catherine Kadair directly supervised all aspects of the editorial process at the Press, doing so in a congenial and highly efficient manner, for which I am grateful. In fact, all those at the Press with whom I have had contact have been most helpful, and, when one is working near the shores of Lake Erie in a land where the 1861–1865 monuments are not to "the glorious Confederate dead," it was a pleasure to hear all those soft southern accents every time I called the Press!

Many others assisted along the way, including Margaret Rawa, Elizabeth Michelle Hill, Eric Romoser, William C. Daroff, David E. Sturrock, William Claggett, Tim Storey, and Renée DeGeorge. Finally, I would like to thank my students at Case Western Reserve University, who have enthusiastically acquainted themselves semester after semester with the politics of this "foreign" region to the south of us and have, in the process, aided me by providing a testing ground for several notions that make their appearance in my opening and concluding chapters to this book.

Alexander P. Lamis
Cleveland, Ohio
December 8, 1998

SOUTHERN
POLITICS
IN THE
1990s

1

THE TWO-PARTY SOUTH: FROM
THE 1960S TO THE 1990S

Alexander P. Lamis

IN the 1990s the American South entered a strikingly new phase in its thirty-year experience with two-party politics. During the first two-thirds of the decade, the Republican party, the once-despised northern party that prosecuted the Civil War and engineered Reconstruction, emerged for the first time—in a stunning advance—as the South's majority party in major state elections. This book tells the story of that remarkable breakthrough and, in the process, comprehensively analyzes the southern two-party system of the 1990s.

The solidly Democratic South, with its roots in racial segregation and the white South's "redemption" after Reconstruction, had, of course, vanished long ago at the presidential level when President Harry S. Truman, a Democrat, introduced his civil rights initiatives prior to the 1948 election. But at the state level the one-party Democratic monolith did not begin to crack until the late 1950s. Then in the sixties it crumbled completely as the national party, over the loud protests of southern Democratic leaders, carried out a Second Reconstruction, a series of eventful departures epitomized in the era's twin legislative capstones, the Civil Rights Act of 1964 and the Voting Rights Act of 1965.

Yet the two-party South that took root between the late 1960s and the late 1980s was full of ironic consequences that more often than not frustrated southern Republican party builders. The GOP handily won the bulk of the region's presidential electoral votes during this twenty-year period, except for the first election of regional favorite Jimmy Carter of Georgia. Below the presidential level, however, a transformed, post–civil rights era Democratic party regrouped and prevented a quick GOP march to majority status.

A necessary prelude to the discussion of the unprecedented Republican gains of the 1990s is a sketch of the complicated southern party system that emerged in the first twenty years of the two-party South, a task I turn to shortly. First, a measure of precision needs to be introduced to facilitate consideration of the region's recent partisan shifts. This is provided in Figure 1, which requires an initial brief explanation concerning its technical construction as well as the historical trends it captures for the early decades.

The solid line in Figure 1 charts Democratic party strength in the South from 1932 to 1996 as measured by a composite of the Democratic vote percentages for three key offices—governor, U.S. senator, and U.S. representative. The measure, devised by Paul T. David of the University of Virginia and appropriately called David's index, is calculated every two years with each office counting a third.[1] In Figure 1, David's index of Democratic party strength (the solid line) is plotted along with the Democratic vote for president (the dotted line), thus permitting the separation of the quadrennial presidential vote from the far more complex process of overall partisan change.

The results of these calculations for each of the eleven southern states are

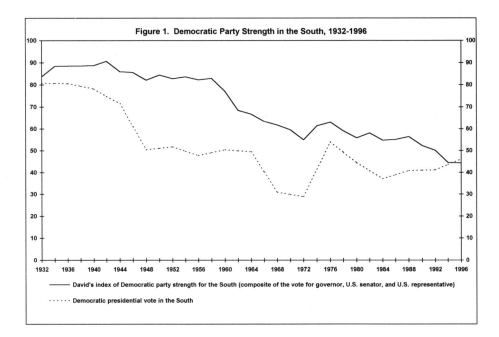

Figure 1. Democratic Party Strength in the South, 1932-1996

——— David's index of Democratic party strength for the South (composite of the vote for governor, U.S. senator, and U.S. representative)

· · · · · · Democratic presidential vote in the South

presented later in this chapter as the diverse state patterns are introduced. The eleven individual state figures show fascinating state-by-state variations in Democratic party strength over the period and serve as invaluable road maps for the book's eleven state chapters. The regional party-strength trend line in Figure 1 aggregates the individual state patterns to offer a vivid picture of the partisan path the South as a whole has followed.[2]

For anyone unfamiliar with the South's political history, the astonishingly high Democratic voting percentages from 1932 through 1958 call out for explanation. How could it be that one party averaged over 80 percent of the vote for these major public offices? What caused such a lopsided partisan outcome? And why did it collapse? Brief answers to these questions will carry the South's partisan story quickly to the 1960s and into the two decades leading up to this book's main focus: the southern party system that took shape in the 1990s.

The explanation for the amazingly high Democratic figures traces directly back to the white South's aggressive defense of slavery in the middle of the nineteenth century and the resulting Civil War. In the aftermath of that bloody armed struggle, the Republican party, which had arisen only in the North during the partisan turmoil of the 1850s, failed in its effort to construct a biracial southern political system that would offer the GOP fertile soil to develop in the conquered region. As the southern states were readmitted to the Union in the years leading up to the Compromise of 1877 and the formal end of Reconstruction, it became increasingly clear that the depth of the white South's antipathy to the party of Abraham Lincoln would not be quickly overcome. Although the Republican party would entertain a series of hopeful southern strategies over the decades, starting during the presidency of Rutherford B. Hayes in the 1870s, by the end of the century white southerners had constructed a one-party system centered on the Democratic party that effectively kept the newly freed slaves politically isolated and in a second-class status.[3]

The overriding purpose of the southern one-party system was the preservation of white supremacy. Its rationale was simple: if whites divided their votes between two political parties, blacks would hold the balance of power and could bargain for an end to racial segregation and discrimination. The commitment among white southerners to this rationale was more intense in the states with the largest percentages of African Americans, but the one-party structure prevailed across the region.[4] (See Table 1 for the percentage of African Americans in each southern state from 1960 to 1990.) To break with Democratic solidarity meant to deviate from white racial unity, and it rarely happened prior to World War II.

The death of the one-party system began in the latter half of the 1940s when

Table 1. Percentage of African Americans in Each Southern State, 1960–1990

State	1960	1970	1980	1990
Mississippi	42.0%	36.8%	35.2%	35.6%
South Carolina	34.8	30.5	30.4	30.1
Louisiana	31.9	29.8	29.4	30.6
Georgia	28.5	26.2	26.8	26.9
Alabama	30.0	26.2	25.6	25.6
North Carolina	24.5	22.2	22.4	22.1
Virginia	20.6	18.5	18.9	19.0
Arkansas	21.8	18.3	16.3	15.9
Tennessee	16.5	15.7	15.8	16.3
Florida	17.8	15.3	13.8	14.2
Texas	12.4	12.5	12.0	11.9

Source: U.S. Census.

national Democratic leaders, in defiance of their southern wing, began to move the party away from dead center on the question of civil rights for African Americans. As Minnesota's Hubert H. Humphrey phrased it during a floor debate at the 1948 Democratic National Convention, "[It is time] for the Democratic Party to get out of the shadow of states' rights and to walk forthrightly into the bright sunshine of human rights."[5] President Truman's civil rights initiatives coupled with the strong platform language concerning the issue at the 1948 convention precipitated the Dixiecrat presidential candidacy of South Carolina governor Strom Thurmond, which denied the victorious Truman the electoral votes of several southern states. While the presidential trend line in Figure 1 shows that 1948 was the end of huge Democratic presidential majorities in the region, the figure's measure of Democratic party strength (David's index) remained in the 80 percent range throughout the 1950s as the region and the nation entered an uneasy period of stalemate on the question that dominated southern politics in that era.

The 1954 U.S. Supreme Court decision declaring public school segregation unconstitutional foreshadowed big changes to come as did the birth of the southern civil rights protest movement in the latter half of the 1950s. But white southern resistance both to the high court's rulings and to the protestors' demands stymied action until the 1960s. Likewise, throughout the 1950s southern Democrats in Congress blocked meaningful civil rights legislation. And because a Republican, Dwight D. Eisenhower, was in the White House during much of the 1950s, the Democratic party could avoid confronting its bitter regional cleavage, a situation that abruptly changed with the election of Massachusetts Democrat John F. Kennedy as president in 1960.

The national deadlock on civil rights was broken during the first half of the ensuing decade. Despite a cautious beginning, President Kennedy employed the power of the federal government to enforce court-ordered integration at several southern universities and to assist civil rights workers. Then in 1963 he introduced a sweeping civil rights bill that would, among other things, outlaw racial discrimination in public accommodations and employment.[6] After Kennedy's assassination, President Lyndon B. Johnson grabbed the mantle of civil rights and skillfully guided the landmark civil rights legislation to passage in 1964 over a last-ditch southern filibuster in the Senate. The end result of these momentous developments for southern politics cannot be emphasized enough. In short, the rationale for the one-party Democratic South vanished, and its demise had been brought about by the national Democratic party.

These events unleashed a torrent of Republican activity in the South. In Mississippi, Republican candidates in 1963 burst forth on the ballot under the slogan "K.O. the Kennedys." In the 1964 presidential election, the Republican party nominated U.S. senator Barry Goldwater of Arizona, who had stood with the southerners in the filibuster against the civil rights bill and voted against the bill's final passage. Goldwater was buried in that year's national landslide for President Johnson, but the Republican standard-bearer carried five southern states—Mississippi (with 87.1 percent of the vote!), South Carolina, Georgia, Alabama, and Louisiana. Goldwater's victory in Alabama swept five Republicans into Congress, an amazing feat for a party that hardly existed in the state before 1964. During the fall campaign of 1964, South Carolina's Strom Thurmond, a Democratic U.S. senator since 1954, dramatically switched to what he called "the Goldwater Republican party." Throughout Dixie in the mid-1960s southerners suddenly found a new political party struggling to get established.[7] Figure 1 graphically displays the result of all this partisan turmoil. From its 83.0 percent perch in 1958, Democratic party strength in Dixie plummets to 63.4 percent by 1966 and bottoms out at 55.0 percent in 1972.

The Republican party's growth was propelled in these early years of the two-party South by two key factors. The first was white southern resentment against the Kennedy-Johnson-Humphrey national Democratic integrationists. Southern Republicans sought to ride this resentment to power by tying their state Democratic opponents to the national Democratic party at every turn, a strategy that frequently lacked credibility given the impeccable segregationist credentials, at least in the early years, of a host of southern Democrats. Examination of these early campaigns is replete with evidence supporting this interpretation. Years after those early campaigns southern Republicans would prefer to forget this aspect of their party's birth in Dixie, as southern Democrats would like not to be reminded of their segregationist past. When I documented the early Republican racial appeal in my book *The Two-Party South*, I was curious how Republicans would react. One of the first reviews of the book was written by a former Republican party activist from South Carolina, Hastings Wyman, Jr., whose treatment of the point is worth quoting at length:

> Throughout the book [Lamis] reminds his readers that a major component of the Republican resurgence in the Old Confederacy was a racist reaction to the civil rights changes that were coming to the South. Not just a racist reaction that Republicans, in the right place at the right time, could take advantage of, but often a reaction consciously encouraged—no, fanned—by the GOP itself.
>
> I look back on the last twenty years of Republicanism in the South and see the progress that the GOP has made. I remember my own bit parts in the drama, and I want to feel pride. Well, I do feel the pride, but this other feeling keeps creeping in—shame. And the Lamis book reminds me of it in chapter after chapter—the role of segregationist issues in Claude Kirk's election as governor of Florida, in Bill Brock's Tennessee Senate campaigns, in Albert Watson's ill-fated gubernatorial campaign (I served as the campaign manager for that one).
>
> I want to say: But those were insignificant details! Our real pitch was for freedom—free enterprise, freedom from governmental interference in the rights of states, of communities, of businesses. And I want to protest that it was the post–World War II economic revolution going on in the South that *really* brought about the growth of the Grand Old Party in Dixie, and that the real racists were the redneck Democrats who voted for Wallace.
>
> But I can't buy my own line. I was there, and I remember: Denouncing "the bloc vote"; opposing "busing" so long and so loud that rural voters thought we were going to do away with school buses; the lurid leaflets "exposing" the integrationist ties of our Democratic opponents—leaflets we mailed in plain white envelopes to all the white voters in the precincts George Wallace had carried. . . .
>
> Well . . . there's nothing we can do to change history. Racism, often purposely inflamed by many southern Republicans, either because we believed it or because we thought it would win votes, was a major tool in the building of the new Republican party in the South.[8]

The second factor propelling the Republican party in the South was its support of conservative economic issues tied to a restrictive view of the role of government. Since the New Deal, outside the South the two major parties had fought over a series of economic-class and role-of-government issues.[9] Owing to the South's one-party system rooted in its goal of preserving white supremacy, the New Deal conflicts had to be played out within the southern Democratic party. Southern economic conservatives in the 1930s, 1940s, and 1950s thus often found themselves in agreement with the national policies of the anti–New Deal Republican party even though they retained their Democratic affiliation for regional purposes. In the 1960s, with the one-party rationale shattered it was now possible for the South to build a Republican party along the lines of those in—for example—Illinois or Ohio. Not surprisingly, it is this aspect of the GOP's party-building strategy that Republicans prefer to emphasize today while downplaying the racial element. In actuality, the twin factors of race and economics were often merged in the heat of the partisan struggle.

As the Republican party began to build at the state level, driven by the white reaction to the end of segregation, the party made its most faithful converts among those attracted by its conservative position on New Deal-type economic-class issues. But it also picked up substantial support from white Democrats angered by their national party's "betrayal" on the race issue. Twisted into the situation was the logical compatibility of conservative economic-class Republicanism with the racial protest. The GOP, as the party philosophically opposed to an activist federal government in economic matters, gained adherents also from those who objected to federal intervention in the racial affairs of the states. The two streams of protest could not be easily separated in the political arena, and the Republican candidates, who recognized that they were beneficiaries of both prongs of reaction, rarely made the effort.[10]

The best exposition of the subtle merger of these twin forces was offered by South Carolinian Lee Atwater eight years before he became chairman of the Republican National Committee after serving as the architect of George Bush's 1988 presidential election victory. It came during an interview while he was a member of President Ronald Reagan's White House political staff:

> *Atwater:* As to the whole Southern stategy that Harry Dent and others put together in 1968, opposition to the Voting Rights Act would have been a central part of keeping the South. Now [the new Southern strategy of Ronald Reagan] doesn't have to do that. All you have to do to keep the South is for Reagan to run in place on the issues he's cam-

paigned on since 1964 . . . and that's fiscal conservatism, balancing the budget, cut taxes, you know, the whole cluster. . . .

Questioner: But the fact is, isn't it, that Reagan does get to the Wallace voter and to the racist side of the Wallace voter by doing away with Legal Services, by cutting down on food stamps . . . ?

Atwater: You start out in 1954 by saying "Nigger, nigger, nigger." By 1968 you can't say "nigger"—that hurts you. Backfires. So you say stuff like forced busing, states' rights, and all that stuff. You're getting so abstract now [that] you're talking about cutting taxes, and all these things you're talking about are totally economic things and a by-product of them is [that] blacks get hurt worse than whites. And subconsciously maybe that is part of it. I'm not saying that. But I'm saying that if it is getting that abstract, and that coded, that we are doing away with the racial problem one way or the other. You follow me—because obviously sitting around saying, "we want to cut this," is much more abstract than even the busing thing *and* a hell of a lot more abstract than "Nigger, nigger."[11]

The strategies of the nascent southern Republican party are only part of the story. Perhaps of greater significance for the first two decades of two-party competition was the remarkable transformation that came to the southern Democratic party in the aftermath of the traumatic events of the mid-1960s. With federal protection, African Americans entered the electorate in large numbers, and they did so as Democrats. Of course, it was natural enough that they should affiliate with the Democratic party since the party's national leaders were the force behind the Second Reconstruction. And, while it was ironic that southern blacks would became part of the former party of segregation, the potential of this large new source of votes was not lost on white southern Democratic politicians as they assessed their altered situation in the latter half of the 1960s.

These leaders—Jimmy Carter in Georgia in 1970 was one of the pioneers—proceeded in the 1970s and 1980s to assemble potent coalitions of nearly all blacks and those whites who had weathered the integration crisis with their Democratic voting inclinations intact. These ideologically diverse, black-white Democratic coalitions became a central feature of the South's politics in the post–civil rights era. They were a key element in blunting the Republican surge in state after state, as the challenging Republicans well understood. For example, a defeated North Carolina Republican gubernatorial candidate commented bitterly in 1968: "You start out with a certain number of Negro bloc votes against you and a certain number of [white] people who vote straight Democratic no matter who the candidate." The chairman of the Georgia Republican party in 1974 described the diverse Democratic coalition that was demolishing GOP statewide challenges in the Peach State similarly: "So what catches us is that you find the [white] conservative rural vote going in voting the straight party ticket, and by the same token you find the urban blacks voting the straight party ticket. And they'd be considered a liberal element, with the South Georgia farmer voting conservative. And yet they're voting hand in hand, and when they do, they're squeezing the lives out of us. And yet there's no tie-in between the two at all. Ideologically, they're as far apart as night and day."[12]

To keep these diverse Democratic coalitions together required considerable political skill, and the white moderate Democratic leaders who arose in state after state provided it. They included, in addition to Carter, Sam Nunn of Georgia, James B. (Jim) Hunt, Jr., of North Carolina, Lawton Chiles of Florida, William Winter of Mississippi, Dale Bumpers of Arkansas, and Richard Riley of South Carolina, to name only a few. They were aided by the benefits that accrued to the Democrats by virtue of their near monopoly on public office through the 1950s—namely a strong Democratic voting tradition (the famous "Yellow Dog" Democrats who, legend has it, would vote for a canine over a Republican) coupled with a storehouse of ambitious, experienced candidates who were already holding office. Further, they had a stroke of luck when one of their own, Carter, was elected president in 1976. And, of course, the Watergate scandal, that national Republican disaster, hurt the GOP in the South as well.

As Figure 1 demonstrates, Democratic party strength reversed its downward movement in 1974, rising to 61.4 percent that year and going up to 63.0 percent two years later when Carter won the White House. It dropped to 59.0 percent in 1978 and then stabilized around the mid-50s for the next ten years, registering 56.4 percent in 1988. The state-by-state figures, which are introduced directly below, offer considerable variation from the regional composite. But the regional view substantiates an important reality of the first two decades of two-party competition in Dixie: The revitalized and restructured post–civil rights era southern Democratic party was not an easy target for the South's rising Republicans.[13] The 1990s, as the regional figure indicates by way of preview, were to be quite different.

THE ARRIVAL OF TWO-PARTY COMPETITION AT THE STATE LEVEL

While the regional overview gives a semblance of cohesion and order, a descent into the messy details of each state's unique blend of traditions, demographics, personalities, and events, among other things, provides a sobering cautionary check on any tendency toward overly broad generalization. Also, since the bulk of this book is dedicated to grappling with just such details from the 1990s, it is wise to consider at least briefly each state's path up to the departure points of the eleven state chapters. The following sketches are aided by individual state versions of the regional Democratic party-strength figure examined above.

South Carolina

Two-party competition at the highest levels came fast and furiously to South Carolina in the 1960s. Senator Thurmond's 1964 switch to the GOP legitimized the party in the Palmetto State and clarified the partisan situation in a unique way. In other southern states, entrenched conservative segregationist politicians, like John C. Stennis and James O. (Jim) Eastland of Mississippi or Herman E. Talmadge of Georgia, remained in the Democratic party and likewise kept many of their supporters from going over to the Republicans. Thurmond was reelected easily as a Republican in 1966 and has been returned by South Carolina voters every six years thereafter, most recently in 1996.[14]

Former South Carolina governor Ernest F. (Fritz) Hollings won a U.S. Senate seat narrowly in 1966 amid the sudden GOP spurt fueled by the race issue. Because his first election was for only two years of an unexpired term, he had to seek reelection in 1968. His Republican opponent did everything he could to hang the label of a national Democrat around Hollings's neck, but the skillful Charleston Democrat used the power of incumbency to the hilt while exercising extreme caution in his voting choices in Washington. In 1967, for example, Hollings voted against the confirmation of Thurgood Marshall to be the first African American associate justice of the U.S. Supreme Court. Hollings was reelected in 1968 and in every election since then through 1992.[15]

The early Republican growth spurred the quick formation in South Carolina of a black-white Democratic coalition, which settled into place in the 1970s and allowed the Democrats to end their rapid 1960s drop in party strength, which is depicted as a virtual nosedive in Figure 2. In states where the GOP rise was much slower, white Democrats were far less prompt in reaching out to their new potential allies; they simply didn't need the votes.

A Republican did win the South Carolina governorship in 1974, but he did so under highly unusual circumstances. The Democratic nominee had been judicially disqualified and his defeated primary opponent substituted in his place late in the campaign. Four years later, in a more normal election, the black-white coalition delivered an easy gubernatorial majority for Democrat Richard

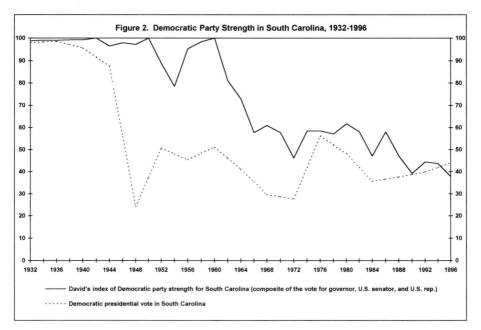

Figure 2. Democratic Party Strength in South Carolina, 1932-1996

——— David's index of Democratic party strength for South Carolina (composite of the vote for governor, U.S. senator, and U.S. rep.)

· · · · · Democratic presidential vote in South Carolina

Riley, who won reelection handily in 1982. The GOP did win several congressional seats, but the party's growth at the state legislative level was glacial. Then came a Republican breakthrough in 1986: winning the governorship narrowly against a united Democratic party. So important is the 1986 election for the spectacular growth of the South Carolina Republican party in the 1990s that this book's South Carolina chapter begins with that election.

North Carolina

As Figure 3 indicates, North Carolina's Democratic party strength in the one-party era was only in the 70 percent range, quite low compared to South Carolina and most other southern states. North Carolina shared these relatively low Democratic percentages from the one-party era with Tennessee and Virginia. In the mountains of these states there were few slaves and the white yeoman farmers there had little sympathy for secession from the Union. A Republican voting tradition took hold in these areas after the Civil War and persisted. These "Mountain Republicans" were a hopeless minority in their states, but they were still a recognizable factor when serious two-party competition emerged in the 1960s.[16]

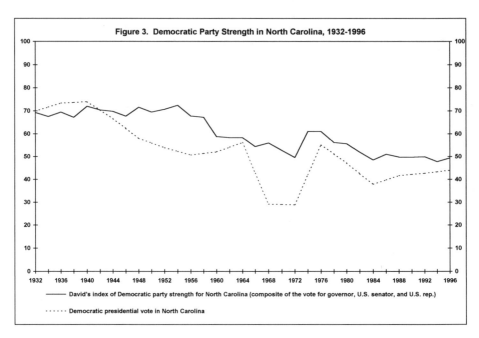

Figure 3. Democratic Party Strength in North Carolina, 1932-1996

—— David's index of Democratic party strength for North Carolina (composite of the vote for governor, U.S. senator, and U.S. rep.)

······ Democratic presidential vote in North Carolina

The disruptions of the civil rights era drove down Democratic strength in North Carolina in the 1960s, as the figure shows. In 1972 the GOP captured the governorship and a U.S. Senate seat, the latter won by a vociferous former Democrat with a segregationist background—Jesse Helms. Helms, an articulate, dynamic social and economic conservative, played an influential role in the North Carolina Republican party's development. After winning relatively easy reelection in 1978, he faced a formidable Democratic challenge in 1984 from Governor Jim Hunt.

Hunt epitomized the white moderate southern Democratic leaders who successfully assembled victorious, ideologically diverse, black-white Democratic coalitions while maintaining beneficial ties to their states' business establishments. A North Carolina newspaperman captured Hunt's appeal:

> He's a very skillful politician, a very skillful coalition builder. . . . He manages a balancing act essentially. He's tough on law and order, which appeals to conservatives. . . . But on the other hand, he appoints a lot of blacks to high, prominent positions—to judgeships. He's very pro-education, pro-public schools, which is kind of viewed as a liberal position. . . .

He talks a good game. When he speaks before black groups, he talks of a new day in North Carolina. He speaks the language of hope, of racial harmony, of working together, of change in racial attitudes. Talk's cheap I suppose, but he is generally perceived by blacks as a friendly politician. When you compare him with the other major political figure in the state, who is Jesse Helms, who certainly raises racial code words all the time in busing and cutting food stamps and in general in a very subtle way the race issue, by comparison Hunt looks good to blacks.[17]

Helms defeated Hunt, 51.7 percent to 47.8 percent, in that titanic Senate election of 1984, probably the most closely watched southern race of the decade. In the shadow of these two dominant politicians, North Carolina witnessed a series of closely contested major elections throughout the 1970s and 1980s, making the Tar Heel State one of the most competitive in the region. Helms and Hunt remained major figures in the 1990s and the fierce North Carolina partisan competition continued, as the North Carolina chapter relates.

Georgia

Two-party competition came suddenly to Georgia with the collapse of racial segregation. The Republican gubernatorial nominee in 1966, U.S. representative Howard (Bo) Callaway, who had been swept into Congress by Goldwater's Georgia victory two years earlier, sought to construct a winning coalition of urban economic conservatives and race-conscious rural and small-town whites. Callaway actually received more votes in 1966 than his segregationist Democratic opponent, Lester Maddox. However, because a third candidate received 7.3 percent, Callaway, who had 46.5 percent to Maddox's 46.2 percent, did not have a simple majority, as required by the Georgia constitution. The choice by law went to the Democratic legislature, which voted Maddox into office. It would be over two decades before Georgia Republicans again mounted a close campaign for governor.

In 1972 another Republican congressman, Fletcher M. Thompson, sought to ride the white backlash to the U.S. Senate. As two historians wrote, Thompson "seized the busing issue, addressing rallies . . . to ban the use of buses to achieve integration. [Thompson] sometimes seemed to be running less against his Democratic opponent . . . than against school buses, [George] McGovern [the liberal 1972 Democratic presidential nominee], and actress Jane Fonda and former Attorney General Ramsey Clark, both of whom had visited North Vietnam and who, according to Thompson, should be charged with treason." To counter Thompson, the Democratic nominee, Sam Nunn, flew to Alabama to receive the endorsement of George Wallace. In the words of a newspaper reporter, Nunn "publicly condemned Carter for refusing to nominate Wallace for President at the Democratic convention. 'George Wallace represents the real views of Georgians,' Nunn said. He echoed Wallace's rhetoric in his attacks on 'judicial tyranny,' his denunciation of school-busing orders. . . . The pseudo-Wallace campaign was enough to counter Thompson's effort to alarm whites with charges that Nunn would received the black 'bloc vote.' " Nunn won with 54.0 percent of the vote to Thompson's 46.0 percent.[18]

Strong statewide GOP challenges faded after 1972. Carter's gubernatorial coalition building, alluded to earlier, was duplicated by a pair of skillful conservative-to-moderate white Democratic leaders who regularly assembled the potent black-white Democratic coalition to retain the governorship easily from 1974 to 1990. As Figure 4 shows, the initial drop in Democratic party strength bottomed out in 1972 at above the 60 percent mark, then soared twenty points to over 80 percent in 1978 and was still resting above 70 percent as late as 1990. A Georgia Republican, Mack Mattingly, did win a U.S. Senate seat in 1980 against a scandal-scarred incumbent who had survived a divisive Democratic primary runoff, but he lost it six years later. In 1990 the Peach State's 10-

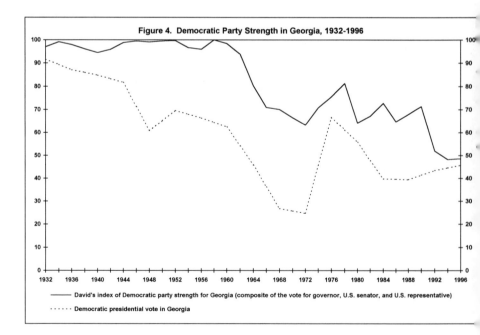

Figure 4. Democratic Party Strength in Georgia, 1932-1996

——— David's index of Democratic party strength for Georgia (composite of the vote for governor, U.S. senator, and U.S. representative)

· · · · · · Democratic presidential vote in Georgia

member U.S. House delegation contained only a lone Republican—Newt Gingrich, the ambitious former college professor who had been elected to a suburban Atlanta seat in 1978.

At the outset of the 1990s, Georgia could still be safely termed a Democratic bastion. That abruptly changed in the new decade, as the Georgia chapter explains and as Figure 4 previews.

Virginia

The conservative political organization of Harry F. Byrd dominated Virginia in the one-party era. Its collapse coincided with the growth of two-party competition in the mid-1960s. Initially, a scion of the Byrd machine, Mills E. Godwin, Jr., assembled a broad coalition as a Democrat to win the governorship in 1965 over Linwood Holton, a moderate GOP nominee in the Mountain Republican tradition.

Four years later Holton, who made no use of the race issue, won the governorship following a divisive Democratic gubernatorial primary. A moderate Democrat, William C. Battle, gained the nomination with Godwin's backing by defeating Henry E. Howell, Jr., a tenacious left-of-center populist with "a base of blacks, labor, white small farmers, and blue-collar workers," to quote a noted authority on Virginia politics.[19] More than a few of Howell's supporters, including African Americans, bolted to the Republican Holton rather than vote for a Godwin-supported Democrat.

In the next few years a fascinating series of events transformed Virginia politics. Howell and his forces captured control of the Democratic party. Although Howell was conscious of the need to build a majority coalition, his strident populism frightened the establishment, which consequently mobilized against him. As part of the effort to stop Howell, former Governor Godwin along with other Byrd Democrats joined the Republican party; Godwin then won the Republican gubernatorial nomination in 1973 and narrowly defeated Howell, 50.7 percent to 49.3 percent, in the general election.

Figure 5 depicts the steady decline of the Virginia Democratic party during this period of partisan turmoil. After Howell was decisively defeated in the 1977 gubernatorial election by another Republican, Virginia Democrats in 1981 nominated for governor a Democrat closer to the moderate-to-conservative tradition of Carter in Georgia or Hunt in North Carolina—Charles S. (Chuck) Robb, who succeeded in assembling an ideologically diverse, biracial Democratic coalition which proved victorious that year and helped propel a Democratic recovery in Virginia in the 1980s.

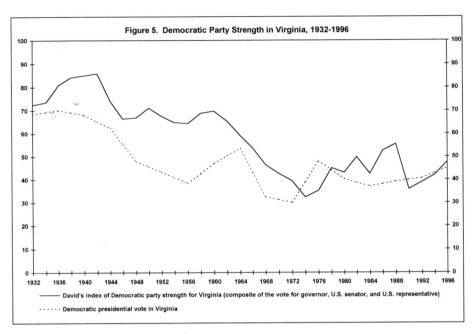

Figure 5. Democratic Party Strength in Virginia, 1932-1996

—— David's index of Democratic party strength for Virginia (composite of the vote for governor, U.S. senator, and U.S. representative)

······ Democratic presidential vote in Virginia

Arkansas

A successful but short-lived Republican challenge in Arkansas in the 1960s followed an atypical southern pattern. Using his personal fortune, Republican Winthrop Rockefeller defeated segregationist Democrats in 1966 and 1968 to win a pair of two-year terms as governor. In both elections he received 90 percent of the votes of African Americans.

Rockefeller was defeated in 1970 by Dale Bumpers, a "New South" moderate Democrat who had won his party's gubernatorial nomination by defeating a comeback attempt by Orval Faubus, the segregationist former Democratic governor who precipitated the Little Rock school integration crisis of 1957. Bumpers went on to the U.S. Senate in 1974 and was succeeded by another popular moderate Democrat, David Pryor. The Republicans who followed Rockefeller in the 1970s were singularly unsuccessful, and Democrats dominated the state as they did in Georgia.

In 1978 Bill Clinton, then the state's thirty-two-year-old attorney general, easily continued the Bumpers-Pryor Democratic gubernatorial victories. But in 1980 a well-financed Little Rock businessman, Republican Frank D. White, narrowly defeated Clinton's first attempt at reelection by capitalizing on several local issues agitating Arkansans. As two newspapermen reported: "Voters saw Clinton as arrogant, aloof, inaccessible or egotistical. The national attention he received [he was portrayed in the press as someone with a bright future in national politics] instead of helping may have hurt him, causing voters to view him as overly ambitious and being more interested in his political future than in them." Two years later Clinton apologized profusely to voters for his errors and reclaimed the governorship. He retained it easily for the next ten years until he was elected president in 1992. Concerning Clinton's 1982 comeback, his Craighead County campaign manager noted: "The people in this county decided that Bill Clinton had learned a lesson. They had spanked him and sent him to his room. They always knew he had the ability and they decided he had matured to the point where they were willing to give him a second chance."[20]

As Figure 6 indicates, Arkansas Democratic strength has taken a roller coaster ride in recent decades. The Rockefeller and White victories mark two dips. When Clinton was reelected governor for the last time in 1990, Democratic party strength had swung up over the 70 percent mark. The Democrats in the 1990s were about to embark, as the Arkansas chapter relates, on yet another downward swing of the roller coaster just as the still youthful Clinton, only forty-six in 1992, departed for the White House.

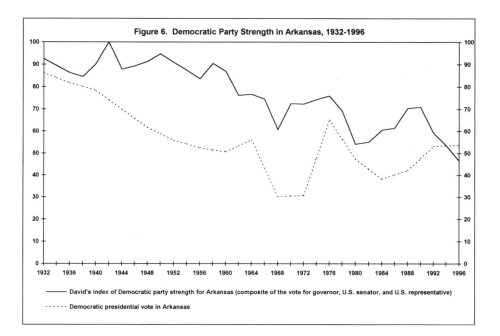

Figure 6. Democratic Party Strength in Arkansas, 1932-1996

—— David's index of Democratic party strength for Arkansas (composite of the vote for governor, U.S. senator, and U.S. representative)

· · · · · · Democratic presidential vote in Arkansas

Tennessee

Tennessee stretches from the Mountain Republican strongholds in the east to the flat, fertile counties near Memphis and the Mississippi River in the west, with their relatively large African American populations. When the era of two-party competition began in the 1960s, the GOP combined early on its traditional strength in the east with a white backlash in the west to win several key statewide elections.

In 1970, for example, Republican U.S. representative Willam E. (Bill) Brock III, heir to the Brock candy-manufacturing fortune, narrowly retired long-term Democratic U.S. senator Albert Gore, Sr., in a campaign during which Brock subtly exploited white racial resentment. Six years later Democrat James R. (Jim) Sasser was able to bring back substantial white support in west Tennessee to narrowly defeat Brock. Sasser, who focused on economic issues, also benefited from Carter's strong Tennessee showing that year in the presidential balloting.

Middle Tennessee, with its relatively strong New Deal Democratic tradition, frequently held the balance of power in statewide elections as the Volunteer State experienced a series of close two-party contests in the 1970s. (See Figure 7.) In 1974 Republican Lamar Alexander, a former assistant in President Richard Nixon's White House, lost the governorship to a Democrat, Ray Blanton, who went out of office four years later in disgrace and eventually went to prison on corruption charges. In 1978 Alexander, a moderate Republican, was elected to the first of two consecutive terms as governor. He was succeeded in 1986 by an unlikely statewide Democratic victor in an era of slick television candidates—a rotund, behind-the-scenes wheeler-dealer with eighteen years' experience in the state legislature, house speaker Ned McWherter. During the first of his two gubernatorial terms, McWherter presided over an atypical, late 1980s southern Democratic burst of strength, which is depicted in Figure 7. The figure also displays the Democratic party's reversal of fortune in the 1990s, which included its stunning triple defeat in the 1994 statewide elections, a topic the Tennessee chapter explores in detail.

Two other important Tennessee politicians deserve mention. Howard Baker, Jr., whose father represented a Mountain Republican congressional district for many years, was elected to the U.S. Senate in 1966 and reelected twice. Along with Alexander, Baker epitomized the more moderate forces in the Tennessee GOP.

When Baker retired in 1984, Democratic congressman Albert (Al) Gore, Jr., who was first elected to the U.S. House in 1976 from a middle Tennessee dis-

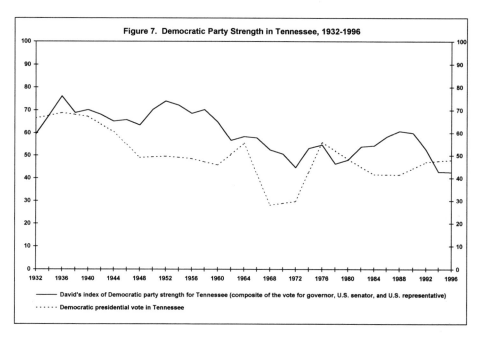

Figure 7. Democratic Party Strength in Tennessee, 1932-1996

——— David's index of Democratic party strength for Tennessee (composite of the vote for governor, U.S. senator, and U.S. representative)

· · · · · · Democratic presidential vote in Tennessee

trict, easily advanced to the Senate fourteen years after his father's Senate defeat. In that 1984 campaign the youthful Congressman Gore, then only thirty-six years old, countered his Republican opponent's attempt to link him to northern Democratic liberals this way: "The old labels—liberal and conservative—have far less relevance to today's problems than efforts to find solutions to those problems. There's no need to rely on an outdated ideology as a crutch."[21] Despite his failed Democratic presidential nomination bid in 1988, Gore overwhelmingly won reelection in 1990 before being elected vice president two years later on the ticket of his fellow "New Democrat" from neighboring Arkansas, Bill Clinton.

Ironically, the departure of Gore and Clinton for Washington in January 1993 set off a sequence of partisan events in their home states that led to major Republican gains over the next few years, as fully described in both the Arkansas and Tennessee chapters.

Alabama

Two years before Goldwater triumphed in Alabama with 69.5 percent of the vote, James D. Martin, a businessman, nearly toppled the veteran Democratic

U.S. senator Lister Hill, a New Dealer, in a 1962 campaign defined by the integration crisis. Martin called for "a return of the spirit of '61—1861, when our fathers formed a new nation. . . . Make no mistake, my friends, this will be a fight. The bugle call is loud and clear! The South has risen!"[22] Martin received 49.1 percent of the vote to Hill's 50.9 percent.

Martin, one of the five GOP congressmen carried into office on the strength of Goldwater's Alabama showing in 1964, hoped to ride the racial backlash into the governorship in 1966, when the segregationist Democratic governor George C. Wallace would be constitutionally ineligible to succeed himself. But the popular Wallace, who had declared in his 1962 inaugural address, "segregation today, segregation tomorrow, segregation forever" and who fought integration of the University of Alabama in 1963 "up to the school house door," decided to run his wife, Lurleen, and the Wallaces prevailed in the 1966 Democratic primary without a runoff. In the general election, Mrs. Wallace swamped Martin, the Republican gubernatorial nominee, 63.4 percent to 31.0 percent. As an Alabama political scientist put it, "No one doubted that Congressman Martin was an Alabama segregationist, but it is hard for a rich man's segregationist to beat a poor man's segregationist."[23]

Wallace, who carried the white backlash nationwide in his third-party presidential candidacy in 1968, dominated Alabama politics for much of the next two decades. The triumph of this Democratic "poor man's segregationist" both prevented the early formation of the standard ideologically diverse, black-white Democratic coalition in Alabama and retarded the early growth of the Republican party. The latter point is starkly portrayed in Figure 8, which shows the rapid post-1958 decline in Alabama Democratic strength ending in the mid-1960s, followed by a rise to above 80 percent in 1974, when Wallace was re-elected to a third term as governor. (He had reclaimed the office himself in 1970).

So powerful had been Wallace's retarding effect on the GOP that in the first post–Wallace gubernatorial election in 1978, a prominent Republican who had been a major fund-raiser for President Richard M. Nixon, Forrest Hood (Fob) James, decided to seek the governorship in the Democratic primaries. James, a wealthy businessman, won the Democratic nomination in a bitter runoff. He handled his ambidextrous partisan past this way: "I was born a Democrat. I was raised a Democrat. During the early 1970s, I strayed away from the Democratic party. In recent years, I've seen the error of my ways. I've come home, and I've come home to stay."[24] The official Republican nominee in 1978 was Guy Hunt, a little-known North Alabama probate judge, who received only 25.9 percent of the vote against James.

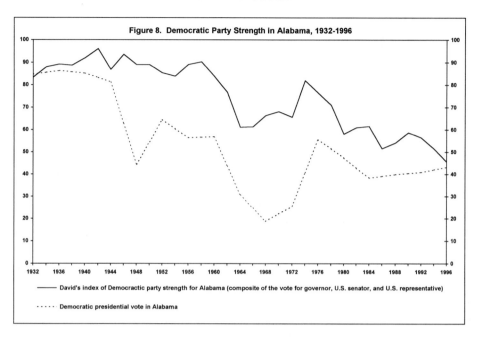

Figure 8. Democratic Party Strength in Alabama, 1932-1996

——— David's index of Democractic party strength for Alabama (composite of the vote for governor, U.S. senator, and U.S. representative)

· · · · · Democratic presidential vote in Alabama

Hunt and James figure prominently in this book's Alabama chapter. Hunt became the state's first Republican to be elected governor as a result of the titanic Democratic intraparty gubernatorial disaster of 1986, which, incidentally, involved another Republican running as a Democrat. The Alabama chapter begins with this pivotal election. James appears in the story of the 1990s because he broke his 1978 pledge about coming home to the Democratic party "to stay" and in 1994 won the governorship a second time but this time as a Republican.

Two further preliminary items need mention. First, in 1980 Alabama elected its first Republican to the U.S. Senate since Reconstruction. He was Jeremiah Denton, a retired navy admiral and former prisoner of war in North Vietnam, who was the beneficiary of a bitter Democratic primary. The Democratic incumbent, Senator Donald Stewart, narrowly lost renomination to James Folsom, Jr., the son of Alabama's legendary post–World War II governor, "Big Jim" Folsom. Folsom and Denton each sought to portray himself as the more conservative candidate in the race with Republican Denton winning this "battle of conservatives" with 50.2 percent of the vote. Interestingly enough, another conservative Democrat, U.S. representative Richard C. Shelby, defeated Denton in the Republican senator's first bid for reelection six years later. Shelby himself would bolt to the Republican party in 1994, when the Alabama GOP was finally on the rise, as the Alabama chapter relates.

A second note in this overview of politics in the "Heart of Dixie," as Alabama license plates proclaim, concerns the fascinating election of 1982. In that year the wily Wallace adapted himself to the transformed political environment of the 1980s by apologizing to blacks for his segregationist past and once again reclaiming the governor's office through three difficult elections, two Democratic primaries and the general election. He won the Democratic nomination with only 50.9 percent of the runoff vote, but vital to that triumph was the astonishing one-third of the black vote that he garnered. In the November election he faced the Republican mayor of Montgomery, Emory Folmar, who had abysmal relations with African Americans. Wallace defeated Folmar with 59.6 percent of the vote to the Republican's 40.4 percent, amassing 90 percent of the African American vote in the November election. Thus in 1982 Wallace won office at the head of the standard post–civil rights era biracial Democratic coalition. It was a new strategy for the former segregationist champion, but by the 1980s it had become the familiar Democratic victory pattern in the South. In winning the last election of his career, Wallace this time ran with, not against, the forces that had transformed the politics of Dixie in his lifetime.

Mississippi

The vehemence of the race issue in Mississippi prevented the early formation of the biracial coalition that was so important for southern Democratic success elsewhere. Instead, white and black Democrats fought each other well into the 1970s, preventing even the formation of a unified Democratic party organization. Also, in the early years white Democratic leaders, many of them former segregationists, turned back the first Republican efforts to win statewide elections amid the white backlash over the integration crisis.

So weak was the Mississippi GOP that it failed to field a gubernatorial candidate in 1971; the white Democratic nominee that year was opposed by an African American independent, Charles Evers, brother of the slain civil rights leader Medgar Evers, who won 22.1 percent, mostly from black voters. The GOP did score a few early gains, however. In President Nixon's 1972 landslide, for example, two young Republicans—Thad Cochran and Trent Lott—won U.S. House seats; both would later advance to the U.S. Senate.

Figure 9 depicts the relatively high levels of Democratic strength through the 1976 election. The figure cannot, however, capture the frustration of black Mississippians with their inability to share fully in the benefits of this nominal

Democratic strength. That frustration became manifest in the 1978 U.S. Senate election. Although black and white Democrats had managed to agree on a unified biracial state party structure in 1976, black voters did not support the party's 1978 white senatorial nominee, whose 31.8 percent of the vote came from the party's white wing. Instead, blacks voted for Evers's second independent statewide candidacy, giving him 22.9 percent. And the Senate seat went to Republican congressman Cochran, who had 45.0 percent. No better example exists of the fragile nature of the black-white Democratic coalition in the Magnolia State at that time and the boost that fragility gave Republicans.

During the 1980s black-white tensions in the Mississippi Democratic party were contained long enough for several key statewide Democratic victories, but Republicans remained confident that the long-term partisan trend in Mississippi favored them. Here is the way Congressman Lott in 1979 phrased the dilemma he saw facing Mississippi Democrats:

> They're in a bind with the national Democrat party. If they subscribe to the national Democrat party's principles, platform, they are clearly going to alienate the overwhelming majority of the white people in Mis-

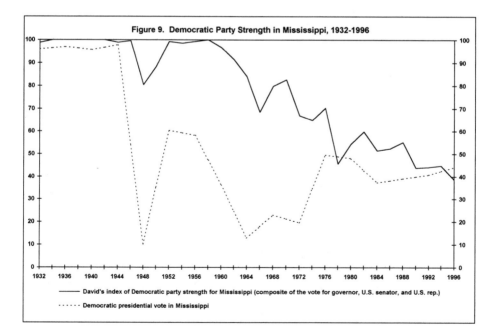

Figure 9. Democratic Party Strength in Mississippi, 1932-1996

——— David's index of Democratic party strength for Mississippi (composite of the vote for governor, U.S. senator, and U.S. rep.)

· · · · · · Democratic presidential vote in Mississippi

sissippi. If they don't do it, they are going to offend the black folks in Mississippi. . . .

So, if they go with the typical national Democrat base, they wind up with blacks and labor and your more liberal, social-oriented Democrats, white people. Put those groups together and they are a minority in Mississippi. . . .

So, they [statewide Democratic candidates] have got to have some of these old redneck George Wallace white voters. If they have these other groups, they alienate that group.[25]

Although Lott may have captured an important element in the state's—and the region's—partisan equation, key Mississippi elections in the latter part of the 1980s provided no definitive answers. The Democratic coalition held together in 1987 to elect a youthful, progressive Democrat, Ray Mabus, to the governorship. But the next year, Congressman Lott himself, who by then had advanced in the Republican House leadership to the number two post, won a seat in the Senate with 53.9 percent of the vote against Wayne Dowdy, a folksy white moderate Democratic congressman with good ties to Mississippi's African Americans.

Those two elections showcased a far more mature party system than existed in Mississippi during the chaotic 1960s and early 1970s. The developments of the 1990s, as covered in the Mississippi chapter, highlight even further the extensive political distance the Magnolia State has traveled over the last three decades.

Louisiana

Louisiana's experience with two-party politics contains several unique features that place the state in a category by itself.[26] Three such elements are the presence of a sizable French-speaking Catholic population, the legacy of Huey P. Long, that "flamboyant advocate of the subversive doctrine of 'Every Man A King' "[27] (as V. O. Key labeled him), and the abolition in the early 1970s of separate party primaries.

The last item, the establishment of an "open primary" system, requires brief explanation. All candidates are listed on a single ballot no matter what their party affiliation. If no candidate gets a simple majority in the first election, then there is a runoff among the top two candidates regardless of party affiliation. Thus, two Democrats or two Republicans could face each other in the second election. The impact of this electoral system is a subject of disagreement, as mentioned in the Louisiana chapter, but no one denies that it has helped set Louisiana apart in its partisan experience.

Early GOP efforts to capitalize on the race issue were blunted by clever Democrats. For example, in the March 1964 gubernatorial election, the victorious Democratic nominee, John J. McKeithen, labeled himself a "one-hundred-percent segregationist" but not a "hater." An early Republican pioneer was David C. Treen, a suburban New Orleans conservative who had been active in 1960 States' Rights presidential electoral slate efforts in Louisiana. He received 42.8 percent of the vote as the Republican gubernatorial nominee in 1972, the last state election before the adoption of the open primary system. The Democratic victor for governor that year and a major force in Louisiana politics into the 1990s was Edwin W. Edwards, a charismatic French-speaking congressman who won in 1972 with, to quote his own description, "a coalition of blacks, farmers, [and] people from South Louisiana of French Cajun descent."[28]

During the 1970s Republican gains were meager except at the U.S. House level. Treen won a congressional seat in 1972 and two others joined him in the next few years. Throughout the 1970s and 1980s Democratic party-strength remained quite high, as Figure 10 indicates.[29] Treen did win the governorship narrowly in 1979 in a bizarre election in which four of his five major Democratic rivals in the open primary ended up supporting him. Four years later former Governor Edwards handily defeated Treen to regain the office for a third time.

A measure of the state's partisan confusion (or to put it less bluntly, its lack of conformity to standard patterns) can be seen from the outcome of the 1987 gubernatorial election, when Edwards sought reelection to a record fourth term. His major competition in the open primary came from a Democrat, Congressman Charles (Buddy) Roemer, who won the governorship when Edwards abruptly withdrew after finishing 5 percentage points behind Roemer in the open primary. A Republican congressman carrying his party's endorsement finished a weak third.

If this doesn't seem confusing enough in partisan terms, consider what happened four years later. Governor Roemer switched to the Republican party to run for reelection in 1991, but the strongest candidate in the 1991 open primary who carried the Republican label (although he was repudiated by the GOP leadership) was neither Roemer nor an "endorsed" Republican but a former Ku Klux Klan leader. The eventual winner was none other than Edwards, still a Democrat although somewhat tarnished by the time he finally secured a fourth term.

The 1987 and 1991 elections—and much more—are fully covered in the

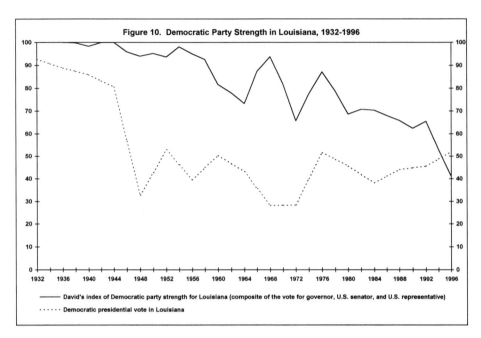

Figure 10. Democratic Party Strength in Louisiana, 1932-1996

——— David's index of Democratic party strength for Louisiana (composite of the vote for governor, U.S. senator, and U.S. representative)

· · · · · · Democratic presidential vote in Louisiana

Louisiana chapter, which admirably accomplishes the difficult task of making sense of this "festival in a labyrinth," as Louisiana politics has been aptly labeled.[30] Amid all the partisan chaos, the 1990s witnessed a sharp drop in Democratic party strength in Louisiana, as Figure 10 indicates.

Texas

In Texas, the southern state with the lowest percentage of blacks, the race issue did not dominate electoral politics, even in the 1960s. Economic issues were of far greater importance in this giant, complex state with a large Mexican-American minority population.

V. O. Key concluded in 1949 that Texas had "developed the most bitter intra-Democratic fight along New Deal and anti-New Deal lines in the South."[31] And the fights between the conservative and liberal wings of the Democratic party persisted into the 1980s, with the former usually in the ascendancy. As a result of the success of conservative Democrats in Texas—Senator Lloyd Bentsen's political career is typical—the challenging Republicans had a difficult time staking out the right-of-center political ground. For example,

Bentsen was first elected to the U.S. Senate in 1970 after he defeated a liberal Democratic incumbent in the primaries and an energetic Republican congressman and future president, George Bush, in the general election.

Texas did give the GOP its first statewide southern victory in the modern era when John G. Tower captured a U.S. Senate seat in a 1961 special election. The seat was vacated by Lyndon B. Johnson after his election as vice president in 1960. Tower had the edge in the election because he had run against Johnson's "insurance" reelection bid the year before and received a surprisingly high 41.1 percent of the vote. Apart from Tower's reelection in 1966 and 1972, the GOP did not win another major statewide election in Texas until 1978, but the party advanced in the large urban areas, especially at the congressional level.

In 1978 Republican Bill Clements, a multimillionaire oil-drilling contractor, narrowly won the governorship after spending several million dollars of his own fortune. Analysis of the voting returns showed that rural, small-town counties, once the core of conservative Democratic strength, were increasingly voting Republican, providing part of the victory margin for Clements. Four years later a conservative Democrat, Mark White, ousted the Republican governor despite Clements's continued lavish campaign spending. In 1986 Clements made a successful comeback, reclaiming the governorship a final time. The ups-and-

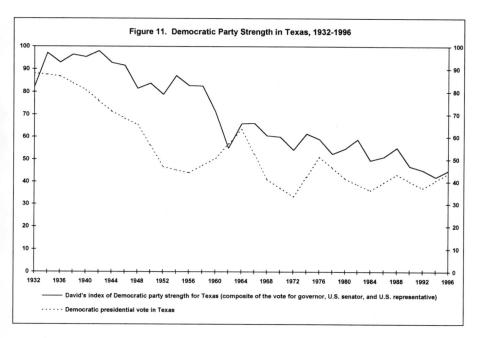

Figure 11. Democratic Party Strength in Texas, 1932-1996

——— David's index of Democratic party strength for Texas (composite of the vote for governor, U.S. senator, and U.S. representative)

· · · · · · Democratic presidential vote in Texas

downs in Figure 11's Democratic-party-strength trend line partly reflect these gubernatorial turnarounds.

Phil Gramm, a former economics professor who had been elected to the U.S. House as a conservative Democrat in 1978, switched to the GOP in 1983 and won a U.S. Senate seat the following year. According to the Dallas *Morning News*, Gramm sought "to appeal to the farm and ranch folks as a 'redneck' rather than [as a] 'country club' Republican."[32] Gramm also tied his campaign to President Reagan's triumphant reelection effort that year.

Throughout the 1980s, Texas Republicans lost more major elections than they won, but each election expanded the party's base. After Clements was defeated in 1982, a West Texas political scientist surveyed the scene and concluded that the GOP's future in Texas was far from bleak: "There is a solid base of more than one million Republican voters in this state, and it tells the Democrats you'd better do things properly, or you're in trouble. The Republicans are going to be winning some offices in the future, and I think it's great the two-party system is alive here."[33] As the Texas chapter shows, this assessment was right on target for the 1990s.

Florida

Staggering population growth over the last half century has shaken Florida loose from its southern political roots. Yet, at the dawn of the southern two-party era in the early 1960s, Florida, despite the steady influx of outsiders and the accompanying changes they were bringing, was still a segregationist state dominated by the Democratic party. Pockets of Republicanism had begun in the 1950s in the retirement communities in St. Petersburg and in other urban areas, but the Florida GOP did not become a statewide threat until the last half of the 1960s.

In the 1966 governor's race, the Democratic nominee, Robert King High, the mayor of Miami, survived a bitter primary runoff in which his opponent, Governor Haydon Burns, attacked him as an "ultraliberal" who is indebted to the "Negro bloc vote." Claude R. Kirk, Jr., the Republican gubernatorial nominee, picked up where Burns left off. As two academic writers recounted the general election, "High had alienated many conservative Democrats in the state with his progressive racial views. . . . [Kirk] criticized High's racial attitudes. . . . Kirk also exploited public dissatisfaction with race riots in the cities, Vietnam, and inflation."[34] Winning with 55.1 percent of the vote, Kirk became Florida's first post-Reconstruction Republican governor. He did especially well in north Florida, a region politically akin to nearby south Alabama and south Georgia.

Two years later, another Republican, Edward J. Gurney, won a U.S. Senate seat in part by labeling his opponent, former governor LeRoy Collins, "Liberal LeRoy" and circulating in the rural areas of north Florida a photograph of Collins walking with Martin Luther King, Jr. Collins, who was considered a racial moderate when he was governor in the last years of legal segregation, had served Presidents Kennedy and Johnson as an adviser on civil rights. At the end of the campaign, the Tallahassee *Democrat* concluded: "It was the civil rights issue that was the undoing of LeRoy Collins. . . . He saw it as an opportunity to lead Florida, and the South, into the mainstream of national affairs. The nation was willing, but Florida and the South weren't."[35]

These early GOP gains were halted in the 1970 elections when two attractive, moderate Democratic state legislators, Reuben Askew and Lawton Chiles, emerged from the primaries with their party's nominations for governor and U.S. senator, respectively. Chiles, a central Florida native who is described as "from the awshucks school of politics," received considerable favorable publicity with a thousand-mile walk across the state. The strongest counties for Askew (who hails from Pensacola near the western end of the Florida Panhandle) and Chiles were in north Florida. Of this strength, Chiles was later quoted as saying, "While Democrats in Florida have voted 'for the man' for years, still, when you get into North Florida areas, they consider themselves Democrats and, if you give them a Democrat they can accept, they'll vote for him."[36]

The Florida Democratic party throughout the 1970s and 1980s generally was successful in offering such acceptable candidates. After Askew's two terms, Bob Graham, a millionaire developer from Miami, won the governorship for the Democrats in 1978 and was easily reelected. Graham had a campaign gimmick that served as well as Chiles's: he worked a hundred days at a hundred different jobs. When his two terms were up in 1986, Graham moved to the U.S. Senate. To get there he defeated Senator Paula Hawkins, a Republican elected in Reagan's 1980 Florida landslide.

The GOP did win the governorship in 1986 after an especially bitter Democratic runoff. The runoff loser, Jim Smith, who later switched to the Republican party, repeatedly blasted the eventual winner and Democratic candidate, Steve Pajcic, as too liberal for Florida. The campaign manager for Bob Martinez, the Republican victor, was jubilant over the intra-Democratic brawl, saying after the primaries. "Jim Smith spent a few million dollars burying the harpoon of liberalism deep in Pajcic's chest, and we're not going to pull it out."[37] When Chiles stepped down from his Senate seat in 1988, U.S. representative Connie Mack, a Republican, narrowly won the post.

Throughout both decades Republican party registration and identification

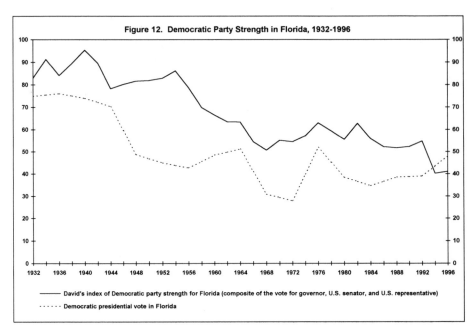

Figure 12. Democratic Party Strength in Florida, 1932-1996

—— David's index of Democratic party strength for Florida (composite of the vote for governor, U.S. senator, and U.S. representative)

······ Democratic presidential vote in Florida

rose steadily as did the party's share of U.S. House and state legislative seats. These gains provided the base for the Florida GOP's takeoff in the 1990s, which is fully explored in the Florida chapter and is previewed in Figure 12.

SOUTHERN POLITICS IN THE 1990S: AN INTRODUCTORY OVERVIEW

By the time of the first elections of the 1990s, then, the Republican party had become firmly established in the South. The Democratic-party-strength figures used so far in this chapter have depicted the GOP's rise indirectly, that is, as the flip side of the Democrats' decline after the breakup of the one-party South. In contrast, Figure 13 plots the Republican growth directly for three key categories of offices, and the trend lines of this figure demonstrate that, despite the party's gains, the southern GOP remained in minority status when the decade of the 1990s began.

Imagine for the moment that Figure 13 stops at 1990, or simply cover the post-1990 portion of the figure with a piece of paper. After the 1990 balloting, the GOP controlled 10 of the region's 33 top statewide offices (that is, of the

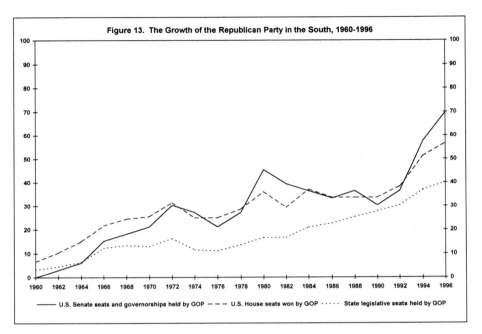

Figure 13. The Growth of the Republican Party in the South, 1960-1996

— U.S. Senate seats and governorships held by GOP   – – – U.S. House seats won by GOP   ····· State legislative seats held by GOP

11 governorships and 22 U.S. Senate seats), or 30.3 percent. The GOP's peak year for these major offices had been 1980, when it controlled 15 of the 33, or 45.4 percent. As late as 1988, it held 12, but the twin 1990 losses of the governorships of Texas and Florida pushed it down to 10. Still, the GOP had held none of them in 1960 or for the preceding four and a half decades.

A second office shown in Figure 13 is the U.S. House of Representatives. In the 1990 elections Republicans won 33.6 percent of the region's U.S. House seats, or 39 of the 116 seats allotted to the eleven states after the 1980 census. The 1986 and 1988 U.S. House elections had yielded the same percentage, which was only a few points below the post-1960 high in this category, reached in 1980 and 1984. As with the major statewide offices, compared to the figures for 1960 (at 7 of the 106 seats then allotted the region, or 6.6 percent), the 1990 percentage represented real progress for the GOP.

Finally, at the state legislative level, the Republicans controlled 27.8 percent of the seats after the 1990 elections. In 1960, the GOP held only 3.3 percent of the South's state legislative seats. In this category the increase had been gradual, rising about 3 percentage points every two years since the mid-1970s.

Now, uncover the post-1990 portion of Figure 13; the GOP leap in the next six years is simply astonishing. After the 1996 elections the Republican party in

Dixie held 23 of the 33 governorships and U.S. Senate seats, a stunning 69.7 percent. In the 1996 elections the Republicans won 56.8 percent of the South's U.S. House seats, or 71 of the 125 seats assigned the region after the 1990 census. Even at the state legislative level the GOP reached 40.0 percent of the seats after the 1996 voting, and by July 1998 more than a score of party switchers plus a dozen or so special and odd-year election victories had pushed the figure up to 41.5 percent.[38]

How did this breakthrough occur? What were its causes and what does it mean for the future of southern politics? Full understanding of the recent developments requires delving into the partisan details in each of the eleven southern states, a task accomplished in Chapters 2 through 12. The remainder of this chapter provides an overview of the political context—national and regional—in which southern politics operated in the 1990s and offers, as well, an introduction to several key elements at work. Then, after the untidy details of the complex state-by-state stories are laid out, Chapter 13 returns attention to broader themes in an attempt to understand the dynamics of southern politics in the 1990s.

The 1990 elections were fought out against the backdrop of the Persian Gulf crisis as a huge American and allied force was assembling in Saudi Arabia to counter Iraq's seizure of Kuwait. During the fall campaign President George Bush, whose already high popularity ratings would soon soar to stratospheric levels after the Gulf War victory in early 1991, barnstormed the nation attacking the "tax-and-spend" liberal Democrats in Congress, calling them "America's biggest and most entrenched special interest." A few months earlier he had reached a budget compromise with the Democratic congressional leaders and in the process had broken his "no-new-taxes" pledge of 1988. "To get an agreement, we had to pay a ransom [tax increases] to get the $350 billion in spending cuts," he asserted on the stump.[39] The President called the "ransom" the price of divided government and urged voters to give him a Republican Congress.

While the party of the president almost always loses seats in midterm elections, Republicans hoped Bush's popularity coupled with an apparently strong economy would reverse the traditional outcome. But the pattern held once more, although nationwide the 1990 Republican losses were modest: nine seats in the House and one in the Senate. The GOP, which had been a minority party in the House since the 1954 elections, would hold 167 seats in the new 102nd Congress compared to 267 for the Democrats. In the Senate the Republicans would have 44 members to the Democrats' 56; Ronald Reagan's 1980 presidential landslide had ended the GOP's twenty-six-year-long minority status in the Senate and the Republicans had remained in control of the upper house until the 1986 elections.

U.S. representative Newt Gingrich of Georgia, the House minority whip, called the 1990 results "a very sobering experience for all of us who thought we had lots of momentum heading into the 1990s," adding that Republicans would now be forced to "reassess where we are going." Gingrich himself in 1990 came within a thousand votes of losing the suburban Atlanta seat he had held since 1978.[40]

The South did not contribute to the GOP congressional setbacks since, as mentioned earlier, the number of southern Republicans in the U.S. House remained the same in 1990 as it had been in the previous two elections. All three Republican U.S. senators up for election, Jesse Helms of North Carolina, Phil Gramm of Texas, and John W. Warner of Virginia, were reelected. Democrats Ann Richards of Texas and Lawton Chiles of Florida did capture their respective governorships from the GOP in high visibility contests, although overall, Democratic party strength in the South (see Figure 1) declined from 56.4 percent in 1988 to 52.1 percent in 1990, reflecting growing voter support for GOP candidates despite the party's failure to win more elections that year. And developments in many individual states, South Carolina, for example, were running favorably in the GOP direction, as the state chapters reveal.

With the exception of Georgia's Jimmy Carter in 1976, Democratic presidential candidates lost heavily in the South from 1968 through 1988.[41] Governor Michael Dukakis of Massachusetts, the Democratic standard-bearer in 1988, received only 40.9 percent of the southern vote to George Bush's 58.3 percent. This compares to Dukakis's nationwide vote of 45.6 percent to Bush's 53.4 percent. Besides being swamped in the South, these Democratic nominees (again excepting Carter in 1976 but not 1980)—Hubert Humphrey in 1968, George McGovern in 1972, Walter Mondale in 1984 and Dukakis—were losers outside the South as well. At the core of these Democratic losses was the party's weakness among the white working class.

Writing in 1991, Thomas B. Edsall and Mary D. Edsall captured the essence of the Democratic problem: "The overlapping issues of race and taxes have permitted the Republican party to adapt the principles of conservatism to break the underlying class basis of the Roosevelt-Democratic coalition and to build a reconfigured voting majority in presidential elections. . . . Race has become a powerful wedge, breaking up what had been the majoritarian economic interests of the poor, working, and lower-middle classes in the traditional liberal coalition. Taxes, in turn, have been used to drive home the cost to whites of federal programs that redistribute social and economic benefits to blacks and to other minorities." In one of their interviews, the Edsalls quote a Chicago carpenter on the point: "You could classify me as a working-class Democrat, a card-carrying union member. I'm not a card-carrying Republican, yet. . . . We have four or five generations of welfare mothers. And they [Democrats] say the answer to that is we need more programs. Come on. . . . It's well and good we should have compassion for these people, but your compassion goes only so far. . . . When you try to pick somebody up, they have to help."[42]

Bill Clinton, the savvy, nationally oriented, veteran Democratic governor of Arkansas, thoroughly comprehended his party's presidential weakness. At a May 1991 gathering of the Democratic Leadership Council (DLC), a group of centrist Democrats, he declared: "Too many of the people who used to vote for us, the very burdened middle class we're talking about, have not trusted us in national elections to defend our national interests abroad, to put their values in our social policy at home or to take their tax money and spend it with discipline. We've got to turn these perceptions around, or we can't continue as a national party." In the words of a newspaper reporter, Clinton, who was the DLC's chairman that year, "argued eloquently throughout the session for a 'new choice' that does not abandon the party's traditional commitment to the poor, particularly poor children, but that is able to sell itself as the advocate of the middle class as well—and thus return to power."[43]

After securing the 1992 Democratic presidential nomination and picking a fellow southerner, Senator Al Gore, Jr., of Tennessee, as his vice presidential running mate, Clinton stuck to his "new Democrat" theme in a brilliant national campaign. One of the Democratic ticket's first television commercials described the two southerners as follows: "They are a new generation of Democrats, Bill Clinton and Al Gore. And they don't think the way the old Democratic Party did. They've called for an end to welfare as we know it, so welfare can be a second chance, not a way of life. They've sent a strong signal to criminals by supporting the death penalty. And they've rejected the old tax and spend politics." As the Edsalls write in a postelection supplement to their book, "In effect, Clinton and Gore contrasted themselves to just the Democratic images that had been at the center of the [winning] campaigns of Richard Nixon in 1968 and 1972, Ronald Reagan in 1980 and 1984, and George Bush in 1988."[44]

This positioning also included a much publicized effort by Clinton to distance himself from Jesse Jackson, the African American civil rights leader and past presidential candidate. At the same time, the Arkansan cultivated "a host of rising black political leaders [such as U.S. representatives John Lewis of Georgia, Mike Espy of Mississippi, Maxine Waters of California, and William J. Jefferson of Louisiana], many of whom were themselves resentful of the way the media and many whites seemed to grant Jackson the exclusive right to speak for the black community." One Detroit-area black politician, Bernard Parker, a Wayne County commissioner, commented on the posturing: "As a politician, I understand why Clinton is playing down [overt policy commitments to the black community]. It's because he is trying to reach white middle America. I'm not bothered by his strategy, I think the strategy is paying off. . . . I am bothered by the racism of this country that forced him to do that."[45]

Of course, the 1992 presidential election involved considerably more than Clinton's much highlighted "New Democrat" shift to the center. President Bush's popularity had plummeted by early 1992 as the economy remained in the mild recession it had entered over a year earlier.[46] With his single-minded focus on economic issues, Clinton benefited from the lingering recession and a general uneasiness about the country's economic direction. And then there was Ross Perot, who attacked both parties for their joint responsibility for mushrooming the national debt by running huge budget deficits year after year.

Although the Clinton-Gore electoral strategy was built on the 1988 base of nonsouthern states Dukakis carried or ran well in, the national Democratic candidates made a strong effort in several southern states beyond their home states of Arkansas and Tennessee, particularly in Louisiana, Georgia, North Carolina, and even Florida. On a visit to Tampa in late October, Clinton told a crowd of several thousand not to let President Bush take Florida for granted: "The economy is in a shambles and yet they say, 'If there's one big state we can depend upon, it's Florida. They'll just knee-jerk and vote Republican.'" He continued, "Know what I think? I think there's a tired old Republican Party that's run out of ideas, energy, direction and compassion, and they ought to be run out of town." Earlier, in Augusta, Georgia, Clinton had sought votes with this appeal: "I have tried to build a new Democratic Party that believes in growth in the private sector, that believes in not bigger government but more effective government, that believes in a partnership between government and business and labor and education." In New Orleans, Senator Gore told a Dillard University rally: "We've been stalled and stuck in a ditch of trickle-down economics. . . . If George Bush went to Hollywood and made a movie, it would have to be called 'Honey, I Shrunk the Economy.' "[47]

For his part, President Bush lambasted Clinton as a "man who has the gall to go around America and promise the moon, when on issue after issue, the sky has fallen in his own backyard." In a campaign swing through five states bordering on Arkansas, Bush attacked Clinton's Arkansas record on issue after issue. "Governor Clinton has more than doubled—you want a horror story, listen to this—he has more than doubled Arkansas state spending since 1983, and he has paid for it by raising taxes that hurt poor and working families the most. My opponent has raised and extended this sales tax repeatedly, and he has opposed removing that tax from groceries." In defense of his own record, he added: "According to Candidate Clinton, the last 10 years have been a nightmare. Well, I've got news for him: it is not true. The Urban Institute back in Washington is not usually sympathetic to me. But listen to what they had to say about the 1980's. 'When one follows individuals, rather than statistical groups defined by income, one finds that on average, the rich got a little richer, and the poor got much richer.' Now that's the truth. Our policies of cutting taxes have spurred growth for all Americans."[48]

Although Clinton's victory with 43.0 percent of the vote to Bush's 37.4 percent was based on states outside the South, the Arkansan did considerably better in the South than any Democratic standard-bearer since Carter. He carried four of the eleven southern states—Georgia and Louisiana plus the ticket's home states of Arkansas and Tennessee. As Table 2 shows, the Democratic presidential percentage in the region was 41.2 percent compared to Bush's 42.6 percent, quite a turnaround from 1988. Perot had a regional average of 15.8 percent compared to his national percentage of 18.9 percent. Texas, Perot's home state, and Florida were his strongest southern states by far; in most of Dixie, Perot's independent presidential bid was far less warmly received than in other regions of the country.

The 39 southern electoral votes the Clinton-Gore ticket won (out of 147 allotted to the old Confederacy) were not critical to the Democrats' electoral college victory with 370 votes, 100 more than the required 270 majority. But this strong national Democratic showing in the South (albeit by two Southern Baptists) is a significant feature of the 1990s regional partisan mix. The state percentages displayed in Table 2 suggest interesting state-level variations soon to be encountered in Chapters 2 through 12. For example, Clinton's relatively close Florida result—Dukakis trailed Bush in the Sunshine State by a whopping 22 percentage points in 1988—encouraged the Arkansan, as reported in the Florida chapter, to make a major effort there in 1996, which he did with good results for the Democrats.[49]

Southern Republicans gained in all nonpresidential categories in 1992, although their successes were modest compared with what would come in 1994. The party won an additional nine seats in the U.S. House, increasing its share of the region's seats from 33.6 percent to 38.4 percent—48 of Dixie's 125 seats. Because the South's population growth exceeded the national average, the region received 9 additional House seats before the 1992 elections.[50] The southern

Table 2. The 1992 Presidential Vote in the South

State	Clinton		Bush		Perot		Total[b]
Alabama (9)[a]	690,080	(40.9%)	804,283	(47.6%)	183,109	(10.8%)	1,688,060
Arkansas (6)	505,823	(53.2)	337,324	(35.5)	99,132	(10.4)	950,653
Florida (25)	2,072,698	(39.0)	2,173,310	(40.9)	1,053,067	(19.8)	5,314,392
Georgia (13)	1,008,966	(43.5)	995,252	(42.9)	309,657	(13.3)	2,321,125
Louisiana (9)	815,971	(45.6)	733,386	(41.0)	211,478	(11.8)	1,790,017
Mississippi (7)	400,258	(40.8)	487,793	(49.7)	85,626	(8.7)	981,793
North Carolina (14)	1,114,042	(42.7)	1,134,661	(43.4)	357,864	(13.7)	2,611,850
South Carolina (8)	479,514	(39.9)	577,507	(48.0)	138,872	(11.5)	1,202,527
Tennessee (11)	933,521	(47.1)	841,300	(42.4)	199,968	(10.1)	1,982,638
Texas (32)	2,281,815	(37.1)	2,496,071	(40.6)	1,354,781	(22.0)	6,154,018
Virginia (13)	1,038,650	(40.6)	1,150,517	(45.0)	348,639	(13.6)	2,558,665
	11,341,338	(41.2)	11,731,404	(42.6)	4,342,193	(15.8)	27,555,738

Source: Richard A. Scammon and Alice McGillivray, *America Votes: A Handbook of Contemporary Election Statistics*, Vol. 20 (Washington, D.C., 1993).

[a]Number of electoral votes is in parentheses.

[b]Voters choosing someone other than Clinton, Bush, or Perot are included in the total. The candidate percentages are based on the total vote.

House gain accounted for the entire 9-seat national gain the GOP made in the U.S. House in 1992.

Republicans in the South scored a net increase of two in major offices when GOP challengers in 1992 retired two first-term Democratic U.S. senators. In North Carolina Lauch Faircloth defeated Senator Terry Sanford, and Paul Coverdell in Georgia edged out Senator Wyche Fowler in an unusual postelection runoff. (Fowler had narrowly led the November 3 balloting, but, because of votes cast for a Libertarian candidate, he did not have a simple majority as then required by Georgia law. As described in the Georgia chapter, the momentum shifted to Coverdell in the three weeks before the second election.) Five other Democratic senators were reelected, all but one—Senator Fritz Hollings of South Carolina—easily. Overall, the U.S. Senate's partisan balance remained the same. North Carolina's former Democratic governor Jim Hunt won a third nonconsecutive term, replacing James G. (Jim) Martin, a Republican not eligible to run again. This Democratic gubernatorial gain was offset by the 1991 Mississippi victory of Republican Kirk Fordice over first-term Democratic governor Ray Mabus. Thus, after the 1992 elections, Republicans controlled 12 of the 33 top southern elective posts, or 36.4 percent. The party continued steady state legislative gains, rising to 30.3 percent after the 1992 voting. And finally, David's index of Democratic party strength declined an additional two percentage points in 1992, registering a fraction above the 50 percent line (50.1 percent, to be exact), which, in retrospect, appears to be a fitting poetic pause at the precipice. (See Figure 1.)

The number of African Americans in Congress from the South more than tripled in the 1992 elections. How this notable development came about and the political and legal controversies that flowed from it and continue to flow from it are important in the current southern partisan configuration. It is useful at this point, then, to delve into the matter, which centers on the creation of black-majority districts. All the state chapters, except Arkansas, Mississippi, and Tennessee, where the issue did not arise directly, consider the topic within each state's special political context, and the following discussion provides background for those segments.

Prior to 1992, black-majority U.S. House districts had been created only in the South's largest cities—Atlanta, Memphis, Houston, and New Orleans[51]— plus one in the rural Mississippi Delta that had been the subject of protracted legal battles in the 1970s and 1980s. Unlike the pattern in the Northeast and Midwest, where blacks live primarily in large cities, southern blacks are a significant presence in rural and small-town areas, a legacy of slavery and the plantation system.[52] In the South Carolina Lowcountry, for example, rural, small-town counties such as Williamsburg and Colleton have large black populations.[53] And, while African Americans make up about a third of the population in Charleston and Columbia, those South Carolina cities individually are too small to alone yield black-majority congressional districts. By linking the predominantly black areas of Charleston and Columbia, however, with heavily black rural counties like Williamsburg and Colleton, a black-majority district can be created. This is exactly what was done to create South Carolina's new Sixth District. In Virginia the new black-majority Third District joined the black neighborhoods of Richmond with those in the Norfolk area and picked up a number of rural, small-town counties in the eastern and southeastern portions of the state. In Alabama, the new Seventh District started in the black areas of Birmingham and then encompassed a large segment of west-central Alabama, including part of Montgomery. In these three states, no African American had been elected to Congress since Reconstruction. In 1992 the new districts produced three: James E. Clyburn in South Carolina, Robert C. Scott in Virginia, and Earl F. Hilliard in Alabama.[54]

A total of twelve new black-majority districts were drawn in the South to go with the five already in existence.[55] And after the 1992 election they produced seventeen African Americans in the U.S. House from the old Confederacy along with a flood of lawsuits challenging the validity of the new districts. Before turning to the litigation, it is useful to examine how this unprecedented number of new black-majority districts came to be created. (Hispanic-majority districts were also created, but, since their importance for southern politics is limited to Texas and Florida, their coverage in the chapters on these megastates is sufficient.)

The new black-majority districts came about because the U.S. Justice Department under the Bush Administration exercised its power to veto redistricting plans in states covered by the Voting Rights Act, thereby forcing states to create the districts.[56] In state after state, Republicans and black Democrats formed alliances to lobby for the new districts. In a May 1992 Washington *Post* article headlined "Black Democrats Are Remapping Their Path to Power: An Alliance with the GOP Aims at Boosting Minority Districts," a reporter wrote: "Republicans will concede black districts to the Democrats for a chance at winning everything else. Putting black Democrats together, they say, will end what they describe as the Democratic Party's practice of creating ready-made constituencies by spreading black voters among several districts." A few months later the New York *Times* quoted the general counsel of the Republican National Committee, Benjamin L. Ginsberg, on the goal of the new departure: "[to end] the Democrats' shameful practice of slicing, dicing and fracturing racial minority communities in order to prop up white incumbents of the Democratic Party." A black Democratic state legislator in Florida summed up his view of the joint GOP-black project this way: "For 40 years blacks have been the party backbone. Now we've come to collect, but all we get is 'thanks but no thanks.' It's time to cut the umbilical cord and learn to feed ourselves."[57]

While a comprehensive consideration of the southern black-majority district controversy is not possible here,[58] a look at the North Carolina and Georgia situations—which became the subjects of landmark U.S. Supreme Court "racial gerrymandering" decisions—conveys the essentials of what happened. Aiming to maximize the number of black-majority districts, the Justice Department turned down as insufficient a North Carolina plan that created only one black-majority district and a Georgia plan that added only one black-majority district to the state's existing one in Atlanta. In order to win Justice Department approval, the North Carolina legislature had to construct a second district, the much-ridiculed Twelfth District stretching from Durham to Charlotte via a path along Interstate 85. (A black politician said of it: "I love the district because I can drive down I-85 with both car doors open and hit every person in the district.") In Georgia a third black-majority district, the new Eleventh District, was drawn stretching from Atlanta to Savannah, including sections of blacks in both those cities and in Augusta as well as in the rural, small-town counties in between. When the Justice Department rejected an early Georgia plan, leading white Democrats criticized the Republican-controlled federal department, contending, in the words of a New York *Times* reporter, that "the Voting Rights Act is being used to create black-majority districts that make nearby districts overwhelmingly white and Republican." The article quoted longtime Georgia house speaker Tom Murphy as saying, "I don't say that it was a conspiracy, but it's obviously an attempt to create more Republican districts."[59]

Then came the lawsuits. Five white Democrats in North Carolina challenged the black-majority districts as unconstitutional "racial gerrymandering." Robert O. Everett, the plaintiffs' lawyer, said the districts are "at odds with the ideals of a democratic society. The Constitution is color-blind; this redistricting is just the opposite and amounts to the use of a racial quota system." Reversing a lower court's dismissal of the plaintiffs' case, a five-to-four U.S. Supreme Court majority in *Shaw v. Reno* in June 1993 sent the case back to the lower court. In her majority opinion, Justice Sandra Day O'Connor signaled the majority's hostility to the new black-majority districts: "Racial gerrymandering, even for remedial purposes, may balkanize us into competing racial factions; it threatens to carry us further from the goal of a political system in which race no longer matters." Two years later, in June 1995, the Supreme Court in another landmark five-to-four decision, *Johnson v. Miller*, struck down Georgia's Eleventh District, declaring that race cannot be the "overriding and predominant factor" in the creation of a district. Any doubt as to the position of the Supreme Court's five-member majority was removed a year later when the court struck down three Texas districts (two black-majority districts and one Hispanic-majority district) along with North Carolina's Twelfth District, which had made its way back up to the high court following the 1993 decision and remand.[60] Based on these Supreme Court decisions, lower federal courts invalidated black-majority districts in Florida and Louisiana, and by 1996 and 1997 challenges had even been brought against the South Carolina, Virginia, and Alabama districts.

"It was based on a lack of reality," commented U.S. representative Melvin (Mel) Watt, the African American elected in North Carolina's Twelfth District, after the Court's June 1995 Georgia decision. Still hopeful then that his district would be upheld, Watt added, "The notion that our nation can be color-blind when the individual members of our nation are not is just foolhardy." U.S. representative Cynthia McKinney, the African American elected in Georgia's Eleventh District in 1992, was characteristically blunt about the situation, to quote a New York *Times* article on her effort to retain her seat in 1996 in a redrawn white-majority district: "Known in both Washington and Georgia as a liberal firebrand, she has referred to her political and judicial antagonists as 'a ragtag group of neo-Confederates' and has asserted that 'the Old South wants to rise again, and it is using the issue of race, as it always has, to keep itself in power.' "[61]

The black-majority district controversy had many ongoing ramifications; so important is the topic that I return to it in Chapter 13. As already mentioned, most of this book's state chapters discuss the "racial gerrymandering" issue as part of their coverage of individual state electoral politics in the 1990s. It is a complex question that is at the cutting edge of southern politics in the 1990s.[62]

The 1994 midterm elections were fought against a backdrop of rising voter disenchantment and pessimism.[63] A late October New York *Times* article based on interviews with party strategists and election analysts described an "anti-Clinton, anti-Government sentiment" that had Democrats more than a little concerned. The article noted that "professionals in both parties said they had never seen so many factors breaking the Republicans' way." A political scientist, Gary Jacobson, was quoted as follows: "I haven't observed an election where there's such a strong general tide. My line for most of this election period has been, 'It's not going to be as bad as it looks for the Democrats.' But I keep having to shift because it looks worse and worse."[64]

When the votes came in on election night, the Republican party won a smashing national victory, capturing the U.S. House for the first time in forty years with a gain of 55 seats, retaking the Senate with an 8-seat increase, and winning a dozen new governorships.[65] The southern component of this GOP sweep was historic in its own right because after the election the party held a majority of the South's U.S. House and Senate seats and governorships for the first time since Reconstruction. Before examining the southern results, brief consideration is in order regarding how President Clinton, the energetic "New Democrat," full of enthusiasm and drive, managed in just twenty-two months to lead his party to such a huge national electoral defeat.

Clinton himself serves as an excellent analyst. Addressing a Democratic dinner in Washington in late September 1994, he said, to quote from a New York *Times* account, that "his efforts to reduce the Federal deficit, increase global trade and rewrite foreign policy had not yet restored optimism about the future—and about his Presidency—because their very nature is to make the future less predictable." Calling this fear of change misguided and irrational, he said the Democratic party had to tackle the issue head-on. "I ask you, if we have a good economy; if we face the challenges of trade and crime; if we have reached out to families who are trying to keep their families together and raise their kids, with the family leave bill and by giving 15 million working families tax cuts; we've put on the table a welfare reform program that is both compassionate and tough—why would anyone think there would be any problem?"

The *Times* reporter paraphrased what the President said next: "Answering his own question, Mr. Clinton suggested that the White House had failed to communicate its successes to some voters, and that others were simply unsettled by global economic changes that might affect their standard of living. Finally, he said that Republicans had taken advantage of both factors to persuade the public that the White House's policies are either ineffective or wrongheaded." The article then quoted Clinton further as saying that, since the voters have "been told for so long that Government can't do anything but mess up a one-car parade, it's hard to imagine that what we do here can make a difference." Citing the recently passed anti-crime bill as an example of positive governmental action, he argued that the prevailing view is wrong and that it was the Democrats' task to convince the voters of this before November.[66]

Missing from Clinton's fall speeches was any mention of the major domestic initiative of his presidency up to then: the ambitious, failed effort to restructure the nation's health care system to see that everyone has access to care at an affordable cost. In an article quoting several liberal Democrats concerning the relationship of their wing of the party to Clinton, Senator Tom Harkin of Iowa observed: "You can't say the health care reform package he sent up here to

Congress is centrist."[67] And therein is a key ambivalence that permeated Clinton's first two years and worked to his political disadvantage. His health care initiative was an important effort to accomplish a major goal on the national Democratic agenda since the New Deal, a scheme that involved heavy government involvement in a large segment of the American economy. Its failure—and Clinton's poor political management of the reform was chiefly responsible for its failure[68]—dashed the hopes of those who believed in the goal he so eloquently proclaimed, and at the same time it gave ammunition to his enemies that Clinton, despite his rhetoric, was indeed a "big government" liberal.[69] Clinton wanted it both ways—to be a "new Democrat" and to be the champion of "those who have less,"[70] who frequently can only be aided by effective governmental action. The performance left him vulnerable, and Republicans rarely missed their target during the fall campaign.

"We're prepared to place our trust in the people to reshape the government. Our liberal friends place their trust in the government to reshape the people." That's the way Georgia's Newt Gingrich, the architect of the House triumph, put the GOP argument in one of his milder charges. Because U.S. representative Robert H. Michel of Illinois, the Republican leader, was retiring, Gingrich, the party whip and Michel's heir apparent, led the 1994 GOP campaign with firm determination to end the Democrats' long rule over the House. Of Gingrich's role in the campaign, Representative Bill Paxon of New York, the chairman of the National Republican Congressional Committee in 1994, said, "He is chief cheerleader, chief fund-raiser, chief recruiter and chief message developer." In October Gingrich assembled over 350 GOP House incumbents and candidates on the Capitol steps to sign a ten-point "Contract with America," promising action on all items—which included term limits, a balanced-budget amendment, and a $500 tax credit for children—within the first one hundred days of the 104th Congress.[71]

Proclaiming his goal to "renew American civilization," Gingrich placed the blame for society's ills on the "counterculture," which, he said, "permeates this Administration." "It is impossible to maintain a civilization with 12-year-olds having babies, 15-year-olds killing each other, 17-year-olds dying of AIDS and 18-year-olds getting diplomas they can't read."[72] When asked at a news conference the morning after his election triumph what his opponents' biggest mistake in the campaign was, he reiterated his chief themes. "The Democrats adopted a McGovernite view of foreign policy and military power, Lyndon Johnson's Great Society structure of the welfare state, and counterculture values. And those three things are so destructive that until the Democratic party weans itself of those and gets back to the basic fundamentals of American civilization, it is going to have a virtually impossible time governing successfully.''[73]

Gingrich's successful effort to nationalize the election was clearly an important factor in the GOP victory, although the "Contract for America" itself probably played only a minor role since the vast majority of the voters never heard of it. A defeated Democratic congressman in North Carolina, David E. Price, a Duke University political scientist, expressed the point well: "It was not so much the contract as the idea that the way to get at Congress and the way to get at Clinton was to vote against your local congressman.''[74]

Figure 13 captures the unprecedented GOP gains in the South. The party picked up 16 U.S. House seats to give it 51.2 percent of the region's seats (64 of 125). Republicans won both U.S. Senate seats in Tennessee. Bill Frist, a physician, defeated three-term Democratic senator Jim Sasser, and Republican Fred Thompson, an actor and lawyer, won the unexpired two years remaining in Vice President Gore's old seat. In 1993, when Senator Lloyd Bentsen, Democrat of Texas, resigned to become Clinton's secretary of the treasury, a Republican, Kay Bailey Hutchison, won a special election to fill the remainder of his term. She was handily reelected in 1994, giving the GOP a net gain of 3 senators to go with their 9 senatorial incumbents. Thus of the South's 22 Senate seats, the GOP held a majority of 12.

At the gubernatorial level, Republicans made a net gain of two in 1994 to go with the victory of George Allen in Virginia the previous year. In Texas George W. Bush, the son of the former president, defeated Governor Ann Richards's bid for reelection. And U.S. representative Don Sundquist of Memphis replaced a retiring Democratic governor in Tennessee. David Beasley, a recent Democratic convert, held the South Carolina governorship for the Republican party; Carroll Campbell, the two-term Republican incumbent in the Palmetto State, was constitutionally barred from seeking reelection. A former Democratic governor, Fob James, won the Alabama governorship running as a Republican; that victory did not represent a GOP gain since a Republican, Guy Hunt, had been reelected to the office four years earlier but had been forced to resign under criminal indictment. Adding in Kirk Fordice, the Republican governor of Mississippi elected in 1991, the 1994 results gave the Republicans six of the South's eleven governorships, a majority for the first time in the twentieth century.

The combined category of GOP governorships and U.S. Senate seats, which totaled 18 as of election night, grew to 19 the next day when Senator Richard Shelby of Alabama, a conservative Democrat, announced he was switching to the Republican party. Thus, after all the election winners were sworn in, the

GOP controlled 19 of the top 33 elective offices in the region, or 57.6 percent. At the state legislative level, Republicans in 1994 made their largest gains since 1966, advancing 6.7 percentage points to control of 37.0 percent of the region's legislative seats.

With the Republicans now in control of Congress, five conservative Democratic members of the U.S. House chose 1995 to switch to the GOP. They were Nathan Deal of Georgia (April); Greg Laughlin of Texas (June); W. J. (Billy) Tauzin of Louisiana (August); Mike Parker of Mississippi (November); and Jimmy Hayes of Louisiana (December). All five were members of the "Blue Dog" group of conservative Democrats in the House, whose ranks of about two dozen were further depleted in 1996 by retirements and defeats. Deal, Tauzin, and Parker were reelected easily as Republicans in 1996. Hayes lost badly in a 1996 Senate bid. And Laughlin, despite receiving the full backing of the Texas Republican hierarchy,[75] failed to win renomination at the hands of an archconservative Republican, Ron Paul, who had been the 1988 Libertarian presidential candidate; Paul narrowly held the seat for the GOP in the 1996 general election.

The U.S. House switches, by far the largest in the post–World War II era, were only one sign of the partisan ferment that engulfed the region after the watershed 1994 elections. Full comprehension of what happened must be delayed until the state chapters, where the stories are told in detail and in the context of each state's pattern of development. These chapters report a rash of party switching at various levels, almost all in one direction: Democrat to Republican. For example, after the 1994 voting, the GOP in South Carolina found itself just short of a majority in the state's house of representatives. Within a week switchers had given the party control, and more converts came along over the following months to solidify its majority. There were also many Republican victories for state executive offices below the governorship throughout Dixie in 1994. Again, these developments must be laid out on a state-by-state basis.

For the moment, it is sufficient to conclude that the 1994 GOP breakthroughs occurred as the result of a combination of two forces: a national electoral tide in which the South contributed at least its share but not much more; and the continuation of the ongoing settling in of two-party competition at a pace accelerated in 1994 by the national Republican tide.

On the national scene, the 1996 elections were played out by the major figures already familiar from 1992 and 1994. Those who were riding high after the November 1994 elections and through much of 1995, however, namely Speaker Gingrich and the other leaders of the Republican-controlled 104th Congress, were put on the defensive by the negative public reaction to the partial shutdowns of the government in late 1995 and early 1996, which resulted from bitter budget disagreements. President Clinton bounced back from the midterm election defeat and found his political footing partly by skillfully adopting portions of the Republican agenda. As the White House political director, Douglas Sosnik, described the situation during the spring of 1996: "The Republicans have given us great gifts. Whether it's shutting down the Government or the revolutionary rhetoric of Newt Gingrich or Bob Dole's inability to articulate a message, they all compound to create a much more favorable environment for Bill Clinton."[76]

Gingrich supported this view, to an extent, in a June 1996 newspaper interview. In the reporter's words, "Mr. Gingrich acknowledged, right at the start, that the Republicans, and especially the House Republicans—himself most prominent among them—had 'overreached in some areas, underrated Bill Clinton's tactical skills and his capacity to come back, and made a lot of clumsy miscalculations.' " Also during the interview, Gingrich called the President "a master of falsehood" who had chosen "carefully managed mendacity as a route to reelection, even if the result is to undermine the nation's civic virtue." In a postelection conversation with reporters, Clinton, in the words of a news account, argued that "the policies enacted in his first two years in office, like his deficit reduction plan and his anti-crime legislation, had come to be appreciated only in 1996. And he cited his ability to work with Congress at the end of the [1996] legislative session as 'the thing that sealed all this.' "[77] And, of course, the economy remained strong in 1996.

Those bipartisan agreements at the end of the second session of the 104th Congress came several months after Senator Bob Dole of Kansas, the Senate majority leader and the 1996 Republican presidential standard-bearer, resigned from the Senate to campaign full time. Despite a vigorous campaign, Dole, who at seventy-three was the oldest man to seek the presidency in the twentieth century as a major party nominee, trailed Clinton in the polls throughout 1996, although Dole had led the president handily in most of the 1995 polls. A Washington *Post* writer concluded the following in a postelection analysis: "By standing up in December [1995] to a Republican Congress that said it preferred closing down the government to giving Clinton his way on the budget, Clinton suddenly seemed decisive. His approval ratings jumped over 50 percent in January and never again fell below that mark. In a head-to-head contest against Clinton, Dole found himself 10 to 15 percentage points behind. And nothing that Dole did throughout the campaign managed to change those numbers in a significant way."[78]

Clinton was reelected with 49.2 percent of the popular vote nationwide,

Table 3. The 1996 Presidential Vote in the South

State	Clinton		Dole		Perot		Total[b]
Alabama (9)[a]	662,165	(43.2%)	794,044	(50.1%)	92,149	(6.0%)	1,534,349
Arkansas (6)	475,171	(53.7)	325,416	(36.8)	69,884	(7.9)	884,262
Florida (25)	2,545,968	(48.0)	2,243,324	(42.3)	483,776	(9.1)	5,300,927
Georgia (13)	1,053,849	(45.8)	1,080,843	(47.0)	146,337	(6.4)	2,298,899
Louisiana (9)	927,837	(52.0)	712,586	(39.9)	123,293	(6.9)	1,783,959
Mississippi (7)	394,022	(44.1)	439,838	(49.2)	52,222	(5.8)	893,857
North Carolina (14)	1,107,849	(44.0)	1,225,938	(48.7)	168,059	(6.7)	2,515,807
South Carolina (8)	506,152	(44.0)	573,339	(49.8)	64,337	(5.6)	1,151,422
Tennessee (11)	909,146	(48.0)	863,530	(45.6)	105,918	(5.6)	1,894,105
Texas (32)	2,459,683	(43.8)	2,736,167	(48.8)	378,537	(6.7)	5,611,644
Virginia (13)	1,091,060	(45.1)	1,138,350	(47.1)	159,861	(6.6)	2,416,642
	12,132,902	(46.2)	12,108,375	(46.1)	1,844,413	(7.0)	26,285,873

Source: Richard A. Scammon and Alice McGillivray, America Votes: A Handbook of Contemporary Election Statistics, Vol. 22 (Washington, D.C., 1996).

[a]Number of electoral votes is in parentheses.

[b]Voters choosing someone other than Clinton, Dole, or Perot are included in the total. The candidate percentages are based on the total vote.

Figure 14. The 1996 Presidential Election in the South by County or Parish

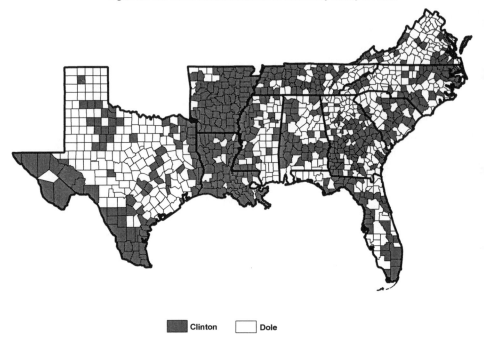

Clinton ▪ Dole ▫

amassing 379 electoral votes, to Dole's 40.7 percent and 159 electoral votes. Ross Perot received 8.4 percent, considerably below his 1992 showing. Clinton again carried four southern states; three of them he had won in 1992—Arkansas, Tennessee, and Louisiana.[79] This time he lost Georgia narrowly but added electoral vote–rich Florida, which he won handily, 48.0 percent to Dole's 42.3 percent.[80] Even with a total of 51 electoral votes from Dixie, Clinton's southern vote was again not decisive. Clinton ran well enough even in the southern states he lost, however, to score a not inconsiderable twenty-year Democratic first in Dixie: Clinton's total popular vote in the South, as shown in Table 3, was just under 25,000 votes ahead of Dole's—46.2 percent for Clinton to 46.1 percent for Dole. The 1996 presidential results are depicted on a county-by-county basis in Figure 14, an illustration that serves nicely as a rough portrait of the areas of strength of both political parties in Dixie by the latter part of the 1990s.

The GOP retained control of Congress in 1996, a feat the party had not accomplished since the 1920s, before Franklin Roosevelt's New Deal began the process of making the Democratic party the nation's majority party. The Republicans gained 2 seats in the Senate, giving them a 55-to-45 margin. In the House they lost 10 seats, reducing their numbers to 226 compared to the Democrats' 208.

Despite a weak presidential candidate and a national congressional outcome that, at best, could be called a stalemate, the southern GOP continued its forward progress. Republicans captured two open Democratic U.S. Senate seats: one by Jeff Sessions in Alabama and the other by Tim Hutchison in Arkansas. In 1995 a Republican (who had been a Democrat right up to the filing deadline), Mike Foster, won the Louisiana governorship. And when Democratic governor Jim Guy Tucker of Arkansas was convicted of Whitewater-related crimes and resigned in July 1996, the Republican lieutenant governor, Mike Huckabee, became governor, giving the GOP a net 1996 increase of four in the category of major statewide offices, boosting its record 1994 total to twenty-three of thirty-three offices, or the staggering 69.7 percent figure mentioned at the beginning of this overview section. Republican U.S. House seats in the South increased by 7 to 71, or 56.8 percent, partly aided by the three Democratic switchers who were reelected as Republicans. GOP state legislative seats continued their upward path, rising 3 percentage points to 40.0 percent after the November 1996 balloting (and to 41.5 percent by mid-1998), as also mentioned above.

There is no question that the GOP's 1996 forward momentum in Dixie came primarily from dynamics within the region, since there was no national tide to share the credit as in 1994. Full comprehension of where the region is going in partisan terms must await the long journey about to begin through the detailed commentaries on each of the eleven states.[81] This venture will introduce various items unexplored so far, such as the growing role of the Christian right in Republican politics, or covered in too brief a fashion, such as racial tensions in the region, which have flared up dramatically from time to time over symbolic issues like the Confederate flag or over issues of greater substance.

These items and much more, along with the personalities who fought the day-to-day political battles on the front lines—the candidates, the officeholders, and their supporters—make their way into the analytical narratives that follow in Chapters 2 through 12. While generalizations coupled with an array of electoral statistics have their place, there is no substitute for acquaintance with the people who engage in the uncertain life of political struggle. They are the ones who have made southern politics what it is in the 1990s, and we turn now to how they behaved and how the voters reacted to them in state after state. We start with South Carolina because its story in the 1990s is one of the most amazing among a host of fascinating partisan state patterns.

2

SOUTH CAROLINA: A DECADE OF RAPID REPUBLICAN ASCENT

Glen T. Broach and Lee Bandy

LATE into the night of November 8, 1994, the citizens of South Carolina, a state once proud of its reputation as a bastion of "Yellow Dog" Democrats, learned that they had narrowly elected Republican David M. Beasley as their new governor. Following on the heels of GOP governor Carroll A. Campbell's two terms, the election of Beasley, a former Democrat, assured Republicans of twelve years of continuous control of the state's highest elective office. But the governor-elect's victory was not the most dramatic departure from the state's Democratic past on this momentous night. Republicans also won six of South Carolina's eight other statewide elective offices, took four of six congressional districts, and captured 60 of the 124 seats in the state House of Representatives. Democratic defections would soon give Republicans 68 House seats and a chamber majority when the new General Assembly took office in January 1995.

The loss depressed Democrats. (See Figure 2 in Chapter 1 for a graphic display of the South Carolina Democratic decline.) Many viewed 1994 as their last stand against a growing Republican party. That Republicans were able to hold on to the governorship and make gains across the state spoke volumes about the fundamental change in the political bedrock of South Carolina. "It was a consolidation of the Republican hold on government office," said Atlanta-based pollster Whit Ayres, a former aide to Campbell.[1]

The story of the GOP's rise from perennial minority to parity and ultimately to control of most of the state's major political institutions is in part a tale of youth, strategic savvy, and organizational energy that enabled the Republicans to position themselves as the party of the future.[2] By contrast, the complacency and organizational ineptitude of the Democrats prevented them from shaking an image as the party of the past and "good ol' boy" corruption. "We lacked the key ingredient: leadership," groused Sam Tenenbaum, a prominent Democratic activist and financial contributor. "We had nothing there to lead us, to articulate us, to market us."[3]

THE EMERGENCE OF REPUBLICAN ASCENDANCY

The reversal of party fortunes is a story of the GOP's gradual but persistent cultivation of the fields of discontent among South Carolina's white voters. Democrats neglected those same fields and paid a price for it. In most elections, at least one in four South Carolina voters is African American, and 90 to 95 percent of those votes are cast for Democrats. This means that Republicans must capture roughly two-thirds of white voters in order to win a majority in a statewide election. Over the years Republicans have found the most fertile ground for their appeals to be among the state's growing suburban middle class and among adherents of the religious right. But the GOP's efforts have yielded statewide electoral majorities only when the party's efforts have harvested conservative white voters in South Carolina's rural areas and small towns. There and elsewhere, the Republican message of social and economic conservatism has resonated with the racial subtext of state politics to yield the GOP's present advantage in the state's electoral politics.

Campbell's successful handling of the governor's office from 1987 to 1995 was a major factor in bringing a great many whites into the GOP. "We saw a dramatic change in the first two years," said pollster Ayres, whose surveys showed that the percentage of whites claiming allegiance to the Democratic party had dropped below 20, while those identifying with the Republicans had risen well into the 40s. "Every now and then, they would break into 50 percent."[4]

The partisan fault lines that by 1994 had thrown up an entirely new South Carolina political landscape first began to open in 1964, when the GOP nominated Barry Goldwater as its presidential candidate and longtime segregationist U.S. senator Strom Thurmond converted to the Republican party. Goldwater's economic conservatism mobilized the incipient Republicanism of the suburbs, and his opposition to the Civil Rights Act of 1964 gave him instant cachet with the state's rural whites. Thurmond, then as now a revered political figure, broke with the national Democratic party on civil rights, a conversion that made it immediately respectable to be a Republican.

Over the next two decades the GOP made minor gains in the General Assembly. Democratic control of redistricting and the emergence of a strongly Democratic black electorate enabled Democrats to limit Republican representation to less than 20 percent of the legislature. As noted in Chapter 1, Democrats also dominated all statewide elective offices until 1974. In that year the Democratic nominee for governor was disqualified, and Republicans were able to cash in on their luck and elect the first Republican governor of the century, Charleston oral surgeon James B. Edwards. Meanwhile, Thurmond continued to win reelection as a Republican, and the party was able to establish itself as the dominant party in three of the state's six congressional districts. The state became strongly Republican in presidential politics, voting Democratic only for Jimmy Carter in 1976.

Notwithstanding the Edwards term as governor and their successes in federal elections, Republicans were unable to present a credible challenge for control of state government until well into the 1980s. Republican General Assembly membership remained a small minority (see Table 4). Democratic governor Richard W. Riley of Greenville, first elected in 1978 and reelected in 1982, placed a strong emphasis on improving the state's system of public education and enjoyed a high level of public approval. Then in 1986 Republicans nominated Campbell, the Fourth District congressman from Greenville, as their candidate for governor. Campbell faced Democrat Mike Daniel, Riley's lieutenant governor, and won a narrow victory, which is viewed in retrospect as the signal event presaging the successes of the South Carolina Republican party in the 1990s.

"It was a real turning point for the Republicans," conceded Don Fowler, former state Democratic chairman and later head of the Democratic National Committee. Unlike the fluke Edwards victory, Campbell's win came in a close, hard-fought contest over a credible Democratic opponent and an outwardly united opposition. It was the first time a Republican had beaten an undivided Democratic party. "Most people going in didn't think we could win. But I felt we could," Campbell said. "I knew it would be extremely tough because we had a sitting lieutenant governor and a governor from my home town. They pulled out everything they had. It was a brutal race. They took me apart at every chance. . . . But the harder they tried to tear me down, the stronger I was."[5]

The Campbell election campaign of 1986 reflects both the issues and the strategic base upon which South Carolina Republicans have been able to build

Table 4. Seats Won by Republicans in the South Carolina General Assembly, 1964–1996

Year	House		Senate	
1964	1	(0.8%)	0	(0.0%)
1966	17	(13.7)	6	(12.0)
1968	5	(4.0)	3	(6.0)
1970	11	(8.9)		
1972	21	(16.9)	3	(6.5)
1974	17	(13.7)		
1976	12	(9.6)	3	(6.5)
1978	16	(12.9)		
1980	18	(14.5)	5	(10.9)
1982	20	(16.1)		
1984	27	(21.7)	10	(21.7)
1986	32	(25.8)		
1988	37	(29.8)	11	(23.9)
1990	42	(33.9)		
1992	48	(38.7)	16	(34.8)
1994	60	(48.4)		
1996	70	(56.5)	20	(43.5)

Sources: Chester Bain, "Partisan Prelude," in William C. Havard, ed., *The Changing Politics of the South* (Baton Rouge, 1972), 631–32; William V. Moore, "Parties and Electoral Politics," in Luther F. Carter and David S. Mann, eds., *Government in the Palmetto State* (Columbia, S.C., 1984), 58; South Carolina Legislative Manual for 1984–1996.

Note: There are 124 house members, who serve two-year terms. Senate members serve four-year terms, except for those elected in 1966, who were chosen for two years under court-ordered reapportionment. The number of senators is 46, except in 1966 and 1968, when the number was increased temporarily to 50. The table does not take account of interim changes due to death, resignation, or elected legislators switching parties, of which the latter was especially numerous after the 1994 elections. The first Republican elected to the General Assembly in the modern era was Charles Boineau, who won a special election in Richland County in 1961. Boineau was defeated for reelection in 1962.

their present strength. A Greenville businessman first elected to Congress in 1978 after serving six years in the General Assembly and two years as an aide to Governor Edwards, Campbell presented himself as the aggressive reformer, saying the state government needed to be overhauled so South Carolina could keep up economically with its southeastern neighbors. He promised to promote business and economic development and attacked the Democrats as having been responsible for budget chaos and numerous tax increases. He stressed consumer issues such as high automobile insurance rates and weighed in on the so-called Democratic "good ol' boy" system in state government by which official positions were routinely exploited for personal gain. Near the close of the campaign he concentrated his attacks on leases for state office space in the Capitol Center, a downtown Columbia building that was being developed at the time by the chairman of the state Democratic party.

Campbell also showed a flair for the dramatic as he emphasized his commitment to fighting crime and drugs by submitting to a drug test and challenging Daniel to do the same. The Democratic nominee refused, showing some political courage in pointing out the complexity of the testing issue. In the end the "Jar Wars" controversy probably mattered little as the election turned on Campbell's ability to maximize Republican strength in the suburbs while making inroads into established areas of Democratic strength in rural South Carolina. Campbell carried traditionally Democratic Anderson County in the upstate by two thousand votes and won several rural counties: Barnwell and Calhoun in the Midlands near Columbia, and Pickens and Oconee counties in the upstate.

"People forget that those rural counties are conservative. As a congressman I represented Union and as a state representative I represented Laurens. Those rural counties were won by a lot of hard work. We targeted them, much to the surprise of the Democrats," Campbell said.[6] It is in counties such as Laurens and Union that the strength of Campbell's rural appeal can be seen most dramatically. Although he lost both counties by narrow margins, getting 48 percent in Union and 49 percent in Laurens, Campbell vastly improved on the GOP showing in 1978, when the Republican nominee, Congressman Edward L. Young, won only 28 percent in Union and 32 percent in Laurens against Democrat Riley, who took the election by a statewide margin of 61.4 percent to Young's 38.1 percent.

In the suburban counties, election returns showed that the well-tuned Republican voter-turnout machine produced astounding results and overwhelming margins for Campbell. In Lexington County (suburban Columbia), 71 percent of those registered turned out to vote, versus 59 percent statewide. Seventy-one percent of Lexington voters cast Republican ballots for governor and Campbell came out of Lexington with a margin of 16,000 votes, 3,000 more than Republican strategists had anticipated. Campbell carried his home county of Greenville by a similar margin of just over 16,000 votes and did almost as well in most other metropolitan counties. By contrast, Democratic strength was greatest in the rural black-majority counties where turnout was consistently below 60 percent of registered voters.

The key to Campbell's winning margin (51.0 percent to Daniel's 47.9 percent) lay in the incursions he made into the Democratic rural strongholds, especially in the predominantly white upstate. It was the defection of white Democrats in these counties, as noted above, that in the end gave Campbell his statewide edge. During the campaign, Campbell said he wanted to break up the "unnatural" and "unstable" Democratic coalition of rural whites and blacks by using wedge issues such as the Confederate battle flag. Campbell supported keeping the banner flying atop the statehouse dome. Daniel avoided directly answering a question about the flag during a debate. At the time, Campbell said in defense of the flag, "It is a part of our heritage [and should remain] as a reminder of where South Carolina has been and how it now has changed." Later, both sides agreed a combination of issues near the end of the campaign, and not the flag, probably pushed things Campbell's way—a Legislative Audit Council report critical of the state tax commission, stories about budget shortfalls, and the "good ol' boy" controversy surrounding the Capitol Center office tower.[7]

Campbell's 1986 victory was very much a personal one as Republican success was largely limited to the highly salient governor's race. Campbell was the only GOP candidate to win statewide office, and the party suffered a loss of one in the congressional delegation when Democrat Elizabeth J. (Liz) Patterson of Spartanburg, the daughter of Olin D. Johnston, a former governor and U.S. senator, won the Fourth District seat vacated by Campbell. Incumbent Democratic U.S. senator Ernest F. (Fritz) Hollings won a landslide victory over Republican challenger Henry D. McMaster, a former U.S. attorney who later became GOP state chairman. In elections for the 124-member state house of representatives, Republicans scored only a modest gain, from 29 to 32 seats (see Table 4). But Campbell's assumption of the reins of the state's highest office provided the foundation for more impressive GOP gains in the years ahead.

The day after his election, Campbell rejected speculation that he would use the governor's office to further the political growth of the state GOP. "I'm going to further the goals of South Carolina and South Carolinians," he said, "and if the Republican Party is furthered by that endeavor, then so be it." Yet it is clear that, unlike Edwards, Campbell was committed to using the governor's office to build the Republican party organization as a continuing major force in the state's politics. A decade later, he said his 1986 election had laid the groundwork to win Republican control of the legislature in 1994. "It served as a catalyst to energize Republicans. Our administration worked hard to get people to switch parties and build and expand the party."[8]

Campbell aides and, begrudgingly, Democrats agree. According to Ayres, "Campbell devoted a lot of time and energy to building the party as well as being a good governor." And, in the view of Crawford Cook, a Democratic consultant and close friend of Senator Hollings, "Campbell was a damn tough guy who got the governor's office and used it to build his party. He did a better job of that than any governor in my memory. Couple Campbell's efforts with what the Republicans have been doing on the national scene and, yeah, that makes the Campbell election a major factor in altering the political structure in South Carolina."[9]

The Republican party organization that first engineered Campbell's victory and was then nurtured by his stewardship was very much the product of the strategic vision and tactical proficiency of Lee Atwater, Campbell's longtime political ally. After helping elect Ronald Reagan president and reelect Campbell to Congress in 1980, Atwater left South Carolina for Washington, installing his youthful protégé Warren Tompkins as executive director of the state Republican party. Throughout the 1980s the South Carolina Republican organization benefited from Atwater's presence in Washington, which resulted in both financial and technical aid from the national GOP. With Campbell preparing to run for governor in early 1986, Tompkins resigned his party office to manage the upcoming campaign. He later became Governor Campbell's chief of staff. The Atwater influence in the campaign is clear in both the careful selection of issues to widen support among white voters and the scrupulous attention to the details of voter mobilization in friendly precincts.

Campbell's fiscal conservatism as well as his attention to reformist issues such as governmental restructuring made him a popular governor with South Carolina's conservative and increasingly middle-class electorate. Ayres contends that "Campbell proved it was safe to vote for a Republican, that a Republican could be a good strong pro-education, low-tax, pro-jobs governor. More than anything else, he made it acceptable to be Republican and vote for a Republican."[10]

As governor, Campbell focused his attention on business development, luring a major BMW automobile plant to the state in 1992 with a giant package of tax incentives. Although he did not promote any new initiatives, he emphasized education as a state budget priority, working closely with then–Arkansas governor Bill Clinton, with whom he had a friendly but competitive rivalry as both men served as New South governors and leaders of the National Governors' Association.[11]

While Campbell was strengthening the Republican organization and building the GOP's image as the party of good government, Democrats were slow to respond to the newly invigorated Republican challenge. The Democratic party coalition of blacks, rural whites, and urban liberals had prospered during Riley's two terms as governor (1979–1987) and seemed to have staved off the Republican challenge engendered by the political upheavals of the civil rights era. But with the governor's office now occupied by an aggressive and popular Republican, state Democrats seemed unable to mobilize their resources in the newly competitive environment. A succession of short-term Democratic chairmen from 1987 to 1990 deprived the party of the continuity necessary to launch the voter mobilization and candidate recruitment activities it needed to counter the Republican threat.

By 1990 Campbell's approval ratings were consistently in the 70 percent range and his reelection was a foregone conclusion, particularly in light of the weakness of the Democrats' response to growing Republican strength. The dearth of Democratic leadership and the party's organizational disarray[12] were clearly revealed by the party's failure to oppose Campbell with a credible opponent, a failure that made it possible for the GOP to concentrate on races for other state offices. With Campbell an apparent shoo-in for reelection in 1990, heavy-hitting Democrats such as Lieutenant Governor Nick A. Theodore, Charleston mayor Joseph P. (Joe) Riley, Jr., and Attorney General T. Travis Medlock chose not to enter the race. Without an organizational leadership willing or able to recruit a credible challenger, the Democratic party's nomination for governor was won by Theo Mitchell, a black state senator from Greenville. Mitchell was opposed in the Democratic primary by freshman state senator Ernie Passailaigue of Charleston, whose campaign was presumably premised on the sole, unstated proposition that the party needed a white, conservative alternative to Mitchell. Mitchell won with 60.1 percent of the vote in a Democratic primary, which turned out only 16.7 percent of registered voters, 43.1 percent of whom were African American. (By contrast, in 1986, 28.5 percent of registered voters, 37.4 percent of whom were African American, had voted in the Democratic primary.)[13]

Hopes were high for a good showing when Mitchell, the first black nominee for governor by a major party in South Carolina, won the right to oppose Campbell. But the Mitchell campaign never turned into anything like the efforts of such southern black candidates as Governor Douglas Wilder of Virginia or U.S. Senate candidate Harvey Gantt of North Carolina. Mitchell stepped into a pit with one much-quoted remark. In late September, Mitchell referred to some prominent blacks who supported Campbell as "house niggers" and "black prostitutes who have sold out their race, their dignity, their honor and their integrity." Campbell used the remarks as the reason for canceling a planned television debate. Despite the urging of influential Democrats, Mitchell refused to apologize for the remark.[14]

Race, which previously may have played a silent role in the Republicans' appeal to white voters, now emerged more openly to the GOP's advantage in the 1990 campaign. The Mitchell candidacy allowed the issue to remain a clear but unspoken component of the election's dynamics, thereby shielding the Republican party and its candidates from any hint of racism or race baiting. It was, according to one African American state legislator, "a gift from heaven for Republicans and made many white moderates embarrassed to be Democrats." Another political observer described the Mitchell candidacy as unfortunately confirming the worst white stereotypes of African American politicians. In the 1970s Mitchell had been implicated in a food stamp scandal. Adding to his difficulties, the Democratic nominee came across on the campaign trail as wooden and inarticulate. (In January 1995, Mitchell was expelled from the state senate after being imprisoned for failing to report a $154,000 cash payment he received from a client who was later convicted of drug trafficking.)[15]

Mitchell got little, if any, support from the Democratic establishment in his general election campaign. With the exception of Senator Hollings, who endorsed him enthusiastically, many prominent party leaders sat on the sidelines. The isolation of the Mitchell candidacy reflected the failure of the Democratic party leadership, both white and black, to act in the interest of the party during a critical period of electoral stress. While Campbell's reelection was virtually assured whoever the Democratic nominee might have been, the abandonment of the gubernatorial campaign by the Democratic leadership reflected a lack of commitment to the party as an institution. The superficiality of the party allegiance of many Democratic officeholders was to be revealed later by the large number of defections to the GOP as Republican strength grew.

Democrats attributed their plight to a lack of leadership, poor candidate training, and a dwindling "farm team." "You've got to train and have people ready to run. You've got to recruit. You've got to raise money," said Democratic activist Tenenbaum. "And more importantly, you've got to have persons in charge who have fire in their belly. People who really have made this important to them personally. We've had decent folks in leadership. But they haven't been willing to throw their body on the railroad tracks. The Democratic party is waiting for the great leader to emerge to lead us."[16]

In many other ways also the Campbell-Mitchell race was over before it began. Mitchell was able to raise and spend only $400,000 (versus nearly $2 million for Campbell), and, forsaken as he was by the party leadership, his campaign was desultory, poorly organized, and unfocused. Fowler, the longtime party leader, said, "I don't think it [the election] had any implication whatsoever beyond the fact that that was just Theo. His campaign was his own campaign and his style." The campaign was a definite contrast from beginning to end. While Campbell's entourage zipped across the state in two planes, Mitchell spent long hours traveling by van, giving the driver directions and toting his own lectern. It was clear to a political scientist who was consulted by Mitchell that the candidate's campaign was sorely strapped for resources and without effective organization.[17] Predictably, Campbell campaigned on a platform of reforming state government with stronger executive control and tougher ethics and disclosure laws, while Mitchell appealed to the poor and downtrodden, calling for more government assistance.

On election day, Campbell was able to plow into normally strong rural Democratic territory in winning 69.5 percent of the vote to Mitchell's 27.9 percent. The governor won all but three of the state's forty-six counties, including seven black-majority counties. Television exit polls estimated that the Republican governor received 14 percent of the vote among African Americans, a milestone for the state GOP.

The weakness of the Mitchell challenge enabled Republicans to concentrate on other statewide races, and their efforts were rewarded with three victories. Republican James M. (Jim) Miles of Greenville unseated a Democratic incumbent as secretary of state, and Commissioner of Agriculture D. Leslie (Les) Tindall, who had been twice elected as a Democrat, won reelection after switching to the GOP. He said he left the Democratic Party because it had "left me."[18]

Most significantly, Republicans captured a major state policymaking office when Barbara Nielsen defeated Democrat Charlie B. Williams, a three-term incumbent, for superintendent of education. Responding to the results of a poll taken in the last month of the campaign that showed Nielsen within striking distance of Williams, state Republican officials began, at Campbell's direction, to mobilize party resources to win the education post. They assigned the party's executive director, Tony Denny, to run her campaign. With a large share of GOP campaign resources at her command and the support of a business community disenchanted with the state education bureaucracy, Nielsen overwhelmed Williams with 55.6 percent of the vote. Reports of a scandal in the Department of Education may have been a key factor in Williams's loss, but former state Democratic chairman Albert McAlister said the loss by Williams "was more a vote against him and against the rate of progress in education" at the time.[19]

Despite their statewide successes, Republicans were unable to score gains in the 1990 election of the state house of representatives. Nevertheless, Republican numbers in both houses of the General Assembly were on the rise for other reasons. The 1988 elections had seen a five-seat Republican gain in the 124-member house from 32 to 37, while Democratic defections and special election victories had placed their number at 42 by 1990. The number of Republicans elected for four-year senate terms in the 1988 elections was 11, slightly less than one-fourth of the 46-member chamber.

The Republican successes of 1990 owed much to the Democratic disarray and disaffection exemplified by the Mitchell candidacy and its abandonment by the party establishment. But many Republicans attributed their appeal less to Democratic ineptness and more to their party's ideological compatibility with South Carolina's political culture. "We and conservative Democrats had a lot of the same beliefs. Conservative Democrats were made to feel comfortable in our party and they came over," Campbell contended in a 1996 interview. "The philosophy of South Carolina is a lot more conservative than the Democratic party. We see that day in and day out. And we continue to win at the local level."[20]

With a Republican president on the ballot for reelection, Republicans were poised for major gains in the contests for state offices in 1992. Their ambitions, however, were to be achieved only in part. South Carolina voters gave President Bush 48.0 percent of the vote to 39.9 percent for Clinton and 11.5 percent for Ross Perot.[21] For the Republican president, this was his second-highest state percentage, matching his showing in Alabama and exceeded only by the 49.7 percent he garnered in Mississippi. Clinton managed to carry twenty-two of the state's forty-six counties, most of them in the less-populated areas of the Lowcountry and in other traditionally Democratic rural areas. As expected, Bush ran well in the suburban enclaves of Lexington and Greenville and in the coastal counties. Exit polls showed a high level of racial polarization. White South Carolinians cast 60 percent of their votes for Bush; black South Carolinians voted 90 percent for Clinton.[22]

Despite Bush's success, Republicans fell short in their 1992 challenge of Hollings, the four-term Democratic incumbent who turned 70 on the first day of the year. Their nominee was former First District congressman Thomas F. (Tommy) Hartnett of Charleston. Hartnett had lost a close race to Nick Theodore for lieutenant governor in 1986. Throughout the campaign, Hartnett and Hollings, two caustic Charlestonians, harshly flailed away at each other. Hollings likened his opponent to the television clown Bozo and called him a hypocrite, a fraud, and at one point accused him of unethical conduct. Hartnett portrayed Hollings as an arrogant, entrenched incumbent who had become insensitive. Toward the end of the campaign, he attacked Hollings for cosponsoring gay rights legislation. "They told more malicious lies," Hollings said of the Republicans. "Lee Atwaterism is alive and well in this state."[23]

On election day, Hollings held firm with a bare majority of 50.1 percent to Hartnett's 46.9 percent. The fact that 3 percent of the vote was divided between two minor party candidates is a small indicator of voter disgust with both candidates, who together conducted one of the most uncivil and acrimonious campaigns in recent memory. During the campaign, Hollings had demonstrated that incumbency had its advantages. The senator raised significantly more money than his challenger and used it to bury his opponent in television advertising.

In the 1992 congressional races, two new members were chosen, each signaling an important new development in the state's politics. Democrat James E. (Jim) Clyburn easily won the Sixth District, the state's new black-majority district that stretches over much of the eastern half of the state, from Charleston through parts of Columbia and into the northeastern counties known as the Pee Dee. Clyburn rolled up 65.3 percent of the vote to become the state's first African American member of Congress in this century. His polls showed him getting 30 percent of the vote among whites and his margin suggests that he may have indeed gotten that much.

But the surprise of election night was Republican Robert D. (Bob) Inglis's upset win over three-term incumbent Elizabeth Patterson in the Fourth District. First elected in 1986 in a conservative, Republican-leaning district, Democrat Patterson had survived two strong Republican challenges by combining effective campaigning skills with a moderate-to-conservative voting record. Inglis, a Greenville lawyer, in making his first bid for political office spent only two hundred thousand dollars, far less than the typical challenger needs to spend to unseat a congressional incumbent. Strongly supporting term limits and promising to serve only three terms himself, Inglis ran a low-visibility, door-to-door "stealth" campaign that apparently lulled Patterson into complacency.

By all odds, the Fourth District should have been represented by a Republican, as it was for eight years until Campbell ran for governor in 1986. But Patterson, a former state senator from Spartanburg, portrayed herself convincingly as a fiscal conservative; for example, the *National Journal* rated her the most conservative Democrat in Congress.[24] Inglis won with 50.3 percent of the vote to Patterson's 47.5 percent. Stunned by her defeat, Patterson blamed it on the Christian Coalition and what she said was its misrepresentation of her stands on abortion, school prayer, and gay rights. (Incidentally, as of mid-1998 Congressman Inglis was mounting a strong challenge to Senator Hollings's effort to win a sixth full term.)

The 1992 elections for the South Carolina senate and house of representatives took place under a post-1990 census redistricting that had been controlled by Democratic majorities in both legislative chambers. These remaps were later thrown out by a federal court and replaced by district lines which, particularly in the house of representatives, worked more to the advantage of Republicans. But even with the first new districting system favoring Democrats, population growth since 1980 in suburban areas and along the coast had brought more Republicans into the electorate, many of them upscale migrants from other states. These demographic changes enabled the GOP to score important gains in the 1992 elections for the General Assembly.[25] In the house, the GOP defeated four Democratic incumbents and gained six seats, bringing their seat total to 50, compared with the Democrats' 73. In the senate, Republicans defeated one Democratic incumbent and picked up two open seats formerly held by Democrats to bring their total membership to 16 in the 46-member body. (See Table 4.) All three Republican senate acquisitions, one each in the suburbs of Greenville, Columbia, and Charlotte, showed the party's increasing reach into the outlying regions of the metropolitan counties.

Democrat Fowler attributed the GOP growth to race and what he called the "revolution in the economy." The booming economy had created a whole new generation of voters in the state who tended to be Republicans, Fowler noted, adding: "And a lot of white people revolted against the perceived policies of the Democratic party on race. And that's a major issue. It has been, perhaps less, but it's still real."[26]

THE 1994 ELECTIONS: A REMARKABLE GOP BREAKTHROUGH

While 1992 saw the GOP make important incremental gains, the elections of 1994 constitute what is now the high water mark of the Republican surge in the Palmetto State. Indeed, the political earthquake that shook the nation that year produced a veritable tidal wave in South Carolina. With the election of Beasley, South Carolina had named a Republican governor for the fourth time since 1974.

In retrospect, the political year of 1994 seems to have begun more auspiciously for the Democrats than for the GOP. With Campbell ineligible for a third term, Democrats appeared to have a surfeit of strong contenders for the state's top office. These included two-term lieutenant governor Nick Theodore, Charleston's youthful, energetic mayor Joe Riley, and Attorney General Travis Medlock. Republicans, on the other hand, seemed to be without a worthy successor to Campbell. The two leading contenders were First District congressman Arthur Ravenel, Jr., considered by many Republican partisans to be too outspoken and too liberal, and Ravenel's congressional predecessor Hartnett, who bore the onus of a loser.

For Republicans, the political equation was drastically altered by Beasley's entry into the race. Beasley had served in the house since 1979 as a Democrat from Darlington County in the largely agricultural and traditionally Democratic

Pee Dee region in the state's northeast quadrant. Something of a wunderkind, Beasley was only twenty-two years old when first elected to the house while a student at Clemson. As a young legislator he developed a reputation for fast living, but eventually became a born-again Christian, married, and began a family. In 1991 he was elected speaker pro tem, a largely honorific office but one which placed its incumbent in a good position to succeed to the speakership. During his final term in the General Assembly, Beasley announced that he was switching to the GOP and would not seek reelection to the house in 1992.

At the time of his switch, Beasley charged that the national Democratic party was headed toward "socialism." He said Democrats were promoting a philosophy that government was the answer to everything, adding, "I believe the government is not the solution for all of man's, for all people's problems." Later, he said, "The Democratic party failed to recognize that its liberal policies were offending pro-family values that southerners maintain. I came to realize that the Democratic party was committed to a liberal agenda that was bad for families and for America. And I came to the realization that this trend was not going to change anytime soon."[27]

The widespread political speculation was that the thirty-five-year-old Beasley would seek the Republican nomination for lieutenant governor as a platform for a later bid for the governorship. But Campbell political aides, concerned that neither Ravenel nor Hartnett would be able to win the general election, urged the former legislator to run for governor. Thus Beasley entered the race with the support of both the party's powerful Christian right as well as the backing of much of the mainstream Republican organization that Campbell had built. He was an immediate favorite to be in a primary runoff against either Hartnett or Ravenel.

In the first primary Beasley came close to winning the nomination outright, getting 47.2 percent of the vote to Ravenel's 31.9 percent. Although Hartnett endorsed Ravenel in the runoff and both mainstream challengers attacked the front-runner for his association with the Christian Coalition, Beasley cruised to a 57.6 percent landslide victory over Ravenel.

Roberta Combs, state director of the Christian Coalition, worked quietly for Beasley. She sat in on most strategy sessions, huddling often with Warren Tompkins and Bob McAlister, products of the Campbell administration and the master strategists of the Beasley campaign. The Coalition provided its mailing list of 75,000 members and manned phone banks for Beasley. These efforts no doubt contributed to the heavy turnout in both the first Republican primary and the runoff, presaging Republican strength in the coming general election. With competitive races for governor on both ballots, Republican participation was 252,000 in the first primary, compared to 257,000 in the Democratic primary. In the runoff, Republican participation actually exceeded that in the Democratic primary, 232,000 to 224,000.[28]

On the Democratic side, Theodore and Riley were locked in an acrimonious struggle that would seriously weaken the party's position in the general election. In the first primary Theodore won 49.6 percent of the vote, just shy of the majority necessary for the nomination. Riley was second with 38.2 percent of the vote, with Medlock a distant third. The Charleston mayor, known throughout his political career for his tenacity, ignored Theodore's near victory and on election night launched a vigorous runoff campaign. With Theodore from Greenville and Riley from Charleston, the runoff had strong elements of the old upstate-Lowcountry conflict that had long been a feature of the state's politics.[29] Much of the Democratic business establishment and party old guard were with Theodore. Riley enjoyed the backing of younger Democrats and the Lowcountry business community.

The son of Greek immigrants, the sixty-six-year-old Theodore had risen from humble beginnings to serve two terms as a state senator and in 1986 was elected to the first of two terms as lieutenant governor. Although Theodore had been identified as a "Young Turk" when he first entered the General Assembly, long service in the state house had given him a reputation as a product of the Democratic establishment and of the "good ol' boy" system, which Campbell had so successfully attacked as unresponsive, wasteful, and corrupt. Theodore had little of the progressive, reformist New South image that Campbell had been able to project. In contrast, Riley was a scion of the Charleston establishment who at fifty-three had served six terms as mayor and was nationally known as a policy innovator in urban development. He had also received considerable positive media exposure during the recovery from Hurricane Hugo, which had devastated parts of the state in 1989.

Theodore won by a razor-thin margin of only 4,000 votes out of 224,000 cast. The Democratic primary not only bitterly divided the party but also produced the nominee least able to counter Beasley's strengths and exploit his weaknesses. Theodore was ill equipped to counter Beasley's youth and reformist image. A preeminent example of the best kind of public servant produced by traditional South Carolina politics, Theodore had developed a reputation for dependability, decency, and the respect for the views of others that was needed to bargain and build coalitions in the General Assembly. Unfortunately, however, his association with traditional Democratic politics undermined the progressive appeal he required to attack effectively Beasley's association with the religious right. Moreover, Theodore's nice-guy image was accompanied by the perception that he was a lightweight, a perception that seems to have been rooted in his manner. He had a circuitous way of answering questions, which made him the target of jokes. Critics called him "Thick Neodore." In a televised debate during the primary campaign, Riley demanded to know how Theodore could run the government when the state auditor had cited him six times for inadequate accounting procedures in his six-person lieutenant governor's staff. Theodore shrugged off the criticism, terming the finding "bookkeeping errors." He added: "I'm not running for governor because I'm the smartest or consider myself smarter than anyone else. I'm running because I can bring people together and help them reach their full potential." Several key members of the business establishment, such as banker Bob Royall, switched from having supported Riley to supporting the Republican Beasley, whom they argued would better continue the reformist image they believed the state had achieved—with consequent payoffs in economic development—under Campbell.[30]

Although his political base was in the religious right, Beasley's general election campaign was conducted primarily on the economic and neopopulist issues that had led to Republican successes in previous elections: cutting back on taxes, reducing the size of government, and getting tough on crime and welfare recipients. He denounced the "good ol' boy" system that had run state government for years, proposing that citizens be allowed to vote on all general tax increases. "South Carolina has been controlled for too long by tax and spend liberals who think that raising taxes and throwing your money around will make problems go away," he proclaimed. He emphasized personal responsibility, warning parents they would be held accountable if their children brought weapons to school. He proposed that welfare benefits be limited to two years, declaring that those who refused to work or be trained for employment can say "farewell to welfare." In an attempt to reassure those worried about the religious right's sway with him, Beasley downplayed social issues and promised audiences that "no group will have undue influence over me."[31] His slogan "Putting Families First" conveyed enough of the message of social conservatism to placate his supporters allied with the Christian Coalition.

Theodore emphasized his record as a fiscal conservative in the General Assembly and proposed a referendum on a state lottery to provide money for education. In seeking to gain support among economic conservatives who were apprehensive about Beasley's social agenda, Theodore emphasized his pro-choice stance on abortion. Tying together his proposal to have the voters decide on a state lottery with his position in favor of a woman's right to choose, Theodore portrayed himself to the voters as "the candidate of choice."[32]

There were a number of important voter groups, including economic conservatives, who had enthusiastically supported Campbell but were unhappy with the choices for governor presented to them in 1994. Beasley's connections to the religious right, his undistinguished career in the General Assembly, and his recent conversion to the GOP made him unattractive to many mainstream Republicans. As one unknown Republican wag put it, referring to Theodore's intellectual reputation and Beasley's evangelical connections, "It has come down to a choice between Elmer Fudd and Elmer Gantry."[33]

Despite his liabilities, Theodore almost pulled out a victory. Beasley won by a narrow margin, 50.4 percent to Theodore's 47.9 percent, the winner running behind all but one of the other six Republicans elected to statewide constitutional offices in 1994. Beasley was less warmly received in the Republicans' key metropolitan base than Campbell had been in 1986. Although Beasley did well in metropolitan and suburban counties, his support there was much less impressive than Campbell's had been eight years earlier. Across the ten largest counties, Beasley ran behind Campbell by three percentage points, 52 percent to 55 percent, in part because of Theodore's showing in the Republican upstate, especially his home county of Greenville. Also, Beasley's position on abortion and his association with the religious right played less well in these more urban and suburban counties than they did in the rural areas of the state.

In fact, Beasley's strength among whites in rural and small-town counties was enough to offset the votes he lost in the traditionally Republican suburbs, thus providing the GOP nominee with his narrow margin of victory. He ran three points ahead of Campbell's earlier showing in these counties, winning 49.5 percent of the vote. This was partly due to Beasley's strength in his home region, the traditionally Democratic Pee Dee, which he carried with just over 51 percent of the vote. But Beasley also did well in some of the other counties of rural South Carolina, particularly upstate, where the population is predominantly white and Christian conservatives are especially numerous. While Campbell carried only seventeen counties, mostly metropolitan, in his 1986 win, Beasley carried twenty-three counties, including the traditionally Democratic upstate counties of Edgefield, Newberry, and Saluda.

The depth of the Republican appeal in 1994 is revealed by GOP victories in other statewide races. The three incumbent Republicans—Barbara Nielsen, superintendent of education; Jim Miles, secretary of state; and Les Tindall, agriculture commissioner—all won landslide victories of 57 percent or more. Newcomer Robert L. (Bob) Peeler, a Gaffney dairyman, captured the lieutenant governor's office with 53.4 percent of the vote, and Republicans elected their first attorney general when Charles M. (Charlie) Condon, a former Charleston solicitor, won with 55.2 percent of the vote. All of these statewide Republican victors ran ahead of Beasley because their candidacies fared better in the Republican suburban base. The only GOP statewide winner to run behind Beasley was Richard A. Eckstrom, who narrowly defeated seven-term Democratic state treasurer Grady L. Patterson with 49.6 percent of the vote to Patterson's 47.1 percent. Like Beasley, Eckstrom was associated with the Christian Coalition.

Democrats won only two statewide constitutional offices. Incumbent comptroller general Earle Morris won reelection to a fifth term with 53.3 percent of the vote over Republican challenger Dell Baker. In the open-seat election for adjutant general, the head of the South Carolina National Guard, Democrat Stanley Spears, easily defeated Republican Thomas Hendrix. Hendrix promised a shakeup of the Guard, a near sacrosanct state institution, and was opposed by the state's political establishment, including many prominent Republicans. In 1995 Spears switched to the GOP, leaving Morris as the only Democrat holding a statewide constitutional office.[34]

In the 1994 house elections, Republicans gained eight seats, winning three open seats formerly held by Democrats and defeating five incumbents. The seats won by Republicans were geographically dispersed across the upstate, midlands, and Lowcountry regions. With the GOP thus two seats shy of a majority, Democrats were no longer able to keep their finger in the dike. Within a week of the election, Representatives Harold Worley of North Myrtle Beach and C. D. Chamblee of Anderson announced that they were switching to the GOP. By the time the house organized in January, 1995, further switches had brought the number of Republicans to sixty-eight, assuring them of control for the first time since Reconstruction.

The Kingfish for the Republicans was Representative William D. (Billy) Boan of Kershaw, who as a Democrat had chaired the influential house ways and means committee. Boan lost his seat as chair when the GOP gained control of the chamber. Former house speaker Bob Sheheen of Camden, a Democrat, remarked, "Billy was obviously very uncomfortable with not being at the table when things were being done." House Democratic leader James H. (Jim) Hodges, a close personal friend, said Boan was making a serious mistake in switching parties. Hodges, who became the Democratic nominee for governor in 1998, said the public would view Boan and other switchers as "opportunists who bailed out on the Democratic Party at a time when it needed them to stand strong. These days I think one of the things people are looking for is consistency in their public officials."[35] Boan's constituents were apparently undisturbed by his defection. He was comfortably reelected as a Republican in 1996.

The Components of Republican Success

The across-the-board Republican electoral successes of 1994 represented a long-awaited and, for the party leadership, much-delayed dividend for the GOP, which by then had clearly established parity with the Democrats in commanding the partisan loyalties of South Carolina voters. Table 5 presents the party identification of South Carolina registered voters surveyed from 1990 to 1996, illustrating remarkable stability in the 1990s. Each sounding found the electorate almost evenly divided among Republicans, Democrats, and independents. Republicans are consistently two to three percentage points ahead of the Democrats in identifiers, with the GOP's high water mark coming in 1994, when almost 37 percent of the sample identified themselves as Republicans.

Table 5 also starkly displays the sharp racial polarization of the South Carolina electorate. As expected, fewer than 10 percent of blacks identify themselves as Republicans. The percentage of African Americans who are Democrats falls within the 60 to 70 percent range, but the percentage of blacks identifying themselves as independents has increased somewhat over the decade, apparently stabilizing at just under 30 percent. Among whites, a partisan consensus has emerged that is almost as impressive as that among blacks. White identification with the Democratic party never edges above 19 percent, while GOP identifiers are consistently 45 percent or more, reaching 50 percent in 1994. Independents constitute from 35 to 39 percent of the white electorate.

These data clearly show that the Republican surge of the 1990s has been based upon the party's strong appeal to white South Carolinians. Since the 1960s, this appeal has been centered in the middle-class suburbs that have sprouted at a steadily increasing rate around the Palmetto State's central cities. In both General Assembly and statewide elections, Republican strength first appeared in the counties that comprise the metropolitan areas surrounding the state's largest cities—Greenville, Columbia, and Charleston. As the orbit of the central cities has expanded and as metropolitan development in neighboring states has spurred development in border counties, Republican voting tendencies have spread accordingly. Thus Republicans now dominate in Oconee and Pickens counties (suburban Greenville), Dorchester and Berkeley counties (suburban Charleston), and in border counties such as York and Aiken (respectively, suburban Charlotte, North Carolina, and Augusta, Georgia). The expansion of the Republican metropolitan base reflects the inexorable growth of southern middle-class society that Earl and Merle Black have identified as central to the recent political development of the South.[36] In South Carolina, this suburban base has been further widened by explosive development in the

Table 5. Party Identification in South Carolina by Race, 1990–1996

	Whites			Blacks			Total		
Year	Dem.	Rep.	Ind.	Dem.	Rep.	Ind.	Dem.	Rep.	Ind.
1990	16%	45%	39%	64%	6%	29%	31%	34%	36%
1992	18	43	39	68	10	22	32	34	35
1994	19	50	31	60	8	33	32	37	32
1996	18	47	35	66	6	29	33	35	33

Source: Institute of Public Affairs, University of South Carolina.

Note: Responses are from a statewide sample of 700–800 citizens given a standard party idenfication question, "Generally speaking, do you consider yourself a Republican, Democrat, Independent, or what?" The institute conducts several such surveys each year; the figures given are from the last survey of each year, usually conducted in November.

coastal counties and an infusion of migrants from other parts of the country to the retirement centers along the coast, such as Myrtle Beach and Hilton Head.

For both suburban middle-class voters and the entrepreneurs and retirees in the coastal counties, the Republican appeal is primarily economic, emphasizing reform and restructuring of state government, cutbacks in state bureaucracy, paring of social programs, and reforms on such consumer issues as automobile insurance. Over and above their liking for these Republican positions, suburban and coastal voters have been attracted to the fresher images of the GOP and its candidates, who have often successfully presented themselves as alternatives to the rural-based Democratic oligarchy that has long ruled South Carolina politics.

Yet from the very beginning this reformist image cultivated by the Republicans has coexisted with a less explicit, more retrograde racial appeal rooted in the state's darker past of oppression and segregation. Racial anxieties have so dominated the state's political culture that V. O. Key saw fit to subtitle the South Carolina chapter of his classic 1949 study "The Politics of Color." It is perhaps inevitable that the Republican appeal to South Carolina whites has had a racial component that belies the party's otherwise reformist image. While the national Democratic party moved from its earlier policy of tolerance for southern segregation to an aggressive stance in favor of civil rights, Republican and third-party alternatives drew their greatest strength within South Carolina's virtually all-white electorate from the Lowcountry and black-belt counties historically most responsive to segregationist appeals. After the reenfranchisement of blacks by the 1965 Voting Rights Act gave rise to a significant African American electorate, especially in the Lowcountry, Republican strength in the predominantly black rural counties of the Lowcountry declined substantially and began to shift to the upstate counties with predominantly white populations.[37]

It is significant that, as noted above, most longtime Republican activists date the party's modern birth to the enthusiasm stirred by Barry Goldwater's 1964 presidential campaign. In South Carolina as in the rest of the Deep South, Goldwater's states' rights message and his vote against the Civil Rights Act of 1964 resonated well with the racial concerns of many white voters. But for South Carolinians the racial reading of the Goldwater message was made especially clear when Senator Thurmond, the archdefender of segregation, switched to the GOP.

Racial concerns have continued to reinforce Republican voting tendencies within the state's white electorate. But by the early 1970s the GOP ceased overt racial appeals and began to nurture a more youthful, reformist image grounded in the ideology of economic conservatism. With many of the state's blacks clustered near the lower end of the socioeconomic scale and firmly in the Democratic camp, this message had an unavoidable, if unintended, racial component for some white voters. And, in South Carolina as in the rest of the nation, the Republican emphasis on government waste and rising crime fit comfortably with white perceptions of black lawlessness and abuse of government largesse funded largely with taxes paid by whites.[38] Moreover, the GOP and its candidates have from time to time more openly played to white South Carolinians' apparent nostalgia for a white supremacist past. Campbell's 1986 declaration of support for the continued flying of the Confederate battle flag over the State House served to express the GOP's sympathy with any latent racial separatist sentiments. And in a flagrant lapse into the demagoguery of the past, Republicans placed a referendum on the flag on the 1994 GOP primary ballot, which produced a three-to-one vote in favor of keeping the secessionist standard above the State House.

It is hard to estimate the precise role that race has played in the development of the Republican party's dominance among white voters in South Carolina. In a state where race and economic status are so closely intertwined, it is difficult to separate the two in the absence of overt racial appeals. As one political scientist observed, the Republican message is framed in economic terms but is interpreted as racial by many white voters, particularly those residing outside of the metropolitan areas. Thus the margin of victory for Republicans in key statewide races can at times be attributed to their ability to reach out beyond the middle-class suburbs and win votes among the less affluent whites in the countryside. Two obvious cases in point are the narrow victories by Campbell in 1986 and Beasley in 1994. One recent study suggests that the racial component of the GOP's appeal is substantial. In a 1994 exit poll of over six hundred voters in Aiken County, fully 78 percent of those who identified themselves as Republicans could be described as "angry whites," agreeing with the statement that "we have gone too far in pushing equal rights in this country."[39]

While Republican candidates have clearly benefited from the traditional racial anxieties of South Carolina whites, GOP electoral strength has also been bolstered by the emergence and growth of religious conservatives as a major force in the state's electoral politics. The Christian Coalition, television evangelist Pat Robertson's grass-roots organization claiming a South Carolina membership of 125,000, is the dominant force within the state Republican party organization. The Coalition's adherents control most county party organizations as well as the state executive committee, and they have a working majority on most major issues that come before the party organization.[40] The Coalition and its allies have been instrumental in promoting the political careers of several prominent GOP leaders, most notably Governor Beasley and Congressman Inglis. The organization's massive voter mobilization efforts have aided numerous GOP candidates. In 1996 the Coalition distributed over a million of its voter guides in twenty-five hundred churches across the state. The guides, ostensibly nonpartisan summaries of candidate issue positions, are distributed the Sunday before an election. They focus primarily on the social issues emphasized by the Christian conservatives, such as abortion and school prayer, but usually also include issues that are part of the more secular Republican agenda, such as term limits, taxes, and gun control.

While Coalition members are in general agreement with other Republicans on most economic and social questions,[41] the group's doctrinaire stance on its own core issues has become a major source of tension within the party. Many Republicans in the party's traditional middle-class constituency oppose the Coalition's position against all abortions, its advocacy of a return to school prayer, and its affinity for perceived threats to public education such as school vouchers. As longtime Columbia-area Republican activist George Shissias puts it, "I didn't know that being a conservative meant that you were anti-woman, anti-child, and anti–public schools."[42]

Other mainstream Republicans may be less passionate in their opposition to the Coalition's policy positions but are nevertheless concerned about the strategic consequences of the Coalition's influence on the party's agenda. These Republicans fear that an overemphasis on social concerns may weaken the GOP's base in the business community and undermine its economic appeal to the state's growing suburban middle class. In addition to disagreements over issues and priorities, the tension between religious conservatives and traditional Republicans also reflects differences in political culture and style. The strength of the religious right is in its mobilization of voters and activists at the grass roots. This grass-roots populist constituency has not always coalesced well with the corporate elite that has provided much of the financial support for Republican campaigns. These differences have been most apparent on the controversy over the Confederate battle flag, which we discuss further below. And some mainstream Republicans complain that Christian conservatives, while contributing virtually no money to the party and its candidates, concentrate most of their energies on capturing control of the party organization rather than on defeating Democrats.[43]

Notwithstanding the reservations of some in the party establishment, the strength of religious conservatives within the GOP has led most Republican statewide candidates to embrace the policy positions of the Christian Coalition. This has given Democrats an opportunity to target issues such as education and choice and thereby make inroads into the GOP's middle-class constituency. To exploit this potential GOP weakness fully, Democrats will have to recruit attractive candidates, invigorate their chronically ineffectual party organization,[44] and prevent tensions within their biracial electoral coalition from erupting into open divisions. They will also have to present a moderate, reformist image to South Carolina's predominantly conservative electorate, a task that may present some difficulties as Democratic party activists have become increasingly differentiated ideologically from their Republican counterparts over the years.[45]

The 1996 Elections: Modest Democratic Gains

In the 1996 General Assembly elections, especially those for the state senate, Democrats made modest gains that seemed to reverse the recent Republican tide. Republicans won 16 seats in the senate elections of 1992, but by the time of the 1996 elections Democratic defections and special elections had brought their number to 21, three short of a chamber majority. The state Republican leadership set its sights on winning a senate majority, targeting several Democratic incumbents in districts regarded as vulnerable to a Republican takeover. But the GOP fell far short of its goal, failing to unseat any Democratic incumbents and scoring only one takeover, that of a seat held by an independent. In a reversal of recent electoral outcomes, it was the Democrats who scored gains in senate elections, picking up two seats to bring their majority from 24 to 26. Republicans suffered a net loss of one seat, dropping from 21 to 20 members.

The 1996 elections for the state house of representatives ended in a virtual draw. Republicans gained two seats, from 68 to 70, but these came at the expense of two of the chamber's three independents. The number of Democrats remained 53. Both political parties declared victory in the 1996 General Assembly elections, but the Democrats, having reversed the recent trend of Republican gains, probably had the greater cause for celebration. As senate majority leader John C. Land III of Manning put it, "We have stopped the bleeding."[46]

Democrats could also celebrate Congressman John Spratt's relatively comfortable 1996 victory for reelection in the Fifth District, which included Rock Hill, Sumter and points in between. Calling the strong showing in 1994 of his Republican opponent, businessman Larry L. Bigham, a "wake-up call," Spratt conducted an aggressive, well-financed campaign to again win over Bigham, this time by a more comfortable margin, 54.1 percent to 45.3 percent. The other congressional incumbents were reelected easily in 1996, leaving the delegation with four Republicans and two Democrats.

However, 1996 also saw the continuation of Republican successes in state-wide elections for federal office. At age ninety-three, Thurmond won reelection to his eighth Senate term, winning 53.4 percent of the vote against Democratic challenger Elliott Springs Close, who had 44.0 percent. Thurmond's margin was his smallest winning margin since he was first elected to the Senate in 1954. The forty-two-year-old Close, an heir to the Springs Mills textile fortune who had never run for public office, tried to make Thurmond's age and fitness for office a central issue. In the end, this was not enough to convince voters to abandon the state's most prominent political institution.

In the 1996 presidential election, South Carolina cast 49.8 percent of its presidential ballots for Bob Dole; only six states gave Dole a higher percentage of their votes, preserving the Palmetto State's reputation as one of the nation's most Republican states in presidential elections. President Clinton received 44.0 percent, with Ross Perot winning only 5.6 percent.[47]

The 1996 General Assembly elections resulted in little partisan change, largely because redistricting, coupled with voting patterns highly polarized along racial lines, had made most districts safe for one or the other political party. As noted above, after the 1990 census state legislative redistricting was controlled by the Democratic majority in both chambers, which, in the traditional manner, adopted a scheme that maximized Democratic representation. This outcome protected the seats of most incumbent white Democrats and only marginally increased the number of black Democrats in both houses. The plan was challenged in federal court by both Republicans and the state NAACP. In 1993 a federal court voided the plan as inconsistent with the minority representation provisions of the Voting Rights Act. An unlikely coalition of Republicans and black Democrats in the General Assembly then passed a plan to remap house districts for 1994 so as to maximize the number of black house members. Inevitably, the plan also increased the number of white Republican districts, leading to both the significant Republican gains of 1994 and an increase in black house membership from 18 to 24.

When the senate redistricted for the 1996 elections, black and white Democrats, apparently chastened by the results of the 1994 elections, held together and pushed through a remapping of existing districts that was less injurious to Democratic interests than the one adopted earlier by the house. Although the alliance between black Democrats and white Republicans in the house had increased the number of African Americans in the chamber, it also helped produce a Republican house majority and a relative decline in influence for black legislators, who were now in the Democratic minority. Blacks found that the new Republican majority was unwilling to cooperate on issues of concern to their constituents. The reapportionment coalition was a "one-issue alliance, a quick marriage and a quick divorce," according to Senator Darrell Jackson. Jackson led the senate effort to ensure that whites and blacks in the Democratic senate majority held together on reapportionment. As a result, the remap gave rise to an increase in the number of African American senators from six to eight, but its more moderate adjustments fell short of maximizing black representation, thereby protecting the seats of more of the chamber's white Democrats.[48] Thus the Democratic successes in the 1996 senate elections, as compared with what happened in the house, are in part attributable to greater cooperation between black and white Democrats in drawing district lines in the senate.

Ironically, parts of both redistricting schemes were invalidated by the federal courts in light of the subsequent U.S. Supreme Court rulings on racial gerrymander. A federal district court ordered the redrawing of six house and three senate districts to bring them into compliance with the new judicial standard. To accomplish this remap, the General Assembly altered the lines of twenty-two house and senate districts, and new elections were held in them in November 1997. Republicans scored two surprising victories, unseating two incumbents, one each in the house and the senate. Both were districts in which the racial composition had shifted from majority black to majority white. And both saw the Republican challenger unseat an African American legislator newly elected in 1996.

The Politics of Color Continues

The redistricting controversies of the 1990s brought to the surface the underlying and enduring tensions between black and white Democrats. They also revealed the fragility of the Democratic electoral coalition on issues that affect directly the racial distribution of political power and advantage. Black Democrats have long observed that their white fellow Democrats, while more than happy to win election to political power with the votes of black citizens, have been more than a little reluctant to share that power once in office. Such sentiments were at the heart of the decision by black house Democrats to bolt their party and strike a deal with Republicans to increase minority representation in the 1994 reapportionment. Although black leaders in the senate refused a similar deal with Republicans for the 1996 redistricting, African Americans still perceive that their role in the Democratic party remains as loyal and dependent followers rather than leaders.

African Americans who have sought statewide elective office in South Carolina have been universally unsuccessful. Only two blacks have won the Democratic nomination for state constitutional office: Mitchell for governor in 1990 and Milton Kimpson for secretary of state in 1994. In both cases the Democratic nominee faced a heavily favored Republican incumbent and credible white Democratic opponents failed to offer themselves for the nomination. In a handful of other cases, African Americans have unsuccessfully sought contested Democratic nominations for state office, most notably the two tries for secretary of state by Jim Clyburn prior to his election to the U.S. House in 1992 from the new black-majority Sixth District. At the time of his statewide bids, Clyburn was state human affairs commissioner and known as a cautious moderate. Yet he failed in 1986 and again in 1990 to wrest the nomination for this relatively minor office from incumbent John T. Campbell, whose "good ol' boy" reputation contributed to his decisive defeat by Republican Jim Miles in 1990.

African American disenchantment with the Democratic party is reflected in a significant drop in black voter participation in the 1980s and 1990s. Trends show that the black proportion of the electorate reached its high point at a quarter of the votes cast in 1984 and 1986, near the end of Democrat Dick Riley's two terms as governor. Since the Campbell victory in 1986, the percentage of blacks voting has gradually dropped, reaching a low of 21 percent in the Republican year of 1994.[49]

Black leaders say that for many African Americans, as long as blacks do not fully share political power, it makes little difference which group of white elites, Democratic or Republican, holds that power, especially when neither offers openly segregationist candidates and there is no "cause" as there was in the salad days of the civil rights movement.[50] Black access to state and federal elective office in South Carolina has so far been limited only to legislative districts in which African Americans constitute a solid voting majority.

Thus far a black candidate has yet to emerge for statewide elective office who can fully overcome the unfavorable stereotypes of blacks and black politicians prevalent among whites. For many whites, black politicians are ipso facto "liberal," a label to be avoided at all costs when appealing for white votes. Moreover, black politicians are viewed by some whites as the products of manipulative political machines within the African American community, trading support for welfare programs and access to government jobs for the automatically Democratic votes of their constituents. According to black leaders, a credible African American candidate for statewide office must work against this stereotype. For example, to win a significant number of white votes, a black candidate has to be moderate to conservative and, in the words of Senator Jackson, "must eliminate all reasons for whites to vote against him other than race."

The effective black candidate who is unassailable on ideological or personal grounds can, according to Jackson, "turn the race issue the other way and appeal to the conscience of South Carolinians." Rickey Hill, an African American political scientist from South Carolina, notes further that the effective black statewide candidate must appeal to migrants from other states and to young voters, asserting that persons in these categories are less wedded to the state's racial past.[51]

The court-ordered changes in the apportionment system that the state is currently undergoing may make the emergence of such a candidate more likely. Some of the African American incumbents whose General Assembly districts have been redrawn will be more dependent than they have been in the past upon white voters to win reelection, increasing the likelihood that black candidates will develop a political style conducive to cross-racial appeals. And there is a possibility that Clyburn's Sixth District will have to be redrawn after the 2000 census to include more white voters if a 1996 court challenge is renewed. The suit, filed by two Florence Republicans, was settled, leaving the black-majority intact, when the state conceded that it had impermissibly used race as the predominant factor in creating the Sixth as a black-majority district. Clyburn, who has done yeoman constituent service and nurtured a cautious, moderate image, would likely be able to win reelection in a district with a substantial black minority. Yet his failed attempts to win statewide office in the past illustrate the constraints confronting black politicians and the limits on their political prospects.

Moreover, recent political developments suggest that any "appeal to conscience," which Senator Jackson says a black candidate must make in order to win white votes, would have a rather short half-life. In early 1997 Governor Beasley made just such an appeal to racial tolerance in urging passage of his proposed Heritage Act, which would remove the Confederate battle flag from atop the statehouse to a memorial on the capitol grounds and permanently preserve all existing Confederate memorials in the state. Beasley based his appeal on a call to South Carolinians to heal racial divisions, but he was rebuffed by the General Assembly and met with a maelstrom of opposition from angry and deeply offended whites.

The flag has flown above the statehouse below the United States and South Carolina flags since 1962. It was placed there by an all-white General Assembly ostensibly in commemoration of the Civil War centennial. But at the height of resistance to the civil rights movement, flying the battle flag in 1962 served equally well to symbolize white South Carolinians' attachment to segregation and white supremacy. Over the years the flag has been an occasional campaign issue, usually raised by pro-flag Republicans to court votes among rural whites. In the General Assembly, black and white opponents of the flag have made attempts to have it removed, but all of these efforts have been unsuccessful in the face of stiff resistance by flag proponents. Beasley is the first sitting governor to advocate taking the flag down. In so doing, he has given the issue a prominence it has never seen before. And he has stirred a furious debate that crystallizes in a single issue the varied cross-currents of race, religion and economic interest that define South Carolina politics in the 1990s.

In his 1994 campaign for governor, Beasley's stump rhetoric emphasized his support for continuing to fly the flag. The governor attributes his turnaround two years later to his faith as an evangelical Christian. In a statewide television address, Beasley told South Carolinians that he came to his decision after much prayer and Bible reading. In his 1997 State of the State speech, the governor tied the Heritage Act to the biblical virtues of "love, joy, peace, kindness, goodness, gentleness, faithfulness, and self-control." Ironically, the religious leaders who have voiced the most enthusiastic support for the governor's position have been priests, rabbis and nonfundamentalist Protestant ministers, including a large statewide coalition of interdenominational clergy. But reaction among the religious rank and file has been mixed. In particular some rural whites felt betrayed by the governor's action and have responded with angry vows to move their support elsewhere in 1998.[52]

Beasley's flag initiative is strongly supported by the state's economic and political establishment. Most of the business community view the continued flying of the flag as destructive of the hard-won New South image that South Carolina has so carefully cultivated as a part of its economic development strategy. Thus the Heritage Act is supported not only by the South Carolina Chamber of Commerce and most business leaders, but also by both Republican and Democratic politicians who have equally strong stakes in encouraging capital investment. The list of politicians supporting the Beasley initiative, many of whom appeared with the governor at a late 1996 press conference to urge General Assembly passage of the Heritage Act, reads like a veritable who's who of South Carolina politics.[53] Supporters included all living former governors: Republicans Edwards and Campbell as well as Democrats Riley, John C. West, and Robert E. McNair. On the list were Senators Thurmond and Hollings (both former governors), U.S. representative Inglis and most of the rest of the congressional delegation. All but one of the politicians currently holding statewide elective office have endorsed Beasley's proposal. The lone holdout is Attorney General Condon. A unified elite usually gets its way in South Carolina politics, yet the house of representatives rejected the Beasley proposal and the senate never took it up. For many white representatives, most of whom are Republicans, the issue raised deeper emotive concerns that transcended their habitual preoccupation with economic development.

Proponents of the flag, led by Condon and Republicans in the General Assembly, assert that the Confederate battle standard is without racial meaning. Instead it is held to be a symbol of valor and sacrifice, commemorating South Carolinians' fight for freedom and states' rights against federal oppression. This assertion coincides well with the ideological opposition to big government shared by a segment of whites, and has enabled those who favor flying the flag to capture the ideological high ground among rank-and-file economic conservatives.

Continued defense of flying the banner starkly reveals the unwillingness of many whites to accept blacks fully as fellow citizens, entitled to the same respect and consideration as the white majority. As the history of South Carolina and the South as a whole vividly illustrates, political symbols, including flags and rallying cries such as "states' rights," have no absolute meaning. Instead, their meaning is constructed in various ways by the varied audiences to which they are communicated.[54] Whites who proclaim the flag as symbolizing valor in the fight for freedom offer one construction of its historical meaning. An alternative, and historically perhaps more supportable, construction of the flag's meaning is current among the state's black citizens, who, unsurprisingly, see the standard as a symbol of racial oppression. To assert that the banner should fly above the statehouse, and presumably wave as a symbol of the state's people, is to ignore the banner's essential ambiguity as well as the historical experience of the African Americans, who make up nearly one in three of South Carolina's citizens. Moreover, it suggests a denial of the state's history of racial oppression and sends a message that South Carolina and its government really belong to whites, and not to blacks. At the very least, it indicates a callous disregard of the reasonable sensitivities of South Carolina blacks that stem from their unique historical experience.

The intensity of the debate over the flag reveals that the economic issues that have dominated South Carolina's political discourse in recent years have yet to displace racial concerns at the core of South Carolina's political culture. In apparent recognition of this central fact of South Carolina political life, Governor Beasley has been careful not to offend the southern nationalism of native whites. He has extolled the flag as a symbol of valor whose "real" meaning has been appropriated by hate groups such as the Ku Klux Klan, a distinction that mimics bumper stickers displayed by flag supporters bearing the legend "Heritage, Not Hate." Yet the governor's position on the flag has cost him with white voters, particularly in the rural areas, who see betrayal in the contrast between his current stance and his stump rhetoric when he campaigned for governor.[55]

The house vote that killed Beasley's Heritage Act in the General Assembly was largely along party lines, with the governor's fellow Republicans, all of whom represent predominantly white constituencies, voting overwhelmingly against taking the flag down. Most Democrats, including all of the chamber's African American members, voted in favor of the governor's position. The near unanimity among Republicans in the house voting belies the sharp divisions the issue has created between the party's business establishment and important elements of its neopopulist electoral base. The GOP state executive committee abandoned plans to have its own members vote on the issue, apparently because the result would have been a virtual tie between the two sides.[56]

The flag issue dramatizes virtually all the conflicts and contradictions of contemporary South Carolina politics, encapsulating the varied forces of tradition and modernity that confront the state as it struggles to free itself from its past and enter the mainstream of American economic and cultural life. Most important, the flag debate clearly reveals that, while contemporary politics is inevitably shaped by the past and its legacy of racial division, the terms of current political discourse fail to confront directly either past or present relations between the races. Although race essentially defines the South Carolina party system, neither Democrats nor Republicans have fully come to terms with the racial differences that plague South Carolina. If nothing else, the flag controversy may bring the issue of race relations to the surface of political debate so that it can be confronted openly and honestly. The outcome of the encounter between South Carolina's past and its present may well determine the state's political future.

3

NORTH CAROLINA: BETWEEN HELMS AND HUNT NO MAJORITY EMERGES

Rob Christensen and Jack D. Fleer

T HE two major candidates in North Carolina's 1990 and 1996 U.S. Senate race were straight out of central casting. There was Republican senator Jesse Helms, the unreconstructed foe of civil rights and the chief tormentor of Tar Heel liberals, being challenged by former Charlotte mayor Harvey Gantt, seeking to become the first black elected to the Senate from the South since Reconstruction. Black versus white. Liberal versus conservative. New South versus Old South. A folksy traditionalist who feels comfortable with Dixie being played at his rallies versus an urbane, Massachusetts Institute of Technology–trained architect and city planner.

Both elections were uncomfortably close for Helms. But Helms and his political lieutenants had been in difficult positions before, and they knew the continued potency of hot-button issues such as race and homosexuality. In the closing days of the 1990 campaign, the Helms campaign began running a TV commercial that featured a pair of white hands crumbling a job application. "You needed that job," said the announcer, "and you were the best qualified. But they had to give it to a minority because of a racial quota. Is that really fair?"[1] In their 1996 rematch, Helms didn't wait so long to uncork his big guns. In September he began running a series of commercials saying that Gantt supported same-sex marriages. Helms also ran ads alleging that Gantt had used his color to get a federal license for a TV station.

The racial-quota commercial may have saved the career of North Carolina's best-known political figure, who won both reelection contests with Gantt. It was also a powerful symbol of the continued mass migration of white North Carolinians from the party of their fathers to the Republican party. But it was not just the old prickly question of race that was transforming North Carolina politics.

North Carolina continued in the 1990s to move into the country's economic mainstream as a fast-growing megastate, with Charlotte becoming one of the nation's leading banking centers and the Raleigh-Durham area emerging as a Silicon Valley with a drawl. Tobacco fields were being plowed under to make room for suburban cul-de-sacs. Barbecue joints gave way to supermarkets where takeout sushi was sold. During the opening of deer season, you'd be as likely to see Broncos or BMWs heading for the countryside as you would pickup trucks. And along with these changes, the Democratic party's grip on politics—which has been slowly loosening since the 1950s—finally gave way.

Nearing the end of the century, the North Carolina GOP controlled both U.S. Senate seats and half of the state's twelve congressional seats. For the first time since horse-and-buggy days, they also controlled the state house of representatives. The party also made historic breakthroughs in the election of Republicans to local political offices.

And yet, the Democratic party was still more vibrant than in such neighboring states as South Carolina, Virginia, and Tennessee. The 1990s saw signs of a revival of the battered North Carolina Democratic party. The Democrats retooled as a party sensitive to the businessmen and bankers in the glass towers, as well as to its traditional constituencies of the poor, working people, and blacks. Its firewall has been Democratic governor James B. (Jim) Hunt. By winning his third and fourth terms as the state's chief executive in the 1990s, he has kept the major part of state government in the hands of Democrats and ensured that his party will be an important force in the twenty-first century.

To a large degree, Helms and Hunt have dominated Tar Heel politics, not just in the 1990s, but in the 1980s and 1970s as well. A modern day Rip Van Winkle who went to sleep in 1977 and woke up twenty years later would need little instruction about who the state's leading political figures were. Helms has satisfied the state's conservative streak—its taste for limited government, a strong military, and traditional small-town values. Hunt has supplied voters' cravings for a competent, largely scandal free state government that has helped keep North Carolina in the forefront of Sunbelt growth.

While Helms is the state's most visible political figure, Hunt is arguably its most influential elected official. During his nearly two decades as governor and lieutenant governor, Hunt has set the state's political tone. A skilled coalition builder and a centrist, Hunt has managed to successfully juggle the interests of corporate CEOs and labor leaders, and liberal urban blacks and conservative rural whites. In doing so, he has helped keep the Democratic party a vital force in North Carolina politics, even as the Republican party continues its extraordinary growth. Hunt's politics are deeply rooted in the Tar Heel Democratic establishment that has for decades been probusiness, supportive of civil rights, and willing to invest heavily in a state university system long considered one of the best in the South.

JESSE HELMS AND THE RISE OF REPUBLICANS

Helms's rise has been a remarkable journey—from son of a small-town police chief in Monroe to chairman of the Senate Foreign Relations Committee. He is arguably the best-known politician North Carolina has ever produced. His TV commentaries of the 1960s presaged conservative talk show host Rush Limbaugh. His election to the Senate in 1972 as an anti-government conservative was a milestone in the advance of southern Republicanism. His sharp-elbowed brand of attack politics made him a pioneer in the age of negative politics. And his willingness to engage in hand-to-hand Senate combat would pave the way for House Speaker Newt Gingrich.

Helms has always been a polarizing figure in North Carolina. Some view him as a mean-spirited bully who never saw a civil rights bill or a program to help either the poor or AIDS victims that he liked. But for thousands of North Carolinians, Helms is seen as a champion of small-town values—a political warrior for fiscal constraint, for untrammeled free enterprise, and for the verities learned at the knees of parents. He is widely admired for his willingness to buck the political odds, for his steadfast convictions, and for his plain, brown-shoes style. His Senate office runs a crackerjack constituent services operation that has helped thousands of Tar Heel residents.[2]

The Helms-Gantt races of 1990 and 1996 had enough star power to attract a rapt national audience. North Carolinians have come to know Helms and Gantt so well that they often refer to them only as Jesse and Harvey. Helms never wins by wide margins, but he always wins. (Helms's largest margin of victory was his 54.5 percent to 45.5 percent victory over insurance commissioner John Ingram in 1978. His closest race was his 51.7 percent to 47.8 percent margin over Hunt in 1984.) He has strong backing from industry, especially from textile and cigarette manufacturers, and a strong following among farmers, particularly embattled tobacco farmers who see him as their champion. "Anybody who has anything to do with the production or the manufacture or sale of to-

bacco who doesn't support Helms needs their head examined," said Gene Lanier, fifty-eight, a third-generation tobacco farmer from the eastern town of
Goldsboro. "He's been our friend for years." Helms does particularly well with
the "gun-rack vote," many of whom are blue-collar workers making a modest
living, toiling on farms, working in textile or furniture factories, or pumping
gas. Helms also enjoys a strong following among Christian evangelicals and
others who are opposed to abortion.[3]

Articulate and polished, Gantt had also come far in his life, which started in
a Charleston, South Carolina, public housing project. He was twice elected
mayor of North Carolina's largest city, Charlotte, which was 75 percent white
and Republican leaning. Gantt had been the first black student to attend Clemson University. Although liberal-leaning generally, Gantt had close ties to many
of the leading business figures in Charlotte, including persons within the state's
giant banking industry.

In both the 1990 and 1996 Democratic primaries, Gantt defeated white
moderates who had presented themselves as more electable alternatives. In 1990
he beat Michael F. (Mike) Easley, a small-town district attorney who would
later be elected the state's attorney general. Gantt won in a runoff, garnering
56.9 percent to Easley's 43.1 percent. Six years later, he defeated Charles (Charlie) Sanders, a cardiologist and former chairman of Glaxo, a major pharmaceuti-
cal manufacturer. Although Sanders spent $1.7 million of his money, Gantt won
by a 52.5 to 41.6 percent margin. Both Easley and Sanders had the backing of
much of the state's liberal white Democratic establishment, including U.S. senator Terry Sanford, who felt it would be difficult to elect a black man to the
Senate.

In his first challenge to Helms in 1990, Gantt ran a competitive race, raising
$7.8 million from liberals across the country. He succeeded for much of the fall
in controlling the debate between candidates—something past Helms opponents had been unable to do. Gantt put Helms on the defensive on issues involving education and the environment. In the closing weeks of the campaign,
however, Helms took control. He ran TV ads accusing Gantt of using his racial
minority status to get a license to start a TV station, then turning around and
selling it. He also ran commercials, featuring a photograph of a bar catering to
homosexuals in Washington, criticizing Gantt for taking money from gays. In
another gambit, the Helms campaign and the state Republican party mailed
125,000 post cards into black neighborhoods warning them of possible voter
fraud and providing misleading information about registration. The state GOP
and the Helms campaign later settled a U.S. Justice Department suit, denying

any wrongdoing but promising not to use any similar "ballot security" program in the future.[4]

Helms has had a pattern of using racially edged tactics and issues in his campaigns, ranging from racial quotas in 1990 to his opposition to the Martin Luther King holiday in 1984. "He does appeal to a nativist, even racist element in the state that has always been there," said Gary Pearce, who is Hunt's key political strategist. "I'm not accusing him of being it. I'm saying he appeals to it. Everyone understands that he appeals to it."[5]

In his rematch with Gantt, Helms relied less on racial cues. But his commercials routinely included photographs of Gantt, and one mailing made by the state GOP included pictures of Gantt with either of the state's two black members of Congress, asking voters if they wanted more of this. When asked about the mailing, Republican officials noted that they made a similar mailing featuring pictures of Gantt and a white congressman. For people such as Thurston Quinn, a seventy-year-old tobacco farmer from Wayne County, race still matters. "I don't think Gantt is capable," Quinn said. "I was born and raised on a farm. I've been around black people all my life. I know there are some smart black people, but Gantt doesn't strike me as one of them."[6] Helms also used the issue of homosexuality extensively in TV ads in 1996, charging that Gantt supports same-sex marriages, homosexual teachers in the public schools, and a gay rights bill.

In many ways, the second Helms-Gantt race resembled the first. Carter Wrenn, a Republican strategist and former Helms advisor, commented: "It was almost the same set of issues. It was almost the same outcome. It was like Star Wars. You had the original and you had the sequel." The major difference was that both Helms and Gantt trimmed their ideological sails for the 1996 election. Both saw the battleground as the moderate, Republican-leaning suburban voters, including many of the seven hundred thousand new voters who had moved into the state since the 1990 election. Many of Helms's original core of supporters were getting older. And many of the new Republicans who moved into the state with corporate relocations did not find Helms's racial tactics and gay-baiting congenial to their own politics. "North Carolina is a state that is changing out from under him in many ways," observed Alex Castellanos, a former Helms media consultant. "There is a generation growing up inside the state that doesn't know him. On the cultural issues, they do not share his views."[7]

Instead of playing the role of conservative iconoclast and holding up dozens of ambassadorial appointments as public policy hostages, Helms, as chairman of the foreign relations committee, began taking on a more constructive role. He worked more closely with the White House and other senators, and helped foster a constructive debate on reorganizing the State Department. He also worked to improve his public image. His office started putting out news releases, something he had rarely done during his Senate career. He began talking more to the news media, and made more personal appearances in the state, often with such leading figures in tow as Secretary of State Madeleine Albright, former secretary of state Henry Kissinger, the Dalai Lama, former president George Bush, and even the ambassador from communist Vietnam.[8] Nevertheless, Helms's role as the chief legislative spear carrier of the New Right was by the mid-nineties being shared with or even eclipsed by other leading conservatives such as Speaker Gingrich.

Just as Helms was moving to the middle, Gantt no longer claimed the mantle of liberalism. His campaign in some ways resembled President Clinton's. Gantt supported welfare reform and the elimination of parole for violent offenders, and spoke often of the need for a return to more traditional values, such as more discipline in the classroom and greater reliance on hard work and religious values. For the most part he championed popular government programs, notably expanded student loan programs. He criticized Helms as a foe of Medicare, the environment, and education.[9] In the final week, former president Jimmy Carter campaigned for Gantt, the first campaign appearance outside of Georgia for Carter since he left the White House.

In the end, Gantt accomplished what he set out to do. He won a majority of self-described moderates as well as a majority of people who had moved into North Carolina since the past election. But it was not enough. Helms defeated Gantt by a margin of 52.6 percent to 45.9 percent. Once again, Helms agnostics—the liberal newspapers, universities, and many in the metropolitan centers—were left scratching their heads at the Helms phenomenon. "I think Jesse is like an old badger," said William Snider, retired editor of the Greensboro *News and Record* and longtime watcher of Tar Heel politics. "He's up in a hole and you can't get at him. He rivals Bill Clinton as a politician."[10]

Despite his victories in 1990 and 1996, the decade provided some hard times for Helms personally. Shortly after defeating Gantt in 1990, Helms suffered a series of illnesses that included a fight with prostate cancer and quadruple bypass surgery. His wife, Dorothy, also had a cancer operation. At age seventy-five, Helms had visibly slowed down by the 1996 campaign. His campaign staff gave him only a light schedule. Helping Helms was the Senate race in neighboring South Carolina, where the then ninety-three-year-old Strom Thurmond won reelection despite being old enough to be Helms's father. In an effort to deal with the age issue, Helms began sporting a button that read, "Thurmond and Helms in '96. Don't waste 200 years of experience."

The 1990s also saw Helms have a bitter falling out with his political organization, which was once known as the National Congressional Club but is now called the National Conservative Club. The Raleigh-based political action committee had begun in 1973 as a vehicle for retiring Helms's campaign debt, but its two chief tacticians, Thomas Ellis and Carter Wrenn, quickly broadened its scope, turning it into one of the nation's largest PACs. The club had pioneered direct-mail solicitations to conservatives around the country—many of them small givers who nevertheless were willing to contribute time and time again. The organization raised $8.1 million for Helms in 1978, $16.9 million in 1984 and $17.7 million in 1990. It also helped save Ronald Reagan's political career by helping him win the 1976 Republican presidential primary in North Carolina.

The club had recruited and conducted Senate campaigns for Republican John East in 1980 and Lauch Faircloth in 1992. But Helms was apparently not happy, having grown dissatisfied with his political lieutenants' constant fund raising. He complained that the club often acted without his authority. There were also personal considerations; Helms was angered when neither Ellis nor Wrenn saved his daughter's job as principal at a private school in Raleigh, where they were both board members. Without the support of its major figure, the Conservative Club hit hard times. The lack of money led to layoffs of most of its staff. It moved to less expensive headquarters outside of Raleigh.[11]

The 1992 Faircloth U.S. Senate campaign may have been the Conservative Club's last hurrah in North Carolina. Faircloth, a wealthy businessman from the small tobacco-belt town of Clinton, had served as a highway commissioner, highway commission chairman, and commerce secretary under Democratic governors Terry Sanford, Robert W. (Bob) Scott, and Jim Hunt in the 1960s and 1970s. Faircloth, who had unsuccessfully sought the Democratic nomination for governor in 1984, had hoped to run for the Senate in 1986. He felt that Sanford, a longtime friend, had broken a private agreement between the two men when Sanford ran for the Senate that year. An angry Faircloth withdrew from the 1986 race.

Sanford, a highly regarded moderate-to-liberal governor in the 1960s, was a former president of Duke University and a two-time presidential candidate. He was elected to the Senate in 1986 with 51.8 percent of the vote to 48.2 percent for a veteran Republican congressman, James T. Broyhill. But his opposition to Desert Storm, the military operation to expel Iraq from Kuwait, had hurt him politically with the state's large military presence. In 1992 Faircloth switched to the Republican party and ran against Sanford with the backing of the Conservative Club. Faircloth promised during the campaign to work for welfare reform, and attacked Sanford as too liberal. Rarely making public appearances, Faircloth ran a barrage of TV ads accusing Sanford of voting similarly to liberal senator Ted Kennedy, of supporting welfare, and of voting to fund the Boston Harbor tunnel. The challenger was helped by Sanford's absence during key weeks of the fall campaign, when he was recovering from heart surgery. That incapacity served to underscore the incumbent's age, which was seventy-five. Faircloth won the election, 50.3 percent to 46.3 percent.

Meanwhile, the Republican party continued its significant growth in North Carolina. For the first half of the century, the North Carolina Republican party had been a party of the western foothills and mountains—a product of anti-secessionist attitudes during the Civil War. But like the rest of the South, North Carolina has in recent decades moved in stops and starts away from Democratic control to two-party competition. Here as in South Carolina, the shift has been caused by numerous factors—a reaction against the Democratic national party's support for the civil rights movement, the leftward drift of the Democratic party, and the division over cultural matters. The GOP has also been helped by an influx of Republican-leaning retirees into the coastal, mountain, and golf resorts as well as former military families' settling near the state's many bases. Republican-leaning corporate executives have arrived from other parts of the country. "It is ironic," says Hunt strategist Pearce. "[The rise of two-party competition] has come about because of what the Democrats did—which is to make the state a mecca for well-educated people who work at research-based companies."[12]

The growth of the Republican party, of course, coincided with racial integration. And racial cleavage lines have helped shape both party's images. As Wilton Duke, past chairman of the Pitt County commissioners, explained, "I've voted Democratic since 1928. But the Democratic party left the white people. When they left, that is what caused the new wave of Republicans." Former secretary of state Janice Faulkner, a Democrat, called race "the moose on the table. The moose comes in and sits on the table with every conversation," she said. "If we are really looking into gaining insight into what is happening, we need to get the moose off the table—the resentments of whites from the days of integration of the schools, the competition for scarce economic development dollars, the increasing cost of entitlement programs."[13]

Jack Hawke, a former state GOP chairman who worked to broaden black participation in the Republican party, had this to say: "One of the disturbing factors is that the parties racially are becoming more polarized to a degree that has hurt the Democrats in terms of white flight. But as the Democratic party shrinks in size and numbers, percentage-wise it becomes more black-dominated.

Republicans have not been successful for a variety of reasons in attracting enough black support to offset the notion that the Democratic party is becoming the party of minorities and the Republican party is becoming the party of the white folks."[14]

Republican registration in the state rose as Democratic registration declined. In just the six years sandwiched between the two Helms-Gantt races, Democratic registration dropped from 63 percent to 55 percent of the total. (See Table 7 for additional registration trends.) "Voting-wise we are getting closer to parity," said Hawke, state Republican chairman from 1986 to 1995. "The big leap that Republicans have made in North Carolina is that it is now socially acceptable to be a Republican. I think if trends continue as they are now, by the year 2000 we will definitely be a competitive, two-party state." He continued: "Where the Republicans lag, and it's going to take a long time to catch up, is in the power structure of the state of North Carolina. By that I mean the university system, the major industries of the state. The leaders all tend to be tied to the Democratic party. It is going to take a long time to break those walls down."[15]

Some walls came crashing down during the Republican landslide of 1994. In that year the Republicans gained a majority of the U.S. House delegation from North Carolina and also won control of the lower house of the General Assembly. In both instances it was the first time the Republicans had earned a majority in this century. Overnight, the congressional delegation went from eight Democrats and four Republicans to four Democrats and eight Republicans. The dramatic change was part of a national anti-Democratic and anti-Clinton mood that resulted in a new Republican majority in Congress. But there were local factors involved that made the GOP gains more sensational in North Carolina than in most other states. North Carolina is the leading tobacco-growing state as well as the leading cigarette manufacturer, and the tobacco industry has always looked to Democratic congressmen to protect the tobacco price support program—a bit of agrarian socialism started by Franklin Roosevelt's New Deal. But in the mid-1990s it was Republicans, under the mantle of less government interference, who were convincing voters along Tobacco Road that they were their best friends.

The 1994 election saw three of the largest tobacco-growing House districts in the country, long Democratic strongholds, go Republican. A fourth district, that included the Winston-Salem home of RJR Reynolds, the giant cigarette manufacturer, also went Republican. Democratic incumbents David E. Price of Chapel Hill, a political science professor at Duke University, and Martin Lancaster of Goldsboro were defeated by Republicans Frederick K. (Fred) Heine-

man and Walter B. Jones, Jr., respectively. (Jones is the son of longtime Democratic congressman Walter B. Jones, who served from 1967 to 1993.) Two seats
where Democratic incumbents retired were won by Republicans David Funderburk of Buies Creek and Richard M. Burr of Winston-Salem.

The Republicans, however, were unable to keep all their gains for long. In
the 1996 elections, Democrats won back two of the seats, giving the North Carolina delegation a six to six partisan split. The Democratic gains were in large
part the result of Republican mistakes. Funderburk was defeated after he was
involved in an automobile accident of which several witnesses told police that
he had switched seats to make it look as if his wife had been driving at the time
of the accident. Democrat Bob R. (Bobby) Etheridge, the state superintendent
of public instruction, won Funderburk's seat with 52.5 percent of the vote.
Heineman was defeated after he defined the middle class as anyone making between $350,000 and $700,000 per year. Former congressman Price was then
able to recapture his old seat, winning 54.4 percent of the vote. The Democratic
winners, Price and Etheridge, were helped by more than one million dollars'
worth of independent expenditures by the AFL-CIO for TV ads, in which both
Funderburk and Heineman were accused of wanting to cut Medicare, among
other things.[16]

Perhaps even more striking than the 1994 Republican gains in Congress was
the GOP's winning control of the 120-member state house of representatives
that year and their retaining control, though by a diminished margin, in 1996,
proving that their initial success had been no fluke. The Republicans also came
very close to winning the state senate in 1994, but lost ground there in the 1996
elections. While North Carolina Republicans had enjoyed success for quite
some time in races for the U.S. House, U.S. Senate, and governor, many Democrats thought the General Assembly was a Democratic stronghold they would
never lose. Table 6 charts the long climb the GOP made to its 1994 state legislative breakthrough.

For the 1994 elections, state legislative Republicans followed the lead of
their counterparts in Congress and issued their own contract with the voters,
which included promises for tax cuts, gubernatorial veto power, and term limits. They also made statewide mailings blaming Democratic legislators for
spending a $1 billion surplus in 1993, rather than using the surplus to cut taxes.
The state house, which had been 78–42 Democratic before the 1994 landslide,
became 68–52 Republican; the state senate narrowly remained Democratic, by
a 26–24 margin, although the GOP achieved a 13-seat gain.

In early 1995, Representative Harold Brubaker, a real estate appraiser and
longtime back-bencher from Asheboro, became North Carolina's first Republi-

Table 6. Party Delegations in the North Carolina General Assembly, 1961–1997

	House (120 seats)			Senate (50 seats)		
Year	Dem.		Rep.	Dem.		Rep.
1961	105	(90.0%)	15	(10.0%)	48	(96.0%)	2	(4.0%)
1971	96	(80.0)	24	(20.0)	43	(86.0)	7	(14.0)
1981	96	(80.0)	24	(20.0)	40	(80.0)	10	(20.0)
1991	81	(67.5)	39	(32.5)	36	(72.0)	14	(28.0)
1993	78	(65.0)	42	(35.0)	39	(78.0)	11	(22.0)
1995	52	(43.3)	68	(56.7)	26	(52.0)	24	(48.0)
1997	59	(49.2)	61	(50.8)	30	(60.0)	20	(40.0)

Source: Department of the Secretary of State, North Carolina Manual, Raleigh, years listed.

can house speaker in a century. (Ironically, the ousted speaker, Democrat Daniel T. [Dan] Blue, had himself made North Carolina political history four years earlier when he became the first African American speaker in the South since Reconstruction.) During the 1995–1996 legislative session the GOP majority in the house and near majority in the senate resulted in a sharp ideological shift in the General Assembly. The legislature became more friendly to business interests, and the state passed the largest tax cut in its history. One casualty of those reductions was the state's taxpayer-financed abortion fund for poor women, the only such fund in the South, which was drastically cut.

The public anger that had been focused in 1994 on the Democratic majorities in both the state and the nation had become more diffuse by 1996 after nearly two years of divided party control on both levels. Furthermore, without any statewide election campaigns in 1994, there was little coordinated Democratic party effort, and the party had been caught by surprise. In 1996, in contrast, the Democrats under the leadership of Governor Hunt, who himself was seeking reelection, were better financed, better organized, and more sharply focused on defending their status. For the first time, Democratic legislators jointly raised hundreds of thousands of dollars, hired consultants and pollsters, and targeted key races.

When the 1996 results were in, house Republicans narrowly maintained their majority by a shaky 61–59 margin. In addition to their house gains, North Carolina Democrats, who were clearly aided by the coattails of their popular gubernatorial victor, widened their slim majority in the state senate to 30 seats compared to 20 for the GOP.

The Republican-promised constitutional amendment giving the governor veto power won voter approval in November 1996. North Carolina had been the only state in the country without a gubernatorial veto—a curiosity that is often attributed to the hatred of colonial Tar Heels for royal authority. The first governor to have the new veto authority was, of course, Democrat Jim Hunt, who began his unprecedented fourth term in January 1997 after his easy reelection triumph.

JIM HUNT AND THE DEMOCRATIC FIREWALL

Like Helms, Hunt is a product of small-town North Carolina. But Hunt's politics took him in a different direction. A corporate lawyer and part-time cattle farmer, Hunt was first elected in 1972 as lieutenant governor—a position that made him the leading Democratic spokesman under Republican governor James E. Holshouser (1973–1977). Hunt was a product of the Sanford organization, a coalition of Democrats who have been moderately liberal by North Carolina standards but have always worked closely with the state's business establishment. He was elected governor in 1976 with 65.0 percent of the vote, and reelected in 1980 with 61.9 percent after pushing through a change in the state constitution to allow governors to succeed themselves. He lost to Helms in his 1984 Senate bid.

After eight years out of office, while Republican James G. (Jim) Martin was governor (1985–1993), Hunt was elected to a third term in 1992 with 52.7 percent of the vote. He defeated Martin's heir apparent, Republican lieutenant governor James C. (Jim) Gardner, a co-founder of the Hardees fast-food chain and a former congressman. Gardner, who received 45.1 percent of the vote, accused Hunt of being both soft on crime and a big spender. But Gardner was hurt by a series of business failures he had suffered in the 1970s. It was Hunt who got the support of most of the state's business leadership, including the major banks, many of whom had supported Governor Martin, the Republican, for the previous eight years. "State government should be run like a business," Hunt said in one debate with Gardner. "But I hope you don't get to run it like one of your businesses."[17]

Returning to office after eight years of practicing law, Hunt seemed more conservative to many observers. "If there is a difference in him, it is his accommodation of business interests with whom he was not perceived in his first tenure as governor to be very friendly," said Faulkner, the former Democratic secretary of state, who has known Hunt most of his life. "With his understanding of his inability to capture that base in his Senate race, he is a wiser man in terms of what drives the economy and what drives the ballot box. Both of those things are money."[18] Hunt had won the election despite his campaign's entanglement in a scandal that soon earned the nickname Scannergate. A low-level Hunt supporter had been listening on her police scanner to telephone calls between Gardner and key supporters that were made on cellular phones. The political intelligence work was discovered when a jilted former boyfriend exposed the Hunt supporter's electronic eavesdropping. Although Hunt was never tied to the operation, a close political adviser and longtime friend, former North Carolina supreme court justice J. Phil Carlton, plead guilty to illegally receiving transcripts of the telephone conversations.

Hunt had always been a middle-of-the-road political figure. He would swing left on such issues as civil rights, increased funding for public education, and North Carolina's tax-supported abortion fund for poor women. But he would swing right on issues like the death penalty and stiff anticrime measures, and in supporting big business. Hunt thus quickly adapted to the country's more conservative mood when he took office for a third term.

Following the Republican landslide in 1994, Hunt proposed the largest tax cut in state history, outflanking even the Republican legislative leaders. The move paid off. Hunt entered the 1996 elections with some of the highest approval ratings of any Democratic governor in the country. He easily defeated Republican Robin Hayes, by a 56.0 percent to 42.8 percent margin, in the 1996 governor's race. Hayes, a state legislator and an heir to the Cannon towel fortune, had upset former Charlotte mayor Richard Vinroot in the GOP primary. The backing of the religious right had assisted Hayes in defeating the more moderate Vinroot.

Hunt's popularity helped keep the Democratic party together during difficult times. Few elected Democrats in North Carolina switched to the Republican party during this period, in contrast to what was occurring in several other southern states, particularly neighboring South Carolina. "Although we have become more Republican, why have we not gone the way of South Carolina, Virginia and Tennessee now?" Pearce asked rhetorically. "The answer is Jim Hunt. He has charted a course in which Democrats can build a coalition of Republican-leaning, moderate-to-conservative business people and traditional, progressive Democratic constituencies—teachers, minorities. There is nothing magical and mysterious about it. It's how Clinton got elected in 1992. It is how he [Clinton] brought himself back in 1995."[19]

Hunt's conservative moves have left some Democrats disgruntled. "A lot of Democrats really detest Jim Hunt," said Chris Scott, a former state AFL-ClO president. "That is because they view him as somebody who does not do what the Franklin Roosevelt Democratic party would have done. But I really admire his skill in reaching out beyond the normal circles that the Democrats travel in." Republicans agree that Hunt has had a major influence. "I think Hunt has been a dominant political figure in North Carolina," Hawke said. "He has been an element in keeping the Democratic party from appearing to be liberal and out of step with the views of the majority of the people."[20]

Hunt's popularity also served as a firewall for other Democratic candidates running statewide. As the Republican base vote has grown in North Carolina, the GOP has come increasingly closer to capturing several down-ticket state-wide offices. For example, a young Republican judge, closely aligned with the religious right, nearly defeated the sitting chief justice of the state supreme court in 1996.

The best known of the Republican candidates for state office in 1996 was former NASCAR racing star Richard Petty, a candidate for secretary of state. In much of rural North Carolina it is Petty, not the late singer Elvis Presley, who is known as the King. Besides his exploits on the stock car circuit, Petty was a businessman and had served sixteen years as a Randolph County commissioner. But he was defeated in 1996 by former state senator Elaine Marshall, a Lillington attorney.[21] Marshall received 53.4 percent to Petty's 45.2 percent. Hurting Petty was an incident during the campaign where he purposely bumped another car that was going too slow for him in the left lane of a road.

Black Democrats made significant gains in the 1990s. As noted above, Gantt twice ran for the U.S. Senate, only to lose to Helms. But in each instance, Gantt captured his party's nomination and ran a strong, competitive race against Helms. Just a month after Gantt's 1990 defeat, Raleigh attorney Blue was elected house speaker, a post he held for four years. The 1990s also saw the election of the first two black members of Congress from North Carolina in the twentieth century. In 1992, Eva Clayton, a veteran public administrator, and Melvin Watt, a Yale-educated attorney, were elected in two black-majority districts that had been created as part of the 1990 redistricting. The North Carolina General Assembly had originally created only Clayton's district, but after the initial plan was rejected by the U.S. Justice Department for failure to comply with provisions of the Voting Rights Act, the legislature carved out Watt's district. Clayton's district was the new First, which zigzagged through the rural tobacco-, peanut-, and cotton-growing areas of eastern North Carolina from Virginia to South Carolina. Much of the area was part of the state's traditional "black belt."

Her district was not nearly as controversial as the newly created Twelfth, a snake-like district that connected the largely urban black neighborhoods along

Interstate 85 from Durham to Charlotte and beyond. Representing that district was Watt, a Charlotte attorney and former campaign manager for Gantt, as well as Gantt's next-door neighbor. The Twelfth, in particular, was the target of national ridicule. As one of the unsuccessful candidates, state representative Mickey Michaux, said of it: "I love the district because I can drive down I-85 with both car doors open and hit every person in the district."[22]

In the landmark 1993 *Shaw v. Reno* case, the U.S. Supreme Court questioned the constitutionality of the Twelfth District, describing it as "bizarre," "uncouth," "irrational," and "extremely irregular," sending the case back down to the lower courts for further review. The dispute eventually returned to the Supreme Court, and in June 1996 the high court ruled that the district constituted racial gerrymandering, but it left the decision on when the legislature had to draw new lines to a three-judge federal panel. Those judges ruled in July 1996 that the lines had to be redrawn by April 1, 1997, thereby permitting the 1996 elections to go forward using the existing districts. In March 1997, the North Carolina General Assembly passed a new congressional districting plan that reduced the influence of race in determining district lines and created no districts with a clear majority of black voters. The new plan had been approved by the Justice Department and a three-judge federal court, but in April 1998, a federal district court ruled that the Twelfth District remained an unconstitutional racial gerrymander and would have to be redrawn, requiring a delay in the 1998 primaries until September. Under the latest plan, the new Twelfth had a black voting-age population of 33 percent, the second highest of the state's congressional districts; the First District's black voting-age population was the highest at 47 percent.[23]

The political effect of the two black districts is a matter of intense dispute. Most white Democratic leaders believe the black districts have weakened the Democrats by depriving white Democrats of a large part of their political base and making the election of Republicans more likely. "The redistricting decision could save the Democratic party in the South," Pearce, the Hunt strategist, said following the 1996 Supreme Court ruling. But many black Democrats see the issue quite differently. Watt argued that the new black districts had little to do with the Republicans winning control of the North Carolina congressional delegation or Congress as a whole in 1994. "There was just a massive shift in the country," Watt says. "This notion that we created the demise of the Democratic Congress is just not true."[24]

Like many other southern states, North Carolina is becoming a reliable Republican state in presidential politics. Republicans have won seven of the past eight presidential contests in the state. Democrat Jimmy Carter defeated Gerald

Ford in 1976 by a margin of 55.2 percent to 44.2 percent. Despite the state's GOP leanings in presidential contests, Democratic presidential campaigns have continued to view North Carolina as a border state that is winnable. In 1992 North Carolina was the only southern state targeted by the Clinton campaign that it lost, although just barely. Bush carried the state by only 20,619 votes. Bush won 43.4 percent to Clinton's 42.7 percent while Ross Perot received 13.7 percent. In 1996, President Clinton and his allies campaigned in North Carolina with a barrage of TV ads in selected regions of the state, hoping to ride Hunt's coattails. But again, North Carolina voters went Republican, giving Bob Dole, whose wife Elizabeth is a North Carolina native, 48.7 percent of the vote to Clinton's 44.0 percent. Perot slipped to 6.7 percent. The President's anti-smoking campaign hurt him in the Tar Heel State, as did his stance on gays in the military, which was unpopular in a region bristling with military bases.[25]

SHIFTING LOYALTIES AND TWO-PARTY COMPETITION

Just as this tour of recent electoral battles in North Carolina depicts the closely competitive nature of two-party politics in the 1990s, an examination of an array of other information—such as party registration data and public opinion surveys—reveals a similar trend. North Carolina is one of only three southern states that registers voters by party, Louisiana and Florida being the other two. As a result, party registration figures provide another window on recent shifts, and they chart dramatically the Democratic decline. (See Table 7.) Three decades ago registered Democrats outnumbered registered Republicans by a ratio of 4.5 to 1. Since then, Republican registration has steadily increased. By October 1998, the ratio of Democrats to Republicans had fallen to less than 1.5 to 1. There were also significant increases in the number of unaffiliated voters.

Likewise, party identification data depict Democratic decline with equal force; see Table 8. Democratic identification has dropped strikingly, from six in ten voters in 1968 to just under one in three in 1996. Republican identification has risen substantially as have those claiming to be independent.[26] In October 1996, the Carolina Poll showed that the portion of the state's voters who identified with the Democratic party (32 percent) was about equal to those who declared affiliation with the Republican party (33 percent). Another fourth of the electorate chose independent status.

Surveys further illuminate voter support for the state's major political parties. (See Table 9.) The base vote of each major state party begins with race—the overwhelming support which Democratic candidates receive from African

Table 7. Registration of North Carolina Voters by Party, 1966–1998

Year	Dem.	Rep.	Unaffil.	Ratio (D/R)
1966	1,540,499	344,700		4.5 to 1
1976	1,840,827	601,897	106,940	3 to 1
1986	2,114,536	836,726	129,728	2.5 to 1
1992	2,313,520	1,217,114	286,069	2 to 1
1996	2,346,952	1,456,599	511,445	1.6 to 1
1998	2,394,935	1,540,836	608,023	1.5 to 1

Source: North Carolina State Board of Elections.

Table 8. Party Identification in North Carolina, 1968–1998

Party	1968	1986	1990	1992	1996	1998
Democrat	60%	51%	40%	37%	32%	32%
Republican	21	30	34	33	33	36
Independent	19	19	17	24	24	22

Sources: Comparative State Elections Project Survey, 1968; University of North Carolina polls, 1986, 1990, 1992, 1996, 1998.

Note: Responses were given to a standard party identification question, "Generally speaking, do you think of yourself as a Republican, Democrat, Independent, or what?"

Americans and the substantial support of white voters for Republican candidates. Throughout the 1990s, generally over 90 percent of black voters cast ballots for Democratic candidates, whether for Harvey Gantt in his two losing U.S. Senate races or for Jim Hunt in his successful quests for third and fourth terms as governor. Given black voters' consistent Democratic voting patterns, a key concern for Democratic candidates is always the level of turnout among African Americans.[27]

Although they support Democrats at a lower rate than Republicans, white voters determine whether Democratic candidates are victorious. A rule of thumb is that a Democratic candidate must receive approximately 40 percent of the white vote in North Carolina in order to win statewide. Looking at major races in the 1990s, only Jim Hunt exceeded this minimum among major candidates, having received 47 percent of white voters in 1992 and 54 percent in 1996. Hunt, the only Democrat to win major office in the 1990s, has been consistently successful in developing a strong biracial coalition to provide the winning margins for his gubernatorial candidacies. Gantt in 1990 and 1996, Sanford

Table 9. Divisions Among North Carolina Voters, 1990–1996

| | U.S. Senate | | | | Governor | | | |
| | 1990 | | 1996 | | 1992 | | 1996 | |
	Gantt	Helms	Gantt	Helms	Hunt	Gardner	Hunt	Hayes
White	35%	55%	38%	62%	47%	51%	54%	46%
Black	93	7	91	8	91	6	89	9
Female	50	50	53	46	56	41	65	34
Male	42	58	43	56	50	50	54	45
Liberal	85	15	83	16	82	15	85	14
Conservative	16	85	19	80	29	61	33	66
Moderate	59	41	57	42	61	37	70	29

Source: Voters News Service, North Carolina Exit Poll, November 1990, 1992, 1996.

Note: Responses in the third panel are to a standard political ideology question, "On most political matters, do you consider yourself 1. Liberal, 2. Moderate, or 3. Conservative?"

in 1992, and Clinton in 1992 and 1996 were less successful among white voters, and were losers in North Carolina. For example, Gantt received 35 percent of the white vote in 1990 and 38 percent in 1996.

Two aspects of the relationship between black voters and the Democratic party deserve particular attention. In recent years, as blacks have gained fuller recognition in the political arena, candidates from that race have been more likely to gain recognition in the Democratic party. In electoral politics, more blacks have been elected as Democrats than as Republicans for positions such as state legislator and county commissioner. And, as previewed above, the first blacks elected to the U.S. House of Representatives in this century from North Carolina were Democrats Eva Clayton and Mel Watt. The only blacks to be elected to statewide offices (Ralph Campbell, a former Raleigh city councilman and the brother of Atlanta mayor Bill Campbell, elected state auditor in 1992, and an associate justice of the state supreme court, Henry E. Frye) were Democrats. The leadership of the Democrats in the state legislature has included several blacks, most prominently former speaker Blue. While the number of black public officials has increased dramatically since the 1965 passage of the Voting Rights Act, as of 1994 blacks held only 14.3 percent of state elected positions although they comprise 22 percent of the state's population and 20 percent of the state's registered voters.[28]

The second component of the relationship between Democrats and black voters is the ongoing debate about representation and legislative districting, as discussed above. The question is whether blacks are better represented when concentrated in a few majority-minority districts or when they are dispersed to affect the elections of a greater number of legislators. The debate presents a dilemma for the Democratic party and its key support group.

While white voters do not concentrate their support to the same extent as blacks, Republican party candidates for a variety of offices have been more likely to receive clear majorities from whites in recent decades. As one would expect, the surveys show that conservative whites are more supportive of Republicans. Moderate and independent whites appear to be more amenable to supporting candidates of either party. For example, one study found that Hunt attracted white voters who were from both the lower and upper ends of the socioeconomic scale with appeals that included moderation of class differences, probusiness policies, tough anticrime measures, racial reconciliation, and a balance between social tolerance and economic conservatism.[29] In the 1990s such positions as welfare reform, concern about increased crime, tolerance for lifestyle differences, and expanded educational opportunities were most successful in attracting support from whites.

Deserving special mention in North Carolina's voting annals are the "Jesse-crats." Traditionally, lower income whites have been more inclined to support Democratic candidates. In North Carolina, however, since the 1970s when Jesse Helms began running for the U.S. Senate, a group of rural, blue-collar, coastal plains and rural Piedmont voters have supported the Republican. Charles L. Prysby's study of the 1990 U.S. Senate race between Helms and Gantt finds that "the appeal of Helms to white voters in rural areas is directly related to the presence of blacks," suggesting that the "Jessecrat" appeal is based in part on race-related issues. In Helms's 1996 election a similar pattern emerged. This relationship seems to be distinctive from that for other Republican candidates in the state.[30]

Table 9 also indicates, not surprisingly, that self-identified liberals consistently provide high levels of support for Democratic candidates, while professed conservatives vote overwhelmingly for Republicans. Avowed moderates, who comprise almost half of the state's electorate, are in contention for the allegiance of the two parties, with the majority going more often than not to Republican candidates. Once again, Governor Hunt's ability to secure support from a larger portion of this bloc of voters contributed to his winning margins. In 1992, he won 61 percent of the moderates and in 1996, 70 percent.

Gender is another demographic factor that helps define differences between the Democratic and Republican coalitions. In the major contests of the 1990s, as Table 9 shows, women consistently voted more for the Democratic candidates than Republican candidates and men voted more for Republican candidates. While the gender gap is not as great as the racial gap, it is consistent and important. Data on North Carolina voters show that men identify more as Republicans and women more often as Democrats.[31]

The issue bases of the gender gap include what some perceive to be "women's issues," such as the right to choice on abortion and improved economic opportunities through affirmative action. Polls of North Carolinians also suggest that major differences exist between men and women on concerns over the level of government spending, continuance of social assistance programs, expansion of quality health care support and government action to restrict violence in films and television. Overall, women appear to favor a more activist government bent on improving citizens' lives. One national analyst of this phenomenon concluded: "By virtually every account, the most important single factor splitting women from men in the voting booth is women's greater confidence in government's ability to help people and their concern about the reduction in services for the young, old and needy."[32]

Socioeconomic status as measured by education and income reveals few consistent relationships to candidate or party preference. Lower-income voters, however, regularly support Democratic candidates at higher levels than upper income voters. An analysis of state voting patterns in the 1980s found that "class polarization . . . among white North Carolina voters is not strong, clear-cut, or consistent across different class measures."[33] The pattern persisted in the elections of the 1990s.

Religion and politics have become more frequently mixed in North Carolina, as well as around the nation. The religious right and especially the Christian Coalition have become well organized and constitute a significant presence in the state. Sim DeLapp, chairman of the North Carolina Christian Coalition, emphasized that the major work of the organization is to "educate" voters on the issue positions of the candidates and to mobilize their voters on Election Day. Voter guides distributed in churches around the state in the weeks before an election are a key vehicle for achieving these twin goals.[34]

Analyses of the relationship of religion and voting preferences in North Carolina suggest that the key factor is the level of religious commitment demonstrated by the voter. In 1992 those who were regular churchgoers were more likely to vote for George Bush than Bill Clinton or Ross Perot. Likewise, whites who identified themselves as "born-again" Christians were more inclined to support the Republican candidate. Similar relationships prevail in the 1992 races for U.S. Senate and governor. In 1996, these patterns were repeated as white voters who considered themselves part of the religious right voted 68 percent to 24 percent for Dole over Clinton, 59 percent to 41 percent for Hayes over Hunt, and 77 percent to 23 percent for Helms over Gantt. These findings suggest that the relationship between the Christian fundamentalist organizations and the Republican party is strong in North Carolina. *Campaigns and Elections* concluded in 1994 that North Carolina was among the eighteen states in which the Christian right was dominant in the Republican party. DeLapp, of the Christian Coalition, pointed to his personal involvement with GOP politics to argue that the Coalition plays a prominent role in the party's organizational battles. Other Republicans interviewed for this chapter, including former Governor Holshouser, were more skeptical of the Coalition's prominence in party affairs.[35]

Place of residence is a final demographic variable that sheds light on Tar Heel voting patterns. As North Carolina has become more urbanized, its seven metropolitan counties have taken on greater significance. They are Mecklenburg (Charlotte), Wake (Raleigh), Guilford (Greensboro), Forsyth (Winston-Salem), Durham, Buncombe (Asheville), and Cumberland (Fayetteville). The first five form a crescent in the Piedmont stretching from the South Carolina border to the state capital, and the latter two lie near the Piedmont region off to the west and east, respectively. The proportion of the statewide vote cast by citizens who reside in these seven metropolitan counties has grown from 15 percent at the beginning of the century to more than a third in the elections of the 1990s. Voters in these counties on average are more affluent than the state as a whole. An examination of the last six gubernatorial elections indicates that whoever wins these key counties, regardless of party, wins the governorship. Thus the top vote-getter in these counties in 1984 and 1988 was the Republican victor, Jim Martin. In 1976 and 1980 and again in 1992 and 1996 the candidate with the top percentage here was the Democratic winner, Jim Hunt.[36]

Party identification is a key influence in how citizens vote. Even though fewer voters are declaring identification, most continue to do so. In elections in the 1990s, the Republican party identifiers have been more consistently loyal to their party than have Democratic identifiers in North Carolina. Since recent statewide polls have revealed an emerging parity among the two parties in identification (see Table 8), this greater loyalty of Republicans has become critical in the outcome of elections for statewide office. It goes some way toward offsetting the Democrats' advantage in party registration.

Another important element is the voting behavior of independent voters. An examination of the major elections of the 1990s shows that Republican candidates consistently attract a majority of the state's independents. Governor Hunt's victories, however, have been aided significantly by his ability to draw large numbers of independents. Other Democratic candidates have done less well with these voters and have not prevailed at the polls.[37]

This excursion through the survey evidence from recent key elections suggests that Republican statewide success in North Carolina is based on a coalition of highly loyal Republican identifiers, majority support among self-proclaimed independents, and modest support from Democrats. Senators Helms and Faircloth amassed this combination in their 1990s elections. Governor Hunt achieved a broader appeal than his Democratic colleagues, capturing more independents, Republicans, moderates, and conservatives in his 1992 and 1996 victories.

Overall, a key feature of North Carolina politics in the 1990s is its competitiveness. Most elections were decided with the victors achieving only modest margins over their opponents. A glance at the state's party-strength figure presented in Chapter 1 confirms this observation. North Carolina in the 1990s was the only southern state to closely straddle the figure's 50 percent line throughout the last ten years. (See Figure 3.) This close competition between the two parties has been building over the last four decades. Since the late 1960s, the majority of major elections have been won by less than 55 percent of the total vote. There is no escaping the conclusion that North Carolina has moved from a modified one-party Democratic state to a competitive two-party state.

While the elections have been competitive and the parties fight hard in almost every contest for major offices, incumbents have been remarkably durable in North Carolina politics. Since neither the Democrats nor the Republicans have been able to lay a convincing claim to being the majority party over an extended period, a different majority has emerged in North Carolina—the "Incumbent Party." In the last quarter century, incumbents in North Carolina have a reelection success rate of three out of four. Incumbents in the state's nine constitutional offices below the governorship, known collectively as the Council of State, were reelected at a rate of 93 percent. For the U.S. House the rate was 91 percent; for the U.S. Senate, 49 percent. In the state legislature, the reelection rate for members of the House was 75 percent, and for the Senate, 71 percent.[38] Moreover, the incumbency advantage is shared by candidates of both parties. Since Democrats have had more incumbents over the years, however, the high incumbency reelection rate has worked to delay the election of Republican candidates, especially in the down-ticket and less visible offices.[39]

The Council of State warrants special consideration for what its recent election patterns reveal about the spread of two-party competition. These nine offices—lieutenant governor, attorney general, state treasurer, state auditor, secretary of state, superintendent of public instruction, commissioner of agriculture, commissioner of insurance, and commissioner of labor—were not immune from the recent partisan trends. Even though only a lone Republican has won a Council of State seat in the last three decades (Jim Gardner's election as lieutenant governor in 1988),[40] races for these nine down-ticket posts have become more competitive. In 1976 the average Democratic winning margin for the council positions was 66 percent, but in 1988 it had fallen to 54 percent and remained there in the 1996 elections. The Democrats' continued control of these offices derives in part from the low visibility of the offices and the contestants, the frequent incumbency of Democratic candidates, and party-line voting influenced by top-of-the-ticket choices. The effort by Republicans in 1996 to attract attention to their slate with a race car folk hero underestimated the sophistication of the voters in regard to these less visible positions.

As electoral competition has spread, North Carolina's political parties have also been transformed organizationally and financially. Both the Republican and Democratic parties now have a more permanent presence in the state with headquarters and professional staffs. Both are receiving significant public money from the North Carolina Political Parties Financing Fund, as well as increased resources from the private sector. These contributions help to sustain the state parties and provide them means to offer more varied services to candidates. Additionally, each party is making a concerted effort to field candidates for offices up and down the ballot. Fewer positions go uncontested. And the two parties are able to provide a greater variety of services to candidates, including issue and opposition research, opinion polling, and advertising advice and support, to name a few.[41]

Turning to future prospects, it is likely that the decade of the 1990s will mark the last hurrah in elective politics for Helms and Hunt. Frail in appearance, Helms seems unlikely to run again in 2002, when he will be 81. Hunt, who was fifty-nine at the start of his fourth term, is constitutionally prohibited from seeking another term as governor in the year 2000, and he has said that 1996 was his last political race.

When Helms leaves the scene, it is far from clear whether the Republicans will be able to continue their mastery of North Carolina's U.S. Senate seats, although they have won seven of the past nine such contests. The next test will be in November 1998 when Senator Faircloth, who has earned a reputation as one of President Clinton's most persistent critics, seeks a second term. A wealthy trial lawyer, John Edwards, won the Democratic senatorial nomination and in mid-1998 appeared to be mounting a strong challenge, capitalizing partly on voter dissatisfaction with managed-care health providers.[42]

Whether the Republican party continues its rapid growth depends in part on the party's ability to hold together its factions and to appeal to middle-of-the-road voters. The GOP ranges from Brooks Brothers–attired bankers sipping fine merlot at the country club to Scripture-quoting fundamentalists who drink nothing stronger than sweet tea. At one point, the GOP seemed ready to break apart. Tensions in 1988 between supporters of George Bush and Pat Robertson, the television evangelist, were so great that a congressional district meeting turned into a brawl requiring law enforcement officers to quell.

Over the years, party power has seesawed between two major groups—the more conservative wing headed by Helms, the National Conservative Club, and the Christian Coalition and the more moderate wing headed by former GOP governors Jim Martin and Jim Holshouser and including chamber-of-commerce Republicans and traditional mountain Republicans. Martin and Holshouser devoted considerable time as governors to building the party's support in the state by developing its organization, raising funds for party operations and campaigns, and recruiting candidates to major offices. But the factional conflict continues. During the eight years Martin was governor, the moderates were in control. But with Democrat Hunt at the head of state government since 1993, control of the Republican party has shifted back to conservatives closely allied with Helms.

In the mid-1990s the North Carolina GOP has been able generally to integrate the Christian Coalition and abortion opponents into their state party with minimal disruption. For example, there was only a modest amount of grumbling in 1996 when Charlotte mayor Vinroot, a moderate Republican, was upset for the gubernatorial nomination by state representative Hayes, who had the backing of the Christian Coalition. "Rather than come in from the outside to take over," Hawke said, "the Christian Coalition leadership came from within the party."[43]

Still, by 1996 the Republican party had taken a definite turn to the political right. At one time, Helms defined the most rightward position in the state GOP. But today Helms is squarely in his party's mainstream. While he won in 1996, most of the other right-leaning Republican candidates, including Hayes, were defeated. Democrats hope the rightward drift of the Republican party will alienate many middle-of-the-road voters just as their own party's leftward drift proved harmful at the ballot box. "To me the question is, which party can take the center," Pearce said. "I think a big part of what happened to the Democrats in the '70s and '80s is that we went so far left, at least the national party did, that we created a vacuum that the Republicans filled. Now they are in danger of going to the right."[44]

Year by year, the Republican voter base grows in North Carolina. Competitive races for U.S. House, U.S. Senate, governor, the Council of State positions, the state legislature and county-level offices seem likely to continue. "I think we are going to be a two-party state for the foreseeable future," Hawke said. "The Democratic party in this state is vital, it's alive, and it's trying to solve its problems. The Republican party is struggling to become equal. I don't see that changing."[45]

At this stage in the state's political development, each major party has assets. The Republican organization has been able to extend its success from top-of-the-ticket races to down-ticket races through increases in its ability to attract candidates to run for offices, the strength of popular gubernatorial and U.S. senatorial candidates' coattails, enhanced organizational resources, and the emergence of a larger and more reliable coalition of voter support that promises candidates a greater future than mere sacrificial lambs. The Democratic party retains the advantages of party registration, historical majorities, and an adaptable appeal that bridges low-income minorities in rural and urban communities and affluent corporate leaders in the business community under an inclusive collection of liberal, moderate, and conservative policy appeals.

In the 1990s neither the Democratic nor the Republican party could lay claim to being North Carolina's clear-majority party. The state does, however, enjoy two strong and competitive parties. And for the foreseeable future, control of political power is most likely to alternate irregularly between them as both short- and long-term forces buttress ongoing political change in the Tar Heel State.

4

GEORGIA: DEMOCRATIC BASTION NO LONGER

Michael Binford, Tom Baxter, and David E. Sturrock

THE political environment of Georgia has changed dramatically in the 1990s. Always strongly Democratic, Georgia routinely elected almost any non-presidential Democrat with ease. Before the 1990s, the few Republican victories in the state were strange anomalies, and they were easily explained as resulting from unusual vulnerability in incumbent Democrats. The state legislature was overwhelmingly Democratic and controlled by longtime party leaders like Tom Murphy, the dean of American legislative speakers, who has wielded his gavel since 1973.

By the latter part of the 1990s, however, significant changes in the political landscape had occurred. Substantial Democratic margins had given way to even competition as the Peach State underwent a quiet but clear evolution. By the mid-1990s, one Senate seat was held by a Republican, eight of eleven U.S. House seats were Republican, all statewide offices were vigorously contested, and the Republican presence in the state legislature was dramatically expanding. The Georgia Democratic party-strength figure in Chapter 1 captures this precipitous decline into the era of fully competitive electoral politics; see Figure 4.

From a calm backwater of Democratic control, Georgia in the 1990s has emerged into mainstream competition between two evenly matched political parties that can take no office for granted. Old political campaigns usually incorporated the local courthouse gang, and candidates could run on slogans like "He's a workhorse, not a show horse." Contemporary campaigns revolve around intensive fundraising, attack ads, and media-savvy candidates like Newt

Gingrich. In the past, there was only one party that served as an avenue for ambitious young politicians; now both are actively recruiting and developing young candidates for office.

Georgia has a history of both flamboyant and colorless candidates serving successfully. Although Georgia lawmakers like Richard B. Russell, Herman Talmadge, and Carl Vinson were nationally known figures in their day, few have been as successful as Gingrich is in gaining media attention. More often Democrats have turned to solid, colorless candidates with large amounts of legislative experience. Sam Nunn may best symbolize this solid, well-respected type of leader, as he gained seniority and respect in the Senate without media hype. Known for his conservative values and cautious approach to political problems, Nunn was without peer in the hearts of conservative Georgia voters, and he ran unopposed in 1990. His decision to retire in 1996 marked the end of an era for Georgia politics.

At the statewide level, Georgia governors have been of the moderately conservative variety for years. George Busbee and Joe Frank Harris, both workhorses, were known as traditional figures with extensive state legislative experience who administered government programs effectively. Negotiating effectively with Speaker Murphy, they governed during times of strong economic growth and enjoyed substantial support from the business community. Murphy, a party stalwart, is a holdover from the days when the state was controlled by rural Democrats who ran the legislature and controlled the governorship. He still runs the Georgia house with a strong hand, but his influence on statewide offices has drastically declined. Furthermore, during the previous era the Democratic party effectively held the reins of power and discouraged strong Republican opposition. As state Republican legislative leader Johnny Isakson explained:

> The Republican [legislative candidate] more often than not in the 1970s and lingering into the 1980s was a disgruntled Democrat who couldn't break through the Democratic machine and went over and ran as a Republican, or they were a fringe person. There were exceptions, but not many. When you started recruiting, when you went to your local banker or insurance executive or lawyer and said, we want you to run as a Republican, and they went to a local party meeting, they said no. Are you going to sit down with Sam Nunn or are you going to sit down with "Machine Gun" Ronnie Thompson? [John Ronald (Ronnie) Thompson, a fiery former mayor of Macon, made his reputation by threatening to have anti-war demonstrators in the 1970s shot: hence the nickname

"Machine Gun" Ronnie]. You're a mainstream guy, what's your answer? I'm going to sit with Sam Nunn.[1]

Republican officeholders were often colorful local politicians like "Machine Gun" Ronnie. These candidates rarely followed traditional political careers and did little to develop the party or to recruit candidates for other offices. Isakson was correct that ambitious politicians consistently chose the Democratic party over the GOP as the path for their careers. By the late 1990s, however, the balance of power had shifted, and many ambitious young politicians saw the Republican party as their best chance for winning office.

THE 1990 ELECTIONS: FAINT GOP STIRRINGS

The 1990 campaign season marked the beginning of a significant change. Even though Senator Nunn ran unopposed for reelection to the Senate, the governor's race was open, and state house minority leader Isakson announced for the Republicans. One of the few of his party with extensive legislative service, Isakson had a statewide network of political relationships and an ability to raise money comparable to any Democratic candidate. He presented the most significant Republican challenge since 1966, when Howard (Bo) Callaway received a plurality of votes (but not the required simple majority) in the governor's race only to have the Democratic General Assembly select segregationist Democrat Lester Maddox as governor.

The 1990 Democratic nomination was strongly contested among four candidates. The one whose circumstances were most like the governors of the previous decade was Representative Lauren (Bubba) McDonald, a small-town hardware store owner and strong supporter of Speaker Murphy. While Murphy's endorsement insured McDonald a base from which to launch his campaign, it also identified him with old-style politics in a year when change seemed the watchword. Another candidate from the legislature, Senator Roy Barnes, was described in one of his television commercials as "a candidate who won't be handcuffed by the politics of the past." A conservative Democrat from increasingly Republican Cobb County, northwest of Atlanta, Barnes favored tough environmental measures to clean up pollution and supported some restrictions on abortion. In an effort to distance himself from other candidates, Barnes promised not to accept any pension from his public service. This claim was to distinguish himself from career politicians like Lieutenant Governor Zell Miller,[2] the eventual winner.

Perhaps the biggest change in 1990 was the candidacy of Atlanta mayor Andrew Young. Young sought to become the state's first African American governor, but he was doubly disadvantaged by his race and his affiliation with urban Atlanta. The rural-urban split, first noted by V. O. Key, Jr., is longstanding in Georgia politics, and rural voters are often skeptical of the help offered by urban politicians. Young was encouraged by the statewide success of a liberal Democratic congressman from Atlanta, Wyche Fowler, who narrowly defeated Republican senator Mack Mattingly in 1986 to recover the U.S. Senate seat formerly held by Herman Talmadge. Also, Young saw the election of Governor Douglas Wilder in Virginia in 1989 as an indication that old voting prejudices were changing. Wilder, however, was nominated under a party convention system, and not a primary system. Young sought to reverse the historical rejection of Atlanta politics and politicians by promising to bring something of the venturesome, world-reaching qualities of the capital city to the state at large. In areas that had not shared in the Atlanta boom years, he promised to serve as an international salesman for the state, luring trade missions and investments statewide. He ran well in urban Atlanta, and surprisingly well in the suburban doughnut of counties around Atlanta, but his efforts did not generate much support in the rural regions of the state. Although he made the runoff against Miller, he was soundly defeated 61.8 percent to 38.2 percent.[3]

The last candidate in the Democratic nomination race was eventual winner Miller, the four-term lieutenant governor from rural north Georgia. He had been a fixture on the political scene since the 1960s, when he was executive director of the Georgia Democratic party. Early in the 1990 race, Miller secured strong financial backing from a group of businessmen, including entrepreneur Virgil Williams and developer Joel Cowan. Still, he was not viewed as a strong frontrunner, and he carried substantial political baggage. In 1980 he had challenged Senator Talmadge in the Democratic primary for Talmadge's Senate seat. The primary had been a bitter and bruising one, which Talmadge won, only to lose narrowly to Republican Mattingly in the general election. Best known as a country music fan and a vocal legislative opponent of Speaker Murphy, Miller often lost legislative battles to the well-entrenched speaker.

Miller's attention had been caught by the similar situation of Pennsylvania politician Bill Casey, who defeated popular lieutenant governor William Scranton III in 1986. As Miller said: "I knew a bit about Casey, and I'd always seen a little of myself in Casey. He had run and been defeated; he was kind of considered a political has-been. He had been around forever like I had, and yet here he was taking on this candidate from central casting, and he beat him. And that impressed me, that a person like that could beat a person like Bill Scranton."

Much of the credit for Casey's upset had been given to a political consultant from Louisiana whom Miller had met a few years before, James Carville. Miller hired Carville and his partner Paul Begala, and together they mounted a campaign unlike any that had been run in the placid years leading up to the new decade. The effort ignored the traditional courthouse gangs and state legislators and relied heavily on media, both earned and paid. Thematically, the campaign omitted Miller's years of government experience and presented him as an outsider who would stand up to Murphy and the political establishment. Miller promised that his would be an administration of new ideas. One of these new ideas, the funding of a variety of educational initiatives from a new state lottery, became the insistent message in the media blitz. Relying on strong financial backing and aggressive fundraising, Miller took his message to the airwaves like no Democratic candidate before him.[4]

The education goals were ideas that Miller, a teacher himself and the son of an educator, hoped would rank him with other southern progressives. Without raising taxes, the new influx of state revenues would be earmarked for a specific set of programs: statewide, mandatory kindergarten; computers in classrooms; and HOPE scholarships for college students. The idea of the lottery to pay for these programs was introduced by Carville, who had made use of the issue before; a lottery proposal helped Carville's candidate in the 1987 Kentucky governor's race, Wallace Wilkinson, bolt past a group of better-known rivals.[5] Earmarking the funds for educational purposes helped undercut opposition to the lottery from conservative religious groups and those skeptical about introducing legalized gambling into the state.

The campaign Miller and his consultants conducted was hard hitting, aggressive, and, like Bill Clinton's presidential campaign two years later, remarkably quick in reacting to new developments. As Isakson, Miller's Republican opponent, said of Carville, "They were so fast, it was like he was in my head, or our heads. I mean, we had leaks from time to time, but they obviously thought out and planned ahead for every single thing we threw at them." Such a quick, highly-charged, combative style stood out in a state accustomed to polite exchanges from legislative insiders. When Miller sharply criticized Young for Atlanta's crime problems, it appeared that the campaign, which was headed for a runoff between these two candidates, might become racially divisive. That it did not owes a great deal to the restraint of both candidates. Miller made a clear effort to include issues that had wide appeal in the minority community.[6] He led the primary with 41.3 percent of the vote to Young's 28.8 percent, with Barnes and McDonald well back at 20.8 percent and 6.1 percent, respectively. As noted above, Miller defeated Young in the runoff. In the general election, minority voters gave Miller strong support, indicating no lingering bitterness over the primary campaign.

Isakson easily won his party's nomination, but his declaration at a debate that he opposed a constitutional amendment banning abortion caused a divisive issue to surface on the Republican side.[7] Largely on the basis of this issue and the support it generated among conservative Christian groups, a relatively un-known anti-abortion candidate, Bob Wood, jumped into the race and finished second, ahead of better-financed opponents. Conservative Christians had by 1990 become a significant part of the Republican coalition, and the abortion issue would be used by Isakson again.

The most dramatic moment of the general election campaign came in an October debate in the Temple, the historic synagogue on Atlanta's Peachtree Street. Miller, again on the attack, seemed to bring Isakson close to tears, accus-ing him of building his political career on his father's successful real estate busi-ness.[8] Isakson felt that the charge backfired and said that this attack was the "big-gest break" of his campaign. Indeed, some appalled Democratic contributors later supported Isakson's 1996 U.S. Senate race. But the incident did not create much voter sympathy, as Miller defeated Isakson 52.9 percent to 44.5 percent. The general election contest did show that Republicans could be competitive with Democrats, both financially and electorally, for the top spot. Isakson had the necessary legislative experience and financial connections to run a profes-sional, media-oriented campaign. Still, while Miller's margin was narrower than previous Democratic winners, it maintained Democratic dominance at the state level.

With Miller's decision to run for the top spot, a number of new candidates sought other statewide offices. In the Democratic race for lieutenant governor, state senator Pierre Howard, a fraternity brother of Isakson's at the University of Georgia, defeated senate colleague Joseph (Joe) Kennedy, another old-style state legislator with strong backing from Speaker Murphy and other influential Democrats. In the general election, Howard—who spent over $2 million on his campaign, almost ten times what campaigns for lieutenant governor had spent in the past[9]—easily defeated Republican newcomer Matt Towery, 62.7 percent to 34.4 percent. The new lieutenant governor and the speaker clashed continu-ally, much as Miller and Murphy had done in previous years, but in the new arrangement Governor Miller and Speaker Murphy proved to be surprisingly cooperative, helping Miller pass several high-profile pieces of legislation.

All during the campaign Miller had emphasized refocusing the Democratic party on economic issues aimed at helping working people. He had long cham-pioned eliminating the sales tax on food, believing that it hurt poor people. He told a June 1991 meeting of the southern caucus of the Democratic National Committee that the party had to "change in fundamental ways" or risk losing "cities and states and seats that we have held for generations." He argued strongly for a return to the economic issues that gave the Democratic party a strong middle-class constituency, rather than the social issues of liberal Democratic activists.[10] The economic recession of the early 1990s put Governor Miller in a tough spot. Lagging state revenues forced him to postpone his proposed elimination of the state sales tax on food and to freeze raises for teachers and state workers. He even suggested furloughs for public employees, including those in the university system. With Murphy's cooperation, he was still able to fulfill several campaign promises, including "boot camps" for young, first-time criminal offenders, tougher DUI laws, and a referendum on the state lottery to fund educational projects.

The speech before the regional party caucus echoed the themes Miller and Carville shared about Democratic politics, and, although it did not receive wide support among party activists, it did arouse the interest of another southern governor, Bill Clinton of Arkansas. This common interest blossomed into a close relationship. Three months later, Clinton showed up at the Governor's mansion in Atlanta after speaking before a Democratic group in the city. As Miller remembered it: "I had gone to his speech that night, and he had frankly wandered a good bit all over the place—I think it was the [Richard] Russell dinner. He [Clinton] said this, I didn't: that he had this weakness of going on too long— and this was after 1988 when he had made that [long Democratic National Convention] speech—and he knew he needed to make his message more concise. And in that vein, somehow I said, well, who you ought to get to help you with that are James Carville and Paul Begala. They sure helped me put some discipline in my campaign and speeches. . . . And he said, well, I'm going to Washington, do you think they'll talk with me? And I said, of course they'll talk with you."[11] The rest is history, for this was the beginning of Carville's involvement with the candidate he would help win the 1992 presidential election.

CONGRESSIONAL REDISTRICTING AND ITS PORTENTS

Georgia's November 1990 congressional elections resulted in no partisan change; the delegation remained as it had been throughout the 1980s—one Republican (Newt Gingrich) and nine Democrats. This situation was to change dramatically in a little over four years. In April 1995, when Democratic congressman Nathan Deal switched to the GOP, there were eight Republican members of the U.S. House from Georgia and only three Democratic members, and all three Democrats were African Americans.

The process that started the fundamental transformation of the Georgia congressional delegation from staunchly Democratic to overwhelmingly Republican began with the 1990 census. As a result of strong population growth, the state was given a new district, the Eleventh. Court rulings made it clear that at least one new black-majority district, joining John Lewis's Fifth District in Atlanta, would probably have to be a part of the new map to meet the requirements of the amended Voting Rights Act. After initial plans were rejected by the Justice Department, with prodding from the Bush administration the legislature drew a second map that created two black-majority districts in addition to Lewis's Fifth: the new Eleventh and the redrawn Second District in southwestern Georgia. The Eleventh stretched from suburban DeKalb County, east of Atlanta, through numerous sparsely populated counties in the old "black belt" region of the state, ending in a narrow finger that reached into inner-city Savannah near the coast. Other fingers reached African American enclaves in Augusta and middle Georgia.[12]

The newly drawn districts offered substantial opportunities for Republicans, who had worked closely with African American state legislators in drawing the new lines. All understood that concentrating African American voters in the two new black-majority districts would likely yield two additional black Democratic members of Congress since African Americans vote overwhelmingly Democratic. The process also reduced the number of African American voters in the surrounding districts, substantially raising the proportion of whites there (a result sometimes referred to, in the inelegant language of the politicians, as "bleaching") and possibly tipping these other districts in the Republican direction.[13]

For Newt Gingrich, the lone Republican in the delegation at the start of the 1990s, the redistricting offered a great opportunity. Since 1978, Gingrich had represented the Sixth District, south of Atlanta, a suburban and formerly rural area with Atlanta's Hartsfield Airport as its economic center. Gingrich had never been entirely secure there, and in the 1990 election had defeated Democrat David Worley by only 971 votes. Worley had effectively attacked Gingrich for accepting a congressional pay raise while voting against federal mediation in a strike against Eastern Airlines, which had devastated the district. The new 1992 map created a safe Republican district, still called the Sixth, in the affluent suburbs north of Atlanta. Gingrich quickly moved to take advantage of this seat.[14]

One of the most vocal members of the Legislative Black Caucus, which pushed for the new black-majority districts, was state representative Cynthia

McKinney. The daughter of well-known civil rights activist and fellow legislator Billy McKinney, she lobbied for creating the maximum number of majority-minority districts, often clashing with white Democratic leaders, who preferred a more moderate plan that would preserve a larger number of more competitive Democratic districts. In 1992 she quickly entered the field of candidates for the Eleventh and ran ahead of an African American state senator to win a place in the runoff. After defeating a white candidate in the runoff, she easily won the general election and became one of seven new members in a Georgia U.S. House delegation radically transformed by redistricting and retirement.

Another African American state legislator, Sanford Bishop, was elected in the Second District after defeating white incumbent Charles Hatcher in a Democratic primary that highlighted Hatcher's 819 overdrafts in the House bank scandal. Two white Democratic state senators, Don Johnson and Nathan Deal, were elected to open House seats in north Georgia. The rest of the seats were won by Republicans: Jack Kingston in the First District, along the coast; John Linder in the suburban Fourth, northeast of Atlanta; and Mac Collins in the Third, which included much of Gingrich's old district. Kingston easily defeated a Democratic newcomer, Barbara Christmas, 57.8 percent to 42.2 percent. In the open seat contest in the Fourth, Linder faced an experienced Democrat in former state senator Cathey Steinberg and won only narrowly, 50.5 percent to 49.5 percent. Collins's victory was much more significant, since he defeated an incumbent Democratic congressman, Richard Ray, 54.8 percent to 45.2 percent. While significantly increasing their presence in the congressional delegation, Republicans still held only four out of eleven seats after the 1992 voting.[15]

THE 1992 ELECTIONS: A MIXED PARTISAN RESULT

At the top of the 1992 ballot, Clinton narrowly eked out a victory, returning Georgia to the Democratic column for the first time since native son Jimmy Carter took the state in 1976 and 1980. Clinton won 43.5 percent of the vote to George Bush's 42.9 percent, with Ross Perot winning 13.3 percent of the vote. Out of 2.3 million votes cast, Clinton's margin of victory was 13,714 votes. The state was accurately seen as a battleground by both sides, and there was vigorous competition for its thirteen electoral votes.[16]

Also in 1992, Senator Fowler sought reelection. A favorite lieutenant of Senate majority leader George Mitchell and highly regarded by Democratic leaders in Washington, Fowler played an important role in the 1990 budget deal that ultimately led to George Bush's difficulties for breaking his pledge to impose no new taxes. In 1991 Fowler sided with the state's senior senator, Sam Nunn, in voting against committing U.S. troops to the war in the Persian Gulf. His support of fellow Georgian Clarence Thomas for the Supreme Court, however, hurt him among many core Democratic groups, especially with women. Fowler's record, as well as a lingering perception of him as a liberal lawyer from Atlanta, made him a vulnerable target and induced Paul Coverdell, a former state Republican leader, to leave his post as director of the Peace Corps in the Bush administration in order to run against him. Despite Fowler's sizable financial advantage and early lead in the polls, the campaign turned into a nasty, hotly contested race to the wire.[17]

An Atlanta businessman with many years in the state legislature, Coverdell had been state Republican chairman and had helped the Bush campaign win the state handily in 1988. He was the best-known and best-funded of the five Republican candidates, but he faced opposition from hopefuls representing new groups in the party, especially the conservative Christians. Coverdell won the GOP nomination by defeating U.S. attorney Bob Barr, who would later win a spot in the congressional delegation, as well as Waycross mayor John Knox, who would return to try unsuccessfully for the governor's office in 1994. Spirited primary competition among Republican candidates was a new phenomenon in a state where previous Republican candidates had often been seen as sacrificial lambs. But this 1992 Republican primary was to be the beginning of a trend, as Table 10 indicates.

When Coverdell entered the race, his prospects appeared to be waning, much like those of Bush, to whom he was often compared. But Coverdell had advantages that Bush lacked. First, he hired an experienced and controversial campaign manager, Tom Perdue, to run his campaign. Ten years earlier, Perdue had engineered Democratic governor Harris's victory by employing a strong no-tax promise and appeals to the religious right. As Harris's chief of staff, Perdue had enjoyed considerable power in state politics and had made a number of enemies, including Fowler. After a series of financial reversals and a divorce, Perdue returned to campaign politics. He made it no secret that he had little regard for Coverdell and was involved in this race largely because of his animosity toward Fowler. Using a corny but effective jingle by seventy-three-year-old Margy Lopp in a television ad, Perdue was able to soften a bitter and personal campaign to bring Coverdell within 36,000 votes of Fowler on election day.[18]

Coverdell's second big advantage was a Georgia statute that required an absolute majority to win statewide office. The presence of a Libertarian candidate, who received 3.1 percent of the vote, prevented Fowler from winning outright. Fowler received nearly a hundred thousand more votes than Clinton, who

Table 10. Primary Turnout in Georgia for Governor and U.S. Senate, 1968–1998

Year	Office	Democratic Party		Republican Party	
		Votes	% of two-party vote	Votes	% of two-party vote
1968	Senator	905,086	96.4	34,121	3.6
1970	Governor	798,650	88.1	107,577	11.9
1972	Senator	716,641	90.1	78,418	9.9
1974	Governor	854,633	94.7	48,022	5.3
1974	Senator	642,144	100.0	Unopposed	
1978	Governor	695,911	96.3	26,605	3.7
1978	Senator	957,687	96.4	24,693	3.6
1980	Senator	1,029,300	95.6	47,138	4.4
1982	Governor	899,990	93.6	61,419	6.4
1984	Senator	888,385	93.0	67,053	7.0
1986	Governor	611,463	100.0	Unopposed	
1986	Senator	626,340	88.8	78,654	11.2
1990	Governor	1,052,315	89.9	118,118	10.1
1990	Senator	Unopposed		No Candidate	
1992	Senator	Unopposed		269,943	100.0
1994	Governor	459,779	60.7	297,221	39.3
1996	Senator	517,697	53.7	446,655	46.3
1998	Governor	486,841	53.8	418,542	46.2

Sources: Richard M. Scammon and Alice V. McGillvray, America Votes: A Handbook of Contemporary Election Statistics, various vols. (Washington, D.C., 1968–   ); Georgia secretary of state primary election summaries.

needed only a plurality to win the state's electoral votes, but the Democratic senator still received only 49.2 percent of the vote and by law was forced into a runoff election against Coverdell, who amassed 47.7 percent in the first round. During the three-week runoff campaign, momentum shifted to Coverdell as the national Republican party poured money into the race and Georgia Republicans, smarting from Clinton's Peach State victory, made the campaign their rallying cry. Overnight, Coverdell's blue and white yard signs sprang up across the north Atlanta suburbs.[19]

Clinton, signaling his debt to Georgia Democrats, campaigned enthusiastically for the endangered senator, but the president-elect's buoyant energy was in stark contrast to an increasingly dispirited Fowler. Two days before Thanksgiving, with turnout down sharply from the general election, Coverdell defeated Fowler by 16,237 votes; the Republican won 50.6 percent of the vote to Fowler's 49.4 percent.

Also in 1992, Congressman Gingrich received an uneasy introduction to his new, supposedly more secure district. Republican state representative Herman Clark had planned to run in the district before Gingrich made his move. He persisted in his primary race and sought to turn the tables on his better-known opponent. He forced Gingrich, who had fanned the flames of the House banking scandal, to admit that he had twenty-two overdrafts and to promise to give up his chauffeur, one of the perks that had come with his position as minority party whip. Gingrich barely defeated Clark, winning the primary by only 980 votes,[20] but went on to an easy victory in the general election, with 57.7 percent of the vote to 42.3 percent for his Democratic opponent.

The following year began with an uncharacteristic political misstep by Governor Miller. The successes of his first two years had been based on a pragmatic, deliberate approach with a moderately conservative agenda. In 1993, he surprised his legislative leaders by calling for dropping the Confederate battle flag from the state flag. With a fiery State of the State speech, he urged the legislature to return to the pre-1956 version of the flag.[21] Long an issue among African American legislators, the flag controversy erupted and spurred protest marches by the Sons of the Confederacy and other fringe groups. It is conceivable that Miller could have built a consensus to change the flag, by stressing especially its embarrassing presence at the upcoming 1996 Olympics, if he had been more careful. But his throwing down the gauntlet in an emotional speech doomed the issue to a short legislative history and a quick defeat.

Miller did not revisit the flag issue after the 1993 session. It was, he said later, a case in which he had disregarded his dictum "not to get involved in things that don't matter in people's daily lives." Lieutenant Governor Howard, who had not been informed of Miller's plans, described it as "a cataclysmic event" that sped along the growing realignment which was to surface in the next election cycle.[22]

THE 1994 ELECTIONS: MAJOR GOP BREAKTHROUGH

By the end of the legislative session, Miller had extricated himself from a 1990 campaign pledge not to seek a second term. He let his intentions regarding reelection be known, and faced only token opposition among the Democrats. Isakson, facing family illness and a difficult business climate as well as the increasing militancy of the conservative Christians in the Republican party, dropped out of the race shortly after entering it. Miller's Republican opponent in the second governor's race of the decade was a type of candidate who frequently popped up among southern Republicans in the 1990s. Like Clayton Williams in Texas and Kirk Fordice in Mississippi, Guy Millner was an up-from-the-bootstraps, successful entrepreneur who aimed for high office in his first attempt at politics. The founder of Norrell Corporation, a large temporary employment agency, Millner was a Florida native who had flourished in Atlanta and had become involved in social, civic, and educational circles. He agreed to pay the college tuition for twenty-one graduates at an Atlanta-area inner city school that he had adopted, and he let it be known that he was interested in politics.[23] Millner introduced himself in an expensive ad campaign and came very close to avoiding a runoff in a crowded, five-candidate field. The second place finisher was John Knox, still supported by the party's religious right; yet Millner, too, had courted the religious right, and with their vote divided, he easily defeated Knox in the runoff.

As Miller and Millner squared off, it was increasingly clear how much Georgia politics had changed from the previous decade. No longer was the contest decided in the Democratic primary; Republicans had more than token candidates to field. The main battle was now a protracted two-party contest, fought over the airwaves and through earned media, and both candidates had the ability to raise large sums of money. Between them, Miller and Millner reported spending $9.2 million in the 1994 contest.[24] Carville, who had become a national celebrity after Clinton's 1992 win, deferred more in this campaign to his partner, Begala, but the Miller campaign's aggressive and quickly-reacting style was the same as in the 1990 race.

Millner was also more aggressive than Miller's earlier Republican opponent. With Clinton's popularity plummeting in the state, the Republican's ads featured a clip of Miller's Democratic Convention keynote address in which he called Clinton "the only candidate who feels our pain," as well as clips of Miller pledging to serve only one term. Millner also raised questions about the financing of a state-run resort in Towns County, near Miller's home town.[25]

In a counteroffensive, Miller accused the Republican of using the federal government's savings and loan bailout to obtain a five-hundred-thousand-dollar break on his Atlanta mansion and wasted few opportunities to call other kinds of attention to Millner's wealth. Millner, in a beginner's gaffe, remarked early that voters would not be seeing him "in many parades on a Saturday down in Vidalia, because that's not where the votes are and that's not where the fundraising will be." To atone, he later met Miller in a debate in the small south Georgia town, where the governor, dressed in a dark business suit, made fun of his opponent's khaki pants and plaid shirt attire as a crude attempt to relate to south Georgia voters.[26]

To underscore his opponent's lack of political experience, what mattered most for the incumbent Democrat was his ability to point to his political successes: the boot camps, tougher DUI laws, and the educational gains from the lottery. The HOPE scholarship program was surpassing projections in its second year. With the extra lottery money, the $66,000 family income cap was removed, thus making all Georgia families eligible. This classic middle-class issue was extremely popular throughout the state, but especially so in the suburban bedroom communities that are traditionally strong areas of Republican support.[27]

The critical importance of this issue became apparent on election day, when Republicans scored numerous upsets while Miller hung on for a very narrow victory.[28] Democrats knew they would have a difficult time beating the popular attorney general Mike Bowers, who had recently changed parties to run as a Republican, but they were shocked when a little-known Augusta principal, Republican Linda Schrenko, defeated incumbent Democratic school superintendent Werner Rogers. Another party switcher, John Oxendine, defeated incumbent Democrat Tim Ryles for insurance commissioner, and Nancy Schaefer, a religious conservative leader, drew 42.5 percent of the vote against Howard, the well-known lieutenant governor. Miller won the governor's race with 51.1 percent of the vote to Millner's 48.9 percent, but his margin of victory dropped from 121,000 votes in 1990 to only 32,555 in 1994.

These 1994 results indicated that Republicans had become equal players in Georgia's lesser statewide contests. Prior to 1990, the GOP had rarely contested, much less won, any of these offices. In 1990, they fielded only three candidates for nine executive and Public Service Commission (PSC) seats, and were competitive in only one of these races. In 1992, however, the Republicans captured an open PSC seat on the same day that Coverdell won his Senate runoff. In 1994, Republicans contested all but one of the down-ballot constitutional offices and won five of them. Thanks to these victories and two midterm conversions, Republicans in 1997 held three of seven executive posts below the governorship and four of five PSC posts.

The 1994 elections, then, were clearly a breakthrough for the Republican party. Building on the success of the Coverdell comeback two years earlier and the redistricting gains at the congressional level, the Republican party ran a full slate of qualified, if not well-known, candidates for statewide offices. Vigorous campaigns involving both the media and old-fashioned organizational fieldwork motivated high turnout and produced a number of Republican successes. Several Democratic candidates were complacent and ran uninspired campaigns, but merely turning out the party faithful and collecting the spillover votes from strong Democratic contenders at the top of the ballot was no longer sufficient to guarantee success. Grassroots activity by conservative Christian groups for Republican candidates, especially Schaefer and Schrenko, helped them take several down-ballot races. Republicans proved they could coordinate their campaign efforts, raise money, field qualified candidates, and, most importantly, win. Democrats learned they could no longer take any office or election for granted.

Nowhere was the growing Republican strength more obvious than in congressional elections. Enthusiastically supporting Newt Gingrich's 1994 call for more Republicans, Georgia voters added three new seats to the party's 1992 gains. Bob Barr, runnerup in the 1992 Republican Senate primary, came back to win the Seventh District by defeating U.S. representative George (Buddy) Darden with 51.9 percent of the vote to Darden's 48.1 percent. Congressman Darden, a moderately conservative Democrat who had weathered several earlier challenges, had supported Clinton's budget package, a decision that was unpopular in his district. Barr had strong support from the religious right and from gun control opponents including the National Rifle Association. Democratic U.S. representative Don Johnson, who also voted for the budget, was soundly defeated in the Tenth District in northeast Georgia by Augusta dentist Charlie Norwood.[29] Norwood captured 65.2 percent to Johnson's 34.8 percent. Both these districts had long been Democratic strongholds despite scattered pockets of "Mountain Republicans."

The most symbolically important seat was won by Saxby Chambliss, a south Georgia lawyer who had organized part of the state for Democrat Pierre Howard in 1990. The Eighth District had been left open by the retirement of popular Democratic representative Roy Rowland. This rural district ran south from Macon to the Florida border, well beyond the Atlanta suburbs. The election of a Republican here by a 62.7 percent to 37.3 percent margin showed that the Republican realignment was sinking deep roots in the state. After north Georgia Democrat Nathan Deal joined the GOP six months after the election, the Georgia congressional delegation was divided along coinciding racial and partisan lines: three African American Democrats and eight white Republicans.[30]

MILLER V. JOHNSON

The 1994 GOP congressional surge was based in significant part on the reapportionment map developed in 1992, and this map became the object of a federal lawsuit that would drastically alter the political landscape before the 1996 congressional elections. Brought by white plaintiffs in the majority African American Eleventh district, the case was heard by a three-judge federal panel, which ruled two months before the 1994 elections that the redistricting plan developed to conform to Justice Department requirements violated the plaintiffs' equal protection rights. The order for new maps was stayed so that the 1994 elections could take place under the old districts, but most observers expected that another redrawing of the boundaries would soon follow.

The U.S. Supreme Court upheld the lower court ruling in June 1995 in the landmark case of *Miller v. Johnson*. Building on the 1993 *Shaw v. Reno* case from North Carolina, the Court held that, while race could be a factor in redistricting, it could not be the "overriding, predominant force in the districting determination." Thus the Georgia redistricting plan was invalidated as an unconstitutional racial gerrymander. In August 1995 the General Assembly returned for a special session to redraw the congressional districts once again, but after four weeks, with an impatient federal judicial panel waiting in the wings, the legislators gave up.[31] The balance in the legislature among Republicans, white Democrats, and African American Democrats was much narrower than in 1991, and resolving their differences proved politically impossible.

Without a legislative plan, the federal court acted quickly and produced a plan in December 1995 that eliminated the African American majorities in both the Second and Eleventh districts.[32] The Second District dropped from 52 percent African American to 35 percent, the Eleventh from 60 percent to 10 percent, and the Fourth District increased from 11 percent to 33 percent African American. The new maps set off a chain reaction of political moves for the upcoming 1996 congressional elections. Congresswoman McKinney chose to remain in the suburban DeKalb County portion of her former district, now reconfigured into the Fourth, a district that included a number of white liberal Democrats from around Decatur and Emory University. The newly configured district was clearly better for a Democrat, and the previous representative, Republican John Linder, chose to migrate to the new Eleventh, which was anchored in suburban Atlanta's Gwinnett county and was considerably more hospitable to a Republican candidate. In effect, McKinney and Linder switched districts, while keeping their core constituencies intact. Saxby Chambliss's home in Colquitt County was taken out of his Eighth District, but he stayed to run for reelection in the district anyway.

While the new map had substantially new boundaries in many districts, it caused no changes in the actual delegation. All the incumbents won in 1996, including Bishop and McKinney, who both now represented white-majority districts. Both defeated white Democratic primary opponents without runoffs, and easily prevailed over their white Republican opposition in the general election. A precinct analysis indicated that each received at least 30 percent of the white vote; furthermore, turnout in the African American areas of the Second and Fourth was very high and cohesive in support of McKinney and Bishop.[33]

THE 1996 ELECTIONS

Newt Gingrich always has a high-profile campaign, and in 1996 he attracted another entrepreneurial opponent, cookie magnate Michael Coles. Much like Millner, Coles was willing to fund his own campaign in large part and made a credible, but ultimately unsuccessful, attempt to unseat the Speaker. Gingrich received 57.8 percent of the vote to Coles's 42.2 percent. The contest was the most expensive House race in the country with combined spending topping $7.1 million. Gingrich reported spending $3.8 million and Coles $3.3 million, including a $2.4 million loan to his campaign.[34] (Incidentally, Coles returned in 1998 as the Democratic nominee opposing Senator Coverdell's first reelection effort; in the interim Coles had served as state Democratic chairman.) Also, Gingrich's seven fellow Georgia Republican congressmen were all reelected in 1996.

The closest race in 1996 was the U.S. Senate election. In the same month that the federal court handed down the new map, Senator Nunn ended a long period of suspense and announced his retirement. He had lost his chairmanship of the Senate Armed Services Committee when the Republicans took over the Senate in 1994, and had grown increasingly uncomfortable with the more strident, partisan tone in Congress. Republicans saw Nunn's retirement as a chance to win a second Senate seat and to emerge as the dominant force in state politics.

This perception of growing Republican ascendancy may have aided Georgia secretary of state Max Cleland, the Democrat who had expressed the most interest in running for the Senate if Nunn retired. Although many Democrats questioned whether Cleland was the strongest candidate, he drew no primary opposition and was able to resign his office in early 1996 to devote himself full time to fundraising and campaigning. Cleland, who had lost both legs and an arm in a grenade accident during the Vietnam war, had served as director of the Veterans Administration in the Carter administration. A popular politician, he had been the Democrats' top vote getter, but some in the party feared he would be vulnerable on several matters, including a wrongful termination case brought by a former employee and an explicit telephone tape made by an estranged girlfriend.[35]

The Republican primary quickly filled with a strong field of candidates, including Millner and Isakson. Both had run effective statewide campaigns and had the ability to raise large war chests. A third candidate, state senator Clint Day, heir to the Days Inn fortune, also had the ability to run an expensive campaign. They all had to compete, however, in a cluttered media environment around the Atlanta summer Olympic games. The primary was held on July 9, before the Olympics began, and the runoff was set for August 6, two days after the closing ceremonies. All these candidates had to attract the attention of distracted voters and a news atmosphere that was allowing little attention to be paid to this campaign.[36]

Many new Republicans had moved into the state since his 1990 campaign, and Isakson found himself running far behind Millner in the early polls. Both Millner and Day were competing for the support of the religious right. Knowing that he lacked support from that wing of the party, Isakson decided on a risky and unconventional strategy. He made an ad with his wife and daughter, reiterating his opposition to a constitutional ban on abortion.[37] By supporting such a ban, he said, Millner and Day were putting women and their doctors in risk of going to jail. While there were pro-choice Republicans in other parts of the country, no candidate produced an ad opposing the amendment, and certainly no southern Republican candidate had been so outspoken against what Isakson came to call the "extremists" in his party. His strategy was in part a reflection of growing frustration among traditional Republicans with the expanding power of religious conservatives in the Republican party. The religious right has had a growing impact on local and legislative races by publishing voter guides to direct conservative voters to the appropriate candidates. Isakson was uncomfortable with the power of these groups and the principles they followed in deciding whom to support:

> You could vote with them all the time because the amendments never were going to pass, or you could do what you thought was right. And I mean, I play politics like everybody else. Sometimes, I'd vote even though I didn't agree with it, just because it would not pass and didn't matter, but when it got to things in the education arena and other areas where it was going to be the wrong thing to do, whether it was going to be a report card issue or not, I just did not vote with them. . . . When I announced for the United States Senate in this race, I knew they would have a candidate. . . . They're in this for political power now and not for moral victories anymore. . . . They're not always wrong, but if you don't always agree with them, you're always wrong.[38]

Millner had learned the importance of having a professional staff in his first statewide effort. To run his second campaign, he hired Tom Perdue, who, after engineering Coverdell's 1992 upset, had run the successful Senate campaign of another wealthy first-time Republican, Bill Frist, winner over veteran Democrat James R. Sasser in the 1994 Tennessee race.[39] Millner also hired John Knox to help attract conservative religious voters. Millner took 41.8 percent of the primary vote to Isakson's 34.8 percent and defeated him 52.9 percent to 47.1 percent in the runoff. But it was a rough and costly victory. The race had grown increasingly bitter as the rivals struggled to get the voters' attention above the Olympic hubbub, and this divisive primary may have cost Millner the general election. Whit Ayres, Millner's pollster, later said hard feelings over the race and its tone reduced the Republican margin in Cobb County, which was Isakson's home and a major source of Republican votes. Millner took only 56 percent of the Cobb vote in November, not enough to overcome the expected Democratic margins in urban Atlanta, and significantly lower than the traditional Republican vote. Many Republican activists and political professionals, including Ayres, believe this difference accounted for Millner's defeat.[40]

The campaign for the general election was tough, too. In addition to the wrongful termination case, Millner attacked Cleland over a letter that had been sent to the Pardons and Parole Board years before requesting parole for the son of a Democratic official. After getting the parole, the son committed a murder. Cleland, like Governor Miller before him, took every opportunity to point out Millner's wealth, including an expensive Florida vacation home with membership in an exclusive, and reportedly discriminatory, country club. The fact that the initiation fee for the country club was more than most Georgians earned in a year brought home exactly how wealthy Millner was. Millner's resources made the race unusually expensive; he spent $9.8 million, and over $6.4 million came from his own wallet. Cleland raised and spent about $2.9 million.[41] He benefited, however, from a united Democratic party and unusually heavy turnout among minority voters in the two challenged districts described earlier. Only 45 percent of the vote was needed to win this time, since the state law requiring a simple majority had been changed after Fowler's defeat two years earlier. Cleland narrowly beat Millner, by 30,024 votes, 48.8 percent to Millner's 47.6 percent. (A Libertarian candidate took 3.6 percent.)

At the top of the ticket in 1996, President Clinton and Bob Dole both made Georgia a battleground state, advertising heavily and making personal appearances in the waning days of the campaign. Dole's narrow victory with 47.0 percent of the vote to Clinton's 45.8 percent made this state one of only three states to switch from Clinton in 1992 to the GOP in 1996. (The others were Colorado and Montana.) The return of some of the Perot voters to the Republican fold was the key to the Republican victory, as the Texan's support dropped from 13.3 percent in 1992 to 6.4 percent in 1996.[42]

GEORGIA'S PARTISAN TRANSFORMATION: AN ANALYSIS

These major elections of the 1990s show a remarkable transformation in Georgia politics, with the state shifting from long domination by the Democratic party to careful balance on a fulcrum, tipping toward first one party, then the other. Indeed, the two parties have attained an almost perfect equipoise in major statewide races. None of the six contests for president, governor, and U.S. senator held from 1992 through 1996 was decided by more than 2.2 percent, with Democrats averaging 48.0 percent and Republicans 47.4 percent. Neither party can take the state for granted, and the comparative quality of each campaign's effort can become the decisive factor.

How did this transformation take place? What were the factors driving it? Earlier research described Georgia's politics as evolving toward two-party competition, and clearly, that evolution has been completed.[43]

The two major factors generating these changes are a dramatic change in the population of the state and the development of a sophisticated Republican party. Demographic shifts provided the raw material, and political leadership converted it into electoral success. By building on growth and gains at the local level and by providing Georgia voters with a consistent chance to behave as Republican voters by voting for Republicans for all major offices, the Republican party has developed into an equal competitor with the Democrats. As these demographic changes continue, the Republican party could become the dominant force in the state, unless the Democrats learn the lessons of their counterparts and adapt to the new conditions.[44]

In 1980, the total population of Georgia was 5,460,000 according to the U.S. census, and by 1990, the state had 6,470,000. This 18.6 percent increase was the fourth highest in the nation. By 1996, the population had increased to 7,270,000, or a gain of 12.3 percent, the greatest percentage change in the South. There were corresponding increases in registered voters from over 2.7 million in 1990 to 3.8 million in 1996. The majority of these increases were in the urban and especially the suburban counties of the state. For example, while registered voters in Fulton County increased 29 percent from 1990 to 1996, suburban Cobb County increased 52 percent, and outpaced Fulton in absolute numbers of new voters. Similarly, DeKalb County increased 36 percent from

1990 to 1996, but adjacent Gwinnett County increased 61 percent and had a greater increase in voters. Many of the new suburban voters were new to Georgia, and many brought Republican affiliations with them. As local suburban governing boards became increasingly Republican and state legislative districts went Republican, the party had a growing basis for development.[45] Future Republican districts wait to be created around the fringe of the Atlanta metropolitan area, where some districts now contain more registered voters than they did people in 1990. Georgia's projected gain of at least one congressional seat after the next census suggests that the party will see promising new opportunities at that level as well.

African Americans' share of the state's registered voters increased from 21.9 percent in 1990 to 24.3 percent in 1996. The changes brought about by new federally mandated "motor voter" registration procedures may have played an important role since 35 percent of all registered African American voters registered after January 1995. In the same period, 25.8 percent of white registered voters signed up. The hotly contested congressional campaigns of McKinney and Bishop may also have spurred African American registration.[46]

The heavy growth in their suburban base helped Republicans recruit more candidates for office and field stronger campaigns for local and statewide office. Republican success underwent a kind of snowball effect owing to the availability of viable candidates for all offices, not just a few high profile races. Perhaps the clearest indication of the growth in Republican voting is the aggregate votes cast for all U.S. House seats. Republican support rose from 33 percent in 1988 to 45 percent in 1990, and, in 1994 and 1996, the party's share reached 54 percent.[47]

Moreover, the Republican base has spread beyond the suburban doughnut surrounding Atlanta. In his narrow Senate victory in 1980, Republican Mattingly carried only 29 of Georgia's 159 counties, while Coverdell's nearly identical margin of victory in 1992 was based on majorities in 75 counties. The same pattern is clear at the gubernatorial level. In 1990 Isakson won only 18 counties, while Millner expanded that base to take 75 counties four years later. Obviously these candidates were making significant gains across the state and taking over 60 percent of the votes in several counties. Furthermore, as Republican strength spreads across the state, more and more counties have become competitive, translating into the election of more Republicans at the local level and in the state legislature.

Parallel growth in voter participation in Republican primaries indicates that both parties are now viewed as viable avenues for electoral success. As long as voters perceived that the key decisions for major offices in Georgia were going to be made in Democratic primaries, few of them saw a reason to cast Republican primary ballots. Apart from stand-alone presidential primaries, Republican primaries in the 1980s typically drew less than 80,000 voters, or about 7 percent of the total primary vote. The 1990 GOP gubernatorial primary, however, drew a record 118,000 voters, and the Senate primary two years later had almost 270,000 voters. In 1996, the Republican Senate primary attracted over 440,000 voters, with 309,000 returning for the runoff. As the Republican party has become more competitive, its primaries have involved between 250,000 and 450,000 voters, roughly forty percent of all primary votes cast.[48] Table 10 shows the rapid increase in Republican primary activity in the 1990s and the party's growing competitiveness in attracting primary voters from the Democrats.

As the data in Table 10 indicate, well into the 1980s the Republican state party was still a minimal force in Georgia politics. Coverdell recalled the state party of those years as having "no funding, no capacity, no muscle: it was kind of like a shell corporation." He remembered state party conventions in these times: "Then as now, we'd have 500 to 1,000 at a state convention. The difference is, back then that *was* the Georgia Republican party; now, that group is a collection that is representative of a much larger whole."[49]

As a result of the expanding base of voter support, Georgia Republicans have been able to increase their fundraising capability, with a 1996 budget approaching $3 million. By contrast, annual state party budgets in the late 1970s were less than $50,000. These increased funds have helped to develop a professional staff for the state party and to provide extensive financial and technical support for individual candidates, especially at the state legislative level. Georgia Republicans have been able to hire a talented support staff partly because more of the state's young political talent now considered Republican politics a good place to lay the groundwork for a political career. For example, three of the staff members hired in the early 1990s had successively served as presidents of the University of Georgia's Interfraternity Council in the 1980s. In earlier times, former Republican party chairman Alec Poitevint noted, "those people went on to Democratic politics."[50]

Republican success in Georgia in the 1990s also reflects the fact that the party has recruited more and better candidates. Many of the winning candidates of 1992 and 1994 were people who had previously lost a race, but received party encouragement to try again. Ayres cited Coverdell's 1992 Senate victory as an event that "energized" Republicans and "showed that Republicans could win" with a direct effect upon candidate recruitment for the 1994 cycle. Ayres pointed to one prominent example of this effect, Eighth District congressman Chambliss: "In 1984, [he] would have run as a Democrat." Nor were established Democratic officials immune to this attraction. At least fifteen elected of-ficeholders switched their affiliation from Democratic to Republican between February 1994 and February 1996. The most notable of these were Attorney General Bowers, Congressman Deal, and Public Service Commission chairman Robert Durden. These successes contrast with the party's earlier recruitment efforts. As late as 1988, Republicans routinely let many statewide and General Assembly seats go uncontested. Poitevint noted that even the promising candidates lacked political seasoning; he said that the party suffered from a history of both "poor candidates and good candidates who were stupid about politics."[51]

Another indication of the growing breadth of Republican support is seen in the evolution of the state legislature. As Table 11 shows, Republicans held only 1 state senate seat in 1960, and they increased by only 4 seats during the next twenty years. They more than doubled their numbers in the 1980s and doubled again in the 1990s. Similar progress was made in the state house, where the GOP increased from 5 seats in 1960 to 20 seats in 1980. Paralleling the senate growth, the 1990s saw a doubling of Republican house members. These gains mean that Republicans in 1997 accounted for 40 percent of the entire General Assembly, putting Georgia exactly at the southern GOP legislative average, as reported in Chapter 1. Republican strength is primarily based in the 16-county Atlanta metropolitan area, where the party now holds 60 percent of all seats. The bulwarks of this support are Cobb and Gwinnett counties, where the GOP holds 28 of 30 senate and house seats. However, Republicans have also made sizable gains in formerly monolithically Democratic middle and south Georgia, and in 1996 won nearly 25 percent of the seats in these regions.[52]

Table 11. Party Representation in the Georgia Legislature, 1960–1996

Year	Senate				House			
	Dem.		Rep.		Dem.		Rep.	
1960	53	(98.1%)	1	(1.9%)	204	(97.6%)	5	(2.4%)
1970	49	(87.5)	7	(12.5)	167	(85.6)	28	(14.4)
1980	51	(91.1)	5	(8.9)	160	(88.8)	20	(11.2)
1990	45	(80.4)	11	(19.6)	145	(80.5)	35	(19.5)
1992	41	(73.2)	15	(26.7)	128	(71.1)	52	(28.9)
1994	35	(62.5)	21	(37.5)	114	(63.3)	66	(36.7)
1996	34	(60.7)	22	(39.3)	108	(60.0)	72	(40.0)

Sources: Senate and House Information Offices, *Official Statistics of Georgia* and *Directory of Members of the General Assembly of Georgia.*

African American Democrats have made smaller, but consistent, gains in the legislature. As at the congressional level, redistricting helped minority Democrats and Republicans at the expense of white Democrats in the state legislature. African American representation in the state senate has increased from 8 to 11 during this time, and the General Assembly has seen an increase from 23 to 32. African Americans now account for about 30 percent of the Democratic officeholders in each branch. With the state continuing to experience population growth, the next redistricting will bring even greater changes in the legislative makeup. Since most of the population increases have been in suburban counties, Republicans could become the majority party in either or both houses after the 2000 reapportionment. Momentum appears to be with the Republican party as the next century approaches.

Republican growth has even reached the chambers of Georgia's 159 county governments, where traditional Democratic courthouse organizations "have been like Stone Mountain" to move. By 1995 Republicans had captured at least 233 elected county offices in Georgia, about 10 percent to 12 percent of the total statewide. Of these, 52 percent were from the Atlanta area with the remainder scattered among 50 counties across the state. Eleven counties, ten in metropolitan Atlanta, have Republican commission majorities. In nine of them the party holds every seat or all but one. Nearly 25 percent of Georgians live in these Republican-controlled counties. Metropolitan counties also account for most of the state's eleven Republican sheriffs and ten district attorneys.[53]

While Georgia Republicans have overcome many of the roadblocks that historically thwarted their party's growth, they must now address other problems that still stand between them and the dominant role they desire. Two of these changes are internal. First, do Georgia Republicans think and act as a governing party? Leading Democrats say no. Agriculture Commissioner Tommy Irvin, a longtime party stalwart, continues to view the Republicans as the "party of against," while state Democratic executive director Steve Anthony says "all they do is stand up and talk about what's wrong without offering any solutions." Surprisingly, some GOP leaders share this assessment. Senator Coverdell believes that Republicans "still [use] the language of the minority," and Ayres asserts that they are still apt to view themselves as "outsiders who stop bad things from happening." According to Coverdell, more effective communication of the party message will dispel this naysayer image. "Communication of [the need for] reduction of the size of government is not an easy thing to do," but it must be mastered if Georgia Republicans are to offer themselves as a party of governance, he argued.[54]

The second major obstacle the Republicans must contend with is factional division. The mobilization of religious conservatives has energized the party's activist base and added new voters to the Republican coalition, but the newcomers do not always mix well with their more secular-minded party colleagues. Strong conservative positions that help a Republican win a contested primary may make the winning candidate appear too conservative and extreme to win in November. Irvin suggests that "good, sensible Republicans are having more trouble with the far right," although Coverdell asserts that this cleavage is "grossly overstated by the media."[55] Coverdell himself, who holds a pro-choice position on abortion, is evidence that a conservative candidate can hold the new Republican coalition together despite deviating from orthodoxy on a particular issue. But Millner's difficulties in 1994 and 1996 underscore the fragility of the relationship between the party's two wings. A major challenge for future elections and new candidates will be to overcome this factional split.

What about the Democratic party? It is clearly changing, with an increase in the number of Democratic voters but with a lower proportion of the overall electorate. The Democratic party is not the clear-majority party it once was, and, if it is to have continued success, it must adapt to the changing environment. Table 12 shows the trends in party identification over the last four years, as measured in a recurring statewide poll conducted by the Applied Research Center of Georgia State University. Democratic identification is declining, and, given the higher rate of participation and cohesive voting shown by Republicans, the parties are at parity with independents holding the balance. These data show a stable pattern for both white and African American voters; very few minority voters side with the Republicans, while the GOP continues to hold a clear advantage among white voters. The sizable number of independents among both whites and blacks indicates the competitive nature of current elections.

For either party to be successful, it must take advantage of short-term forces, such as attractive candidates and appealing issues. The lottery and the HOPE scholarships were just such appealing issues having broad support among independents and middle-class Republicans. Republican pollster Ayres noted that Miller prevailed against the 1994 GOP tide because of his sponsorship of the lottery-based HOPE scholarships. This program "peeled away suburban white, middle-class Republicans who want to send their kids to UGA [the University of Georgia] or Georgia Tech."[56] Indeed, Millner in his 1994 bid received only about 55 percent of the suburban vote, well below what Republicans have needed to win statewide. Attractive candidates must be able to distinguish themselves with such broadly appealing issues.

Within the state, the Democratic party has lagged behind the Republican

Table 12. Party Identification in Georgia by Race, 1992–1996

Year	Whites			African Americans			Total		
	Dem.	Rep.	Ind.	Dem.	Rep.	Ind.	Dem.	Rep.	Ind.
1992	26%	32%	36%	64%	5%	24%	35%	26%	33%
1993	26	31	32	69	3	20	37	24	29
1994	26	30	35	60	4	30	35	34	23
1995	25	31	32	52	3	33	31	25	32
1996	24	31	35	56	6	28	32	24	33

Source: Applied Research Center poll, Georgia State University.

Note: Responses were given to the following question: "Do you usually think of yourself as a Democrat, a Republican, or an Independent?" Data exclude those who "don't think in those terms."

party in using sophisticated technology to help candidates and in developing an aggressive and successful direct mail campaign to raise funds. Anthony, the Democratic party director, acknowledges "being behind the curve," but he said the party is making significant improvements by establishing a research department, promoting ties with local Democratic officials, actively encouraging the upgrading of county organizations, and undertaking the hitherto unnecessary task of candidate recruitment.[57]

Republican gains obviously threaten Democratic control of the state. For Democrats to retain that control, they can no longer rely upon their "night-and-day" alliance of blacks and rural whites. Democratic support from rural and small-town whites has diminished sharply in the 1990s, while Republican-friendly suburbs cast an ever-increasing share of the statewide vote. The erosion of Democratic strength among non-metropolitan whites seems to result from a combination of ticket splitting and generational replacement. Speaker Murphy contended that older voters have remained loyal Democrats because they "remember the Depression," while Ayres and other Republicans argued that Democratic loyalties are much weaker among voters under the age of forty-five.[58]

Nevertheless, the 1994 Miller and 1996 Cleland victories offer a blueprint for a refashioned night-and-day strategy, one which requires taking a significant bite out of the Republicans' suburban Atlanta doughnut. The goal is not to win these counties in statewide contests, but to shave Republican suburban margins enough to allow Democratic majorities in Atlanta proper (the doughnut's "hole"), smaller urban areas like Augusta and Macon, and black-majority rural counties to put their candidates over the top.

The best recipe for this containment strategy would mix a continued Democratic credibility on economic conservatism, with the ability to be seen as more moderate (although not especially liberal) on such social issues as abortion. This approach is essential if Democrats are to gain a sympathetic hearing from recent arrivals from the North. While there may be some truth to Irvin's lament that these new Georgians have "no appreciation for Jeffersonian Democrats," Anthony believes that their inherited Yankee Republicanism may wane with prolonged exposure to Georgia's moderate-sounding Democrats and bluntly conservative Republicans.[59] If 1994 and 1996 are to be examples, a divisive Republican primary is also helpful.

In many ways, the transformation of the Democratic party in Georgia reflects the changes that are taking place in the national party. Both were once dominant, majority parties that could win elections by turning out the party faithful and minimizing party defections. Both are now evenly matched with Republicans, and their electoral success depends on attractive candidates, issues that cut across party lines, and revitalized coalitions among core groups and supporters. The resources and the quality of the campaign effort can be crucial. By recasting the party as a moderately conservative middle-class party with strong support among African Americans, Democratic leaders like Miller and Cleland have been successful in close elections. Black candidates such as Bishop and McKinney have also motivated core supporters and attracted enough white votes to stay in office. Such strategies may be what is required for the Democrats to be viable competitors in Georgia and across the nation.

A key test for both parties lies in the upcoming 1998 state elections. It is entirely possible that the state will have a new governor, lieutenant governor, and house speaker in place by 1999, and that at least two of them will be from the Atlanta metropolitan area. They may well be Republicans. Personalities aside, the strategic and thematic attention of the 1998 campaigns were likely to be centered on the suburban Atlanta doughnut, in vivid contrast to the rural versus urban focus that once dominated Georgia politics.

Republicans originally viewed Mike Bowers, who resigned as attorney general in order to seek the governorship, as their leading candidate, and they believed he was conservative enough to rally rural whites who are dissatisfied with the Democrats. He seemed moderate enough to minimize Republican defections in the doughnut, but his recently admitted ten-year affair with a secretary while he was attorney general raised serious doubts about his candidacy. His strong "straight arrow" image as a tough law enforcer was seen as slightly hypocritical, and Republicans, long gloating over President Clinton's fidelity problems, came to realize that marital fidelity is not a partisan issue. Guy Millner, who views his two close defeats as similar to a startup business operating in the "red" before beginning to turn a profit, entered the contest and became the GOP frontrunner. In the July 21 first primary Millner won the nomination, securing just over 50 percent of the votes and barely avoiding a runoff with Bowers, who surprised observers by garnering 40 percent of the vote despite his personal difficulties. Bowers insisted on a recount before he would concede defeat. Clint Day, another wealthy candidate mentioned earlier, and Mitch Skandalakis, the chairman of the Fulton County Commission, battled each other for the Republican nomination for lieutenant governor in an August runoff, with Skandalakis the eventual winner. The GOP fielded a full slate of statewide candidates in 1998, several of whom had the advantage of running as incumbents.

On the Democratic side, Lieutenant Governor Pierre Howard was considered the frontrunner for governor, but his sudden early withdrawal led to a hotly contested race. State representative Roy Barnes, who ran for governor in 1990, won the Democratic nomination after the first primary when the second-place finisher, Secretary of State Lewis Massey, citing the need for party unity, declined to insist on a runoff even though Barnes fell about a percentage point short of the required 50 percent of the vote; Massey had trailed Barnes with 28 percent of the votes. The 1998 statewide Democratic ticket was notable for containing its first three African American nominees. Thurbert Baker, a black legislator from suburban DeKalb County, was appointed attorney general by Governor Miller when Bowers resigned. In a conscious slate-building effort by Miller and other party leaders, Baker won the Democratic nomination for a full term without a challenge. Two other African Americans won statewide Democratic nominations: Michael Thurmond for secretary of labor and Henrietta Canty for insurance commissioner. Their candidacies had the potential to stimulate turnout among African Americans in the fall.

In front of the Woodruff Arts Center in Atlanta is a huge metal sculpture by Alexander Calder. Massive steel plates are carefully balanced so that small changes in the wind cause the sculpture to move gently and turn. The current balance between the two parties in Georgia is quite similar: two large, massive forces, delicately balanced so that small changes can cause dramatic shifts. In such a precarious situation, every action can have a significant consequence both within the state and beyond its borders. Georgia has been one of the nation's premier partisan battlegrounds in the 1990s, and the next census should confirm its emergence as a megastate. If it has come to look much more like America in the late twentieth century, the reverse is equally true. In the last fifty years, Georgia has shared with the nation and the world the leadership of Martin Luther King, Jr., Jimmy Carter, Andrew Young, John Lewis, and Newt

Gingrich. It has helped reshape our media environment through CNN and has highlighted the region as international host for the 1996 Olympics. What is, and what will be, happening in Georgia politics as the last decade of the twentieth century ends is as good a predictor as any of the course of American politics— not just southern politics—in the early years of the twenty-first.

5

VIRGINIA: REPUBLICANS SURGE IN THE COMPETITIVE DOMINION

Margaret Edds and Thomas R. Morris

THE state that V. O. Key called "a political museum piece" was by the 1990s transformed.[1] The quaint political customs that had accompanied one-party, machine politics in the era of Harry F. Byrd, Sr., had been replaced by intense two-party competition and, in many major races, personality-driven politics. Cookie-cutter candidates who in bygone days sprang from rural court-houses and the inner circle of the Byrd machine had been replaced by men, and occasionally women, whose mates or fortunes or escapades had brought them fame. Most Virginia voters remained moderate-to-conservative in ideology, but the epicenter of state politics had shifted from small towns and farming communities to suburban enclaves, where mores and political interests often seemed more aligned with those of mid-Atlantic states than with the Old South. Increasingly, statewide candidates looked to the once-ignored Washington, D.C., suburbs as the mother lode of money and votes. An economy dependent on agriculture, manufacturing and the federal government was acquiring a faster-paced, global cast with an influx of high-tech industries. Chamber of Commerce types were heralding the rise of "The Silicon Dominion."

Meanwhile, Virginia politics drew an ever broader audience. "We used to be a little ol' state whose elections didn't mean much to anybody but us," said C. Richard Cranwell, a Roanoke lawyer and Democratic majority leader in the House of Delegates. "That's changed."[2] The defeat of Chesapeake televangelist Pat Robertson in the 1988 presidential race gave birth to the Christian Coalition, a grassroots organization aimed at enacting his conservative political and social agenda. As the Coalition's influence spread nationally, climaxing with the 1994 Republican congressional revolution, religious conservatives also tightened their hold on the Virginia Republican party. Tensions grew as the new activists sought to stamp their imprimatur on a party once dominated by economic conservatives.

The 1989 election and subsequent four-year term of L. Douglas Wilder, the nation's first elected African American governor, also brought widespread attention to Virginia. That a grandson of slaves had risen to power in a former Confederate state prompted scrutiny of his unique victory and turbulent term. Less lofty, but equally intense interest attended the 1994 U.S. Senate race between Democratic incumbent Charles S. (Chuck) Robb and Iran-Contra figure Oliver L. North. Robb's personal foibles, including admittedly "not appropriate" relationships with women other than his wife, were pitted against North's professional ones, including a conviction—overturned on technical grounds—for obstructing Congress.[3] Virginians squirmed as their staid image was tarnished by tabloid revelations and late-night talk show jokes. Despite spending almost $20 million, easily a record for a Virginia campaign, North was unable to turn the rabid devotion of his followers into an electoral majority. "Oliver North was way too much of a hot-button personality," concluded Anne B. Kincaid, a longtime Republican activist and leader in the state's right-to-life movement. "He did a beautiful job of articulating the Republican conservative themes, but for some it was a matter of, was he a liar?"[4]

Throughout the 1990s, Virginians sent mixed messages about their partisan affiliations, although, as the turn of the century approached, Republicans were gaining the upper hand. After electing three straight Republican governors between 1969 and 1977, voters had swung back to their Democratic roots in the 1980s. In three elections, culminating with the Wilder race in 1989, Democrats swept the state's highest offices—governor, lieutenant governor and attorney general. But in 1993, disillusioned by Democratic infighting, attracted to an energetic Republican nominee, and experiencing the frustrations with "politics as usual" that erupted in the national elections a year later, Virginians elected Republican George Allen to the governorship by the most lopsided margin of any gubernatorial nominee in more than thirty years. Four years later, with Allen's popularity high, the state economy booming, and Republican candidates coalescing around a pledge to end the hated property tax on cars and trucks, Republicans swept the state's three highest offices. The Virginia party-strength trend line[5] in Chapter 1 depicts this up-and-down pattern; see Figure 5.

In federal elections Virginians voted with a decided Republican bent. Only once between 1948 and 1996 did a Democratic presidential nominee carry the state; that distinction went to southerner Lyndon B. Johnson in 1964. In 1976 Virginia was the only southern state to back Republican Gerald Ford over Georgian Jimmy Carter, although the vote was close, 49.3 percent to 48.0 percent. In U.S. Senate races, Republican John Warner was reelected three times. Only the nomination of the controversial North prevented the state's second Senate seat from slipping into Republican hands in 1994. On the U.S. House side, Virginia delegations tilted to the Republicans during the 1970s. By 1980 the GOP had reached record strength, claiming nine of the state's ten seats. But Democrats gradually fought back in the 1980s, and by 1990 the congressional split favored them by six to four. When redistricting expanded the state delegation to eleven in 1992, Democrats captured the new seat. And even against the Republican tide of 1994, while Republicans were picking up sixteen House seats across the South, Virginia Democrats lost only the new seat won two years earlier in northern Virginia. Thus, the delegation retained a Democratic majority—six Democrats to five Republicans. "The thing that I am most proud of is not only the defeat of Ollie North," said Mark R. Warner, a northern Virginia businessman who made a fortune in cellular phones before serving as chairman of the Virginia Democratic party from 1993 to 1995. "Everybody talked about Robb and North, but nobody talked about the fact that six out of seven of our congressional candidates won in 1994, and no other southern state got close to that."[6]

As the 1990s progressed, Democratic control of the legislature gradually evaporated. For a decade many analysts had predicted that it was only a matter of time until one or both houses would be in Republican hands. While there was steady movement in that direction, however, the change was longer in coming than many had expected. Between 1967 and 1989, GOP representation in the 40-member senate rose by only 4 seats, from 6 to 10. Growth was more substantial in the 100-member house, where GOP numbers grew steadily from 14 in 1967 to 39 in 1989.[7] The early 1990s brought the party to the edge of dominance, as Republicans moved to within three seats of a senate majority in 1991 and four seats of a house majority in 1993. See Table 13.

Many expected the long awaited breakthrough to come in 1995, but after record spending and months of campaign vitriol, the parties battled almost to a draw. Democrats retained a 52–47–1 majority in the house. In the senate, Republicans picked up two seats, achieving a 20–20 tie. (These legislative elections are discussed in greater detail below.) The even split resulted in a power-sharing arrangement that gave the Republicans unprecedented clout. But with a tie-breaking vote on most matters resting with the Democratic lieutenant governor, total success still eluded the GOP. Republicans put the best face on the

Table 13. Party Representation in the Virginia Assembly, 1985–1997

	Senate (40 seats)			House[a] (100 seats)		
Year	Dem.		Rep.		Dem.		Rep.
1985	32	(80.0%)	8	(20.0%)	65	(65.6%)	33	(33.3%)
1987	30	(75.0)	10	(25.0)	64	(64.6)	35	(35.4)
1989	30	(75.0)	10	(25.0)	59	(59.6)	39	(39.4)
1991	22	(55.0)	18	(45.0)	58	(58.6)	41	(41.4)
1993	22	(55.0)	18	(45.0)	52	(52.5)	47	(47.5)
1995	20	(50.0)	20	(50.0)	52	(52.5)	47	(47.5)
1997	19	(47.5)	21	(52.5)	50	(50.0)	49	(49.0)

Source: Virginia Votes.

Note: The 1997 figures reflect the results of special election victories by Republicans shortly after the 1997 elections.

[a]A long-time conservative independent, Lacy Putney of Bedford, served throughout this period, and in 1989, a write-in candidate defeated the Democratic incumbent, served as an independent for that term, and was reelected as a Democrat in 1991.

outcome. "A few more 'defeats' like this one, and we'll control the legislature," quipped J. Scott Leake, executive director of the Republican legislative caucus. But there was also acknowledgment of some disappointment. "We were all more optimistic when we made the big gains of the 1980s," said M. Boyd Marcus, Jr., the most prominent GOP campaign consultant in state elections. "We squeezed all the easy ones out of the system. The reason the Democrats hold on to the House of Delegates is their rural House members. It's very difficult to beat an incumbent in those areas."[8]

At the start of the 1998 session, Republicans gained long awaited control of one chamber and near parity in the other. After GOP governor-elect James S. (Jim) Gilmore III lured two Democratic lawmakers into positions in his administration, prompting a series of special elections, Republicans secured a 21–19 edge in the senate, and in the house they occupied 49 seats to the Democrats' 50 with a long-serving conservative independent rounding out the membership of the 100-seat chamber. House Democrats used their tiny edge, plus the fact that three newly elected Republicans had not been formally certified by the state board of elections, to push through the reelection of Democratic house speaker Thomas W. Moss, Jr., on the assembly's opening day. In a remarkable display, Republicans banged their desks, shouted, and turned their backs in protest as the Democrats worked their will. A day later, however, with the body's lone independent siding with the Republicans, thus giving the GOP 50 votes,

House Democrats agreed to a historic power-sharing arrangement. The under-standing, creating parity on committees, was scheduled to last for four years, provided neither side acquired more than a 55–45 majority. A similar power-sharing arrangement, signed after senate membership reached a 20–20 tie in 1995, remained in effect there. The combination meant that Virginia was unique among the states in having power-sharing arrangements in place in both houses of the legislature.[9]

As a new century approached, both Republicans and Democrats were pre-dicting healthy, two-party competition well into the next decade. "I don't know that you'll ever have a dominance again between Republicans and Dem-ocrats. I think that's good," said J. Randy Forbes, a state delegate and attorney from Chesapeake, soon after his election as chairman of the Republican party in the summer of 1996. "I think dominance creates arrogance, and I think that would be true whether it's Democrats or Republicans. And I think arrogance is probably the thing that people dislike most about politics. What I think we'll see is a constant movement between the parties."[10]

THE 1989 ELECTIONS: A HISTORIC OUTCOME

As Democrats approached the gubernatorial race in 1989, they were more con-cerned than arrogant. The economy was relatively good, and the party had been in control of the state's highest offices for a generally successful eight years. But the Democratic nominee was about to test all the old assumptions about the ability of African Americans to win statewide office in the South. Doug Wilder, a Richmond attorney and veteran member of the state senate, had already pricked a pinhole in conventional wisdom. Winning the office of lieutenant governor in 1985, he had proven that his heritage was not an insurmountable hurdle with voters. Still, the magnitude of his accomplishment was captured in the title of a book documenting that election, *When Hell Froze Over.*[11] Winning a part-time, largely ceremonial office, however, was far different from becom-ing governor of one of the nation's most prosperous and rapidly growing states.

Republicans approached the election with quiet confidence. A combination of liberal votes in the state senate, several personal or professional snafus, and the race factor would make Wilder unacceptable to a majority of Virginians, they believed. The Republican primary field had been narrowed to three candi-dates: J. Marshall Coleman, a former attorney general whose early populism had evolved into a more doctrinaire conservatism; former U.S. senator Paul S. Tri-ble, Jr., who had declined to run for reelection in 1988 in the face of a potentially grueling battle against Chuck Robb; and Stanford E. Parris, a former congressman and wealthy northern Virginia real estate investor. One early internal GOP poll gave Trible 44 percent support, Coleman 15, and Parris 10.[12]

Over the next few months, those numbers changed dramatically. Beaten down by the unrelenting, two-pronged assault of his competitors and several missteps of his own, Trible became the victim of front-runner's disease. His steady erosion in the final weeks of the campaign fueled his opponents' energy. Coleman, whom voters deemed the more attractive alternative, was the beneficiary of that decline. Cutting into Trible's strength in Tidewater and northern Virginia, he squeaked past Trible, winning 36.8 percent of the vote. Trible had 35.1 percent and Parris had 28.1 percent. (Virginia no longer requires a runoff if no candidate has a simple majority.)

One issue that did not separate the three candidates was abortion. All three took a hard-line view, reflecting the growing power of the religious right within the Virginia Republican party. Coleman, who had once been pro-choice, joined the other two in saying that abortion was acceptable in only one instance—to save the life of the mother. Even in cases of rape and incest, it was wrong, he said. That view, almost certainly essential to Coleman's winning the Republican nomination, became his Achilles heel in the fall general election. On July 3, 1989, the U.S. Supreme Court ruled in *Webster v. Reproductive Health Services* that states could restrict abortions beyond limits set in 1973 in *Roe v. Wade*. The ruling set off jubilation in some quarters, but it produced shock in others. Seizing the moment with trademark boldness, Wilder focused on Coleman's extreme position on rape and incest and on the question of who decides whether an abortion is appropriate—individual women or the government?

"What you have to do is put yourself in the place of the woman affected," Wilder admonished Coleman at their first debate. "I guess I can more readily identify with that because I have two daughters. I can't imagine any situation where they would be victimized by crime, by rape, and that government would say to them, or to me as their father, that they could not or should not be in some degree of destiny as to what happens to their future." Later, a widely praised ad captured the argument more concisely. As footage of a statue of Thomas Jefferson filled the screen, an announcer intoned: "In Virginia we have a strong tradition of freedom and individual liberty—rights that are now in danger in the race for governor. On the issue of abortion, Marshall Coleman wants to take away your right to choose and give it to the politicians. He wants to go back to outlawing abortion, even in cases of rape and incest. Doug Wilder believes the government shouldn't interfere in your right to choose. He wants to keep the politicians out of your personal life."[13]

On election day, the dual pulls of Wilder's abortion position and the state's desire to break free of old stereotypes outweighed reservations about Wilder, giving him the narrowest of victories. The day was not without drama that highlighted racial divisions. Moments after the polls closed, television announcers released the results of exit surveys taken earlier in the day. They projected a 10-percentage-point victory for Wilder. Instead, when all the ballots were counted (and recounted three weeks later), the difference between Wilder and Coleman was an infinitesimal 6,741 votes, 50.1 percent to 49.8 percent. Analysts speculated that many voters had lied when they said they had voted for Wilder. For some, race apparently was paramount.

Assessing what had produced Wilder's historic election years later, Coleman's former campaign manager cited race, abortion, and personality. "People voted for Doug Wilder to make history," said Boyd Marcus. "But it crystallized on personalities more than anything. Marshall came across as not very believable, Wilder as one more place to show change." Ultimately, many said, credit for the victory rested at Wilder's door. "Chief among them would be the political savvy and skill of Doug Wilder himself," said state delegate Jerrauld C. Jones, one of Virginia's leading young African American politicians, in evaluating the reasons for Wilder's win. "You just couldn't quarrel with the fact that he was well qualified, and then when you combined that with the personal skill that he had, that's what allowed it."[14]

The euphoria that Wilder's election produced among Democrats was short lived. Within months, the new governor had snubbed some longtime party workers with his appointments and infuriated prominent Democratic legislators by what they perceived to be slights. Buffeted by the state's worst fiscal crisis since the Great Depression and by the unpopularity of his September 1991 decision to campaign for the presidency, Wilder achieved a midterm low in popularity for a sitting governor. In a January 1992 public opinion poll by Mason-Dixon Opinion Research, Inc., only 32 percent of those surveyed approved of his performance.

Substantive accomplishments—particularly Wilder's skillful handling of the fiscal crisis that hit the state soon after he took office—were overshadowed by his personal style. He could be amiable and charming in one setting, vindictive and combative the next. "If Doug Wilder hadn't been so confrontational, he might be spending his final weeks as governor enjoying the praise Virginians traditionally reserve for fiscal conservatives instead of the barbs that go with being the most unpopular chief executive in memory," wrote Warren Fiske, political writer for the Norfolk *Virginian-Pilot*, at the end of Wilder's term.

"But," Fiske added: "if Doug Wilder hadn't been so confrontational, he never would have been governor."[15]

Such was the paradox surrounding Wilder's historic term. Seeking to explain the complex character of a man who evoked both admiration and loathing among Virginia voters, Jerrauld Jones turned as did many others to Wilder's often gutsy and lonely path to the top. Despite their racial and political ties, Jones was not unfamiliar with Wilder's ire. He and other members of the legislative black caucus had expected a cozy relationship when Wilder became governor. That did not occur. "He didn't draw us into an inner circle or kitchen cabinet," said Jones. "There were people who just couldn't fathom that he didn't communicate with us that way."[16]

Jones theorized that Wilder, as governor, was unable to divorce himself from the man who for years had defied history and convention to claw his way past racial barriers. "I just think you have to understand, maybe, that the Doug Wilder who arrived here in this institution in 1969 was denied a shoeshine right across the street. The same Doug Wilder who in 1976 was looking to run for statewide office, the lieutenant governorship, all of a sudden here comes a Chuck Robb out of the blue, says, 'No, no. I'm going to be your next lieutenant governor.' . . . And then, meetings held behind his back to prevent him from getting in the race and getting on the ticket. You know defeat after defeat after defeat of issues near and dear to his constituency's heart. . . . You have to put a real historical, longitudinal analysis on Doug Wilder to help understand why it is that he did not have the legislative honeymoon relationship."[17]

The style that prompted compassion in Jones produced fury in some others. "Everything was a slight when it wasn't meant to be a slight," said one longtime party activist. Describing the infighting that emerged between Wilder and other Democratic leaders, including Robb and Attorney General Mary Sue Terry, he noted: "It was such a cycle. Doug would do something crazy. Chuck and Mary Sue did equally knifey things, but the whole power structure was [saying], 'There goes that crazy guy again.' . . . His modus operandi was, 'I'm going to stick 'em even more.' "[18]

A more dispassionate assessment came from Mark Warner, who took over the party chairmanship in 1993. "The Democratic party of Virginia entered the 1990s with tremendous optimism. We had just set Virginia and national history with the election of Wilder. Our margins in the General Assembly were still fairly strong. Wilder was the third leg of the Robb-Baliles-Wilder [gubernatorial] chain. That almost immediately started to break down as the governor and the legislature had their series of battles, and from a party standpoint, institutional inner tensions in the party, papered over in 1987 and 1989, all sort of broke open in 1991.''[19]

The 1991 legislative elections were a wake-up call for Virginia Democrats. Republicans had made steady gains in the 140-member body over the last several decades, but both chambers remained firmly in Democratic control. As the electioneering began, however, it was clear that Democratic candidates faced more than the usual problems. Not only was the economic news dour, not only was there a rising tide of Republicanism across the South, but the antics of the state's top Democratic officeholders—Robb and Wilder—were wearing thin.

As 1991 progressed, Robb was struck by an escalating series of crises. In the mid-1980s, newspaper stories had focused on his links, while governor, to a fast-living crowd in Virginia Beach. Among the set were known drug users and individuals later convicted of serious drug crimes. Despite the proven connections and the persistence of additional rumors, Robb easily won election to the U.S. Senate in 1988, and even was mentioned on short lists of possible future presidents. Most voters seemed to accept Robb's statement that he had never knowingly been in the presence of illegal drugs.

But by the spring of 1991, the carefully woven image was unraveling. A former Miss Virginia USA came forward to allege that she had had an affair with Robb while he was governor. The politician who presented himself to Virginia voters as a ramrod-straight Marine and who won office on the coattails of his wife, Lynda Bird Johnson Robb, had a secret side, said Tai Collins, whose story and photographs eventually wound up in *Playboy*. Meanwhile, a television news magazine show, *Exposé*, aired a piece again linking Robb to drug users and illicit sex. And in May a private detective—who later turned out to have been bankrolled by Republicans—published a scandalous account of alleged cocaine use by the senator himself. Robb continued to deny any drug connections, but acknowledged that Collins had given him a nude massage in a New York hotel room.

The worst was yet to come. In an effort to divert attention from the senator's mounting problems, Robb aides leaked to the press copies of an illicitly obtained cellular phone conversation. In it, Wilder chortled with a supporter over Robb's troubles and pronounced his old rival politically finished. As it turned out, the leak was not only a political miscalculation but an illegal act. By July, three aides had resigned and a grand jury investigation was underway. The queries resulted in convictions of the aides on minor charges. Only two last-minute grand jury appearances by the senator seemed to save him from indictment also. It was nineteen months before the grand jury dissolved.[20]

Just as the 1991 legislative elections were heating up, Wilder further fueled voter fury by announcing that he would seek the presidency. His absences from the state intensified, even as budgetary woes were worsening. On election day, voters exacted a price. Despite the advantage Democrats should have gained through legislative redistricting, Republicans went from 10 to 18 seats in the 40-member senate. Seven Democratic senators were defeated. No GOP senators lost, and Republicans won 5 of the 9 open seats. In the 100-member house, the GOP gained 1 seat for a century high of 41. The small house gain was more impressive when pitted against the fact that Democrats had effectively stripped Republicans of seven seats during redistricting. Table 13 illustrates the dramatic GOP senate breakthrough in 1991. (Two years later the Republicans in the house would advance again.) Hearing the message from the legislative results, Wilder withdrew from the presidential race in January 1992.

The 1992 elections were quieter and more predictable. Virginians continued their long-term pattern of voting Republican in presidential elections, despite the presence of two southerners on the Democratic ticket. Republican George Bush won 45.0 percent of the vote; Democrat Bill Clinton, 40.6 percent, and Ross Perot, 13.6 percent.[21] In races for the U.S. House of Representatives, Democrats expanded their 6–4 majority, picking up the new northern Virginia seat created by redistricting, as mentioned earlier.

THE 1993 ELECTIONS: REPUBLICANS WIN THE GOVERNORSHIP

Leading the Democrats into the 1993 statewide elections was Mary Sue Terry, a small-town lawyer and businesswoman, set apart only by gender from the conservative, business-oriented males who had traditionally run the state. During two terms as attorney general, Terry had methodically lined up support from much of Virginia's financial and social elite. Early polls showed her leading Republican George Allen by 55 percent to 28 percent.

Allen, a former state delegate and congressman who had handily won a three-way convention nomination battle, brought to the table an engaging personality, a plan for upheaving government-as-usual, and a degree of gusto learned on the football field from his father, legendary Redskins football coach George Allen. Armed with far more enthusiasm than cash, the Allenites feared Terry would sew up the election with an early television assault that would brand her opponent as an extremist. Little known by the general public outside of his home district, Allen was vulnerable to being defined politically by his opponent.

In what was later viewed as the critical mistake of her campaign, Terry did not attack. As the summer wore on, Allen began to gain ground with his promises to abolish parole, reduce government spending, and reform welfare. Terry was less visible on the campaign trail, appearing at times to be more interested in grooming for governor than winning an election. "Mary Sue Terry took it for granted really until the end of the summer, took it for granted in a big way," said Michael E. Thomas, Allen's campaign manager and later a member of his cabinet.[22]

Nor was the Allen camp impressed when Terry finally began unloading her arsenal. Her call for a five-day waiting period for handgun purchases was more placebo than strong medicine when it came to fighting crime, they believed. Internal polls confirmed that voters saw the abolition of parole and truth in sentencing as more solid solutions.[23] Moreover, the Allenites gleefully believed that Terry's bow to gun control was undercutting the rural base that had sustained her in previous elections.

Confirmation that they were correct came in late August when the seven-thousand-strong Fraternal Order of Police endorsed Allen. The action was a stunning rebuff to Terry's crime-fighting credentials after seven years as attorney general. It cemented Allen's designation as the anticrime candidate. Republicans saw the moment as a turning point in the campaign. "From that point on, I felt we would set the agenda," Thomas said.[24]

Nor was a perceived lack of toughness Terry's only problem. The results of Democratic infighting cropped up at every turn. "There was an arrogance of power, a cult of personality, across the way," said one prominent Democratic leader, recalling the period. "The party had ceased being a party as much as it was a group of factions, and the factions were all interested in advancing their own personality leader."[25]

With the animosity between Robb and Wilder dominating headlines, Terry opted to distance herself from both. One unintended result was her failure to capitalize on what should have been a Democratic strength: the fact that Virginia essentially had been well managed and prudently progressive, despite the wars of personality and the tough economic times. Twice during Wilder's term, *Financial World* had named the state the fiscally best run in the nation. Virginia was one of only two states to come through the early-1990s recession without raising taxes.

Not only did Terry soft-pedal those selling points, but Wilder wasted no time in highlighting the gaffe. At times during the Wilder administration, his relationship with Terry had been barely cordial, and the strain showed. By late September, Wilder was questioning why more was not being said about the accomplishments of his administration. And he second-guessed a variety of other actions by Terry. Voters cared more about the economy than gun control, he said, urging her to shift her message. A campaign ad in which she promised not to coddle inmates with cable service and color televisions was "hyperbole. . . . Let me say here and now the state doesn't furnish those things to inmates," he said.[26]

The result of campaign missteps, Democratic disarray, and Allen's focused assault was a steady erosion of Terry's support. Allen won the most lopsided victory for governor by any candidate in 30 years, winning 58.3 percent of the vote to Terry's 40.9 percent. Allen won 59.9 percent of the suburban vote, while Terry carried the central cities by a dismal 52.5 percent. Turnout in predominantly black precincts was only 50.5 percent, according to Larry Sabato, a University of Virginia political scientist and a leading authority on Virginia politics. Allen attributed his victory to a "grassroots campaign where people were more involved than power brokers or the establishment." He also portrayed himself as a new kind of Virginia leader, as schooled in the temperament of the West— where he grew up—as of the South. "I like the traditions of the South. I've got Western blood in me also, and that's a more independent approach than what you'd find from just pure Southern," said Allen, who campaigned in cowboy boots, chewed tobacco, and decorated his office with animal skins. "There's an independence of thought and an antipathy to government constantly pestering people."[27]

What did not become evident until a year later was that Allen's victory was also a precursor of the national election results in 1994. "That was a harbinger of things to come in 1994," said former Democratic governor Gerald L. Baliles, who served the term between Robb and Wilder.[28] Like the congressional revolutionaries led by Georgia's Newt Gingrich, Allen was charting a new course away from the predictable pattern of steady investment in state infrastructure needs followed for three decades by his predecessors. Wilder also had broken with that mold, but it was unclear whether his actions were dictated more by philosophy or economic necessity.

Another element of change occurred in the 1993 elections when the Republican party picked up 6 seats in the House of Delegates, bringing the GOP total to 47, just four seats shy of a majority. (See Table 13.) In 1993 the GOP had nominated more candidates for the 100-seat lower house—77—than ever before in the modern period. Since the entire senate was elected for a four-year term in 1991, there was no change during this election in the senate balance of 22 Democrats and 18 Republicans.

Allen took hold of his office with whirlwind speed. Within a year he had led the legislature in abolishing parole and establishing truth-in-sentencing guidelines, established a host of study committees on revamping government, and proposed a $2.1 billion tax cut plan for the 1995 legislature. Democrats at first seemed dazed by the onslaught. Even their victory in the 1994 U.S. Senate race seemed to bring little comfort in the face of what many Democrats feared was merely the state version of a conservative revolution in American politics.

THE 1994 ROBB-NORTH SENATE SLUGFEST

The Senate matchup in 1994 among Robb, North, and Marshall Coleman—who resurfaced as an independent candidate with Republican U.S. senator John W. Warner's backing—was unparalleled in state political annals for its sound and fury. Wilder also played a brief role as a candidate, before dropping out owing to insufficient support. The final spending tally topped $26 million, making it one of the most expensive Senate races in American history. The charismatic North drew throngs of ardent campaign supporters, while only Democratic loyalists embraced Robb with enthusiasm. Despite backing from the popular Warner, Coleman was never able to distinguish himself in voters' minds from the person they had rejected in gubernatorial races in 1989 and 1981. In the end, most analysts agreed that the outcome said less about the politics and philosophy of Virginia than about which man's foibles the public was more willing to tolerate. "It was totally personality," observed Marcus. "The reason Chuck Robb was in such trouble to begin with was him personally. He addressed the problem by having a candidate run against him who was even more mired in his own personal foibles."[29]

In both parties, alternative candidates tried to save the state from calamitous campaigns, but failed. Robb was opposed by Virgil H. Goode, Jr., a state senator and conservative populist from Rocky Mount; Sylvia L. Clute, a Richmond lawyer with a history of promoting women's equity issues in the state legislature; and Nancy B. Spannaus, a backer of political extremist Lyndon LaRouche. None of the challengers proved able to widen his or her base much beyond a core group of voters disgusted with Robb. Goode, who eventually won 33.9 percent of the primary vote, came closest.

The major distinction of Goode's campaign was his decision to air the most pointedly negative television ad of the season. "Ollie North will ask Chuck Robb about his parties with prostitutes and drug criminals, involvement in what Robb's own staff described as sexual activity with young girls," an announcer intoned. "Why give Ollie North this chance?" Release of the ad was accompanied by the distribution of explosive memos, written by former Robb staffers who—in a damage control effort—had attempted to investigate the charges against the senator. In one memo, a former staffer listed four women who allegedly engaged in sexual activities with Robb. One was listed as being twenty years old. Ages of the other three were not given. The Robb campaign termed the ad "character assassination."[30] Despite the potent material, Robb won 57.9 percent of the primary vote. His financial clout and the longstanding loyalties of many Democrats to him and his wife were too significant to overcome.

Republicans opposed to North's nomination rallied around James C. (Jim) Miller III, an economist and former budget director in the Reagan administration. Miller's credentials were solid and his style became less wooden as time passed, but he was no match for the charismatic North. Despite laments from party moderates that an available Senate seat was being tossed away, GOP delegates voted 55 percent to 45 percent to nominate North at a convention in Richmond. The crowd responded to North with messianic fervor as he accepted the nomination, promising to lead a grassroots assault on evil in the federal government. Equating his mission to that of U.S. troops storming Normandy, he vowed, "This time the beachhead we seize is not on some distant shore. It is across the Potomac. . . . This time there is only one hill we must take, Capitol Hill." With us-versus-them clarity, he declared a cultural war on promoters of abortion rights, homosexuals in the military, and big government. "Whose side are you on?" demanded North.[31]

Throughout the summer, however, North seemed to take pains to soften his image, opening his doors to reporters, shaking thousands of hands, and speaking with earnest conviction about the problems facing America. He seemed less threatening than thoughtful, less zealous than committed. Meanwhile, as Democrats fretted, Robb was spending most of his time in Washington, attending to Senate business. "I have a sense of timing, and ultimately I'm going to succeed or fail based on my own sense of what to do and when to do it," countered Robb in typically stubborn defiance of those who insisted that he should be more visible. "I was never a sprinter. I'm a long-distance man."[32]

The relative calm of the summer was destined to evaporate. By October Robb was hinting at mental instability on North's part, and the former Marine colonel was homing in on Robb's foibles and the evils of Washington. "It's time we had a senator in Virginia who cared more with a passion about the people of Virginia than . . . about trying to govern his own passions," North argued in one particularly memorable speech in Richmond. Referring to President Clinton as a "flip-flopping, anti-defense yahoo from Little Rock," he went on: "What Chuck Robb and Bill Clinton are doing to the armed forces of this nation is nothing short of a fundamental betrayal of the men and women that they're in office to represent." Meanwhile, Robb drew ominous conclusions from a series of campaign-trail misstatements by North. Robb began alluding to North's mental state by referring to "Ollie's World." "I can't imagine anyone being able to continue to (tell) those lies without some sense of self-delusion. I think the problem here is deeper or more serious than has been discussed," he said. By mid-October, the charges and countercharges were on television. On October 12, North began airing an ad touting the fact that Robb had gotten a nude massage from a beauty queen and had frequented parties in Virginia Beach where cocaine was allegedly used by other guests. Robb's response ad bore the tag line: "Oliver North—People are starting to wonder if he knows what the truth is."[33]

The most damaging assault on North's credibility came several weeks later from an unexpected source. In her first sustained interview in three years, former First Lady Nancy Reagan took on North. "I know Ollie North has a great deal of trouble separating fact from fiction," Mrs. Reagan told an audience in New York. "And he lied to my husband and lied about my husband, kept things from him that he should not have kept from him." Other former Reagan associates had already disavowed North, including former secretary of state George Shultz, former secretary of defense Caspar Weinberger, and former CIA director William Colby. Reagan himself had issued a statement during the nomination battle saying that he was getting "pretty steamed" about North's insistence that Reagan had authorized the Iran-Contra arms-for-hostages deal. But the timing of Nancy Reagan's comments and their unequivocal message elevated them into one of the campaign turning points. North's response was necessarily muted. "My mother told me a long time ago never to get into a fight with a lady," he said.[34]

Disaffection among a substantial bloc of Republicans, Coleman's success in splitting the GOP vote, and Wilder's eleventh-hour decision to campaign heartily for Robb among African American voters all contributed to the senator's narrow reelection. Virginians, exhausted and embarrassed, cast 45.6 percent of their votes for Robb, 42.9 percent for North, and 11.4 percent for Coleman.

In the U.S. House races, Virginia Democrats showed remarkable staying power, given the success of Republicans across the South in 1994. Of seven incumbent Democrats, only one—Delegate Leslie L. Byrne, who had been elected two years earlier in the newly created Eleventh District in northern Virginia—was defeated, as noted above. The split of six Democrats (five whites and an African American) and five Republicans remained intact after the 1996 House elections.

The story of the survival of white moderate-to-conservative Democratic congressmen in Virginia is a remarkable one, virtually unparalleled in the South outside of Texas. This is all the more noteworthy because nearly a decade-and-a-half earlier—in 1980—the Virginia delegation had consisted of nine Republicans and one Democrat. The Democrats' return occurred gradually, one election at a time, owing partly to Republican infighting, partly to Democratic success in recruiting moderate-to-conservative businessmen to carry their banner, and partly to the power of incumbency in Virginia. The shift occurred primarily in the 1980s as moderate Democratic governors Robb and Baliles led the state. Among those elected were Owen B. Pickett of the Second District, a Virginia Beach certified public accountant who scored heavily among voters in urban Norfolk while cutting usual Democratic losses in the suburbs; Norman Sisisky of the Fourth District, a wealthy bottler from Petersburg who combined liberalism on racial issues with conservatism on many others; and Frederick C. (Rick) Boucher of the Ninth District, an Abingdon attorney who repeatedly outhustled and outmaneuvered Republican opposition.

Even though Virginia's congressional map was dramatically changed by 1990s redistricting, state voters proved unwilling to oust such representatives from office merely to satisfy national political trends. During redistricting, the General Assembly placed the additional district awarded Virginia due to population growth—the Eleventh District—in northern Virginia, giving the region three seats. The Democratic legislature with Governor Wilder's encouragement also created the black-majority Third District, stretching from Hampton Roads to Richmond. History was made in 1992 when the first African American in this century, state senator Bobby C. Scott, was elected in the Third and the first woman ever sent to Congress from Virginia, Delegate Byrne, was elected in the Eleventh.

In drawing the three congressional district lines in northern Virginia, the legislature balanced the Eleventh more or less evenly between the two parties while tilting the existing two districts in favor of the area's Democratic and Republican incumbents, James P. Moran in the Eighth District and Frank R. Wolf in the Tenth District, respectively. In 1994, Republican Thomas M. (Tom) Davis defeated Byrne with 52.9 percent of the vote to the Democratic incumbent's 45.3 percent. Thus, after only two years Virginia once again had an all-male congressional delegation.

In early 1997 a three-judge federal panel struck down the black-majority Third District on the grounds it was racially gerrymandered. The court concluded that the General Assembly had gone too far in its efforts to create a safe African American seat, as evidenced by the "bizarre and tortured shape of the district" variously described in state newspapers as a "grasping claw" or a "squashed salamander." In order to achieve a district with a 64 percent African

American population, the legislature had anchored it in the Tidewater cities of Norfolk, Suffolk, and Portsmouth. The district meandered 225 miles northeast through black-majority Charles City County to the African American portions of the racially divided state capital. The noncontiguous portions of Hampton and Newport News included in the district were connected, in the words of the court's opinion, "only [by] the open water of the Chesapeake Bay and the James River." In February 1998 the Assembly adopted a redistricting plan supported by the entire Virginia congressional delegation. The plan makes the Third District more compact but still leaves it with a majority of African Americans. The district, which stretches from Norfolk and Portsmouth to Richmond, is 54 percent black, 10 percentage points lower than the old Third.[35]

Despite holding on to the Senate seat and losing only one of their seven U.S. House seats, Democrats arrived in Richmond for the 1995 Assembly fearful that their future was in jeopardy. The national Republican majority headed to Congress underscored the popularity of Allen's proposed $2.1 billion tax cut, they felt. Over the next several weeks, however, resolve stiffened as Democrats realized the impact that some of Allen's proposed cuts would have on education and social services. There was also a growing sense that bowing to the popular executive's demands would only hasten their own party's demise.

The Democrats' distaste was heightened by the fact that they had never taken George Allen seriously when he was a junior member of the House of Delegates a few years earlier. Those same Democrats had gerrymandered him out of his congressional seat, won in a 1991 special election, by pairing him with a fellow Republican, an act that had made Allen's decision to run for governor an easy one. Perhaps it was his youthful exuberance for Jeffersonian conservatism and his smoldering resentment toward legislative Democrats that prompted Allen in his inaugural address to characterize the legislature as "a citadel of special interest" controlled by "stolid, status quo, monarchical elitists." Furthermore, he said, "In recent times, the will of the people has been frustrated by an unholy alliance of manipulative, well-heeled interests, entrenched bureaucrats and political opportunists." Later that year at the Republican convention at which North was nominated, Allen talked of "knocking [the Democrats'] soft teeth down their whiney throats," a comment he subsequently admitted he should not have made.[36]

THE COMPETITIVE PARTISAN BALANCE OF 1995 AND 1996

Little wonder that the 1995 legislative session became one of the most contentious in memory. The governor had laid down the gauntlet; both parties were fully aware that control of the legislature was at stake. Differences with the house leadership prompted the governor to deliver his televised "State of the Commonwealth" address from his office rather than the traditional lower house chamber. Tension escalated from there, and when the votes finally were taken, virtually all of Allen's tax and spending cut proposals were killed. The governor seemed momentarily stunned, but vowed that retribution would come later at the polls. The response, the governor eventually concluded, had been the result of an organized effort, planned in conjunction with a political consultant, to undermine GOP initiatives. "Once you saw that they were all following the plays that were being called by these consultants, then it all made sense. Then we had a revelation."[37]

Some others, however, felt Allen's statement was misguided. "It would be far different in Virginia, in my judgment, had the Republicans not been too cocky in the nomination of Oliver North or too cocky in the broadsides of George Allen," Wilder said. "That cost them a Senate seat and it cost them control of the legislature unquestionably in my judgment."[38]

Governor Allen's effort to make the 1995 legislative elections a referendum on his agenda raised the stakes of the midterm campaign to a new level in Virginia. Both Democrats and Republicans viewed the races as a climactic moment in the GOP's long march to supremacy. Armed with what he believed to be the popularity of his tax and spending proposals, Allen took to the campaign trail with a vengeance, forming his own fundraising political action committee and spending more time boosting local candidates than any chief executive in memory. Democrats also girded for battle. Key legislative leaders and Democratic activists met regularly throughout the spring, charting a strategy that would focus on education and Allen's alleged efforts to undo progress.

The end result, after combined spending of over $20 million, was a GOP gain of two seats in the state senate. Republicans defeated two of the Democratic senators who survived close races in 1991, including the majority leader, Senator Hunter Andrews of Hampton. Two other Democratic senators were also defeated, and Republicans picked up a Lynchburg seat previously held by a Democrat. All five districts had a history of voting Republican in statewide races. Similarly, three Republican incumbents were defeated in districts with a Democratic electoral orientation. Thus, in 1995 the Senate districts had almost sorted themselves out along predictable partisan lines. Overall, the election left the Virginia senate split 20 to 20, requiring a power-sharing arrangement. In the 1995 elections for the House of Delegates, the GOP made no gains, again finishing four seats short of a majority, even though the party put up another record number of candidates—85, five more than the Democrats. House Democrats in 1995 demonstrated the capacity to wage a vigorous, coordinated campaign on an issue that worked in their favor—education.

The 1996 legislative session was a comparatively peaceful one by the standards of a competitive legislature. Governor Allen shifted course following the elections, acknowledging that relations with Democratic legislators had become too contentious. Adopting a more conciliatory tone, he acknowledged the political realities confronting a lame-duck governor presiding over a divided government. His cooperative approach mirrored the stance increasingly being adopted at the time at the national level. Addressing the members of the legislature's money committees prior to the 1997 session, Governor Allen reminded them that the voters "didn't send us down here to bicker. They sent us here to work together."[39] As he began the final year of his term, Allen's approval rating was 65 percent, making him the state's most popular political figure. He reminded voters of the comprehensive reforms of the state's criminal justice and welfare systems and was given credit for the enactment of a strict parental notification law on abortion.

Although the 1995 legislative elections did not constitute the long-sought GOP breakthrough, they were symbolic of the degree to which Virginia had become a competitive, two-party state.[40] Further evidence that the state's political center lay somewhere in the moderate-conservative zone came seven months later as Republicans nominated a candidate for the U.S. Senate in June 1996. Activists in the GOP's conservative wing who had been infuriated by John Warner's opposition to North in 1994 were determined to punish the senator for that disloyalty. They coalesced around Jim Miller's second campaign. Opposition to Warner galvanized further when North, just days before the primary, openly backed Miller. The National Rifle Association also beat Miller's drum, as did the Christian Coalition in its pre-election voter guides. But it was the GOP's right wing, not Warner, that was in for comeuppance when voters went to the polls. Outdoing all predictions, Warner captured 65.6 percent of the vote to Miller's 34.4 percent.

Republicans won both of the statewide races in the 1996 elections even though the results in each case were closer than expected. Senator Warner survived a well-financed media blitz by his opponent and a lackluster general election campaign on his own part to win reelection to a fourth term with 52.5 percent of the vote to the Democratic nominee's 47.4 percent. Buoyed by his easy primary win, Warner underestimated his opponent, Mark Warner (no relation to the senator), a former Democratic party chair quoted earlier. The senator's overconfidence showed early in the campaign when, with typical flamboyance, he predicted to the editorial board of the *Virginian-Pilot* that Mark

Warner, while losing, would win points for courage in "taking on the king." A joint appearance at a Labor Day parade in Buena Vista seemed to set the tone for the ensuing campaign. The younger Warner jogged the parade route, pouring sweat as he bounded from one outstretched hand to another. "I'm the underdog; I've got to work harder," Mark Warner explained. But John Warner, who glided down the street on the back of a power-red convertible, dismissed his opponent's drive. "He's trying to run off a little nervous energy, I guess," the senator said.[41]

The Democratic nominee, who had never held elective office, spent over $10 million of his own fortune, by far the largest amount expended personally by a Virginia candidate for any office. Senator Warner, who was outspent 5 to 1 in the general election, complained that the outlay was excessive and "un-Virginian." But the senator's efforts to respond to his opponents' attack ads were frustrated when it was revealed a photo featured in one of the incumbent's television ads had been doctored to superimpose the head of Mark Warner on the body of Senator Robb, who was shaking hands with Wilder. In fact, Mark Warner was at the event pictured in the ad standing a few feet behind Senator Robb. John Warner fired his advertising agency, let most of the Democratic attacks against his voting record go unanswered, and limped to victory on Election Day.[42]

The 1996 presidential race was the closest since Gerald Ford's narrow victory over Jimmy Carter in 1976. Published polls showed President Clinton leading Bob Dole throughout the summer and into October. "Clinton has a better chance of carrying Virginia than anybody since Lyndon Johnson," predicted Norfolk Treasurer Joe Fitzpatrick, a former Democratic party chair, in early August. The Virginia Democratic party, euphoric to find the state undecided in October of a presidential election year, brought President Clinton in for a rally in Springfield (in northern Virginia) attended by prominent Democratic officeholders, including the U.S. Senate nominee. As one of the founders of the Democratic Leadership Council along with Chuck Robb, President Clinton was not nearly as threatening to Virginia voters as previous Democratic presidential nominees had been. To many Virginians, Clinton was nationalizing the biracial, centrist strategy used so successfully by Virginia Democrats in the 1980s. President Clinton ran strongly in the state's urban corridor stretching from northern Virginia to Tidewater, losing there by less than one percentage point. Statewide, Clinton improved his 1992 showing to come within two percentage points of Dole; the Republican won 47.1 percent of the vote to Clinton's 45.1 percent, with Ross Perot at 6.6 percent. To Larry Sabato, the results were significant: "It is no longer difficult to imagine a set of circumstances that would produce the first Democratic [presidential] victory in Virginia since 1964: a candidate with fewer personal flaws than Clinton, a GOP split down the middle between fiscal and social conservatives, and pro-Democratic electoral conditions such as those that prevailed in 1992 and 1996. Continued population growth in northern Virginia will fuel this increased competitiveness, as southern, rural Virginia—more conservative by nature—loses still more influence proportionately."[43]

Dole benefited from enduring tendencies in the Virginia electorate that have worked to the advantage of Republican nominees for years. Democratic successes at the state legislative and congressional levels as well as Clinton's strong showing, however, suggest those Republican advantages can be overcome. The Virginia electorate, especially in the northern half of the state, has increasingly responded more like a Middle Atlantic state than a southern state. The overwhelming vote from that part of the state for Wilder is a case in point. Even though the Republican ticket won statewide in 1996, the strong showings by President Clinton and Mark Warner as well as the continuation of a Democratic majority in the congressional delegation were impressive.

All the congressional incumbents won reelection easily in 1996, allowing Democrats to maintain their 6–5 edge in seats. Democratic state senator Virgil Goode won the open Fifth District seat in Southside vacated by Democrat L. F. Payne, who left office to run for lieutenant governor in 1997. Goode might have been the only Democrat who could have held the seat for his party in what was the heart of the racially conservative Byrd organization's terrain. Goode, who pulled an incredible 86.9 percent in his home county of Henry, won with 60.8 percent of the vote against the same Republican opponent who held Payne to 53.3 percent in 1994, George C. Landrith. A flamboyant orator with a reedy hill country drawl, Goode proved a far more effective campaigner in his native district than he had been running statewide against Robb in 1994. Once elected, Goode promised to join the conservative Democratic Blue Dogs caucus.

Further examination of the 1996 Virginia voting patterns reveals interesting trends that are consistent with those in other major statewide elections. Slightly over 60 percent of the total 1996 presidential vote in Virginia was cast in the suburbs. That total was up from 51.2 percent in the 1985 gubernatorial election. Not surprisingly, the suburban vote has grown at the expense of the rural vote. From 1985 to 1996 the rural proportion of the vote declined from 31.7 percent to 21.8 percent. Meanwhile, the central city percentage of the total vote has remained fairly consistent at 17 percent to 18 percent over the eleven-year period; exceptions were a significant increase in 1989 (22.5 percent) inspired by the Wilder candidacy and a dip in 1992 (13.7 percent).[44] In 1996, Clinton carried the central cities decisively, and his Republican opponent won the suburbs comfortably. The rural areas yielded a narrow margin for Dole. With variations, these patterns of vote distribution have been reflected in other statewide elections during the 1990s, illustrating the stability of partisan patterns in Virginia. In 1994, North ran well in the rural areas but lost the election when he barely carried the suburbs, falling well below the expected showing for a winning Republican candidate. Two years later, John Warner's reputation as the person who had thwarted North's chances contributed to a narrow loss of the rural areas to his Democratic opponent and a stronger-than-usual showing for a Republican in the central cities.

THE 1997 ELECTIONS: CLEAN REPUBLICAN SWEEP

As the 1997 statewide races approached, analysts and strategists on both sides of the political divide expected a competitive election. Virginia remains the only state in the union not allowing its governors to succeed themselves; while not precluding governors from sitting out a term and running again, the one-term policy eliminates incumbency as a factor in gubernatorial contests. It also renders it more difficult for a party to hold the governorship in Virginia's competitive political environment. Political positioning for the nomination begins early in both parties. Following the 1993 elections, it soon became apparent that Jim Gilmore, the Republican attorney general, and Donald S. Beyer, Jr., the Democratic lieutenant governor, would run against each other for governor in 1997.

Beyer and Gilmore brought contrasting experience, style, and agendas to the 1997 campaign. A successful northern Virginia Volvo dealer, Beyer had gained his first elective office when he won the lieutenant governorship in 1989. A personable campaigner who laced his speeches with self-deprecating humor and erudite phrases, Beyer exuded a love of ideas and a philosopher's temperament. His nondoctrinaire approach to problem solving appealed to moderates, but put him on what liberal Democrats regarded as the wrong side of such issues as welfare reform. His willingness to compromise with Republicans led those critics to question the depth of his commitment to some traditional Democratic principles. Only the Christian conservatives seemed to regard Beyer with any personal distaste, their antipathy stemming from Beyer's 1993 aggressive, winning campaign against their favorite, Michael Farris, a former Moral Majority state leader and home-schooling advocate.

By contrast, Gilmore's experience was as a U.S. Army intelligence officer, a prosecutor in a suburban Richmond county, and a one-term attorney general.

Intense and exacting, he was far more engaged by public policy debates than by campaign-trail chitchat. Critiqued as a rather humorless campaigner, Gilmore was nonetheless known as a caring administrator, well-regarded by both Republicans and Democrats within his staff. Although Gilmore had not emerged from the Christian-right portion of the party, he had solid support from Pat Robertson and other members of the Christian Coalition. In his 1993 campaign (which had resulted in a win with 56.1 percent of the vote), he had been successful in weaving the often-warring Republican factions into a united front. He remained loyal to the Allen administration, but appeared to be subtly distancing himself from some of the more controversial elements of the term, including Allen's environmental record.

In the race for lieutenant governor, Democrat L. F. Payne began as a strong favorite over Republican John H. Hager. Payne had represented the conservative and largely rural Fifth District in Congress for four terms. He offered the sort of bipartisan appeal that Democrats hoped would keep their fortunes alive in the future, even if Virginia should continue to shift to the political right. Hager, a retired Richmond tobacco executive and longtime party activist, had a compelling personal story. Decades earlier, he had contracted the polio virus from his infant son and had spent much of his adult life in a wheelchair. He had the disadvantages, however, of never having held elective office and of having made several impolitic statements, including the claim that tobacco is not an addictive substance.

There was no early favorite in the race for attorney general. The Democratic nominee, William D. Dolan, was well known in state legal circles and was a managing partner in a large northern Virginia law firm. His opponent, Republican Mark L. Earley, a prominent state senator from Chesapeake, had been a floor leader in a variety of highly publicized reform movements, including the abolition of parole, the revamping of welfare, and the overhaul of the juvenile justice system. He also was the leading legislative spokesman for pro-life forces in abortion debates, and on several other issues he was considered to be the voice of Christian conservatives in the assembly. That designation was a mixed blessing. It meant that he would have a strong base of support,[45] but no prominent member of the Christian conservative movement had won statewide office in Virginia, even though Farris and North had tried in 1993 and 1994.

Gilmore launched his gubernatorial campaign with an announcement of priorities: first, hiring four thousand new teachers; second, creating a merit-based college scholarship program, and third, eliminating the property tax on cars and trucks valued at $20,000 or less. That "third priority" quickly became the focus of the campaign. Gilmore's somewhat complex plan, including a five-year phase-in of the reduction, was reduced to a three-word slogan, "No Car Tax," on yard signs and bumper stickers that blanketed the state.

Beyer, who had hinted early on that he might endorse major spending for schools and roads, first responded that Gilmore's car-tax proposal was irresponsible. Briefly, it appeared that the 1997 election would become a referendum on investment versus tax cuts. But in a July debate, Beyer flip-flopped, laying out his own plan for car-tax reduction. The Democrat proposed a $250-a-year maximum tax credit to offset the property tax levy on vehicles, a plan that drained less money from the state treasury than Gilmore's. It also was harder to understand, however, and did nothing to help individuals who were too poor to pay income tax. The end result was that the plan appeared to disappoint both those who wanted tax relief and those who didn't. The tax cutters preferred Gilmore's plan because the benefits were greater. Those pushing for investment were disappointed that Beyer seemed to have forfeited the high moral ground.[46]

Throughout the summer and fall, Beyer attempted unsuccessfully to focus public attention on other issues. His billing of himself as "the education candidate" held promise, but his major proposal—raising teacher's salaries to the national average—proved less popular than Gilmore's plan to hire more teachers. Similarly, Beyer's attempt to rally support by attacking Gilmore's position on abortion and links to Pat Robertson apparently backfired. Exit polls suggested that relatively few voters were motivated by those issues and that, among those who were, about as many voted against Beyer as for him.[47]

On election day the GOP scored a clean sweep, winning all three of the statewide posts, a first for the party in Virginia. Gilmore won with 55.8 percent to 42.6 percent for Beyer, whose showing was the second worst of the century for a Democratic gubernatorial nominee, surpassed only by Terry's dismal performance four years earlier. As Sabato noted, "Jim Gilmore won virtually everything—almost every group and every region." Most stunning, perhaps, was Beyer's defeat even in his home region of northern Virginia, where car-tax rates were among the highest in the state and where many personal property tax bills came due just before the election. Gilmore seems to have benefited from the defection of African American voters, at least some of whom appear to have been persuaded by Wilder's decision to remain neutral in the contest. African Americans comprised 12.5 percent of those voting in 1997, an unusually low figure, and Gilmore received about 19 percent of that vote, higher than usual. About 17 percent of the African Americans who voted said they were influenced by Wilder's neutrality.[48]

The closest of the three races was the contest for lieutenant governor, where, until the votes were counted, Democrats felt they still had a fighting chance.

Even so, Gilmore's momentum proved too powerful for even the well-positioned Payne to overcome, and Hager won comfortably with 50.2 percent to 45.1 percent. The election of Mark Earley as attorney general with 57.5 percent to Dolan's 42.4 percent carried overtones beyond a single election. Winning endorsements even from both the moderate *Virginian-Pilot* and the more liberal Washington *Post*, Earley showed that it is possible for a religious conservative activist to be elected in Virginia, particularly if the candidate's credentials extend beyond issues identified with the religious right.

DEMOCRATIC AND REPUBLICAN INTRAPARTY CLEAVAGES

Apart from the strengths and weaknesses of individual candidates and events unique to each electoral cycle, the modern Democratic and Republican parties in Virginia can best be understood in terms of the ruinous factionalism that has invaded both their nomination processes. Democrats were plagued by the prolonged feuding between Wilder and Robb, whereas Republicans differ philosophically, especially on social issues. The 1994 Senate contest, for example, underscored the various schisms. Democrat Wilder and Republican Coleman ignored the outcomes of their respective parties' nomination contests and ran as independents. Wilder eventually dropped out and endorsed Robb; as a result, Robb received the overwhelming support of Wilder supporters, without which he would not have won. Coleman remained in the race and was at least partially responsible for the disastrous defection of Republican voters that doomed North's candidacy; North won only three-fourths of the Republican vote. Gilmore's success in 1997 can be attributed in part to his ability to unite the often-warring factions within his party. Meanwhile, Beyer had the disadvantage of Wilder's defection.

A momentous change in the modern Democratic party in Virginia was the abandonment of primaries to nominate candidates for statewide offices. Not since 1977 have Democrats nominated their gubernatorial candidate in a primary. In that year, the fiery liberal Henry Howell was the nominee, losing his third consecutive race for governor and prompting book chapter titles such as "Virginia: Transformed by a 'Loser.' "[49] The 1981 Democratic move to a less divisive state nominating convention system, coupled with Robb's moderate image, made it respectable for many of the state's voters to be "Virginia Democrats" again, and the electoral fortunes of the party soared. Ironically, it was the cooperation of Robb and Wilder that made possible the centrist biracial coalition that led to Democratic victories in the 1980s. In 1985 the Democrats unified their diverse constituencies with a ticket that included an African American (Wilder) and a woman (Terry). That year Gerald Baliles, a white Democrat, was elected governor. The second step in the unification march was the election of Wilder as governor and the reelection of Terry as attorney general in 1989. The hat trick for diversified tickets was to be the election of Terry as governor. Just as Terry had stepped aside and allowed Wilder to be nominated without opposition in 1989, Beyer in 1993 ran for reelection as lieutenant governor, thereby ensuring Terry's uncontested nomination.

Virginia Democrats have strictly adhered to the practice of uncontested nominations in harmonious conventions since 1985. Consistent with that practice, Beyer automatically became the Democratic gubernatorial nominee at the 1997 state convention when no candidate filed to run against him. Likewise, when no one filed against them, Payne officially became his party's choice for lieutenant governor and Dolan, the unsuccessful 1993 Democratic candidate for attorney general, became the ill-fated 1997 nominee for attorney general. As this slate was developing, Wilder, in comments that previewed his later stance of neutrality in the gubernatorial election, questioned whether an all-white-male Democratic ticket could win. "If you want to think of healing," wrote Wilder in a letter to Beyer in mid-December 1996, "it would be well to start 1997 with a Democratic slate of candidates which don't represent retrogression." Wilder's secretary of education, James Dyke, an African American, seriously explored the possibility of seeking the lieutenant governor's nomination before announcing his decision not to run. The names of two minority legislators, Delegate Jerrauld Jones of Norfolk and Congressman Bobby Scott, had also been mentioned as possible candidates for attorney general. In the wake of the defeats in the 1997 elections, some Democrats suggested that the party was suffering because of the lack of competition in the nominating process. One of the options being debated in 1998 was a return to primary elections.[50]

Unlike the post-Howell Democratic party, Republicans have witnessed intense and often bitter contests for statewide nominations. The 1994 state convention in Richmond epitomized the divisive struggles of the modern Republican party. Almost fourteen thousand delegates crowded into the Richmond Coliseum where North won 55 percent of the vote on the first and only ballot. It was the largest Republican convention yet, but, unfortunately for the Republicans, not the only divisive one in recent years.

The history of the Virginia Republican party over the past fifteen years is the struggle of the Christian right for acceptance. The division in the 1990s between Christian social conservatives and traditional economic conservatives can be traced to the 1981 state convention, when Virginia Republicans appeared to be on the ascendancy. Marshall Coleman was poised to run against Chuck Robb for governor. Guy O. Farley, Jr., a former Democratic legislator and candidate for the Republican nomination for lieutenant governor, attracted the active support of Christian conservatives. In a bitter, tumultuous state convention, the party leadership warned of a Moral Majority takeover if Farley was nominated. Farley eventually withdrew, throwing his support to a third candidate whose nomination displeased the traditional economic conservatives.[51] Bitterness from this convention lingered in the party for years.

In the 1990s the factional strife between the Christian right and the more moderate Republicans was exacerbated by a dispute between Governor Allen and the state party chairman. The new governor was convinced that Patrick McSweeney, the chairman, had withheld critical party support and funds from him during the summer months when he had trailed Terry in the polls. Once elected, Allen's forces attempted to remove McSweeney, but failed to get enough votes in the state central committee to do so. McSweeney had been elected to a four-year term at the 1992 state convention with the active support of the Christian Coalition, which constituted a sizable bloc on the state central committee.[52] The situation of divided leadership handicapped the Republican party until Allen's hand-picked choice, Delegate Randy Forbes, was elected party chairman in 1996.

There was an unusually high level of animosity between the Christian right and those conservative and moderate Republicans who supported Senator Warner. The Christian right dominated the state conventions in 1993 and 1994 and was instrumental in the nomination of Michael Farris for lieutenant governor and North for the Senate. Constituting as many as one-third of the delegates, the home-schooling advocates spearheaded a 60 percent majority vote for Farris in 1993 against a pro-choice woman.[53]

Senator Warner's nonendorsement of Farris and active support of Coleman's independent Senate bid in 1994 reopened the old party wounds from the previous decade. Farris's defeat in the 1993 general election (he received 45.5 percent of the vote) was a bitter disappointment rationalized as attributable to Warner's position and the hard-hitting negative campaign of the popular Democratic incumbent, Beyer. Farris retaliated by charging, "We've got a sickness in our party and that sickness is named John Warner."[54] McSweeney, viewed as an unusually pugnacious party chair, challenged Warner's Republican credentials to become chair of a Senate committee, snubbed him at GOP functions, and orchestrated a straw poll at the 1996 state convention that gave Miller 75 percent of the vote ten days before the Republican primary.

For his part, Warner was out of the country when North was nominated, and in 1996 he did not attend either the state convention in June or the national convention in August. Meanwhile, Governor Allen remained neutral in the bitter 1996 Republican primary, labeling it "an intra-squad scrimmage." He praised Warner's record in the Senate and described the senator as "almost an uncle" to him, while empathizing nonetheless with those Republican activists embittered by Warner's apostasy.[55]

Even before Earley's 1997 election as attorney general, Christian conservative activists could take solace from the key role they played in energizing the substantial majorities received by Allen and Gilmore in 1993.[56] Moreover, two of their number landed high positions in the Allen administration. Although Allen did not run for governor as a proponent of the Christian right's social issues, his policies were in line with the movement's goals. His support of parental notification, charter schools, and an "opt-in" provision for Family Life Education became election issues in some legislative districts in 1995.

Interrupted only by the gubernatorial primary of 1989, the long string of Virginia Republican conventions ended in 1996. John Warner invoked a state law permitting incumbent federal officeholders nominated in a primary to require the same method for renomination. Party activists anxious to deny Warner's renomination challenged the state law but were foiled by an opinion from the Republican attorney general, Gilmore, who refused to find the primary option unconstitutional. Frustrated by Warner's success in pressing for a primary and concerned about federal approval of registration fees charged delegates to GOP nominating conventions,[57] the party leadership reluctantly voted to use the primary method to nominate its statewide candidates in 1997. Since a Virginia primary is open to any registered voter, the Christian conservatives, whose influence was magnified in state conventions, had to share the nomination process with rank-and-file Republicans, not to mention Democrats and independent voters choosing to participate. The change undercut their strength. Still, in the low-turnout Republican primary for attorney general in 1997, the Christian conservatives' candidate, Earley, won with 36 percent of the vote in a four-person contest.

In summary, Democratic resurgence in the 1980s gave way in the 1990s to a new competitiveness that permeated state legislative races and even affected winning margins in presidential contests. These developments led analysts to refer to the Old Dominion in recent decades variously as the "New Dominion," the "Dynamic Dominion," and, perhaps most appropriately for the late 1990s, the "Competitive Dominion." As the decade wore on, Republicans gained the advantage, sweeping the three top statewide offices in 1997 and achieving power-sharing arrangements in both houses of the legislature. Thus, the decades-long struggle of the GOP to establish a two-party system at all levels in Virginia came to fruition in the last gubernatorial election of the century. With the new millennium drawing near, Republicans were poised, absent a return of their earlier schisms, to advance even further. In an electoral system that brings the voters to the polls every year and that eliminates the possibility of an incumbent governor running for reelection, Democrats could count on early opportunities to recoup their recent losses, and they were hopeful of being able to do so. Meanwhile, Virginia's largely conservative, suburban voters remain the chief beneficiaries and guarantors of the state's current vibrant and dynamic two-party system.

6

ARKANSAS: CHARACTERS, CRISES,
AND CHANGE

Jay Barth, Diane D. Blair, and Ernie Dumas

ARKANSAS politics in the 1990s has been both a throwback to the past and a window to the future. Reminiscent of traditional southern politics, election alliances and outcomes were often influenced by intense personal rivalries and singular, sometimes bizarre, dramatic episodes. In other respects, especially with regard to the increasing acceptability—though until 1996 still-infrequent occurrence—of Republican victories, new partisan political patterns were clearly unfolding. Overshadowing and affecting everything else that occurred in Arkansas politics in the 1990s, however, was the historic election and reelection of a native son, Bill Clinton, as president.

THE "BIG THREE" AND DEMOCRATIC DOMINANCE

As prelude to the 1990s it is important to understand that in the post-Reconstruction era no state has had a deeper attachment to, nor elected its officials more consistently and exclusively from, the Democratic party than has Arkansas. Arkansas was the last of the southern states to enter the Republican presidential fold (in 1972); had never elected a Republican to the U.S. Senate; had sent a grand total of two Republicans to the U.S. House; and only two Republicans had been elected governor: Winthrop Rockefeller in 1966 and 1968, and Frank White in 1980.[1] While Rockefeller's two victories broke the spell, they came about largely by virtue of support from newly enfranchised black voters and disaffected progressive Democrats. When these two groups returned to their Democratic traditions with Governors Dale Bumpers (1971–75), David Pryor (1975–79), and Bill Clinton (1979–81 and 1983–92), Republicans reverted to their distinctively minor-party status.

While traditions, demographics, and some unique electoral arrangements all combined to perpetuate Democratic dominance, perhaps the most important factor discouraging Republican growth in contemporary Arkansas was the combined personal popularity and political skill of the "Big Three" of late-twentieth-century Arkansas politics: Bumpers, Pryor, and Clinton.[2] All three were elevated by the Arkansas electorate from the governorship to national office: Bumpers to the Senate in 1974, Pryor to the Senate in 1978, and Clinton to the presidency in 1992.

Beginning with Richard Nixon in 1972, then Ronald Reagan in 1980, and even more decisively with President Reagan in 1984 and George Bush in 1988, Arkansas had finally joined the rest of the South in favoring Republicans in presidential contests. Reagan's personal popularity plus the appeal of the themes emphasized in his campaigns (less federal government, less crime, lower taxes, more family, more God, more patriotism) went a long way toward making the Republican label more legitimate, more respectable, indeed—in presidential races—positively preferable in Arkansas.[3]

However, the Big Three at the top of the statewide Democratic ticket (as they were thirty-six times between 1970 and 1994, since the Arkansas governorship was for a two-year term until 1986) presented a formidable bulwark against any significant trickle-down effects of Republican presidential popularity. The moderately progressive positions they took helped mediate what may have seemed the ideologically inappropriate stances of the national party, and their extensive campaign organizations insured a healthy turnout by those most likely to vote Democratic. As Little Rock Democratic political consultant and party activist Ron Oliver put it: "These were three individuals [who] are very good at creating and nurturing personal relationships. . . . The Democratic party has really piggy-backed on the personal organizations of these three men."[4]

Although allies with overlapping bases of support, the three men operated separate political organizations and displayed significantly different personal styles. As Little Rock political consultant Sheila Bronfman, a Democrat, explained: "Pryor and Clinton especially developed their own entire network separate from the Democratic party in this state. Pryor has the 'Pryor family list.' Pryor has always worked that extremely well. . . . [Pryor and Clinton] have their own county coordinators in every one of the 75 counties. . . . They have a huge, huge list of people whom they have continued to work over and over and over. David Pryor has that football tent [at University of Arkansas home games] every year two or three times. Whenever you get a mailing, they don't make it a 'mass mailing.' You get something that you feel is very personal."[5]

Pryor's organization is reinforced by a personal style that, in the words of Richard Fenno, "must be seen to be believed." Fenno recounted: "To come off the road and sit with him for an hour in a Little Rock hotel lobby and eat an evening meal with him and some friends in a Little Rock steakhouse is to experience a steady flow of exchanges with people . . . who stop by to say hello, introduce themselves, discuss a mutual friend, share a reminiscence, ask for an autograph, leave a problem, give advice, or tell a story. . . . It would not be correct to call them interruptions or intrusions, for the senator is as eager to make contact as they are." On the other hand, as political consultant Bronfman put it, "You can't beat Bill Clinton for charisma . . . and then you back that up with an organization that's really strong." It is Bumpers who has the least well developed organization. Instead, according to Bronfman, "His speaking style has always motivated people. . . . He appeals to that higher level, to the best of people. Bumpers is a *statesman*."[6] Whatever their distinctive political skills, these three dynamic politicians created a barrier against GOP development in Arkansas. In the 1990s this bulwark began to crumble.

The 1990 elections really began on July 28, 1989, when Democratic congressman Tommy F. Robinson, standing by President Bush's side at the White House, announced his decision to switch to the Republican party. "The hard fact is," he said, "that there is and will be no room for conservative southern Democrats in today's National Democratic Party." Furthermore, in the colorful language for which he had long been noted and which Lee Atwater hoped would reverberate among rural "Yellow Dog" Democrats, Robinson observed: "I could no longer stomach staying in a party run by the likes of Ted Kennedy and Jesse Jackson. . . . The Arkansas Democrat is nothing like the national Democrat. They're hard-working people, they believe in God and motherhood and chivalry and apple pie, and the eastern liberals have pointy heads and they carry big briefcases around with nothing inside but ham sandwiches."[7]

The announcement had been encouraged and orchestrated by Atwater as part of Operation Switch, and, clearly seeing in Robinson's red-meat appeal exactly what the national GOP needed to detach other Arkansas Democrats from their traditional loyalties, the party ran statewide television ads featuring the White House event. According to Skip Rutherford, state Democratic chair at the time, "Lee Atwater was very much wired to Tommy. . . . Atwater was the one person who saw Bill Clinton as the foe to beat George Bush. Atwater . . .

recognized that taking the governorship was critical to building the Republican party in Arkansas. So Atwater had two objectives: to wound or cripple Bill Clinton and to build the Republican party. Tommy Robinson was the vehicle, and at the time Atwater was associated with him, Robinson was an extremely popular politician. Atwater never dreamed there would be a Republican primary."[8]

Within months, however, not only had Atwater's health begun failing, but the 1990 Republican gubernatorial nomination had become far more complicated. Sheffield Nelson, another lifelong Democrat, had resigned after twelve years as chief executive officer of Arkansas Louisiana Gas Company in 1984 with hopes of seeking the governorship in 1986. When Clinton decided to seek reelection, Nelson busied himself in civic endeavors but then announced his gubernatorial intent in June 1989 (though not yet specifying from which party he would seek the nomination). When Nelson announced in August that he also was switching parties, the flavor of the resulting clash was characterized by Mark Shields as "at least a miniseries, a morality play and maybe even a novel, teeming with treachery, vengeance, ambition, busted friendships and truly colorful characters." Shields went on to describe concisely the bizarre dynamics of the showdown:

> In 1982, Nelson, as chief executive officer, approved a gas-lease sale that proved so disadvantageous to Arkla [Arkansas Louisiana Gas Co.] that the company eventually had to repurchase the leases at a cost of $146 million. The happy beneficiary of this deal was a friend of Nelson's named Jerry Jones, who used his proceeds to fulfill a fantasy by buying the Dallas Cowboys football team. Jerry Jones' closest boyhood and manhood friend had been, you guessed it, Tommy Robinson, whose campaigns Jerry Jones helped to bankroll. . . . But by attacking Nelson for the leases that made Jerry Jones truly rich, Robinson has made Jones his ex-best friend. Jerry Jones now backs Sheffield Nelson. Robinson is backed by Jack Stephens, a multi-millionaire Arkansas investment banker who wants to punish Nelson. Why? Jack Stephen's partner and brother, Witt, gave young Sheffield his start at Arkla, and their relationship turned bad and ugly over some of Nelson's management moves there.[9]

While the questionable business practices of the gas company were a constant issue in the race, Robinson drew enthusiastic audiences, especially in rural areas, and much media attention. One reporter summed up his typical stump speech: "We've got inmates on death row sitting there with central air conditioning while our children sit in classrooms where they can't learn because it's too hot. . . . We've got crack dealers in junior high schools. . . . I'm not gonna consolidate any schools. . . . We're being taxed to death."[10]

Robinson eventually carried fifty-six of seventy-five counties. Nelson, however, won the Republican primary with 54.3 percent of the vote. This anomaly primarily reflects the dominance of Democratic candidacies for thousands of substate offices. In most counties the Nelson-Robinson matchup was the only contest in the Republican primary, and few voters were willing to sacrifice their vote on all other choices to express a preference in the Republican contest. So while Robinson, as he had proudly predicted, "stomped" Nelson in Woodruff County, that gave him a margin of exactly 7 votes (13 to 6), while Nelson piled up large numbers in the Republican and densely populated northwestern counties and, significantly, in Arkansas's largest metropolitan county of Pulaski (Little Rock).[11] Another peculiarity of Arkansas's election system was relevant here: In the absence of party registration, crossover voting is entirely legal, and at least in Robinson's home of Pulaski County Democrats wanting to punish him for his party-switching perfidy and fearing Robinson's appeal in a general election clearly did so.[12] Rutherford recalled, "Because I was identifed with the Democratic party myself, I couldn't cross over and vote for Nelson myself, but I encouraged lots of people to do so."[13]

One other Arkansas election oddity is significant here. Until 1996, primaries in Arkansas were financed by parties themselves, using the sizable revenue from steep filing fees to pay for election workers and vote-counting machinery. With numerous Democratic candidacies, the Democratic party could afford to open many polling places, whereas the Republicans were often hard pressed to provide even one polling place per county, an inconvenience discouraging to all but the most dedicated.

The Democratic gubernatorial nomination, originally expected to be highly contested, produced much more limited fireworks. Attorney General Steve Clark, who had announced in January, by spring was being investigated for allegations of spending state money for luxurious dinner dates and trips, and by November had been convicted of felony theft by deception. Jim Guy Tucker, a former attorney general (1973–1977) and congressman (1977–78) who had spent the 1980s building a private fortune in real estate and cable television, announced his gubernatorial intent in February.

Bill Clinton, having served ten of the previous twelve years as governor, was indecisive about running for another term. While there is no evidence that the Clintons seriously mulled the option, rumors surfaced that Hillary Rodham Clinton might run for the office. According to Gloria Cabe, the 1990 Clinton campaign manager, Dick Morris, who had made a deal with the national Republican party to work for Bill Clinton only "as long as he was running in the state," that is, not for the U.S. Senate, "got permission to work for Hillary if she ran." Less than three months away from the primary, on March 1, Clinton scheduled an announcement of his 1990 plans. Cabe remembers, "We had invited his supporter list to the Capitol for the announcement and they didn't know what the announcement would be."[14] Clinton announced for another term.

Following Clinton's declaration that he would seek reelection, Tucker decided he would seek the lieutenant governorship nomination instead. Off-the-record interviews with Clinton operatives indicate that they did make overtures to Tucker confidantes on the issue of Tucker leaving the governor's race. "Our story to him was that you're going to get beat, it's going to be destructive to the party. We'd help him pay off whatever costs he had incurred to date and help him with his campaign effort. And I think we did get something like $25,000 for him."[15] Speculation, however, that Clinton and Tucker made a pact in 1990 that if Tucker would move to the lieutenant governor's race, Clinton would run for president in 1992, leaving Tucker the governorship, seems unfounded. As Cabe said, "That's absolutely BS."[16]

In seeking a fifth term, Clinton kept a previous pledge not to challenge incumbent Democratic senator David Pryor. The formidably popular Pryor thus remained unopposed in either the primary or the general election.

In the general election campaign, Nelson continued a theme used to no avail by Clinton's challengers in the Democratic primary: "Ten Years Is Enough." The Republican challenger also portrayed Clinton as a liberal tax-and-spender whose expensive education initiatives had produced few results. While Nelson strongly hinted at ethical improprieties and sexual misconduct on Clinton's part, the state press, after some investigation, did not publicize the issue—a decision likely based on the fact that the particular charges were being made by a disgruntled former state employee who had been fired after making calls to raise funds for the Nicaraguan Contras on state telephones.[17] Nelson's bitterness about the press's "noncoverage" of what he felt were legitimate campaign issues helps to explain his activity in spreading unflattering stories involving the Clintons to the national press in the years that followed.

Clinton's hold on Arkansas voters was wearing thin in 1990. His winning percentages in both the Democratic primary (54.8 percent) and the general election (57.5 percent) were his slimmest victories since 1982. Still, the election outcomes suggest that while the Republican party was making significant gains elsewhere in the South, by 1990 it was still struggling for legitimacy in Arkansas.

The Republicans' biggest disappointment was Asa Hutchinson's unsuccessful bid for the open attorney general's office. Hutchinson had the Democratic nominee, Lieutenant Governor Winston Bryant, on the ropes late in the race. But, as Richard Bearden, state GOP executive director, remembers, "At the very end, Asa simply ran out of money. You had so much money being sucked up by the governor's race." In addition, because Hutchinson lacked the money to respond on television, he reacted to Bryant's charges that Hutchinson, when a U.S. attorney, had not thoroughly investigated a drug-trafficking ring that had made use of a small airstrip in Mena, by filing a lawsuit for libel. Bearden admits that Hutchinson's using the courts rather than counterpunching had its costs. "Asa did not really come across as looking like a strong candidate [by filing the lawsuit]."[18]

The high hopes that accompanied Robinson's dramatic announcement had ended in this reality: The Republicans could not capitalize on widespread anti-incumbent sentiments to defeat a controversial governor seeking his fifth term; they could not even find a candidate willing to take on an incumbent U.S. senator; the congressional seat surrendered by Robinson to make his unsuccessful gubernatorial bid was recaptured by the Democrats (returning the delegation to the three Democrat-one Republican split that had become customary since Republican John Paul Hammerschmidt's victory in northwest Arkansas's Third District in 1966); and, finally, Republican strength in the state legislature remained at 4 of 35 state senators and only 9 (down from 11) of 100 representatives. Indeed, in eastern Crittenden County, an independent whose death was announced three weeks prior to the election still beat a Republican candidate for a seat on the Quorum Court, the county's governing body. Only in the presidential contest, it seemed, could Arkansas Republicans count on statewide success, and in 1992, courtesy of native son Bill Clinton, even this victory was to be denied them.

A NATIVE SON PRESIDENT, BUT IRONIC CONSEQUENCES AT HOME

When Bill Clinton announced his presidential candidacy on October 3, 1991, his chances for victory seemed remote at best, even in Arkansas. In June 1991, a hypothetical match between him and President Bush showed an overwhelming Bush victory, 65 to 27 percent, with Bush's job performance rating a seemingly impervious 81 percent. One veteran Democratic state legislator, when asked in the late summer if he would support a candidacy by his governor said, "Right now I have some reservations. I'm a Democrat and I usually support the Democratic candidate, but . . ."[19] An Arkansas poll taken immediately after Clinton's presidential announcement still showed Bush ahead, 53 percent to 40 percent.

But as the 1992 campaign unfolded, with national Republicans harshly deriding Arkansas as a way of attacking Clinton, the state began rallying round. One of us wrote elsewhere: "As the campaign progressed, it became increasingly clear to the people of Arkansas that it was they themselves—their state, their lifestyle, their economic well-being, their educational attainments, their environment, indeed their intelligence in consistently reelecting Clinton—that was being questioned."[20] Presumably, the citizens of any state would arise in patriotic defense against perceived slurs from "strangers," but for Arkansans, the slight, which began in the primary and then escalated into a major campaign theme in the general election, reopened sensitive psychic wounds of long duration. Arkansans are acutely aware of and highly resentful and defensive about the state's longstanding national reputation for poverty, provincialism, and general backwardness.

Despite increasingly explicit warnings from state Republicans, the Bush campaign's onslaught on Arkansas escalated, culminating in Bush's statement that what worried him most was for Clinton to "do to America what he did to Arkansas. . . . We do not want to be the lowest of the low." Especially infuriating was a television ad depicting Arkansas as the land of the living dead complete with a lightning storm illuminating a dead tree in a desert, with a vulture sitting in its barren branches while the announcer intoned: "And now Bill Clinton wants to do for America what he's done for Arkansas. America can't take that risk."[21]

For Arkansas Democrats, 1992 was a dream come true. Bronfman, who coordinated the Arkansas Travelers, a group of Clinton supporters who traveled to other states to sing the praises of their governor, said: "While it was happening, it energized this state like nothing had ever done before. . . . It brought people out of the woodwork. . . . We raised more money here than any state per capita has ever done. . . . The numbers down at headquarters were huge. . . . It was massive."[22]

Unsurprisingly, Clinton's winning margin in Arkansas, 53.2 percent of the popular vote, was his largest percentage in any of the fifty states. Bush, who had carried fifty-two of Arkansas's seventy-five counties and received 56.4 percent of the popular vote in 1988, was reduced to six counties (all in the mountains of northwest Arkansas, an area of GOP support since the Civil War era) and 35.5 percent of the vote in 1992. Perot received 10.4 percent.

All other political events in the state in 1992 were overshadowed by the

Clinton candidacy. Dale Bumpers, seeking his fourth term in the U.S. Senate, was challenged by a surprise opponent in the Democratic primary: Julia Hughes Jones, longtime Democratic state auditor. Even in the "Year of the Woman," however, Jones drew little support from women's groups or indeed many others; Bumpers won the nomination decisively with 64.5 percent.

Despite attempts by his Republican opponent to tar him as a Kennedy-clone liberal leftist, Bumpers defeated Mike Huckabee, former president of the state Southern Baptist Convention, by nearly the same margin (60.2 percent) as in his 1986 victory (62.3 percent) over Asa Hutchinson, who by this time was chairing the state Republican party. A public poll just over a year before the 1992 general election had shown Bumpers leading Huckabee 70 percent to 12 percent. Huckabee gained some traction, however, as he traveled the state promoting a conservative populist message. He focused on term limits, the veteran Bumpers's out-of-state fundraising and perks as a senator, including "the mother of all pension plans," expansion of the death penalty (including for those who knowingly transmitted the AIDS virus), and a return to traditional moral values. In an emblematic line on the campaign stump, Huckabee said, "When I was in school they passed out Gideon Bibles. Today, they pass out condoms."[23] In addition, Vice President Dan Quayle, Senate minority leader Bob Dole, and singer Pat Boone stumped and raised money for Huckabee in the state.

Then the Huckabee campaign had a bad month of August that stymied its momentum. First, in a disclosure that directly contradicted Huckabee's populism, Federal Election Commission records showed that the Huckabee campaign had paid more than six thousand dollars to Huckabee's one-man company for campaign media services and that Huckabee's wife was the highest paid campaign staffer. Second, the Arkansas-bashing at the Houston GOP convention, where Huckabee addressed the delegates, provided fodder for Arkansas Democrats. Huckabee's remarks there had been tame, but other Republicans went after the state. Most remembered by Arkansans was Marilyn Quayle's comment to the Texas delegation: "Do we want our country to look like Arkansas?"[24]

Democratic strength at the congressional level was evident in the First (Northeast) and Second (Central) Districts as well, where Republican candidates received only 30.2 percent and 25.8 percent of the vote respectively. Such a lopsided margin in the First District was particularly noteworthy because the Democratic victor was a thirty-two-year-old woman, Blanche Lambert, the first woman to enter Arkansas's congressional delegation other than by the widowhood route, and because she had eliminated twelve-term congressman Bill

Alexander—a man for whom she had once worked as a receptionist—in the Democratic primary. Lambert ran something of a stealth campaign, but as she drove the district she met voters who were infuriated by Alexander's bounced checks and other expressions of perceived arrogance. She claimed repeatedly, "I'll promise you one thing. I can sure enough balance my checkbook."[25]

Also tarnished by the House Bank scandal and also falling in the primary was the seven-term congressman from the Fourth (Southern) District, Beryl Anthony, Jr. Anthony's overdrafts at the House Bank were much less numerous than Congressman Alexander's and far fewer than those of Robinson—who led the House with 998—but opposition from both the National Rifle Association and the state AFL-CIO forced him into a runoff with Secretary of State W. J. (Bill) McCuen, who ultimately won the nomination.

Leftover bitterness by Anthony supporters undoubtedly contributed to the Republicans' biggest prize in 1992: Jay Dickey, a businessman and political novice, became the first Republican ever to win a congressional seat from south Arkansas. Because the Fourth District contains the state's highest percentage of blacks (27 percent), and black voters in contemporary times have overwhelmingly voted for Democratic candidates, Democrats had routinely won this district by margins of 70 percent or more. Dickey, however, who included on his campaign literature coupons for free tacos at his Taco Bell franchises, made the case that the controversial McCuen (who later ended up in prison for criminal activities while secretary of state) would embarrass the state in Washington. The veteran McCuen was brazenly overconfident, saying, "I don't need to debate him to win."[26] Mistakenly, state Democrats consoled themselves that Dickey's victory with 52.3 percent of the vote was a fluke that could be remedied in the future.

In complete contrast to Dickey's district is the northwest Arkansas Third District, held by Republican John Paul Hammerschmidt for twenty-six years (1967–1993). Here in the Ozark uplands, economic boom, affluent (and often northern) retirees, religious fundamentalism, a minute (2 percent) black population, and the traditions of southern Mountain Republicanism have combined to form an increasingly Republican stronghold. Hammerschmidt's eventual successor, Tim Hutchinson (Asa's older brother, a Bob Jones University graduate like his brother and a Christian school founder and Baptist minister), had made his first political mark in 1984 by unseating an eighteen-year Democratic veteran for a Benton County state legislative seat. Although both the Republican nomination and the general election were sharply contested (including an election-week personal appearance by presidential nominee Clinton in behalf of Democrat nominee John Van Winkle), neither Hutchinson's primary win nor his general election victory (the latter with 50.2 percent of the vote) was unexpected.

The outcome of the 1992 congressional races meant a rare even split between Republicans and Democrats in the U.S. House delegation. It also meant that Arkansas, which had once specialized in congressional seniority, was represented by three first-termers and a second-termer in the U.S. House.

State and local offices remained overwhelmingly Democratic. Despite post-census redistricting, Republicans gained only one seat in the state house (for a total of 10 of 100 seats) and one seat in the state senate (for a total of 5 of 35 seats). Aside from Dickey's anomalous Fourth District victory, it seemed to be another year of Democratic dominance as usual, with the particular satisfaction for state Democrats of seeing their own Bill Clinton recapturing the White House for their party. Nevertheless, Democrats might well have paid heed to an old Ozark saying: when your cup runneth over, you better watcheth out. Buried within the sweet fruits of Clinton's presidential victory were some of the seeds of Democratic dissolution.

The intensity of the Clinton campaign left Arkansas Democrats with something of a political hangover in its aftermath. As Bronfman put it, party activists were "dry" emotionally, financially, and in terms of time committed to politics, after the inauguration. The new president, unintentionally of course, weakened the state Democratic party by taking with him to Washington some of his most able operatives and potentially strong statewide and congressional Democratic candidates. In particular, Clinton had traditionally run up amazing margins in the state's predominantly black precincts, a strength based mainly on organization: "[Clinton operatives] Rodney Slater, Bob Nash, and Carroll Willis were . . . using churches . . . the only thing that was really organized in the black community to key into African American politics. Willis was really comfortable doing that and was building all the time, bringing in new blood."[27] All three of these men went with Clinton to Washington.

It had not been organization alone, however, that had brought about the tremendous success in the black community; also now missing was Clinton's deep personal connection to rank-and-file African Americans throughout the state. As a Democratic party strategist commented: "Clinton is the *only* one who can have that appeal, and it's not that easy to transfer . . . because it's such a personal appeal. People have met him; he's been in their churches; he's been in their houses. He's come to their organizational dinners. He's invested a lot of time in connecting with [African Americans]."[28] Both Clinton and his unique organization in the black community were gone. Simultaneously, some of President Clinton's earliest policy initiatives—most notably gays in the military and gun control—complicated constituent relations for Democratic officeholders throughout the South, including Arkansas.

Perhaps most notably, when Clinton became president, Lieutenant Governor Jim Guy Tucker ascended to the governorship, thereby creating a vacancy in the lieutenant governorship. After some wrangling over the election process, that post was won in a July 1993 special election by Republican Huckabee. Ironically, then, Clinton's presidential victory had facilitated the first Republican victory for statewide office since Frank White's 1980 upset of then-governor Clinton, and one of only five Republican victories for statewide office in twentieth-century Arkansas up to then.

Democrat Nate Coulter, a party activist and lawyer from Little Rock, had gained his party's nomination after an impressive primary campaign in which he introduced himself to voters by focusing on the adoption of teenage curfews and an audit of state government. He ran a vigorous grassroots campaign. "I went more places and did more things for that kind of election," Coulter remembered later, including visiting small-town newspapers and developing relationships with Democratic county officials around the state.[29] It clearly mattered also that the thirty-three-year-old novice had worked for both Bumpers and Clinton. Coulter used their separate, yet overlapping, organizations to gain a significant lead over 1990 Clinton primary opponent Tom McRae—a candidate who made it easier to motivate the Clinton people—in the first primary, then to defeat him easily in the runoff.

Huckabee, the GOP's 1992 U.S. Senate nominee and past president of the 490,000-member Baptist convention (a decidedly political position in the era of division between moderates and conservatives in the denomination), avoided primary opposition, then defeated Coulter narrowly (50.8 percent) in the July 27, 1993, general election. Though it was not fully recognized at the time, this election would have major ramifications on the state's politics for the rest of the 1990s. "Watershed, wasn't it?" commented a Democratic loyalist wistfully three years after the fact. Republican Richard Bearden agreed: "It was a huge boost for our party, in light of the fact that 6 or 8 months previously we'd been devastated by the election of Bill Clinton. . . . In terms of energy, enthusiasm, and fund-raising ability [it was] a tremendous boost to our party. . . . It really put our party on the road to where we are today."[30]

Democrats attributed Huckabee's victory to uniquely favorable circumstances: greater name recognition than his Democratic opponent, and especially the dynamics of a small-turnout special election which attracted Huckabee's hungrier and more committed Republican and religious following more than it did the business-as-usual Democrats. Two past Democratic chairs intimated that the then-popular governor Tucker, concerned that a victorious Coulter would quickly challenge him, sat on his own organization. Jerry Russell, longtime campaign consultant for candidates of both parties, placed some blame on Coulter's own organization, saying: "In 1993 [a Coulter consultant] told Nate Coulter that they didn't need to court the black vote because the black vote had nowhere else to go. Yea, they do. They can go home. They did. . . . If they had done the work, Nate would be governor today."[31]

While recognizing the roles of some misallocation of resources and a talented political opponent, Coulter focused on the weakness of his own television advertising campaign in the general election. "I think if our media had been a little bit more effective that would have made the difference." In particular, the Coulter campaign failed to directly respond to Huckabee's most damaging charges, that Coulter was simply the latest product of the "Democratic machine." The Coulter advertisement that received the most criticism centered on Huckabee's putting his wife, Janet, on the campaign payroll. While the criticism was on Huckabee's management of his campaign, Huckabee successfully refocused the issue as an "attack" on his wife with a response ad featuring a passionate Huckabee speaking directly to the camera with his pained wife at his side. This refocusing succeeded in portraying Coulter as a man taking an unfair shot at an opponent's wife. As Bronfman says, "You don't do that in Arkansas."[32]

While the race is appropriately seen as more of a Democratic loss than a Republican victory, Huckabee did use very effectively an "outsiders vs. insiders" clean-up-the-system motif in his paid media. Such reform themes mesh nicely with longstanding strains of Arkansas populism, and they neatly tap into contemporary voter anger at and mistrust of government. Huckabee's chief consultant in his 1993 victory was Dick Morris (the same Dick Morris who later achieved notoriety as Clinton's fallen political adviser). Clearly, Morris knew Arkansas well, and—after Huckabee's victory—he publicly touted his winning strategy as follows: "A southern Republican must separate himself from the country club and high society ethic with which his national party is associated and stake out ground as a rural populist. If the spin in a southern state is rich/poor, the Republicans will lose. But if we can make it insider/outsider we win. Huckabee ran an ad which said Arkansas was run by a political machine. . . . 'A political machine runs Arkansas . . . it caters to its special-interest friends. There is one set of rules for them and another for the rest of us. . . . We can unplug the machine on July 27th and empower the people.' "[33]

In addition, nothing could have served state Republican interests more than the Whitewater investigations, another negative legacy for state Democrats from their native son's presidential victory. Regardless of what is ultimately determined to have been done by the Clintons, a big-budget, broad-authority, highly skilled investigative team began subjecting a broad array of past private and public transactions by Arkansas activists (most of them, naturally, Democrats) to exhaustive scrutiny.

Giving further validation to the increasingly popular Republican theme that the political system constituted one huge cesspool in need of total draining were two other factors, one small and personal, one huge and systemic. The first was Sheffield Nelson, who, still smarting from his 1990 defeat by Clinton, carried on the campaign by other means. Nelson served as a major source of the anti-Clinton stories that ultimately found their way into the tabloid press and assorted investigative bodies.[34] The major factor, which continues to reverberate in Arkansas politics, is the October 1991 takeover and closing of the traditionally Democratic *Arkansas Gazette* by the traditionally Republican *Arkansas Democrat*. The *Democrat-Gazette*, as the paper called itself after the *Gazette*'s demise, carried on a non-stop anti-Clinton editorial campaign. The fact that it became the state's only daily statewide newspaper with significant circulation (175,000 daily) has been—according to many observers—the most significant weapon in the emerging Republican party's arsenal. Indeed, many interviewees without being prompted cited the demise of the *Gazette* as a key change in the state's political landscape. As a prominent political writer observed in 1992, "Now that we've endured a general election in Arkansas with only one statewide daily newspaper, we can reasonably conclude that the real winners of the vaunted newspaper war were the Republicans."[35]

In November 1994 Arkansas was touched by the "seismic shocks" that turned Congress over to Republican control for the first time in forty years and that reverberated throughout the South, but the state was not transformed by them. All four incumbent congressmen held their seats, but by significantly different margins. Republican Tim Hutchinson recaptured by 67.7 percent the Third District seat he had narrowly won in 1992. Republican Jay Dickey's 51.8 percent win in the Fourth District, against a united Democratic party and a strong candidate, state senator Jay Bradford, was an even more potent indication of Democratic slippage since this was the seat Democrats had confidently expected to recapture. Dickey came home often to a district that had felt neglected during the Anthony years and comforted voters with his folksy practice of using his House office as his bedroom while in Washington. He was rewarded with reelection in a race that likely was decided by the national GOP tide.

As for the two Democratic incumbents, Ray Thornton's 57.4 percent win over an inexperienced Republican challenger in the Second District was unimpressive compared to his 74.2 percent margin in 1992; and the now-married Blanche Lambert Lincoln's fall from 69.8 percent to 53.4 percent over another Republican novice in the once safely Democratic First District was especially encouraging to Republicans. One of the statistics most frequently and proudly cited by state Republican chairman Hutchinson in the election's aftermath was that, for the first time in Arkansas, a majority of votes in the congressional races had been cast for Republicans. Considering that it was not until 1982 that all four congressional seats were even contested in the general election, his elation was understandable.

Equally heartening to Republicans was Lieutenant Governor Huckabee's reelection, which was not only by a greater margin (58.6 percent compared to his special election 50.8 percent) but was much more geographically extensive as well (67 of 75 counties compared with 32 in 1993). In the campaign Huckabee ran safe advertisements focusing on crime issues and his bipartisan approach to state government. State senator Charlie Cole Chaffin, Huckabee's Democratic opponent, ran short of money and was remembered in political circles for an unintentionally funny television advertisement she aired late in the campaign. In it a plaid-shirted Chaffin faces the camera holding a shotgun and touts her support for gun freedom. The ad closes: "This's one of my shotguns. It's a Remington Model 1100 twenty-gauge magnum with an invector choke. Second Amendment rights don't need to be taken away; criminals do. Gun control, no; criminal control, [Chaffin loudly chambers a round] yes!"

Compared to what was happening elsewhere in the South in 1994, these were marginal gains. Importantly, unlike the situation in other southern states, the Democratic primary remained the center of action during the nomination process. In 1994, for instance, nearly eight times as many voters participated in the Democratic primary—without a governor's race—than in a GOP primary with a neck-and-neck finish in the gubernatorial contest.[36]

In terms of actual offices and power, Democrats in 1994 remained firmly in control. Governor Tucker, having secured the Democratic nomination without a primary contest, was easily elected to the office he had previously gained by succession, winning 59.8 percent of the general election vote and carrying all but two of Arkansas's 75 counties. The Republican victim once again was Sheffield Nelson, whose narrow (50.8 percent) Republican primary win employed tactics (including last-minute highly dubious charges against his chief opponent, state senator Steve Luelf, run exclusively on religious radio stations) which, as in 1990, left a deeply divided party and an unelectable nominee.[37] "A good candidate would have beaten Jim Guy," political consultant Jerry Russell observed.

In particular, Tucker, described by Russell as a "cold fish," lacked the strong personal political skills of the "Big Three," particularly the governor he had replaced.[38] As a Tucker associate related: "To look at the mechanics of campaigning, I think Clinton set a standard in Arkansas that was very difficult for Tucker and others to follow, because Clinton would show up at *every* fish fry, at *every* Democratic party event, at *every* bake sale and shake every hand until he'd shaken them all. . . . Clinton is obviously the consummate politician and Tucker *abhorred* those politicking days."[39]

Still, Tucker was perceived as having run the state competently during his short term. And, according to Yates, Tucker's campaign director, "He managed to keep from [irritating] any major groups." But, most important, he was facing Sheffield Nelson. Yates commented: "It's just incredible how much people disliked [Nelson]. I guess it was the combination of the campaign that Clinton ran in 1990, the [gas lease purchase] stuff that was still out there, Jerry Jones being very high profile and a lot of people associating him with Jones and the Cowboys. . . . People would bring that up. They'd say, 'You know that should be *our* football team because we paid for it.' It was surprising how many kept that thing in their mind, but it was kept in the public consciousness because of the Cowboys. Our media strategy was designed to push those buttons on Nelson."[40]

Nelson did attempt to take advantage of an ethical cloud over the governor and the potentially resulting chaos for the state government, going so far as to place a cutout of Tucker's face in the witness box in an advertisement that closed with the sound of a jail door slamming. While the ad was prescient, it did little good for the disliked Nelson in November 1994.

All five of the other statewide elected positions were filled by Democrats. As has been typical in modern Arkansas politics, the Republicans failed to even offer a candidate for two of the offices: state treasurer and land commissioner. Attorney General Winston Bryant, who had squeaked by in 1990, won 80.5 percent of the vote against a party-switcher who spent most of the campaign dealing with his prosecution and trial on wife-beating charges. A veteran state legislator from south Arkansas, Gus Wingfield, won 63.0 percent against another former Democrat in the race for state auditor. The closest of the three races was for secretary of state. There, the former mayor of Little Rock (a primarily ceremonial post), Sharon Priest, defeated a third former Democrat, longtime state auditor Julia Hughes Jones, with 52.5 percent of the vote.

The results in these three contested races showed the dubiousness with which Arkansas voters have treated Republican candidates who have switched parties, something that has not been the case in other southern states where the

GOP has used former Democrats to quickly build farm teams. In addition, the races for these five offices demonstrated that in Arkansas the real action in down-ticket races is still more likely to be in the Democratic primary. In all three contested races, the Democratic victors had significantly more difficulty winning their primary elections than in winning the general election. Bryant had to defeat Senator Pryor's son, Mark, a state legislator from Little Rock. Wingfield defeated another south Arkansas Democratic state house member with only 51.8 percent of the vote. Finally, Priest pulled off the biggest upset of the year by defeating the longtime secretary of state, Bill McCuen, in a runoff.

While Republicans contested more state legislative seats than usual in 1994 (43 general election contests compared with 37 in 1992, 31 in 1990, and 13 in 1988), Democrats remained firmly in control of both houses of the General Assembly with 88 of 100 house seats and 28 of the 35 seats in the senate, a net gain of four for the Republicans. As of 1994, while there were glimmers of hope for the Republicans, more had stayed the same than had changed in Arkansas politics.

Signs of Change as the "Big Three" Depart

Democratic retirements for the 1996 campaign cycle in the state opened up opportunities for Arkansas Republicans. First, David Pryor, arguably the most politically popular of the "Big Three," announced his retirement. In late 1995, another Democratic veteran officeholder, Second District congressman Ray Thornton—who later sought and won a seat on the state supreme court— announced his retirement. Then, in January 1996, Representative Blanche Lambert Lincoln, who had planned to run for reelection while pregnant, decided not to run after all when she found out twins were on the way. (Incidentally, she reentered the political arena in 1998, winning the Democratic nomination for the U.S. Senate seat being vacated by the retiring Bumpers.) As a result of the retirements, for the first time since Reconstruction no Democrats were running for reelection to seats in the House. After it was all over, Arkansas would have its least seniority in Washington in 122 years.

Almost as rare was an open U.S. Senate race, a circumstance that ordinarily would have unleashed the ambitions of Democratic stars bridled by the protracted tenures of Clinton, Bumpers and Pryor. But the long-dominant party suddenly found that it had no stars. It had been decapitated by Clinton's leapfrog to the White House, the Democratic primary upsets in the congressional delegation in 1992, and the criminal prosecutions of Tucker and Attorney General Steve Clark.

From the outset, the party's candidate seemed ordained, by default, to be Winston Bryant, the attorney general. Lieutenant Governor Huckabee would be his Republican opponent, and Bryant, a lusterless politician who had built a reputation over twenty-four years for workmanlike competence and honesty in four yeoman political offices, struck most people in the party as a poor match for the personable former preacher. While Bryant had lost only once in ten campaigns, his doubters were legion. He had little organization, the fealty of supporters other than labor unions was soft, he had never raised much money, he had a knack for leaving his vanquished foes frustrated and enraged, and for a man who was celebrated for his dullness he had collected a panoply of powerful enemies. Although Bryant had served innocuously for ten years in the largely ministerial offices of secretary of state and lieutenant governor, in his first term as attorney general after his election in 1990, he managed to nettle nearly every major economic interest. His office fought rate increases for the major utilities, sued polluting industries, sued to halt timber harvesting in sensitive national forest lands, and accused doctors and other providers of Medicaid fraud.[41] Such actions guaranteed that serious opponents would not lack for campaign money.

Though Bryant's bland personality and oratorical ineptness were his signature, the clutch of opponents he drew in the Democratic primary offered poor contrast. Kevin Smith, a freshman state senator from Stuttgart, struck out on a thousand-mile walking tour of Arkansas and was rarely heard from again until his weary concession statement. Sandy McMath, the quixotic son of a postwar governor, Sid McMath, spent little but his own money, mostly on cheaply produced Medicare infomercials on obscure cable television channels. Bill Bristow of Jonesboro, an angular Harvard-educated lawyer with an impressive client list, sharply receding hair, and an even thinner voice, boasted, "I'm not slick and polished with blow-dried hair." He took some courageous stands in the race, but, aside from the support of some upscale progressive voters, never made headway outside of northeast Arkansas. State Senator Lu Hardin of Russellville, a lawyer and college business teacher, was the serious opposition. Hardin was known as the nicest, friendliest man in the legislature. Though socially conservative, he tried not to offend liberals and brokered compromises on social issues. He had nearly always voted with Governor Clinton, particularly on tax increases.[42]

Hardin made the Democratic primary runoff with Bryant, and the campaign turned nasty. Both men spent the three-week runoff period accusing each other of publishing vicious negative ads that distorted their records. Bristow and

Smith endorsed Hardin; so did the *Democrat-Gazette*. Hardin appealed to Democrats to support him because his strength in the Republican-voting mountains and his conservative politics would cut away Huckabee's strengths. And Hardin did carry the Republican strongholds of northwest Arkansas. But Bryant received 53.6 percent of the vote statewide, easily carrying his home territory of south Arkansas, most of the Mississippi Delta and much of central Arkansas. (Incidentally, Hardin switched to the Republican party in September 1997.)

Since his election as lieutenant governor in the special election of 1993, Huckabee had been the heir to the Republican nomination. He was a popular speaker at national assemblies of religious conservatives, but back in Arkansas he maintained a centrist philosophy, which had served Clinton so well, and he struck a chord of reasonableness and bipartisanship. Huckabee had said he would never run against Pryor, and he implied that people might expect him to be something like the beloved Democrat in Washington. But he provided messages to conservatives not to expect business as usual. In radio spots about the time of his Senate announcement in October 1995, he said he would be going to Washington to represent the "people who get up at 6 in the morning, fix a sandwich for lunch and come home at dark worn out . . . [who are] tired of paying taxes for those who get up at 10 o'clock, watch Oprah all afternoon, and cruise the streets at night." By the summer of 1996, Huckabee's image of pristine virtue had taken a few dents, and Democrats were a bit emboldened. A bipartisan vote of the state ethics commission, acting on complaints of election law violations, concluded that the lieutenant governor had "acted unreasonably" in soliciting $91,000 in campaign contributions during a period in which he was barred from fundraising for a future campaign. The solicitations were ostensibly to pay off an old campaign debt of about $17,000. The commission ruled that he had filed inaccurate campaign reports and misused campaign donations.[43]

All of that was forgotten overnight in late May 1996, just a week before the first primary to choose Huckabee's Democratic opponent, when the federal jury in the Whitewater trial of Governor Tucker and Jim and Susan McDougal came in. Tucker was convicted of two felony counts involving mail fraud and a conspiracy to deceive federal regulators. Saying "the people of the state should not be put through this," Tucker, a few hours after the verdict, announced at a news conference that he would resign the governorship on or before July 15.[44]

Saying he was called to place duty before "personal desire," Huckabee formally abandoned the Senate race on May 30. During the next six weeks, Huckabee began assembling a staff and Tucker prepared to leave office, including delivering a farewell speech to the state legislature. Then, on the day appointed for the transition, perhaps the most bizarre series of events in contemporary Arkansas political history occurred. Tucker was scheduled to resign at noon; Huckabee would take his oath two hours later. At 1:55 P.M., however, with Huckabee's Republican supporters having filled the statehouse gallery for the swearing in, Tucker called Huckabee and told him that he had decided to stay governor pending the federal judge's decision on whether he deserved to be retried. Soon thereafter, Tucker sent a letter to the legislature, which was read to the assembled crowd, saying that he was giving Huckabee power only "until my disability shall cease." He and his wife left the Capitol to the sounds of boos, hisses, "liar," and "You are a disgrace to the whole state."[45]

Republican Bearden described the chaotic scene in the house chamber: "There were 1,100–1,200 people who'd waited for hours to see Mike Huckabee sworn in as governor, and I think at some point . . . if he'd said, 'Folks, grab a chair and break a limb off, we're going to go storm the Governor's Mansion,' I think those . . . people would have followed him down to the Governor's Mansion, broken through the gates and taken control. It was a very volatile, angry [crowd of] people." After Huckabee announced to the crowd that he would address the state later in the day, strategy sessions between Huckabee, his staff, and key legislators began. At one point Tucker sent the senate president pro tem a letter resuming the full powers as governor. Then, during the evening news, Huckabee returned to the house chamber to state that, if Tucker's resignation was not received by the next morning, he would call the legislature into session to begin impeachment proceedings. Soon thereafter, Tucker issued a letter of resignation and Huckabee took the oath of office five hours behind schedule.[46]

Huckabee's withdrawal from the U.S. Senate race left the Republicans without a prepossessing candidate, and a Democratic nomination that many thought not worth having suddenly had enormously inflated value. Asa Hutchinson, the former United States attorney who, like Huckabee, had previously challenged Bumpers, had wanted the GOP nomination. He had resigned as state chairman of the party to be ready in case Huckabee did not run. But national GOP officials thought his older brother, Tim, the U.S. representative from northwest Arkansas, was the better candidate. Tim Hutchinson, who had only a token Democratic opponent in his Third District, at first invited support for a Senate bid, then shocked GOP officials by declining to run. The maverick Republican congressman from Democratic south Arkansas, Jay Dickey, formed an exploratory committee for the race, but he had irked the Hutchinsons and party regulars both in Arkansas and Washington. State senator John Brown of Siloam Springs announced he was running, and after the Republican Senatorial Campaign Committee, the GOP national headquarters, and state Republican leaders, including Huckabee, urged him to run, Tim Hutchinson reconsidered.[47] A Republican caucus certified the consensus, and brother Asa was awarded the Third District congressional nomination.

Aside from the presidency, no race was more important to national Republicans than the Senate seat of President Clinton's home. The money and the fury of the effort suggested the importance the GOP attached to the race, but Arkansas voters were singularly unexcited. Hutchinson, the operator of a religious broadcasting station, was a marginally more interesting campaigner than Bryant. Poking fun at the attorney general's lack of eloquence and charm was the most popular topic of political columnists, but Hutchinson enjoyed only slightly better press.

If the candidates were personally boring, their television ads were not.[48] Bryant attacked Hutchinson as a stooge of Newt Gingrich who had voted with the speaker 96 percent of the time and who had joined the Republican effort to slash $270 billion from Medicare. Hutchinson said Bryant was a liberal who was frightening old people and who would go to Washington and fatten the national debt. But other than Medicare, education spending and abortion (Bryant favored a woman's right to choose but opposed late-term abortions; Hutchinson opposed abortion under any circumstances), their postures on major issues didn't seem to voters to be so far apart. Both favored a balanced budget amendment and opposed higher taxes and gun control.

A turning point came in September, when the Arkansas Supreme Court chastised the attorney general's office because an assistant attorney general had missed deadlines for filing an appeal of lower-court rulings on evidence in two pending criminal cases at Fort Smith. The Democrat-Gazette said the failure made it likely two murderers would not be convicted. Bryant apologized, fired the assistant and said he had instituted procedures to prevent its happening again, but the controversy dominated the campaign for a month. Bryant's reputation for workaday competence was sullied, and his lead vanished. While public polls showed different leaders, in none of them did either candidate have a lead greater than the margin of error through the home stretch of the campaign.[49]

A week before the election Hutchinson said the race boiled down to "who would least embarrass the state." For many, that seemed to sum up the race. But, two factors late in the campaign may have been key to the ultimate Hutchinson victory. First, the Bryant campaign had demonized Hutchinson for months as a Gingrich clone who would slash Medicare. Hutchinson may have been humanized for Arkansas voters, however, when his son was badly injured in an automobile accident and the campaign was temporarily suspended by both sides in the final days of the race. Second, while major Democratic candidates in Arkansas almost always enjoy a financial advantage, the money dried up for Bryant and it came in barrels for Hutchinson in the closing weeks. In the last fifteen days of the race, Hutchinson outspent Bryant nearly five to one, and that did not include the heavy independent and Republican soft-money expenditures, for which there was no accurate accounting.[50]

The voters chose Hutchinson by 52.7 percent to Bryant's 47.3 percent. In the end, the negative advertisements in the campaign likely did have one big impact: fewer people voted for United States senator than even for lieutenant governor, an uneventful race well down the ballot where little was at stake.[51] Election returns showed another ominous reality for Arkansas Democrats; the suburban counties surrounding Little Rock had suddenly become a GOP stronghold. Combining majorities in these counties with the traditional Republican strongholds in the quickly growing northwest counties could overwhelm Democratic majorities in the more stagnant eastern and southern counties and in Little Rock proper.

The Republicans began the season with unconcealed optimism that they might capture the entire congressional delegation except the seat of Senator Bumpers, which was not up until 1998. Despite the original sense that he was an accidental victor, voters in the traditionally Democratic Fourth District had become accustomed to Jay Dickey's slightly daffy pronouncements[52] and admired his occasional independence from the Republican leadership. And in 1996 the Democrats did not field a serious candidate against him. The Democratic candidate was Vincent Tolliver of Lake Village, a twenty-nine-year-old black writer, an enigmatic candidate, eschewing campaign events and avoiding reporters.[53] Dickey won handily with 63.5 percent.

Republicans had controlled the Third District since 1966 by widening margins, Bill Clinton's close losing race in 1974 having provided the only real contest for the Democrats. Tim Hutchinson, who succeeded Hammerschmidt in 1992, was certain of reelection before he decided to run for the Senate. The sacrificial Democratic candidate was Boyce Davis of Lincoln, a lawyer and publisher of a small weekly newspaper. When the Republicans handed the nomination to Tim's brother Asa, Democrats rued their failure to field a strong candidate. Davis dropped out of the race seven weeks before the election, saying he had neither the money nor time to run a good race. A hasty and buoyant Democratic convention nominated Ann Henry, a fifty-four-year-old lawyer, business professor, and Democratic activist who was a longtime friend of the Clintons, whose wedding reception had been held in her home. Henry and her husband, a former state senator, plumped down $130,000 of their own money, raised more than $300,000 in a few weeks and matched Hutchinson's spending. Betsey Wright, Clinton's legendary political aide during his Arkansas reign, went to the Ozarks to run the campaign. Henry hit the Republicans hard on Medicare—retirees are a high percentage of the electorate in the mountains—and education, while Hutchinson said their basic difference was over the balanced budget amendment.[54] He favored one, she didn't. Henry generated the first serious Democratic challenge in the Third District in a generation, but in the end voters stuck with the Republican. Hutchinson received 55.7 percent of the vote to Henry's 41.8 percent.

In the farming regions and hill towns of northeast Arkansas, one of the most blighted regions in the country, voters returned just as naturally to the Democrats. Republican Warren Dupwe of Jonesboro had come shockingly close (46.6 percent) to Lincoln in the First District race in 1994, and this time he was better financed. The Democrats also had a nasty primary. The Democratic nomination was supposed to go to Marion Berry of Gillett, a farmer who resigned as President Clinton's agriculture liaison to run, but he got a stiff challenge from Tom Donaldson, a smart, good-looking deputy prosecutor from West Memphis. Donaldson criticized Berry because his family used multiple corporations to fatten their federal crop subsidies. Berry was overmatched in debates, but he had an advantage in money and political connections. In a runoff, the more conservative Berry won. In the fall, Dupwe and Berry ran boilerplate party campaigns. Dupwe embraced the Republican agenda, tax and spending cuts and a balanced-budget amendment; Berry condemned Republican Medicare reductions, opposed tax cuts until the country balanced the budget, and praised the minimum wage increase enacted by Congress in 1996.[55] The sprawling district went handily to the Democrat by a 52.8 percent to 44.3 percent margin.

In the Second District of central Arkansas, with its burgeoning capital suburbs and bustling media which reach the entire state, three Democrats and six Republicans filed for the congressional seat. On the Democratic side, prosecuting attorney Mark Stodola of Little Rock was the favorite. John Edwards, a young aide to Senator David Pryor, began running early. Vic Snyder of Little Rock, an iconoclastic Democratic state senator, entered the race at the deadline. Snyder, a doctor at two family clinics and a lawyer who eschews fundraising until ninety days before any election, had refused to enroll in the legislative pension system and regularly introduced legislation to repeal the state law that criminalizes homosexual activity. Stodola depended on his name recognition, longtime party activity, and superior money to carry him, and he got 48 percent in the first primary. In gentlemanly and respectful forums in the runoff, Stodola delineated his slightly more conservative stances on issues. But Snyder won the nomination, showing that having more passionate support in low-turnout run-offs is vital.

The easy Republican nomination winner was Bud Cummins, a businessman and a rising Republican star. The young bachelor had modeled for hot tub ads (a *Democrat-Gazette* columnist called him "Bud the Stud") and charmed youthful crowds. Cummins, who buoyantly embraced every Republican dogma, charac-terized his opponent as a dogmatic liberal, although Snyder sometimes strayed from Democratic stands on economics and criminal justice. But it was on social issues that Cummins tried to frame the race. Snyder spent the campaign ex-plaining his efforts to repeal the sodomy law, his votes against flag-burning laws, and his opposition to restrictions on women's reproductive choices (even on late-term abortions), to federal legislation allowing bans on same-sex marriages, to school-prayer amendments and to balanced-budget amendments.[56] TV com-mercials said Snyder would be "Wrong for America. Worse for Arkansas," and showed a weary Snyder with his head in his hands.

A heavy barrage of TV and radio attacks in the final two weeks brought Cummins close. In the last week, however, Cummins likely went too far when on a television interview he said that the "liberal" Snyder had "chosen a philos-ophy to pursue . . . [that] kind of leads to socialist, kind of leads to communist." The charge gave Snyder, a marine who served in Vietnam, a great opportunity to remind voters that "Communists tried to kill me."[57] In compiling his win-ning 52.3 percent of the vote, Snyder carried most Little Rock precincts by lop-sided margins. Cummins, who received 47.7 percent of the vote, won the growing suburban communities all around the capital, even Saline County south of Little Rock, where the votes of industrial unions once assured Demo-crats lopsided victories, and left the clear message that the district would not again be safe for the Democrats.

There was one other domino effect of Huckabee's ascension to the gover-norship: another vacancy in the office of lieutenant governor. A namesake from the Arkansas past, Winthrop Paul Rockefeller, the son of the former GOP gov-ernor, received the Republican nomination without opposition. The Demo-cratic party state committee, feeling pressure from Governor Huckabee to avoid a costly primary at taxpayer expense, chose to select its nominee at a state con-vention. Charlie Cole Chaffin, the party's losing candidate for lieutenant gover-nor in 1994, defeated four challengers to win the nomination.

Coming off an embarrassing showing in 1994, Chaffin had tremendous dif-ficulty in raising money. While raising money is always problematic, such is cer-tainly the case when running against a Rockefeller. However, the chain-smoking Rockefeller provided an opening for Chaffin as he made few public appearances during the campaign, an issue Chaffin harped on, particularly after Rockefeller failed to attend the lone statewide televised debate. In his television advertisements, Rockefeller stressed the power of his name in recruiting new industry to Arkansas. Unlike most Republicans, Rockefeller attempted to make inroads into the state's African American community.[58] And the efforts seem to have had some impact; for example, in one predominantly black Little Rock precinct where Clinton defeated Dole by an amazing 649 to 5 margin, Rockefeller won 99 votes to Chaffin's 555.

Chaffin's tenacity as a campaigner made what should have been an easy GOP victory a close race. The outcome was not certain until the day after the election. Rockefeller won the office with 50.6 percent of the vote. For only the second time in the modern era, the Republican party had control of two state constitutional offices.

While the victory in the lieutenant governor's race was a boost for the GOP, the party was once again disappointed by its absence of gains in the state legislature. After January special elections to fill vacancies in both chambers, the GOP had gained a net of two seats in the house (to 14 out of 100) and stayed steady with only 7 members in the 35-member senate. The results were particularly surprising in that the highly popular Governor Huckabee had become involved in the legislative campaigns through writing letters, cutting radio spots, and handing the remains of his U.S. Senate campaign fund to the state party for the purpose of electing more Republicans to the legislature. After the election, the state GOP executive director could only say, "Man, it's frustrating."[59]

Oddly, considering its historic nature, for most of the year the reelection campaign of the state's native son president was overshadowed by the other dramatic political events. While the end result was essentially the same, with Clinton easily winning the state's six electoral votes, turnout fell eight percent from November 1992, slightly more than the national drop. At least in his home state, the 1996 Clinton campaign lacked the intensity of that of 1992 for several reasons. For one thing, rather than being centered in the famed War Room in Little Rock's old *Arkansas Gazette* building, it was run out of Washington. Also, the glory of the 1992 Clinton election had faded for many Arkansans who had themselves been under legal assault or had friends who were sent into debt by legal bills. A more general pall was cast over the state by the dark side of the first Clinton administration since most of the ethical questions had some relationship to the Clinton years in Arkansas. As state house speaker Bobby Hogue said, "It's a sad time, a sad time for Arkansas. A shadow has been cast over the state, and we really don't deserve that." As one national observer described the new stereotype, "Every Arkansan is now instantly suspect as a crook or an incompetent."[60]

Interestingly, however, the events surrounding Whitewater, including the convictions of Tucker and the McDougals, had little impact on the President's popularity in the state. Indeed, one public poll late in the election cycle showed that Whitewater special prosecutor Kenneth Starr was exceedingly unpopular in the state: 49 percent of Arkansan voters rated him unfavorably; only 19 percent favorably.[61] President Clinton did make three trips home in the year before the election. First, in December 1995, Clinton came home to salute the retiring Senator Pryor at a fundraiser for the state Democratic party. Then, just after the Democratic National Convention, Clinton came home to the Old State House in Little Rock to symbolically begin his general election campaign. Finally, in an attempt to aid Democratic congressional and state candidates, the President held an airport rally in Little Rock on the weekend before the general election.

Conceding Arkansas from the outset, Republican Bob Dole did not travel to the state. A planned visit in early August was aborted when verdicts in a Whitewater-related trial in Little Rock were imminent; Elizabeth Dole filled in for her husband at the event. Arkansas Republicans also took a pass on campaigning aggressively against the home-state president.

On election day Clinton carried the state with 53.7 percent of the vote, his best showing in the South. However, this time six other states—Massachusetts, New York, Illinois, Maryland, Rhode Island, and Hawaii—gave Clinton a larger percentage of their votes. (In 1992 Arkansas had led the fifty states.) Still, on election night, Bill Clinton was back home for the final electoral victory of his life. Standing in front of the Old State House, he told the celebrating crowd: "There is no person in America tonight who feels more humble in the face of this victory than I do. Fifty years ago, when I was born in a summer storm to a widowed mother in a small town in the southwest part of our state, it was unimaginable that someone like me could have ever become President of the greatest country in human history. It has been, for me, a remarkable journey, not free of failure, but full of adventure and wonder and grace. I have worked hard to serve, but I did not get here on my own."[62]

Clearly, a key retardant to a movement in the Arkansas electorate toward the Republican party has been the presence of Clinton, Pryor, and Bumpers. The departure of the first two politicians (and the retirement of Bumpers in 1998) removed this key barrier to future GOP success. The state's demographics also bode well for the GOP. Northwest Arkansas and the suburbs of Little Rock are simultaneously the state's fastest growing areas and the most Republican parts of the state. As mentioned above, the *Arkansas Gazette* also is gone as a daily defender of progressivism in the state. Continuing media coverage—in both the state and national press—related to the series of scandals known collectively as Whitewater also will likely assist Arkansas's Republican party as it promotes a message of political reform.

Moreover, Huckabee has shown hints of the kind of personal dynamism seen in the Big Three. One longtime Clinton watcher says, "[Huckabee] is, like Bill Clinton, hard to dislike in a personal meeting."[63] And, while his governorship since the July 15, 1996, swearing in has had its ups and downs, his handling of that day's crisis was universally praised. If he were to remain as governor for an extended period of time—making use of the significant power over appointments—and to govern successfully, Republicanism in Arkansas could become cemented.

Finally, one 1992 election outcome—lost in the frenzy over the presidential election—has potentially much to do with strengthening state Republican chances. The Arkansas electorate, by a 60 percent margin, adopted a term-limits initiative. Although the term limits it imposed on members of the U.S. Congress were subsequently struck down by the U.S. Supreme Court as unconstitutional, the limits on state officeholders remain and should prove highly consequential. The two-term limit on state executives means many future openings in the seven state constitutional offices, and the two- and three-term limits respectively in the state senate and house will provide countless future legislative opportunities for the traditional "out" party.

While these elements favor acceleration of Republican growth, other key factors point to continued problems for the GOP. Most basically, while a majority of Arkansas voters may now be open to voting for Republicans, that party must be able to offer these voters quality "products." As of 1997, the Democratic party, despite its recent problems, still contained most of the state's political talent. They may not be candidates of Big Three quality, but they are considerably more numerous than the limited talent pool of the state's GOP. Things may be changing, however, in that individuals entering the political arena now see new models of political success in the GOP. As Democratic political consultant Bill Paschall puts it: "With Mike Huckabee at the top, they see that someone can be successful running as a Republican. . . . It is a viable alternative for them and I sense that young folks [now] look hard at both parties."[64]

Another potential problem for the Republican party is the hints of division within it. Despite their shared backgrounds in the religious conservative movement, Huckabee and the Hutchinson brothers have long had a difficult relationship.[65] And the state's other Republican congressman, Jay Dickey, has had deep differences with Asa Hutchinson in particular. For a small party, the state GOP has a surprising amount of internal tension.

Of course, the future of the state's politics resides in the attitudes of younger voters who are now entering the electorate and the young persons who will decide to run for public office. Throughout the South survey evidence shows that young people, especially males, are more than willing to embrace the Republican party, and this trend is present in Arkansas.[66] Still, it is important to keep in mind both that Arkansas has always had a populist tendency underlying its political culture and that the race issue has not had as much potency in Arkansas as in some other southern states. Certainly, the Arkansas GOP has more reason for optimism than at any point in this century, but its growth potential in the near future contains real limits.

7

TENNESSEE: A PARTISAN BIG BANG AMID QUIET ACCOMMODATION

Philip Ashford and Richard Locker

THE evening of November 8, 1994, was a particularly sweet one for Republicans in Tennessee. After eight somnolent years, the party rode the tide of the voter resentment of 1994 to capture the governor's office, both U.S. Senate seats and a majority of the U.S. House delegation. Within a year, the Republicans also gained a nominal majority in the state senate after two lame-duck Democrats switched parties.

It was, in short, the Big Bang of political progress for the Republicans, a moment when the stars were uniquely aligned for Republican success. All the factors for success were present—a united party, attractive Republican candidates and weaker Democratic ones, and a mood of voter disenchantment with the Clinton administration. The Republicans took advantage of those opportunities skillfully and banked their most successful election night in the state's history. "Tennessee was the scene in 1994 of the most thoroughgoing political revolution in a politically revolutionary year," proclaimed the *Almanac of American Politics*.[1]

For the Democrats, the defeats of one night undid the party's successful resurgence in the 1980s from Republican gains in the 1970s, when Republicans found themselves similarly in control of the governor's mansion and both Senate seats. (See Figure 7 in Chapter 1 for a depiction of several decades of partisan swings.) While there was a great temptation on the Democratic side to write the whole thing off as a giant voter tantrum, there was also clear evidence to suggest that the Democrats' hold as the voters' default choice was waning and the state was entering an era of solid two-party competition.

The question that the Republican victories left unanswered was whether the party was building an enduring structure for success in the state or whether the high tide of 1994 was just an oddity. The 1996 election did not put enough on the table to be a worthy test of the durability of the Republicans. For much of the past century, the history of Republican politics in Tennessee has been one of accommodation with the Democratic leadership except when the Democrats through ineptitude, chicanery, or disunity have left the door open for the Republicans. At less promising times, party elites found it easier to make their peace with the ruling Democrats because, after all, while politics is a matter of great principle, business is business.

As one looks at Tennessee's politics in the 1990s, several basic themes emerge:

• In spite of Republican gains, the basic partisan geography of the state that dates back to the Civil War remains intact. To the extent that those traditional identities have been eroded, this erosion is most visible in the fast growing urban and suburban areas. There is also evidence of the enduring influence of race in the Republican gains, particularly in Memphis and west Tennessee.

• Democrats in Tennessee had largely succeeded in establishing a separate identity from the national party, which is attractive in this moderately conservative state. While the Democrats retain a certain residual loyalty, however, they have been vulnerable to a growing pool of swing voters who refuse to vote for "yellow dogs."

• Party elites continue to view the parties as instruments for personal, ideological or group ends rather than objects of loyalty, and their flexibility here has been important in determining electoral outcomes.

A man standing in Mountain City in the northeast corner of the state would, if he were only a casual observer of U.S. geography, be surprised to learn that he was closer to Canada than he was to the state's largest city, Memphis. The very length of the state has left it room for many strains of politics, whose original outlines were set by the Civil War and which persist today in muted form. What has made the progress of the Republicans in Tennessee different from that of other southern states is that the post–civil-rights-era growth of the party started from a higher plane, giving the party long experience as a significant, but ultimately losing, minority. While Tennessee was clearly a part of the segregationist South, there was much less profit in trying to ride the race issue in the state. While it is true that many of the counties in cotton-growing west Tennessee voted for the Dixiecrats in 1948, it is equally true that in east Tennessee the race issue had no bite because it just didn't seem relevant to the backcountry whites who lived in counties with few if any black citizens. Even in more solidly Democratic middle Tennessee, the black population was small by southern standards.

Tennessee was the last and most reluctant state to leave the Union in 1861. The state's mountainous eastern section was dominated by small landholdings that were unsuitable for slave labor, which translated into opposition to secession. While east Tennessee has thus been enduringly Republican since the aftermath of the Civil War, theirs has been the more moderate stripe of Republicanism that has produced politicians like former senator Howard Baker and his protégé, Lamar Alexander, who did not advance their careers by riding the tide of resentment stirred by the civil rights struggles of the 1960s. This base of Republican strength provided a core vote for the party to build on once the Solid South started to crack and traditionally Democratic parts of the state began to realign.

The development that made the Republicans a force to be reckoned with in Tennessee was the emergence of the Republican party in Memphis and surrounding Shelby County in the 1960s. The Shelby Republicans were the other kind that the South has produced. Energized by the presidential candidacy of Barry Goldwater in 1964, conservative activists took control of a vestigial and largely black Republican apparatus and built an organization that was more ideological, more conservative, more organized, and more disciplined than the hereditary Republicans to the east.[2] The development of the Republicans in the west made possible a string of successes in the 1970s, including the election of Winfield Dunn (1971–1975) and Lamar Alexander (1979–1987) as governor and William E. Brock as senator (1971–1977). As Alexander's term ground to a close, however, much of that progress had slipped away.

DEMOCRATIC RESURGENCE FROM THE MID-1980s TO THE EARLY 1990s

The 1986 Tennessee gubernatorial election was important in setting the context for Republicans in the 1990s. Winfield Dunn's status as a former governor allowed him in 1986 to preempt several younger Republican hopefuls, and he conducted an energetic and well-funded campaign. He was haunted, however, by lingering resentments over issues from his first term as governor, particularly among Republicans in the upper east Tennessee area. Although that area had delivered Dunn his widest margins in 1970, he soon fell from favor over an array of local issues; the citizens there were disappointed that the first Republican governor in 50 years did not seem to be redressing the grievances they felt against Dunn's line of Democratic predecessors. A particularly sore point had been Dunn's opposition to the creation of a medical school at East Tennessee State University, a course vigorously opposed by leaders of the University of Tennessee medical school, which is in Memphis, Dunn's home. The school ultimately got built, through the cooperation of Democratic leaders and Republican congressman James O. Quillen, and Quillen retained a longstanding enmity to Dunn.[3]

Meanwhile, house speaker Ned McWherter, a folksy conservative Democrat from Weakley County in west Tennessee, captured the Democratic nomination in a bitter primary by running to the right and judiciously fanning white racial resentment in rural west Tennessee. His opponents were Nashville mayor Richard Fulton, a labor Democrat who had established himself as a progressive by being one of four southern congressmen to vote for the Civil Rights and Voting Rights Acts, and Public Service Commissioner Jane Eskind, a wealthy liberal with strong ties to the powerful political organization in the Memphis black community led by U.S. representative Harold E. Ford.

During the primary, McWherter went on a two-day blitz through courthouse squares and crossroads general stores in the rural western counties, calling on the largely white crowds to give him a big majority to offset Eskind's backing from Congressman Ford in the "inner city." The campaign swing, later known in the state's political folklore as the tour of the "Redneck Express," touched off a storm of controversy in Memphis, particularly embarrassing McWherter's black supporters.[4] McWherter's own internal polls, however, showed his rural white support consolidating in the wake of the controversy and allowing him to capture a solid victory over Eskind, 42.5 percent to 30.5 percent. Fulton, who had trouble extending his appeal beyond his middle Tennessee base, trailed with 25.7 percent of the vote. (Unlike all other southern states except Virginia, Tennessee does not have a runoff primary.)

The general election challenge for McWherter was to reunify the party after the divisive primary, particularly with regard to black voters naturally skeptical of rural conservative Democrats and concerned about the tone of the primary campaign. The centerpiece of his effort was a circuitous three-day, thousand-mile "unity" bus tour of the state, reaching from Bristol in the northeast to Memphis in the southwest and accompanied by most of the leading Democrats, including Eskind, Fulton, and Senators Albert Gore, Jr., and James R. Sasser. Ford handled the arrangements for the culminating rally at the Peabody Hotel in Memphis. Similarly, on the final Sunday before the election, Ford and Eskind escorted McWherter on a blitz through the key black churches in Memphis.[5]

During the fall, McWherter also benefited from Dunn's woes in the east. Although Quillen publicly announced a reconciliation with Dunn, the former was widely suspected of quietly undermining the Republican nominee. By contrast to the cold shoulder Dunn got from Quillen, west Tennessee Republican congressman Don Sundquist, with future statewide plans of his own, took Dunn along on his regular campaign bus tour of the sprawling Seventh District and even allowed Dunn to be the featured speaker at each of the campaign stops. (Sundquist had no serious opposition.)

Much of the campaign debate focused on which candidate could portray himself as best able to continue the perceived progress of the Alexander years, and, as a consequence, McWherter and Dunn did not sharply differentiate themselves on the issues. The final days of the campaign boiled down to each man trying to raise questions about the various financial wheelings and dealings of his opponent, but to no apparent effect. McWherter ultimately scored a 54.2 percent to 45.7 percent victory, including powerful majorities in the rural areas, where his traditional southern folksiness proved attractive, underscored by the campaign slogan "He's one of us."[6] He also captured nearly 53 percent of the vote in Quillen's First Congressional District, where Dunn had won 70 percent in 1970.

Following Dunn's 1986 defeat, the Republicans entered a dormant period as a force in statewide politics. Much of the disappointment centered around the party's small but critical third wing: the Nashville-money Republicans. While the Republicans have made much more limited strides in gaining power in middle Tennessee, greater Nashville is the home to many of the key players in the party who can give and raise money. These include men like former U.S. ambassador to France Joe Rodgers and real estate developer Ted Welch, both past Republican national finance chairmen, whose temperature readings do much to determine which candidacies will be dead on arrival at the election commission and which will have a chance of being disposed of by the voters. In 1986 Republicans had given until it hurt for Dunn, who raised over six million dollars, and much intraparty recrimination followed when the financial effort was not rewarded with victory.

In 1988 the Republicans had no stomach for an all-out effort in the major statewide race. Democratic senator Sasser, who was first elected in 1976 and who captured easy reelection in 1982, ended up facing Bill Andersen, a moderate young lawyer and West Point graduate from Kingsport in upper east Tennessee who entered the statewide race after failing to nudge Quillen into retirement. Quillen made his annoyance at young Andersen known and worked to undercut him, much as he had undermined Dunn two years earlier.[7]

Although Andersen was generally perceived as intelligent and articulate, his campaign never took off. He tried to present himself as a champion of the working man with progressive views on the environment and employee business ownership, but he declined to thump on the usual red-meat social conservative themes.[8] This approach had little appeal in west Tennessee, and it was widely perceived that the Senate race was all just positioning for a future race for Quillen's seat. Andersen received little help from the party hierarchy, and Sasser was able to lie back and conduct a successful imperial candidacy. He received 65.1 percent of the vote and carried all but one of Tennessee's 95 counties, a county in Quillen's district, which may have given Andersen some satisfaction.

In spite of the debacle at the Senate level, Republicans easily carried the state for George Bush in the presidential race, the third straight presidential election victory in Tennessee for the Republicans. This was not much of an achievement, however. As local campaign officials acknowledged after the race, Democratic candidate Michael Dukakis wrote the state off early, providing scant resources and little campaign time, even though it had been Walter Mondale's strongest southern state in 1984. Dukakis ended up running slightly behind Mondale's performance, losing the state with 41.5 percent of the vote to Bush's 57.9 percent.[9]

Apart from the presidential level, Tennessee Republicans entered the 1990s with little going their way. After the reverses of the 1980s, they had no momentum and not many candidates. Because so few positions in Tennessee are filled by the choice of the voters, there are few stepping stones to higher office. In the early 1990s, only the governor and the three members of the regulatory Public Service Commission were elected statewide with various other state constitutional positions such as lieutenant governor (chosen by the state senate) and attorney general (chosen by the supreme court justices) filled indirectly. (In 1995 that number was whittled down to one—the governorship—when Governor Don Sundquist convinced the legislature to abolish the PSC and replace it with the Tennessee Regulatory Authority, with three appointed directors.)

Congressional seats offer a good platform for candidates with statewide aspirations, but here the Republicans faced a logjam in 1990. For more than two decades, two of the three seats had been held by Republicans Quillen (First District) and John Duncan (Second District), the two hoary stalwarts of Republican politics, who sat in their mountain fiefdoms unwilling to lead, follow, or get out of the way. Duncan died in 1988, but was succeeded by his son, John, Jr. With neither seat occupied by a candidate with broader ambition, that left only Congressman Sundquist from the Memphis suburbs (Seventh District) with the stature to be a formidable statewide candidate—and in 1990, a statewide race was not on Sundquist's personal timetable.

The year 1990 dawned as a promising time for Democrats, however. In the two statewide races that year, the party had popular incumbents seeking second terms in McWherter and Senator Gore. McWherter had coasted through a largely controversy-free first term, gaining small accomplishments bounded by small ambitions. He focused on redesigning the road-building program approved in Alexander's last year and on shifting Alexander's prison program from focusing on early release of inmates to building more prison capacity. He also redeemed a campaign pledge to create a medical care program for the indigent by pioneering a way of using "donations" from hospitals to manipulate federal Medicaid regulations to produce more matching funds, which were then shoveled back to contributing hospitals on terms roughly reflecting the hospitals' original contributions.[10]

Gore had been elected in 1984 by stressing his ardor as a "raging moderate" and keeping a healthy distance from the national ticket in a race in which his opponent taunted him in three debates about his unwillingness to even mention Mondale's name. During his abortive presidential campaign in 1988, he had been pulled away somewhat from his cautious moderation by the need to court labor and northern liberal votes, but in spite of the exigencies of running as a national Democrat he had largely held on to his reputation as a man in step with the sentiments of the state.

Thus the Democrats came into the 1990s without lingering open wounds and having gone through the unifying exercise of rallying around a favorite son's presidential campaign. There was, however, one nasty little rift that may have presaged troubles to come: the unpleasantness over the state senate, where the Democrats held a comfortable 22–11 seat edge over the Republicans.

After the 1986 elections, many of the senate's Democrats were chafing under the long tenure of John Wilder as senate speaker, a post that carried the additional title and responsibility of lieutenant governor. Since first being chosen in 1971, Wilder had held the job longer than anyone in the state's history, and many of his colleagues thought it was time for him to go. Wilder, a wealthy Fayette County planter and lawyer, had aggravated some of his Democratic colleagues as insufficiently liberal, insufficiently partisan, too cooperative with Alexander's Republican administration and too firmly entrenched in the paths of their individual ambitions. He also bothered some as entirely too eccentric with his penchant for talking about the cosmos and other otherworldly concerns.[11]

Three weeks in advance of the senate Democratic caucus that would select the party's nominees for senate leadership posts, a group of fifteen Democrats held a publicized meeting to lay plans for dumping Wilder and his key lieutenants and apportioning those posts among other party members. The meeting proved a fatal misstep. Wilder used the occasion as pretext to stage his own preemptive strike, gathering six remaining Democratic senators loyal to him into a coalition with the Republicans to retain his hold on the speakership.

After besting the nominee of the regular Democratic caucus, which he and his allies declined to attend, Wilder then proceeded to reorganize the senate along lines reflecting his personal coalition, stripping his detractors of their key committee assignments and chairmanships and turning over some committee chairmanships to Republicans. For his two key supporters, Senators Milton Hamilton and Bob Rochelle, whom the Democrats had stripped of their re- spective positions as majority leader and Democratic caucus chairman, he cre- ated the new positions of "senate leader" and "deputy speaker." For his betrayal of the party, the state Democratic executive committee denied Wilder a dele- gate slot for the 1988 national convention, but Wilder suffered no other conse- quences. He patched together another winning coalition in 1989 after the main- stream Democrats recruited Hamilton to change sides and challenge Wilder's leadership. Since then, Democrats have thrown in the towel in their attempt to dislodge the Wilder coalition, which was still in place in 1998.

What is striking about the whole battle is how little it had to do with partisan politics and how much with personalities and ambitions. The Wilder coalition may have looked a little more conservative and a little more probusiness than the regular Democratic party, but it also included two of the senate's most lib- eral members, African Americans John Ford, the brother of Congressman Har- old Ford of the Ninth District in Memphis, and Avon Williams, who had been one of the key figures in the civil rights struggle in Nashville during the 1950s and 1960s. The opposition to Wilder may have appeared a bit oriented toward the labor–trial lawyer bloc in the senate, but it also included some of that bloc's most ardent foes. What seems to be the chief lesson here is that the Democratic party is secondary to the personal interests of those involved, a point made clear by the switching coalition components in the 1989 reprise.

The other striking aspect of the process is the relative docility of the Repub- licans, who contribute the lion's share of the votes to Wilder but who are clearly the junior partners in the arrangement. This has remained so even as the Re- publican portion of the senate has grown. When two Democrats switched par- ties in 1995, in an episode discussed again below, Republicans gained nominal control for the first time since Reconstruction, and Wilder remained speaker.

In the 1996 elections, Democrats regained control, 18 to 15, and afterward the Democratic caucus elected Wilder to a fourteenth two-year term as speaker, despite his having campaigned on behalf of Republican senators.[12]

The struggles in the senate, however, were just a smudge on the otherwise bright Democratic prospects in 1990. McWherter, a shrewd businessman with considerable charm and a fleeting exposure to higher education, had made a fortune in beer distribution and trucking. This background helped him gain a public reputation as a good manager of state government operations able to re-duce waste and increase efficiency. Such attention to governmental detail was widely perceived as necessary after the more creative period of leadership under Alexander.

As the 1990 gubernatorial election approached, McWherter's polling num-bers were solid and leading Republicans were disinclined to challenge him. The Nashville business wing of the Republican party was comfortable with his lead-ership and felt that he was a man its members could do business with. Indeed, he was probably more fundamentally conservative than Alexander except on the few reflex issues where Democrats are obliged to lean left and Republicans to lean right. In other words, for Republicans, McWherter was a very non-threatening figure. He had built his political career around a fourteen-year stint as speaker of the house, a position in which he had been mainly a broker and technician who got things done in the backroom. Much of Alexander's success as governor had hinged on winning over McWherter, whose support was criti-cal to passing Alexander's school, road-building and prison programs. "Ned was strong," observed Republican activist Randle Richardson, who served as state party chairman during the 1994 election cycle. "Ned was what Tennessee was about. The swing vote in this state is still the rural white vote; Ned is a rural white conservative. He talked the language of Tennessee. When I'd go to East Tennessee, people—Republicans—would say Ned talks our language."[13]

If the Republican leadership had reason to suspect him, it may have been owing to some of his friends. He was popular with the teachers' union—the Tennessee Education Association—and the Tennessee State Employees Associa-tion, largely because he had been attentive to their bread-and-butter issues while staying out of the more bruising philosophical issues. Organized labor was similarly comfortable with him, although his support for labor was muted. Overall, McWherter kept a respectable distance from the things that really ag-gravated Republicans, such as progressive taxation, repeal of right-to-work laws, and major social welfare initiatives.

So after a handful of better known Republicans, principally state senate Re-publican leader Ben Atchley of Knoxville, opted out of challenging McWherter's 1990 reelection, the ultimate challenger was Dwight Henry, a first-term state representative who had previously served as mayor of Cookeville, a medium-sized city midway between Nashville and Knoxville. Henry was neither well known nor well financed, and his race seemed like a rerun of the Andersen campaign of 1988. Largely ignored by the party's chieftains, Henry tried to stir public interest by making the race a single-issue affair, staking out a firm no-income-tax stand and hammering away at McWherter's refusal to rule out either a state income tax or a tax hike to fund the massive education plan he promised to deliver after the election.[14]

Hit with what would have been a volatile issue if Henry had had the money for a serious campaign, McWherter's organization decided to remove whatever threat he constituted by distributing to reporters opposition research about the Republican's personal financial affairs. Henry had filed for bankruptcy a decade earlier after a children's clothing store he operated with his wife, Nyoka, failed with $139,000 in debts. To make matters worse, a small radio station he owned had neglected to file its corporate tax returns for four years.[15] The leaked financial documents made for a crushing series of revelations that left Henry constantly on the defensive, unable to raise money and shift the focus back to McWherter and his repeated unwillingness to discuss the issue of income tax. Henry thus became the first major party Tennessee gubernatorial nominee in the television age unable to afford a single TV commercial. With only days left in the campaign, Henry tried to diversify his campaign by calling for a state lottery, parental choice in the public schools their children attend, and free college tuition for high schools students who perform well.

In what limited campaigning he did, McWherter touted the accomplishments of his first term, including road building, health care and housing for the poor, economic development, and improved teacher pay. His central goal appeared to be to avoid any discussion of a state income tax, which contrasted with his 1986 race, when he had flatly ruled out that possibility. Declining to debate, McWherter confined his campaign to appearances with Democratic legislative candidates in largely staged events filled with Democratic partisans not likely to raise the dreaded T-word. He avoided discussing how he would pay for the education plan, and finally began airing his first TV commercials— positive, biographical messages—two weeks before the election.[16]

The primary reason for Henry's defeat, however, was probably his abandonment by leading Republican power brokers. McWherter worked out an early accommodation with key Republican fund-raisers and leaders, many of whom quietly supported the income tax as a necessary source of stable income for the state to promote economic growth. That accord resulted in many of the leading

Republicans sitting on their hands and, consequently, starving any Republican challengers. "I visited with the governor and he indicated he had visited with a lot of the [Republican] leadership and they weren't going to support anybody opposing him," recounted Welch, the key Nashville fund-raiser and GOP national committeeman. "He and I had dinner at the [governor's mansion] and he wanted to know what my position was. I told him I had been trying to locate a first-tier candidate to run against him and if I found one, I would back him but I would not try to find somebody who was not first tier—and if someone like that announced, I would not be a vigorous fund-raiser for them."[17] As a consequence, Henry was only able to raise $125,000 for the campaign, chiefly from a handful of large contributors not previously active in state Republican politics. McWherter raised $3 million, but spent only $900,000.[18]

When the dust cleared, McWherter had won with 60.8 percent of the vote to Henry's 36.6 percent. While the margin was decisive, it was weak enough to suggest that a stronger, better-financed candidate than the feeble Henry might have at least given McWherter a bit of a bloody nose. In his concession speech on election night, Henry assailed the traditional big-money GOP financiers who refused to back his candidacy and accurately predicted what was underway within the party. "You've witnessed the beginnings of a rebuilding of the Republican Party in Tennessee—not just a reshuffling of the Republican Party of old but a dynamic new Republican Party of the grass roots, not the wealthy elite who held a grip on our party but a new Republican Party to oppose—not lie in bed with—the Democrat Party."[19]

In the U.S. Senate race, Republican performance was barely perceptible. Gore was tremendously popular in the state, having captured over 60.7 percent of the vote in his first effort in 1984. While Republicans regularly claimed that his popularity would slip once the voters got to know him and he was forced out of the liberal closet, no signs of any such thing were visible even though the 1988 presidential nomination campaign had, as mentioned above, tugged him somewhat to the left. In any case, Gore was still very attentive to his popularity and his perceived status as a moderate. He insisted on maintaining his schedule of conducting at least two open meetings for constituents in every county every year in what an amateur Freudian might say was an effort not to fall victim to the charge that he had deserted the state, a notion that probably contributed to his father's 1970 Senate defeat after thirty-two years in Congress. "Gore raised a lot of money in preparation for the race. He was concerned that the Republicans would try to put a lot of money into a campaign by someone to bloody him up and possibly damage him for [a presidential race in] 1992," recalled Eugene (Chip) Forrester, who managed Gore's campaign that year.[20]

What Gore ultimately faced was much different. William Hawkins, a former economics instructor, defeated the usual array of chronic candidates (it only takes twenty-five signatures to get on the ballot for a statewide race in Tennessee) to win the Republican primary and then conducted a desultory campaign, mostly in small towns in east Tennessee, focusing on economic issues and libertarian perspectives. Hawkins received no significant help from the party apparatus and raised less than $12,000. "Because Gore is such a visible target because of his presidential ambitions, I figured people would want to help take him down a peg or two. I guess people really thought he was invincible."[21] When he attacked Gore, largely by press release, the theme was always that the senator was "too liberal" for Tennessee. Gore, who had raised over $2 million for the race, ended up spending only about half of it, mostly on a thirty-minute campaign program that aired in each of the state's media markets and a single sixty-second ad that also ran statewide. In the end, Gore captured 67.7 percent of the vote and swept all 95 counties in the state—making him the first Senate candidate to do so in modern times.

The contests for the U.S. House, where Democrats held six of the state's nine seats, yielded more of the same. No incumbent congressman had been ousted from his seat in Tennessee since 1974, when Republican Dan Kuykendall lost to Harold Ford after the black-majority Ninth District was created in Memphis. In 1990 there were no open House seats, and all the incumbents were reelected without serious challenges. All in all, 1990 in Tennessee was a year without political hoopla, aptly symbolized by McWherter's decision to forgo a ceremonial inaugural culminating in a ball, saying a big party was inappropriate with the Gulf War looming. It appeared that the 1992 election cycle would be duller still, with no statewide races scheduled.

But as the events unfolded, the aftermath of the 1990 vote stirred up considerable ferment in both parties. Good to his word, McWherter came forward with a major education reform package, driven in part by the expectation of a state supreme court ruling on a lawsuit by small rural counties intended to force greater equalization of school funding. Most of the education plan was pulled off the shelf from the standard remedies of the Tennessee Education Association—smaller class sizes, discretionary funds for teachers, more planning time—combined with more use of classroom technology and revised funding formulas to assist small school districts. What it lacked was any kind of dramatic component to capture the public imagination as Alexander had done eight years earlier with his push for merit pay for teachers. What it included—dangerously—was a plan for funding based on a general income tax. Not surprisingly, that component caused considerable agitation.

There followed two years of bitter legislative fighting over the education re-form plan with McWherter ultimately giving up on the income tax and sup-porting a half-cent increase in the sales tax. McWherter blithely declared vic-tory, but the matter was a bitter pill for many who held out higher hopes. McWherter's income tax proposal was meant to end one of the state's grosser inequities, the collection of sales tax on groceries. Instead, the rate, including local options, was pushed up to a typical level of 8.25 percent in most counties with the tax on groceries still in place. In addition, the half-cent increase did not come anywhere near to funding the whole plan. Therefore, McWherter took the sales tax revenue, applied it to a scaled down version of the whole program, and promised to phase in the balance of the program over the next half-dozen years.

While the fight over the education program diminished McWherter person-ally and undermined the Democrats, it also put significant strains on the Repub-licans, with the party getting into bitter fights as to how to play the role of the opposition. The central figure in this battle was the state's young party chair-man, Tommy Hopper, who favored a scorched-earth battle with the Democrats every inch of the way and who wanted to cast the Republican party in a popu-list role that eschewed its dominant image as the party of the rich and powerful in favor of one as a party made up of cultural conservatives who mostly wanted to get the government off their backs. Hopper found many allies from the downtrodden Republican ranks in the state house of representatives, which Re-publicans had controlled for only two years (1969–1970) since Reconstruction. Moreover, he appeared in tune with the sentiments of growing numbers of sub-urban Republicans, who may not have been interested in the gamesmanship of politics but were certainly not interested in paying a general income tax. He was sharply at odds, however, with much of the state's business elite, many of whom supported the education initiative and the tax plan.

The rift was on display when a group of seventeen prominent Republican leaders (including many of those previously involved in the 1989 pre-campaign accord) held a press conference to assert their support for McWherter's educa-tion program and the income tax as a mechanism for funding it. The endorse-ment was problematic for Hopper, who had been trying to make opposition to the income tax the cornerstone of Republican legislative campaigns for 1992. In August 1991, Hopper gave an interview to the *Nashville Scene*, an alternative weekly known for its harsh caricatures of the rich and powerful. Apparently thinking his words would never see print, Hopper slipped into the lingo of the *Scene*: "The real elitists are the 17 moneypigs, not one of whom currently has children in the public schools," he said. "They say they're concerned about education, and they are. But there's also a lot of the moneypig mentality behind it. They want their business taxes reduced—there's a second agenda there."[22]

Hopper's comments set off considerable discontent among the party's elite ranks, whom he had thought he could get away with ignoring in his effort to build a rank-and-file party because the wealthy business Republicans had no other vehicle besides the party for advancing their agendas. While Hopper had the firm backing of the executive committee of the party, largely made up of the party's rank-and-file activists, he did not have the support of the party's major contributors. They were apparently reluctant to give money to anyone who re-paid their generosity by referring to them as "moneypigs." Tensions among the wings of the party continued, especially after the Republicans produced disap-pointing returns in the 1992 legislative races, which had ostensibly been what Hopper was focusing on. Hopper was eased out as party chairman with an at-tractive settlement.[23]

Apart from the rift within the Republican party, what saved the Democrats in the elections of 1992 after the tumultuous legislative sessions of 1991 and 1992 was, quite simply, good news at the top of the ticket. There wasn't much at stake in 1992—no Senate or gubernatorial contest—but the hard feelings went away as the party coalesced in the fall around the candidacy of Arkansas neighbor Bill Clinton for president and Tennessee's own Al Gore for vice presi-dent. The Clinton-Gore ticket carried Tennessee with 47.1 percent of the vote to George Bush's 42.4 percent; Ross Perot trailed at 10.1 percent of the vote.[24]

The congressional races produced little excitement; only one incumbent, Democrat Marilyn Lloyd, of the Chattanooga-anchored Third District, had a close race. Lloyd edged out Republican Zach Wamp, 48.8 percent to 47.5 per-cent. For the state legislature, Republican hopes of gains were partially stymied by the artful job of redistricting that the Democrats had put together. Six Re-publican house members found themselves reassigned to districts with other in-cumbent Republican lawmakers. Partly as a result, the Democratic majority went from 56–43 to 63–36. On the state senate side, the Republicans picked up one seat to trim the Democratic margin to 19–14, with the Wilder coalition left in firm control. The clout of the Republicans in the coalition gave them more say in how senate districts were redrawn and probably helps explain why they did not suffer the same kinds of losses as their house colleagues.

The major consequence of the 1992 elections was the resignation of Gore from the Senate, opening up the opportunity to appoint a successor until a spe-cial election could be held in 1994 for the last two years of Gore's term. Mc-Wherter's choice was between appointing a caretaker to hold the seat until the people could vote or naming someone with the expectation that the person chosen would be able to run and hold the seat. There was no shortage of possibilities for this latter category, although none was more aggressive about making his interest known than U.S. representative Jim Cooper of the Fourth District, a sprawling swath of rural counties running from southwest of Nashville to northeast of Knoxville. The owlish Cooper, a Rhodes Scholar and the son of former governor Prentice Cooper, was a political moderate with close ties to the business community. He had first gained prominence when he decisively won his House seat in 1982 in a much-watched contest with Cissy Baker, whose father Howard was then the Senate majority leader.

McWherter's own first choice, however, was U.S. representative John Tanner, a conservative Democrat from rural west Tennessee who was just beginning his third term in the House after a long term in the state legislature. Tanner, who was emerging as a leader of the congressional Democrats' "Blue Dog" faction, had the kind of conservatism and rural charm that gave him the look of someone whom Republicans would have a tough time ousting. He was comfortable with much of the state's cultural conservatism while being somewhat more middle-of-the-road on economic issues. Tanner, however, did not feel ready to give up his safe Eighth District House seat and rejected McWherter's offer.[25]

McWherter then gave the job to his deputy, Harlan Mathews, who had been frustrated in his bid for a Clinton administration appointment in spite of his yeoman service raising money for the Clinton campaign. A longtime veteran of state government who had served as state finance commissioner and state treasurer before taking the position as McWherter's main operative, Mathews was clearly not a prospect for election, never having run for office and being virtually unknown outside political circles. That fact was brought home when McWherter—under criticism in his own party for not appointing someone who could hold the seat—then announced his support for Cooper for the Democratic nomination in 1994. The move was vintage McWherter, putting him on two sides at once, and it largely preempted any other Democrat from seeking the nomination.

Republicans, meanwhile, were putting their house in order for the 1994 races, which now stacked up as a kind of Super Bowl with both Senate seats and the governorship on the ballot and with three of the nine congressional seats likely to be vacant. Republican prospects looked strong enough to stir enthusiasm. After twelve years in Congress, Sundquist, who had been positioning himself for a statewide race, was the prohibitive favorite for the gubernatorial nomination. For the two years remaining in Gore's Senate term, Nashville lawyer Fred Thompson was gearing up to run. Thompson, a Baker protégé, had first attracted attention in 1973 as Republican counsel to the Senate Watergate committee and had carved out an interesting second career as an actor. For the other Senate seat, a group of six lesser known aspirants stepped forward for the more formidable task of challenging Sasser, who was preparing to seek a fourth term. That field quickly narrowed down to a contest between Nashville heart surgeon William F. (Billy) Frist and Chattanooga developer Bob Corker, who waged a spirited contest before the more conservative Frist prevailed in the August primary.

Frist is the brother of Dr. Thomas Frist, Jr., the founder of the Nashville-based Hospital Corporation of America, which prior to its acquisition by Columbia Health Systems was the nation's largest private hospital company. While Billy Frist had apparently absorbed some of the family's billion-dollar-plus fortune by osmosis, he had devoted his career to the active practice of medicine and his personal wealth did not measure up to that of his brother or his father, who had also played a major role in the founding of the hospital company. Frist, a political novice who had not bothered to register to vote until he was thirty-three, brushed aside family objections to take on what appeared to be a hopeless race. Frist himself noted after he captured the seat that many Republicans had told him he could not win the primary, much less the general election.[26]

"His daddy didn't tell him not to do it," contended his campaign manager, Tom Perdue. "His brother, whom he worships, advised him not to do it. And from his brother's perspective, he was right: Bill had never really been involved in politics. . . . But Bill saw something there that not a lot of people saw. He saw an opportunity and a vulnerability and a chance to make a difference." Frist met Perdue in June 1993, at a seminar in Washington for Republicans who were considering running for the Senate. Perdue had managed Republican Paul Coverdell's upset of Democratic senator Wyche Fowler in Georgia the previous year, and Frist saw a parallel between the liberal Fowler and Sasser in Tennessee. "Frist really thought, in 1993, that if he put his mind to it, he could win the nomination and beat Sasser. He had no polling; it was just a feeling he had," said Perdue.[27]

The Democratic lineup, meanwhile, was set from the start on the Senate side with Sasser and Cooper, but was much more open on the gubernatorial side. A number of leading Democrats flirted with the race before opting out. The absence of big names attracted some other longshots into the race, and one year before the election, the Democratic race looked like a wide-open scramble. That was before the other shoe dropped. In November 1993, Mathews, with Sasser's clandestine backing, persuaded Nashville mayor Phil Bredesen to enter the governor's race. Bredesen, a health care multimillionaire who had been elected mayor of the state's capital in 1991 after two failed political bids liberally financed with his own money, had scouted out a campaign for governor earlier in the year before ultimately announcing in May that he would not seek the governorship. He reentered the race with Mathews's overt endorsement and the widely rumored private ones of Sasser and McWherter.

Bredesen ultimately cruised to a decisive primary victory, capturing 53.0 percent of the vote against a half-dozen active candidates. Sundquist grabbed 83.3 percent of the vote against a thinly funded right-wing candidate. Primary night should have offered a warning to the Democrats of impending troubles. Tennessee has no party registration, and typically two-thirds of the voters take part in the Democratic primary even in years when the Democratic slots at the top of the ticket are uncontested, a reflection of residual party loyalty and more numerous and interesting down-ballot races on the Democratic side. This time primary participation was split much more evenly with only 53.6 percent of the voters taking part in the Democratic primary. Because of his lopsided margin, Sundquist, with 386,696 votes, actually outpolled Bredesen, who received 284,803 votes. Also in the primary, Frist bested Corker by polling strongly in middle Tennessee.

THE SMASHING REPUBLICAN VICTORIES OF 1994

The fall campaigns tempt one to paraphrase Tolstoy: All winning campaigns are alike, while losing ones are lost in their own special way. The Republicans fielded well-funded candidates backed by a unified party and a fairly consistent message; the Democrats were undone by their individual problems. In Sasser's case, long service in Washington took its toll. As chairman of the Senate Budget Committee and a supporter of President Clinton, Sasser had been pushed into a visible role on a number of tough issues, including the 1993 deficit reduction package and the assault weapons ban. Frist hammered at Sasser as an out-of-touch, old-fashioned, big-spending liberal with a huge taxpayer-financed pension, closing his campaign ads with the tag line, "18 years of Jim Sasser is enough," and promising "to transplant that bleeding heart liberal."[28] Perdue said Frist's tracking polls indicated that Frist had passed Sasser about ten days before the election and Sasser had never caught up, adding that the "mood of the country played a role" in Frist's victory.

Another factor, Perdue said, was Frist's commitment to the race, in terms of his willingness both to campaign hard and to spend his own money. Frist also received the strong support of the National Rifle Association. Although Sasser did not have a particularly strong gun-control record, he had supported the assault weapons ban. The NRA ran anti-Sasser television ads featuring spokesman Charlton Heston, who also campaigned with Frist. The latter's politicking was as organized and driven as a military unit; from the start of the campaign through the primary, Frist never took his eyes off Sasser as the target, even as his primary battle with Corker tightened. Exploiting the public's lack of understanding that most congressional votes are routine, he repeatedly accused Sasser of "voting with Ted Kennedy 86 percent of the time."[29]

By the time the Senate finally adjourned in October, freeing Sasser to campaign full time, Frist had already defined him in the eyes of the voters. He had concurrently presented himself as for term limits, a balanced budget amendment, a cut in the capital gains tax rate, and line-item veto authority for the president—and against cuts in defense spending. The Frist campaign sent out wave after wave of direct mail advertising—reportedly totaling nearly three million pieces—"targeting gun owners, abortion opponents, conservative Christians, healthcare providers, tobacco farmers, and any other group that might be dissatisfied with Sasser past, present or future," according to the Memphis *Commercial Appeal*. Election day polling indicated Frist won big with most of these groups, racking up gun owners 2–1 over Sasser and white Christian conservatives 3–1.[30] In the last two weeks, Frist and a caravan of supporters crisscrossed the state in a campaign bus he dubbed the "Frist Force Victory Tour."

Sasser's campaign rarely seemed to click, featuring in the early going much-ridiculed ads of the senator riding around in a police car (as if he did it often) and revealing Sasser's apparent reluctance to talk about the contributions of the Democratic party. On the stump toward the end, he emphasized that if he won he would likely be chosen Senate Democratic leader, a post from which he would be able to deliver even more for the state than he had as Budget Committee chairman. To this, Frist responded, "Jim Sasser is talking about clout. Jim Sasser is talking about Washington. Bill Frist is talking about people out there trying to earn a good wage."[31] Even the promise of more pork seemed to strike many voters as mere business-as-usual in Washington. For example, Frist carried traditionally Democratic Coffee County in southern middle Tennessee, where Sasser had a few days earlier staged a big campaign rally in support of a proposed $2.5 billion wind tunnel project at the Air Force test facility there, which he promised to help deliver upon his reelection. Clinton, who carried Coffee in 1992, would win it again in 1996.

More than the other Democratic senatorial candidate in 1994, however, Sasser kept the organized part of the Democratic constituencies in line—teachers, trial lawyers, minorities, labor unions and liberals. He also picked up some rather unusual support. During the last week, the dean of the Republican congressional delegation, Quillen, campaigned with him in his home district, praising their work together as a "team for upper East Tennessee." And the conservative Nashville *Banner* gave him its editorial support. Despite his role as Budget Committee chairman, he couldn't match in campaign contributions the amount the wealthy Frist was willing to spend—or loan—his own campaign: upwards of $3.7 million. But for all that, Sasser just didn't get the votes;[32] one suspects the reason was the accumulation of time and enemies. Frist crushed Sasser with 56.4 percent of the vote to the incumbent's 42.1 percent.

Cooper, on the other hand, entered the race with a large lead in various polls, and Thompson's campaign got off to a rocky start as he replaced two campaign managers before persuading his Washington-based political consultant, Bill Lacy, to move to Nashville and run the operation full time. The *Tennessee Journal*, a weekly political newsletter with Republican connections, wondered in late spring what was wrong with the Republican's campaign. Indeed, throughout the primary, Thompson never seemed to get much traction. When an ill-funded Christian right-wing candidate picked up 34 percent of the vote in the August primary, Thompson looked like the weakest of the three statewide Republican nominees.

But Lacy's presence and Thompson's decision to call on Tom Ingram—a top political aide to Alexander when he was governor—for advice were laying the groundwork for a dramatic shift in the candidate's fortunes after the primary. Immediately after the August vote, Thompson parked his Lincoln, shed his lawyer attire, donned blue jeans, cowboy boots, and a western-style khaki shirt, and rolled out what would become the symbol of his campaign: a red extended-cab pickup truck. The costume and the prop remained in place for the duration of the race and made their reprise in his successful 1996 reelection campaign. The transformation to "Ol' Fred" was one of the most remarkable political makeovers in history.

Although the truck was universally slammed by the press, its "contribution to this campaign—its absolutely enormous contribution—was making Fred comfortable as a candidate, making him feel in touch, making him have fun," Lacy said in retrospect. Ingram agreed. Before the truck, Thompson was "miserable and not performing well," he said.[33] After Thompson's appearance in eighteen motion pictures from 1985 to 1993, the election of 1994 was his most successful performance and is testimony to his skill as an actor. And at a craggy 6 foot 6, Thompson made a striking contrast to the soft-spoken, bookish Cooper.

For his part, Cooper largely self-immolated, laying the seeds of his own destruction by crossing the president early on. Cooper gained national attention with an alternative to Clinton's health care plan, the key element of which was his refusal to support Clinton's goal of universal health insurance coverage. Cooper's efforts did considerable damage to the Clinton plan, and they earned him the Washington-orchestrated enmity of organized labor. "They [labor] weren't much good at helping us, but they were sure good at screwing Cooper," observed an official of another campaign.[34]

Cooper, who called himself a "maverick," conservative, independent Democrat, later attempted several clumsy appeals to right-wing constituencies—such as calling for the impeachment of an anti–death penalty federal judge in Nashville—and largely succeeded in driving away a good part of the Democratic coalition while failing to gain anything from the other side. Polls showed that the momentum began to shift toward Thompson in September, and it never stopped. In October, as his own campaign fell further and further behind, Cooper finally put aside his determination to run a "positive" campaign and started attacking Thompson and his contrived image. Most of the attack focused on Thompson's Washington lobbying career in the 1970s and 1980s, which had slacked off at least somewhat as Thompson gained more movie roles in the early 1990s.

Using the theme "The Hunt for Fred in October"—a takeoff on one of Thompson's most popular movies, *The Hunt for Red October*—Cooper hammered daily at his opponent's lobbying career. Thompson had earned half a million dollars lobbying from 1975 through 1993, but the bulk of it came in the years after the GOP won control of the Senate in the 1980 elections, when his political mentor, Senator Baker, was majority leader.[35] Cooper contrasted Thompson's new country-boy image to the Thompson who owned a Pennsylvania Avenue condominium.

Thompson didn't have to hit back very vehemently, but when he did, he criticized Cooper for voting for the $30,000 congressional pay raise of 1989, which also banned honoraria. In his own platform, Thompson called for twelve-year term limits for Congress, pay cuts for its members, cutting congressional sessions down to half a year, and allowing members to hold jobs at home. On the campaign trail, Thompson was more of a celebrity than a political candidate. He would pull the truck, trailed by its caravan of supporters, into a Wal-Mart parking lot, and women would swoon. On a few occasions, the candidate, whose divorce had let him become something of a midlife bon vivant, even brought along his ex-wife to campaign with him. A *Commercial Appeal* account reported: "At every stop, people touched him, snapped pictures of each other with him, asked for his autograph and offered their babies for him to admire. One woman in Dickson got him to autograph his picture on a campaign poster and told him she intended to hang it in her bedroom." When it came time for rhetoric, Thompson climbed into the truckbed and proclaimed, "What this country needs is a good housecleaning in Congress." "The key decision was to attack Congress, not President Clinton. We had a pretty good idea that Congress was not going to repair its reputation before the election," Lacy said.[36]

In the end, Thompson—who raised and spent the least amount, $3.5 million, of any of the statewide candidates that year—won with the biggest victory margin, 60.4 percent to Cooper's 38.6 percent, sweeping every demographic group except blacks. "I am convinced today more than ever before that it had more to do with something other than just partisan politics and who is president of the United States. People feel alienated from their government. People feel alienated from the people's branch of government and if the professional politicians don't understand that, they're sure going to," he said in his victory speech.[37]

The closest of the major 1994 races was the governor's contest, where Bredesen was the only Democrat who started behind and gained ground during the race. Largely through Mathews's intercession, much of the McWherter organization was pulled together around the state in support of Bredesen, and Bredesen also got the backing of organized labor and the teachers' union. Some other traditional Democratic constituencies, including the state employees and trial lawyers, sat out the race, and a number of well-known Democrats (many of them losers from the August primaries) defected to endorse Republican Sundquist. "Our PAC did not give to either candidate in the governor's race. I think it was felt that both Bredesen and Sundquist came from business backgrounds and didn't offer anything for us," said John Summers, executive director of the Tennessee Trial Lawyers Association.[38]

The governor's race set a Tennessee record of $21.3 million in campaign spending, far eclipsing the previous record of $15 million in 1986. Bredesen threw about $6.5 million of his own wealth into the race, most of it in the closing weeks when the TV ad wars were intense. Overall, the Democrat spent $9.6 million, compared to Sundquist's $7 million.[39]

It was often difficult to tell the two apart in terms of their campaign rhetoric. Both voiced support for the death penalty and opposition to taxes. The two differed more by degree, except on the issue of abortion; Sundquist proclaimed himself pro-life, while Bredesen professed to be pro-choice. "Generally in Tennessee, you don't find candidates stressing philosophical differences as much as they do for national office. But these two here probably come across more alike in a policy sense than any two in the last 20 years," observed William Lyons, a University of Tennessee political scientist.[40]

So rather than a referendum on the state's direction, the race revolved around "trust" and character. Bredesen's TV ads bashed Sundquist's congressional votes against increases in the minimum wage and for a congressional pay raise and accepting perks, speaking fees, and trips from special interest groups. Sundquist accused Bredesen of flip-flopping on such issues as public funding for abortion and school privatization. Ultimately, Sundquist narrowed his focus to taxes, warning that Bredesen could not be trusted not to raise taxes, which he had done as mayor. And Bredesen zeroed in on Sundquist's service on the board of directors of a not-for-profit retirement complex in Memphis called Kirby Pines, whose residents had filed a lawsuit charging the board with negligence in protecting their assets. (Once the case was ultimately decided, after the election, Sundquist claimed vindication.)[41]

The election was also notable in one other aspect: both the candidates were northern-born men (Sundquist in Moline, Illinois, and Bredesen in New Jersey but having grown up in rural upstate New York) who moved to Tennessee as adults and gained business and political success.[42] Indeed, it was the first time since Pennsylvania-born Democrat William Carroll was sworn in as governor in 1821 that Tennessee was assured of a governor not born either in the state or a neighboring southern state.

Sundquist won the election with 54.3 percent of the vote to Bredesen's 44.7 percent, benefiting significantly from the 1994 Republican tide. Republicans acknowledged that they were wary down to the wire that their success was attributable to a big Republican sweep. Sundquist recalled: "Even on the Thursday before the election when [aide] John Bakke talked to the infamous Dick Morris [a Sundquist consultant in 1994], and Dick Morris had the results of our last poll, and it showed my positives going up and Mayor Bredesen's negatives going up, I was nervous. Morris said the election was over. I didn't even want to talk about it."[43] How much the major races may have been shaped by the general voter anger at Democrats might be indicated by the outcome in the Public Service Commission race. Democrat Sara Kyle, a niece of former governor Frank G. Clement, won the post on the three-member utility regulatory board by a 52.2 percent to 45.1 percent margin over Tom Watson, a token candidate who did not wage an active campaign. Republicans had routinely conceded the PSC to the Democrats, and token candidates had typically received from 35 percent to 37 percent. Watson's showing indicates a Republican surge of 8 or 9 percentage points. Applying that figure recklessly, one might conclude that in a more temperate year, while Thompson would still have bested Cooper, Bredesen would have won and Frist and Sasser would have battled down to the wire.

All three statewide Democratic candidates, Bredesen, Cooper, and Sasser, took comfort in asserting that their losses were part of a national political earthquake that none of them could have predicted or withstood, even with the most money, the best organizations, and the best political breaks. "If the margin here had been something like two points, then you could say, 'If we'd only done this, or gotten more voters to the polls, or whatever.' But there was just a cold wind coming out of Washington," Bredesen said. Sasser added: "What occurred was a political earthquake. Voters absolutely demanded change and there's not much a political campaign can do about that."[44]

Along with the three statewide successes, and as part of the nationwide congressional GOP victory of 1994, Tennessee Republicans transformed their long-standing minority status in the state's U.S. House delegation (6 Democrats to 3 Republicans) into a 5 to 4 majority. They did it by winning two open seats; in the process they nearly ousted an incumbent Democratic congressman. Republican Van Hilleary won Cooper's old House seat in the Fourth District that was considered to be slightly Democratic-leaning. Hilleary, a thirty-five-year-old Rhea County textile executive and Gulf War veteran who had run unsuccessfully for the state legislature in 1992, won 56.6 percent of the vote. And Zach Wamp captured the Third District seat that he had nearly won in 1992 against the incumbent, Lloyd, after the latter decided to step down in 1994. Wamp, a thirty-six-year-old Chattanooga developer and real estate broker and a former Hamilton County Republican party chairman, secured 53.3 percent of the vote in a district that was viewed as Republican-leaning.

In addition to winning the statewide Public Service Commission seat, Democrats also took solace in the fact that they retained control of the state legislature after the 1994 election even though they lost a total of one senate and four house seats. Except for a brief 17–16 GOP majority in the senate which resulted from two members switching parties in September 1995 (discussed directly below), Democrats have maintained numerical majorities in the legislature for nearly three decades, and the 1990s opened with them holding a 22–11 margin in the senate and a 58–41 majority in the house. The Republican quest for seats was sharply thwarted in the house by the Democratic-drawn redistricting plan after the 1990 census. For example, house Democrats combined the districts of eleven house Republicans—plus one maverick Democrat who promptly switched parties—into six districts. The GOP has been able to make larger inroads in the senate, where its numbers had steadily increased until finally, in September 1995, jubilant Republicans gained control of the Tennessee senate for the first time since Reconstruction when Democrats Milton Hamilton of Union City and Rusty Crowe of Johnson City switched parties, giving the

GOP the 17–16 edge mentioned above. The midterm switch had little practical impact, however, because Republicans had already shared power, including committee chairmanships, under the Democratic-Republican coalition put together by senate speaker John Wilder eight years earlier. Moreover, the GOP majority was short-lived: in the 1996 legislative elections, Democrats regained a senate majority, 18–15, although Wilder retained the speakership, as mentioned earlier and detailed below. The Democrats also increased their majority in the house to 61–38.

The 1996 Elections: Partisan Stabilization

Following the Democratic debacle of 1994, the main question for 1996 was to be the degree to which the Democrats would be able to bounce back. With two of the three top offices not on the ballot, however, there were limits to what they could hope to achieve. Overcoming the effects of his aggressive stance on tobacco in a major tobacco-growing state, Clinton—aided by the presence of Gore on the ticket—carried the state in the 1996 presidential election by a relatively narrow 45,000 votes.[45] Polling data showed Clinton comfortably ahead of Senator Bob Dole for most of the year before the race tightened in October.[46] Clinton received 48.0 percent to Dole's 45.6 percent with Ross Perot at 5.6 percent. The Democratic standard-bearer's performance closely mirrored his victory pattern of four years earlier.[47]

Thompson's 1996 reelection bid was a repetition of his 1994 victory over Cooper, complete with his mobile stage prop, the red pickup truck. Unlike Cooper, however, the senator's 1996 opponent, Tipton County lawyer Houston Gordon, actually campaigned on Democratic themes, but the outcome was unchanged. Thompson added a percentage point to his first victory margin, capturing 61.4 percent of the vote. Asked about Thompson's big margin, the defeated Democrat said, "He was strong, he hadn't been there very long, he has a great personality, he has a commanding personality." Gordon added that the mixed results of the elections in Tennessee—in favor of the Democratic White House while reelecting a Republican senator—indicated that "Tennesseans are moderate, they want the government to work well, and, by and large, they are tired of the blame-giving and name-calling." Thompson said the voters' mood was different from two years earlier, when there "was a broad-based, mutual consensus that we wanted a change. Anger is not the feeling I came away with two years ago. I thought it was concern. I think the concern is still there—but it's more of a long-term, fundamental concern [about the nation's future]."[48]

The Democrats did manage to win nominal dominance of the state senate, although Wilder remained firmly in control based on his support on both sides of the aisle. Wilder, who had raised a significant campaign war chest in anticipation of a Republican primary challenge in his district, ended up unopposed when Sundquist interceded to forestall the Republican challenge. Wilder then used his campaign funds to give contributions to all incumbent senators seeking reelection regardless of party and to the senate caucuses of both parties.[49]

Also in 1996, the Republicans managed to consolidate their hold on the two congressional seats picked up in 1994, keeping the GOP's five-to-four majority in the state's U.S. House delegation. Wamp was reelected in the Third District with 56.4 percent of the vote. In the rural Fourth District, Hilleary captured 58.0 percent of the vote, despite being targeted by organized labor,[50] which ran numerous ads criticizing him for opposing a minimum wage increase and supporting Republican budget-cutting efforts.

While the Democrats gained some ground, the basic accomplishment of 1996 was stabilization. The party's nose dive was halted, but the process of regaining altitude remained ahead. See Figure 7 in Chapter 1 for a graphic depiction of this partisan pattern.

All in all, the great upheaval of 1994 in Tennessee and subsequent consolidation in 1996 underscores the manner in which Tennessee politics is somewhat different from other southern states. Lyndon Johnson's famous observation that the passage of the 1964 Civil Rights Act was likely to cost the Democratic party the allegiance of the South for thirty years has not exactly been true even while it was prophetic. At the presidential level Johnson was right on the mark; at the state level the southern Democratic edifice was so large and so entrenched that it has required a thirty-year campaign for Republicans to topple it. Race was the wedge that first opened the door to steady Republican progress in Dixie, but over time the process became more complicated.

What has been different in Tennessee is that the Republicans scored their triumphs early and then the Democrats won the state back in a protracted struggle culminating in the election of McWherter in 1986. Because the Republicans started from a higher plane in the late 1960s, the first flush of gains was enough to put them in charge of a significant array of public responsibilities. The early gains also put the Democrats on notice that things would not remain the same and that the Democratic party would need to adapt to new realities. The victories of Sasser, Gore, and McWherter were triumphs for a more moderate state party that took care to distance itself from the national Democratic party.

By the 1980s survey data indicate that the traditional ties of the voters to either party were substantially reduced. Hence it was possible for Tennessee

Democrats to fashion a new period of success, albeit one that was also vulnerable to the volatile moods of the voters. "Probably nothing helped the Republicans more than the fact that Walter Mondale and Michael Dukakis were the presidential nominees in 1984 and 1988," said Richard Lodge, who served as Democratic party chairman for much of the 1980s. "They cut loose a lot of people who had been traditional Democratic voters and left the party pared down to its core, the basic interest groups that make up the party: labor, urban progressives and blacks, trial lawyers and teachers."[51] It is easy to forget that, while Dukakis and Mondale were drubbed by 270,000-plus margins, Jimmy Carter carried the state in 1976 and lost it to Ronald Reagan by less than 5,000 votes in 1980. In that context, Clinton's victories look less like an aberration and more like a statement that the state is available to Democrats as long as the Democrats field candidates within the moderate range. "The Republicans were successful in 1994 in nationalizing the election," observed Lodge. By contrast, he noted, no one to date has quite figured out a way to interject Newt Gingrich or Teddy Kennedy into races for the state house of representatives.

An examination of election returns shows that vestiges of the traditional regional alignment remain in place even as the state's politics has changed. The broad-stroke portrait of east Tennessee as Republican against Democratic middle and west Tennessee is still roughly true, although west Tennessee is much less firmly so. Bredesen's vote in 1994 is typical and illustrative. He received 36 percent of the vote in east Tennessee, 53 percent in middle Tennessee and 46 percent in west Tennessee en route to a 44.7 percent statewide vote.

This is, of course, an oversimplification for a changing, complex state. Given the fairly monolithic support of black voters for the Democratic party, for example, greater black participation masks the defection of white voters from the Democratic party in west Tennessee. Even weak Democratic candidates typically poll 85 to 90 percent of the black vote in statewide races. As a result, Shelby County, which includes Memphis, has remained competitive in statewide elections even as the vote became more racially polarized. In west Tennessee counties with black populations of greater than 30 percent, Democrats averaged 54 percent of the vote in major statewide races from 1988 to 1996. By contrast, in middle Tennessee counties where blacks make up less than two percent of the population, Democrats secured about 54 percent of the vote, highlighting the relative weakness among white voters exhibited by Democratic candidates in west Tennessee in the modern era.

The other important demographic change in the state has been the rise of the suburbs and the corresponding development of a suburban Republican party quite different from the party's financial hierarchy. Just as the 1950s and the 1960s marked the major movement of citizens from small towns and rural areas to the major cities, the 1980s and 1990s were marked by a countermovement to the adjacent suburbs. In Nashville for example, the population grew moderately while adjacent Rutherford, Williamson, and Sumner counties were among the state's fastest growing locations. This produced suburban rings that are whiter and more Republican—although not necessarily more affluent—than the core cities they surround. The political center of gravity is moving slowly toward the suburbs. As areas that are the embodiment of change, the suburbs are the areas where traditional loyalties are most shaken, which, of course, works to the disadvantage of Democrats. New people in new areas make new judgments. The Republicanism they have spawned tends to be less ideological, more economic, and more socially tolerant than the state's traditional Republican party.

Overall, in suburban counties, Democrats averaged 47.8 percent of the vote in key statewide elections from 1988 to 1996, compared to 49.9 percent statewide and 51.3 percent in the Big Four urban counties. It was in these suburban areas that Hopper hoped for Republican gains and Republicans made their most significant advances in the state legislature.

While the Republicans clearly scored a major breakthrough in 1994, the party still remains in the grip of its elite rather than the rank-and-file, although this is somewhat less important now that the Republicans have major statewide officeholders again. While the gains of the party have been dependent on the changing sentiments of working class voters, particularly the cultural conservatives who used to stand by the Democrats as the party of the New Deal, the golden rule of politics remains in force: Those who have the gold make the rules. The absence of elite support thwarted any rank-and-file inclination to take on incumbent Democrats in 1990. It was also true to a degree in 1994 in the challenge to Sasser, with Frist's personal wealth allowing him to ignore the early coolness of party moguls.

Many leading Republicans explain away the long dry spell as indicative of McWherter's personal appeal and the party's own lack of candidates. "We didn't have anybody in the wings," recalled Randle Richardson, the party operative who succeeded Hopper as chairman in 1993. But it is also clear from the willingness of the Republican party's money-raising elite to strike a deal with McWherter where the center of gravity in the party lies. "I think Governor McWherter did a good job of co-opting our contributors," Sundquist said. "That's not criticism; that's respect. What better way not to have an opponent than to have people who might support your opponent support you. He did so because he had an agenda that was conservative, and he was perceived by the business community as having been a very good governor. Obviously, I heard about the tension [within the party], but I understood it."[52]

Looking to the future, the Republicans still hold many of the high cards as the Democrats try to work their way back. Senator Frist has also shown considerably more moderation in office than he did during the campaign.[53] Thompson was always more moderate and even broke with Republicans early on tort reform issues (Thompson is a trial lawyer by profession). Sundquist has largely avoided controversy with a modest legislative program and after two years in office seemed reasonably popular, racking up a 66 percent approval rating in one poll.[54]

Democratic success hinges on hitting the right note in Tennessee, which several of its recent major candidates have failed to do. For example, Sasser's responsibilities in Washington had transformed him into that least loved of all southern political figures, the national Democrat. The mix that seems to work for Democrats in Tennessee is one of cultural conservatism with a leftward tilt on pocketbook issues; Sasser was merely seen as a tool of Democrats in Washington. Bredesen's failure was largely one of cognitive dissonance. He tried to run as a moderate contemporary southern Democrat, but stumbled over reality with many voters who couldn't forget that he came from upstate New York, went to Harvard, and had moved to Tennessee only in 1975.

It is also clear, however, that the Democratic party retains vitality in the state despite the recent GOP advance.[55] Thus, by the latter part of the 1990s one could say with confidence that a strong, if complex, system of two-party competition had settled in throughout Tennessee.

8

Alabama: The GOP Rises in the Heart of Dixie

Patrick R. Cotter and Tom Gordon

For several weeks after the November 5, 1996, election, a large wooden sign stood outside the Alabama Republican party state headquarters building in Birmingham's Southside. On the sign, in large block letters, were three words: "Thank you, Alabama." For Alabama Republicans, the 1996 election had given them much to be thankful for and plenty of reasons to be optimistic about the 1998 cycle. For the state's Democrats, the election had produced considerable cause for alarm. The GOP had won every statewide race on the 1996 general election ballot, including hard-fought contests for an open U.S. Senate seat and a Democratic-controlled state supreme court seat. Its booty also included two open U.S. House seats, three other appellate court posts, and more gains for its candidate farm system at the county level.

Moreover, the 1996 election had significance beyond the ballot box because it ratified and built upon historic Republican breakthroughs in the 1994 election, when the GOP won the governor's chair and seven other statewide offices, boosted its ranks in the state legislature and at the county level, and prompted a number of sitting Democratic officeholders to trade their "Yellow Dog" pins for elephant tusks. Between the 1994 election and March 1998, fifty-three Democratic officeholders, including one of the state's two U.S. senators (Richard Shelby), along with the secretary of state and two appellate court judges, jumped ship to the GOP. Republican officials boasted that no other state except Texas had a higher number of party switchers over the same period.

In January 1997 the state GOP gathered in Mobile to celebrate its successes, and in a moment of rhetorical exuberance, party chairman Roger McConnell said his troops had "awakened the Democrats," adding: "What we need to do is chop their head off." Two months later, less than half of the 250 state Democratic executive committee members listened quietly in a Montgomery hotel conference room as their highest ranking elected official, Lieutenant Governor Don Siegelman, said the party was broken and needed repairs. "In the last 10 years, we've gone from a majority party to a minority party," the grim-faced Siegelman said.[1]

One can't deny that the recent political numbers in Alabama indicate a Republican trend. Owing to victories and party switches in the last two election cycles, the GOP held, as of mid-1998, a majority of the state's constitutional offices, including the governor's chair and the attorney general's seat. Republicans also held both U.S. Senate seats and five of the state's seven U.S. House seats, majorities on the state's board of education and court of criminal appeals, and were only one win away from a majority on the court of civil appeals. The GOP occupied three of nine seats on the state supreme court, which the party has long viewed as being much too friendly to plaintiffs' trial lawyers. Republicans hoped to win a majority when three of the high court's seats were up for election in November 1998. Some Republicans also believed that enough switches and wins in the 1998 general election could even give them a majority in the 35-member state senate, where they held an all-time high of 14 seats, and they expected to gain more ground in the house, where they held 36 of the 105 seats as of mid-1998.

These trends are a far cry from just ten years ago, when Republicans were not much of a presence in state politics and seemed dependent, for the electoral gains they did achieve, on Democratic fumbles and freak political accidents.

The Republican millennium, however, has not necessarily arrived. Democrats still held legislative majorities and most of the local offices around the state. And though Bill Clinton failed to carry the state in 1996—no Democratic presidential contender has won Alabama since Jimmy Carter in 1976—the president's late-October visit to Birmingham gave the GOP a scare because it put most of the major Democratic candidates either ahead of or in striking distance of their GOP opponents. "Had the election been held two weeks earlier, many of the races that we lost, conceivably we could have won," party chairman Joe Turnham told his fellow Democrats at their March 1997 meeting. Two months earlier, in a quiet moment after his vow to decapitate the Democrats, GOP chairman McConnell himself told of the panic Republicans had felt upon seeing the polling numbers for their candidates after Clinton's Birmingham visit.

"There's no big bad Republican party," McConnell said. "We've got a lot of work to do."[2]

REPUBLICAN GROWTH AND DEMOCRATIC STUMBLES

More than ten years ago, few would have forecast that Alabama's political landscape would be as dramatically changed as it is today. But that was before the 1986 gubernatorial election, which proved to be the last campaign in which most voters believed that whoever won the Democratic nomination was certain to become the state's next governor. From the mid-1960s to the mid-1980s, the Republican party had gradually become a presence in the state, as related in the Alabama preview section in Chapter 1. But the GOP's growth had come in fits and starts, and by the mid-1980s its overall influence was still only marginal.

At the start of the 1986 election season, Republicans were mindful of their past defeats and publicly de-emphasized the governor's race.[3] Their top priority was the reelection of their first-term U.S. senator, Jeremiah Denton. But by the year's end, those early assumptions had been turned upside down.

The story of the 1986 election begins, as does much of postwar Alabama politics, with George Wallace. By positioning himself as both an economic populist and a racial and social conservative, Wallace dominated state politics for more than two decades and became an important actor on the national stage. In retrospect, many Alabamians would agree that Wallace stunted the state's two-party development by remaining a Democrat. Throughout his career, he railed against federal bureaucrats, federal judges, and the federal government in general, calling them tyrannical, unnecessarily intrusive, and worse. In early 1986 Wallace was in the last year of his fourth gubernatorial term, the last one won at the head of the standard ideologically diverse, black-white Democratic coalition (as mentioned in Chapter 1). Although eligible to run yet again, he had suffered during the first three years of this term bouts of illness linked to the 1972 assassination attempt that had partially paralyzed him, and there was considerable public concern over who was actually running the government. With his popular standing in decline, Wallace, in April 1986, went to the house chamber in the state capitol and tearfully bid the state "a fond and affectionate farewell." His retirement set the stage for the deep and rancorous partisan conflict that followed in that momentous election year.

Eventually, this conflict would crystallize into a primary battle between Lieutenant Governor Bill Baxley and Attorney General Charlie Graddick for the Democratic gubernatorial nomination. Baxley, a former attorney general and the more liberal candidate, was supported by the key Democratic party power groups—the Alabama Education Association, labor unions, plaintiffs' lawyers, and black political action groups such as the Alabama Democratic Conference. Graddick, a former Republican and district attorney who had switched to the Democratic party in order to have a political career outside his home county of Mobile, was a tough-talking type whose strong support for the death penalty had earned him the nickname of "Charcoal Charlie." Though nominally a Democrat, Graddick had kept his distance from the party, and he entered the primary with the backing of business groups and Republicans who already had conceded the general election to the Democrats.

Amid charges of racism, marital infidelity, dishonesty, and tax evasion, Baxley and Graddick waged a particularly nasty runoff campaign. At the end, Graddick claimed a narrow 8,756-vote victory out of the more than 930,000 votes cast in the second primary. Baxley and his supporters refused, however, to accept Graddick's victory. Instead, they filed an official challenge alleging that Graddick had violated party rules by encouraging Republicans who had voted in the GOP's first primary to "cross over" and vote in the Democratic runoff. An endless series of court rulings and party committee hearings ultimately led to a decision that Graddick had in fact violated party rules and would be replaced as the Democratic nominee by Baxley.

The Democratic party's seemingly undemocratic action of removing Graddick, the top vote getter, in favor of Baxley created an uproar and shifted public attention and support to the Republican gubernatorial nominee, Guy Hunt, a longtime Republican activist and a former probate judge in the north Alabama county of Cullman. Hunt, a Primitive Baptist minister and a onetime Amway salesman with a high school education, had also been the GOP nominee in 1978 and had lost the governorship by more than 350,000 votes to Democrat Forrest Hood (Fob) James; Hunt received only 25.9 percent of the vote to James's 72.6 percent. (Like Graddick, James, a wealthy Opelika businessman, was also a former Republican.)

During the fall campaign, Hunt stayed above the controversy that the aftermath of the Democratic runoff campaign had generated. Trying to focus on traditional Democratic issues, Baxley offered proposals to deal with the state's financial problems. He also questioned Hunt's qualifications and whether the Republican candidate had been forced from his previous federal job for politicking. The Democrats also poked fun at their opponent's Amway background and tried to get reporters to focus on some supposedly sizable debts that Hunt owed.

The bitter crossover issue from the runoff, however, remained at center stage, largely because of Graddick, who mounted a write-in campaign, with-drawing only shortly before the general election. In the end, the Democratic party's apparent disregard of majority rule in substituting Baxley as its nominee was too much for Alabama voters. Hunt, with 56.3 percent of the vote, became the state's first Republican governor since Reconstruction.

Hunt's victory was not accompanied by additional major shifts in Alabama politics. No other Republican candidate was elected to statewide office in 1986. Indeed, the GOP's candidates for offices such as lieutenant governor, secretary of state, and state treasurer lost by large margins. Furthermore, the GOP added only slightly to its state legislative holdings, increasing its seats from just 13 to 16 in the 105-member house and going from 4 to 5 seats in the 35-member senate.[4]

Also, Senator Denton, who started 1986 as the GOP's top reelection priority, narrowly lost his seat to U.S. representative Richard Shelby, a conservative Democrat. Shelby criticized Denton for allegedly favoring reductions in Social Security and for paying insufficient attention to local problems. While Social Security proved to be a potent election-year issue for Democrats around the country and no doubt hurt Denton, also damaging, if not more so, were his eccentric personality and lack of fundamental, grassroots-oriented political skills.

Hunt's 1986 gubernatorial victory changed Alabama politics. In subsequent campaigns, the state's news media would no longer concentrate its attention on the Democratic nominating process as if it were the final step in electing a gov-ernor and other officials. Moreover, now that it had a demonstrated chance for victory, the Republican party found it easier to recruit potentially successful candidates. Hunt added to this pool by making hundreds of board and commit-tee appointments around the state and filling vacancies in various elected offices. And these candidates, now that they were considered serious challengers, found it easier to obtain the financial and other resources needed to conduct modern campaigns.

Hunt began his 1990 reelection campaign immediately upon taking office. He made numerous public appearances, took considerable credit for various ac-complishments, and promoted himself extensively. Substantively, the accom-plishments of the Hunt administration were limited, but that situation was not surprising given the small number of Republicans in the legislature. Laws were passed to curb crime and civil liability lawsuit damages, and Hunt also claimed considerable success in promoting the state's economic development. Alto-gether, the apparent Republican momentum in the state in conjunction with the governor's high level of popularity suggested that he would be difficult to beat.[5]

Despite Hunt's strong position, five major candidates entered the 1990 contest for the Democratic gubernatorial nomination. These were state senator Charles Bishop; U.S. representative Ronnie Flippo; Paul Hubbert, executive secretary of the Alabama Education Association (AEA); former governor James, and Don Siegelman, who was then the state's attorney general. During the primary campaign, the Democratic candidates focused on the need for better leadership, economic development, environmental protection, tax reform, and better public schools. Most notably, in contrast to previous elections and reflecting the changed partisan situation in the state, conflict among the Democratic candidates during the campaign was muted.

Hubbert, who in twenty years had molded AEA into one of the state's most formidable political organizations, used support from its statewide network and other Democratic base groups to finish atop the primary with 31.5 percent of the more than 740,000 votes cast, about seven percentage points ahead of Siegelman. In the runoff, Hubbert emphasized the need for leadership and his record of accomplishment as leader of the AEA. Siegelman, who based much of his campaign on the need for a state lottery and his desire to raise taxes on rich timber barons as a way to fund the public schools, followed the fairly typical runner-up strategy of attacking the pacesetter.

Specifically, Siegelman labeled Hubbert as the candidate of special interests and raised questions about his opponent's real commitment to better schools, as opposed to better conditions for schoolteachers. Siegelman also indirectly raised the issue of race by highlighting Hubbert's close ties to Joe Reed.[6] Reed, Hubbert's second-in-command at AEA, is the authoritarian and highly effective head of the Alabama Democratic Conference, the state's oldest black political organization, whose election year endorsements have been much coveted over the years by Democratic candidates who pay substantial sums to get out the black vote.

Although Siegelman tried to capitalize on Reed's controversial image, Hubbert won the runoff with 53.6 percent of the more than 577,000 votes cast. Hunt, meanwhile, had coasted to the GOP nomination in a three-candidate primary, winning nearly 120,000 of more than 125,000 votes cast.

Hubbert's victory was a remarkable achievement. At the beginning of the campaign, because of his association with the AEA, unions, and past party misfortunes, he was seen as one of the more liberal of the Democratic candidates. This meant that he would likely do well among traditional Democratic groups. And to reinforce his base, Hubbert continued to support some liberal social welfare initiatives. During the campaign, he made such statements as this: "We need better schools, we need to have infant mortality addressed, we need to have rural hospitals reopened and primary health care facilities provided. We all want better jobs for our young people. There's so many things we can agree on, we need to move forward on those fronts."[7] He argued for improved environmental protection and attacked the low taxes paid by large timber companies.

To broaden his appeal to less partisan voters, whose support was necessary for statewide victory in the general election, Hubbert focused on issues that made it difficult to label him a liberal. He pointedly echoed catch phrases Wallace had made famous, saying, "I'll stand up for Alabama." He accused the state government of coddling inmates in air-conditioned prisons, and called for a return to work camps where prisoners would "earn their keep." He took an ambiguous but essentially pro-life position on abortion. He opposed additional taxes and instead urged more efficient government programs. "People want no new taxes until they are convinced we are spending taxes wisely," Hubbert argued. He called for reform in the state's welfare programs, advocating workfare instead of welfare.[8] Additionally, Hubbert addressed the "union" issue directly and in doing so reinforced his own image as a competent leader. He said that as head of the AEA, his job was to look out for teachers, and he had done that job well. As governor, he said he would have a different job, different constituencies, and look out for the public as a whole.

Finally, Hubbert's own conduct during the campaign was also directed at addressing his liberal image. He continually stressed his connection to the average Alabamian. He adopted a 4-H motto ("Take the best and make it better") as his campaign theme. He talked about his rural background, his religious convictions, and the financial difficulties he had experienced as a beginning teacher.

Hubbert's successful campaign to position himself near the political center won him the Democratic nomination and meant he would be a difficult opponent for Governor Hunt. Adding to Hubbert's strength was the fact that he entered the fall campaign as the head of a united Democratic party. Fulfilling a pre-election agreement with his runoff opponent, Siegelman traveled to Hubbert's headquarters on runoff night and pledged his support. Flanked by Siegelman and surrounded by a number of other Democratic officials, Hubbert said, "For those misguided souls who think the Democrats are not together, they've got another thought coming in November."[9]

Still, as a personally popular incumbent officeholder, Hunt held the advantage as the fall campaign began. To overcome this deficit, the Hubbert campaign set out to tarnish Hunt's image and thus persuade voters it was time for a change. One way Hubbert did this was to release his past tax records and challenged Hunt to do the same, an action designed to raise questions about Hunt's personal finances. During and following his unsuccessful 1978 gubernatorial campaign, Hunt had gone deeply into debt, almost to the point of bankruptcy. Following his unexpected election in 1986, his debts were largely paid off. Democrats thought there were possible ethical and legal issues in these activities. But Hunt's popular image, particularly the view that the Primitive Baptist preacher, farmer, and family man was personally honest, meant that frontal attacks on the governor were unlikely to have credibility.

Thus the Hubbert campaign was greatly assisted by a Montgomery *Advertiser* story that documented what had happened to Hunt's debts after the 1986 election. Based on a reading of Ethics Commission forms, the story said, Hunt had owed at least $700,000 in April 1986. By April 1989, Hunt's debts had been reduced to less than $100,000. Hunt called the newspaper story "totally inaccurate" and said he would not release information about his personal taxes. "You wouldn't want to disclose yours, so I have no intention of disclosing mine."[10]

Unfortunately for Hubbert, his good luck did not last. In what turned out to be the most important event of the campaign, the *Advertiser* soon retracted its story. Mathematical errors and an incorrect reading of documents made the story inaccurate, the *Advertiser* said. Other stories about Hunt's debts would appear later in the campaign,[11] but the issue would never become very important. The *Advertiser*'s retraction made the cost of pursuing it too high. As a result, questions about Hunt's character never took center stage.

While touting his record, Hunt milked further political benefits from the official stops and ceremonial trips that came with being governor. But he also became an aggressor, something he had shied away from during the Democrats' Baxley-Graddick brawl of 1986. For example, one Hunt campaign ad sought to tap voter resentment of various national Democratic bogeymen, citing the AEA's endorsement of Walter Mondale in Alabama's 1984 presidential primary, its coendorsement of Jesse Jackson and Albert Gore in the 1988 primary, and its support for eventual nominee Michael Dukakis that year. Based on the company Hubbert keeps, the ad said, he "might be a good governor of Massachusetts." By contrast, the ad went on, "Governor Hunt's for Alabama. He's on our side."[12]

Another part of the Republican campaign involved labeling Hubbert as a special interest politician. The GOP pointed out Hubbert's ties to groups such as the trial lawyers and the toxic waste and gambling industries. The Hunt campaign particularly stressed the ties between Hubbert and Reed's ADC, running two television ads showing a cigar-smoking Hubbert seated in the back seat of a car with Reed. In response, Hubbert said Hunt was running a "campaign that's just got racism dripping from it. . . . If sitting beside a black man as two of his ads have portrayed me doing disqualifies me from being governor of Alabama, I don't want to be governor," Hubbert said. "Alabama has seen enough of that and it's time for that sort of foolishness to end."[13]

Still another facet of Hunt's campaign involved challenging Hubbert in what should have been the Democrat's strong point, education. Hubbert was not really interested in better schools, just more for teachers, Hunt argued. "The problem with education has been some of the trenchmen in the education community," he said. "They have created the problem. They have stuck their heads in the sand and said education is as it should be. . . . Anybody who has been on the scene for the last 20 to 25 years, and if there haven't been any improvements made, they are probably part of the problem." The Democrats replied with a television spot that said Hunt was misleading voters. "Guy Hunt saying Paul Hubbert is opposed to quality education is like saying Colonel Sanders is opposed to chicken. It's just not true."[14]

Finally, in the closing days of the campaign, in a move reminiscent of George Bush's hard-hitting 1988 presidential campaign against Dukakis, a Hunt television commercial told voters that Hubbert was a card-carrying member of the National Education Association. This organization, and by extension Hubbert, favored, according to the Hunt campaign, "letting homosexual teachers stay in the classroom." Voters were told that the NEA also opposed drug testing of drivers and an English language–only constitutional amendment.[15]

Altogether, the net effect of the campaign was a draw. The race had started with Hunt slightly ahead, and it ended the same way. When the votes were counted, Hunt won a second term by a close 52.1 to 47.9 percent margin.[16]

Hunt's victory proved to be quite personal. No other Republicans running for state office were elected. GOP casualties included incumbent secretary of state Perry Hand, whom Hunt had appointed to fill a vacancy resulting from Democrat Glen Browder's having won a special election for the U.S. House. Nor did the overall partisan balance in the state legislature change. Rather, the Democrats gained one seat in the state senate and the GOP added one in the house. Overall, the GOP's legislative numbers were slightly larger than four years before. In the house, it now held 23 of the 105 seats, compared with the 16 it had after the 1986 election. Over the same period, its number of seats in the 35-member senate had gone from 5 to 7.

At the federal level in 1990, there was no change in the partisan makeup of Alabama's congressional delegation. Incumbent Democrat Howell Heflin coasted to a third U.S. Senate term, taking 60.5 percent of the vote against Bill

Cabaniss, a businessman and state senator from the state's wealthiest city, the Birmingham suburb of Mountain Brook. Heflin characterized his record as progressive and conservative, and there was truth in that. For part of his tenure in the Senate, he had been more supportive of the Reagan administration than any other Democrat. He had incurred the wrath of environmental groups for blocking for years the expansion of an Alabama wilderness area after loggers complained the expansion would cost thousands of jobs. At the same time, he had voted against Reagan's nomination of Judge Robert Bork for a Supreme Court seat. Cabaniss had a hard time finding holes in Heflin's massive reelection armor. He tried vigorously attacking the incumbent's environmental record and vote against Judge Bork, and claimed Heflin's support of a 1990 civil rights measure would force employers into adopting minority-hiring quotas to prevent litigation. But as those attacks fell largely on deaf voter ears, Heflin, who was not exactly poor himself, was poking fun at the button-down Cabaniss's upper-class background, likening him to those "Gucci-clothed, Mercedes-driving, Perrier-drinking, Aspen-skiing, rich-society Republicans who don't eat broccoli." He was also outspending Cabaniss by $3.4 million to $1.8 million.[17]

One important change in the 1980s resulted from various Voting Rights Act–related court cases that mandated the replacement of at-large voting arrangements with single-member districts. The new districts produced dramatic jumps in the numbers of African Americans elected as state legislators, city council members, county commissioners, and county school board members. When the 1990s arrived, the state had more than 700 black elected officials, one of the nation's highest totals, and the pressure was on to fashion a district that could elect a black congressman.[18] In 1992 such a district emerged—west central Alabama's Seventh—in a federal court-approved redistricting plan. Incumbent Democrat Claude Harris retired, and Earl Hilliard, a state senator from Birmingham and a close ally of the city's black mayor, Richard Arrington, won the Democratic nomination and easily bested a GOP challenger to become Alabama's first African American congressman since Reconstruction.

But setting the table for Hilliard's historic victory proved costly to Democrats because it made two other congressional districts more Republican-friendly. The redrawn Seventh District took in chunks of black voters from southeast Alabama's Second District, which had been held, sometimes precariously, by Republican Bill Dickinson since 1964. The new Seventh took an even larger number of black voters from the Birmingham area's Sixth District, which had been held more comfortably for ten years by Democrat Ben Erdreich. As a result, the Second's voting-age population went from 27 percent to 24 percent black, and the Sixth's went from 31 percent to 9 percent.

When Dickinson retired, Enterprise businessman Terry Everett kept the Second District seat in Republican hands by defeating state treasurer George C. Wallace, Jr., the son and namesake of the state's only four-term governor, by a narrow margin, 49.5 percent to 47.9 percent. In the redrawn Sixth, after a tough and negative campaign, Democrat Erdreich was unseated by suburban lawyer Spencer Bachus, a former state legislator, state school board member, and Alabama GOP chairman. Bachus won 52.3 percent of the vote to Erdreich's 45.0 percent. The chair of the state Democratic party, Bill Blount, explained the outcome of the congressional elections by saying: "This whole thing came to pass because a Republican three-judge panel drew the districts to favor Republicans."[19]

The 1992 U.S. Senate race was even less of a contest than Senator Heflin's romp in 1990. Democratic senator Shelby, whose votes tended to please conservatives much more than the loyalists in his own party, easily defeated an underfunded and little-known Republican businessman, Richard Sellers, with 64.8 percent of the vote. Many Republicans, pointing to Shelby's conservative voting record in Congress, were not dismayed by his election; Shelby had voted against his party's majority 55 percent of the time, more than any other Democratic senator.[20]

In 1992 Alabama saw its closest presidential contest since 1980. President George Bush, who had walloped Democrat Michael Dukakis with nearly 59.2 percent of the vote in 1988, won the state again by a margin of 47.6 percent to 40.9 percent over Bill Clinton, with 10.8 percent going to Ross Perot. The closeness of Bush's Alabama margin was a hint of his vulnerability elsewhere, and the state had actually looked winnable for Clinton for a time during the fall. The Democratic standard bearer did not visit the state, but Bush made two stops to keep it in his column.[21]

While the 1992 campaign was running its course, some unprecedented events were unfolding in Montgomery, all of which would play roles in the historic election outcomes of 1994. One of them was a criminal investigation of Governor Hunt. Soon after his second inaugural, questions about Hunt's personal finances had returned to the news, and in September 1991, the state ethics commission ruled that Hunt's use of state airplanes for trips on which he was paid for preaching at Primitive Baptist churches may have violated the law. Attorney general Jimmy Evans, a Democrat, began to investigate, and shortly before the end of 1992 a Montgomery County grand jury indicted the governor for, among other things, taking $200,000 from his 1987 inaugural fund for his personal use. In April 1993, after a trial of more than two weeks, a state court jury in Montgomery convicted Hunt of misusing the inaugural funds. Hunt thus became the first governor in Alabama history to be removed from office by a criminal conviction.[22] He was succeeded by Democratic lieutenant governor James E. (Jim) Folsom, Jr., the son of one of Alabama's most colorful governors, James E. (Big Jim) Folsom, a hard-drinking, backslapping hulk who freely admitted he had stolen money—but to help the people—while in office.[23]

The 1994 Elections: GOP Earthquake

In taking office, the younger Folsom, whose reserved personality rendered him the opposite of the garrulous father he resembled, became the front-runner to be elected to the post outright in 1994. But the circumstances of Hunt's unprecedented removal—following his prosecution by a Democratic attorney general—gave Republicans a potent political issue. "I think the Republican party can thank Jimmy Evans for showing what a one-party system can do to the people," Hunt said a few years later. "Such arrogance, and people said, 'This is not what we want.' "[24]

Other issues, involving education reform, industrial development, and Folsom's own ethics would also play a significant role in the election. In March 1993, Montgomery County circuit judge Gene Reese ruled that Alabama's public school system was unconstitutional since it did not provide all the state's schoolchildren with an adequate education. He later ordered the state to develop a plan to remedy the situation. Upon taking office, Folsom sought to draw up a remedy. Opposed by an unusual alliance of Paul Hubbert's AEA, the militantly anti-tax Alabama Farmers Federation, and conservative Christian groups, the plan failed in the legislature in 1994, but even as it did, Folsom claimed leadership and commitment to education reform.

In September 1993, Folsom added an economic development feather to his election cap. The automaker Mercedes-Benz announced it would build a three-hundred-million-dollar plant in Tuscaloosa County. Nationally, this was the industrial catch of the year, and Folsom had worked hard to get it. Though there was some grumbling as to whether he had given away the store in the process, he touted it often during his election bid.

Even before he was propelled into the governor's chair by Hunt's ethics conviction, Folsom had been planning to run for governor in 1994. So, too, had the 1990 Democratic nominee, Paul Hubbert. Everyone anticipated the Folsom-Hubbert Democratic primary showdown would be a war, but Folsom's education reform and Mercedes recruitment efforts made him a difficult target. Furthermore, Hubbert could not count on as much black support as in 1990, partly because shortly after taking office Folsom had ordered the state to drop its appeal of a court ruling that said the Confederate battle flag did not belong above the state capitol dome, where it had flown since 1963.

Black leaders and black lawmakers had been calling for the flag's removal for years, saying it recalled Alabama's Jim Crow days and had been a symbol of racist defiance toward federal civil rights initiatives. Even some leading Republicans, such as Montgomery mayor Emory Folmar, said the flag was hurting the state's image and harming its economic development efforts. Most whites said the flag should remain where it was because it was a worthy symbol of a worthy heritage and that they had given enough ground to blacks already. In January 1993, following a suit by African American legislators, a state judge ruled that an 1896 state law prohibited any flag but the United States and state banners to fly above the dome. Hunt had appealed the ruling, but, shortly after succeeding Hunt, Folsom dropped the appeal, saying the flag issue was hurting the state.[25]

The one potentially useful area open to Hubbert was to raise questions about Folsom's character. There was much to discuss. Since he had taken office, Folsom's name, or those of his relatives or political associates, had been linked to a number of dubious dealings. These included allegations about government-funded jobs held by Folsom's wife and mother; free work and materials for the improvement of his home; a purported gift of $25,000 in cash from a state senator in return for a choice committee assignment, and help by others in paying his personal bills.[26] Hubbert sought to exploit these problems, but faced difficulties because he, too, was a Montgomery insider with a reputation of being an effective operator in the shadowy world of the state's legislative and executive politics.

On primary day, Folsom won 54.0 percent of the more than 703,000 votes cast. He garnered sizable black support in some areas, including Jefferson County, where he had the endorsement of Birmingham mayor Arrington's powerful political machine. On primary night, he linked his own accomplishments with a campaign theme song made famous by his father, telling the state's voters, " 'Y'all Come,' come home to a state that is first in economic development, come home to a state with a first-class education system for all of its children."[27]

By 1994, despite feeling dispirited in the immediate aftermath of Hunt's removal from office, the GOP did not lack for candidates who wanted to topple Folsom. The three leading contenders for the nomination were former governor James, who joined the Republican party when he declared his intention to run; Montgomery businessman Winton Blount; and Mobile state senator Ann Bedsole. James, who had served one gubernatorial term (1979–1983) as a Democrat,[28] entered the Republican primary on the last day of qualifying and did so in person at state GOP headquarters as former governor Hunt and other Republican notables looked on approvingly. No such approval came from his competitors, particularly Bedsole and Blount, who would criticize James's lack of consistent party credentials as well as his record as governor.

Blount, whose wealthy businessman father had been postmaster general under President Nixon, mounted a well-financed campaign, focusing on the need for change in Alabama politics and his status as a political outsider. Bedsole, the first woman elected to the Alabama senate, also advocated political reform and a new direction in Alabama politics. "I want to change the way things have been done," she said. "I don't want to see our state government just rock along as it has. Fob James is saying, 'Elect me and I'll do it again.' I'm saying elect me and I'll make sure we don't do it like we have in the past."[29]

James, meanwhile, stressed the need for honest government, tougher stances against crime and a steadfast opposition to any tax increases, particularly for education reform. "We've got enough money to do everything that government should do," he said shortly after qualifying.[30] There wasn't a lot different in the James message from what the other candidates were saying. Despite his wealth, he was rather down-home, sporting a comb-over that barely concealed his bald spot, seeming anything but suited to designer clothes and speaking in a style much more redneck and proletarian than silk stocking. That style, along with his higher name recognition and campaign organization, helped him easily lead the GOP gubernatorial primary with 39.5 percent of the 212,471 votes cast.

That style also was just one of the contrasts between himself and Ann Bedsole, whose 25.6 percent of the vote was just enough to edge Blount (24.4 percent) for the runoff spot with James. Candid and well-heeled, Bedsole was pro-choice on abortion. That made her anathema to Christian conservatives, who already were moving toward James because of his opposition to gambling and abortion and his support for school prayer. To the added dismay of many conservative Republicans, Bedsole had also voted for the Folsom education reform plan, to which James was resolutely opposed. Not surprisingly, the runoff was no contest, as James took 62.4 percent of the 208,571 votes cast.

In the general election Folsom seemed to have an edge in money, substantial business support, and such assets as Mercedes and his efforts at education reform. Folsom continued to stress those assets and to remind voters why James had been unpopular during his gubernatorial term as a Democrat, although some of the things he faulted James for were due to tough economic times beyond a governor's control. "Fob James failed to balance the state budget three out of four times," one Folsom TV spot said. "James mismanaged state prisons so badly, 277 hardened criminals were set free on one day. Folsom's new law locks violent juveniles behind bars. Under James, unemployment was the highest in the nation. Under Folsom, a record number of Alabamians have jobs."[31]

Meanwhile, James generally kept to the script that had put him through the primary, but in the final weeks he began focusing on the character issue. He had plenty to work with, and a few weeks before the November election, he got another issue when newspapers wrote about Folsom's use of state gambling magnate Milton McGregor's plane to take a family vacation in the Caribbean in the spring of 1993, not long before Governor Hunt's own fall from grace on an ethics charge. About twenty days after his return, Folsom had asked legislators to support a McGregor-backed bill to allow slot machines and other electronic gambling devices at the magnate's two tracks. A James campaign ad said that Folsom had "a checkered past" and "faces possible indictment." Another said that "Alabama has a lot of things to be proud of, but state government is not one of them. Fob James: An honest government for a change."[32]

The ethics issue was clearly worrying the Folsom brain trust, a campaign insider said after the election. Even before the news broke about the airplane trip, the campaign's pollster told Folsom and other chief strategists that the candidacy was already bleeding because of ethics-related matters. Another big disclosure, the pollster warned, could cause a hemorrhage.

A few days before the election, new allegations surfaced about Folsom's links to a defunct and controversial state agency set up as a funnel for legislators' political pork appropriations. A bookkeeper said in an affidavit that about $200,000 in tax money from the agency had been set aside for Folsom, an accusation he heatedly denied. Folsom's legal adviser and campaign treasurer, John Tanner, also had received money from the agency, which originally bore the somewhat laughable name, the Center for Quality and Productivity. James said the center would have closed sooner had Folsom taken action against it, adding that the governor's race had "boiled down to an issue of corruption and cover-up."[33]

The 1994 Alabama election was, of course, contested against the backdrop of a national campaign that brought an end to forty years of Democratic control of the U.S. House. For much of the fall, it seemed that the train might bypass Alabama. Weeks before the election, state Democratic party executive director Al LaPierre suggested that the GOP "might fold up their tent and move."[34]

It was not to be. A strong voter turnout for change, coupled with a dropoff among likely Democratic supporters, helped James win the governorship by the extremely narrow margin of 50.3 percent to 49.4 percent. For the year, James had spent about $3.2 million to Folsom's nearly $8.2 million. In winning his nearly 605,000 general election votes, he carried just twenty-three of Alabama's sixty-seven counties. But many of them were vote-rich and populous. Furthermore, through local elections and party switches, some had become GOP hot spots. For example, James not only carried the state's most populous county of Jefferson (Birmingham), but also Shelby, its fast-growing, solidly GOP neighbor to the south, and St. Clair, Jefferson's neighbor to the east. And as James was winning St. Clair, Republicans took total control of the county's five-member commission. James also won Montgomery County and bordering Elmore and Autauga, and Madison County, home to high-tech Huntsville, and bordering Limestone and Morgan counties.

The James victory was part of a larger state political earthquake in which Republicans won seven statewide offices, more than twice the number they had won previously for the entire century. Republican candidates unexpectedly won the largely invisible contests for state auditor and agriculture commissioner, and even a state appeals civil court seat in which the GOP contender had raised only a hundred dollars.

After a nearly year-long legal battle over disputed general election absentee ballots, Republican Perry Hooper, Sr., gained the Alabama chief justice's post over Democratic incumbent Sonny Hornsby. It was generally assumed that if the disputed ballots had been counted, they would have given Hornsby a winning margin. Both a Democratic circuit judge, Gene Reese, and the majority-Democratic supreme court had basically ruled the votes were lawfully cast. A federal judge ruled otherwise, but the Democratic state court rulings gave Republicans another issue—"the Democrats are trying to steal the election"— which they would use again in another supreme court race in 1996. "A lot of people turned out in reaction to the absentee [issue]," said former lieutenant governor Jere Beasley, one of the state's best-known plaintiffs' lawyers and a longtime Democrat. "Democrats took a terrible blow in that fight."[35]

The most notable down-ticket victory for the GOP in 1994 was state attorney general Evans's lopsided defeat at the hands of Jeff Sessions. Sessions was a former U.S. attorney whose nomination for a federal district judgeship had been derailed in 1986 because of allegations that he had made racially insensitive remarks and because of a vote-fraud probe his office had prosecuted in some of the same parts of the state where many disputed absentee ballots were cast in the Hooper-Hornsby race. By and large, the attorney general's race was low key, but as the election drew near, Evans stepped up his attacks on Sessions, questioning his opponent's record as a U.S. attorney and calling him "a paper-pushing federal bureaucrat" with few if any courtroom skills. In turn Sessions suggested Evans "was part of the political establishment" that needed new faces.

But his aces in the hole were the ethics controversies that swirled around Folsom, particularly those that came late in the campaign, and voter sentiment that Evans had not been as vigorous in going after Folsom as he had been toward Hunt.[36] In the election, Sessions won with 56.9 percent—nearly 667,000 votes, a total larger than any other statewide GOP candidate.

Boosted by anti-incumbent sentiment plus a redistricting scheme designed to give blacks enough house and senate seats to mirror their 25 percent share of the state's population, Republicans gained eleven seats in the state legislature. In doing so, they knocked off several prominent Democrats, including one of the house's most powerful members, ways and means chairman Taylor Harper of Grand Bay. Another casualty was onetime house speaker pro tem Jim Campbell of Anniston. In 1990, when he had won a fourth house term, Campbell's district had been about 60 percent white and 40 percent black. In 1994 his district had become nearly 90 percent white, and votes that had gone to him in the past had become part of a black-majority district. In other parts of the state, some veteran Democrats decided not to run for reelection when they saw themselves in redrawn districts more likely to vote Republican or for an African American primary opponent.[37]

The day after Folsom, Evans, Campbell, and other Democrats were jolted by defeat, Alabama's junior U.S. senator Richard Shelby added his own aftershock to the earthquake by announcing he was switching to the GOP. "I thought there was room in the Democratic Party for a conservative Southern Democrat such as myself. . . . But I can tell you there is not," Shelby said. His move was not surprising to many of his fellow Democrats. Over the years he had annoyed them by casting conservative votes while soaking up funds and votes from traditional Democratic constituencies. "He was a Republican in everything but name," said Bobbie McDowell, a Jefferson County legislator. "I think it's slapping thousands and thousands and thousands of Alabamians in the face who voted for him as a Democrat," declared state party chair Bill Blount.[38]

As the months passed, there were more aftershocks. Besides receiving a warm vocal endorsement from George Wallace, Jr., the GOP welcomed into its ranks two more state legislators, the president of the public service commission, a criminal appeals judge, and a scattering of local officials including, on one day, ten judges from the state's most populous county, Jefferson. The judges, who hailed from Republican-leaning Birmingham suburbs, promised that the way they handled cases and conducted themselves on the bench would not change, but they obviously felt it was politically advantageous to run under the Republican label. A few months earlier, they had received letters from the county GOP's candidate recruitment chairman urging them to switch and suggesting that those who didn't join soon could face political consequences.[39]

While the anti-incumbent, anti–Bill Clinton sentiment that swept the nation can help explain some of the GOP's Alabama gains, it was not necessarily the dominant factor. As Democrats pointed out repeatedly afterward, their major losers were tainted. Folsom, as already mentioned, was under an ethical cloud that would not lift until years later when state and federal investigations cleared him of any wrongdoing. Attorney General Evans also paid dearly for the well-publicized financial mess that he had made of his office, and his standing in voters' eyes only worsened when Folsom gave him funds to help straighten out the mess.[40]

Two other Democratic losers, Agriculture Commissioner A. W. Todd and the nominee for state auditor, Charley Baker, a former administrative assistant in the auditor's office, had also drawn criticism for their conduct while on the public payroll. Todd, who was seventy-eight, had come under fire for hiring two of his grandchildren for state jobs. He also had hired Governor Folsom's mother, Jamelle, as an agricultural inspector. Baker had been hired as an administrative assistant by the outgoing auditor, Terry Ellis, who had fired him in 1993, charging that Baker and his family members had made thousands of dollars' worth of personal calls on state phones.[41] Similarly, incumbent chief justice Sonny Hornsby, along with Evans, had been criticized for secretly agreeing to a plan to add more blacks to the state's appellate courts, and Republican and probusiness types had argued vigorously for replacing Hornsby to make the supreme court less sympathetic to plaintiffs' lawyers.

Adding to the Democrats' case were the easy victories for two of their "untainted" candidates, Lieutenant Governor Don Siegelman and Secretary of State Jim Bennett. Siegelman had gotten his repeatedly stated campaign wish that his fellow Democrats and others would help him put a political stake through the heart of his underfunded and controversial Republican opponent, the former attorney general and 1986 Democratic gubernatorial contender Charlie Graddick. On election day, Siegelman was the state's top vote getter, receiving 732,285 votes, 62.3 percent of the ballots cast.[42] (Siegelman was the Democratic party's 1998 nominee opposing Governor James's reelection bid.)

In the secretary of state's race Bennett had a tighter but still clear win over Republican Vickie Gavin. Gavin was an anti-abortion and party activist making her first bid for office. Bennett was a veteran legislator whom Folsom had appointed to the secretary of state's post in 1993. Both campaigned on the need to further reform political fund-raising and the voting process, and the few issues raised by Gavin concerned some past Bennett bankruptcies and his future political ambitions. Bennett won with 53 percent of the vote. His $100,000 plus in expenditures was more than twenty times what Gavin could muster.[43]

In each of the contested statewide races except the Sessions-Evans race for attorney general, the Republicans had been outspent by their Democratic opponents. Overall, the Democrats raised almost $17 million and spent nearly $19 million. The GOP candidates raised nearly $6 million and spent about $6.5 million.[44] Despite the funding gap, the Republicans won 7 of the 15 statewide races in which they had competed against the Democrats, and their numbers reached record levels in the state legislature. They now had 31 seats in the 105-member house, and 12 in the 35-member senate. Party switches boosted their senate numbers by two and their house membership by four over the next three years.

Meanwhile, both parties made leadership changes. Mobile County Republican chairman Roger McConnell, who had helped direct GOP successes there, replaced Elbert Peters as state party chairman, arguing that the party could have done even better in 1994. On the Democratic side, party chairman Blount stepped down and was succeeded by Auburn businessman Joe Turnham. The son of a veteran Democratic legislator, Turnham hoped to give the party a new image and better prospects in 1996.

THE 1996 ELECTIONS: HIGH STAKES PARTISAN DRAMA

Overall, the 1994 Republican victories were an important advance for the GOP, but whether they would continue was the subject of considerable speculation. Events of 1995 soon added to the anticipation and increased the 1996 stakes. Two of the state's most prominent Democrats, three-term U.S. senator Howell Heflin and fifteen-term U.S. representative Tom Bevill, from north Alabama's Fourth District, both said they would retire after 1996. Then another Democratic incumbent, U.S. representative Glen Browder, created a vacancy in east central Alabama's Third District when he decided to try for Heflin's seat. In addition, another north Alabama Democratic congressman, the Fifth District's Bud Cramer, was considered vulnerable because he had barely beaten his Republican opponent in 1994.

These three open-seat federal contests enabled Alabama to play an unusually prominent role in the 1996 elections. In past presidential election years, the state had largely been ignored because of its relatively small size (nine electoral votes) and the perception that it was almost solidly Republican in presidential contests. Indeed, the state hadn't supported a Democratic presidential nominee since Jimmy Carter in 1976. But in 1996, with the competitive campaigns for the open Senate and two House seats, with Bill Clinton being strong enough nationally to go into states not recently hospitable to Democratic presidential nominees, and with GOP nominee Bob Dole having to fight to keep his base states, Alabama had its day in the presidential spotlight.

That spotlight shone on October 24 when Clinton came to Birmingham (thus making his first Alabama visit since the 1992 primary campaign) and Dole visited Montgomery. The focus of both visits was decidedly on national rather than state politics. Still, polls following the Clinton visit showed Democrats in many of the state's major races, particularly the federal ones, either ahead or as party chairman Turnham said, "in play." In the end, Dole pulled ahead, winning the state with 50.1 percent of the vote to Clinton's 43.2 percent; Ross Perot was a distant third at 6.0 percent.[45]

In the 1996 U.S. Senate race, both parties experienced multicandidate primary elections. For the Democrats, the leading candidates were Russellville state senator Roger Bedford, Congressman (and former political science professor) Glen Browder from Jacksonville, and Natalie Davis, a Birmingham Southern College political science professor, Democratic activist, and pollster. Relatively few differences emerged among them during the campaign. Bedford, however, had the best-financed effort. A virtual nonstop campaigner since he had won a state senate seat in 1982, the northwest Alabama native was legendary—and the butt of many jokes—for his eagerness to go anywhere to court any group of voters, even in nonelection years. In 1990 he ran for attorney general despite being stricken with lymph cancer. He recovered and turned his battle with cancer into an often tear-filled part of his stump speech both in 1990 and in subsequent campaigns. In 1996, Bedford had lined up the support, or at least the cosupport, of such important Democratic groups as organized labor, plaintiffs' trial lawyers, and the state's largest black political organizations. With this long-cultivated backing, Bedford led the primary and then easily defeated Browder by 61.6 percent to 38.4 percent in the runoff.

The field was more crowded on the Republican side, where seven serious candidates qualified. The front-runner from start to finish was Attorney General Jeff Sessions, and the other candidates knew they were seeking the second spot in a GOP primary runoff. A former Eagle Scout who had led an idyllic childhood in a south Alabama hamlet named Hybart, Sessions was a popular public official, and he ultimately won the nomination by defeating a former Democratic state legislator, Sid McDonald, a millionaire businessman, in the runoff. Key factors in McDonald's defeat were his own past Democratic candidacies and his more recent contributions to Democratic candidates such as Folsom. "The things he [McDonald] says today sound consistent with the Republican agenda, but just a few months ago, you know, he was associating with people who didn't agree with that," Sessions argued.[46]

The campaign between the backslapping, energetic Bedford and the more reserved Sessions was a no-holds-barred affair, with accusations—largely televised—flying like mud pies in a Three Stooges comedy. Overall, though, both candidates generally followed the script used by Democratic and Republican congressional candidates nationwide, and each also vowed to take "a good dose of Alabama common sense" to Washington. In keeping with the national Democratic strategy, Bedford tried to link Sessions with the unpopular U.S. House speaker, Newt Gingrich, charging that Sessions would join Gingrich and other budget-cutting extremists in the Congress, and also reminded voters of Sessions's alleged remarks that had derailed his federal judgeship nomination. Bedford also tried to protect his right flank, calling himself a conservative Democrat and staking out positions against abortion, gay rights, and gun control. "You can either go off and work for Alabama values and work on a bipartisan approach as I have done as a state senator under Democratic governors and Republican governors," Bedford said, "or you can sign up with the extremism of the Republican Party, which I think is harmful to the senior citizens and future of our children in Alabama."[47]

Sessions, in turn, called Bedford a "liberal" and sought to link him to such national Democratic bogeymen as Clinton and Ted Kennedy and to such prominent state Democrats as Mayor Arrington of Birmingham and Joe Reed. He also vowed to trim back government, overhaul the welfare state, and push for the return of prayer to public schools. He added that he would do nothing to hurt entitlement programs like Medicare. "We're not going to gut those programs, but protect them for senior citizens."[48]

Despite all the candidates' national issue–linked rhetoric, the Senate campaign may have turned on a much more localized issue. In the campaign's final weeks, it was revealed that Bedford had used his state senatorial position to obtain a grant to run a water line to some south Alabama property that he and others were using as a hunting lodge.[49] When his staff got word that the Sessions campaign was looking into the matter, Bedford told them it wouldn't be damaging. When the news broke, he dropped fifteen points in his own poll. "That didn't pass the smell test," a supporter said later. Bedford had a hard time answering the water-line charge and focusing voter attention on other issues. This happened partly because Sessions continued his practice of largely avoiding joint appearances with any of his opponents. The general election campaign's only debate occurred, without benefit of statewide television coverage, in the middle of a Friday afternoon about a month before election day.

The campaigns in the state's competitive congressional races, for the Third, Fourth, and Fifth Districts, were near carbon copies of the U.S. Senate contest. Each involved a heavy emphasis on who better represented Alabama values. Each also involved claims and denials about who was most closely linked to national figures like Kennedy and Gingrich. What was most notable about these campaigns as well as the Bedford-Sessions race was the large amount of money spent and the involvement of parties, party committees and independent groups.[50] In the Senate race, Bedford and Sessions raised more than $7 million and spent most of it, with Sessions's share of the spending about $800,000 more than Bedford's. During the last two weeks of October, Sessions raised slightly more than $1 million, compared to Bedford's $274,000.

In the end, 1996 proved to be a very good year for Republicans in Alabama. Not only did Dole carry the state, but Sessions also won by a fairly comfortable margin of 51.9 percent to 45.7 percent.[51] In the two open congressional seat contests, the Republican candidates (Robert Aderholt in the Fourth and Bob Riley in the Third) won narrow victories. Aderholt, who received 50.0 percent of the vote, won despite being outspent by Democrat Bob Wilson, who received 48.3 percent of the vote. Riley, meanwhile, narrowly outspent Democrat Ted Little and won with 50.9 percent of the vote to Little's 46.9 percent.

In the Fifth District, incumbent Bud Cramer was the only Democratic bright spot, winning with a surprising 55.7 percent of the vote over Wayne Parker, the son-in-law of House Ways and Means chairman Bill Archer, a Texas Republican. Parker had nearly toppled Cramer in 1994, but the incumbent, a former Madison County district attorney who raised a little more money than his GOP challenger, no doubt helped himself by taking the positions of the "Blue Dog" coalition, a small group of conservative House Democrats.

While savoring its federal victories, the GOP also reveled in its substantial gains at the state and local level. Its biggest prize came in the roughest statewide campaign, the battle for the Place 1 seat on the Alabama supreme court. The race paired one-term incumbent Democrat Kenneth Ingram and GOP challenger Harold See, a University of Alabama law professor who had narrowly missed defeating another Democratic associate justice in 1994. The aggressive nature of the campaign raised considerable controversy. Ads portrayed See as a skunk, a Chicago outsider bent on taking away the right to trial by jury, and morally unsuitable for the high court because of past marital problems. Many thought that this type of name-calling was inappropriate for a judicial election. Much of the criticism was directed at Ingram, who ended up losing to See by a 52.8 percent to 47.2 percent margin. After the election, several unsuccessful Democratic candidates remarked that the anti-See ads may have cost them dearly in their own elections.[52] Overall, the Ingram-See race consumed more than $4.3 million in either candidate-raised cash or donated services, according to the candidates' own disclosure forms. The total was more than four times what Hooper and Hornsby had spent in the heated race for chief justice just two years earlier, and it did not include hundreds of thousands of dollars that other groups spent separately on behalf of either Ingram or See.

Not surprisingly, the mid-1990s GOP breakthrough caused more state and local Democrats to jump the fence. In Autauga County north of Montgomery, where Republicans took control of the county commission in the general election, the county's district attorney, state representative, sheriff, and coroner turned to the GOP in the ensuing months. During the same period, Bradley Byrne of Mobile, a lifelong Democrat who had been elected to the state board of education in 1994, made the switch, giving the GOP a five-to-four edge on the school board. Byrne's switch had been preceded by that of another Democratic board member, Dutch Higginbotham, and was followed by Secretary of State Jim Bennett's decision to join the GOP.

CONTINUED COMPETITIVENESS OR ONE-PARTY REPUBLICANISM?

Overall, the results of recent elections show that a high degree of party competition has developed in Alabama in the 1990s. Both political parties have won recent statewide elections. Many of these contests, particularly those for governor, have been quite close. Republicans have made important gains in down-ticket state offices and in the state legislature. Still, Democrats continue to hold a strong majority in the legislature. Similarly, while there is no roster of county government officials by party, an examination of election results indicates that Democrats still predominate, though the number of Republicans is increasing.

The close partisan division currently found in Alabama politics is reflected in the distribution of party identification among the state's citizens. Since the mid-1980s, the exact balance of Democrats and Republicans has shifted several times. Generally, however, there has been roughly an equal number of Democratic and Republican party identifiers among Alabamians. In 1996, for example, 34 percent identified as Republicans and 36 percent as Democrats. A number of Alabamians do not identify with either party. In 1996 independent status was claimed by 29 percent.[53]

The current competitiveness of Alabama's politics is also indicated by the images which the state's citizens have of the two parties. When asked which party would do "the best job" in different issue areas, Alabamians, by a 60 to

20 percent margin, believe that Democrats are most likely to care for the have-nots of society. Likewise, by a 53 to 29 percent margin citizens say Democrats are more likely to protect the environment. In contrast, the Republican party is seen as the more likely to hold down taxes (34 percent Democrat, 47 percent Republican), maintain traditional values (31 percent Democrat, 45 percent Republican), fight crime (31 percent Democrat, 47 percent Republican), and maintain a strong defense (27 percent Democrat, 56 percent Republican). On other important issues, such as improving education (45 percent Democrat and 38 percent Republican) and economic prosperity (33 percent Democrat and 45 percent Republican), neither party is seen to have an advantage.

On a more general note, Democrats are viewed as the party most likely to attend to the needs of the poor (66 to 20 percent), blacks (62 to 19 percent), and women (56 to 23 percent). The GOP is perceived as the party of the upper class (70 to 18 percent). Perhaps most important, Alabamians are divided on which party is most likely to look out for the interests of the middle class (44 percent Democrat, 38 percent Republican) or "people like you" (43 percent Democrat, 35 percent Republican).[54]

Several forces have contributed to the current competitiveness of Alabama's partisan politics.[55] Included among these are the nonpolitical demographic and economic changes experienced by the state.[56] As the state's population has become whiter, more urban and suburban, and more middle class in terms of education and income levels, so too has it become more Republican.

Also important to the development of party competition has been the manner in which the state's politics has been conducted. In particular, Democratic errors such as the Baxley-Graddick disaster have been an important source of Republican growth. "It has been the Democrats' folly and not necessarily the Republican vision that got us to this point," said former state GOP executive director Marty Connors. Similarly, longtime Democrat Victor Poole observed, "We Democrats just have a history of pulling that pistol and shooting the big toe."[57]

The GOP's introduction and exploitation of social issues has been another source of the increase in party competition. Some, although not necessarily all, believe that the most important of these issues has been race. According to this view, Republicans, whether they like it or not, have drawn support from voters who harbor antiblack sentiments or who view the Democrats as too influenced by black political groups. The belief is illustrated by the observations of Pete Mathews, a retired legislator, former public service commissioner, and longtime Montgomery lobbyist who was elected to office as a Democrat. According to Mathews, many of those who cast their lot with Republicans "do not like black people. I don't give a [expletive] who tells me they do. I'm telling you they don't. And that's who they perceive as controlling the Democratic party and they're right."[58]

One result of this racial division is that sharp differences exist in the party identifications of black and white Alabamians. For most of the last decade, a clear plurality of white Alabama citizens have identified themselves as Republicans. During this same period, Democratic party identification among blacks has generally exceeded 80 percent. Another result of the racial division is that Republican candidates typically make little effort to gain black votes, and those who do generally fail. In the 1996 election, Sessions, whose 1986 nomination for a federal judgeship, as mentioned above, had foundered in the Senate because of accusations he was racially insensitive, never made a strong pitch for black voters. Third District winner Bob Riley did make an effort to attract black supporters, but did not receive much in return. Riley opened a headquarters in predominantly black Macon County, and even had Oklahoma's J. C. Watts, one of the then two black Republicans in the U.S. House of Representatives, campaign for him. The November election results showed, however, that Riley received only a small portion of the district's black votes.[59]

Neither party has made a concerted effort to reduce the racial polarization found in the state's politics. Indeed, recent campaigns often include actions that broaden the division. For example, shortly before the 1996 general election, Democrats circulated a flier that said a victory for Sessions would be a victory for the Ku Klux Klan. Similarly, McConnell, the state GOP chairman, who has said he wants to boost black support for and participation in the party, has been told by some of his county chairmen, especially those in rural and small-town areas, that they would pay an economic and social price for reaching out to blacks in their areas.[60] They fear that by recruiting black GOP candidates they will make some white Democrats angry and as a consequence their businesses and social status could suffer.

The connection with African Americans has not, however, been the only issue-related reason Democrats have lost their position of dominance. More generally, Democrats have, at least in the minds of some voters, become an unresponsive party of unrepresentative "special interests." Former state senator John Baker, who chaired the Democratic party from 1985 to 1990 and spent part of that time trying to reduce the control of various groups over the party's governing body, said the party's loss of strength in recent years has caused it to become "more of a coalition-based party than it was before." In 1994 and in some other years, those constituency groups have not insisted "on high standards for [those] who they nominate . . . and those nominees don't succeed in the fall," Baker said, refering to candidates who were tainted by ethical and other problems.[61]

Recently Democrats have attempted to overcome this image of being out-of-touch. In these efforts, however, Democrats were clearly playing catch-up to an agenda set by Republicans. For example, in 1996 the party tried to portray itself as one with a centrist outlook, adopting a platform with heavy doses of family values commentary and a tolerant nod towards the various viewpoints within party ranks on such hot issues as abortion. To counter the one million-plus state voter guides distributed before the election by the fast-growing Christian Coalition, the party distributed its own faith and values sheets to show how religious beliefs guided its candidates.[62]

Then during the regular legislative session in 1997, after Governor James vowed to use the National Guard if necessary to allow a state judge, Roy Moore, to continue posting the Ten Commandments in his courtroom, Democratic lawmakers—with backing from Lieutenant Governor Siegelman—proposed a state constitutional amendment that seemed straight out of the GOP playbook. The amendment would have required public school teachers to read a prayer each day, lead classes in the pledge of allegiance, and hold discussions on the links between the nation's Judeo-Christian heritage and its governing institutions. In the same legislative session, Democrats successfully pushed two measures to limit late-term abortion. To the open dismay of some Republicans, the chief sponsor of these measures was none other than Roger Bedford, who was eyeing yet another campaign. "I was a Christian long before the Democratic Party got involved in this," Bedford said the day James signed the measure into law. In another move that brought chuckles from Republicans, Siegelman said he supported fingerprinting welfare recipients.[63]

Even the state's Democratic majority on the supreme court showed signs of a different attitude toward civil liability damage suit. In May, the high court reduced to $50,000 a $2 million verdict against BMW for repainting a new sedan sold to a Birmingham doctor in a case that became a centerpiece in Alabama's tort reform debate. The doctor had sued BMW after learning the automaker had repainted the car to cover acid-rain damage. A state court jury had originally awarded him $4 million. The state supreme court had reduced that to $2 million, but the U.S. Supreme Court ruled that even that amount was "grossly excessive."[64]

Democrats also showed signs of taking the fight to the GOP. Siegelman openly questioned the fairness of James's tort reform proposals, which failed to pass the legislature. Others vowed to fund children's programs despite the governor's staunch opposition to any new taxes.[65]

For his part, James has picked up where he had left off when last governor, fighting the courts and the federal government on a number of fronts, as most Alabama governors had done since the late 1950s. Among other things, James challenged—so far unsuccessfully—Judge Reese's ruling that the state public school system was unconstitutional. He also challenged as unreasonable and too costly a federal court settlement to provide better care for the state's foster children. He also pushed an education funding plan that proved costly to some of the state's wealthier—and Republican-represented—school districts.[66] Democrats were hoping their centrist efforts would resonate with Alabama voters, but James's resolute backing of both Judge Moore's Ten Commandments and his pretrial courtroom prayers seemed to be popular.

While the current competitiveness of Alabama's electoral politics is obvious (see the Democratic party-strength trend line in Figure 8 in Chapter 1), whether the state will remain politically balanced is far from certain. Some observers believe that party competition will remain strong in Alabama. Paul Hubbert, the two-time Democratic gubernatorial candidate and one of the state's most knowledgeable political observers, has argued that "there's no question the Republican party is now as strong as the Democratic party." But Hubbert added: "I don't think the Republicans now have a lock on people's loyalty. I think they now have the opportunity to present [candidates] who will win with good campaigns." Others, like Pete Mathews, disagree, believing instead that the state is moving in a decidedly Republican direction: "We're going to be a Republican state—you can bet on that."[67]

Several characteristics of the state's current politics point to the continuation of party competition. These include the relatively even balance in Democratic and Republican identifiers, the fact that neither party can claim the allegiance of a majority of the state's population, and the mixed images of the Democratic and Republican parties. Added to these is the fact that Republicans are as capable of making electoral blunders in the future as Democrats were in the past. Other factors point in the Republican direction. These include Republican triumphs in the two most recent elections, the real possibility that Democratic-related groups will continue to promote their own narrow interests, and the continued racial political polarization in a state in which blacks make up roughly a quarter of the population.

Which of the two scenarios, continued competitiveness or one-party Republicanism, proves to be the future direction of Alabama's politics is an open question. One fact likely to be particularly important in the future is the relative ability of the parties to recruit electable candidates. In this regard, the number and quality of officeholders who switch to the Republican party in the near term will be crucial. Similarly, the number and quality of new faces recruited by each party will also be important. Recent GOP victories have given Republicans, for the first time, a respectable farm team from which to select candidates. In contrast, some Democrats are wondering where their future candidates are going to come from. Former Democratic executive director LaPierre explains that for years, "Democrats were recognizable faces voters were comfortable with. Those names are not there anymore, and there's nobody out there that they're comfortable with."[68] Finally, the relative ability of the parties to govern will be a crucial factor. Recent GOP successes have, for the first time in more than a century, made Republicans responsible for operating state government. How well they perform this role in the eyes of Alabama's voters will undoubtedly affect their party's fortunes.

9

MISSISSIPPI: FROM PARIAH TO PACESETTER?

Stephen D. Shaffer, David E. Sturrock, David A. Breaux, and Bill Minor

THE public life of Mississippi underwent striking changes during the 1990s. The Republican party finally emerged as a successful competitor for political leadership in the state, while the long-dominant Democrats showed impressive resilience in adapting to the new competitive environment. In turn, these developments and related changes have, quite improbably, established Mississippi as an innovator whose example has exerted a positive influence far beyond its borders.

In retrospect, it is now clear that the 1970s and 1980s were a period of difficult but salutary transition from the segregationist, atavistic, and violent political culture that had long stigmatized the state in the eyes of the rest of the nation. Even neighboring southerners had long found it comforting to proclaim, "Thank God for Mississippi," as the state's backwardness made their own conditions look positive by comparison. But in the 1990s Mississippi slipped quietly into the regional mainstream.

The Democrats' iron grip on the state had begun to weaken as early as the 1964 presidential election. By the 1970s Republican candidates were often competitive, and sometimes victorious, in U.S. Senate and U.S. House races, and in the 1980s the party was so effective in capitalizing on the national Democratic party's liberal image that the Magnolia State appeared to be reliably Republican in presidential contests. That in his first reelection bid, in 1984, Republican senator Thad Cochran won 60.9 percent of the vote against popular former governor William Winter illustrated the great strides the GOP had made. Meanwhile, Mississippi's Democrats had successfully adapted to the enfranchisement of African American voters (35.6 percent of the state's population in 1990) by building a biracial coalition that had elected a "New South" governor in 1979—Winter—and even in the late 1980s was delivering strong Democratic margins in statewide executive branch races, powerful domination of the state legislature, and control of every county courthouse.

The complex and interesting story of political change in Mississippi in the 1990s is best understood by first examining the 1987 gubernatorial election. Democrats had good reason to be confident. Their biracial coalition had produced comfortable majorities in three consecutive gubernatorial contests, holding both conservative and moderate Republican challengers to no more than 45 percent. Ray Mabus won the Democratic nomination on the strength of his youth (he was thirty-nine years old), leadership experience (he had been one of the architects of Governor Winter's Education Reform Act), reformer credentials (as state auditor he had investigated allegations of corruption in local government), and blue chip academic credentials (Harvard Law School). He promised that if he was elected, "Mississippi will never be last again." His Republican opponent was Tupelo businessman Jack Reed, who had strongly supported Winter's educational reforms while serving as chairman of the state board of education and who in the 1960s had offered one of the few prominent public calls for racial tolerance and moderation in the state. Both candidates agreed on the need for further educational and governmental reforms and for continued diversification of the state's economy.[1]

Mabus outspent Reed by $2.9 million to $1.8 million and was elected with 53.4 percent of the vote. Reed's 46.6 percent was the best Republican showing for governor in this century, and his conservative views on social issues like abortion and school prayer enabled him to make inroads into the state's more conservative, traditionally Democratic rural areas. Nevertheless, his association with the increasingly conservative national Republican party helped ensure a huge margin among black voters for Mabus, who carried all of the state's black majority counties.

The 1990 midterm congressional elections also provided a benchmark. The state's six incumbents all won easy reelection, despite a national trend that produced an unusually high number of defeats and close calls for incumbents. Republican U.S. senator Cochran, whose 45.1 percent plurality victory in 1978 marked the modern Mississippi GOP's first nonpresidential statewide victory, had worked to cultivate a moderate image by backing such Mississippi-friendly programs as food stamps, rural housing, and aid to black colleges. These efforts bore fruit in 1990, when he was elected to a third term without opposition. Also unopposed was the House Veterans Affairs Committee chairman, G. V. (Sonny) Montgomery, a conservative Democrat who had represented eastern Mississippi's Third District since 1966.

The state's other four Democratic House incumbents cruised to victory with 65 percent and better against lightly regarded Republican opponents. Of particular note was Mike Espy's 84.1 percent reelection romp in the Second District, centered in the Mississippi Delta. Espy, an African American with a liberal voting record, generated powerful crossover appeal to white voters by combining a handful of high-profile conservative stands—notably opposition to gun control—with aggressive efforts to aid such local interests as the burgeoning catfish industry.

THE 1991 ELECTIONS: GOP GUBERNATORIAL BREAKTHROUGH

When Mississippians turned their attention to state elections in 1991, however, they displayed a very different mood. "Incumbent" and "establishment" were labels that proved to be handicaps, not assets. The state's voters threw scares into both the incumbent governor and lieutenant governor in the Democratic primary election and turned out both in November. In addition, a blunt-talking first-time Republican candidate upset his party leadership's choice—a statewide officeholder who had recently switched parties—in the primary and went on to win the governor's office in the general election. These results were harbingers of the anti-incumbent, anti–career politician mood that was to erupt with such force in elections across the nation in 1992 and 1994.

Governor Mabus entered his reelection race with a mixed record of success. Although he had reallocated $180 million of state money to public education, his BEST (Better Education for Success Tomorrow) program had died in the legislature in 1990 when Mabus's centerpiece for its funding, a state lottery, was killed after massive opposition by the Mississippi Baptist Convention. Mabus had also tacked on a plan to tax video poker and raise some user fees with no success. Without funding in sight, lawmakers weren't about to launch a big, new program. Further challenges were posed by the 1990–1991 recession, which reduced state revenues. Mabus stood by his election pledge to avoid tax increases, maintaining, "I don't think that Joe Six Pack wants his taxes raised." This forced a number of painful budget cuts, the most notable of which denied pay raises to teachers and state employees for two straight years.

While the powerful antigaming Baptist lobby was concentrating on stopping the lottery, from a wholly unexpected direction a seemingly innocent "local" bill passed the senate, opening the door for riverboat casinos to operate out of Natchez to bolster that city's tourist economy. In the house, a few shrewd lawmakers doctored the bill to cover all counties on the Mississippi River and let the riverboats remain in port, even without engines. By then, the Mississippi riverboat casino bill had enough headway to cruise through both branches. Because it had a local option provision, lawmakers could take the heat. Left out of the riverboat bill, Gulf Coast lawmakers immediately began clamoring to get in on the same deal, resulting in a special session later in 1990, to include counties bordering the Gulf of Mexico. No one realized that they had launched what would become a bonanza floating casino industry.

Mabus encountered further political difficulties in the spring of 1991, when his veto of a 24-hour waiting period for abortions was easily overridden by the legislature. Even Mother Nature made Mabus's life difficult: his administration's decision to halt nearly all Delta flood-control projects pending completion of an environmental impact study provoked an irate response from some Delta residents when record spring rains caused the flooding of more than two million acres and two thousand buildings in the region.

Enter Democratic primary challenger Wayne Dowdy, a former congressman from the Fourth District (Jackson and southwest Mississippi), who had been defeated by Republican Trent Lott for an open U.S. Senate seat in 1988. Dowdy, a self-styled populist, had proven himself a skilled practitioner of modern-day Mississippi coalition politics by championing such issues as the extension of the Voting Rights Act, Social Security, and labor union concerns without alienating conservative voters, thereby winning four terms in a previously Republican district.

This track record, combined with a folksy, down-home demeanor, made Dowdy well positioned to build a diverse "Save Us from Mabus" coalition of rural conservatives, educators, and state employees. Dowdy's campaign, however, was poorly funded and relied heavily upon the support of family members rather than professional consultants. He compensated with intensive old-style politicking heavy on rallies and personal campaigning, which was guided by the goal of shaking hands "with everyone in Mississippi." The challenger also sought to capitalize on endorsements from such prominent Democrats as former governors Bill Waller and Bill Allain, and former gubernatorial candidates Mike Sturdivant and Maurice Dantin. By late June, a Mason-Dixon poll reported Mabus led his scrappy challenger by only four points.[2]

Befitting a race whose differences were largely stylistic rather than ideological, the content of the Mabus-Dowdy contest was frequently personal and sometimes downright petty. The flavor of the campaign was on vivid display during the contenders' stump speeches at the Neshoba County Fair in early August. Contrasting Mabus's reputation for arrogance with his own carefully cultivated workingman's image, Dowdy quipped, "The 'ruler' claims to be the only farmer in the governor's race. I guess he was president of the Future Farmers of America chapter up at Harvard." The challenger also linked Mabus's budget problems to his reputed presidential ambitions with this gibe: "When our present ruler took office, the New York *Times* and other Eastern newspapers referred to him as the Boy Wonder. Now I understand—Wonder what the boy did with that surplus. Wonder where that boy issued all those bonds." Underscoring dissatisfaction with the Mabus administration with a word play on Mabus's 1987 campaign slogan, Dowdy pledged that under his administration, "Mississippi will never be lost again. . . . The past four years have just been a disappointment for our state."[3]

Mabus responded to Dowdy's criticisms: "My Democratic primary opponent said in June in Meridian . . . Mississippi will not realistically be able to compete with California. Be ashamed, Wayne, be ashamed. Dowdy the doubter. Wayne, you stayed in Washington too long. You've given up on Mississippi." Mabus also chided Dowdy for his congressional attendance record and accused him of being a remnant of an "old guard" that placed self-interest above the interests of the state. The incumbent sought to frame the campaign in these terms: "Do we go forward or back? Do we hope or do we give up? Do we trust the people of this state to run this state or do we give it back to the powerful few?"[4]

Many black leaders found it difficult to choose between two candidates they had long considered allies. In late July, Congressman Espy aired radio commercials backing Mabus because of state gains in education, health care, and jobs, but quickly pointed out that his endorsement was "not anti-Dowdy at all. It was pro-Mabus." Three days before the primary, the influential Greenwood Voters' League, a largely black political action group in the Delta, endorsed Mabus in "a close call," because "Dowdy's record is almost as good." League president David Jordan applauded Mabus "because he's worked very closely with black people and promoted them to key positions."[5]

Mabus's five-to-one spending advantage enabled him to dominate the airwaves, and on primary night he won renomination with 50.7 percent of the vote. Dowdy received 41.2 percent and 8.1 percent went to a political novice, George (Wagon Wheel) Blair.

While the Democrats squabbled, the Republicans appeared poised to nominate forty-three-year-old state auditor Pete Johnson, a former Democrat. The grandson and nephew of two Democratic governors, Johnson appeared to take his new party's nomination for granted as he focused his summer television ads on Mabus. He faced a serious challenge in the primary, however, from Kirk Fordice, a fifty-seven-year-old construction executive from Vicksburg. Fordice, a blunt-talking conservative whose Republican activism began during the 1964 Goldwater campaign, skillfully stirred up voters' discontent with career politicians: "Let's take Petey first. I'm not a professional politician like he is. You put Petey, Rayboy, and Wayne in a sack and shake them up and dump one out—it doesn't matter who—and you've got a professional politician who sings and dances to the same tune." A Fordice TV ad displayed Mabus's and Johnson's faces side by side as a narrator asked, "What's the major difference between Ray Mabus and Pete Johnson? There isn't any. They're both career politicians." The camera then turned to Fordice, who proclaimed his backing of term limits and concluded: "If you want another slick politician, vote for Mabus or Johnson. If you want a change, vote for me."[6]

Fordice further contrasted his brand of hard-nosed conservatism with Johnson's milder approach by rejecting the possibility of further tax increases, opposing racial quotas, and questioning the work habits of state employees. Fordice was also outspoken on education issues, blasting Johnson's education proposals as "a back-door request for a tax increase." He advocated parental school choice and weeding out incompetent teachers, and asserted that "with the limited resources that we have [the state has] no business supporting eight universities."[7]

On primary night, the little-known first-time candidate stunned Mississippi's political establishment by leading Johnson 44.7 percent to 43.4 percent, with pro-life businessman Bobby Clanton winning 11.9 percent. State GOP leaders were delighted that their party's primary turnout had risen from 18,853 in 1987 to 63,561 in 1991 (an increase of 237 percent), though that total was still dwarfed by the 726,465 votes cast in the 1991 Democratic gubernatorial primary. Fordice's feisty, populist conservatism was probably a selling point among the small GOP primary electorate, where party activists enjoyed disproportionate influence. In a 1991 survey of Republican activists, 37 percent called themselves "very conservative," 48 percent were "somewhat" conservative, and only 15 percent labeled themselves as "moderate" or "liberal."[8]

Each candidate tried to seize momentum in the runoff campaign by showcasing endorsements from prominent Republicans. Johnson touted the support of 1987 GOP gubernatorial nominee Jack Reed, who called for "an inclusive, not exclusive party," and saw Johnson as better able to attract Democratic and independent votes. Meanwhile, third-place finisher Clanton praised Johnson for having the "strongest position on abortion." Fordice countered with the support of 1975 and 1979 gubernatorial nominee Gil Carmichael. Although he had long been viewed as a party moderate, Carmichael lauded Fordice as "one of the pioneers in the Republican Party in Mississippi," who had "been working in the vineyards for a long time. . . . He's earned the chance to run."[9] In the October 8 runoff, Fordice routed Johnson with 60.6 percent of the vote to his opponent's 39.4 percent.

In the general election campaign, Fordice used some of his relatively limited funds to more fully introduce himself to Mississippians. In one spot he spoke directly to his anti–career politician theme: "I'm a private citizen, just like you. The politicians have raised hundreds of thousands of dollars in out-of-state money to attack me on television because I stand for change, and career politicians fear change more than anything else. Well, they should be afraid . . . you and I have the opportunity to take Mississippi back from the political hacks." Another ad showcased welfare reform. While the viewer saw interspersed images of busy construction workers and a cheerful black mother and daughter shopping for clothes, the narration praised workfare, which "puts welfare recipients to work with jobs that benefit Mississippi. It gives them real jobs and real training," and "gives people futures of hope." Fordice also emphasized economic development.[10]

Despite Fordice's strong campaign, Mabus appeared to enjoy the advantage as election day drew closer. Since the primaries, he had raised more money than Fordice by a two-to-one margin, run a series of television ads promoting his BEST program and other achievements, and received strong words of support from the Jackson *Clarion-Ledger*, the state's largest newspaper. The paper endorsed Mabus as having the "vision necessary to lead the state" and to "push reform" and "finish the job he has begun," while dismissing Fordice as having "no real new ideas" and an "apparent lack of concern for education." Although Mabus held an eleven-point lead in a late poll, the survey found 24 percent of likely voters undecided, a disturbing sign for any well-known incumbent.[11]

On November 5, Mississippians made clear their unhappiness with the status quo by electing their first Republican governor since 1874. Fordice's late surge won him 50.8 percent of the vote, while Mabus's 47.6 percent represented a drop of nearly six percentage points from his 1987 showing. Independent Shawn O'Hara received the remaining 1.6 percent. Observers attributed the upset primarily to voter distrust with politics and politicians. Columnist Sid Salter maintained that the "winds of change" sweeping Mabus to office in 1987 had turned into a "hurricane of voter frustration and mistrust" four years later. In a statewide syndicated column, one of the authors of this chapter cited Mabus's elitist image, "lack of a common touch," and lack of "rapport with the rednecks," which made the average voter feel that he was "not one of us." Also, the column continued, the governor was ill-served by his "egghead advisors who would never tell the emperor when he didn't have clothes on [and who] did virtually nothing without first running a poll."[12]

Some Democrats, including national chairman Ron Brown, alleged that Fordice attempted to appeal to racial resentments by using the issues of job quotas and welfare reform. Republican U.S. senator Cochran rejected these charges, arguing that Fordice had run a "campaign against career politicians . . . based on an anti-incumbent theme," while President George Bush spoke of a "good, clean race on fundamental issues." If racial themes were in play in the 1991 campaign, they did not trigger a heavy turnout among African American voters. In fact, turnout in the black-majority Delta lagged behind 1987 levels. Speaking at the state NAACP annual convention, national executive director Benjamin Hooks chastised the mostly black audience for voter apathy that had helped elect a Republican governor: "Our brothers and sisters in the past had sense enough to vote for the lesser of two evils."[13] Black enthusiasm for Mabus may also have waned because his budget cuts closed some charity hospitals and because he attempted unsuccessfully to replace Ed Cole, the first black state Democratic chairman, with a white female campaign supporter.

Magnolia State voters' discontent with the status quo was also the determining factor in the contest for lieutenant governor, which in Mississippi is a position of significant power. The holder of this office presides over the state senate and wields the power to make committee appointments and refer bills to committees. Incumbent Democrat Brad Dye, whose long career included stints as a state legislator and assistant to U.S. senator James Eastland, was respected for his effectiveness as a legislative leader, but his reputation for backroom politicking and cozy relations with statehouse lobbyists made him a tempting electoral target in a year when voters appeared tired of "politics as usual." Primary challenger Ken Harper, a state senator from Vicksburg, charged that Dye had contributed to "gridlock" over such reforms as initiative, referendum, and regulation of lobbyists, while Dye's battlefield embrace of these reforms during a speech at the Neshoba County Fair struck many as opportunistic and insincere.[14]

In keeping with the spirit of Mississippi politics in 1991, the candidates' television advertisements soon featured personal attacks. Harper took Dye to task for spending $850 of taxpayers' money for a leather office chair while supporting a tax increase, and the usually courtly Dye accused Harper of improperly benefiting at public expense by doing legal work for three government bodies while a state senator.[15] Harper's support from organized labor and the state teachers' association helped him match the incumbent's campaign war chest of $221,000.

Dye survived the primary with a narrow 51.5 percent to 48.5 percent margin over Harper. With race a nonissue in the campaign, Dye was able to carry 20 of the 24 black-majority counties, in addition to 36 of the 58 majority white counties. Yet Harper's hard-hitting campaign had clearly bloodied Dye, giving people reasons to vote against him and making him vulnerable to yet another "reformer" in the general election.

Although he had just recently become a Republican, state senator Eddie Briggs was unopposed in his new party's primary and devoted his summer television campaign to introducing himself to the voters as a "fresh new face in Mississippi politics," notwithstanding his two terms in the senate as a Democrat. Once Dye had won his primary, Briggs trained his fire on the three-term incumbent by painting him as a captive of "the tired, old, worn politics of the past," chiding him for failing to release his tax returns, for refusing to debate, and for abusing a loophole that enabled him to draw both his own salary and that of the governor's while serving as acting governor in the governor's absence.[16] He also charged Dye was a roadblock to such reforms as term limits, initiative, and referendum, and promised to make the senate more open and democratic.

Although Dye was philosophically and stylistically different from Mabus, he too fell victim to the state's "throw the bums out" mood. Mississippians punctuated their taste for change by electing the first Republican subgubernatorial executive officer in the twentieth century, as Briggs defeated Dye 49.5 percent to 41.5 percent, with a black independent, former state senator Henry Kirksey, claiming 9.0 percent.

Democrats retained their historic hold on the remaining executive offices, winning all six races by comfortable margins. The failure of the Republicans even to field a candidate to succeed recent convert Pete Johnson in the auditor's contest was a telling sign of the GOP's shallow talent pool. Republicans did show some vigor in legislative elections, where they won 32 of 174 senate and house seats, or 18 percent of the total membership in 1991. The GOP had been struggling to gain a serious presence since 1967, when they elected their first 3 members in modern times. That small band had grown to only 8 seats (4 in each chamber) by 1979, and reached 16 (9 percent of all seats) in 1987.

Vigorous Two-Party Competition, 1992 to 1994

Electoral activity for state offices in Mississippi normally goes into a hiatus following a gubernatorial election, since all executive and legislative posts are elected on the same four-year cycle. A 1991 federal district court ruling, however, held that newly adopted legislative district lines could be used only for that November's elections and directed the legislature to produce new senate and house boundaries in time for a November 1992 special legislative election. The three-judge panel held that the 1991 redistricting failed to meet federal Voting Rights Act standards for promoting minority electoral influence. The legislature responded in the spring of 1992 with new plans that created 50 black-majority districts (38 in the house and 12 in the senate), which were accepted by the plaintiffs, the Justice Department, and the federal district court panel.

The new districts largely achieved their intended results: black candidates won 32 house seats (26 percent of that chamber) and 10 senate posts (19 percent). These gains represented a major breakthrough for African American representation, which had begun in 1967 with a lonely pioneer, Representative Robert Clark, had seen its first two senators elected twelve years later, and had grown incrementally from 10 percent to 14 percent of the legislature's 174 seats between 1979 and 1991.

The new lines, which had been promoted by an alliance of black and Republican legislators, not only created more black-majority districts but rendered many neighboring seats "whiter" and more Republican. Not surprisingly, Republicans registered gains in the 1992 elections, when their senate strength rose from 9 to 13, and their house delegation increased from 23 to 27. These inroads occurred chiefly in urban areas, particularly along the Gulf Coast, in open seats vacated by retiring white Democrats, and through incumbents switching parties.

Republican ranks were also bolstered by seven Democratic legislators who switched parties during Fordice's first year in office. Significantly, six of them were able to win reelection under their new colors in the 1992 special election. Fordice played an active role in that year's legislative elections, campaigning and raising funds for more than a dozen Republican candidates. This activism prompted many Democratic lawmakers to consider how the party could protect its traditional domination of the legislature. House Democrats soon formed an informal Democratic caucus, but the group found it difficult to exert any real power, largely because of fears that a more activist legislative agenda and enforcement of party discipline would spark further defections to the GOP. Also, no comparable organization was formed in the senate. Legislators continued to

vest the power of making committee assignments and designating chairmanships with the house speaker and lieutenant governor (even under the Republican Briggs), and each chamber's leader selected chairmen from both parties.[17]

As the 1992 presidential election began, few national observers expected
Mississippi's seven electoral votes to be seriously contested since Republicans
had won over 60 percent of the vote in the state in 1984 and 1988. Because of
voter anxiety about the economy and because their ticket boasted two candidates from neighboring states, Governor Bill Clinton of Arkansas and Senator
Al Gore of Tennessee, Democrats sensed that Mississippi might be in play in
1992. Aiming for a major upset, Clinton stumped in Jackson six days before the
election, attacking President Bush for belittling his southern roots and accusing
the President of appealing to the "worst in us." Mississippi Republicans strove
to paint Clinton as a liberal who was out of step with the state's values and
lacked the character to serve as president. Fordice blasted Clinton as "a liberal,
Democrat, draft-dodger, philanderer," and charged that Gore embodied the
"left-wing, tax-and-spend, big-government thinking that has stifled the United
States Congress." President Bush visited the state twice, blaming the "grid-
locked Congress" for stalling his economic agenda and pledging a "domestic
war" against joblessness modeled after the successful Cold War. For all their efforts, Democrats were not able to pull off any surprises in Mississippi. In fact,
the state was Bush's best in the nation, giving him 49.7 percent to Clinton's
40.8 with Ross Perot trailing at 8.7 percent.[18]

While Mississippians had given incumbent Democrats a rough time in 1991,
they were willing to reelect their all-Democratic U.S. House delegation with
little fuss in 1992. Four were reelected with vote shares of between 63.2 and
81.2 percent. The exception was eighty-two-year-old Jamie Whitten from the
northeastern First District, who had "temporarily" stepped down from his
chairmanship of the powerful Appropriations Committee because of health
problems. Republican Clyde Whittaker, a former mayor of Tupelo, received
enough national party support to wage a very competitive race. But the incumbent's campaign placed heavy emphasis on his decades-long success in delivering federal benefits to "every county in our district," and he won an unprecedented twenty-seventh term, albeit with a career-low 59.5 percent.[19]

Some Mississippians returned to the polls in the spring of 1993, thanks to
newly elected president Bill Clinton's nomination of Second District congressman Mike Espy as secretary of agriculture. Two African American Democrats
quickly mobilized significant support in the race to succeed Espy: Hinds
County supervisor Bennie Thompson, a twenty-four-year veteran of local elective office and an outspoken liberal, and Mike Espy's brother, Henry, a success-

ful businessman and chairman of the National Conference of Black Mayors, who sought to build a biracial coalition in the manner of his brother's earlier campaigns. Although Republican Hayes Dent, a white thirty-one-year-old Fordice aide, led the all-candidate primary with 34.4 percent, he entered the runoff as the clear underdog to Thompson, who had garnered 28.7 percent in the first round, eight points ahead of Espy. Thompson skillfully mobilized the black vote by raising fears of GOP hostility to their interests, warning: "If you vote for my opponent, it's like the chicken voting for Colonel Sanders." Probably no one was surprised when Thompson won the runoff with 55.2 percent. This figure closely matched the district's black voting age population of 58 percent, which had been increased by five percentage points in the 1991 redistricting. During the campaign, Thompson, known for his confrontational style, called the 1993 election a "litmus test of whether the party survives. . . . The party faithful must be willing to back African American candidates as well as white candidates."[20]

The 1994 congressional elections in Mississippi bore strong resemblance to recent previous cycles, with one historic exception. U.S. senator Trent Lott, who had emerged as a Republican leader in his first term in the Senate, won a second term by defeating would-be "giant killer" Ken Harper 68.8 to 31.2 percent. Three Democratic House incumbents won with accustomed ease, although the national Republican tide did reduce their victory margins from earlier levels. In the Delta, Congressman Thompson won his first full term, widening his victory margin by five points over his 1993 special election showing.

In the First District, Jamie Whitten's decision to bring down the curtain on his record-setting fifty-three-year House career set the stage for spirited primaries in both parties. On the Democratic side, state representative Bill Wheeler successfully exploited house speaker Tim Ford's weaknesses to score an upset primary victory. The Republican primary illustrated the generational switch of whites from the old Democratic party to the modern GOP, as well as the party's increasingly conservative makeup. State senator Roger Wicker emphasized the fact that his father, a popular longtime officeholder in northeast Mississippi, had been a conservative Democrat "who would be a Republican [were he in office now]."[21] His runoff opponent, twenty-seven-year-old Cochran aide Grant Fox, apparently made some inroads by depicting Wicker as a "closet liberal," and held him to a 53 percent to 47 percent victory in the runoff.

In the general election, Wheeler styled himself as the workingman's candidate who would stand up for the rural residents of the district, while Wicker claimed to be the conservative who would rein in the size of government and preserve small-town ideals. Wheeler emphasized his conservative views on social issues and vowed to protect Social Security and Medicare, while Wicker sought to link the Democrat with "big labor," "liberal special interests," and "more of the same in Washington." The latter theme seemed to resonate as well in Mississippi as anywhere in the year of the Republican tsunami, and Wicker romped to a 63.1 percent to 36.9 percent victory.

The elections from 1991 through 1994 resulted in unprecedented electoral reversals for Mississippi's Democrats. The Fordice and Briggs victories indicated that the party's skillful coalition balancing was no longer sufficient to retain control of state government; Cochran and Lott's reelection romps raised serious questions about the Democrats' ability to regain lost territory; and Wicker's easy takeover of the Whitten congressional seat reminded them that the advantages of incumbency could last only so long as their incumbents did.

Perhaps most disturbing, the Republicans' electoral breakthroughs were accompanied by dramatic gains in party identification. Fueled by a large shift among self-identified white conservatives, 38 percent of Mississippi whites considered themselves Republicans by 1994, while only 21 percent remained Democratic; see Table 14. Meanwhile, Republicans failed to make significant inroads among African Americans, even among those blacks who called themselves "conservative" because of deep religious convictions or views on social and moral issues.[22]

Despite these developments, Mississippi Democrats could take comfort from the growing pains that Republicans were enduring as they operated the levers of power in Mississippi for the first time. Governor Fordice learned that his assertive, take-charge manner did not guarantee he would always set the state's agenda. For example, the Democratic legislative majority, aided by some defecting Republicans, overrode his veto of a one-cent sales tax hike in 1992 on the grounds that public education needed protection from further recession-induced budget cuts. The newly ascendant Republicans also showed they were just as capable of intramural bickering as the Democrats were. While Fordice was hunting big game on an African safari, acting governor Briggs expanded Fordice's call for a special legislative session to include a streamlining of the death penalty appeals process, thereby prompting Fordice supporters to accuse the Republican lieutenant governor of a "power grab."

THE 1995 AND 1996 ELECTIONS

Unlike his predecessor, Fordice was able to run for reelection in 1995 with the advantage of a strong economy and a bulging state treasury fed by the newfound

Table 14. Party Identification in Mississippi, 1990–1996

Party	Whites				African Americans			
	1990	1992	1994	1996	1990	1992	1994	1996
Dem.	36%	29%	21%	22%	74%	73%	72%	68%
Ind.	28	26	41	35	19	20	25	26
Rep.	36	45	38	43	7	7	3	6
N =	(395)	(351)	(412)	(386)	(172)	(163)	(189)	(179)

Party	All Mississippians				White Liberals			
	1990	1992	1994	1996	1990	1992	1994	1996
Dem.	47%	43%	37%	37%	38%	41%	39%	24%
Ind.	26	24	36	32	27	24	43	45
Rep.	27	33	27	31	35	35	18	31
N =	(567)	(514)	(601)	(565)	(101)	(54)	(76)	(56)

Party	White Moderates				White Conservatives			
	1990	1992	1994	1996	1990	1992	1994	1996
Dem.	50%	40%	20%	30%	31%	19%	13%	14%
Ind.	26	34	51	43	28	22	34	29
Rep.	24	26	29	27	41	59	53	57
N =	(61)	(112)	(119)	(118)	(232)	(174)	(196)	(195)

Source: Statewide opinion polls conducted by the Social Science Research Center, Mississippi State University.

Note: Responses were given to a standard party identification question, "Generally speaking, do you consider yourself a Democrat, Republican, Independent, or what?" To determine ideology, the respondents were asked: "What about your political beliefs? Do you consider yourself very liberal, somewhat liberal, moderate or middle of the road, somewhat conservative, or very conservative?" Ideology was recorded by combining "very liberal," and "somewhat liberal" into the "liberal" category, and combining "very conservative" and "somewhat conservative" into the "conservative" category.

riverboat gaming industry. By then four counties on the Mississippi River and two Gulf Coast counties had taken advantage of the 1990 local option bill, and by the mid-1990s Mississippi was in third place only behind Nevada and New Jersey (Atlantic City) in dollars spent on gaming. By 1996 more than two billion dollars a year from the riverboat casino industry were turning over in the state's economy, outstripping even King Cotton. Opinion polls indicated, however, that Mississippians were only mildly impressed with the governor's performance in office, with one survey reporting a favorable to unfavorable ratio of only 55 percent to 44 percent.[23]

The 1995 gubernatorial race was the first in memory for which the primary election was a mere footnote. Fordice was renominated with 93.8 percent in a Republican primary whose turnout reached 126,018, a 98 percent increase over the 1991 contest. Since Democrat Dick Molpus also faced minimal opposition in his party's primary, the candidates were able to begin drawing general election battle lines early in the year. Molpus had developed a reputation as a reformer while serving as secretary of state, leading the push for initiative, referendum, and stricter regulation of lobbyists. He had also worked with Ray Mabus to craft Governor Winter's landmark Education Reform Act in the early 1980s.

The first real sparks of the campaign flew when Molpus, perhaps inadvertently, called attention to Fordice's 1993 comment that he and his wife Pat were enduring "irreconcilable differences" in their marriage. On at least one occasion in early 1995, Molpus had used the same phrase to describe his ideological differences with the governor, a choice of words that ensured another serving of the personality conflicts and political theater that Mississippians were accustomed to sampling during campaign season. At a joint appearance with Molpus before a business leaders' conference in April, Fordice entered the room hand-in-hand with his wife, spoke of the "unbelievable high points" and "low points" in their married life, and then turned to Molpus and upbraided him for taking "a thinly veiled cheap shot at [their] 40-year marriage." In response, Molpus claimed that Fordice had incorrectly interpreted his remarks, and forswore any further interest in the subject: "Your personal life . . . is not part of this campaign." Not surprisingly, this episode dominated news coverage of the early phase of the gubernatorial contest.[24]

As usual, the summer phase of the campaign was dominated by the candidates' appearances at the Neshoba County Fair. Fordice criticized the recent movie *Mississippi Burning* for its depiction of the 1964 murders of three civil rights workers in Neshoba County, and indirectly chided Molpus for his 1989 public apology for those events. "We need to speak positive Mississippi," he asserted, and called attention to the state's improved race relations and large number of black elected officials. Molpus responded that he had "apologized then" to "the mothers, fathers, brothers, and sisters" of the victims, and would "make no apology to you about that [now]."[25]

Molpus devoted much of his fall campaigning to a critique of Fordice's performance on education, claiming that leading educators had called the governor's PRIME proposal (calling for school choice, local control, and merit pay for teachers) "a recipe for disaster" and featuring his wife Sally, herself a former teacher, in a television spot on that issue. Shortly thereafter, Fordice guaranteed the press another field day when he mimicked Mrs. Molpus's remarks and suggested that Molpus had used his wife to present an "untruth." Mississippians were subsequently treated to the elevating spectacle of their leading public officials vowing to take each other "to the woodshed."[26]

In addition to the state's prosperity and his own favorable job approval rating, Fordice enjoyed a sizable financial advantage, outspending Molpus $3.16 million to $2.38 million. On November 7, these factors helped the Republican become the first Mississippi governor to win a second consecutive four-year term. His 55.6 percent to 44.4 percent victory over Molpus was built on strong support from white voters, as he carried 51 of 58 white-majority counties. By contrast, Molpus swept the impoverished Delta, and won 21 of 24 black-majority counties across the state, a pattern that closely matched the geography of the 1992 Bush-Clinton contest. These results indicated that V. O. Key's analysis of a Mississippi divided between a conservative Delta and a populist "hill country"[27] had been stood on its head. The post–Voting Rights Act enfranchisement of African Americans had ensured that the Delta would be a bulwark of support for liberal Democrats.

Partisan observers debated the extent to which racial issues shaped the outcome of the 1995 gubernatorial election. Some Molpus supporters alleged that Fordice's discussion of education, crime, welfare, and taxes were couched in terms that invited white voters to see them as racial issues, while others questioned the Molpus campaign's judgment in airing a final-weekend spot on black radio stations which claimed that "Fordice wants to put folks like you and me [in] the back of the bus."[28]

Fordice supporters rejected such analyses and argued that Fordice's record in office, especially on the economy, was the key determinant. State Republican chairman Mike Retzer also gave some credit to the governor's provocative personality: "Kirk is generally misunderstood by the North Jackson 'chablis and brie' crowd, and very well understood out in the countryside. He is probably . . . the right kind of candidate for this state, more populist; some of the edges are a little rough, but he is sure enough genuine, [a] businessman, no compromise . . . and a lot of people like that."[29]

If Retzer's analysis is correct, then the overall results of the 1995 Mississippi elections offered poetic justice, because Fordice's victory was largely personal, not partisan. The state Republican party had undertaken a major anti-incumbency campaign against Democratic lawmakers, and some party leaders even dared speculate in public about the prospect of a Republican majority in the senate.[30] The GOP, however, gained only two seats in the house (for a new total of 34 of 122 seats, or 28 percent), and actually lost one in the senate (now 18 of 52 seats, or 35 percent). Also, Republicans again failed to establish themselves as a competitive force in lesser statewide elections. Although they fielded a full slate of statewide candidates for the first time, Republicans averaged only 32.7 percent in four races against Democratic incumbents, and pulled only 39.0 percent and 39.9 percent in open contests for secretary of state and agriculture commissioner.

The party's biggest setback came with the defeat of first-term Republican lieutenant governor Briggs. Fordice and his backers had questioned the more moderate Briggs's commitment and effectiveness in pushing the Fordice agenda in the senate, and early in 1995 the governor called for a "real" conservative to challenge Briggs in the Republican primary. Briggs responded by threatening to run for governor as an independent, thereby jeopardizing Republican control of both offices. Fordice and Briggs subsequently engaged in a public fence-mending, but the personal and ideological bad blood cast a cloud over Briggs's reelection prospects.

His Democratic opponent was two-term state senator Ronnie Musgrove. A self-styled "conservative," Musgrove was well positioned to unify his party's disparate coalition because of the close relations with black and teacher organizations he had built during his tenure as chairman of the senate education committee. Musgrove sought to put Briggs on the defensive by contrasting their respective views on education and juvenile crime, charging that on the latter issue Briggs had done nothing "for three years." The Democrat also blasted the incumbent for failing to debate or release his tax returns, and alleged he had personally profited from a "sweetheart timber deal."[31]

Briggs sought to unite Republicans and paper over his differences with the governor by advocating a return to prisoner 'chain gangs,' a tightening of welfare laws, and statewide expansion of the WorkFirst program, "so that if you want help from the taxpayers, you're going to have to work for it." Briggs continued to draw criticism, however, from some conservatives who questioned the sincerity of his 1991 party switch and charged he had used his senate powers to undercut pro-life legislation. For other Republicans, the real cause for dismay was the general ineffectiveness of Briggs's campaign, epitomized by his failure to spend $100,000 of his campaign funds.[32] Musgrove's advantage in unifying his party's coalition was probably decisive, and the Democrat avenged his party's loss of the office four years before with a 52.7 percent to 47.3 percent triumph.

During the 1996 presidential campaign in Mississippi, the Democrats emphasized a variety of Clinton administration initiatives, including deficit reduction, family medical leave, the increase in the minimum wage, and restrictions on the sales of handguns and assault weapons. Mississippi GOP supporters of the Dole-Kemp ticket tried to paint a contrast of character between the two presidential nominees and to suggest that the Democratic ticket was more liberal than its moderate-sounding campaign rhetoric. Election night did not start out well for Mississippi Republicans, as Clinton led the count for most of the evening. A late surge for Dole delivered him the state's electoral votes, but his 49.2 percent to 44.1 percent margin was the weakest Republican presidential showing in Mississippi in twenty years. Ross Perot again ran poorly, garnering only 5.8 percent.[33]

When Mississippians cast their votes for the U.S. Congress in 1996, they again rewarded incumbents for their labors, giving strong margins to all five officeholders who sought reelection. For the first time, however, this practice meant good news for Republicans, as their party claimed three of those returning lawmakers. Senator Thad Cochran's affable manner, careful attention to state issues, and relatively nonideological tone continued to wear well with Mississippi voters, as they granted him a fourth term by a 71.0 percent to 27.4 percent margin over Democrat James (Bootie) Hunt, a retired farmer and factory worker.

The two Republicans winning reelection in House races also appeared to benefit from an occasional willingness to place district interests above strict party or ideological loyalty. Roger Wicker consolidated his party's new hold on the First District with a 67.6 percent victory. Republicans were also watching a "freshman" of a different sort in the Fourth District. After serving seven years in the House as a Democrat, Mike Parker had become a Republican in the fall of 1995. Parker, who said his moderately conservative views were no longer welcome in the national Democratic party, demonstrated that his political strength transcended party lines with a 61.2 percent win over an African American Democrat, Kevin Antoine.

Two Democratic incumbents also fared well, perhaps aided by the best Democratic presidential showing in Mississippi since 1980. Facing a black conservative Republican challenger for the second time, Second District Democratic congressman Bennie Thompson improved his vote share to 59.6 percent, a six-point gain from 1994. Emphasizing the federal money and projects he had brought into the district, Thompson campaigned for white as well as black votes. He received "respectful, even healthy applause and friendly handshakes" from white Rotarians in Clarksdale, while planter Mike Sturdivant, Jr., hosted a reception for Thompson and lauded him for being "very supportive of the ag issues [and] flood control, and . . . interested in creating jobs."[34]

In southern Mississippi, voters again frustrated Republicans' hopes of reclaiming the Fifth District from Gene Taylor, a leader of the Blue Dog group of conservative House Democrats. Even more than his Republican counterparts, Taylor was accustomed to distancing himself from his party when district interest or constituent opinion required it. In 1995 Taylor had voted "present" (rather than for Democrat Richard Gephardt) for Speaker of the House. Taylor campaigned on the defense contracts he had delivered to Pascagoula's Ingalls shipyard, as well as other local issues, and defeated a former Republican state legislator with 58.3 percent of the vote.

Mississippi did feature one open seat contest in 1996, thanks to the retirement of conservative Democrat G. V. (Sonny) Montgomery, who had represented eastern Mississippi's Third District since 1966. Nine Republicans filed for the primary election, spurred on by the fact that the Third had become Mississippi's most Republican district in recent presidential elections. While the candidate most identified with the Christian Coalition finished third in the first round, the primary runoff was also a contest to determine who the more reliable conservative was. Bill Crawford, a Meridian civic leader, was assailed by Chip Pickering for having supported the election of Democratic gubernatorial hopeful Mabus in 1987. Pickering had two connections that proved unbeatable: his father, now a federal judge, who had been a leading Republican figure in the 1970s, and his former boss, Senator Trent Lott. These assets fueled Pickering to a 56.5 percent win. Democrats had less success trying to cash in on pedigree when they nominated John Arthur Eaves, Jr., whose father had run three times for governor. Eaves claimed that he too was "very conservative," but the district's increasingly Republican electorate apparently preferred the genuine article, and Pickering breezed to a 61.4 percent victory.[35]

While 1996 was a year of vigorous electoral activity, one episode in Mississippi politics stood alone for compelling human interest, drama, and mystery. On election day, November 5, Governor Fordice was involved in a one-car crash that nearly cost him his life. The accident occurred on Interstate 55 about 110 miles north of Jackson. Fordice, who had become separated from his security detail, was returning to Jackson from Memphis when he drove off the road and crashed into a wooded area at about 5 P.M.

When the governor's Jeep Cherokee left the highway, the vehicle flew forty feet into a gully and slammed into two trees before landing upside down in flames. Several commercial truckers, seeing the burning wreckage, extricated Fordice. The truckers, aided by a nurse who also stopped to help, worked nearly forty-five minutes to keep him alive until an ambulance from Grenada could reach the site. Only at the Grenada hospital did his identity become known. Accompanied by two doctors, Fordice was transferred by ambulance (helicopters being grounded by weather conditions) to the University Medical Center in Jackson.

His chest had been crushed, his heart bruised, and one lung had collapsed, necessitating a tracheotomy to restore his breathing. There were fractures of several ribs and his back. Also, his left ear had been nearly severed. Hospital authorities later revealed that Fordice had nearly died while in the trauma facility that night. The governor remained in the hospital for five weeks, two of them in critical condition, and underwent several operations.

Mississippians immediately began to speculate that Fordice had traveled to Memphis to visit a woman with whom he had been romantically linked in 1993, when he had announced that his thirty-seven-year marriage to his wife Pat was in serious jeopardy. Speculation was further whetted by the news that Mrs. Fordice, with whom he had reconciled, was traveling in France at the time of the accident. During the early stages of Fordice's recovery, Mississippi journalists were reluctant to aggressively investigate his whereabouts on the day of the wreck. But a few days after the incident, the Memphis *Commercial Appeal* and a Jackson television station reported that Fordice had been seen lunching that day with an unidentified woman at an upscale restaurant in suburban Germantown. Accompanying the story were photographs of the restaurant and interviews with the manager and a waiter who said that Fordice and the woman shared a glass of wine and held hands.

In general, journalists were inclined to give Fordice the chance to explain, when he was able, where he had been, with whom, and why, in the hours preceding his near-fatal accident. A weakened, uncharacteristically subdued Fordice made his first public appearance on January 12 to deliver a brief State of the State address to a joint session of the legislature. In humble tones, he devoted most of his remarks to acknowledging the truck drivers and nurse who helped save his life at the accident scene, as well as the medical personnel who attended him at University Hospital.

On the following day, meeting with reporters for the first time since the accident, Fordice had regained his customary sharp tongue and quick temper. He declared he had "absolutely no memory" of his activities on November 5 prior to his wreck. He refused to entertain any questions about the circumstances of his solo journey to Memphis, or whom he had been with. Even if he did remember, he made clear it was "no one else's business."

Two reporters who regularly cover the Fordice administration came down hard on the governor's apparent evasions in subsequent commentaries. Reed Branson, Jackson correspondent for the *Commercial Appeal*, observed that "it is uncharacteristic of this detail-minded engineer not to offer up some possible explanation" of his Memphis trip. Bobby Harrison, Jackson correspondent for the Tupelo *Daily Journal*, commented: "I find it hard to give him the benefit of the doubt on the memory issue." Since Fordice had been so outspoken in the past about Bill Clinton's alleged indiscretions and had accused state lawmakers of partying and chasing women, Harrison wrote that, because of the strong public perception that Fordice had "sneaked off to Memphis to see another woman," he was no longer in a position to offer himself "as some type of moral leader."[36]

Months later, Fordice remained adamant about not discussing his whereabouts on November 5, 1996. Rather than being remembered in Mississippi political history for serving as the first Republican governor since Reconstruction, many believed that Fordice's "Memphis incident" and his refusal to deal publicly with the events of that day would become his best-known legacy. More immediately, they called into question his ability to exercise effective leadership for his state and his party.

In its own way, the Fordice accident offers an apt punctuation to the narrative of Mississippi politics in the 1990s. It may be overstatement to call the 1990s the "Fordice era" in Mississippi, but he has clearly been the dominant personality, if not always the most influential force, in the recent public life of the state, and he is certainly the most visible symbol of the two-party system that finally took root in Mississippi in the 1990s. As prospective successors in both parties jockey for position to succeed him in the governor's mansion at the dawn of the twenty-first century, the time is ripe to assess how Mississippi politics has changed during the 1990s. Figure 9 in Chapter 1 offers a handy illustration of part of the Magnolia State's partisan path, specifically the steady decline in recent years of Democratic party strength, at least as measured by Paul David's index.

ANALYSIS: TRENDS AND PARTISAN CHALLENGES

Our review of the last decade of Mississippi political life reveals three major trends, each of which may hold implications for the rest of the South and beyond: the emergence of the Republican party as a broadly based, highly competitive force in both state and federal elections; the ability of Mississippi Democrats to adapt, and potentially even thrive, in the two-party era; and the continuing challenge of building harmonious race relations in the state with the nation's most troubled racial history.

Why were Mississippi voters, after frustrating a generation of Republican efforts in the state, finally willing to trust the GOP with significant political power in the 1990s? Probably the most important factor was the massive realignment of party identification that occurred among white Mississippians in the early part of that decade. Statewide surveys conducted by Mississippi State University's Social Science Research Center indicate that what had been a dead heat (both parties claimed 36 percent of identifiers) in party preference among whites in 1990 switched to a 16-point GOP advantage in 1992, widening to 21 points in 1996. See Table 14. Not surprisingly, white conservatives—who account for about a third of the state's voters—led this exodus, as an already significant Republican advantage among these voters (10 percentage points) ballooned to forty percentage points by 1992. Moreover, moderate whites were also traveling in this direction. What had been a 26-point Democratic lead among this bloc— which comprises about a fifth of Mississippi's electorate—had turned into a 9-point Republican margin by 1994, although Democrats were able to recoup some of their losses among this group in 1996.

Moderate-to-conservative voters who were adopting the Republican label in large numbers for themselves were presumably also willing to cast Republican votes for an increasing number of offices, which would help explain the across-the-board growth in the GOP's electoral performance in the 1990s. Less clear is why this large swing in voter loyalties occurred, particularly over such a short period. Possibly the election of a Republican governor in 1991 validated the party as a feasible vehicle for political action for those voters who had long been sympathetic but were reluctant to cut their ties with the party that had dominated Mississippi politics for the previous century. A second possibility is that the voters' dissatisfaction with the status quo, so powerfully reflected in Mississippi elections in the early 1990s, may have eroded, at least for the short term, the voters' perception of the Democrats as the natural governing party of Mississippi. The Republicans' success in exploiting anti-incumbency and anti– career politician sentiments in both federal and state campaigns between 1991 and 1994 lends credence to this notion.

Some state Republican leaders endorse a third possibility, that national trends and personalities have undermined the ability of Mississippi Democrats to insulate themselves from the liberal image of their national party. Former state GOP chairman Clarke Reed views his party's gains in Mississippi as an evolutionary process sparked by a variety of issues: "defense [and] the social issues are pretty hot down here. You know there are more churches in Mississippi per capita than anywhere else. . . . The liberal excesses on social issues have really helped us a lot too." Current party chairman Mike Retzer agrees with Reed's analysis and adds that the national parties are more ideologically distinct today than in the 1960s: "Obviously, the Republican party is a right-of-center party, and the national Democratic party is a left-of-center party, being fritzed at this moment by a President who is willing to adopt Republican positions to ensure his re-election. . . . But that's only temporary. I mean, if you look at the overall structure of the national Democratic party, it is far more liberal than it's ever been, and [with] fewer southerners."[37]

A final explanation would be the expansion of the Republicans' candidate pool, which was significantly strengthened by an infusion of party-switching Democratic officeholders in the 1990s. This development, long hoped for by Mississippi Republicans, was highly significant, as it reinforced the historically thin ranks of Republican elected officials, especially in the legislature, and also served as a leading indicator of where conservative politicians in Mississippi thought they would be best able to pursue their political careers.

This migration began in 1992, Fordice's first year as governor, when seven Democratic legislators became Republicans. At least thirty-five other Mississippi elected officials followed suit between July 1993 and April 1997, according to the Republican National Committee. This haul included four state senators, seven state representatives, and a geographically diverse assortment of county and city officials. The most notable of this group was Representative Charlie Williams of Senatobia, chairman of the house ways and means committee and a prospective Republican candidate for governor in 1999. Another switcher, Representative Tommy Woods of Byhalia, probably spoke for most of his fellow converts when he observed "my district has really turned Republican. I have been voting that way, and I'm very conservative." The GOP's biggest catch by far was, as mentioned above, Congressman Parker, whose conversion followed the November 1995 state elections. At least one Democratic leader, state party executive director Alice Skelton, believes these Republican conversions mask an underlying GOP weakness: "The Republican party is obviously not growing their candidates over there, and the only way they can field candidates for governor is to switch them."[38]

The Republican success in Mississippi has had significant consequences for the national Republican party. By 1995 Senators Lott and Cochran had risen to the number two and three posts in the Senate Republican leadership and were the only contestants to succeed Bob Dole as majority leader when he resigned from the Senate in June 1996 (a vote that Lott won 44 to 8). Three years earlier, Haley Barbour, a longtime Mississippi Republican leader and himself an unsuccessful Senate candidate against Democratic incumbent John Stennis in 1982, had been elected chairman of the Republican National Committee. The big national GOP gains in the 1994 midterm elections occurred under Barbour's tenure. Mississippi's emergence as a major source of Republican leadership in Washington is impressive evidence that the state has become part of the national political mainstream and is helping to set the national agenda.

Mississippi Republicans have much to celebrate as they review their accomplishments in the 1990s, but their enthusiasm should be tempered by recognition of at least five challenges they must confront, and resolve, if they are to establish themselves as the state's dominant party. Two of these concern their ability to groom strong leaders. First, can they translate their numerically large gains in the number of offices held (especially at the legislative level) into producing attractive, electable candidates for statewide office? Second, can they continue to attract defections from the ranks of elected Democrats? Johnson's 1991 loss to Fordice remains an object lesson to prospective party switchers not to underestimate the risks of changing their party colors in midcareer.

Third, Republicans now face significant coalition management challenges of their own. While the party has benefited from the influx of conservative Christian activists into their ranks, the newcomers have not always meshed easily with more secular-minded Republicans. The two blocs frequently differ over the emphasis the party should place on social issues like abortion and school prayer, though not necessarily on the substance of those issues. These tensions are not going to disappear in the foreseeable future.

Fourth, Republicans are not likely to become the "normal" majority party in Mississippi so long as they continue to face massive rejection from African Americans, who account for over a third of the state's voting age population. In 1996, Republicans trailed Democrats in party identification among this group by 68 percent to 6 percent (see Table 14), and the party's candidates have received similarly meager support from black voters.

Fifth, while Mississippi Republicans are not likely to depart dramatically from the conservative agenda that has served them so well in recent elections, they do need to decide how they should best present their message to the voters. The electorate's disgruntlement with the political status quo that fueled Republican gains in the early 1990s has abated, and the party's many electoral successes make it harder for GOP candidates to present themselves as outsiders. The contentious, often angry demeanor for which Governor Fordice is so well known may have outworn its welcome with Mississippians as the decade nears its end, and Republicans will soon need to determine the tone and manner in which they speak to the voters in the post-Fordice era.

For Mississippi Democrats, the 1990s were by no means all bad news. Poll data from Mississippi State University surveys indicated that a large majority of Mississippi voters called themselves "moderate," or "somewhat conservative," suggesting that the conservative tide of the period still left Democrats some running room. Also, Mississippians were supportive of spending on education and highway programs that were seen as improving the quality of life in the state, while remaining conservative on social issues such as crime and family values.[39]

Probably the major source of encouragement for Mississippi Democrats in the 1990s was the emergence of a cohort of young, politically adroit statewide officeholders. In fact, the party's sweep of the seven subgubernatorial statewide executive offices in 1995 may prove to exert more influence over the near term direction of Mississippi politics than any other single event. One of these officeholders, Attorney General Mike Moore, has likened the group to the heroes of the Hollywood movie *The Magnificent Seven*.[40] Their success as candidates and high visibility in office suggest that these leaders have put the Democratic party in position to maintain its hold on executive branch offices for the next four to eight years, possibly regain the governorship in 1999, and even pose serious challenges to the Republicans' hold on U.S. Senate and U.S. House seats.

Moore drew national attention in 1994 when he filed the first state suit seeking reimbursement from the tobacco industry for smoking-related Medicaid expenses. The vast majority of other states have followed Mississippi's lead. In his bid for a third term in 1995, Moore swamped a black Republican by winning 76.4 percent. His campaign naturally showcased his anticrime credentials, but also emphasized mentoring programs for at-risk youth and other efforts to keep youngsters away from drugs. One of his television spots gave prominent display to the Bible as a backdrop to a message promoting personal responsibility. For good measure, Moore also called attention to his conservative streak on social issues in his third term, during which he defended a new state law permitting students to initiate and lead prayer in the public schools against a lawsuit filed by the American Civil Liberties Union.

Lieutenant Governor Musgrove has used his new position to promote education and anticrime programs. For example, in 1997 he led a successful coalition of lawmakers in overriding Fordice's veto of a bill designed to correct educational funding inequities across the state. He scored points with social conservatives by using his power in the senate to help pass a law placing additional restrictions on abortion providers. Another rising star for Mississippi Democrats was Eric Clark, who was elected secretary of state in 1995. Showing activism not always associated with this largely custodial office, Clark cajoled the legislature to implement the federal motor voter bill.

While they can cheer the skillful actions of their statewide officeholders, Mississippi Democrats must address several serious challenges if they are to maintain their viability. The most important, and most complicated, of these is the ongoing task of coalition management. Mississippi Democrats must work to preserve their appeal to the broad mix of the state's voters, but at the same time they can't afford to take for granted their base of blacks and white liberals, who account for roughly 40 percent of the Mississippi electorate (see Table 14). Leslie B. McLemore, an African American political science professor whose independent candidacy in the Fourth Congressional District in 1980 drew votes from a white Democratic nominee and helped elected a Republican, offered this warning: "I don't think we can get much more conservative without reverting back to the Mississippi of pre-1965 or pre-1960. . . . How conservative can the body politic get without totally excluding black people and poor people and other progressive people in this state?"[41]

The delicacy of the Democrats' balancing act is underscored by the survey data presented in Table 15. The findings indicate that white and black Democrats disagree significantly on social issues. For example, on affirmative action white Democrats and Republicans (who are nearly all white) register an almost identical view, which is overwhelming disapproval. A solid majority of black Democrats, by contrast, favor affirmative action. On the death penalty white Democrats are considerably closer to Republicans than to black Democrats. But on economic issues such as government's responsibility to provide jobs, the need for spending to aid the poor, and government's role in providing social and economic help for minorities, black Democrats are far closer to white Democrats than they are to Republicans. In fact, on these bread-and-butter questions, white Democrats occupy a middle position between their black fellow partisans and Republicans. When elections turn on economic issues, it is obviously easier to maintain Democratic unity than when social issues rise to the fore. These fascinating attitudinal differences highlight the challenges that face the leaders of Mississippi's biracial Democratic coalition.

A recent episode illustrates both the problems black-white divisions can cause within the party and the efforts that white Democrats are prepared to make to mitigate those tensions. In early 1996 Governor Fordice nominated four white males to the state college board, a move that would leave the twelve-member board with only two blacks and two white females. When a specially convened senate subcommittee rejected the nominations, Fordice, noting that the panel had not questioned the candidates' credentials, charged that the Democrats were trying to "enforce a quota system." When a subsequent Fordice bid to make interim appointments under the color of his constitutional emergency powers was challenged in court, Attorney General Moore testified in support of the black plaintiffs, asserting that no emergency existed and that the governor could not reappoint nominees who had already received legislative rejection.

Table 15. Political Views of Mississippi Partisan Blocs, 1996

Political Issue	White Dem.	Black Dem.	Rep.
Death Penalty for Murder			
Favor	58%	23%	73%
Oppose	42	77	27
N =	(76)	(111)	(176)
Affirmative Action			
Favor	17%	68%	19%
Oppose	83	32	81
N =	(78)	(120)	(176)
Fed. Socioeconomic Aid to Blacks			
Favor	68%	94%	39%
Oppose	32	6	61
N =	(77)	(119)	(173)
Jobs and Living Standard Ensured by Fed. Gov.			
Favor	61%	97%	47%
Oppose	39	3	53
N =	(82)	(119)	(176)
State and Local Spending for Poor			
Favor	61%	82%	39%
Oppose	39	18	61
N =	(82)	(118)	(172)

Source: 1996 statewide poll conducted by the Social Science Research Center, Mississippi State University.

Note: The issue questions were worded as follows: 1) "For someone who is convicted of murder, do you generally favor the death penalty, life in prison without parole, or a jail term that is shorter than the rest of someone's life?" Life without parole and a shorter jail term were classified as opposing the death penalty. 2) "Do you agree or disagree with the following statement: Because of past discrimination, blacks should be given preference in hiring and promotion." 3) "Do you agree or disagree with the following statement: The federal government should make every effort to improve the social and economic position of blacks and other minority groups." 4) "Do you agree or disagree with the following statement: The federal government should see to it that every person has a job and a good standard living." 5) "As you know, most of the money government spends comes from the taxes you and others pay. For each of the following, please tell me whether you think state and local government in Mississippi should be spending more, less, or about the same as now. How about programs for the poor?"

Eventually, the senate's higher education committee turned down the nominees on a near party line vote, with only one white Democrat joining the five Republicans in support of the nominations.[42] Fordice then selected a new group, which included a black male and a white female, who received senate confirmation without fanfare. This episode is significant because it indicates that white Democratic leaders have an acute sensitivity to the issues of greatest concern to their black colleagues, and a willingness to take some political risks to support them on those issues.

In view of the racial and ideological tensions inherent in their coalition, it is essential for Mississippi Democrats to produce candidates who can appeal to all major factions within the party, yet also attract middle-of-the-road independent and Republican voters. Their success in 1995 indicates they can field white candidates who fit this bill. Several recent examples suggest the same formula can also work for black candidates. In 1996 Fred Banks, an African American, won election to a full term on the state supreme court in a white-majority district. In the spring of 1997, Harvey Johnson won election as Jackson's first black mayor by upsetting the incumbent white Democratic mayor in the primary, and then winning 69.5 percent of the vote against a conservative white businesswoman in the general election. In Vicksburg, like Jackson a city with a 50–50 black-white voter balance, former mayor Robert Walker, an African American, regained his post with a 60.1 percent victory over the white independent who had upset him four years earlier.[43] In each case, the winning black candidate was able to frame his campaign as a referendum on performance (either positively or negatively), rather than ideology or race.

The ability of African American Democrats to win office is very important for the Democrats' coalition management task. It offers recognition of, and validation for, black voters' sustained, and usually monolithic, support for white Democratic candidates. At the same time, there is increasing evidence that these electoral breakthroughs can occur without alienating the white voters the party needs to win. Indeed, it is now plausible to speak of the day when an African American, presumably but not necessarily a Democrat, can win statewide office in Mississippi.

Coalition management also means looking after the health of the "party in government." Here too, Democrats have found signs of encouragement during the 1990s. A notable example comes from the first Fordice term, when most white Democratic legislators joined their black colleagues to override the governor's veto of a bonding bill that contained the customary 20 percent set-asides for "socially and economically disadvantaged individuals."[44] While Fordice labeled the set-asides as "discriminatory" and "outdated," Democratic lawmakers had some success in shifting the public focus of the bill from race to economic development, a strategy consistent with their ongoing need to knit together their coalition on economic issues. In 1996, Lieutenant Governor Musgrove made his own contribution to maintaining the Democrats' coalition within the legislature when he appointed eight African American committee chairmen in the senate, a huge increase from one the previous session,[45] though he also honored the recent practice of bipartisan appointments by naming five Republican chairmen.

Another challenge confronting Mississippi Democrats is to position themselves at a distinct but not disloyal distance from the more liberal national party in order to appeal to the sizable number of nonliberal whites in the electorate. State Democratic leaders contend that their party has positioned itself shrewdly in this regard. For example, Alice Skelton asserted in regard to the Democrats' winning statewide executive candidates in 1995: "Their message resonated with the voters [because] they dealt with real pocketbook issues [and] you saw Mississippi Democrats talking about Mississippi issues." By contrast, she said, "the themes in a lot of the Republican campaigns were national themes." At a Starkville "beans and greens" dinner, Secretary of State Clark maintained that all victorious Democrats in 1995 had embraced beliefs in "family virtues, respect for life, prudent stewardship of public finances," and expanding educational and economic opportunities for all Mississippians. In sum, he said, Mississippi Democrats "are not wild-eyed, left-wing radicals . . . We're everyday people."[46]

Republican leader Clarke Reed doubts the Democrats will remain successful at strategic positioning for much longer. He envisions an increasingly liberal state Democratic party helping to elect Republicans. "What's happened is, we [Mississippians] have lucked out. We've had some moderate Democratic governors, but those days are gone. . . . There won't be such as that again. They'll all be very liberal, just like their party. So the days of the moderate Democrat are over . . . except for maybe on the local level."[47]

Overall, race relations remain an important element in Mississippi politics. It is difficult to overstate the progress the state has made in this area in recent decades, a point Eric Clark expresses this way: "My opinion is that in the quarter century between 1965 and 1990 Mississippi made more progress in human relations than virtually any place else in the world." Yet, the division between whites and blacks still lies at the heart of the dynamics that shape life in Mississippi at the close of the twentieth century. As this narrative has shown, nearly every election campaign and public policy debate is sooner or later likely to be viewed through the prism of race. Even the development of significant two-party competition, usually considered a healthy indicator of democratic vitality, appears to be interpreted by many Mississippians as a racially driven phenomenon. Democratic insurance commissioner George Dale is concerned that for many voters, "when you think of the Democratic party you think of blacks and when you think of the Republican party you think of whites. I think that's wrong." State Democratic executive director Skelton attributes that perception to her party's allowing the Republicans "to control the dialogue [earlier in the decade], especially with the press and the general public, and they painted us as a black party, even though our membership and our voting districts did not demonstrate that." Republican state chairman Retzer, noting the racially divisive 1996 state Democratic convention where African Americans were elected to all three of the party's top positions, responded: "They're painting themselves. I have nothing to do with it. I'm taking care of my own deal. I want [us] to be painted as Mississippi's party."[48]

What can Mississippi's political leaders do to ameliorate the remaining racial divisions in the Magnolia State? Several strategies seem plausible. First, continue to search for what Clark calls "common ground" solutions for such issues as education, economic conditions, and human relations. Such consensus is problematic given the ideological differences between blacks and whites (see Table 15 above), but creative risk-taking by leaders from both races might do much to promote the perception that there are common interests binding together a large and diverse majority of Mississippians.

Second, white political leaders have an ongoing responsibility to send signals of good will and openness to the black community. As noted above, white Democrats have a long head start over their Republican rivals. But for both parties, careful attention to the fine points of language, tone, nuance, and symbolism would likely help reduce the psychological distance between the two races. On this point Clark observed, "If folks are disrespectful of the progress that we've made or irresponsible about the future of our state, then people who want to throw bombs can have a very bad effect." On the Republican side, Clarke Reed makes a similar point about the wisdom of avoiding racially divisive messages and actions: "The white people don't like . . . this polarizing thing, you know. They're still conscious of [the state's] old image, which has gotten better and used to be bad, so I think it would really backfire if you did that [stir up racial division]."[49]

Third, the parties should continue to foster coalition building. Of course, this has been the Democrats' forte since the 1970s, but Republicans should be alert for opportunities here. One way for the GOP to cultivate a more open-minded reception from African American voters would be to recruit credible black Republican candidates and run them in contests they can win. Any suc-

cess they achieve on that front would also help erase the image of racially polarized parties, which in itself would be a healthy development.

Answers to immediate questions about the future of Mississippi politics must
await the 1999 state elections, since the 1998 elections were expected to be a
quiet interlude. Although Congressman Parker in the Fourth District announced his retirement, all four of the state's other incumbent congressmen
were likely to win comfortable reelection. By contrast, the 1999 elections
promised to be hotly contested from the governorship on down.

Whatever the outcome of the 1999 elections, it is clear Mississippi will enter
the twenty-first century a vastly different place than the one V. O. Key depicted
in the late 1940s. Half a century later, our narrative reveals a state whose political
life is distinctive for the dramatic empowerment of its long-disfranchised black
citizens, vigorous competition between two resourceful and dynamic parties,
and a diverse issue agenda shaped by a variety of forces and interests. These
transformations mean that once-scorned Mississippi now deserves recognition
as a source of leaders, strategies, and ideas that offer much to the nation in the
late 1990s and into the new century and beyond.

10

Louisiana: Still *Sui Generis* like Huey

Edward F. Renwick, T. Wayne Parent, and Jack Wardlaw

Huey Long once described himself as *sui generis*—one of a kind—a term that applies as much to the state Long ruled and its continuing political development as it does to the populist legend himself.[1] Although Louisiana lies in the South, it is unique among its neighbors. The Bayou State's traditional southern food, southern drawl, and Baptist religion in the north are counterpoised by spicy New Orleans cuisine, Cajun French, and Catholic High Mass in the south. The state has a unique election system and a history of flamboyant politicians from Huey Long and Earl Long to Edwin Edwards and David Duke and their different brands of populism. It should come as no surprise, then, that the path of Republican advance in most of the South has not been followed here. Louisiana's experience with two-party politics can best be described by using Huey Long's term—sui generis.

Louisiana's similarity to other southern states regarding politically important characteristics is evident. Its population is 30.6 percent African American, second only to Mississippi; its per capita income is $14,279, higher only than Arkansas and Mississippi; and the rate of high school graduation is 58.5 percent, higher only than South Carolina. Yet Louisiana has at least two politically important demographic differences: it is both more Catholic and more urban than most of its neighbors. The estimates of those identifying themselves as Catholic range from 32 percent to as high as 48 percent. While the relationship between Catholicism and voting Democratic has declined significantly in recent decades, due at least in part to shared Republican and Catholic pro-life stances on abortion, surveys in Louisiana show that white Catholics remain more likely to vote Democratic than white non-Catholics, a vital point we return to below.[2]

If the impact of Louisiana's Catholicism on the state's two-party politics is sometimes difficult to gauge, the impact of the other unique characteristic of Louisiana's population mix is easier to understand. Louisiana's population is 68.1 percent urban, over twenty percentage points higher than Mississippi's. Although some of Louisiana's urban voters are located in the fairly suburban and Protestant cities of Baton Rouge and Shreveport, New Orleans—which accounts for 11.8 percent of the state's population—is the urban center with the strongest impact on Louisiana politics. For example, in 1996 Democrat Mary Landrieu carried the city of New Orleans by 100,353 votes while winning that year's U.S. Senate election by only 5,788 votes statewide.

Add to this population mix a unique election system and a history of flamboyant populists, and the Louisiana story becomes complicated. The Louisiana Democratic party's tenacity in the midst of Dixie's Republican hurricane is the result of this mixture of circumstances and traditions that define Louisiana as a one-of-a-kind southern state. Republicans have enjoyed successes, though, largely owing to many of the same forces at work throughout the region: racial polarization, the appeal of the GOP's probusiness message to growing and prosperous suburban residents, and the appeal of cultural conservatism in the more rural, less prosperous areas of the state.[3]

Spurred on by these factors, Republican progress is impressive. (See Figure 10 in Chapter 1 for a depiction of recent Louisiana partisan trends.) In 1995 the GOP was able to elevate a popular former Democrat, Mike Foster, to the governorship with 63.5 percent of the vote. After the 1996 elections Republicans controlled five of the state's seven seats in the U.S. House of Representatives, up from only three of eight in 1990. Republicans have been able to win elections in almost every area of the state except the city of New Orleans. And the GOP enjoyed a surge in party voter registration from 1 percent in the early 1960s to 21 percent in 1998. (See Table 16.) U.S. representative Robert L. (Bob) Livingston, a leading Louisiana Republican, said he expects that percentage to continue to grow: "I think we are destined to be the majority party here and throughout the South."[4]

The Democrats, for their part, have held their own during this period of Republican surge. Democratic U.S. senators John Breaux and Mary Landrieu are the South's only all-Democratic U.S. Senate team; Democrats hold six of eight statewide elective offices; both houses of the legislature are firmly in Democratic hands (see Table 17), and Democratic presidential candidate Bill Clinton carried Louisiana comfortably in 1992 and with a twelve-point landslide in 1996. Republicans have noticed the tenacity. David Treen, who in 1979 was

Table 16. Voter Registration in Louisiana by Party, 1963–1998

Year	Dem.	Rep.
1963	98.5%	1.0%
1967	97.8	1.6
1971	96.7	2.2
1975	95.2	3.0
1979	89.5	5.3
1983	83.5	9.1
1987	77.5	14.0
1991	73.5	18.1
1995	68.4	20.0
1998	62.9	21.4

Source: Louisiana Commissioner of Elections.

Table 17. Party Representation in the Louisiana Legislature, 1964–1998

Year	House		Senate		% GOP
	Dem.	Rep.	Dem.	Rep.	
1964	103	2	39	0	1.4%
1968	105	0	39	0	0.0
1972	101	4	38	1	3.5
1976	101	4	38	1	3.5
1980	95	10	39	0	6.9
1984	91	14	38	1	10.4
1988[a]	86	18	34	5	15.3
1992[a]	88	16	34	5	14.6
1996	78	27	25	14	28.5
1998	80	25	26	13	26.4

[a]Additionally, there was one Independent elected in each of these years.

Louisiana's first elected Republican governor, said: "It's frustrating. I'm disappointed that we haven't been able to elect a U.S. senator, while our neighbors in Texas and Mississippi have two each."[5]

LOUISIANA'S UNIQUE ELECTION SYSTEM

Part of the reason for Louisiana's distinctiveness in party competition is its unique open primary law. In the open primary, all candidates regardless of party affiliation run against each other, and if no candidate gets a majority in the first election, the top two vote-getters proceed to a runoff. While the runoff almost always pits a Democrat against a Republican, there have been a few instances where two members of the same party have faced each other in the final election.

The origins of the open primary system date back to 1972, when the newly elected Democratic governor, Edwin Edwards, exhausted from the rigors of the previous system, obtained the cooperation of the legislature to establish the procedure, making the state's elections different from anywhere else. Before the new plan went into effect in 1975, Louisiana had a three-stage election process: a partisan first primary, runoffs if necessary, then a general election between the Democratic and Republican nominees. Edwards did not like the old system because the Republican candidate almost never had first primary opposition and the Democratic candidate normally had a first and second primary fight. Edwards saw the Republicans as "sitting back as scavengers and waiting to move into the ranks of the losers and stirring up continued hatred among the disillusioned and the unhappy . . . whose candidates did not win in the Democratic primary."[6]

Although unintended by Edwards, the open primary may have spurred the growth of the Republican party. Before this time, the real election was in the Democratic primary. Republicans had no chance in the general election. Thus, anyone who failed to register as a Democrat was effectively disenfranchised in state politics. "In the early days, the open primary system probably helped the growth of the GOP," according to Quentin Dastugue, a former longtime Republican state representative. Dastugue pointed out a current drawback of the system as he sees it: "The open primary leads to extremists being the runoff candidates. None of the five Republican congressmen in Louisiana could get elected statewide because they could not get into a runoff. They are seen as more moderate, not extremists."[7]

Republican congressman Livingston agrees with Dastugue. Livingston said he believes the open primary system was instrumental in moving the party "from nonexistence to existence," but that the system is now "counter-productive" because "good solid candidates from the mainstream . . . get shunted out" and, instead, "we get the fringes." A former state Republican chairman, William (Billy) Nungesser, takes another view of the open primary: "It would be a big mistake to change. If it were changed, moderate Democrats would more often get nominated." Nungesser said this would be disastrous for the GOP, adding, "Republicans can't beat moderate or conservative Democrats in Louisiana."[8]

Both points ring true. The open primary system helps Republican registration, but hurts the party's role in elections.[9] Under the open primary law, voters can register as they wish and still participate fully in the process. But it has also caused a blurring of party lines, and it left Republicans powerless to prevent maverick candidates like David Duke, a former Ku Klux Klan leader, from running under the GOP banner. Candidates' names go on the ballot according to the way they register to vote, regardless of the wishes of the party organization. Louisiana Republicans have tried to deal with this problem by holding nominating conventions, a strategy Livingston labeled a "disaster." Indeed, in the 1990 U.S. Senate race, the 1991 governor's race, and the 1995 governor's race, the GOP convention "nominee" withdrew before the election. Dastugue, who was the GOP convention's designated nominee for governor in 1995 but withdrew during the campaign because of a lack of money, observed, "Nobody needs the party machinery to run for office . . . because it has been so useless in the past."[10]

Many in both parties would like to change the open primary system, but the individuals who have to make the change, legislators and the governor, were elected using this system. Governor Foster articulates the prevailing view. "I like the open primary. Without it, I probably wouldn't be governor."[11]

THE 1986 SENATE AND THE 1987 GOVERNOR'S ELECTIONS

If only one major candidate from each party is running, the open primary can function much like a general election system. The best example of this came when veteran Democratic senator Russell B. Long retired in 1986, giving rise to the first competitive two-party U.S. Senate race in Louisiana's modern history. This was a reasonably stable election with few surprises or colorful characters, and served as a rather calm prelude to the more volatile and convoluted party politics of the 1990s. U.S. representative John B. Breaux, a moderate Democrat from southwest Louisiana, was in a runoff with a moderate Republican U.S. representative from Baton Rouge, W. Henson Moore, who was initially favored to win.

Democrat Breaux successfully exploited the state of the economy to his own political advantage. The Republicans held the White House, and Louisiana was in the depths of a recession caused by the collapse of oil prices in the early 1980s. Breaux continually attacked his Republican opponent over the state's economic woes, often telling a story about a conversation in which one voter says to the other: "You know, they told me six years ago that, if I voted for the Republicans and the Republican party, things would start picking up. You know something, they were right. I voted for the Republicans. Last month, they picked up my car, my truck, my house and my boat."[12]

The Republicans, on the other hand, created another problem for themselves by running a "ballot integrity" program aimed at scrutinizing black voters to see if they were properly registered. The Republicans didn't extend the program to white voters. Blacks were incensed, which increased black turnout and helped Breaux win. Moore led in the first primary with 44.2 percent of the vote to Breaux's 37.4 percent, but Breaux won the runoff with 52.8 percent to Moore's 47.2 percent. Sixty-one percent of the whites, according to exit polls, supported Moore, but he needed at least two-thirds of the white vote to be victorious.[13]

The next major statewide race, the 1987 governor's election, illustrates the more common impact the open primary law has had on party politics. In that year, the Republicans had another chance for a substantial win when Democratic governor Edwin W. Edwards sought reelection to an unprecedented fourth nonconsecutive term. Much of Louisiana politics in the 1970s and 1980s revolved around the wins and losses of this powerful governor, first elected in 1971–1972 and reelected in 1975. The state constitution barred him from a third successive term in 1979, but he roared back to the governor's mansion in 1983 by crushing the one-term incumbent Republican, David C. Treen, with 61.9 percent of the vote to Treen's 36.8 percent.

Edwards had an advantageous political birth. He was born in Marksville, near the geographic dividing line between north and south Louisiana, of a Cajun Catholic mother and a Protestant father. Early in life, Edwards was a Nazarene minister. Later, when he married his first wife, he became a Catholic. From Edwards's first foray into politics, running for the city council in Crowley, up to 1987, he had never been defeated in seventeen elections. Part of the reason for his success was his skill at using humor. For example, Edwards handled stories about his womanizing by saying the only way he could lose the 1983 gubernatorial election was to be caught in bed with a live boy or a dead girl. When running against Treen, Edwards said of his Republican opponent: "He's so slow, it takes him an hour and one-half to watch *Sixty Minutes*."[14]

Edwards's third term was dominated by legal troubles. He was indicted for selling hospital and nursing home permits in which he "illegally used his influence" regarding some applications. He was tried twice; the first trial ended in a hung jury. He was finally acquitted in the third year of his third gubernatorial term. Over the years Edwards had been the target of thirteen federal investigations, ranging from suspected sale of state positions to his first wife Elaine's allegedly accepting a $10,000 gift from Tongsun Park, a South Korean business-man. Between 1981 and 1984, according to testimony given at his 1985–1986 federal trials, Edwards had amassed $2 million in gambling debts. Indeed, a debt collector for a gambling casino said he had picked up $780,000 in cash in suit-cases from the governor.[15] In addition to his legal troubles, Edwards had pushed through a $750 million tax increase. The combination had destroyed his popularity.

Charles (Buddy) Roemer, a Democratic congressman from Shreveport, decided to run against the troubled incumbent. Roemer was born into a well-known political family. In fact, his father was very close to Edwards, heading up the Division of Administration during Edwards's first term. Buddy Roemer, who had been elected to Congress on his second try in 1981, had a conservative voting record and frequently disagreed with his party's House leadership. He was an outsider in an insider's profession.

Several other candidates also saw Edwards as vulnerable and joined the race. Congressman Bob Livingston was the only Republican, while secretary of state Jim Brown and U.S. representative W. J. (Billy) Tauzin were major Democratic candidates along with Roemer and Edwards. Everybody wanted to get in the runoff with Edwards because they thought the electorate would go for anyone but the governor.

In the open primary, Roemer received 32.7 percent of the vote, Edwards 28.3 percent, and Livingston 18.6 percent. Facing the likelihood of defeat, Edwards withdrew from the second election, ceding the governorship to Roemer. A maverick who talked of reforming state government had thus broken the Edwards hold on Louisiana Democratic politics, or so it seemed after the 1987 balloting. The Republicans were simply left out.

Despite losing the 1986 Senate race and being shut out of the governor's runoff in 1987, the Louisiana Republican party as the 1990s began had brighter prospects than the results of those two statewide elections seemed to indicate. Edwards's Democratic coalition had been shattered. And even though he was a Democrat, Governor Roemer was severely at odds with the state's Democratic establishment. Further, the GOP could claim one statewide victory in 1987, the election to the lieutenant governorship of Paul Hardy, a former Democrat. Hardy, a Catholic Cajun, gave up his position as Louisiana's secretary of state to run for governor in 1979 as a Democrat. He did not make the runoff, but he endorsed the eventual GOP winner, David Treen, and accepted a post in Governor Treen's administration. He switched to the Republican party and in 1987 was victorious in his race for lieutenant governor. Also, the son of former Democratic governor John J. McKeithen (1963–1971), Fox McKeithen, who had originally been elected secretary of state in 1987 as a Democrat, switched to the Republican party in 1990.

Moreover, the GOP could claim three members of Congress out of the eight then allocated to the state. When Henson Moore gave up his congressional seat in 1986 to run for the U.S. Senate, Richard H. Baker, a Democratic state representative who had switched to the Republican party in 1985, won the job with 51.0 percent of the vote. In 1986, Clyde C. Holloway, a Republican businessman, was elected to a vacant U.S. House seat previously held by a Democrat. Holloway's opponent in the runoff was a black female Democrat who received 48.6 percent of the vote to Holloway's 51.4 percent. The third Republican member of Louisiana's U.S. House delegation as the 1990s began was Livingston, who had first been elected to Congress from a New Orleans suburban district in 1977 in a special election necessitated by the resignation of a then newly elected Democratic congressman who had been indicted for election fraud. Adding to Republican optimism was the fact that Ronald Reagan and George Bush had carried the state comfortably in three straight presidential elections in the 1980s.

In sum, the Republican party in Louisiana had made real progress, and prospects appeared reasonably hopeful for the party to unseat incumbent Democratic U.S. senator J. Bennett Johnston in 1990 and to win the 1991 governor's race.

ENTER DAVID DUKE: THE 1990 SENATE AND 1991 GOVERNOR'S ELECTIONS

Senator Johnston appeared vulnerable. In 1988 he had positioned himself to make a run for Senate majority leader—a position he lost to George Mitchell, a Democrat from Maine—and in the process had taken political stands that may have improved his image among his more liberal Senate colleagues but that did not sit well with his more conservative Louisiana base. Johnston's most risky center-left gambit was his highly visible decision to galvanize southern Democratic opposition in the Senate to the confirmation of Judge Robert Bork for a position on the U.S. Supreme Court; Johnston's actions effectively defeated Bork and left bitter lasting memories in the minds of Louisiana conservatives.

At this juncture, the Republican party's worst nightmare became a reality. David Duke, the former Klansman, entered the 1990 Senate race as a Republican and quickly emerged as Johnston's principal opponent. A New Orleans native, Duke had been operating on the outer edge of politics since the 1970s, running unsuccessfully for public office as a fringe candidate. He was best known for his tenure as grand wizard of the Ku Klux Klan and as a Nazi sympathizer, the latter during his days at Louisiana State University. Duke, who became head of the Klan in 1975, had a long fascination with racism. Interestingly, he welcomed Catholics and women to the Klan. In 1980 he resigned from the Klan and formed a new organization, the National Association for the Advancement of White People. He then largely disappeared from public view until 1988, when he ran for president as a Democrat. For the 1988 general election he became the presidential nominee of the Populist party, and after that election he became a Republican. Thus, within a single year Duke had been a Democrat, a Populist, and a Republican.[16]

Duke's political fortunes took an upward turn in 1989 with a special election for a vacancy in the Louisiana house of representatives from Metairie, a nearly all-white New Orleans suburb. Though there was some doubt that he met the residency requirements, Duke entered the race, for an open seat in a Republican district. Thirty-five percent of the district's voters were registered Republicans, and George Bush had received 78 percent of the vote there in the 1988 presidential election. With the media wanting to interview him at every turn because of his notoriety amid a weak field of candidates, Duke led the open primary, receiving a third of the vote. In second place was John Treen, brother of former governor David Treen, who received 19 percent of the vote. Although Ronald Reagan did a radio spot for Treen, few others came to his defense in the runoff. Duke won with less than 51 percent of the vote but still 227 votes ahead of Treen. Eighty percent of the top third of Republican registration precincts (the most consciously partisan, mainstream Republicans) went with Treen while 80 percent of the top third of the Democratic registration precincts supported Duke.[17]

Although he had been in the Louisiana house less than a year, Duke next announced his intention to run for U.S. senator. He entered the race against Senator Johnston and Ben Bagert, Jr., the official Republican nominee. In his campaign speeches Duke preached that the poor and minorities received too much assistance from the government and that the middle class did not get enough, instead being forced to pay for programs to assist the poor. As the election neared, national Republican leaders, fearing bad publicity from having a former Klan leader running as their Senate candidate, became nervous. President Bush denounced Duke. Then Republican leaders prevailed upon Bagert to withdraw, hoping to have Johnston win outright in the first election, thus avoiding a potentially embarrassing runoff.[18]

In the beginning of the campaign, Johnston had positive TV commercials stressing how much he had done for the voters of Louisiana, but as the campaign came into the final stretch, there was nobody on TV but Duke. He was the subject of both his own and Johnston's commercials.

A pre-election poll showed that on nonracial issues, there was no great difference between all voters, Duke voters, and white voters. But there was a difference on the race issue. Eighty-seven percent of Duke's voters in the survey said the government sponsored too many programs giving too many benefits to minorities. About two-thirds of Duke's voters opposed minority set-asides, and three-fifths of his backers said the civil rights laws had gone too far. Forty-six percent of his voters would not give any governmental help to minority groups. Another, earlier poll showed that voters overall, however, did not feel comfortable with David Duke. Forty-one percent of the voters felt comfortable with Johnston but only 29 percent with Duke. Duke's racist past defeated him, but it was a close call. Johnston won reelection in the first primary with 54.3 percent of the vote to Duke's 44.5 percent, with other candidates picking up the few remaining votes. Fifty-five percent of Louisiana's white voters cast ballots for Duke,[19] who carried twenty-five of the state's sixty-four parishes, including Senator Johnston's home parish of Bossier and former governor Edwards's birthplace, the parish of Avoyelles. For the GOP, the disastrous prospect of a former Klan leader who claimed GOP affiliation winning a U.S. Senate seat had failed to materialize, but the ordeal was nonetheless a serious setback.

With Duke's strong showing in defeat, the stage was now set for the 1991 governor's race. The day after the Senate election, Quentin Dastugue, the veteran Republican legislator, predicted: "I can't see [Duke] beating anyone [for governor, but] he could make the runoff but couldn't win it." Not taking Dastugue's advice, Duke followed his defeat for the Senate by announcing for governor, declaring, "I'm a Populist like Huey Long, but we need a Huey Long in reverse."[20]

Governor Roemer was vulnerable. In 1987 he had run on a platform of starting a revolution in Louisiana, but had been unable to get things off the ground. "Roemer, in his first legislative session, had a golden opportunity," Billy Nungesser, the former state GOP party chairman, recalled. "That session of the legislature would have let him do anything he wanted."[21] Roemer wanted to change the educational system and initiate fiscal reform, but he waited until later in his term to try to make these changes. He accomplished neither. Regarding education, the teachers wanted additional money for salaries but did not want to be subjected to a performance evaluation process, while the politicians did not want to change the management structure of education in Louisiana with its resulting patronage.

Roemer's "revolution" had toppled three-term governor Edwards, but Roemer was unable to build a firm, lasting, dependable base of political support for his ideas. This became evident in a 1989 statewide referendum on Roemer's other major initiative—a fiscal reform program. He had proposed an ambitious plan to restructure the state's tax system away from sales taxes, which bear most heavily on poor people, to increased income taxes, which are more progressive. The oddity of this election was that Roemer's upper-income allies—who would have had to pay more taxes under the plan—voted for it while blacks, influenced by Edwards and African American leaders, who feared they could not control Roemer, voted no.[22] To add to his woes, Roemer, with the governor's race under way, vetoed one of the strictest anti-abortion bills passed in the United States. In a first, the Louisiana legislature overrode his veto, dramatically undermining his authority as governor.

Although Roemer was an avid poker player, he had run initially as an opponent of gambling, reflecting his fundamentalist Protestant congressional district in north Louisiana. By the time he ran for reelection, however, the legislature had legalized the lottery, gambling cruise ships, and video poker. Since gambling was not popular with many of his original supporters from north Louisiana, this created more headaches for him. And in addition to his political woes, Roemer had personal troubles that became obvious when his second wife left him and filed for divorce. In an effort to deal with his crises, the governor brought an old family friend who was a Baptist minister to live in the governor's mansion with him. Roemer started wearing a rubber band on his wrist, and during an address to the legislature related how he had asked his staff to wear rubber bands on their wrists and flick them whenever they had a hostile thought. This comment caused the governor to become the butt of many jokes.

Late in his first term, Roemer participated in secret talks with President Bush and White House chief of staff John Sununu, leading to Roemer's decision to switch to the Republican party. Not being aware of these talks, various Louisiana Republicans were discussing who would challenge Democrat Roemer for the governorship. They decided among themselves, according to Nungesser, to unite behind one candidate. The discussions were ongoing with no decision having been reached on who that candidate would be when Roemer began his own talks with state Republican leaders.

When the governor asked Nungesser to meet with him after an initial inconclusive gathering, Nungesser asked why, and Roemer replied, "I am going to change [party affiliation]. I want you to support me." Nungesser answered that he had to "meet with all of the other possible Republican candidates who have been considering running against you. I can't agree to support you now without meeting with them and getting their support." This did not go over well with the governor, and words were exchanged.[23]

Roemer scheduled a Sunday evening reception to announce his party switch to his supporters before the planned public announcement. To discuss the situation, Nungesser set up a meeting in Baton Rouge prior to the reception for the Republicans who were considering running against Roemer. Nothing was agreed upon at this meeting except to go to the governor's reception. At the mansion, Roemer told them, "I am announcing and I hope no other Republican runs against me." None of them, however, promised Roemer not to run. The meeting did not go well. Roemer finally said, "I am the governor and I am going to switch." He then strode into the reception and made his announcement, saying he was a social liberal and an economic conservative. While listening to Roemer characterize himself as less than a total conservative, Nungesser began to edge away from the group of Republicans who were standing behind the governor as he spoke, and he left the mansion before the speech was over.[24]

In another meeting with Roemer several days later, Nungesser asked Roemer to meet with Congressman Holloway, a Republican who was considering a gubernatorial campaign, telling the governor that Holloway "doesn't want you to run [as a Republican]." The conversation, according to Nungesser, became agitated, and Roemer "called me a son of a bitch," adding, "I don't need you or [David] Treen." As Nungesser related the session: "We were seated in front of a glass table, and Roemer was pounding the table so hard that I got up and moved. I did not want him to break the table. We were cursing and screaming at each other."[25] Roemer and Holloway did not work out their differences, and the Republicans selected Holloway, who was backed by the Christian right, as their "official" candidate for governor. Thus Roemer became the first sitting governor of Louisiana to switch parties, but it was a partisan marriage made in hell. Instead of enjoying the support of a unified party guaranteeing him a runoff position, newly minted Republican governor Roemer faced two other Republicans, Holloway and Duke.

In addition to Duke, Holloway, and Roemer, the 1991 gubernatorial election featured the flamboyant, determined Edwards, back for a final try at winning an unprecedented fourth term. He declared: "I have a mission. It is to prove that I was right four years ago, that he [Roemer] was lying about me and that he could not do what he said he was going to do." While Edwards put on an energetic campaign, Roemer appeared detached, not even bothering to politick on weekends. Some people believed Roemer did not want to win. Working in Edwards's favor was the fact that he knew how to get along with the legislature, a political skill that voters could appreciate, and that there had been good economic times during much of his tenure as governor.[26]

Republicans believed that Edwards, a Democratic party legend who had survived two trials but had never convinced the public of his complete innocence, was a beatable candidate. As it turned out, the three Republican candidates together polled 64 percent of the vote in the open primary, an indication that a united GOP might have prevailed in 1991. As it also turned out, the three Republicans trailed Edwards in the open primary balloting; the former governor received 33.8 percent of the vote. Duke won the coveted runoff position, garnering 31.7 percent of the vote. Roemer finished third with 26.5 percent, and the "official" GOP candidate, Holloway, trailed badly at 5.3 percent. The day after the election, Roemer claimed, "David Duke beat me, not Edwin Edwards. He beat me in my home territory."[27]

Duke now faced Edwards in the "runoff from hell"— a former Klan leader against a former Democratic governor whose popularity had dwindled. Edwards's once-dominant Democratic populist coalition was no more; his camp now consisted of the black community and a handful of Democratic diehards. As for the GOP, the open primary had left the party in a shambles. Even though Duke was running with Republican after his name, party leaders from Roemer and Treen on down hastened to disavow him.

The runoff campaign centered on the state's economic future, and the momentum switched to Edwards. The tenor of the campaign was captured in a widely distributed bumper sticker: "Vote for the Crook. It's Important!" Edwards suddenly became the establishment's candidate. "Every time I've been in the running," the former governor observed, "there's been some other guy who the newspapers, the country club types, and the so-called good government types thought was better than I was. Well, it sure feels good to be the good guy for a change." The press went all out for Edwards. James Gill, a columnist for the New Orleans *Times-Picayune*, wrote, "This column regrets any observation over the years that could have been construed as implying that Edwards is a corrupt, cold-hearted, skirt-chasing, gambling-addicted demagogue, a champion of polluters and crooks and a reckless administrator who left the state in shambles four years ago."[28]

The state's economic future was the basis of the *Times-Picayune*'s front-page editorial endorsing Edwards. "Many conventions," the editorial stated, "the economic lifeblood of our metropolitan area . . . will [pull out if Duke wins]. Many of the nation's top athletes will stay away from Louisiana." Voters were scared. In a statewide poll taken shortly before the election, 75 percent of all voters and 82 percent of whites were more concerned about what Duke would do in the future than about what Duke had done in the past.[29]

Edwards won the election with 61.2 percent to Duke's 38.8 percent. The turnout was extremely heavy. Duke received 51 percent of the vote in white precincts, far short of the 70 percent of the white vote he needed to win. A key goal of Edwards's campaign strategists was to bring the Roemer voters into their fold, and they succeeded. An exit survey showed that 75 percent of voters who supported Roemer in the October primary voted for Edwards in the November election. According to voters in a postelection survey, the economy and potential loss of business were the most important reasons given by Edwards voters for supporting the former governor, while the welfare system came out on top as the reason given by voters supporting Duke. As the dean of Louisiana political consultants, Jim Carvin, said, "Pocketbooks overrode emotions."[30]

Comparing the governor's race with the 1990 Senate race showed Duke's support falling significantly in the urban areas of New Orleans and Baton Rouge. In rural north Louisiana, an area known for its three P's, "Pine Trees, Poverty, and Protestants," Duke's support increased, while it remained about the same in rural south Louisiana.[31]

Overall, the 1991 election was a complete disaster for the Republican party. For the second year in a row, it seemed the GOP had snatched defeat from the jaws of victory in a major statewide election. Besides losing the governorship, Republican lieutenant governor Hardy and a GOP candidate for insurance commissioner, Peggy Wilson, were defeated. Even Secretary of State Fox McKeithen barely held on to his post, becoming the only statewide Republican survivor. Duke had clearly wounded the Louisiana GOP.

The election further damaged the Republicans' dimming hopes of winning the presidential race in Louisiana for a fourth consecutive time. President Bush seriously contested Louisiana in the 1992 election even though the state was still in the midst of a recession and the Democratic candidate, Bill Clinton, was the governor of a neighboring state. Louisiana had last voted for a Democratic presidential nominee—Georgia's Jimmy Carter—in 1976. Bush and Clinton campaigned in Louisiana often during the fall, giving the Bayou State more attention than it had received since the disputed Hayes-Tilden election of 1876. Native son James Carville ran the Clinton campaign, which didn't hurt Clinton's effort in Louisiana. Clinton carried the state with 45.5 percent of the vote to Bush's 40.9 percent and Ross Perot's 11.8 percent. Clinton's Louisiana victory, especially when contrasted with Bush's substantial pluralities in Mississippi and Alabama, illustrates the tougher road Republicans face in this one-of-a-kind southern state. Once again, urban, Catholic, African American New Orleans was a key component in the Democratic victory. Clinton carried Orleans Parish by 81,242 votes and won the entire state by 82,525 votes.[32]

DEMOCRATIC PARTY CONFLICTS:
THE 1995 GOVERNOR'S ELECTION

The Democrats' return to prominence was to be short-lived. The political misfortunes that befell the GOP owing to intraparty splits were overshadowed in the 1995 governor's race by a similar problem within the Democratic party. The 1995 gubernatorial election campaign began taking shape in June 1994, when, during an address to a joint session of the legislature, Edwards delivered a bombshell. He announced his retirement from politics.

Edwards's departure drastically changed gubernatorial politics. One Democratic candidate, state treasurer Mary Landrieu, had been gearing up to run against him, but she was planning to run as an anti-Edwards reform Democrat. There was no political heir on the horizon who seemed likely to pull together the old Edwards coalition of blacks, organized labor, Cajuns, teachers, and small farmers. Amid the confusion in both political parties, two major candidates-to-be drew little notice. One was Mike Foster, an obscure Democratic state senator from south Louisiana, whose grandfather, Murphy Foster, had been governor from 1882 to 1890. Foster was considered a probusiness conservative—hardly a populist—and had ties to the pro-Edwards senate leadership. Picking up on a hot-button populist issue, Senator Foster pushed through the legislature a bill allowing private citizens to carry concealed weapons. Edwards vetoed it, but the resulting publicity made Foster something of a hero to National Rifle Association partisans.

The other virtually unnoticed candidate was U.S. representative Cleo Fields of Baton Rouge, one of the state's two African American congressmen; he represented a new black-majority district that had been the subject of repeated legal challenges and would likely not be available to him in 1996. Edwards's retirement opened the way, for the first time in Louisiana's modern era, for a serious black candidacy for governor, and Fields planned to be that candidate.

On the Republican side, two high-profile candidates, Duke and former governor Treen, both decided not to run. Quentin Dastugue, who was the official Republican nominee, found himself short of money and withdrew, as mentioned above. It suddenly appeared that Roemer, who was extremely unpopular with party regulars and the Christian right alike but who had hopes of a comeback, might be the only major Republican candidate. Clearly a vacuum had been created.

Foster moved quickly to fill the void. In the political maneuver of the decade, he changed his party affiliation from Democrat to Republican at the same time he qualified to run. What looked like a desperate gamble turned out to be a masterstroke. For the rest of the campaign, Foster played down the probusiness conservatism that had marked his senate career and played to both the Christian right and the Duke voters. When Duke endorsed him, he refused to disavow the endorsement.[33] He attracted Christian right followers with a no-compromise anti-abortion stand. And he added another "populist" touch by advocating an initiative-and-referendum plan by which voters could place proposed laws and constitutional amendments directly on the election ballot.

On the Democratic side, racial politics took center stage. Landrieu was popular with black voters and had received solid black support in her earlier campaigns. Her father, Moon Landrieu, had been an ally of blacks as mayor of New Orleans in the 1970s and later served in President Carter's administration. But Landrieu was facing something that no white Democrat had to deal with in modern times—a serious black candidate. Fields's aim was to unify black voters around his candidacy, at least enough of them to put him into the runoff. It was no easy task. He attracted few campaign contributors. Most observers felt that even if he did make the runoff, he was unlikely to win the general election against Roemer or Foster in a state where black voters then constituted 28 percent of the electorate. Black politicians were in a dilemma. They needed a sympathetic Democrat in the governor's mansion to replace Edwards, but they feared retribution from their constituents if they failed to stand up for a black candidate. Outside the New Orleans area, most chose Fields; in the city they were split, some with Landrieu and some with Fields. Ed Murray, a black state representative from New Orleans, said, "I supported Landrieu in the primary when she ran for governor. I didn't think Cleo could win."[34] New Orleans mayor Marc Morial, perhaps the state's most powerful black elected official, issued a dual endorsement of Landrieu and Fields.

The racial split in the Democratic party came to a head in the final days of the campaign, when Landrieu, campaigning in heavily black New Orleans, urged voters to support a Democrat who could win the runoff. Fields accused her of playing "the race card in the black community. . . . [She is] saying if you vote for a black person you're voting for a Republican. I'm sick of that."[35] By raising the issue that a black candidate could not win, Landrieu contributed to a racial split in the Democratic party.

The results of these shifts in both parties showed up clearly in the open primary results. Foster finished first with 26.1 percent of the vote, dropping fellow Republican Roemer down to fourth place at 17.8 percent. Fields, riding a strong black vote, edged Landrieu out of the runoff by less than a single percentage point, 19.0 percent to 18.4 percent.

The outcome of the runoff was a foregone conclusion. Apart from the intangible factors surrounding his race, Fields, who had a liberal voting record by Louisiana standards, could not unite Democrats behind him. Even Edwards did not campaign for him, and Landrieu, piqued over what she regarded as unfair racial tactics by the Fields camp in the primary, declined to endorse him.[36] The general election was, in many ways, a mirror image of the Edwards vs. Duke runoff of 1991. This time, the Democratic candidate was unacceptable to elements of his own party, while the newly minted Republican had no such problem. In the runoff between Foster and Fields, partisanship had little impact. Fields was black and Foster was white. Fields was too liberal, Foster not too conservative. Foster came from south Louisiana, which had produced a four-term governor. Foster was not French, Cajun, or Catholic, but he was from the heart of Cajunland. Even if Fields had been white, Foster would have done well in south Louisiana. The result was a landslide for Foster, 63.5 percent to 36.5 percent for Fields.

Fields's loss to Foster illuminates a major problem Louisiana Democrats face. Senator Jon Johnson, a longtime black Democratic state senator, explained: "African Americans are a major portion of all Democrats. Until we elect one or two African Americans to statewide office, most of us who are Democrats will not think there is fairness and equity in the Democratic party." The consequences of this frustration among black officials, according to Representative Murray, is "racial division in the Democratic party. Cleo Fields's race crystallized it. You can feel it at party functions."[37]

The results of the 1995 election finally gave the Republicans their first major statewide victory in sixteen years. They increased their representation in the legislature by twenty members, even though they remained a minority (see Table 17). A Republican was elected second in command in the house of representatives. The 1995 elections left the Republicans with an outwardly unified party going into the 1996 federal elections.

THE 1996 SENATE RACE: A COMPLEX PARTISAN SLUGFEST

When Johnston in 1995 announced his intention to step down after twenty-four years in the Senate, the Republicans seemed better positioned than the Democrats to claim his seat. With racial division within their party running high in the wake of the 1995 governor's runoff, Democrats faced the possibility of meeting a similar fate in the 1996 Senate election. Senator Breaux took an active role on the Democratic side. He managed to talk Fields and the state's other black congressman, U.S. representative William J. (Bill) Jefferson of New Orleans, out of the contest, and to talk Mary Landrieu into running. Former governor Edwards, however, detested Landrieu, who had planned to run against him for governor in 1995 if he had chosen to run again. Edwards opposed Landrieu's candidacy and convinced black leaders to support Attorney General Richard Ieyoub of Lake Charles, a moderate Democrat. Landrieu, who had been talked into running by Breaux before Ieyoub emerged, remained in the race, giving the Democrats two major candidates.

Meanwhile, the Republicans were having unexpected difficulty in settling on a candidate. Congressman W. J. (Billy) Tauzin, a conservative from Thibodaux, would have been a leading candidate in either party. He switched to the GOP in 1995, but he surprised many by taking himself out of the Senate race, leaving no clear contender on the Republican side. Early in 1996, the GOP convention chose as its U.S. Senate nominee the darling of the Christian right, state representative Louis (Woody) Jenkins of Baton Rouge, whose main claim to fame was to have pushed through the legislature the strongest anti-abortion law in the nation, one that allowed for no exceptions for rape or incest but only to save the life of the mother. The measure was vetoed by then–Republican governor Roemer. Jenkins, who had been in the house since 1972, was well known in the legislature for holding up plastic models of fetuses at various stages of development. His base of support was "the network . . . made up of home-schooling advocates, opponents of abortion, and Amway distributors (Jenkins is an Amway distributor)."[38] On the other hand, Landrieu had been a pro-choice advocate strongly endorsed by Emily's List, a leading national pro-choice women's group.

In addition to Jenkins, the Senate race drew a large GOP field, including Duke. Unfortunately for Republican hopes, there was no clear leader among the six of their party in the race. In early surveys, all GOP candidates were mired in single digits. A few weeks before the September 21 primary, there was a breakthrough—but on the Democratic side. The *Times-Picayune* revealed that Ieyoub had diverted campaign money from his previous race for attorney general to his own use, some of it to carpet his new home in Baton Rouge. He immediately dropped in the polls, leaving Landrieu out front. As the primary approached, panic began to set in at high levels in the Republican party. It was bad enough that the party seemed on the verge of blowing another golden opportunity to pick up a previously Democratic seat in the Senate from the South. It was even worse that the party could suffer the humiliation of an all-Democratic runoff, which might keep Republican voters away from the polls in the general election, thereby damaging the chances of presidential nominee Bob Dole in Louisiana. But it was a third scenario that truly struck fear into the hearts of GOP leaders: a Duke-Landrieu runoff coinciding with the 1996 national elections. That would have created the worst possible publicity for the GOP nationally.[39]

To prevent such a disaster, former governor Treen, the "grand old man" of the Louisiana GOP, tried to get the five Republican candidates other than Duke to agree to this scheme: a poll would be taken privately to see which of the five would be the strongest candidate against Landrieu in the general election. Treen would then meet with the five to decide who would stay and who would go. Although some candidates appeared ready to go along with this plan, one or two refused. The effort appeared dead and then collapsed completely when one candidate released a confidential memo from Treen about the scheme and called the plan a backroom deal.[40]

Days before the primary, the unity effort was revived by the man with the most to lose from any national GOP debacle: Congressman Livingston, by now chairman of the powerful House Appropriations Committee. Failing to get anyone out of the race, Livingston endorsed Jenkins and urged other GOP leaders to join him in an effort to boost Jenkins into the runoff, or at least keep Duke out of it. The strategy worked better than the Republican leaders hoped. Livingston's endorsement was followed by Treen's, then by all but one of the other Republican congressmen (Baker was the exception). Apparently Republican voters were simply waiting for a signal to settle on one of the five non-Duke GOP candidates. When the signal finally came, they flocked to Jenkins, pushing him to the head of the open primary balloting with 26.2 percent of the vote. Landrieu followed with 21.5 percent, just ahead of Ieyoub's 20.4 percent. Duke limped home in fourth place with 11.5 percent, but his presence in double digits indicated that, without the Republicans uniting behind one candidate, there was a possibility he may have made the runoff.

Both parties entered the runoff with problems. Landrieu made the runoff but had not closed the racial divide within the Democratic party. Nor was she able to make peace with Ieyoub, who was upset by the Democratic party's failure to come to his rescue with TV ads to counteract the bad publicity over his campaign funds. Ieyoub sat out the runoff, never endorsing anyone. The black vote was another problem for the Democratic candidate. There was lingering resentment in the African American community over Landrieu's failure to endorse Fields in 1995. At an appearance with Vice President Al Gore at historic black Southern University in Baton Rouge, Landrieu was booed.[41] Although

Fields gave her a limp endorsement, he cut no TV or radio ads for her. But Landrieu had strengths. She had the good luck to be on the ticket with President Clinton, who was riding a wave of economic prosperity that made him popular with Louisiana voters. It was clear from the beginning that Clinton would carry Louisiana. And helping Landrieu ease the racial rift was the solid support of both Mayor Morial and Congressman Jefferson. Morial's New Orleans political organization helped bring black voters to the polls for Landrieu.

Jenkins, meanwhile, was having unity problems of his own. He said after the primary that he would win the election because, if one totaled up the Democratic (Landrieu-Ieyoub) vote, it came to only 45 percent, while the vote for the six Republicans totaled about 55 percent. But it wasn't that simple. Jenkins had a solid base in the Christian right, but he had to win over the economic conservatives and social moderates, many of whom were made very nervous by the Christian Coalition. A problem with Jenkins's math was that the candidates were facing a much larger electorate in the November 5 presidential election than in the September 21 primary. Turnout rose from 50.1 percent of registered voters to 70.5 percent.

Jenkins's intended "bridge" to the economic conservatives was a plank to abolish the Internal Revenue Service and the entire income tax system, replacing it with a national sales tax. While Jenkins insisted that the level of the proposed sales tax would be about 16 percent, Landrieu skillfully used this issue against him, producing a staff report from a Republican-led U.S. House committee saying that the rate would be at least 32 percent. The tax issue blew up in Jenkins's face, and the campaign got dirtier as the weeks dragged on.

Just as she appeared to be pulling ahead, Landrieu suffered a last-minute bombshell. With just days to go before the vote, retired New Orleans archbishop Philip Hannan held a news conference to warn Roman Catholics that, because of the pro-choice stands of Clinton and Landrieu on the abortion issue, it would be a sin to vote for them.[42] Two bishops from Catholic south Louisiana immediately distanced themselves from the archbishop's statement, advising their congregations that "political responsibility does not involve religious leaders telling people how to vote. . . . [This] would, in our view, be pastorally inappropriate, theologically unsound, and politically unwise."[43]

Landrieu eked out a narrow victory, defeating Jenkins by 5,788 votes, 50.1 percent to 49.9 percent. Landrieu won despite Archbishop Hannan's attack on her pro-choice position, Ieyoub's refusal to endorse her, and Fields's weak, late endorsement. Against all the odds, she was able to get the support of enough African Americans and Catholics to win.[44] Jenkins claimed that the outcome was tainted by fraud and launched a protracted, yet ultimately unsuccessful, battle to have the U.S. Senate call for a new election.

Landrieu had benefited from a strong Democratic presidential turnout and vote for President Clinton as well as the presence on the ballot of a local-option gambling issue. Voters in each parish with legalized gambling were asked to determine the fate of riverboat casinos (and, in New Orleans only, a land-based casino) and video poker machines. Predictably, gambling interests, intent upon protecting themselves, poured millions of dollars into TV and radio ads and into election day get-out-the-vote activities, much of it in black precincts. Despite Landrieu's troubles with Fields, when African Americans voted, they tended to vote not only for gambling but for the Democratic ticket of Clinton and Landrieu as well.[45]

The presidential contest was a sideshow compared to the U.S. Senate race. President Clinton's victory in Louisiana was never in doubt. The Dole campaign, however, did not write off Louisiana, with Dole making five visits to the Bayou State. The president received 52.0 percent of the vote to Dole's 39.9 percent and Perot's 6.9 percent.[46] For the seventh presidential election in a row, Louisiana had gone with the winner.

Although Republicans lost to Clinton and Landrieu in 1996, the GOP could look with satisfaction at its increased strength in the state's U.S. House delegation by the mid-1990s. In 1986 there had been only three Republicans to five Democrats in the state's then-eight-member delegation. As mentioned earlier, the Republicans were Congressmen Livingston, Baker, and Holloway. When Congressman Roemer, then still a Democrat, was elected governor in 1987, he was replaced by a Shreveport Republican, Jim McCrery, making the partisan split four to four as the 1990s began. Owing to slow population growth after the oil industry collapsed in the 1980s, Louisiana lost one of its eight House seats. The redistricting plan adopted for the 1992 elections forced two of the Republican congressmen, Baker and Holloway, into the same district with Baker the winner, thus reducing the GOP contingent to three of the new seven-member delegation.

Under pressure from the Bush administration's Justice Department to create a second black-majority district to go with the New Orleans black-majority district created in the 1980s, Louisiana responded with the Fourth District, which elected Cleo Fields in 1992. The district, which was 63 percent black and encompassed all or portions of twenty-eight of Louisiana's sixty-four parishes, had a Z shape and was quickly dubbed the "Mark of Zorro" district. It was short-lived. Several white north Louisiana residents successfully challenged the district in federal court, claiming that it was an unconstitutional racial gerrymander.

The Fourth District was then revised. The second plan created a wedge-shaped configuration stretching almost three hundred miles, taking in all or part of fifteen parishes and having a 55-percent black voting-age population. Fields won reelection in this district in 1994, but the same plaintiffs from the earlier case challenged his new district. Once more, they won. The districting plan adopted for the 1996 elections contained no district outside of New Orleans with more than a 30 percent black population. Fields, unsuccessful in his 1995 gubernatorial bid, chose not to seek reelection to Congress in 1996. (Incidentally, Fields won a state senate seat in a special election in December 1997.)

In the meantime, the partisan division of the state's U.S. House delegation did not change in the 1994 elections because all seven incumbents—four Democrats and three Republicans—were reelected. After the Republicans captured control of Congress in 1994, two of the four Louisiana Democratic congressmen—Billy Tauzin and James A. (Jimmy) Hayes—switched to the new majority party. Thus, as the 1996 elections approached, the House delegation consisted of five Republicans and two Democrats. (In addition to Fields, the other Democrat was the African American Jefferson of New Orleans.) Much of what had been Fields's old district had been reconfigured into a white-majority district (the Fifth District) encompassing the northeastern corner of the state; it was won in 1996 by a Republican, Dr. John Cooksey of Monroe. In 1996 Congressman Hayes did not seek reelection to the House as a Republican, running instead for the Senate that year and finishing a distant fifth. His seat was won by a white Democrat, Chris John, a former state representative from Crowley (hometown of both Edwards and Breaux).

In 1996, then, the Democrats took back the seat they had lost when Hayes switched parties, but the GOP captured a redrawn district that could be thought of as Fields's old seat. Since Republicans Livingston, McCrery, and Baker and new-Republican Tauzin were reelected in 1996 with little or no opposition, the delegation stayed at five Republicans to two Democrats, a considerable overall improvement for the GOP.

In fact, the GOP successes at the congressional level—albeit partly propelled by a party switch and redistricting—coupled with Foster's 1995 gubernatorial victory and Jenkins's narrow 1996 loss boosted the party's strength as shown by David's index; see Figure 10 in Chapter 1. Given the often blurred partisan patterns described in this chapter, Figure 10's unambiguous picture of significant recent Democratic decline is striking.

Even while Louisiana Republicans were advancing, they were plagued by continuing intraparty conflict between the Christian right and the more moderate elements of the party. The battle reached such an absurd level that the GOP state chairman actually filed suit against the Republican governor and the state's five Republican congressmen. In 1997 the legislature unanimously passed a bill adding six new members to the Republican state executive committee. The Christian right held five of the existing seven seats on the committee. Adding the new members would likely shift the majority from the Christian right to the moderates. Mike Francis, the party chairman and a member of the Christian right, not only sued to have the law overturned, but he called on state senator John Hainkel, the chairman of the Republicans in the legislature and a strong supporter of the law, to resign his chairmanship, accusing him of "treason." In a letter to Hainkel, Francis wrote, "You have wreaked havoc on your own party long enough: I will not stand for it another day." When the lawsuit was filed, Hainkel commented that he was "totally amazed and flabbergasted" by it. "These people must be crazy. Their opposition borders on insanity. . . . Nobody is going to give the party any money with foolishness like this."[47]

CONCLUSION: A VOLATILE, COMPETITIVE PARTISAN FUTURE LOOMS

As the end of the 1990s approached, Louisiana remained divided by geography, race, ethnicity, religion, political affiliation, and intraparty wrangling. Consequently, coalition building is the number-one priority of Louisiana politicians. Since there is no natural majority, a coalition of usually disparate parts must be assembled to create a winning combination. The Democrats must put together most African American voters and enough whites to get their 50-percent-plus-one vote, while the Republicans need approximately two-thirds of the white vote statewide to win an election, assuming they get less than 10 percent of the black vote. It has been easier for the Democrats to get the blacks (28.9 percent of the electorate) and one-third of the statewide white vote than it has been for the Republicans to pick up two-thirds of the white vote. For one thing, 36 percent of Louisiana's whites in a 1996 statewide survey viewed themselves as Democrats. See Table 18, which also shows that 34 percent of the state's whites identified with the Republican party; 28 percent picked the independent label. Thus, if a statewide Democratic candidate can hold the bulk of these white Democratic identifiers and most of the Democratic-leaning black electorate, a Republican faces a stiff task amassing a simple majority in a head-to-head contest, even if the GOP settles on a unifying candidate.

A further problem for the Republicans, as seen in Table 19, is that 34 percent of the somewhat conservative whites and 48 percent of the moderate whites call

Table 18. Party Identification Among Whites in Louisiana, 1996

Party	State Total	Acadiana
Democratic	36%	48%
Republican	34	26
Independent[a]	28	25
N =	(548)	(120)

Source: State survey of 750 registered voters conducted February 23–29, 1996, by Edward F. Renwick.

[a]Figures do not total 100 percent because of rounding and don't know/refused responses.

Table 19. Ideology of Louisiana Whites by Party, 1996

Party	Lib.	Mod.	Somewhat Conserv.	Very Conserv.
Democratic	61	48	34	15
Republican	3	17	41	61
Independent[a]	35	33	24	25
N =	(38)	(195)	(172)	(128)

Source: State survey of 750 registered voters conducted February 23–29, 1996, by Edward F. Renwick.

[a]Figures do not total 100 percent because of rounding and don't know/refused responses.

themselves Democrats. Only 55 percent of all whites think of themselves as being either somewhat or very conservative. It is therefore a daunting task for a conservative Republican to defeat a moderate Democrat. Incidentally, Table 18 illuminates how Acadiana (the French Catholic region) gives the Bayou State its unique slant on the typical southern mix. White voters in Acadiana were 48 percent Democratic, or twelve percentage points higher than all Louisiana whites. Only 26 percent were Republicans, giving the Democrats a 22-point edge over Republicans in this region. Also, 44 percent of the whites in Acadiana identified themselves as conservatives and 43 percent said they were moderates, not much of an advantage for conservatives in this critical swing region.

At present there is a potentially divisive racial disagreement within the Democratic party's black-white coalition and a tense ideological divide within the Republican party, which claims virtually no blacks. Because of these splits, neither party can be viewed as the automatic favorite in major statewide races. As our narrative has demonstrated, much depends on the type of Democratic and

Republican candidates who emerge from the open primary into the final election.

To conclude, it is instructive to learn how several partisan observers view the situation. "For the Republicans, the deeper underlying problem for the party," according to Ray Teddlie, a leading Louisiana political consultant, is that the GOP "is an overwhelmingly white party in a state that has a substantial black population. It is difficult for such a party to avoid being tarnished by suspicions of racism. I think that is a hindrance. Republicans are going to have to develop programs and messages that attract significant support from black voters if the Republicans are going to win statewide elections."[48]

State insurance commissioner Jim Brown, a white Democrat who has run unsuccessfully for governor but has won statewide races for secretary of state and insurance commissioner (twice), commented: "Louisiana is still a Democratic state. It's probably the most Democratic state in the Deep South. A Democratic candidate in a statewide race in Louisiana starts out with a base of a 30 percent black vote, and that's a tremendous advantage. The AFL-CIO isn't what it used to be, but organized labor is still more of a force in Louisiana than most southern states. You have the teachers and a lot of local elected officials. The Democrats still run this state." Ed Murray, the African American legislator quoted earlier, agreed with Brown: "Louisiana is a Democratic state. No question about it."[49]

Republican secretary of state McKeithen disagreed. "I think the GOP is in the ascendancy. The Republicans have the momentum and the Democrats do not. One reason is that the Republicans have been able to attract a lot of the old populists, the blue-collar Democrats who now vote and register Republican."[50]

And then there's David Duke's view: "I think the Republican party's coming on in the state. . . . The Republican hierarchy is very ineffective. Very ineffective." The Democratic party, Duke continued, is "losing ground with the white voters. The Democratic party is becoming the party of minority interests. . . . [It is controlled by] the black bloc vote." The Republican party, by contrast, he added, is becoming the party of "traditional majority interests."[51]

As the comments of these participants in the political process reveal, in Louisiana neither party seems to have the upper hand. A volatile, highly competitive partisan future beckons. And given the Bayou State's penchant for charting a singular path, much like its most famous political leader, Huey Long, the safest prediction of all is to expect the unexpected.[52]

11

TEXAS: REPUBLICANS GALLOP AHEAD

Richard Murray and Sam Attlesey

TEXANS gave Harry S. Truman 66.0 percent of their presidential votes in 1948, easily his strongest showing among the forty-eight states. And with Democrats sweeping every other federal and state elected position, no state from the old Confederacy seemed safer for the Democracy as midcentury approached. But that was not in fact the case. Just four years after Truman's triumph, GOP presidential nominee Dwight Eisenhower bested Adlai Stevenson in the Lone Star State by more than six percentage points, and doubled this margin in 1956. Indeed, presidential Democrats have won just one substantial victory in Texas since Truman—native son Lyndon B. Johnson's landslide over Barry Goldwater in 1964. Republicans have carried Texas in eight of the last twelve presidential elections, usually by large margins.

On election night in 1996, Governor George W. Bush, whose Connecticut Yankee parents had moved to Texas the year of Truman's victory, told a cheering Austin rally, "I think the message to Texans is our state is Republican, and proudly so." He continued, "It does look like an overwhelming night for Republicans statewide."[1]

Governor Bush certainly had bragging rights. His state, alone among the top ten electoral vote venues, had gone solidly for Bob Dole and Jack Kemp. Senior U.S. senator Phil Gramm had been reelected by a comfortable margin, along with all nine other Republicans on the statewide ballot. The Texas senate, a Democratic bastion as late as the 1980s, seemed certain to end up with a 17–14 Republican majority after special elections in December and January. And Republicans had reduced the Democratic edge in the 150-member house of representatives from 26 to 14 seats. Local Republicans also won most countywide contests in Harris (Houston), Dallas, and Tarrant (Fort Worth) counties, the largest urban centers in the state. The GOP's long march from electoral oblivion in 1948 seemed finally crowned with success in 1996.

How did this transformation occur? Specifically, why did Texas, often described as a "must win" state for presidential Democrats through the 1980s, swing so decisively into the Republican White House coalition over the last twenty years? And what enabled Republicans in 1996 to translate, at long last, their top-of-the-ticket appeal into second tier state and local victories?

The factors underlying Republican gains are complex, and the partisan shift is not complete by any means. As the December 10, 1996, special runoffs in two competitive congressional districts showed, Democrats still have life in Texas and are far from ready to concede the nation's second largest state to the Republicans. We return to the latter point at the conclusion of this chapter, but the first order of business is a brief sketch of the rise of the modern Republican party in Texas, followed by a detailed examination of the state's partisan battles of the 1990s.

General elections in Texas, below the presidential level, were humdrum through the 1950s. Few Republicans ran for statewide, congressional, legislative, or local offices, and those who did were not taken seriously. Voter interest and turnout in general elections were well below Democratic primary levels. Things began to change when a young college professor, John Tower, won a special election runoff in 1961 and became the first Republican to represent Texas in the U.S. Senate since Reconstruction. Democrats wrote off Tower's win as a fluke, but he held the seat through three tough reelection fights in 1966, 1972, and 1978. When he retired, recent GOP convert Phil Gramm won the seat in a landslide.

Despite being wiped out in the Goldwater debacle, Texas Republicans reestablished a few beachheads around the state in 1966, and ran strong races for governor in 1968 and 1972. Former governor John Connally switched parties in 1973, and the conservative exodus accelerated after moderates and liberals gained control of the state Democratic party and convention in 1976.[2] Divisions within that party contributed to another and more important GOP statewide upset win in 1978 when Dallas businessman William P. Clements edged past the favored Democratic gubernatorial nominee, Attorney General John Hill.[3] Texas governors have limited legislative powers, but their appointive duties provide excellent opportunities for party-building, which Clements made effective use of.

Three general factors helped the Republicans close the gap with the Democrats in Texas during the 1970s and 1980s. First, the Texas GOP benefited, like their fellow Republicans across the South, from the growing perception that the Democratic party was too liberal, too pro–labor union, too accepting of gays and lesbians and feminists, and too supportive of big government and high taxes. Racial politics in Texas matters less than in the Deep South states, but the Democrats paid a price with Anglo voters for the overwhelming support African Americans and, to a lesser degree, Mexican Americans gave Democratic nominees from the White House to the courthouse. This disaffection with the ancestral party was crystallized in the presidential campaigns of the 1980s when the Democratic nominees, Jimmy Carter, Walter Mondale, and Michael Dukakis, were widely viewed by Texas Anglos as out-of-the-mainstream liberals hostile to the traditional values of Texans. By contrast, GOP nominees Ronald Reagan and George Bush were popular with most Anglo Texans.[4]

Second, the national alliance between the religious right and the Republican party paid big dividends in Texas in the late 1970s and 1980s. Texas has a high percentage of evangelical, fundamentalist, and Pentecostal Christians who endorsed this alliance, and relatively few Jews, liberal Protestants, or secular voters who might be offended by it. Christian conservatives brought a new voter base to the state party and helped cut traditional Democratic margins in blue collar and small-town Anglo areas.[5]

Third, rapid economic growth attracted sizable numbers of white middle- and upper-middle-class voters to the booming suburbs around Dallas, Houston, Fort Worth, and San Antonio. Unlike other new immigrants, they registered and voted, and they mostly voted Republican. The direction and magnitude of this shift can be seen in the four U.S. Senate general elections Democrat Lloyd Bentsen was a candidate in between 1970 and 1988 in Collin County, Texas. In 1970 the county, northeast of Dallas, was still largely rural, small-townish, and Democratic. Bentsen carried the county by 1,774 out of less than 13,000 votes in 1970 over a strong opponent, future president George Bush. Bentsen faced weaker opponents in each subsequent race, but he lost Collin County by 3,920 votes in 1976, by 7,922 votes in 1982, and by 11,094 votes in 1988. In this last contest, more than 90,000 votes were tallied in Collin County.

The consequences of these developments[6] are strikingly evident when we track changes in party identification from the late 1970s to early 1990. As Table 20 shows, the Democrats held a huge edge in partisan self-identification (Texas does not have registration by party) among registered voters in 1978, outnumbering Republicans by 48 percent to 19 percent. This deteriorated rapidly after 1982, to the point that by the spring of 1990, voters were about equally divided

between Democrats, Republicans, and independents. (Party identification figures for the 1990s are shown below in Table 25.)

While partisan attachments were shifting, another long-term change was occurring in the electoral process: the declining importance of the Democratic
primary in Texas politics. Historically, the Democratic primary was the route to
office for serious state and local candidates. As such, in nonpresidential years it
drew far more voter interest and participation than did general elections. As the
data in Table 21 show, in 1950 almost 1.1 million votes for governor were cast
in the Democratic primary, compared to less than 400,000 in the general election, a ratio of 2.75 primary voters to each November participant. But that proportion steadily dropped so that by the 1980s the Democratic primary–general
election vote ratio was less than .40 in nonpresidential years. Texas had become
a two-party state, at least in high-profile contests.

Down-ballot Democrats, however, retained their dominance in the 1970s
and 1980s. In 1978, Republicans won just 4 of 24 congressional seats and only
improved to 8 of 27 in 1988. Results were equally lopsided in the legislature.
The GOP claimed just 22 of 150 state house seats in 1978, and 57 of 150 in
1988. The state senate changed even less, with only 4 Republicans among 31
victors in 1978, and 8 of 31 in 1988. And fewer than 15 percent of local officials
elected on partisan ballots were Republicans as the 1980s ended.

THE 1990 ELECTIONS: MISSED OPPORTUNITY FOR THE GOP?

Heading into the 1990 election cycle, Texas Republicans were optimistic about
converting their growing voter base into elective success in a nonpresidential

Table 20. Party Identification in Texas, 1978–1990

Year	Dem.	Rep.	Ind.	None/Other
1978	48%	19%	32%	1%
1980	45	22	31	2
1982	46	22	31	1
1986	40	26	33	1
1987	39	23	38	1
1989	33	28	38	1
1990	34	33	33	1

Source: Surveys conducted by the Center for Public Policy, University of Houston.

Note: The question asked was, "Generally speaking, do you think of yourself as a Republican, a
Democrat, or an Independent?"

Table 21. Total Votes Cast for Governor in Texas Democratic Primaries Versus General Elections, 1950–1986

Year	Dem. Primary	Gen. Election	Ratio (Dem./Gen.)
1950	1,086,564	394,747	2.75
1954	1,350,752	634,784	2.13
1958	1,317,516	789,865	1.67
1962	1,447,106	1,567,731	.92
1966	1,255,397	1,425,705	.88
1970	1,543,500	2,235,520	.69
1974	1,519,715	1,654,992	.92
1978	1,777,858	2,369,584	.75
1982	1,257,480	3,191,088	.39
1986	1,095,345	3,441,460	.32

Source: Mike Kingston, Sam Attlesey, and Mary G. Crawford, *The Texas Almanac's Political History of Texas* (Austin, 1992).

year. But before they could expand their position, the GOP had to defend Senator Gramm's seat and hold the governorship. The former task seemed easy. Gramm was popular with voters and had a big campaign war chest, and his Democratic opponent, Hugh Parmer, was a relatively unknown state senator with little fund-raising potential. The 1990 governor's race presented more of a problem. The Republican incumbent, Bill Clements, had won back the job he had lost in 1982 only to be plagued by a combination of character and political problems throughout his second term. He was not a candidate for reelection.

Seven Republicans, including four serious contenders, filed for the March primary. Former congressman Kent Hance of Lubbock was an early favorite. He had run a strong statewide primary race for the U.S. Senate in 1984 as a Democrat, had finished second to Clements in the 1986 Republican gubernatorial primary, and enjoyed a strong financial base. Dallas lawyer Tom Luce and Houston businessman Jack Rains also had substantial support in their respective metropolitan areas. The fourth contender was Clayton Williams, a multimillionaire west Texas oilman, rancher, and business owner whom Texans had seen featured for several years in ads for his fledgling long distance phone company, Claydesta.

Despite his lack of political experience and establishment backing, Williams broke the race open in the fall with an advertising blitz. Spending $8 million of his personal fortune, he presented himself as a plain-speaking, successful businessman who would have convicts "busting rocks" when he became governor. Using colorful imagery associated with his hero, John Wayne, Williams defined himself as a political outsider who would restore the lost greatness of the Lone Star State. By the time his less heavily funded opponents began their media advertising, Williams had seized a wide lead in public opinion polls that he would not relinquish. He ended up taking 60.8 percent of the 855,231 votes cast in the March primary.

One small cloud did appear in Williams's blue campaign sky a few days after his smashing primary victory. The candidate invited a number of reporters to the spring roundup at his west Texas ranch. Shut in one morning by bad weather, he "joked" with his journalist guests that the inclement conditions were like rape—"if it's inevitable, just relax and enjoy it."[7] The widely publicized remark was not found amusing by all Texans, especially women of various partisan persuasions.

Texas Democrats went into 1990 determined to both regain the governor's chair and preserve their state and local preeminence. Two prominent state officials had been pointing to the governor's race for years. Attorney General Jim Mattox had a deserved reputation as a fighter for the downtrodden in the Texas legislature, the U.S. Congress, and for the last seven years as attorney general. He felt his strong record of service to African Americans, Hispanics, women, organized labor, and liberals had earned him the right to the Democratic nomination.

State treasurer Ann Richards did not agree. She knew Mattox and his record; she and her former husband, liberal attorney Dave Richards, had been friends and political allies of Mattox for years, and Dave was now working for Mattox in the attorney general's office. Ann Richards might concede that Mattox had more impressive credentials, but she sensed those mattered little to voters, and she believed she possessed assets he lacked. She was a rising star in national feminist circles and enjoyed wide popularity with state Democratic voters. Unlike Mattox, she had made few enemies while climbing the political ladder. Her life story, which included overcoming alcoholism, a painful divorce, and breaking into the "good ol' boys club" of Texas politics, resonated with many Texans. Her national stature and renowned wit earned her a coveted keynoter spot at the 1988 Democratic National Convention in Atlanta, where her sharp barbs at prospective GOP nominee and fellow Texan George Bush brought down the house. State Republicans were infuriated by Richards's remark, "Poor George, he can't help it, he was born with a silver foot in his mouth,"[8] but Democratic voters applauded her humor.

Democratic leaders knew the potential for a bitter Mattox-Richards collision, but hoped the pair's long friendship and mutual interest in taking back the governor's office would restrain them. Hopes for a peaceful primary were reduced when former governor Mark White, by then a Houston lawyer, decided to also enter the primary in the fall of 1989. White had backing from some well-heeled supporters, but he had virtually no organization in the field to compare with those of Mattox and Richards. Like Clayton Williams, he would have to depend on paid media advertising, but, unlike the Republican, White was a well-known politician with considerable baggage who lacked the ability to outspend his competitors down the stretch.

The Democratic race started slowly, with Richards holding a modest lead over White in published polls and Mattox lagging in third place. The attorney general, frustrated by the lack of support he was getting from groups he had championed for years, knew he would have to turn up the heat on Ann Richards. He got the opportunity after the first televised candidate debate in January 1990. Dallas television reporter Cindy Kennard asked Richards if she had ever used illegal substances. Richards declined a direct answer by saying she had used no "mind-altering chemicals" for ten years. At a second debate, when Richards deflected the same question, Mattox pounced. Addressing her, he pressed the issue: "Ann, Mark and I have known you a long time, *and we understand why you don't want to answer the question*. At least eight times reporters have asked you to respond—and that's only the Democratic primary. If you were the nominee of this party, the Republicans will not be so gentle. Clayton Williams will do more than just bust rocks. He'll bust our party. Regardless of how much you think it will hurt you, you need to respond and answer the question in the primary. Because it has become the biggest question in this campaign."[9]

Richards stuck to her position and endured a press feeding frenzy that echoed Mattox's demand. Her lead in the polls plummeted. White was the initial beneficiary as Richards's soft support drifted to the former governor rather than the aggressive attorney general. Richards did not waver, then hit back hard at both her opponents in a March 5 press conference and a follow-up thirty-second television ad. She accused White and Mattox of "lining their pockets" while holding public office.[10] The charges stuck, particularly to White, when press stories raised new questions about his financial dealings in and out of office. Running out of advertising money and lacking a field organization, his campaign collapsed the last week before the March 13 primary.

Mattox, who had built up a campaign war chest of $4 million during his tenure as attorney general, made his closing move with a huge television buy in late February and March that presented him as the only alternative to the damaged Richards. Richards barely held a lead on primary day with 39.0 percent of the 1,487,260 votes cast, compared to 36.7 percent for Mattox. White, denouncing Richards for her "Himmler" tactics, got just 19.2 percent.

Texas, like most of the other southern states, requires a runoff when no primary candidate gets a majority, so Richards and Mattox had to fight on another month. It would be, as Richards foresaw, "a mud wrestling contest."[11] To win, Mattox had to keep the focus on Richards's alleged drug use. This he did in free and paid media. Mattox's escalating charges that his opponent had used cocaine and other illegal drugs while holding public office were aired on the CBS network program *Face the Nation* and given space in every major national newspaper. But when the attorney general could not produce supporting evidence, the attacks eventually backfired with Texas voters. Richards's core supporters held firm, her field organization got out their vote, and she won 57.1 percent of the 1,122,734 votes cast in the runoff.

Democrats were relieved to see the primary war end, but they also knew that Richards had been badly damaged after ninety days of being pounded on the drug issue by the press and Mattox. Her favorability rating with her party was barely 50 percent, and in the entire electorate it was around 30 percent after the runoff while her unfavorability rating soared above 50 percent.[12] Now she would have to face the well-funded Clayton Williams, who had sailed through the Republican primary with barely a glove laid on him.

The Republican nominee's colorful outspokenness, an asset in the primary, gradually became a liability in the general election campaign. Williams had followed up his roundup rape joke in April by volunteering that he had, as a youth, visited houses of prostitution along the Mexican border. This was, he noted, "part of the fun of growing up in West Texas," and that "the houses were the only place you got serviced then." In a July interview with *U.S. News and World Report*, he meant only to explain his earlier meaning, but instead dug himself a deeper hole: "In the world I live in . . . you talk about the bull servicing the cow. I was trying to find a nice, polite term for f—ing."[13]

Throughout the summer the Texas Republican party and Williams kept up a steady stream of harsh attacks on Richards as a liberal, soft-on-crime, pro-abortion feminist, while dubbing her an "honorary lesbian" for taking gay and lesbian endorsements. Despite Williams's huge lead in the polls, Richards held her fire, convinced that swing voters would decide late in the campaign for whom they would vote and determined that her campaign would have enough money to match Republican spending down the stretch.

Richards got some help in August when the Dallas *Morning News* and the Houston *Chronicle* ran investigative stories critical of Williams's business dealings over the years. Many of the companies he founded had not made money, and half had been sold or dissolved, often after litigation. But the stories seemed to have little immediate impact. A Houston *Chronicle* poll taken September 6–10 showed Williams holding a 48 percent to 33 percent lead.

In early October, Richards finally hit Williams with a series of hard television ads attacking his alleged shady business dealings. Williams was outraged and promised to "head and hoof her and drag her through the dirt." He confronted Richards at a rare joint appearance before the Greater Dallas Crime Commission. After telling a companion, "Watch this," Williams went up to Richards and declared, "I'm here to call you a liar today."[14] The treasurer, taken aback, responded, "I'm sorry, Clayton," and offered her hand. Williams refused to shake, blasted Richards as a liar again, and stormed away in full view of live television cameras.

The GOP candidate thought his frontal attack was the right approach, but Williams's staff knew better and increasingly tried to keep him away from reporters. Press relations deteriorated as the easygoing cowboy of the primary morphed into a boorish Bubba in the general election. Women voters were especially distressed at his personal attacks on Richards. By late October, Richards had a clear lead among female voters and trailed by single digits overall. Poll movement was not so much Richards moving up in voter standing but Williams declining. The question seemed to be which would be the least popular by election day.

Williams was still in a position to win, if he could avoid further self-inflicted wounds. He could not, making two more missteps in the last week before the general election. Williams had voted an early absentee ballot, but could not recall when asked by reporters how he had voted on a constitutional amendment dealing with the powers of the office he was seeking. He claimed his wife had told him how to vote on it, and he had forgotten her advice. Then, after months of fending off Richards's demand that he join her in releasing his income tax returns, Williams volunteered that he had paid no federal income taxes in 1986. For a very wealthy businessman running in a state mired in an economic slump, that was not a helpful comment.[15]

Richards won with 49.5 percent of the record 3,892,746 votes cast; Williams received 46.9 percent and nearly all the rest went to a Libertarian. The Voter News Service exit poll showed a sharply polarized race along gender lines. Williams won a near landslide among males, taking 55 percent of their votes; but Richards did even better among women, getting 61 percent of the major-party female vote. Williams ran better in rural and small-town Texas than any previous Republican gubernatorial candidate, but lost the usually Republican big urban counties. Suburban women, including Republicans, voted for Richards in large enough numbers to offset Williams's strong showing in nonmetropolitan counties. Richards rolled up large majorities among black voters (91 percent) and Hispanics (75 percent), while Williams led among whites by 57 percent to 43 percent.

Williams's big mouth certainly contributed to his losing the election, but considerable credit also goes to Richards and her campaign.[16] The candidate survived one of the roughest primaries in modern American history and did not crack under great pressure. She raised over $13 million for the primary and general election campaigns, which enabled her to compete in the most expensive governor's race in U.S. history (Williams spent $21 million, and other candidates more than $16 million in the primaries). Richards's grass-roots organization came through for her in both primaries and the general election, helping her become the first woman governor of Texas elected on her own merits. Her late surge also was helped by favorable national conditions. In October and November 1990 the national economy was slowing, and voter movement at the margins was swinging toward the Democrats as economic worries deepened. Richards and other Democrats in Texas were not swimming against a national tide on November 6, 1990.

Republicans could take some solace from the overall results of the Texas elections. Senator Gramm overwhelmed his underfunded opponent, state senator Parmer, with 60.2 percent of the vote, and Kay Bailey Hutchison won the open treasurer's position Richards was leaving. Hutchison, a former state legislator, would find her new position an excellent platform to mount a campaign for higher office, much as the governor-elect had just done. The GOP took another statewide post when recent party convert Rick Perry, a West Texas legislator, upset an outspoken populist Democrat, Agriculture Commissioner Jim Hightower.

But in the open-seat contests for the important positions of lieutenant governor, attorney general, and comptroller of public accounts, the Democrats' superior bench strength paid dividends. Longtime comptroller Bob Bullock won the powerful lieutenant governorship, assuring continued Democratic control of this efficacious leadership post in the state senate. State senator John Sharp, a conservative Democrat from Victoria, won the vacated comptroller position, and state representative Dan Morales of San Antonio became the first Hispanic attorney general in the state's history.

Elsewhere the parties fought to an absolute draw. In the U.S. congressional elections, Democrats retained their 19–8 majority. There was no change in the Democrats' 23–8 Senate majority, and 93–57 state house edge. Aside from losing a winnable governor's race, the failure to make significant state legislative gains in 1990 was particularly painful for Republicans, because Democrats would keep their big redistricting advantage heading into the 1991 legislative and congressional redistricting process.

The 1992 and 1993 Elections: The GOP Gains Ground

The 1992 election cycle began in January 1991 when the legislature convened for its 140-day biennial session. Members faced the usual thorny issues of funding the budget, dealing with an exploding prison population, and tackling inequities in public school finance. But they also had to redraw the electoral districts for their respective houses and the U.S. House. Big changes had to be made. With three new congressional seats coming to Texas because of population gains, at least a dozen of the twenty-seven old U.S. House seats would have to be greatly altered.

Political considerations also dictated major realignments. Hispanics, who had been 21 percent of the state's population in 1980, were 26 percent in 1990, and their leaders were insisting on a bigger share of the representational pie. Republicans, angry over having received a much higher percentage of votes cast than congressional and legislative seats won, were determined to block Democratic gerrymanders in the 1990s. Blacks wanted to protect their representational gains from the 1971 and 1981 redistrictings and secure the first black congressional seat in the Dallas–Fort Worth area. Anglo Democrats, holding majorities in all three bodies that had to be redistricted, were vulnerable, especially since most population growth in the 1980s had occurred in Hispanic south Texas, Latino urban neighborhoods, and Houston and Dallas suburbs that usually voted Republican up and down the ballot.

Republican hopes for a better outcome in 1991 than in the previous redistrictings rested on three factors. First, there had been promising exploratory talks in Texas, as in other southern states, between GOP strategists and minority members about making common cause against the Anglo Democrats in the redistricting process.

Second, the Voting Rights Division of the U.S. Department of Justice, headed by George Bush appointee John Dunne, was signaling that departmental approval of new district maps would in large part hinge on a maximum effort to create majority-minority districts in the South and other areas under the special provisions of the Voting Rights Act. And that maximum effort, the Justice Department made clear, would include aggressive mapping techniques, down to the census block level. Republicans and Democrats knew that that approach could strip out minority neighborhoods often vital to the survival of urban white Democrats in Congress and the legislature.

Third, the local federal district courts in Texas and the regional appellate court (the Fifth Circuit) were dominated by Reagan and Bush appointees with strong conservative and Republican pedigrees. If the legislative Democratic majorities lost control of the process to the courts, they would be in a heap of trouble.

In light of these conditions, it is somewhat surprising that Texas Anglo Democrats were able, in two of three cases, to secure plans that both protected their incumbents and passed Justice Department scrutiny. *The Almanac of American Politics* gave its "Phil Burton Award" to the 1991 Texas congressional plan. Like Congressman Burton's famous (or infamous) 1981 California plan, which locked up a large majority of the state's 46 congressional seats for the Democrats, the Lone Star State's plan was honored "for its creatively drawn lines in unlikely places; for the convoluted boundaries of its districts which, snakelike, seem to be threatening to swallow each other; for the ingenuity with which white urban Democrats, long dependent on black votes, were given districts where Democratic rural counties were substituted for urban black neighborhoods."[17]

The award-winning plan was developed by an aide to Dallas–Fort Worth Democrat Martin Frost, one of the most endangered incumbents. One key to selling the deal was creating three majority-minority districts with the newly gained seats. Two of these were crafted to meet the political interests of Dallas state senator Eddie Bernice Johnson, an African American who chaired the senate committee on congressional districting, and state senator Frank Tejeda of San Antonio and south Texas. The third was tailored for Houston Hispanics, in the form of a majority Mexican-American district in central Harris County. Apart from these three, the task of Frost staffer Bob Mansker was to design realigned districts that the twenty-seven incumbents, including eight Republicans, could sign off on. Ironically, he could do this only by using the districting procedures the Justice Department was promoting for other reasons. So the odd shaped districts created in Texas not only increased minority representation, but also preserved incumbent interests—a very different result from what had occurred in Georgia and North Carolina. The Republican-minority coalition technique did not operate in Texas, because, as Houston city councilman Ben T. Reyes, a longtime Hispanic leader active in redistricting negotiations, observed in late 1995, "The Republicans wanted too much. We got a better deal by working with the Democrats."[18]

The plan for the Texas house of representatives was equally creative in stringing together minority urban neighborhoods to preserve Democratic incumbents. To get the support of black legislators, the final map had to protect African American house members in Harris, Dallas, and Tarrant counties. This was not easy because overall black population growth had slowed in the 1980s, and segregated inner city wards that were the bases for these members had lost much of their populations to suburban areas. To get sufficient populations in each black district, most had to be extended, very creatively, deep into suburban areas. The next problem was accommodating Hispanic interests. This required sacrificing one Anglo Democratic district in Harris County to get a third majority Mexican-American seat, but other urban white members, Democratic and Republican, were protected by the new lines. Population patterns assured the shift of several other seats from Anglos in west and north Texas to Hispanics in south Texas.

Texas senate Democrats were unable to duplicate a timely plan that protected incumbents of both parties and addressed minority needs, and they lost control of the districting process to a three-judge federal court. That panel of Republican appointees drew and imposed their own state senate plan, which put six of the twenty-three incumbent Democrats at risk. Republicans finally had one favorable set of districts for the 1992 elections.

With redistricting settled, at least for 1992, and with no major statewide offices at stake, attention shifted to the upcoming presidential election. Throughout 1991, Texas pundits, like their national counterparts, assumed George Bush would breeze to the Republican nomination and likely reelection in November. One indication of the president's perceived strength came in the fall of 1991 when popular Democratic senator Lloyd Bentsen, who in 1970 had beaten George Bush for a U.S. Senate seat in Texas, declined to run for president in 1992. With other prominent national Democrats also passing on the race, Bush entered the fourth year of his presidency in a strong political position, even as economic growth lagged and his personal approval ratings were declining from their stratospheric levels after Desert Storm.

On the Democratic side, Governor Bill Clinton of Arkansas became the front-runner when Governor Mario Cuomo of New York finally decided in December 1991 that he would not be a candidate for his party's nomination. Texas was a key state for the relatively unknown Arkansan. Clinton's strong Texas ties were forged in 1972 when he managed the doomed effort of George McGovern in the state. Over the course of that campaign, Clinton got to know the state's politics and its Democratic politicians. He made lasting friendships with many, like liberal leader Billie Carr, a Democratic National Committee member from Houston, and Garry Mauro, the Texas land commissioner who agreed to organize the state for Clinton's presidential campaign. Clinton also had a warm relationship with fellow governor Ann Richards, who seemed to harbor no presidential ambitions for herself.

By January 1992, when the Gennifer Flowers story broke in the national press, Commissioner Mauro and other Texas FOBs (Friends of Bill) had already put together a strong network of state supporters and financial contributors. When Flowers went public with her story of a twelve-year affair with Clinton, the candidate was immediately engulfed in a media feeding frenzy much as Gary Hart had been in 1987 when his involvement with Donna Rice was revealed. Taking lessons from the Hart campaign meltdown, Clinton was determined not to lose control of his schedule and instead to fight through the swarming media and take his case to the primary voters.

Senior Clinton supporters and financial contributors met with the candidate at a critical strategy session in Washington on January 23, 1992. Among those present was a Houston lawyer and FOB, Bill White, who had been organizing a Texas fund-raiser for the governor the following week. White recalled: "The decision was made for the President to go on Sixty Minutes after the Super Bowl on Sunday. Without getting into specifics, but in understandable language to any adult, he and Mrs. Clinton would make it clear they had had marital problems, but they had worked through them, and they would leave it to the American people to decide whether or not this disqualified him for the presidency. Then, he would resume his planned schedule the next day, which was a Southern day, ending at the Houston fund-raiser."[19]

In journalist Joe Klein's semifictional bestseller, *Primary Colors*, the scandal-ridden southern governor breaks off New Hampshire campaigning and flies to Los Angeles for a critical fund-raiser. In fact, Governor Clinton came to Bill White's event in Houston on January 27 to replenish his nearly depleted war chest. The governor's Texas friends came through, and he netted $150,000 to fund paid media in the critical closing weeks before the New Hampshire primary. Texas dollars were critical to the Comeback Kid's strong second-place finish behind New England regional favorite Paul Tsongas of Massachusetts.[20]

After finishing a respectable second in New Hampshire, Clinton headed south in early March. His big win in Texas on March 10 (65.6 percent of 1,482,675 total votes) keyed a sweep of the southern primaries on Super Tuesday and gave him a commanding delegate lead over his remaining rivals, former senator Tsongas and former California governor Jerry Brown. Tsongas dropped out of the race two weeks later and Clinton, though dogged by the national media's focus on character issues of sexual infidelity and draft dodging, had won a clear majority of the delegates by the close of primary season on June 2.

While Clinton and Bush were locking up their respective party nominations, another presidential contender from Texas, Dallas billionaire Ross Perot, began hinting that he too might enter the fray. When queried about his future plans by TV talk show host Larry King, Perot coyly signaled he could be talked into running as an independent.[21] Not all Texans were surprised by Perot's edging into the presidential race. Perot had long displayed a taste for high profile projects that put him in the limelight. His involvement in one such project, resolving the Vietnam War POW/MIA issue, brought him into conflict with Vice President George Bush during the Reagan administration. Few noticed when Perot bitterly criticized Bush during his 1988 campaign, but his undeclared candidacy in 1992 immediately moved him into the national spotlight. As Perot set about organizing a run for president across the nation, he focused his attacks on the president, not the struggling Arkansas governor, in the spring of 1992. That strategy worked in May and June when the feisty Texan moved into a virtual tie with President Bush in national opinion polls. Bill Clinton trailed both by ten points or so.

In a way that virtually no analyst at the time expected, Perot's fresh campaign and aggressive style made the race a referendum on Bush's domestic presidency and deflected interest from Clinton's character problems. Perot then did Clinton a second big favor by abruptly withdrawing from a race he had never officially entered on July 16 and issuing a semi-endorsement of the governor just as he was accepting the nomination of his party in New York. As the only alternative to the diminished Bush, Clinton surged into a wide lead over the incumbent by the end of July.

Clinton's unexpected rise in the polls meant the Republican National Convention in Houston was critical to GOP hopes of getting back into the race. Unfortunately, when the convention was planned, the expectation was that it should shore up Bush's right flank to prevent defections to Perot in a three-way race. Now the problem was cutting into Bill Clinton's big lead before the fall campaign began. The opening night lineup starring Pat Buchanan and Pat Robertson was designed to steady wavering conservatives, not to woo back moderates and independents drifting to Clinton. Nor was the "family values" theme President Bush and Vice President Quayle emphasized in their acceptance speeches. The president's approval and trial heat numbers improved a bit after the Houston convention, but Clinton still led in all national polls, and there were few good opportunities left to tighten the contest.

Clinton's selection of Tennessee senator Al Gore for his running mate suggested he might emulate Jimmy Carter's "southern strategy" of 1976 and 1980 to win an electoral college majority. Instead, as one observer noted, the party's all-southern ticket "only skirmished in Dixie, and instead marched north to victory."[22]

Local observers like Billie Carr say Clinton badly wanted to take the fight to Bush in Texas. Clinton visited the state a half dozen times in 1992 and polls showed after Perot reentered the race in early October that the Democratic ticket had a real chance in Texas. But in the end, the highly disciplined Clinton campaign team persuaded their candidate to stick with their game plan of concentrating media buys in twenty states with targeted appeals to particular groups. Texas was not on the list. Bush, even with or behind Clinton in all big states, had little choice but to pour time and money into Texas. Bush and Perot advertised heavily in Texas (Bush spent $5 million, Perot even more), and it paid off as both moved up and Clinton stalled out in the last days of the campaign. On November 5, Bush got 2,496,071 votes (40.6 percent) to Clinton's 2,281,815 (37.1 percent). Perot ran a strong third with 1,354,781 (22.0 percent).[23] Strategically, one could argue that Clinton won the Texas game by forcing Bush to expend resources here, leaving the GOP with less for the battleground states of Ohio, New Jersey, Michigan, Pennsylvania, and Wisconsin, where Clinton won his electoral college majority.

National exit polls showed Perot voters would have divided about evenly between Bush and Clinton had he stayed out of the race. There can be little doubt, however, that he drew votes away from Bush in Texas and kept the race close. Table 22 presents a summary of presidential vote patterns and turnout in the five largest urban counties of Texas. Turnout was far above the overall average in upscale Republican areas, but the usual GOP vote share was down in these areas because Perot took a good part of the white middle- and upper-class vote. By contrast, Perot got virtually no black votes and few from Hispanics, so he did not substantially reduce the big Democratic advantage among minority voters.

Ironically, what was bad for President Bush helped other Republicans on the ballot, because Perot's independent candidacy drew record turnouts in white, conservative areas. These extra votes went mostly to Republican candidates in nonpresidential contests further down the ballot. This skewed turnout helped Republicans win three of the seven statewide elections and a majority of local contests in big urban counties.

The congressional results, with one exception, went as predicted, with incumbents winning reelection and the three new majority-minority districts electing Democrats (although the Twenty-Ninth District in Harris County, a majority Hispanic area, elected an Anglo, Gene Green). Republicans picked up a south Texas seat when Henry Bonilla, a television anchor in San Antonio, de-

Table 22. Turnout and Presidential Vote in Urban Texas for the 1992 General Election

Urban Precinct Group	Mean Voter Turnout	Mean Presidential Vote		
		Bush	Clinton	Perot
Affluent whites	87%	65%	19%	16%
Middle-class whites	83	51	26	23
Lower-middle-class/blue-collar whites	75	34	41	25
Hispanics	49	16	72	12
Blacks	57	3	96	1
All precincts	73	40	41	19

Source: Data compiled by the Center for Public Policy, University of Houston, from official returns, Office of the Secretary of State, Texas, for precincts in Harris, Dallas, Tarrant, Bexar, and Travis counties.

feated Congressman Albert Bustamante, who was under federal indictment. The effectiveness of the Democratic districting plan can be seen when one looks at the congressional votes versus seats won by party in 1992. The Democrats contested 28 districts and won 2.81 million votes; Republicans contested 27 districts and won 2.69 million votes. The Democrats won just 51.1 percent of the two-party vote, but 70 percent (21 of 30) of the seats.

The story was repeated in the Texas house of representatives. Republican candidates got a record number of total votes, but won just one net seat, giving them 58 to 92 for the Democrats. The state senate, elected under the Republican court-ordered plan, was a horse of a different color. Republicans gained four seats and came close in two other cases, cutting the Democratic majority from 23–8 to 19–12.

If the 1992 elections started with redistricting in 1991, they extended into 1993 as a consequence of Clinton's general election victory. The president-elect's first Cabinet nominee was Senator Bentsen for secretary of the treasury. His confirmation created a vacancy to which Governor Richards could name an interim senator, but a special election open to all comers was required within ninety days. Richards had trouble making up her mind in December and January, but eventually settled on former congressman and then–railroad commissioner Robert Krueger. Krueger had run a strong race for the Senate against Tower in 1978, but had finished third in the Democratic primary when he ran for the same seat in 1984. The latter race turned out to be more indicative of his voter appeal in 1993 than the former contest.

Twenty-three candidates filed against the new senator in a May 1 special election. Krueger's vulnerability was suggested by the entry of two Democrats with some appeal, wealthy Dallas businessman Richard Fisher and former Raza Unida party leader Jose Angel Guitierrez. Krueger's main competition came from three Republican contenders, Congressman Joe Barton from the Dallas area, Congressman Jack Fields from Harris County, and state treasurer Kay Bailey Hutchison. As mentioned above, Hutchison had won the open seat contest to replace Richards in 1990, not a particularly good year for statewide Republicans. She benefited in 1990 from a strong base in the numerous Republican women's clubs across Texas, and she would again in 1993. Neither did it hurt that she was the only female among the six major contenders.

On May 1 Hutchison ran slightly ahead of the interim senator, taking 593,338 votes to Krueger's 593,239 (each had 29.0 percent of the vote). Since the combined Republican vote was 60 percent to 40 percent for the Democrats, Krueger was given little chance in the June 5 runoff. Krueger's campaign tried a variety of tactics, such as TV ads poking fun at his aloof image, but nothing clicked with voters. On June 5, 1993, Hutchison won 67.3 percent of the runoff vote.

This Democratic debacle, just seven months after Clinton had spent little money in Texas but had still run a close second to George Bush, resulted from several factors. First, Republicans traditionally run very well in special elections in Texas. These contests draw small turnouts, and GOP voters participate in much higher numbers than Democrats. Over 6 million people voted in November 1992, compared to about 1.5 million in June 1993. Second, the Clinton administration's early performance was especially unpopular in Texas where issues like gays in the military and tax hikes riled substantial numbers of voters. The special election gave these voters a convenient venue, nearly four years before the next presidential election, to vote against the Clinton administration and its policies. Third, Krueger's self-deprecating ads were right; he was a much worse candidate than Hutchison. Together, these added up to a rout comparable only to the 1972 McGovern defeat among Democratic losses in Texas.

THE 1994 ELECTIONS: TEXAS JOINS NATIONAL GOP TIDE

Texas Democrats were understandably concerned about the drubbing Hutchison gave Krueger, but party leaders were relatively confident they could again hold off the GOP in 1994 when all major state offices were up for election. Hopes even for regaining Bentsen's Senate seat were rekindled when Senator Hutchison was indicted by a Travis County grand jury just after the Senate runoff for allegedly abusing her previous office of treasurer. The indictments, sought by local district attorney Ronnie Earle, a Democrat, alleged that Hutchison had used treasurer employees for political purposes and had destroyed some computer files while Earle's office was conducting its investigation. These misdemeanor charges were based largely on the testimony of disgruntled former employees, including Sharon Ammann, the daughter of former governor John Connally. She and others complained they had been personally mistreated by the Texas treasurer. When the indictments and employee complaints were publicized, Senator Hutchison's job approval ratings fell sharply, and it seemed likely she would draw strong opposition, possibly even in the Republican primary, when she ran for a full six-year term in 1994.

Governor Richards entered the 1994 election cycle in somewhat better shape for reelection. Texas had led the nation in job growth since 1991, and unemployment was down on her watch. The character issues that dogged her through the primaries and general election in 1990 had faded as no new controversies flared about her private life. Politically, Richards steered a cautious, centrist course as governor, trying to position herself for reelection. The governor strongly backed the North American Free Trade Agreement (NAFTA) and worked to attract and keep businesses and industry in the state. Inheriting a serious budget shortfall, Richards helped push through a state lottery and signed a corporate income tax. When Lieutenant Governor Bullock, however, proposed a personal income tax as the long-term solution to Texas's continuing revenue shortfalls, Richards quickly opposed the idea and Bullock dropped it.

Governor Richards also signed a jerry-rigged compromise public school funding plan to reduce disparities in local school support among districts. This "Robin Hood" plan, which shifted property tax revenues from wealthy to poor districts within the state, pleased few, but it did—in contrast to previous legislative efforts to address inequities in school funding—pass muster with the Texas supreme court. The governor stuck to her guns on abortion rights, rejecting a parental consent requirement for teenagers. And she vetoed a concealed-weapons act strongly supported by the National Rifle Association and other gun rights advocates. Her centrist policies drew fire from the left and right. Liberal Ronnie Dugger, publisher of the *Texas Observer*, asked: "Where, oh where, oh where, is the leadership of Gov. Ann Richards? A New Texas, indeed. . . . This is an abdication of leadership." Conservative Jack Rains, an unsuccessful gubernatorial candidate in 1990, gave her "an 'A' on rhetoric and an 'F' on matters of substance." Policy issues aside, the governor used her considerable appointive powers to strengthen her liberal, feminist, and minority bases by naming far more women and minorities to state boards and commissions than any previous state executive. On balance, Governor Richards's policies, appointments, and conduct in office suited Texans. At the end of 1993 she enjoyed the highest job approval rating of any governor since Connally, who left office in 1969.[24]

Other major Democratic incumbents like Bullock, Comptroller of Public Accounts John Sharp, and Attorney General Dan Morales also enjoyed positive job ratings and seemed in a strong position to win reelection in 1994. Republican leaders recruited Cameron County judge Tony Garza to run against Morales but did not encourage challengers to Bullock or Sharp.

The competitive U.S. Senate race that appeared likely in 1993 fizzled out early in 1994. Three potentially strong Democratic challengers filed against Hutchison, but with the help of Senator Gramm and the GOP establishment she avoided a significant opponent in the Republican primary. The most prominent Democrat to enter the race was former attorney general Mattox, now short of campaign funds but well known to Texas voters after his slugfest with Ann Richards in the 1990 primary for governor. The junior senator's perceived vulnerability also drew six-term Democratic congressman Mike Andrews into the race. A moderate from Houston with a seat on the powerful House Ways and Means Committee, Andrews hoped his good relations with Texas business and professional groups would enable him to fund a statewide media campaign. Dallas businessman Richard Fisher, who had finished fifth in the 1993 special election with 8.1 percent of the vote, also filed for another run at Hutchison. He foreswore PAC contributions, emphasized his willingness to spend his own money for the race, and touted his status as an outsider who had advised Ross Perot during the latter's on-off-on campaign in 1992.

Just as the Democratic rivals began to engage each other in February 1994, Travis district attorney Earle's case against Senator Hutchison collapsed. In a surprising and somewhat bizarre move, Earle dropped all charges when the presiding judge refused to rule on a pretrial motion sought by the district attorney on the admissibility of evidence his office had seized in a June 1993 raid on the treasurer's office. His abrupt action suggested to many a political setup by an ambitious partisan Democrat, who ended up more damaged by the indictment than his target, Senator Hutchison.

With the senator legally exonerated, interest in the Democratic primary dropped. The first casualty of Hutchison's political recovery was Congressman Andrews. His fund-raising stalled after the dismissal of charges, and he could not afford a paid media campaign to expand his support beyond Houston. He ran a poor third against the better-known Mattox and the better-funded Fisher. The latter, who ended up spending about two million dollars of his personal fortune, beat Mattox 53.6 percent to 46.4 percent in a light-vote April runoff.[25]

In contrast to the hotly contested 1990 gubernatorial primaries, both parties rallied behind consensus candidates in 1994. On the Democratic side, Governor Richards drew a single, unknown, unfunded Hispanic opponent. Despite these huge handicaps against the formidable Richards, Gary Espinoza took 22.2 percent of the 1,036,944 votes cast in the March Democratic primary. (Another unknown but ambitious Mexican American, high school civics teacher Victor Morales, noted that result with considerable interest, as the 1996 election season would show.)

Republicans united behind George W. Bush, the eldest son of the forty-first president. Bush had modest elective experience himself, having run a losing 1978 congressional race against Kent Hance in west Texas. But George W., as he is called to distinguish him from the former president, had been a close adviser in his father's campaigns and was well known in Republican circles as a part owner (2 percent) and president of the Texas Rangers baseball team. Like Richards, Bush drew a single, unknown opponent, but he dispatched his challenger with 93.3 percent of the 557,340 primary votes.

One other Republican primary result is worth noting. Tony Garza, recruited by state Republican leaders to provide a Republican challenger to Attorney General Morales, ran fourth in a four-person primary contest. His poor showing reflects the fact that the GOP primary electorate in Texas is overwhelmingly Anglo and conservative, making it difficult for the party to nominate minority candidates when alternatives are available.

With the U.S. Senate race generally conceded to Hutchison and no prominent Republican challengers for other state offices, attention focused on the 1994 governor's race. The contest had star power. The silver-haired grandmother governor was the best-known woman in American elective office. Her opponent was the energetic, attractive scion of the state's most famous political family. The race also had some qualities of a grudge match, given the bad blood between Ann Richards and the Bushes since her 1988 Atlanta speech.

Both Richards and Bush entered the race with strong positive ratings, and each had considerable fund-raising abilities. Richards could tap a national base of supporters and would get strong backing from a bevy of successful Texas trial lawyers. Bush could count on the usual Republican sources, with especially strong backing from the trial lawyers' opponents—medical doctors, insurance companies, small businesses, and manufacturers. In the end, the candidates would raise and spend about $15 million each on their campaigns.

Aside from equal financing, Richards and Bush ran very different campaigns in 1994. The governor's reelection effort was eerily reminiscent of President Bush's failed campaign in 1992. Richards chose not to run on her defensible record and never spelled out for voters why they should elect her to a second term. Like the president two years earlier, the governor seemed annoyed that she had to endure a competitive reelection against an opponent that she considered unqualified for the job. Given that mindset, perhaps it is not surprising that Richards sought to make her opponent the issue, partly through personal attacks and partly by emphasizing his questionable business dealings.

On the personal side, Richards staffers and supporters routinely derided George W. Bush as the "scrub," and she publicly called him a "jerk" at one point in the campaign. Richards hammered away at Bush's lack of elective experience and then turned her media attacks on allegedly shady business deals her opponent had been involved with over the years. Bush had been connected to several failed business ventures, some of which had been investigated by government authorities.[26] These investigations, however, had produced no charges or "smoking gun" findings that could be turned against him. Consequently, the Richards barrage had little impact on voters, in contrast to her closing attacks on Williams's business record in 1990.

To no one's surprise, Ross Perot injected himself into the 1994 campaign in its closing days. While he urged his supporters to "give the Republicans a chance" to run Congress after forty years of Democratic control, he endorsed Governor Richards over the son of his arch-rival, former president Bush. Like most political endorsements, Perot's made little difference to most Texas voters.[27]

Bush ran a focused, issue-oriented, positive campaign modeled more after Clinton's 1992 effort than his father's. George W. turned out to be both more sophisticated and more energetic a candidate than George Herbert Walker Bush, and he proved capable of sticking to his basic game plan. The Republican nominee avoided personal attacks on Richards, while skillfully exploiting her weaknesses on issues with selected groups of voters. For example, criticism of the "Robin Hood" school finance plan was targeted to upscale suburban districts that lost money in the transfer process. To energize gun rights advocates, Bush endorsed the concealed weapons bill Governor Richards had vetoed. And he attacked Richards and the Democratic legislature for not dedicating all lottery proceeds to public school funding as many voters had wrongly assumed would be done when they approved the scheme. Bush appealed to religious right voters by endorsing the parental notification bill for teenage abortions that Richards opposed, and he skillfully turned Governor Richards's comments to a Texas Girls State Convention audience into a "family values" issue. The governor, in a June 1994 address, had warned the young ladies, "I cannot tell you what a pitfall it is to count on Prince Charming to make you feel better about yourself and take care of you." She went on to add that the prince often ended up with a "beer gut and a wandering eye." Bush claimed her remarks denigrated men and added, "the leader of the state ought to be optimistic and positive, and this (speech) is extremely negative. Throughout the speech, evidently there was a gnashing of teeth and complete consternation about marriage."[28]

By selectively emphasizing such issues, Bush pulled together a formidable coalition of economic and cultural conservatives and moderates. Late polls showed a close race, but Bush won the largest gubernatorial majority in twenty years, getting 2,350,994 votes (53.5 percent) to Richards' 2,016,928 (45.9 percent). Bush got a half million more votes than Williams had received in 1990, while Richards gained only about 90,000 additional votes. Network exit polls showed Bush won by a wide margin among men, as had Williams earlier, but he also cut Richards's margin among female voters. Suburban Republican women who had deserted the GOP nominee in 1990 came home in 1994. That reversed the result in the large urban counties of Bexar (San Antonio), Dallas, Harris (Houston), and Tarrant (Fort Worth). Richards won these counties by 68,461 votes against Williams, but lost them by 110,721 votes to Bush. The vote was strongly polarized along racial and ethnic lines. Richards won 97 percent of the African American vote and 78 percent of the Hispanic vote, but Bush had a 63 percent to 36 percent advantage among non-Hispanic whites.

Things played out as polls since spring had indicated in the U.S. Senate race, with Hutchison cruising to a vindicating victory (60.8 percent) over Fisher (38.3 percent). The senator outspent the challenger by almost two to one as he proved unwilling or unable to emulate his mentor Perot's spending spree of 1992.

In other high-visibility statewide races, Texas Democratic incumbents got sufficient ticket-splitter votes to resist the strong GOP tide in the state and nation in November 1994. Lieutenant Governor Bullock actually got more votes (2,629,497, for 61.5 percent) than anyone on the ballot. Comptroller Sharp garnered 55.5 percent of the vote, with Attorney General Morales and Land Commissioner Mauro winning by solid, if closer, margins. Of course, they were all helped by the fact that their opponents were relatively unknown and had less money than the Democratic officeholders.

The underlying strength of the Republican tide is more evident when we look at the low profile contests where voters knew little save the partisan identity of nominees. In down-ballot statewide races, Republicans won seven of eight contests, and missed winning the treasurer's position by just 24,567 out of 4,145,981 votes cast.[29] The same pattern can be seen in large urban counties where down-ballot races are largely decided by the party cue. In populous Harris County, Republican judicial nominees won forty-eight of fifty contested races, often by wide margins. All Democratic judicial nominees with opponents were defeated in races in Dallas and Tarrant counties.

In the 1994 congressional voting, Texas Republicans fell short of their historic national sweep, while the GOP nationwide netted 55 seats. In the Lone Star State, just two Democratic incumbents lost—the 21-term veteran Jack Brooks in the Ninth District and 3-termer Bill Sarpalius in the Thirteen District. That left the Democrats with a 19–11 advantage, although that dropped to 18–12 when Congressman Greg Laughlin of the Fourteenth District changed parties after the November election. Congressional Democrats were fortunate that, although a federal court ruled in August 1994 that the three majority-minority districts created in Houston (the Eighteenth and Twenty-Ninth) and Dallas (the Thirtieth) were unconstitutional, it was too late in the election cycle to make changes. Thus, the 1991 lines were used in 1994. The Democrats survived not only because of favorable districts, but also because of the ability of high-profile incumbents to win split-ticket voters just as statewide Democrats like Lieutenant Governor Bullock were able to do.

At the state legislative level, 1994 was a good if not great year for the Republicans. Despite an incumbent-friendly house map, the GOP picked up five seats to cut the Democratic margin to 87–63. Two more Republican senators were elected, narrowing the Democratic edge to 17–14.

Despite the survival of prominent statewide Democrats other than Governor Richards, of most congressional Democrats, and of Democratic majorities in the Texas legislature, 1994 was a breakthrough year for Texas Republicans. After January 1995, with the governorship and both U.S. senators, they held all three top elective positions in the state. All three members of the powerful Texas Railroad Commission, which regulates the energy and trucking industries, were also Republicans, as was a majority of the Texas supreme court for the first time since Reconstruction. And the fifteen-member State Board of Education also had a first-time Republican majority. Only a handful of local countywide Democratic elected officials were left in the three most populous counties of Harris, Dallas, and Tarrant. The GOP had added depth to its breadth in the 1994 elections.

To sum up, the 1994 Texas elections were driven by a variety of forces: state issues, candidates, campaigns, and districting patterns. In some cases, like the lieutenant governor and congressional races, the advantages went mostly to Democrats. In the governor's race, Republicans benefited by race-specific factors. But national factors also played a very big part in the 1994 Texas electoral story. We note the obvious point that 1994 was the best election year for the national Republican party since 1946. The striking and, to many, surprising national Republican surge in 1994 reflected a convergence of long-term and short-term forces that combined to give Republicans a great advantage across the country. A partial list of these factors would include the declining standing of the Democratic-controlled Congress; disappointment in President Clinton's failure to even get a vote on his comprehensive health care reform bill; the fusion of economic conservatives angry at Democratic tax hikes with religious and cultural conservatives who had come to view the president as akin to the antichrist; and a game plan that nationalized the 1994 elections, brilliantly executed by Newt Gingrich and his House allies. The late U.S. House Speaker Tip O'Neill would have been wrong about 1994: All politics is *not* local.

Historically, partisan electoral surges like the 1994 Republican tide are rare and are often followed by declines as marginal-seat gains are lost back when more normal circumstances prevail. Texas Democrats could thus hope for a comeback, while saying it could have been worse in 1994. As Bob Slagle, the state Democratic party chair, noted, "Texas Democrats fared far better than Democrats in many other states."[30] Republicans recognized their triumph in 1994 was incomplete, but believed they were clearly on a path to be the dominant party in Texas before the end of the twentieth century.

THE 1996 ELECTIONS: A MIXED PARTISAN RESULT

A number of factors favored Texas Republicans going into the 1996 elections. Their new governor had worked well with the Democratic-controlled legislature in 1995 and had gotten most of his program enacted into law. His personal popularity and job approval ratings eclipsed the high marks Governor Richards had enjoyed and far exceeded those of Bill Clements, the only other modern-day Republican governor. By contrast, President Clinton's poll ratings in Texas continued to lag well behind his anemic national numbers throughout most of 1995. Texas would be a difficult state for the Democratic presidential campaign to contest, much less win, in 1996.

Texas Republicans were also encouraged by the possibility that Senator Gramm would be the party's nominee in 1996. The state's senior senator had been pointing to the race for years, solidifying his Texas base, building a national organization and fund-raising network second to none, and defining himself in the Senate to the right of majority leader Bob Dole, the front-runner. Gramm would also be running for reelection in 1996, using the "LBJ law" passed by the legislature in 1959 to allow Lyndon Johnson to run for the presidency and reelection to the U.S. Senate in 1960.

Additionally, there seemed a better than even chance the Democratic congressional plan passed in 1991 might be eliminated before the 1996 general election. The U.S. Supreme Court was reviewing the three-judge panel's 1994 decision that the new majority-minority districts were unconstitutionally drawn on a racial basis. If a new plan were imposed by federal judges, Republicans could likely expect better opportunities for congressional gains in 1996.

Sensing opportunity after their success in 1994, Republicans attacked Texas Democrats from the courthouse to the White House in 1996. For the first time in history, the party had chairs in every county, so GOP primary voting could be held in all 254 counties in Texas. Republicans recruited candidates for all nine of the statewide positions up for election in 1996. A half dozen Texas senate Democratic seats were targeted in the hope of gaining at least two to win a legislative majority for the first time since Reconstruction. And with a new battle cry, "76 in '96," the party planned to vigorously contest about twenty house districts in hopes of taking control of that 150-member body as well as the senate.

On the Democratic side, worried incumbents led by Lieutenant Governor Bullock and Comptroller Sharp staged a coup in 1995 and forced Slagle, the longtime party chair, to resign. He was replaced by Bill White, the Houston lawyer who had organized the successful 1992 Houston fund-raiser for Clinton and more recently was a senior administrator in the U.S. Department of Energy. White had his work cut out for him. One sign of the Democrats' problems was their inability to recruit a candidate for a Texas supreme court position. Consequently, for the first time in more than a century, a Republican was assured of winning a statewide general election.

White went to work, nonetheless, with gusto, declaring the Democrats were "back with a vengeance. We're not on the defensive, we're on the rise." A more sober assessment was made by veteran Texas court of criminal appeals justice Frank Maloney, who would be the highest ranking Democratic incumbent on the statewide ballot. The Democrats, he noted, "have come down an awfully long way in Texas politics."[31] The Democratic decline through 1994 is captured graphically in the Texas party-strength trend line in Figure 11 in Chapter 1.

On the plus side for the Democrats, the stinging defeats in 1993 and 1994 had unified the party in a fashion not seen since 1982, when their candidates swept all statewide offices. Republicans, in contrast, were finding that electoral success could aggravate internal divisions within the party.

The basic schism in the Texas Republican party, like a number of others around the country, is between the traditional mainstream conservative and moderate elements of the party, and the energetic religious right, Christian Coalition wing. The latter were convinced it was their efforts that had brought the Republican victories of the 1990s, and they now wanted their place at the table when policy decisions were made. The party establishment, represented by Governor Bush and Senators Gramm and Hutchison, were not eager to embrace the conservative cultural and social agenda the religious right favored. So fault lines opened and widened inside the Republican party.

Infighting between the religious right and establishment Republicans had been going on for years in party precinct, county, and state conventions, with the Christian conservatives routing the regular Republicans in the 1990s. After the 1994 elections, conflict increased when a number of candidates identified with the Christian right won in the party primary and then prevailed over Democrats in November. Intraparty conflicts were particularly bitter on the state education board, where newly elected Republicans led by Donna Ballard of the Woodlands, a new suburban area north of Houston, became increasingly critical of Governor Bush's appointed education commissioner, as well as board president Jack Christie, a moderate Republican from Houston. Christie had to rely on votes from the Democratic minority on his board to hold off the militant Republicans.[32]

As internal tensions rose within the Texas GOP, Republicans lost momentum nationally in late 1995 and early 1996 after the budget showdowns with President Clinton, who showed surprising strength by the spring of 1996 after being widely written off as a political corpse in 1995. In the meantime, the stock of "revolutionary" congressional Republicans, led by Speaker Gingrich, plummeted. The national Republican tide of 1994–95 seemed to have ebbed, although in Texas the President's unpopularity with many Anglo voters largely persisted.[33]

The decline of congressional Republicans was one factor that doomed the well-financed presidential campaign of Senator Gramm. Despite his well-heeled coffers, Gramm had to bow out of the race after being upset by Pat Buchanan in early tests in Alaska and Louisiana, followed by a poor showing in the February Iowa caucuses. With the collapse of his presidential campaign, Gramm returned to Texas to defend his Senate seat, now more at risk after his embarrassing presidential performance.

Incumbent Democratic congressmen Jim Chapman from east Texas and John Bryant from Dallas had given up their seats to seek the Senate nomination. Attorney John Odam of Houston was also in the race. And there was a fourth candidate, a pickup truck–driving political newcomer Victor Morales. As mentioned above, the high school civics teacher had marked the relatively strong showing of an unknown Hispanic against Governor Richards in the 1994 Democratic primary. Perhaps he could do even better as an active candidate in 1996 who shared a surname with Dan Morales (they are unrelated), twice elected attorney general of Texas.

Running his primary campaign from his kitchen table and repeatedly responding that he did not know the answers to many current questions, Morales astounded political observers when he ran first, taking 36.1 percent of the vote, in the March 1996 Democratic primary. His runoff opponent, Congressman Bryant, gathered most endorsements from party leaders, while Morales continued his Washington outsider campaign by stumping the state in his white Nissan pickup. Victor Morales won the April runoff with 51.2 percent of the vote, partly due to name confusion with the attorney general, but also because he aroused the sleeping giant of Texas politics, the Hispanic vote. Postelection analyses showed Hispanics accounted for nearly half the runoff electorate, and Victor Morales got almost all their votes.[34]

Aside from the surprising Senate nomination, the 1996 Texas primaries produced little drama and news coverage. Bob Dole swept to an easy win in the presidential primary, but that was the expected result after his primary victories in the preceding weeks. And President Clinton took over 90 percent of the Democratic vote in his uncontested drive for renomination. There was, however, one interesting aspect of the 1996 party primaries. As Table 23 shows, for the first time in history, the Texas Republican primary drew more votes than the Democratic primary. In a state where there is no registration by party, this is an indicator of relative party strength. As such, it signaled that the minority party had at long last achieved parity or even surpassed state Democrats.

The 1996 Texas presidential campaign was in many ways a rerun of 1992. President Clinton still had a deep personal desire to win Texas, as evidenced by his three campaign swings across the state, which ended with a rally in the shadow of the Alamo on the last weekend of the contest. And, as in 1992, state polls showed a close race, perhaps with a Democratic lead after the conventions. But Clinton had a much bigger national lead over Dole, and that dictated a paid media strategy focusing on winnable battleground states as the Democratic campaign had done in 1992. Once again, Texas was not on the list.

For reasons less clear, the Republicans gave little attention to Texas in 1996. Dole made only a couple of token stops in the state, and there was little local organizational effort on behalf of the GOP ticket. Nevertheless, since Dole was trailing badly across most of the country, he was forced, as President Bush had

Table 23. Turnout in Democratic and Republican Primaries in Texas, 1976–1998

Year	Dem.	Rep.
1976	1,481,645	460,574
1978	1,812,846	158,403
1980	1,377,769	526,769
1982	1,318,663	265,769
1984	1,463,449	336,814
1986	1,096,552	544,719
1988	1,767,045	1,014,956
1990	1,487,260	855,231
1992	1,482,075	797,146
1994	1,036,944	557,340
1996	923,244	1,018,689
1998	664,532	596,839

Source: Texas Secretary of State.

been in 1992, to make national media buys in a vain attempt to close the gap with President Clinton. It did not work, but it meant the Dole-Kemp campaign would have a Texas advertising effort up in the closing days of the campaign while Clinton-Gore would not.

Ross Perot, trying to repeat his strong showing of 1992, offered Texans another presidential option. But the luster was off the Dallasite in his home state. Nonetheless, with the public money he received based on his 1992 finish, Perot would again have a major paid media campaign running in Texas in the last weeks of the campaign. Perot's ads once again attacked the president, but this time his sharp elbows were aimed at Bill Clinton, not George Bush, and his focus was on Clinton-Gore fund-raising abuses, not Republican mismanagement of the economy. National polls and postelection analyses showed the presidential race tightened in the last days as Dole finally gained a little ground after the press became focused on questionable Democratic fund-raising from Asian sources. Nationally, the gap was still too large for Dole to catch up, but in Texas he moved ahead at the end and won with 48.8 percent to Clinton's 43.8 percent.

Perot, who had taken 22.0 percent of the Texas vote in 1992, got just 6.7 percent in 1996, well below his national average of 8.4 percent. But Perot's candidacy hurt President Clinton in Texas in 1996, just as his 1992 candidacy had hurt President Bush. Perot's savage closing attacks on the president and first lady, mentioning possible felony indictments, drove voters away from Clinton.

The Texan's vote support dried up to virtually nothing in Republican areas, so he did not split the conservative white vote as had been the case four years earlier.[35]

With Texas playing a secondary role in the presidential contest, media attention was on newcomer Victor Morales's bid to unseat Senator Gramm. Morales was Texas's first Hispanic nominee for the U.S. Senate, but he came into the general election with no money, no professional consultants, and political experience limited to one term on his hometown of Crandall's city council. Nonetheless, Texas Democrats had rallied behind him after his runoff victory. They promised to help as much as he wanted, but most recognized the "weird freshness" of his candidacy meant they had to "let Victor be Victor. Keep on trucking."[36] He vowed to do just that. Standing on the bed of his truck at the June Democratic state convention, Morales told thousands of the faithful, "I am you."

National and even international media began to play up this David versus Goliath contest in the Lone Star State. Some reporters cast him as a 1996 version of "Mr. Smith Goes to Washington," others as the truck-driving Don Quixote. The publicity was not lost on his opponent. Senator Gramm sent out a fundraising letter saying the unfair "media lovefest" Morales was enjoying underscores "just how critical and how competitive this race really is."[37]

Despite positive media exposure in the nation and abroad, the Morales campaign stalled in Texas in the summer and early fall. The newcomer's fresh outsider status helped him in an anti-incumbent, anti-Washington era, as it had Paul Wellstone in his upset Senate victory over Rudy Boschwitz of Minnesota in 1990. But Senator Gramm avoided the mistakes of his former colleague and ran a careful campaign that took Morales seriously, avoiding demeaning personal attacks and using his huge financial edge to raise doubts about his Hispanic challenger.

While Gramm avoided mistakes, Morales made several. After the runoff, he was slow to reach out to major Hispanic leaders across the state, apparently piqued that many had not supported him in the spring. He did not mobilize the Hispanic leadership, because he planned to take his campaign directly to the people. Unfortunately, without funding in place for a major media effort, the retail politicking Morales continued all summer wore him down but failed to reach the vast majority of voters in a huge electorate spread across an enormous state. Morales had counted on significant national assistance, and some was promised after the runoff. But with President Clinton not running paid media in Texas, and polls showing Morales 15 to 20 percent behind Senator Gramm,

Democratic Senate strategists channeled their limited funds to other states with closer races and less expensive media markets.

Gramm, flush with "a politician's best friend, ready money,"[38] could run unanswered TV and radio ads defining Morales as a liberal supporter of affirmative action, same-sex marriages, and tax increases, and an opponent of a balanced-budget amendment and immigration and education reform. After sixteen weeks of such negative advertising, Morales's negative ratings rose from 18 percent in June 1996 to 35 percent in October, according to the Harte-Hanks Texas Poll.

For his own part, Morales made a major tactical error when he declined to debate Senator Gramm on September 29, 1996. The challenger understandably wanted a debate closer to the general election, but by turning down the opportunity Morales lost his one chance to appear side-by-side with his adversary. He also gave the senator's campaign an opening to attack him for ducking the debate. Morales made another rookie mistake when he attacked U.S. representative Henry Bonilla of San Antonio, the state's lone Republican Hispanic congressman, as a person who "reminds me of the people when I was growing up that we called chocolate chips, coconuts . . . white on the inside, brown on the outside."[39] The candidate apologized for the personal slurs, but lasting damage was done to his image as the untainted challenger.

In light of these adverse conditions—no presidential paid media in Texas, a very well funded, sharp opponent, no money for TV buys until the last days of the campaign, and an amateur candidate prone to mistakes—it is surprising Morales held Gramm to 54.8 percent of the vote, while taking 43.9 percent himself. This was a far better performance than Gramm's Anglo opponents had made in 1984 (41.4 percent) or 1990 (37.4 percent). And Morales achieved this without a huge Hispanic turnout. Hispanic registration totaled over 1.5 million by November 1996, but turnout among registered voters in heavily Mexican American counties and precincts was below 40 percent, compared to a statewide average of 58 percent.[40]

Another important election story developed in Texas when the U.S. Supreme Court released its decision on July 13, 1996, upholding the lower federal court decision that three Texas congressional districts were unconstitutionally drawn in 1991. The case was sent back to the three-judge panel in Houston for a remedy. The federal panel rejected Attorney General Morales's argument that it was too late in the election cycle to take action for the 1996 general election. Instead, the court announced in August that the unconstitutional districts had to be reformed before the November election and, since the state had refused to act, the court would impose its own plan for the 1996 elections. Their map redrew thirteen of the thirty Texas congressional districts in and around Dallas–Fort Worth and Houston.

The court-ordered plan smoothed out the boundaries of affected districts and reduced minority populations in the Eighteenth, Twenty-Ninth, and Thirtieth Districts, but did not drastically alter the partisan makeup of the redrawn electoral units. Republicans did have a better shot at the Twenty-Fifth District, represented by freshman Democrat Ken Bentsen, who lost heavily black precincts in Fort Bend County. And the changes figured to indirectly benefit Republican Steve Stockman in the Ninth District, even though only a minor adjustment was made in the local boundaries.

This possible benefit to Stockman came because the court created a different set of election rules for the redrawn districts. In these thirteen districts, the March-April primary results were thrown out and a new "open primary" was ordered on November 5, the day of the general election. Any eligible person could file in the open primary by paying a $2,500 fee, and all candidates would run together. If no one received a majority, a runoff between the top two finishers would be held December 10, 1996. Given the Democratic bent of the Ninth District, Stockman would probably lose to a single Democrat in a high turnout presidential election, but if he could advance from a multicandidate open primary to a special runoff in which turnout would likely be much lower, the congressman might well win reelection.

Twenty-seven of the thirty Texas congressional districts were decided on November 5, with Democrats winning fifteen and Republicans twelve. The GOP was also assured of a thirteenth seat because Republicans ran 1–2 in the Eighth District open primary to replace the retiring Jack Fields. Elsewhere, Stockman and Jefferson County tax assessor Nick Lampson, a Democrat, faced each other in the December runoff, as did Democratic congressman Bentsen and Dolly Madison McKenna, a Republican businesswoman, in the Twenty-Fifth District. If Republicans could take both runoffs, a distinct possibility given GOP successes in Texas special elections over the years, the Texas delegation would be split fifteen to fifteen in the 105th Congress.

That did not happen, and the results are a cautionary lesson to those sure that the Republican party is the wave of the future in Texas. Stockman was defeated by Lampson in the Ninth District, in part because of high turnout among minority voters. Lampson won 52.8 percent of the vote to Stockman's 47.2 percent. But the congressman, a favorite of the religious right and gun rights advocates, also failed to get sufficient support from moderate Republicans and independents who had voted for Bush and Hutchison in 1994 and Gramm in 1996. The reverse situation existed in the Twenty-Fifth District, where Dolly Madison McKenna lost to Bentsen by a surprising 57.3 percent to 42.7 percent margin after Christian conservatives urged their supporters to stay home, preferring a pro-choice Democrat to a pro-choice Republican. The fragility of the Texas Republican coalition was also evident in the Eighth District, where Republican state representative Kevin Brady fought four bitter 1996 elections before finally defeating Republican physician Eugene Fontenot, a self-financed ardent foe of abortions. Brady won the intra-Republican December 10 runoff with 59.1 percent of the vote to Fontenot's 40.9 percent. Therefore, after the 1996 elections Democrats retained a majority of the state's U.S. House delegation, 17 to 13.

The 1996 Texas legislative results were more favorable to Republicans. The "76 in '96" campaign fell short, but the GOP gained five net seats, cutting the Democratic advantage in the Texas house of representatives to 82–68. In the 33-seat senate, Republicans won 15 seats on November 5 and then picked up a sixteenth in a December special election. In a January contest to replace a Democrat elected to Congress, the GOP won its seventeenth seat and thus attained majority status in one of the state's legislative bodies for the first time since Reconstruction.[41] Table 24 documents the two-party shifts in legislative strength since 1974.

Most pleasing to Republicans was the sweep of the eight statewide contests for judicial and state commission seats, usually by wide margins. Those results gave the GOP 20 of the 28 statewide offices in 1997. Just seven years earlier

Table 24. Party Representation in the Texas Legislature, 1974–1997

Year	Senate		House	
	Dem.	Rep.	Dem.	Rep.
1975	28	3	134	16
1977	28	3	131	19
1979	27	4	128	22
1981	24	7	115	35
1983	26	5	114	36
1985	25	6	98	52
1987	25	6	94	56
1989	23	8	93	57
1991	23	8	93	57
1993	18	13	92	58
1995	17	14	89	61
1997	14	17	82	68

Source: Legislative Reference Library, Austin, Texas.

Democrats held a 21–7 advantage. As the defeated justice Maloney had warned, his Democrats had come down "an awfully long way."

Both Democrats and Republicans could find something positive in the 1996 Texas elections. Democrats successfully defended their congressional majority, losing just one net seat in the face the retirements of six incumbents and the imposition of a late redistricting plan with special rules for nearly half the seats, thus surviving an election where no statewide Democratic candidate had a significant media budget. The presidential race was close until the end, and Senator Gramm was held to his lowest general election victory margin by a candidate who could not advertise on television until the last week before voting. The party still had a solid majority in the state house, where only one Democratic incumbent lost to a Republican. In addition, more than 70 percent of local officials remained Democrats in 1997.[42]

Republicans like Governor Bush could justly retort that they won Texas in 1996, taking the presidential electoral votes, holding their U.S. Senate seat, winning every statewide election, and gaining a Senate majority. And where they did not win majorities, they made gains in the Texas House and the Texas delegation to the U.S. House.

The elections we have reviewed in the 1990s chronicle the transformation of Texas from an occasionally presidential Republican state to one solidly in the GOP electoral vote column and leaning Republican in statewide contests. Democrats are still competitive in statewide elections under favorable circumstances, but their strength is in sub-state elections where they hold 17 of 30 congressional seats, 96 of 181 legislative positions, and a sizable majority of local partisan offices.[43]

THE FUTURE OF TEXAS POLITICS

Will the Republican advance continue? Perhaps, but we expect GOP gains, if any, will be modest for two reasons. First, the Texas Republican party has pretty much cashed in electorally on the attitudinal gains it made with Anglo voters in the late 1970s and 1980s. As Table 25 shows, a series of Harte-Hanks Texas Polls taken in the 1990s show virtually no net partisan movement. Roughly equal numbers of Texans describe themselves as Republicans, Democrats, or independent/other. This static situation reflects, in our view, the passing of the conditions that drove the Republican gains in previous decades.

More specifically, the immigration of white, conservative, upscale workers slowed greatly after the state's economy turned down in the late 1980s and is less

Table 25. Party Identification in Texas, 1990–1997

Year	Dem.	Rep.	Ind.	Other
1990	32%	31%	31%	2%
1991	29	30	33	4
1992	31	28	31	6
1993	27	28	31	5
1994	27	31	29	8
1995	26	31	28	9
1996	29	29	27	13
1997	30	31	25	9

Source: The Harte-Hanks Texas Poll.

Note: The question asked was, "Would you describe yourself as a Republican, a Democrat, an Independent, or none of these?"

likely to resume as other parts of the country are now enjoying strong economic growth. The conversion of religious conservatives to the Texas Republican party is also largely complete: few Democrats remain among politically active white evangelical and fundamentalist Texans. And nationally, the party of Ronald Reagan and George Bush has become the party of the less visible and less popular Trent Lott and Newt Gingrich. On the Democratic side, President Clinton, despite his personal unpopularity with many Texans, is clearly closer to Lone Star State voters than was Walter Mondale or Michael Dukakis.

A second reason we do not expect further major Republican gains in upcoming elections is that it will be hard for the GOP to have better-participating state electorates than it enjoyed in 1994 and 1996. National studies have shown that, while turnout was predictably lower in 1994 than the previous presidential election, conservatives were highly motivated to go to the polls and vote a straight Republican ticket.[44] Following the usual pattern, voter turnout was higher in the state and nation in 1996 than in the 1994 midterm elections, but it was very low for a presidential contest. This dropoff was especially sharp in Texas, where the 1996 turnout was down 11 percentage points from 1992, compared to a national drop of 8 points. The relatively small presidential turnout was again skewed toward conservative, Republican voters, a phenomenon quite pronounced in Texas, where a postelection analysis by the University of Houston's Center for Public Policy showed turnout dropped much more sharply in Democratic voting urban precincts than in Republican areas.[45] These data suggest Texas Republicans probably had as large an advantage in selective voter turnout in 1994 and 1996 as they can expect to get. Democrats, by contrast, have considerable opportunity for improvement.

If Texas politics has reached a new plateau with Republicans advantaged in statewide elections and Democrats in better shape in district elections, where do things go from here? Both parties obviously have opportunities to improve, or diminish, their appeal to voters. Nationally, Republican control of Congress brings responsibility for shaping domestic policy, while President Clinton can use the bully pulpit to define what the Democratic party stands for. Within Texas, Governor Bush can set a course for his party, while state Democrats, who still have most of the legislative power, can support or oppose the governor's direction.

The most immediate problem Republicans have is holding their religious conservative–mainstream conservative coalition together now that they wield real power in Texas. When these wings split, as in the December 1996 congressional runoffs, Republicans usually lose. Democrats have become more unified in the face of Republican successes, but they must find ways to mobilize their voters in blue-collar and minority neighborhoods or they will continue to lose statewide elections in Texas.

Heading into the 1998 general elections, each party's success seemed to depend on turning out its base voters. That will not be easy. With no primary contests for governor or U.S. senator (neither Gramm nor Hutchison was up in 1998), combined turnout in March 1998 was just 11 percent of registered voters, the lowest since Texas adopted primaries at the turn of the century. Fall turnout was also anticipated to be very low, partly because Governor Bush was expected to easily defeat his Democratic opponent, Land Commissioner Mauro. Despite an evident lack of voter interest, both parties had much at stake in 1998, and polls showed close races for several open statewide offices. Most crucial was the contest for the powerful lieutenant governor's post being vacated by Bob Bullock; in that contest, Democratic comptroller John Sharp faced Republican agriculture commissioner Rick Perry. Elsewhere, Democrats were targeting three Republican state senate seats in an effort to regain control of the upper house, while Republicans were vigorously contesting twenty state house seats.

Fifty years ago, V. O. Key, Jr., noted in his classic study *Southern Politics* that his native Texas was different from the other states of the old Confederacy. "The Lone Star State is concerned about money and how to make it, about oil and sulfur and gas, about cattle and dust storms and irrigation, about cotton and banking and Mexicans." At the end of the twentieth century Texas is still more concerned about economic issues and less about black–white conflicts than the rest of the South, but Key's home state is different in other ways today. The state has become much more metropolitan with a better-educated and wealthier population than is the case in the region as a whole.[46]

Texas is also very different from the rest of the South and the nation, excepting California, in one other important respect. It is fast becoming a much more Hispanic and less Anglo state. That trend began accelerating in the 1980s when the Hispanic, mostly Mexican American population, grew from 21 percent to 26 percent while the Anglo percentage dropped from 66 percent to less than 60 percent. The African American share was unchanged at 12 percent.

Texas demographer Steve H. Murdock and his colleagues at Texas A&M University recently published a monograph analyzing the present and future transformation of the state's population.[47] They note that the Anglo population is aging and producing a smaller and smaller share of live births in Texas. By contrast, the much younger Hispanic population is more fertile and continues to grow by immigration. Those patterns will drive the Anglo population down toward 50 percent in the 2000 census, with the Hispanic population rising above 30 percent. By 2030 Murdock and his colleagues foresee a Texas population that is 45.9 percent Hispanic, 36.7 percent Anglo, 7.9 percent African American, and 9.5 percent Asian and other.

Politically, the impact of Hispanic growth began to happen within the Democratic party in the 1980s with the rise of Mayor Henry Cisneros of San Antonio and the election of Attorney General Dan Morales in 1990. But the most dramatic evidence of the coming change was the unexpected success of Victor Morales in 1996. This unknown, inexperienced, and underfunded candidate swept to victory over established Democrats in the Senate primary and gave Senator Gramm a closer race than pundits forecast. Victor Morales's relative success is not a fluke; it is a harbinger of things to come.

To be sure, Hispanic political progress has been slow, and formidable barriers remain to translating population growth into electoral success. In 1996 Hispanics made up 30 percent of the state's population, but they were only 16 percent of the registered voters and cast about 12 percent of the total general election vote. Still, that was a record, and every year more Hispanic citizens come of voting age, more register, and more turn out. The underlying demographic shift is so massive that it is inevitably transforming the Democratic party and the general political climate in Texas.

Democrats will enter the twenty-first century with initial advantages in appealing to the awakening giant of Texas politics. Most elected Hispanics are Mexican American Democrats, and recent Republican actions in Congress—for example, on immigration and affirmative action—have driven this voter group further from the GOP.[48] But Governor Bush and other Republicans know the arithmetic. The Texas Republican party of the future cannot grow, indeed cannot remain competitive, by continuing to mobilize conservative Anglo voters. It must compete with the Democrats for a substantial share of the increasingly minority electorate. That competition, when it occurs, will profoundly alter Texas politics.

12

FLORIDA: A VOLATILE NATIONAL MICROCOSM

Joan Carver and Tom Fiedler

SEVERAL years ago Florida's tourism promoters settled on a slogan they thought captured the state's attitude: "The rules are different here," it went, conveying images of barefoot walks in a high-heeled world, days with no neckties and nights with no bedtime. However effective the slogan was in luring visitors may not be known, but it agrees with the conclusion of many political scientists who have analyzed Florida's politics since World War II. This, they say, is "the different state," located in the South geographically but not quite a part of it politically.[1] The Sunshine State is, in fact, less a part of any region than it is composed of the parts of many regions. The reason for this peculiarity is simple: newcomers.

Surging population growth has been one of the defining forces of Florida's politics throughout the twentieth century. Between 1950 and 1990 over 10 million people joined the state's relatively modest 1950 population of 2.8 million, pouring into the peninsula from the Midwest, the Northeast, the Mid-Atlantic, and, of course, from neighboring states in Old Dixie. An additional 1.2 million have been added during the first five years of the 1990s, putting Florida's population in 1996 at 14 million and making it the fourth largest state in the union. By the 1990s, this demographically diverse state could be fairly described as a microcosm of the nation.[2]

Florida's bellwether role is reflected in its population statistics, which indicate an ethnic and racial mix mirroring that of an increasingly diverse nation: as of 1996, African Americans made up an estimated 14.4 percent of the population and Hispanics 14.2 percent, the latter figure up from 12.2 percent in 1990.[3] Meanwhile, Florida is one of the leading recipients of new immigrants, both legal and undocumented. The mobility of the nation is also magnified. In 1990 over two-thirds of the population had been born outside the state. And trends here foreshadow the graying of America, with 18.7 percent of the population over 65, considerably above the national average of 12.8 percent.[4]

With population growth and shifting has come political change. As the number of registered voters increased from 2.7 million in 1968 to 6.0 million in 1990 to 8.1 million in 1996, party affiliation and party loyalty were transformed. Democrats lost their preeminence as Republicans and independents gained in number. In 1970, 72.4 percent of the registered voters were Democrats and 25.4 percent Republicans; by 1998, the party division was 45.2 percent Democratic and 40.1 percent Republican. In a trend suggestive of a restless electorate, those registering as independents or with minor parties increased from 2.2 percent to 14.7 percent in the same period. (See Table 26.)

Polls suggest that Republicans and independents constitute an even greater proportion of the electorate than voter registration figures indicate. In 1995 the

Table 26. Voter Registration in Florida, 1970–1998

Year	Dem.		Rep.		Other		Total
1970	2,024,387	(72.4%)	711,090	(25.4%)	61,523	(2.2%)	2,797,000
1971	2,162,185	(71.7)	777,261	(25.8)	76,485	(2.5)	3,015,931
1972	2,394,604	(68.7)	974,999	(28.0)	117,855	(3.4)	3,487,458
1974	2,438,580	(67.3)	1,035,510	(28.6)	147,166	(4.1)	3,621,256
1976	2,750,723	(67.2)	1,138,751	(27.8)	204,834	(5.0)	4,094,308
1978	2,812,217	(66.7)	1,178,671	(27.9)	226,299	(5.4)	4,217,187
1980	3,087,427	(64.2)	1,429,645	(29.7)	292,649	(6.1)	4,809,721
1982	3,066,351	(63.0)	1,500,031	(30.8)	299,254	(6.2)	4,865,636
1984	3,313,073	(59.4)	1,895,937	(34.0)	365,462	(6.6)	5,574,472
1986	3,214,753	(57.1)	2,038,831	(36.2)	377,604	(6.7)	5,631,188
1988	3,264,105	(54.0)	2,360,434	(39.0)	422,808	(7.0)	6,047,347
1990	3,149,747	(52.2)	2,448,488	(40.6)	432,926	(7.2)	6,031,161
1992	3,318,565	(50.7)	2,672,968	(40.9)	550,292	(8.4)	6,541,825
1994	3,245,518	(49.5)	2,747,074	(41.9)	567,006	(8.6)	6,559,598
1996	3,728,513	(46.1)	3,309,105	(41.0)	1,040,259	(12.9)	8,077,877
1998	3,697,981	(45.2)	3,278,543	(40.1)	1,205,056	(14.7)	8,181,580

Sources: Florida Department of State, Division of Elections, *Elections Online,* http://election.dos.st; Florida Department of State, *Official Elections Returns,* November 5, 1996, p. 5.

Note: All figures are as of October of the year except for 1970, 1974, and 1998, whose figures are of August, September, and May, respectively.

annual policy survey conducted by the Survey Research Center of Florida State University found only 27 percent of the electorate identifying as Democrats with 39 percent as Republicans and 34 percent independents. A comparison of 1980 and 1995 survey data indicates that while there was an erosion of Democratic support in virtually all categories of voters, the greatest losses came among the youngest voters, male voters, and those in the northern part of the state.[5]

By the 1990s Florida had clearly moved from the status of a one-party Democratic state to that of a highly competitive two-party state, although one with a tilt to conservatism and the Republican party. For a depiction of this pattern, see the Florida party-strength trend line in Figure 12, Chapter 1. By the end of 1996 Republicans held one U.S. Senate seat, three of the six Cabinet seats, fifteen of the twenty-three U.S. House seats, controlled both houses of the state legislature, and held an increasing number of local posts.

The state's newfound partisan competition is not homogeneously spread among the counties; political change has come not only through realignment, but also through migration. One of the factors that makes Florida a national microcosm is that different parts of the state have been populated by transplants who share a common political heritage. Manning J. Dauer, the late University of Florida political scientist, found it useful to divide the state into three geographic areas: north, central and south. More recently, dividing the state into five regions, each with distinct political cultures, seems to make sense. The Miami *Herald* termed these five the "inner states of Florida": Dixie (north Florida); the Linchpin (central Florida); the Gold Coast (southeast Florida); the Barbell (southwest and east central Florida); and Forgotten Florida (the rural, inland counties south of Orlando).[6] (See Table 27 for the placement of Florida's sixty-seven counties into these five divisions.)

Dixie, the state's upper tier, which is home to the highest percentage of both native-born southerners and African Americans, is the area most like the South culturally and economically; the region shows high Democratic party registration combined with conservatism and a propensity to vote Republican, especially in national elections. The Linchpin, the fast-growing counties of the Interstate 4 corridor stretching down the coast from Jacksonville to Orlando and Tampa, is the most volatile region politically, with registration almost equally divided between Democrats and Republicans. The Gold Coast (the Fort Lauderdale-Palm Beach-Miami megalopolis), the most culturally and ethnically diverse part of the state, is home to liberal Jewish and ethnic retirees from the Northeast as well as to conservative Hispanic and Cuban immigrants; it is the region that is most liberal and the most supportive of Democratic candidates. The Barbell counties of southwest Florida, with many Republicans transplanted

Table 27. Party Registration and Voting by Region in Florida, 1990–1996

Region[a]	Voter Reg. in 1996			Pres. Election of 1992			Pres. Election of 1996			Gubern. Election of 1990		Gubern. Election of 1994	
	Dem.	Rep.	Other	Dem.	Rep.	Perot	Dem.	Rep.	Perot	Dem.	Rep.	Dem.	Rep.
Dixie	58.2%	32.4%	9.4%	36.2%	41.9%	21.5%	41.1%	47.5%	10.8%	54.3%	45.7%	48.0%	52.0%
Gold Coast	48.9	36.9	14.2	48.2	36.4	15.2	59.4	33.5	6.7	62.7	37.3	59.3	40.7
Linchpin	43.6	43.1	13.3	36.1	42.8	21.1	45.5	44.8	9.7	56.0	44.0	47.9	52.1
Barbell	34.3	52.8	12.9	32.6	43.6	23.5	41.0	47.8	10.6	48.3	51.7	45.8	54.2
Forgotten Fla.	70.6	23.3	6.1	34.9	39.7	25.3	44.1	41.2	14.3	56.1	43.9	47.9	52.1
Florida	46.1	41.0	12.9	39.0	40.9	19.8	48.0	42.3	9.1	56.5	43.5	50.8	49.2
Florida—No. of People (Millions)	3.729	3.309	1.040	2.073	2.173	1.053	2.547	2.245	.484	1.995	1.535	2.135	2.071

Source: Division of Elections, Department of State, Tallahassee, and Miami *Herald*, September 15, 1996.

Note: The 1992 and 1996 Democratic candidate was Bill Clinton. The 1990 and 1994 Democratic gubernatorial candidate was Lawton Chiles. The 1992 Republican presidential candidate was George Bush; the 1996 candidate was Robert Dole. The 1990 Republican gubernatorial candidate was Bob Martinez; the 1994 candidate was Jeb Bush. "Other" includes voters registering as no party and with minor parties. The percentages are of the total vote and may not total 100 because of rounding and, in the case of the presidential elections, votes cast for minor parties; thus in 1992 .03 percent and in 1996 .05 percent of the electorate voted for minor party candidates.

[a]*Dixie (north Florida):* Counties of Alachua, Baker, Bay, Bradford, Calhoun, Columbia, Dixie, Escambia, Franklin, Gadsden, Gilchrist, Gulf, Hamilton, Holmes, Jackson, Jefferson, Lafayette, Leon, Levy, Liberty, Madison, Marion, Nassau, Okaloosa, Putnam, Santa Rosa, Sumter, Suwannee, Taylor, Union, Wakulla, Walton, and Washington. Total registered voters in October 1996: Democrats, 684,163; Republicans, 380,308; no party and other, 110,055.

Gold Coast (southeast Florida): Counties of Broward, Dade, Monroe, and Palm Beach. Total registered voters in October 1996: Democrats, 1,119,531; Republicans, 847,195; no party and minor parties, 324,869.

Linchpin (central and northeast Florida): Counties of Brevard, Citrus, Clay, Duval, Flagler, Hernando, Hillsborough, Lake, Orange, Osceola, Pasco, Pinellas, Polk, St. Johns, Seminole, Volusia. Total registered voters in October 1996: Democrats, 1,509,091; Republicans, 1,494,804; no party and minor parties, 461,670.

Barbell (southwest Florida): Counties of Charlotte, Collier, Highlands, Indian River, Lee, Manatee, Martin, St. Lucie, and Sarasota. Total registered voters in October 1996: Democrats, 371,356; Republicans, 572,148; no party and minor parties, 139,867.

Forgotten Florida (south-central Florida): Counties of DeSota, Glades, Hardee, Hendry, and Okeechobee. Total registered voters in October 1996: Democrats, 44,372;

from the Midwest, serve as the Republican stronghold in the state. In Forgotten Florida—the counties around Lake Okeechobee that were bypassed by the state's rapid growth—Democratic party registration is high. But, as in the northern part of the state, voters often select Republicans for higher office. Table 27, which contains voter registration data and recent gubernatorial and presidential election results by the regions, displays the political differences among the five inner states of Florida.

MAJOR STATEWIDE ELECTIONS FROM 1990 TO 1996: COMPETITION GROWS

When 1990 dawned, the Republican party of Florida should have looked toward the new decade with the utmost anticipation. In the 1980s, more than 950,000 voters had joined the party's ranks, nearly bridging the yawning gap that had separated it from the Democratic party for all of this century.

Republican governor Bob Martinez, despite a rocky term and weak poll numbers, was preparing for reelection by collecting a record amount of money. The party was encouraged by trends as far down the ballot as the county level. For example, while the Republican party could claim a majority on just a half dozen of Florida's sixty-seven county commissions in 1980, eleven were under Republican control by the end of the decade. And the electorate seemed to be moving in the GOP's direction. In 1988 Republican Connie Mack III had captured the U.S. Senate seat that became vacant when veteran Democrat Lawton Chiles, citing burnout from his years of public service, declined to seek reelection. At the time, Chiles's retirement seemed cause for GOP celebration, but that attitude was to change during the 1990 election for governor.

For U.S. representative Bill Nelson, a Democrat with deep family roots in Brevard County near the futuristic structures of the Kennedy Space Center, the new decade seemed the time to make the move he had dreamed about since high school. Even before the New Year, Nelson announced his intention to give up his congressional seat after twelve years in order to challenge Governor Martinez. A boyishly handsome, Yale-educated multimillionaire, Nelson had gained considerable fame for becoming the first nonscientist civilian to go into space aboard the shuttle Columbia, just one mission ahead of the ill-fated Challenger. He was also a proven vote-getter, having cruised to reelection year after year in a conservative district known for leaning Republican in all other aspects.

The path to the Democratic gubernatorial nomination had been cleared by a seeming fluke. When Chiles retired from the U.S. Senate in 1988, two men who otherwise appeared aimed for the 1990 governor's race—Insurance Commissioner Bill Gunter and U.S. representative Kenneth (Buddy) MacKay—shifted course and jumped into the Democratic primary to succeed Chiles. MacKay won the nomination, but narrowly lost in the general election (50.4 percent of the vote to 49.6 percent) to Mack, the Republican nominee, a defeat that, at the time, appeared to end MacKay's political career. Gunter, too, announced his retirement from politics. Only one other viable candidate challenged Nelson for the Democratic gubernatorial nomination: State senator George Stuart, Jr., a Harvard man who had earned a reputation as an environmentalist in Tallahassee. Through the end of 1989 and into the spring of 1990, the pair scrapped to earn the nomination. The major difference between the two appeared to be which man was more liberal on abortion rights, but all differences soon proved irrelevant. Lawton Chiles, who had spent 1989 seeking succor as a scholar at Florida State University's LeRoy Collins Center, had become fascinated by events in Eastern Europe as Communism fell and men like Vaclav Havel emerged to lead new nations, and had consequently experienced a revival of his own political ambitions.

In March 1990, Chiles had been invited to address a seminar in Chicago about the reasons for his disenchantment with the U.S. Senate. In preparing for that speech, he found inspiration in words delivered by Vaclav Havel, the new president of Czechoslovakia. According to the Miami *Herald*'s account, Chiles delivered his own interpretation to the students on March 16, sounding very much like a man about to reenter the public arena:

> When Vaclav Havel was asked how quickly and thoroughly he wanted to emulate the West's dog-eat-dog free-market system, he smiled and demurred and said Czechoslovakia would develop something in between, something that better nurtured the human spirit.
>
> This has been the message of my inner voice. That there is a spirit upon the land. A spirit that rejects the mindless dedication to self and celebrates a commitment to others. A spirit that celebrates our religious, moral and ethical traditions. That encourages cooperation and the ties that bind. That redefines work as the quiet contribution to the good of all and not merely self-advancement.[7]

This inner voice was to become well known in the weeks to come. On April 12, Chiles, sixty, and his newly named running mate, Buddy MacKay, fifty-seven, who had agreed to also emerge from retirement, appeared on the capitol steps in Tallahassee and began what they called a different kind of campaign for the governorship, one where donations would be limited to $100, where there would be no pollster and no media advisers. Within weeks, Stuart folded his tent and endorsed Chiles. Nelson slugged on, hoping his multimillion-dollar bank account and media-savvy ways would enable him to prevail. He even gingerly attacked Chiles, raising questions about whether the former senator's admitted bouts with depression and dependence on the drug Prozac disqualified him from serving.

Voters weren't biting. Chiles and MacKay did, indeed, run a different campaign, one that resembled a nonstop seminar on policy ideas. Their television ads were almost literally homemade, with Chiles appearing before the cameras reciting a script he had written with his wife, Rhea. Nelson's high-tech version didn't stand a chance. Chiles buried him, collecting over two-thirds of the Democratic vote in the primary.

Governor Martinez, meanwhile, had his own primary to worry about, although it was not much of a battle. His main competitor was former state senator Marlene Woodson-Howard, whose major concern was that her opponent was putting too much money into prison building and not enough into education. There was little doubt that Martinez did carry significant baggage into his reelection. He had infuriated voters by reneging on his 1986 pledge not to back new taxes, just months later proposing an expanded sales tax on professional services. Then almost as quickly, he abandoned that proposal and left stranded many GOP lawmakers who had agreed to go along with him on the tax. His department of transportation nearly collapsed in fiscal chaos. And he finally did push through a tax on alcoholic beverages, which became known as the "Governor Bob" beer tax. But no issue hurt him as much with voters as his attempt to be the first governor in the country to implement strict obstacles to abortion after the U.S. Supreme Court gave states more power to limit the procedure. Martinez called the legislature into special session and proposed such measures as mandatory waiting periods and parental notification. The Democrat-controlled legislature took just two days to kill the package and adjourn itself, leaving Martinez looking powerless.

By the summer of 1990, however, the governor had recovered some footing. The legislature had gone along with his ambitious prison-building program, which helped as a campaign issue. And he earned points with environmentalists by establishing a trust fund to buy and protect endangered lands. He easily defeated Woodson-Howard and some lesser known candidates, then turned to face Chiles in what seemed a mismatch. Chiles had emerged with the Democratic nomination virtually broke and still promising to hold contributors to $100. Martinez had about $11 million.

In the end, the money hardly mattered. Whatever questions people may have had about Chiles's health were dispelled in debates, which the Democrat dominated. Martinez also hurt his cause by choosing a relatively unknown sheriff from the Keys, J. Allison DeFoor II, as his running mate. DeFoor, although considered progressive and a strong environmentalist, was outmatched by MacKay, whom *Florida Trend* magazine had once called the man most qualified to be governor.

On election day, the Democratic ticket trounced the Republicans, winning 56.5 percent to 43.5 percent. Moreover, GOP hopes of capturing the state senate and several local offices were dashed in the landslide. Exit polls and county returns revealed that Martinez's loss was attributable as much to a lack of support from Republicans—especially women, who didn't forgive him for his antiabortion stance—as to dramatic backing for Chiles.[8] In a host of solidly GOP counties, such as Manatee and Sarasota, Martinez collected fewer votes than he had gotten four years before. His strongest support came from southwest Florida, with Chiles's from the Gold Coast and the counties in which the University of Florida and Florida State University are located.

The 1990 gubernatorial loss cast a pall over the GOP's dream. A former chairman of the Republican National Committee, Frank Fahrenkopf, lamented, "This reverses the tide that we've had running for us for the past 10 years." Added Alvin From, director of the Democratic Leadership Council: "Florida was the fastest-moving Republican state in the country. What this shows is that if a Democrat can win there, a Democrat can win anywhere."[9]

Under Florida's constitution, executive power is shared among the governor and the elected cabinet, whose six members are power centers unto themselves. Turnover is rare as long as an incumbent, always bankrolled by many of the interests he or she regulates, seeks reelection. In the 1990 races five of the incumbents did just that, and won in mostly lopsided contests. The cabinet's two Republicans, Treasurer–Insurance Commissioner Tom Gallagher and Secretary of State Jim Smith (a party-switcher who had earlier served as a Democratic attorney general), coasted to new terms, Gallagher with 57.2 percent of the vote and Smith with 59.4 percent. The victories gave both men encouragement regarding their next moves—toward the governor's mansion—four years down the road. The cabinet's three incumbent Democrats, Attorney General Bob Butterworth, Education Commissioner Betty Castor, and Comptroller Gerald Lewis (who oversaw the state's banks) sailed to additional terms, Butterworth without opposition. Castor was the top vote-getter statewide, winning 65.8 percent of the vote, while Lewis won 59.5 percent of the vote.

There was real action, however, for the remaining post, commissioner of agriculture. Incumbent Doyle Connor, a Democrat, had announced his retirement after thirty years in the position. As a result, the Republican party had an opportunity to pick up a seat and, for the first time in history, have equal strength with the Democrats in the cabinet. But the Democrats put up a tough contender—former senate president Bobby Crawford, a citrus grower from Polk County. Aided by urban and suburban voters who favored his strong environmental record, Crawford defeated Charles Bronson, a cattle rancher from Brevard who had called for less regulation, with relative ease, taking 55.4 percent of the vote.[10]

The 1992 presidential election in Florida proved to be the most seriously contested national race since 1976, when Jimmy Carter carried the Sunshine State for the Democrats. In the 1988 presidential election, George Bush so dominated the Florida electorate that Democrat Michael Dukakis pulled out virtually all his staff and resources six weeks before the election. Florida had also gone heavily for Republican Ronald Reagan in 1980 and 1984, causing many political analysts to label the state solidly Republican in presidential elections. Governor Bill Clinton of Arkansas didn't believe them. He and his running mate, Senator Al Gore of Tennessee, brought their campaign bus into Florida for a swing that drew massive media attention. After Hurricane Andrew flattened much of south Dade County, Clinton and his wife toured the area, media in tow, promising help if he were elected. The Democratic candidate also courted conservatives in Miami's Cuban-American community. And in the week before election day, he appeared at a huge outdoor rally in downtown Tampa, an important swing area.

President Bush and his vice president, Dan Quayle, responded in kind. The president made a personal visit to the hurricane-ravaged area, and Quayle had a bus trip of his own in central Florida. Complicating the equation was the presence of independent Ross Perot, the Texas billionaire, whose anti-politics style drew thousands of enthusiasts to rallies in Orlando and Tampa. On November 7, 1992, Florida voters stayed in the Republican column—but barely. Bush won 40.9 percent to Clinton's 39.0 percent; Perot matched his national showing with 19.8 percent.[11]

Also on that November day, Democratic U.S. senator Bob Graham crushed his GOP opponent, Bill Grant, an outcome that came as no surprise, not even to Grant. Just a few days before the vote, when polls showed him facing a three-to-one loss, Grant told a Miami *Herald* reporter: "He's the best politician in the state. Hell, that's the problem. I think he's sincere."[12] Graham had established himself long before the 1992 contest as a giant among the state's politicians. Born to wealth and power in Miami in 1936, the son of a former state senator and land baron, Graham was educated at the University of Florida and Harvard law school. His heart seemed always in public service, starting in the state house, moving to the state senate and, in 1978, winning a long-shot bid to become governor. His gimmick involved changing his name from D. Robert Graham to simply Bob, and working one hundred ordinary jobs around the state to prove he wasn't just a rich boy playing politics. His campaign was conducted under the tutelage of a masterful image-maker, Bob Squier, who had earlier helped Jimmy Carter become president. Graham won easy reelection as governor in 1982, setting himself up to challenge incumbent U.S. senator Paula Hawkins, a Republican, in a titanic 1986 race. Despite the best efforts of the GOP that year, including several direct appeals from President Reagan on Hawkins's behalf, Graham won, 54.7 percent to 45.3 percent.

When the year approached for Graham's reelection to the Senate, the Republican party's rising and established stars looked elsewhere. Finally, Phil Gramm, the Republican senator from Texas who headed the GOP's senatorial campaign committee, persuaded Grant, a former Democratic congressman who had switched parties in 1989 and then lost reelection the following year, to give it a try. He gamely agreed, but his campaign had little sting, few allies, and a perpetually empty treasury. Grant traveled the state in his own Jeep Wagoneer trying to build the case that Graham hadn't done enough to cut the federal deficit. But if voters cared about the issue, they didn't blame Graham, who responded with commercials showing off his grandchildren. Grant got almost no help from his party, which wrote the race off as a losing cause. Graham won with an impressive 65.4 percent of the vote.[13]

The 1994 races for governor, the cabinet seats and the U.S. Senate illustrate the increasingly competitive nature of Florida politics, the tendency of voters to ignore party labels, and the variations in candidate strength in the different regions of Florida. By the summer of 1993, Governor Chiles was in trouble. The media knew it; his party knew it; a pack of Republicans knew it well enough to have launched campaigns to replace him. It seemed everybody knew it—except Chiles. A Mason-Dixon poll at the time had concluded that only 27 percent of likely Florida voters gave the Democratic governor positive marks for his performance. When one of the authors confronted the governor with a list of negative statistics over lunch one day and demanded to know whether Chiles agreed he was in deep trouble, the governor put on his best poker face and deadpanned: "You're absolutely right. There's no way I can win. I guess I should give up now. Have we decided what we're going to order?"[14]

The governor's confidence didn't deter challengers. In the summer of 1993, Miami businessman Jeb Bush (his real name is John Ellis Bush), second son of the former president, announced that he would challenge Chiles. Although the young Bush had never sought elective office before, he had served a stint as Governor Martinez's secretary of commerce. And his political credentials were stellar: not only had he run his father's campaigns in Florida, both as president and vice president, but he had been the Republican party chairman of Dade County and a cochairman of Martinez's 1986 and 1990 campaigns. Bush had lived in the state since 1980, when he moved to Miami to run his father's first Florida primary campaign. In an interview before his formal announcement, Bush tried to define his goal: "I am not going to get elected because I am the son of George and Barbara Bush. In fact, I will probably face some automatic opposition because some people will not like what my dad has done. . . . I want [people] to see that there is more to me than my name."[15]

Although early polls showed that Bush would be a formidable challenger, he quickly drew opposition from an all-star field of Republican candidates. They included Secretary of State (and former attorney general) Smith of Tallahassee; state senator Ander Crenshaw of Jacksonville, who had become the first Republican ever to serve as president of the Florida senate; Treasurer–Insurance Commissioner Gallagher, a Miamian who had run unsuccessfully in 1986; and Tallahassee lawyer Ken Connor, an activist in the anti-abortion movement and a favorite of many Christians conservatives. For the most part, the Republican primary campaign was gentlemanly, shepherded along by state GOP chairman Tom Slade of Jacksonville, who was quick to step in to referee any spats that could split party forces. The group appeared together in a record twenty-five debates around the state. But the order barely changed: Bush held a commanding lead from the start, while Smith and Gallagher battled for second spot.

In an unusual move, Gallagher and Smith shared the cost of a campaign ad raising questions about one of Bush's real estate deals that wound up enmeshed in the huge savings and loan bailout. And in the closing days, Gallagher aired another ad noting that he had won endorsements from nine Florida newspaper editorial boards while Bush hadn't collected any. Said the ad, "The score in the Republican primary is nine to nothing." An announcer, reading from one of the editorials, described Bush as "shallow" and unready for the state's top job. Smith's attacks became even more personal, as he increasingly dismissed Bush as a rich kid running on his father's coattails.[16]

The rough attacks didn't seem to matter. Bush and his running mate, state representative Tom Feeney of Orlando, collected 45.7 percent of the primary vote to 18.4 percent for Smith and his running mate, Barbara Sheen Todd, who finished a distant second. For seventy-two hours Smith tried to rally support from the other also-rans in the hope of leap-frogging Bush to the nomination.

But the numbers appeared too daunting, and he opted not to call for a runoff. "You can't run from reality," Smith told reporters the following Saturday morning, wiping away a tear. "It's important that the party come together so that we not spend the next three weeks chewing each other's legs off." He pledged his support to Bush and the stage was set for the final showdown.[17]

Governor Chiles, meanwhile, with 72.2 percent of the vote, had made quick work of his primary challenger, a maverick candidate named Jack Gargan of Cedar Key, who had hoped in vain that disaffected voters would rally to his impoverished candidacy. Chiles's win, however, gave him no momentum. Several polls showed Bush holding a solid lead over the incumbent. But rather than send panic through the Democratic ranks, the polls appeared to embolden the candidates, who mounted an uncharacteristically tough and personal campaign against both Bush and Feeney. MacKay, in an interview, explained the jolt: "They say that seeing the shadow of the hangman's noose tends to concentrate the mind. Perhaps that's what we needed."[18]

For the next seven weeks, Chiles and MacKay rarely discussed their own record, choosing instead to relentlessly attack Bush. They questioned his competence in business (raising again the specter of the savings and loan scandal); his judgment in choosing a deeply conservative running mate aligned with the Christian Coalition (in one stream of attacks, the Democrats accused Feeney of having advocated abolishing Medicare); his attitudes toward women (the Republicans were adamantly anti-abortion); and, finally, his purported involvement in shadowy business practices.

Bush fired back, alternating ads between those that outlined his positions on such issues as education and crime and those that pounded Chiles for being soft on criminals. The sharpest ad featured the mother of a teenage girl who had been abducted and murdered many years before. The killer had averted the death penalty through court maneuvering. In the Bush ad the girl's mother blamed Chiles for the fact that the execution hadn't taken place, implying that he opposed the maximum penalty. The allegation rankled the governor, who told reporters that Bush was taking a page from his father's 1988 campaign attacks against Democrat Michael Dukakis in which he had used the case of Willie Horton, a Massachusetts convict who, after being let out of prison on furlough, raped and tortured a Maryland woman.[19]

Chiles's best opportunity to respond came during the third and final debate of the campaign, held in Tampa on November 1. It was also the only debate held at night and televised statewide during prime viewing hours. And it was held at a time when most statewide polls showed the race growing too close to call. Moderator Tim Russert of NBC's *Meet the Press* raised the death-penalty issue early in the confrontation, asking Bush to justify running the ad. Bush attempted to make his case by implying that Chiles has been "liberal on crime" and hadn't yet acted on ten other death warrants. Chiles seemed barely able to contain himself when it was his turn. His voice was filled with a cold fury as he stared at his opponent and said, "All my political life I have supported the death penalty; as governor I have executed eight men. I hold the phone as they walk into the death chamber. I give the last command before they pull the switch." As Bush stood mute, Chiles wagged a finger and chided the Republican for airing the ad at all: "You knew it was false. You admitted it was false," he said. "And I am ashamed that you would use the loss of a mother in an ad like this." The Republican, who seemed flustered by the force of Chiles's words, never gained the offensive. By the end, the sixty-four-year-old Democrat seemed to dominate the stage, even drawing on a bit of Florida folklore to liken himself to a "he coon," the oldest and wisest raccoon in a pack, who knows how to outwit the hunters.[20]

Chiles won by nearly 64,000 votes out of 4.2 million cast, 50.8 percent to 49.2 percent. Although Bush carried most of the state's sixty-seven counties, he lost by huge margins in Dade (his home county), Palm Beach, and Broward counties, which offset Republican margins elsewhere. In Broward alone, for example, Chiles emerged with a surplus of over 120,000 votes. Exit polls also showed that the Republican's views on abortion rights hurt him in many GOP strongholds along the Gulf Coast.[21] Although Bush carried such counties as Collier, Manatee, and Sarasota, he didn't get the margins his strategists had expected.[22] Voter turnout jumped 10 percent over 1990. Among those contributing to the increase were senior citizens and blacks, the latter energized by Chiles and by Doug Jamerson's unsuccessful attempt to become the first elected African American commissioner of education.

Remarkably, Chiles was the only large-state Democratic governor to win election in the 1994 nationwide Republican wave. Postelection analyses suggested that he could attribute his success in part to the presence on the same ballot of a proposed constitutional amendment to allow casino gambling in Florida. Proponents of gambling spent more than $15 million in their unsuccessful effort. A big part of that was to get two groups to the polls that gambling strategists thought would favor their cause: blacks and senior citizens. Ironically, they succeeded in getting those groups to the voting booth—but they cast ballots against more gambling. While they were at it, however, these historically Democratic blocs voted heavily for Chiles. Slade, the state Republican chair, later lamented this turn of events: "The casino [campaign] was the one thing we had no control over."[23]

Until the 1990s, campaigns for state cabinet races were generally staid and predictable affairs, mere undercards for gubernatorial and other contests. The first Republican didn't arrive until Jim Smith, who had served two terms as attorney general as a Democrat before switching parties, was elected secretary of state in 1988 to fill the uncompleted term of retiring George Firestone. Incumbents had historically coasted to reelection unless under the cloud of scandal. In 1994, however, the cabinet would become one of the battlegrounds of the war between the two parties for dominance in state government.

Democrats held four of the six seats. Attorney General Butterworth, Comptroller Lewis, and Agriculture Commissioner Crawford were seeking reelection, and Education Commissioner Jamerson, who had been appointed to fill the unexpired term of Betty Castor (who had resigned to become president of the University of South Florida in Tampa), hoped to stay on and become the first African American elected to the cabinet. The two Republican-held seats were those of Treasurer–Insurance Commissioner Gallagher and Secretary of State Smith. But both had resigned, as mentioned above, to make their unsuccessful bids for the GOP gubernatorial nomination, providing Democrats with two more chances to maintain dominance.

Working for the Republicans, however, was the continuing growth in voter registration, a well-financed state party organization adept at identifying and recruiting good candidates, and a restless electorate unhappy with government in general. With the exception of the attorney general's race, where Butterworth appeared unassailable, the Republican party mounted a widespread offensive to take over the Florida cabinet for the first time—and came remarkably close.

The race for education commissioner quickly evolved into the most watched of the contests. Two other African Americans had served in the cabinet, but only as appointees who didn't later seek election. Only one African American had ever won statewide election in Florida; in 1976 supreme court Justice Joseph Hatchett, who had been appointed to the state's highest court to fill a vacancy, succeeded in winning his seat. (Since then, Florida's constitution has been changed to eliminate direct election of appellate judges.)

An expert at school financing, Jamerson, a burly ex-teacher, was a six-term state legislator from St. Petersburg when appointed by Governor Chiles. Republicans sought to portray the Democrat as a captive of the state's powerful teacher unions—a strong weapon in this union-averse state. The GOP pick was Frank Brogan, superintendent of schools from affluent Martin County and a former school principal. Brogan evoked the fresh-scrubbed earnestness of a choir boy, and his no-nonsense approach to dealing with the teacher unions while squeezing taxes had made him a rising star in his home county. The contest became largely a referendum on schools with those defending the status quo aligned with Jamerson and those opposing it—and calling for radical changes, such as tuition tax vouchers—rallying to Brogan. The campaign took on a slight racial overtone in the eyes of some when Brogan ran unusual TV ads in the final days featuring ten-second sound bites of Jamerson. Critics said the ad seemed designed to ensure that Jamerson's race was widely known, which might hurt him among conservative whites.[24] Although the state's black voters turned out heavily, it wasn't enough to save the incumbent. Brogan won easily, 53.4 percent to 46.6 percent, to become the state's first Republican education commissioner.

After incumbent Republican Smith declared his intention of leaving the office of secretary of state to run for governor, Democrats expressed confidence that they could capture this seat with an up-and-coming star named Ron Saunders, a veteran legislator from Key West and a favorite with environmentalists and progressives. Saunders, a fifth-generation Floridian, easily won his party's nomination and seemed a solid bet for the general election. But his opponent was an equally popular Republican, Sandra Mortham, a financial consultant from Largo, near St. Petersburg, who had been the house Republican leader for the preceding two years. In that post she assembled a young and politically ambitious staff that laid the groundwork for her statewide race. Mortham also defused one of the major issues the Democrat could use against her by declaring her support for abortion rights. At the same time, she held the conservative wing of her party by taking strong stands against gun control—an issue because the secretary of state is responsible for licensing gun users. Mortham won 52.4 percent to 47.6 percent.

The race for treasurer-insurance commissioner, too, was seen as a golden opportunity for Democrats after Gallagher attempted to move up. The party fielded one of its stars, former congressman Nelson, the handsome multimillionaire from Florida's Space Coast who had lost his bid for the Democratic gubernatorial nomination to Chiles in 1990. Nelson had spent the intervening years practicing law. But as soon as the treasurer's seat became open, he jumped back into politics, collected $2 million—the legal maximum for the cabinet post—and regained his old form. Nelson's opponent, Tim Ireland, a thirty-six-year-old, four-term state representative from Fort Myers, ran a creditable race. But Nelson wasn't to be denied a return to office, and he captured the cabinet seat which had been in Republican hands, 51.7 percent to 48.3 percent.

The race for agriculture commissioner should have been the equivalent of a six-inch putt for Democratic incumbent Crawford, facing his first reelection. A central Florida farmer and a former state senate president, Crawford faced token

Republican opposition from little-known Frank Darden. Things shifted when Darden bowed to pressure from state GOP chair Slade and quit the race in mid-September, a week after the first primary election. Slade then got the state GOP executive committee to draft Jim Smith, the outgoing secretary of state who had just suspended his race for governor in the face of certain defeat at the hands of Jeb Bush. The switch, which Democrats labeled a "back-room deal," became the campaign's major issue and hurt Smith among hard-core Democrats. And Smith, the owner of a large plantation north of Tallahassee, failed to convince Florida farmers that he understood their issues. Still, the contest was close and Slade's gamble nearly paid off; Crawford squeaked to reelection by 51.0 percent to 49.0 percent. The defeat appeared to signal the end of Smith's eighteen-year career in public office. "I think, realistically, it's all over," Smith told a Miami *Herald* reporter. "It's very disappointing. Life will go on."[25]

If any cabinet Democrat looked vulnerable on the eve of the 1996 campaign, it was Lewis, the twenty-year veteran comptroller from Miami and dean of the cabinet. He had been investigated (and cleared) by a grand jury, and faced calls for his impeachment by state legislators, who questioned his vigilance during the savings and loan scandals. Yet Lewis won the Democratic primary easily and appeared headed for easy reelection against a neophyte GOP-challenger, Robert F. (Bob) Milligan. What this Republican lacked in electoral combat, however, he more than made up for in real combat. Milligan had recently retired from the U.S. Marine Corps as a three-star general, the second highest-ranking officer in that branch of the military. He had commanded Marine Corps forces in the Pacific and overseen logistical needs in the Persian Gulf War. The contrast between Lewis's troubled leadership and Milligan's stellar military record proved too great for the Democrat to overcome despite outspending the Republican by nearly ten to one. Milligan became the first Republican comptroller in Florida history, defeating Lewis 51.0 percent to 49.0 percent.

The attorney general's race was the most lopsided of all the 1994 statewide elections, a tribute to the political prowess of incumbent Democrat Butterworth and to his vote-rich base of Broward County. Seeking a third term, Butterworth easily defeated former Dade County circuit judge Henry Ferro, capturing 57.5 percent of the vote to Ferro's 42.5 percent.

When the dust had cleared at the cabinet level, the parties were tied with three seats each, marking a Republican gain of one seat. Although the GOP did not win the majority it sought, it could take comfort from the close contests its nominees ran in two of the three races it lost. Only Butterworth gave the Democrats a solid cabinet victory. The narrowness of the victories in five of the six races reflected the highly competitive nature of Florida politics in the mid-1990s.

The U.S. Senate election of 1994 offered a sharp contrast to that year's closely contested gubernatorial and cabinet races. Republican Connie Mack, namesake of the legendary baseball owner and manager (real name: Cornelius McGillicuddy), had been a little-known three-term congressman from Fort Myers when he ran in 1988. That outcome, against Buddy MacKay, which was mentioned above, was so close that it took absentee ballots to push Mack over the top. In the ensuing six years, however, the boyishly handsome, ideologically conservative former banker had risen in stature and in the hearts of Floridians. The August 1994 issue of *Florida Trend* magazine summed up Mack's chances neatly in an article about the race under the headline: "Home Free . . . Now his re-election is assured."[26]

Yet despite the seemingly lopsided nature of the 1994 U.S. Senate race in Florida, it drew attention across the nation because the Democratic nominee, Hugh Rodham, was the younger brother of First Lady Hillary Rodham Clinton. Rodham, a bear of a man nicknamed "Huge Rodham" by his staff, had no direct political experience. He had moved to Miami in 1980 after a stint in the Peace Corps in Latin America, intent on starting a career in the law. Over the years he had risen to become an assistant public defender and, by virtue of his White House connections, a fixture on the Democratic party circuit. Still, when he announced his intention to challenge Mack, many thought him foolhardy and Republicans thought him merely a fool. Slade, the GOP chair, showed up at Rodham's campaign kickoff to tell reporters that the candidate was "nothing more than Billy Carter with a law degree."[27] On election day, Mack—who had spent most of the campaign traveling in other states to give his money to more needy Republicans—administered a mercy killing, collecting 70.5 percent of the vote to Rodham's 29.5 percent. If the Democrats could take solace in anything, it may have been in knowing their party's level of bedrock support.

In 1996 President Clinton, perhaps driven by his close 1992 race in the Sunshine State, made an all-out effort to win Florida, devoting extensive attention to the state. Three of his Cabinet members—Attorney General Janet Reno, Treasury Secretary Robert Rubin and Environmental Protection Agency administrator Carol Browner—hailed from Dade County. Clinton also made good on his 1992 promise of hurricane relief; staged the Summit of the Americas in Miami, the largest gathering ever of Latin American heads of state; appeared at several Florida functions, political and ceremonial; and became the first sitting president to address the Florida legislature. He also courted Governor Chiles, Lieutenant Governor MacKay, and other prominent Floridians. And Clinton made it clear that he believed Chiles's blueprint for winning in 1994 was the right formula for him. Like Chiles, the president would run a campaign with four pillars: senior citizens (he was helped by the ham-fisted attempts by the Republican-led 104th Congress to slow the growth of Medicare); pro-choice women; African Americans; and environmentalists.[28] As early as the summer of 1995, he began airing television ads in key markets to turn around negative perceptions. Regardless of what the numbers showed about Republican growth in the state, Clinton appeared convinced that the votes were there for him to become the first Democratic presidential standard-bearer to carry Florida in twenty years.

Despite his links to the state (he owned a condominium in Bal Harbour, just north of Miami Beach), Senator Bob Dole of Kansas, the Republican nominee, seemed curiously apathetic about the threat from Clinton. He spent several days at his oceanfront condo during a crucial week in October, mostly in seclusion. Just days before, Clinton had swept the state from south to north, hitting eleven cities in three days. When Dole did campaign, his audiences were often preselected and small. State party workers privately despaired, and their pessimism was justified. Clinton won Florida's twenty-five electoral votes with 48.0 percent of the vote to Dole's 42.3 percent. Ross Perot finished with 9.1 percent. An exit poll conducted for the Miami *Herald* demonstrated that Clinton fulfilled his equation flawlessly, winning heavy margins among women, voters over age sixty, and minorities.[29] Ironically, the same electorate provided Republicans a historic triumph in the elections for the Florida legislature.

Two-Party Competition Expands Downward

State Legislative Level

From the mid-1980s through the mid-1990s, the GOP advanced tenaciously at the state legislative level. In 1994 the party captured control of the senate for the first time. Then in 1996 the Republicans not only added a seat to their senate majority but also won a narrow majority in the state house, giving Florida a GOP-led legislature for the first time since Reconstruction. Table 28 charts the GOP's path to this mid-1990s breakthrough.

When the control of rural northern counties over the legislature was broken in 1967 by a court-mandated reapportionment, the Republican share of seats in the senate jumped from 5 percent to 42 percent and in the house from 9 percent

Table 28. The Growth of Republican Strength in the Florida Legislature, 1958–1996

Year (Nov.)	Senate No. of Seats Dem.		Rep.		House No. of Seats Dem.		Rep.	
1958	37	(97.4%)	1	(2.6%)	92	(96.8%)	3	(3.2%)
1960	37	(97.4)	1	(2.6)	88	(92.6)	7	(7.4)
1962	37	(97.4)	1	(4.4)	90	(94.7)	5	(5.3)
1964	42	(95.5)	2	(4.5)	102	(91.1)	10	(8.9)
1967[a]	28	(58.3)	20	(41.7)	80	(67.2)	39	(32.8)
1968	32	(66.7)	16	(33.3)	77	(64.7)	42	(35.3)
1970	33	(68.8)	15	(31.2)	81	(68.1)	38	(31.9)
1972[b]	25	(62.5)	14	(35.0)	77	(64.2)	43	(35.8)
1974[b]	27	(67.5)	12	(30.0)	86	(71.7)	34	(28.3)
1976[b]	30	(75.0)	9	(22.5)	92	(76.7)	28	(23.3)
1978	29	(72.5)	11	(27.5)	89	(74.2)	31	(25.8)
1980	27	(67.5)	13	(32.5)	81	(67.5)	39	(32.5)
1982	32	(80.0)	8	(20.0)	84	(70.0)	36	(30.0)
1984[c]	32	(80.0)	8	(20.0)	77	(64.2)	43	(35.8)
1986[c]	25	(62.5)	15	(37.5)	75	(62.5)	45	(37.5)
1988[c]	23	(57.5)	17	(42.5)	73	(60.8)	47	(39.2)
1990[c]	23	(57.5)	17	(42.5)	74	(58.3)	46	(38.3)
1992	20	(50.0)	20	(50.0)	71	(59.2)	49	(40.8)
1994[c]	19	(47.5)	21	(52.5)	63	(52.5)	57	(47.5)
1996[c]	17	(42.5)	23	(57.5)	59	(49.2)	61	(50.8)

Sources: Richard M. Scammon and Alice V. McGillivray, *America Votes: A Handbook of Contemporary Election Statistics,* various vols. (Washington, D.C., 1956–); *Journals of the House of Representatives* (Florida); *Journals of the Senate* (Florida).

Note: Between 1958 and 1970, the Senate grew from 38 seats to 44 to 48, and the House from 95 to 112 to 119. The Senate's current size of 40 and the House's size of 120 date from 1972.

[a]Election held in March. The results of the November 1966 election were nullified by the Supreme Court, and a new legislature was elected under a new apportionment plan.

[b]One Independent (Lori Wilson) was elected to the Senate in 1972, 1974, and 1976.

[c]The party division is as of the November general elections. The ratio of Democratic to Republican members sometimes changed in the period between elections due to resignations, deaths, and changes in party affiliation. Years in which such change occurred in the house were 1985 (76 Dem. to 44 Rep.), 1989 (72 Dem. to 48 Rep.), 1991 (73 Dem. to 47 Rep.), 1997 (55 Dem. to 65 Rep.), and 1998 (54 Dem. to 66 Rep.); in the senate, 1985 (30 Dem. to 10 Rep.), 1991 (22 Dem. to 18 Rep.), 1995 (18 Dem. to 22 Rep.), and 1998 (15 Dem. to 25 Rep.).

to 33 percent.[30] Initially, Republican successes came primarily in the south and central areas of the state, but by the 1990s the party was competitive throughout the state.

An examination of how the GOP came to control the Florida legislature in the mid-1990s reveals more than a little about the current dynamics of politics in the Sunshine State. The immediate story of the Republican legislative triumph of the mid-1990s starts with failure as the decade of the 1990s opened. Motivated partly by the desire to maximize GOP influence on the upcoming redistricting, the Republicans made a major, though unsuccessful, push to win control of the legislature in the 1990 elections.[31]

Reapportionment issues dominated the legislature for the next two years. Despite their majority position, Democrats had difficulty controlling the redistricting process. Various conflicts erupted involving efforts to protect incumbents, gain partisan advantage, and create majority-minority districts. The players included African Americans, Hispanics, women, incumbents, Republicans, and Democrats, all seeking to gain or, at a minimum, not be disadvantaged by the new lines. African American members were divided; some cooperated with the Democratic leadership, while others joined Republican leaders to maximize the creation of black-majority districts.[32]

The plan adopted was indicative of the diversity of the state; it included eight house and two senate districts with a black voting-age majority and nine majority-Hispanic districts in the house and three in the senate. Peter Wallace, the chair of the house reapportionment committee in 1992 and the house speaker from 1994 to 1996, characterized the Republican strategy as follows: "It was, I think, a cynical manipulation. . . . [T]he Republican party figured out that, if it could siphon traditional Democratic voters out of Democratic districts, it could improve its successes and that is what the creation of a number of minority districts, particularly African American districts, accomplished." When asked about the reapportionment process in an interview, Slade, the Republican state party chair, observed, "The blacks and Republicans have joined together in an unholy alliance to do in the white Democrats, and we have succeeded. We have been spectacularly successful."[33]

The reapportionment plan, which survived a lengthy court battle, did, in fact, increase opportunities for Florida's diverse population to win office. African Americans, Hispanics, and women all benefited, gaining seats in 1992. Republicans too profited, winning three additional seats in both the house and the senate. The resulting party division was 71 Democrats to 49 Republicans in the house, while the senate was evenly divided, 20 to 20.[34]

Two years later in the 1994 elections Republicans again made gains, captur-

ing the senate with 21 Republicans to 19 Democrats. The defection by a conservative Democrat to the Republican party a few months later made the split
22 to 18. The Republicans picked up 8 seats in the house, narrowing the division to 63 Democrats and 57 Republicans. The GOP won 3 open seats that had
been held by Democrats and defeated 6 incumbent Democrats while losing only
1 open seat it had held. The strong anti-incumbent mood of the electorate and
the 1994 national GOP tide were factors contributing to the outcome.

Going into the 1996 election, Slade expressed the GOP confidence: "I don't
think there is any question that the Republicans will control the House and
maintain control of the Senate. We have a better message, better candidates, and
competitive resources. The Republican party presents the vehicle for change."
Leading Democrats showed equal confidence. Lieutenant Governor MacKay
praised the quality of the 1996 Democratic legislative candidates: "I believe we
have as good a team and as good an effort as has ever happened in Florida. So
. . . [in] the sophistication that has gone into recruiting candidates, showing the
candidates how they could win, using polling techniques and so forth to try to
convince the strongest candidates to run . . . [we've] done a good job in catch-
ing up [with the Republicans]."[35]

Despite the lieutenant governor's optimism, the Republican party had two
advantages at the outset in achieving its objective in the house: fewer incumbents were retiring from office—one Republican compared with twelve Democrats—and the Republicans challenged more incumbents. Republicans targeted nine of the twelve open Democratic seats and eleven Democratic
incumbents.[36] These were hotly contested races with clear differences between
the candidates apparent in a number of the races; among the issues dividing candidates were school vouchers, abortion, environmental controls, and taxes.

Governor Chiles campaigned throughout the state for Democratic legislative candidates, while Republican candidates benefited not only from state party
funds but from national party spending. An analysis of campaign finance reports
by the Miami *Herald* revealed that the Republican senatorial campaign committee paid for a barrage of attack ads in the last two weeks labeling Democrats
unfit for office, which may have been the decisive edge in several close elections. A seven-term Democrat who lost by 2,300 votes said the ads were "significant if not decisive," adding, "All of the ads were very, very negative. I was
depicted as a liar and a thief."[37]

Republicans narrowly achieved their goal, defeating two Democratic incumbents, both of whom had won by less than two percentage points in 1994,
and winning two open seats Democrats had held. The result: GOP control of
the house, 61 to 59. Republicans elected their first speaker in modern Florida

history, Daniel Webster, an Orlando conservative identified with the Christian right. (An ominous sign for Democrats: by May 1998, the Republicans had gained five additional seats, four from Democrats who switched parties and one in a special election. This made the party division 66–54.)

The Florida senate posed an even more difficult challenge for the Democrats. Republicans held 11 of the seats that were not up for election in 1996, and, of the 21 seats that were to be filled, 6 of the Republican incumbents were not challenged. Thus, Republicans, certain of 17 seats before the election, needed to win only 4 of the 11 contested seats to maintain their control. They won 6 of the 11 seats, giving them a net gain of one, and a 23–17 continuing majority.

U.S. House Elections

An analysis of elections in Florida at another level—for the U.S. House—casts further light on the political dynamics of the state, especially its increased partisan competitiveness. Florida's first post-Reconstruction Republican congressman, William Cramer, was elected in 1954 from a St. Petersburg–centered district. As the state's population surged, the number of congressional seats allocated to Florida increased correspondingly after each census—from 12 in the 1960s to 15 in the 1970s to 19 in the 1980s to 23 in the 1990s. Each reapportionment led to an increase in Republican representatives as new districts were created, district lines redrawn, old loyalties disrupted, and longtime incumbents resigned to seek higher office or retired.[38] The Republican share of seats rose from 25.0 percent in 1970 to 65.2 percent in 1996 with the Republican gains coming by winning open seats and not by defeating incumbents, who were nearly always reelected.

Following the 1988 elections, Democrats and Republicans were nearly balanced; Democrats held ten seats, Republicans nine. Two events in 1989 put the GOP into majority status on Florida's House delegation: Democrat Bill Grant switched to the Republican party and a Cuban-American Republican woman won a special election. Ilena Ros-Lehtinen, a GOP state legislator, became the first Hispanic and only the second woman to be elected to the U.S. House from Florida when she won the seat left vacant by the death in May 1989 of Claude Pepper, a liberal Democrat and champion of the elderly. The Democratic candidate, Gerald Richman, who was Jewish, responded angrily to a statement by the Republican national chairman that the seat belonged to a Cuban-American: "This isn't an Anglo seat, it isn't a Jewish seat, it isn't a Cuban-American seat. It's an American seat."[39] (In fact, the seat, with somewhat different district lines, would become one of those designated in the 1992 reapportionment as a Hispanic seat.) Ros-Lehtinen won with 53.0 percent of the vote. Exit polls showed that 90 percent of Hispanics voted for Ros-Lehtinen, while 96 percent of African Americans and 88 percent of non-Hispanic whites supported Richman. Ros-Lehtinen's victory coupled with Grant's shift left the Florida delegation at eleven Republicans and eight Democrats as the 1990s began.

Democrats gained one seat in the 1990 elections when Grant, the party switcher, lost. The other seventeen incumbents who sought reelection were successful. Grant was defeated by Douglas (Pete) Peterson, a retired air force colonel and a former Vietnam POW. Peterson received 56.9 percent of the vote to Grant's 43.1 percent, despite being outspent by nearly three to one. Voters in the Second District, which included the state capital and Florida State University, had the highest percentage of Democratic registrants (80.8 percent) in the state.

Because of reapportionment, the context of congressional elections changed significantly between 1990 and 1992. The reapportionment was complicated by the issue of minority representation and the presumed mandate to create minority-access districts. While the Florida legislature had been able to draw state house and senate lines, it became hopelessly deadlocked on congressional districting. In fact, a recent study describes the Florida struggle over congressional apportionment as "titanic" and as reaching "levels of partisan acrimony unparalleled in anyone's memory." In a special session senate agreement on a plan broke down when two conservative Democrats defected and joined Republicans, creating a 20–20 deadlock. Some of the intra-Democratic party tension is captured by the remarks of Corrine Brown, an African American member of the Florida house at the time of the redistricting who was subsequently elected to Congress from the Third District. She said in a 1996 interview:

> Politics [is the reason the legislature could not agree on the congressional lines]. Well, I'll never forget. We had a meeting [with Speaker] T. K. Wetherall, who . . . called all the black members together. . . . [H]e said that we have always had good relationships [between] Democrats and blacks, and we are not going to have the same formula that they have around the country [that is, Republicans and blacks cooperating to create the maximum number of black-majority districts]. And he said we are going to give you all one seat and we are going to give the Hispanics two. And so everybody was supposed to be happy with that, but I couldn't understand it. If you look at the population, we should have close to four seats in Florida—not one, not two, not three—if they hadn't been draw-

ing them funny to keep us from power. And so that is when the blacks and Hispanics got involved in a lawsuit to get the courts to draw the districts. . . . we were asking for four seats.[40]

When the senate deadlocked, a panel of three federal judges, brought into the reapportionment dispute by the lawsuit Brown mentioned, drew the congressional lines. The judges adopted a plan that created three black-majority districts and two Hispanic districts. The black-majority district located in north Florida, the Third (later won by Brown), was one of the more bizarre in shape in the nation, linking predominantly black neighborhoods in fourteen counties and running 250 miles from Jacksonville to Orlando in what was likened to a "bug splat" because of its erratic wishbone shape. Ironically, in 1996 the same federal court panel, following subsequent U.S. Supreme Court precedents holding that race could not be the predominant reason for drawing districts, ruled two-to-one that the district the panel had initially drawn was an unconstitutional attempt to ensure the election of an African American. Then, the state legislature, under court mandate to modify the Third District lines by May 1996, developed a plan replacing the wishbone shape with a straight Jacksonville to Orlando district that had the effect of reducing the black voting age population from 50.6 percent to 42.3 percent. The other two black-majority districts, located in south Florida—the Seventeenth, won in 1992 by Carrie Meek, and the Twenty-Third, won the same year by Alcee Hastings—were never challenged in court.[41]

A comparison of the ratio of Democrats to Republicans in the districts before and after the 1992 court-drawn reapportionment suggests that the Republicans benefited from the rearrangement of the lines. Although there was only a small change in the ratio of Democratic to Republican registration in the 1990 to 1992 period (see Table 26), there was a substantial change in the number of districts with a Republican plurality. In 1990 six of the nineteen districts (32 percent) had a plurality or majority of Republican voters; in 1992 ten of the twenty-three districts (44 percent) had at least a plurality of Republicans. The reapportioned districts were, however, closer to the voter registration ratios.

Fundamental issues of representation emerge in the Florida reapportionment dispute. Did African American voters benefit more from having three of their own representatives than from having influence in a greater number of districts? The Florida reapportionment plan concentrated black voters in the three districts mentioned above, each with over 50 percent of the population black, but at the same time the number of districts with over 15 percent of the population black dropped from eight to four (including the three black-majority districts).

The benefits of ensuring the election of several African American representatives by concentrating black voters in a few districts must be weighed against the costs of losing influence overall and perhaps contributing to the election of more Republicans and the adoption of policies that do not reflect the concerns of African Americans.[42]

The 1992 elections following the reapportionment brought a further strengthening of the Republican position with the party division changing from ten Republicans and nine Democrats to thirteen Republicans and ten Democrats. Once again victories came not by defeating incumbents but by winning in open seats or newly created seats. Thirteen incumbents, eight Republicans and five Democrats, ran for reelection and won, although three of the five Democratic victories were by narrow margins. In the ten districts with no incumbent owing to retirements or the creation of new districts, Republicans and Democrats each won five seats.

The 1992 reapportionment had an impact not only on the partisan composition of the congressional delegation but also on its gender, ethnic, and racial makeup. Prior to the 1992 elections no African Americans from Florida had been elected to the House of Representatives in the twentieth century, while there had been only two women (one 66 years earlier) and one Hispanic (Ros-Lehtinen, who was also one of the two women). The delegation following the 1992 elections included three African Americans, two Hispanics, and five women (two of the women were African American—Corrine Brown and Carrie Meek—and one Hispanic). All were easily reelected in both 1994 and 1996.

The increased competitiveness of the state in 1992 was reflected not only in more Republican victories but also in the narrow victories of some longtime Democratic stalwarts. Both Earl Hutto, who had represented the Pensacola area since 1978 and was one of the most conservative Democrats in the U.S. House, and Sam Gibbons, a staunch liberal from the Tampa area who had been first elected to the House in 1962, saw their comfortable majorities of earlier years erode, with Hutto taking only 52.0 percent of the vote and Gibbons 52.8 percent. The narrowest victory in the House elections was that of Jim Bacchus, a moderate Democrat elected in 1990 to the seat that Bill Nelson had held in the conservative Melbourne–Cape Canaveral area. Bacchus won just 50.7 percent of the vote.

The 1994 elections resulted in further erosion of the Democratic position; the congressional balance following the November balloting was 15 Republicans to eight Democrats, a two-seat gain for the Republicans. Incumbency remained a major advantage. Twenty of the 23 incumbents (eight Democrats and twelve Republicans) ran for reelection and all won, most with relative ease.

Democrats let nine Republican incumbents go unchallenged while only two Democrats—African Americans Meek and Alcee Hastings—had no opposition. (Hastings had been initially elected in 1992 following a bitter primary battle focusing on his impeachment and removal as a federal judge.)

The three open seats, two of which had been held by Democrats, were won by the Republicans. The vulnerability of the Democrats in these districts had been foreshadowed in the narrow victories in 1992 of Hutto in the First (northwest Florida) and of Bacchus in the Fifteenth (Space Coast). Hutto's successor, Republican Joe Scarborough, won 61.6 percent of the vote against conservative Democrat Vince Whibbs. In the Fifteenth, Republican David Weldon, a physician who called for banning abortions and phasing out welfare, defeated his pro-choice Republican-turned-Democrat opponent, Sue Munsey, 53.7 percent to 46.1 percent.

The congressional delegation remained fifteen Republicans to eight Democrats following the 1996 elections despite Republican efforts to increase their seats. In 1996 all fifteen Republican incumbents and five of eight Democrats ran for reelection and all won. At the direction of the National Republican Congressional Campaign Committee,[43] Republicans had candidates in every race while Democrats, in contrast to 1994 when they let nine seats go uncontested, had candidates in all but three of the districts. The Florida Democratic party's executive director, Scott Falmelen, elaborated: "We actually fielded a candidate in every district with the exception of three, the two that are currently held by Hispanics in South Florida and those were left vacant by design. We did not want to field candidates there and have them boost the Hispanic turnout. Tillie Fowler [the Republican representing northeast Florida's Fourth District] was the only one where we tried to recruit and couldn't find a candidate."[44]

The decision in 1996 of three Democratic incumbents not to run again led to early predictions that the Democrats would have difficulty holding these seats. They did, however, win all three with comfortable margins, benefiting from the level of Democratic registration in their districts, among the highest in the state, and perhaps from the Clinton campaign effort in the state. Jim Davis, running for the seat that Congressman Gibbons was giving up, exceeded Gibbons's 1994 margin, winning 57.9 percent of the vote against the same candidate who had run against Gibbons in 1992 and 1994.

Democrat Alan Boyd, vying to replace Pete Peterson, who had stepped down after two terms, won 59.5 percent of the vote in the Second District, which included Tallahassee. Boyd, who had served in the Florida house since 1989 and had chaired the house Democratic conservative caucus, stressed his support for welfare reform and balancing the budget. Boyd had the advantage of both registered voters and dollars; Democrats constituted 71.5 percent of the district's registered voters, and he outspent his opponent by over four to one.

In the heavily Democratic Broward County, Robert Wexler, a former state senator, won 65.6 percent of the vote in a campaign that drew clear lines between the two candidates. Wexler's platform included health care, the cushioning of children from the impact of welfare reform through food vouchers, increased support for child care, and the taxing of the sugar industry to clean up the Everglades, while his Republican opponent, Beverly (Bev) Kennedy, ran on Newt Gingrich's 1994 Contract with America, which she claimed to have helped write.

The congressional race that received the most national attention was that of Corrine Brown, whose black-majority Third District had been redrawn under court order, dropping the black voting age population to 42.3 percent and raising the issue of whether a black candidate could be elected from a white-majority district. Brown was aided by the fact that her white Republican opponent, Preston James Fields, was a little-known lawyer who had never held political office and by her far-larger campaign chest ($298,000 to $38,000). Campaigning on the theme "Corrine Cares" and building on her work for senior citizens, veterans, and her constituency, she won easily with 61.2 percent to Fields's 38.8 percent. Brown received 95 percent of the vote in predominantly black precincts, but only about a third of the vote in white precincts.[45] In 1998, all 23 incumbents sought reelection, and only five (three Republicans and two Democrats) had major-party opposition. Corrine Brown, who had come under attack on ethics issues, was one of the two Democrats facing a challenge.

The U.S. House delegation that represented Florida in the 1990s was polarized ideologically along party lines. In earlier years the Democratic party encompassed both conservatives and liberals with the variation dependent at least in part on the region of the state they represented. Party loyalty was also relatively low then. The emergence of the Republican party led to more ideologically cohesive parties than in earlier years as conservative Democrats left the Democratic party for the Republican party, black voters gained influence in the Democratic party, and the constituencies of both parties became more homogeneous. Using the ratings of the *National Journal*, the average score on liberalism for Florida's eight Democratic representatives in 1996 was 78 percent with a range from 67 percent to 92 percent. In that same year, the composite liberal score for the state's fifteen Republicans was 29 percent with a range from 15 to 45 percent, the two GOP Hispanic representatives—Ros-Lehtinen and her south Florida colleague, Lincoln Diaz-Balart of the Twenty-First District—registering at the upper end of the scores.[46]

The Local Level

By the 1990s the Republican strategy of building the party from the top down was realizing notable success at the local level. A comparison of the party affiliation of county sheriffs, most of whom are elected in Florida, is indicative of the changing local partisan situation. In 1980, fifty-eight of the sixty-seven sheriffs were Democrats and six were Republicans, located in those counties that had the strongest Republican base in south Florida. (Three did not take a party label.) By 1996, twenty-five of the sixty-seven listed their party affiliation as Republican.[47]

Further insight into the local ferment can be glimpsed by an examination of the 1995 elections in Jacksonville–Duval County, which has a consolidated city-county government. Although Duval County voter registration in 1995 was 58.5 percent Democratic, 34.4 percent Republican, and 7.1 percent Independent, both George Bush in the 1992 presidential election and Jeb Bush in the 1994 gubernatorial contest had won a plurality of the county's voters, and a majority of its state legislative delegation was Republican.

The 1995 mayoral campaign marked a partisan turning point for Jacksonville. There were six contenders, only three of whom had the resources and recognition to wage serious campaigns: two former mayors, Democrats Jake Godbold (1979–1987) and Tommy Hazouri (1987–91), and Republican John Delaney, a young lawyer who had served as chief assistant to the Democratic mayor Ed Austin (1991–95).

The former mayors brought a good deal of baggage with them. Hazouri had angered the business community as mayor through his actions and words, calling the business leaders of the community "fat cats." When he sought a second term in 1991, he was narrowly defeated by Austin in a primary race that was highly polarized. Austin, who became a Republican after leaving office, carried middle-class and more affluent suburbs and Hazouri black and lower-income areas of the city. While Godbold was popular as mayor, his administration had been subsequently tainted by corruption charges and the conviction of several of his key aides.

Delaney, a former Democrat, had been recruited to run by Tom Slade, the ubiquitous state GOP chair, who had also suggested the theme of the campaign, "It's time for a new beginning."[48] The Republican party spent over $200,000 in support of the Delaney candidacy. The campaign was a bitter one. After being eliminated in the first round of voting, both Hazouri and Harry Reagan, a former city councilman running for mayor, endorsed Delaney over former mayor Godbold despite the fact they were Democrats. In the second round of voting,

Delaney eked out a narrow victory (50.9 percent to 49.1 percent) over Godbold in a highly polarized election that roughly split the city into haves and have-nots.[49] The city council elections left the Democrats in control with ten seats to the GOP's nine. In September 1996, a little more than a year after the election, two of the Democrats announced their change of party registration. The council balance shifted to eleven Republicans and eight Democrats, giving the GOP control of the council for the first time in the twentieth century.

At the same time that Jacksonville elected its first modern Republican mayor, it also elected the first black sheriff in the state, Nat Glover, a Democrat. A number of prominent citizens backed Glover, a well-trained undersheriff, and a highly professional advertising campaign emphasized his qualifications. He won a majority in the first election, taking 55.4 percent of the vote compared to 24.3 percent and 20.3 percent received by his two white opponents. In contrast to the polarization in the mayor's race, the winner in the sheriff's race had support across all sectors of the community.[50]

While the circumstances of these two elections for mayor and sheriff were unique to Jacksonville–Duval County, similar interesting local variation could be found throughout Florida as two-party competition spread to the local level and as voters demonstrated a willingness to ignore party labels in making decisions.

KEYS TO THE FUTURE: POLITICAL PARTIES AND PUBLIC POLICY CHOICES

The changing role of the political parties as institutions is another factor contributing to the increased competitiveness of elections in the Sunshine State. Florida's party system in the past was defined as a "no party system masquerading as a one party system." V. O. Key, Jr., in 1949 concluded that Florida is "not only unbossed, it is also unled." Throughout most of this century both the Democratic and Republican party organizations were weak and faction-ridden. It was not until the mid-1970s that the two parties established permanent headquarters in Tallahassee. By the 1990s, however, both parties, which reported having party officials in all sixty-seven counties with offices in the larger counties, were judged to be among the better organized in the nation. In contrast with earlier years, by the mid-1990s the Republicans had moved from having a less pervasive county organization than the Democrats to having, according to Slade, "some semblance of organization in every county." He went on to suggest the importance of the state organization to the local organizations, noting:

"We have some gee-whiz technology that will help us in campaigns at every level. We have so much precinct-by-precinct information that we're about to enter information overload. We can target each precinct and craft a message for each one."[51] The Democrats, for their part, were also strengthening their organizations in the 1990s, boosted by the efforts of Governor Chiles and other Democratic leaders, as touched on below.

Slade, whose career stretches from his service as a state senator in the 1960s to his reelection as party chair in 1997, is a strong, if sometimes controversial, party leader. He has aggressively recruited candidates and on occasion pushed his favorites to the forefront; for example, as mentioned above, Slade took an active role in the 1994 gubernatorial primaries. Despite this type of strong leadership at the top, the party continues to suffer from the division between its conservative and moderate wings.

While divisions between religious fundamentalists and party moderates created some battles for control over the Republican county organizations in the 1988–1990 period, these seem to have been resolved by the mid-1990s. Although members of the Christian right continue to serve on some county executive committees, Slade said that if the fundamentalists controlled any of the county organizations in 1996, he was not aware of it. Nonetheless, the continued involvement of the Christian Coalition with the Republican party has tilted the GOP further to the right. In 1996, the Coalition had about 175,000 members and supporters in Florida and a small state headquarters staffed by four people. Max Karrer, the state chairman of the Coalition, indicated that there was some overlap with the Republican party, noting, for example, that Coalition members were active in the Republican presidential nomination process in the state. The Coalition's principal political activities in the mid-1990s were the distribution of both legislative score cards and the results of polls taken of candidates on key issues.

Karrer, a physician, explained that during an election "the most effective thing we do is to poll candidates on where they stand on the issues [and place an asterisk when there is any difference between a politician's actual voting record compared with what the candidate says]. We distribute this to the churches, 380 churches in Duval, for example—it is very effective. We do not officially endorse candidates; we try to get information to the voters." He suggested that congressmen and legislators are very sensitive because they want a good rating, and, by way of example, he noted: "If Tillie [U.S. representative Tillie Fowler, Republican of the Fourth District] is going to vote against us, I'll get a call explaining it."[52] The Christian Coalition in 1995 and 1996 joined the Catholic bishops and Southern Baptists to lobby the legislature for a family-oriented Contract for Florida.

The growing strength of the Republican party organization has had the effect of bringing greater cohesion to the Democratic organization. Gaining control of the governor's office in 1990 and of the presidency in 1992 bolstered Florida's Democratic party's organizational strength and resources. Nonetheless, its organizational resources still lag behind the Republicans; for example, the Republican state chairmanship is a full-time paid position while the Democratic chair's position is unpaid and part time.

The Democratic party has suffered in the past from divisions between the more liberal and more conservative components of the party as well as between elected officials and party officials. In 1992 the governor's choice for party chair was rebuffed as party activists stuck with the incumbent chairman, Simon Ferro, a Cuban-born lawyer from Miami. But Ferro realized his future wasn't bright if he stood in Chiles's way. Citing the need to spend more time with his family, Ferro stepped aside, clearing the way for Chiles's favorite, Terrie Brady, a leader in the state teachers' union. Under the governor's leadership, a little-noticed bill was passed in 1995 that solidified the position of state and federal elected officials in the party by increasing their voting power on the Democratic Executive Committee.[53]

The Democratic party in Florida faces the difficult problem of coordinating its disparate coalition groups: traditional white southerners, often quite conservative on social and foreign policy issues; African Americans, one of the most liberal voter blocs; union members (although not a major force in Florida), often liberal on social issues; the ethnic and Jewish voters of southeast Florida, more liberal on many issues than the majority of Floridians; and strong local political machines in some areas. As an increasing number of more conservative voters drop their allegiance to the Democrats, the party is torn by conflicting pressures. Should it emphasize its liberal roots or should it appeal to moderates who want lower taxes and less government and focus on building alliances between liberal and moderate factions? A former Democratic party chair, Charles Whitehead, reflected on one aspect of the party's problems, saying, "Some Southerners feel that the Democratic Party has been taken over by minorities." He went on to suggest that, while Democrats still have a strong black base, the white vote may be slipping.[54]

In May 1998, with the party in turmoil, Terrie Brady resigned as Democratic state chairman. African Americans were angry over the removal of state representative Willie Logan of Opa-Locka, a black, as the next house Democratic leader (known as speaker-designate), and his replacement by a white woman legislator, Anne Mackenzie. While party leaders cited Logan's failure to raise money and recruit candidates for the upcoming elections, Logan said he was told by members of the Democratic house caucus that there was concern about what an African American leader could do to get them elected in conservative white districts. All fifteen black house members walked out of the caucus at the time of the vote ousting Logan, with one calling the action "blatant racism." Subsequently, a number of black leaders in the state denounced the Democratic party and indicated they would steer black voters away from blind support for Democrats. Frustrated by her failure to end the dispute, Mackenzie resigned the house Democratic post in mid-July 1998, and several black legislators sought the job, but not Logan.[55] Republicans were quick to reach out to the disaffected black Democratic leaders. Adding to the Democrats' woes, the Republican candidate for governor in 1998, Jeb Bush, was far ahead of their own gubernatorial nominee, Buddy MacKay, both in the early polls and in fundraising. Faced with these difficulties, the Democrats turned to their south Florida base, selecting Mitch Caesar, Broward County party chair and longtime Democratic activist, to head the troubled party.[56]

An organization separate from the Democratic party but important as an influence on party leaders and elected officials during the 1990s is the Florida Democratic Leadership Council. Established in the mid-1980s by then-senator Chiles and other leading Democrats and modeled on the national DLC, it was not until 1993 that the Florida DLC was put into place structurally. The organization was initially headed by Jon L. Mills, a former speaker of the Florida house and the director of the Florida Policy Institute. Its board of directors includes the Democratic state party chair. The Florida organization was by 1995 the third largest in the nation and had been, according to Mills, singled out by the national DLC as a model for other states to follow. Describing the organization's goals, Mills said the DLC "is looking for creative solutions that are acceptable, logical, and not easily defined as left wing or right wing—which is really hard to get. I mean we joke about this. . . . [I]t is hard to have a moderate revolution because it is easier to generate enthusiasm with radical comments whether it be left or right."[57]

In the 1990s two ideologically distinctive parties had thus emerged with party structures significantly stronger than in earlier decades. While there was still plenty of factionalism within both parties, the divisions of earlier years were less serious—with the possible exception of intra-Democratic controversy over the Logan ouster—partly because the movement of conservative Democrats into the Republican party has given greater homogeneity to both parties.

Florida politics is shaped not only by parties and candidates but also by the political beliefs and policy preferences of its citizens. One of the most significant attitudinal factors that has conditioned policy-making in Florida for many years is the tendency by many of its new residents to view someplace else as "home" and so to reject the concept of a long-term commitment to the state.[58] The annual policy surveys done by Florida State University's Policy Sciences Center shed light on the attitudes and policy preferences of the citizenry. Perhaps most striking is the lack of confidence in public officials and the erosion of confidence over time. In 1980, 44 percent of the respondents assessed the Florida legislature as doing a good or excellent job; by 1995 the good/excellent rating had dropped to 28 percent.

The most important problems cited by citizens year after year are crime, immigration, education, and the economy. Citizens indicate by a strong majority that they prefer maintaining services to reducing taxes, but at the same time they hold that Florida's major taxes are too high and overwhelmingly reject the establishment of a state income tax. They have also voted for various constitutional limitations on additional taxes in the past decade. Such contradictory views—favoring government services but opposing the taxes that pay for the services—pose problems for those charged with making public policy. On the basis of his 1993 surveys of Florida voters, Lance deHaven Smith holds that Florida's public life is parochial and uncivic because political leaders, who misperceive the public, have often avoided the tough issues and the media has given little attention to the complexity of the problems facing the state.[59]

Understanding Florida's politics is no easy task because Florida behaves in many ways not as one state but as several states. And if there is a single factor that dominates Florida's politics, it is change. Driving that change has been the continuing influx of new people, bringing their own ideals, values, and traditions. The extraordinary growth that began in the 1950s continued through the 1990s, adding numbers and diversity to a body politic recognized as "different politically" as early as Key's classic study of southern politics in the late 1940s. Florida has moved from what was essentially a no–party, multifactional, fragmented politics to a competitive two-party politics today. Florida, which Key suggested almost fifty years ago was "scarcely a part of the South," was clearly by the 1990s no longer a part of the traditional South in a political sense; its politics was closer to the politics of other high-growth megastates.[60]

A surface examination of the electoral results of the 1990s would seem to suggest that Florida is still in the era of factional, every-man-for-himself politics—a Democratic governor, a Republican state legislature, a Democratic U.S. senator and a Republican one, both elected overwhelmingly. In fact, the volatility today comes not from the absence of organized parties or the absence of voters with a strong adherence to their particular parties, but rather from the high percentage of independent voters who add volatility to every election. Survey data and the estimates of party leaders suggest that 20 to 40 percent of the electorate falls into the independent category.[61] These voters, increasing in number, will be the swing voters in future elections, moved by issues and candidate appeal, and ensuring continuing volatility to Florida politics.

Florida promises to be a microcosm of the nation's future, not only in its volatile partisan politics, but also in how it meets the major policy challenges facing it and the country. With a strong low-tax philosophy, enshrined in constitutional provisions and laws, Florida's leaders will be forced to confront the problems posed by the growth and diversity of its population:[62] protecting the environment against overdevelopment; assisting the needy elderly; assimilating a high percentage of immigrants, and providing educational facilities for increasing numbers of students, to cite just the most obvious.[63] These issues will provide the substance of the politics of Florida's next decade.

13

SOUTHERN POLITICS IN THE 1990S

Alexander P. Lamis

A̲T the end of our long journey through partisan life in the eleven southern states in the 1990s, this concluding chapter seeks to highlight the key elements in operation as the two-party South entered its current, mature phase of development. Although it is always a dangerous oversimplification to attempt to reduce a complex reality to a few central tendencies, the dramatic events that occurred in southern politics in the 1990s can perhaps best be understood as embodying the rapid confluence of twin, related movements. First, the ongoing settling in of two-party competition in the region took a sudden spurt forward during the decade, especially during the 1994 elections and their aftermath. Second, the arrival of a mature two-party system throughout the South finally reunited the region with the nation's political mainstream, a process containing important implications for the future.

The first half of the chapter examines the intraregional developments by surveying the nature of the two-party structure now in place in Dixie, a task that requires drawing together many of the diverse elements uncovered in state after state by our expert teams of journalists and political scientists. The second half seeks to place the South in a national context and to shed light on how the process of national electoral change has grown dramatically in importance—as witnessed in the 1994 elections—in what once was a region singularly isolated from such trends. The latter task involves dealing with the elusive realignment concept in a way that meaningfully captures the dynamic forces of change now in operation in the nation and the region.

THE TWO-PARTY SOUTH IN THE 1990S

Perusal of the last years of the Democratic party-strength figures for each of the southern states (Figures 2–12 in Chapter 1) reveals the remarkable path of GOP growth throughout the region in the 1990s. Only the Virginia figure shows the GOP losing a little ground, but there the Republicans started the decade higher than the southern norm, and besides, the figure doesn't include the 1997 Republican success in the Old Dominion. In North Carolina the even partisan balance found in the 1980s continued fairly steadily at the 50 percent line through 1996. In the other nine states, the party strength measures show marked Democratic decline in the 1990s. Overall, the regional Democratic strength percentage, as previewed in Chapter 1, fell from 52.2 in 1990 to 50.1 in 1992 to 44.6 in 1994 and to 44.3 in 1996.

These figures, of course, only measure the high visibility offices, as was discussed when David's index was introduced in Chapter 1. The state chapter narratives encompass many more offices and indicators of party strength. Thus, the story as it unfolds in the state chapters reveals a fuller portrait of GOP gains—in state legislative races, in "down-ticket" statewide elections, and, where possible, at the local level. For example, in South Carolina in 1994 the GOP won six of the eight statewide constitutional offices and picked up a seventh through a party switch the following year.[1] In Florida, as late as 1980 58 of the state's 67 sheriffs were Democrats; by 1996, 25 of the 67 sheriffs were Republicans. Voter registration by party is required in only three southern states, but in all of them—Florida, North Carolina, and Louisiana—the Republican party scored notable advances.

Another method used in the state chapters to trace GOP growth is to compare voter turnout in each party's primary. In Texas in 1996, a little over 95,000 more people participated in the Republican primaries than the Democratic ones; see Table 23 in the Texas chapter. In Georgia in the 1990s, Democratic primary participation plummeted in relation to the GOP, although the Democrats still outdrew their Republican competitors in the Peach State; see Table 10 in the Georgia chapter. In the 1994 contested gubernatorial primaries of both parties in South Carolina, the Democrats drew a few thousand more voters to the first primary and the Republicans did the same for the runoff. For a region where politicians still active today can remember the time when winning the Democratic primary was, in the standard phrase, "tantamount to election," these are remarkable developments.[2]

While Republican strength has grown in the 1990s, the party coalitions discussed in the state chapters do not differ markedly from those that took hold during the first two decades of the two-party South. The well-known racial divisions appear when southern voters in the 1990s are asked in surveys about their party identification; such findings were reported in several of the state chapters. For example, Table 5 in the South Carolina chapter and Table 12 in the Georgia chapter report that the percentages of blacks identifying with the Republican party in those states were mostly in single digits. Among whites the same tables show that Republicans had a narrow edge in Georgia and a significant lead in South Carolina. For the region as a whole, 34 percent of white southerners identified with the Democratic party in 1996, up three percentage points from 1990 but far down from the 61 percent recorded in 1960. Republican party identification among white southerners stood at 31 percent in 1996, down several percentage points from a high reached in 1994 but still notably higher than the 21 percent registered in 1960. The region's African Americans overwhelmingly identified with the Democratic party.[3]

Voter exit polls from the 1996 elections, shown in Tables 29 and 30, substantiate further the continued existence of these racial divisions in elections. In 1996 most blacks voted Democratic, while Republicans generally won a solid majority among whites. As Table 29 shows, President Clinton received 36 percent of the vote among white southerners and 87 percent among black southerners; Senator Dole won 56 percent of the region's whites but only 10 percent of its African Americans. Similar patterns appear in the eight 1996 U.S. Senate elections depicted in Table 30. There was also a considerable gender gap in the region, as in the nation, in 1996; Clinton scored about 10 percentage points better among women than among men.

Subcategory breakdowns from a typical southern state in 1996, Georgia, provide a glimpse into other divisions visible in the region's electorate. For example, exit polls disclosed that 69 percent of those in Georgia making less than $15,000 voted for Clinton with only 21 percent for Dole; among those making over $100,000, Clinton received 31 percent to Dole's 63 percent. Seventy-five percent of Georgia voters who said they were liberals voted for Clinton in 1996, 14 percent for Dole. Among conservative Georgians the figures were reversed: 72 percent for Dole and 21 percent for Clinton. Clinton did better among Georgia's moderates in 1996, winning 56 percent to 36 percent for Dole. Perot's percentages among the ideological categories were virtually the same— about 7 percent. Among Georgia whites who said they were members of the religious right, 79 percent voted for Dole and 12 percent for Clinton. Georgia whites who said they were not part of the religious right gave Clinton 57 percent of their votes compared to 35 percent for Dole. For Perot, there was little

Table 29. Exit Poll Estimates of the Vote for President by Race in the South, 1996

State	Whites			Blacks		
	Clinton	Dole	Perot	Clinton	Dole	Perot
Alabama	28%	63%	8%	89%	10%	—
Florida	43	48	9	87	10	3
Georgia	30	59	9	92	6	1
Louisiana	33	57	9	94	4	2
North Carolina	37	55	8	91	7	1
South Carolina	28	65	6	88	8	4
Tennessee	43	50	6	90	9	1
Texas[a]	31	61	6	88	8	3
Virginia	40	52	7	89	9	2
South[b]	36	56	8	87	10	3

Source: Voter News Service based on questionnaires completed by voters at polling places throughout the South.

[a]Texas Hispanics supported Clinton by 76 percent to 16 percent for Dole.
[b]Includes Kentucky, Oklahoma, and West Virginia.

Table 30. Exit Poll Estimates of the Vote for Senator by Race in the South, 1996

State	Whites		Blacks	
	Dem.	Rep.	Dem.	Rep.
Alabama	33%	66%	85%	12%
Arkansas	45	55	—	—
Georgia	38	60	85	12
Louisiana	32	68	91	9
North Carolina	38	62	91	8
South Carolina	33	66	79	21
Tennessee	35	64	79	19
Texas[a]	31	68	79	19

Source: Voter News Service based on questionnaires completed by voters at polling places throughout the South.

[a]Texas Hispanics supported the Democrat (Morales) by 79 percent to 20 percent for the Republican victor (Gramm).

difference; he received 9 percent among white religious right voters and 7 percent from those whites who were not part of the religious right.

This sketch of the divisions in the southern electorate, provided by the survey data, illuminates only a part of the partisan picture in Dixie. The state chapters give lots of other revealing information concerning the region's partisan coalitions. If we look first at the Republicans, two notable trends emerge: the strength of the GOP in the region's growing suburbs as well as the party's growth in once-heavily Democratic rural and small-town areas; and the often bitter struggles within the Republican party between economic conservatives and social or religious conservatives.

The growth of the suburbs coincided with the South's impressive economic advances since World War II. For example, per capita income in South Carolina in 1940 was 51.6 percent of the national average; it increased to 63.4 percent by 1960. By 1990, the Palmetto State's per capita income had risen to 81.1 percent of the national average. The South Carolina experience was on the low end of the southern average, with four states below it in 1990 and six above it; Florida and Virginia were the regional pacesetters, as was Texas before the oil bust of the 1980s.[4] This economic expansion spawned, in the words of Earl Black and Merle Black, a "new middle class" composed of those "with professional, technical, managerial, administrative, sales, and clerical positions." In 1940 only 30 percent of white southerners held such jobs; by 1980 more than 55 percent did.[5]

Many of these people in the new middle class found homes in the suburbs and were receptive to the conservative economic message of the Republican party. As the writers of the Texas chapter put it, "Rapid economic growth attracted sizable numbers of white middle and upper middle class voters to the booming suburbs around Dallas, Houston, Fort Worth, and San Antonio. Unlike other new immigrants, they registered and voted, and they mostly voted Republican." The Tennessee chapter authors articulate the same theme this way: "Just as the 1950s and 1960s marked the major movement of citizens from small towns and rural areas to the major cities, the 1980s and 1990s were marked by a counter movement to the adjacent suburbs. . . . This produced suburban rings that are whiter and more Republican. . . . New people in new areas make new judgments." The Georgia authors highlight the significance for the GOP of Atlanta's burgeoning suburban "doughnut." The South Carolina chapter ties "the Republican surge of the 1990s [to] the party's strong appeal to white South Carolinians . . . centered in the middle-class suburbs that have sprouted at a steadily increasing rate around the Palmetto State's central cities." The Virginia writers report that "the epicenter of state politics had shifted from small towns and farming communities to suburban enclaves." Similar items appear in other state chapters as well.

Likewise, significant GOP gains in rural and small-town areas were found throughout Dixie. For example, when Carroll Campbell won his narrow gubernatorial victory in South Carolina in 1986, a triumph that was crucial to the GOP's rapid rise there during the next ten years, he did so by making unprecedented "incursions . . . into the Democratic rural strongholds, especially in the predominantly white upstate." "People forget that those rural counties are conservative," Campbell told one of the authors of the South Carolina chapter in a 1996 interview devoted to assessing Republican growth in the Palmetto State. In noting that "Democratic support from rural and small-town whites has diminished sharply in the 1990s," the authors of the Georgia chapter point out that recent GOP statewide nominees regularly win majorities in 75 of the Peach State's 159 counties, compared to only 20 or 30 before the 1990s. Although this arena draws less attention and is hard to follow given the small numbers of people living in each unit, the quiet partisan struggles that are fought in the rural, small-town counties will be at the forefront of the next generation of partisan growth, especially in the less populous southern states where metropolitan suburban Republican strength can carry the GOP only so far.[6]

Everywhere in Dixie the advancing Republican party is divided between adherents who are motivated primarily by economic conservatism and those who are more interested in an array of conservative social and cultural issues. The latter group is closely identified with the Christian Coalition and commonly labeled the religious right or the Christian right. Most of the state chapters contain at least some discussion of this cleavage. For example, in Texas the infighting reached high visibility when newly elected Christian-right Republicans on the state education board clashed with the Republican governor's appointed education commissioner; in fact, the education board chairman, a moderate Republican, had to rely on votes from the board's minority Democrats to block his fellow Republicans. In Georgia, a prominent mainstream Republican, Johnny Isakson, expressed his frustration with the Peach State GOP's religious right this way: "They're not always wrong, but if you don't always agree with them, you're always wrong."

Despite the tensions, the religious right has contributed significant organizational might to the GOP and has been able, in the words of one study of the movement, "[to get] conservative Christians to the polls in support of Republican candidates in many key races." The current phase of the movement grew out of the unsuccessful GOP presidential nomination campaign of televangelist Pat Robertson in 1988. Drawing on his base of supporters, Robertson in 1989 created the Christian Coalition. In a detailed survey of the movement, *Campaigns and Elections* magazine reported: "The Coalition is a grassroots organization with over 450,000 members and almost 1,000 chapters located in all 50 states. Led [through 1996] by Ralph Reed, the Coalition organizes local chapters, trains activists and potential candidates, provides voter 'information,' and supplies resources for mobilizing voters."[7]

Within the Republican party, the Christian conservatives' chief asset is organizational ability; their members turn out for local party meetings and as a result have become influential in the GOP's party structure in many states. In fact, *Campaigns and Elections* investigated the level of Christian right strength in state Republican organizations and concluded that it was dominant in eighteen states, including 8 of the 11 southern states. Two others—Arkansas and Mississippi—fell into the next category of thirteen states where the faction's influence was viewed as substantial (above 25 percent but below a majority). Only Tennessee was in the grouping of nineteen states where the influence was classified as minor. While the survey shows that the Christian right movement is very important to the southern GOP, it also indicates that the phenomenon is national in scope. Among the ten nonsouthern states that fell into the dominant category were California, Minnesota, Oregon, and Iowa, states with political traditions quite different from the southern patterns studied in this book—that is, quite different until recently, as the last part of this chapter suggests.[8]

Although the Christian Coalition is a leading force in the GOP's religious right faction, the movement itself does not exhibit complete uniformity. An authority in this area, John C. Green, cautions: "Just keep in mind that certain social issues aren't necessarily synonymous with the Christian Right. For example, some Catholics are adamantly pro-life but they would take great umbrage in being lumped in with the Christian Right. And of course, the Christian Right is not monolithic. Many evangelicals, for example, can't stand Pat Robertson."[9] Regardless of the cohesiveness of the religious right, as the GOP continues to grow in the South, management of this intra-GOP factional split poses a serious challenge for the party. In our chapter on Virginia, Robertson's home state, these cleavages in the 1990s have been most dramatically displayed along with the positive side of the Christian right's affiliation with the GOP.[10] The authors of our Georgia chapter offer a useful summary assessment that captures the dilemma facing the GOP: "The mobilization of religious conservatives has energized the party's activist base and added new voters to the Republican coalition, but the newcomers do not always mix well with their more secular-minded party colleagues. Strong conservative positions that help a Republican win a contested primary may make the winning candidate appear too conservative and extreme to win in November."

Turning to the issue of race in southern politics in the 1990s, one confronts a complex of issues that entangles both parties in a variety of subtle and not-so-subtle ways. These racial crosscurrents appear throughout the state chapters. Within the region, the issue was aptly characterized in the North Carolina chapter as "the moose on the table," a quote from that state's white former Democratic secretary of state, Janice Faulkner. "The moose comes in and sits on the table with every conversation. If we are really looking into gaining insight into what is happening, we need to get the moose off the table—the resentments of whites from the days of integration of the schools, the competition for scarce economic development dollars, the increasing cost of entitlement programs." Southern blacks might well accept the analogy, but their listing of resentments would be different, flowing as they would from being on the receiving end of discrimination in the era of segregation and earlier. Such is the historical legacy the current political system confronts.

Black-white relations in the southern party system fall into two related categories: between the two parties and within the biracial Democratic party coalition. On the former, Jack Hawke, onetime North Carolina GOP chairman, told one of the authors of the North Carolina chapter: "One of the disturbing factors is that the parties racially are becoming more polarized to a degree that has hurt the Democrats in terms of white flight. But as the Democratic party shrinks in size and numbers, percentage-wise it becomes more black-dominated. Republicans have not been successful for a variety of reasons in attracting enough black support to offset that notion that the Democratic party is becoming the party of minorities and the Republican party is becoming the party of white folks." In the Alabama chapter, a retired former Democratic official, Pete Mathews, puts the issue more bluntly: "[Many Republicans] do not like black people. I don't give a [expletive] who tells you they do. I'm telling you they don't. And that's who they perceive as controlling the Democratic party and they're right."

These notions and others like them seek to express the reality of the partisan racial division as these observers honestly see it. Such comments like Hawke's and Mathews's have on occasion led to the prediction that eventually the South will have a nearly all-black Democratic party to go with its nearly all-white Republican party. In my view this is not going to happen, and this book's eleven state analytical narratives substantiate my assertion. Certainly racial tension between the two parties is unlikely to end anytime soon, probably not until many more blacks participate in politics through the Republican party, which may be a decade or more away but will happen someday. In the meantime, the bulwark against a racially polarized party system is the continued existence of the black-white southern Democratic coalition. And the state chapters do not portray the coalition as on the road to extinction. The biracial alliance is clearly under considerable pressure and undergoing change in the face of the rapid Republican rise of the 1990s, but, taking the region as a whole, the biracial Democratic coalition is very much alive today, although it has had to confront its own set of intraparty racial tensions.

Black-white tensions in the southern Democratic party surface from time to time. Their most visible manifestation is found in the controversy over the creation of black-majority districts, which was introduced in Chapter 1 and which is discussed again directly below. But the tensions appear in other areas as well. They were visible in Louisiana when Cleo Fields, a black Democratic congressman, received weak support among white Democrats in his losing 1995 gubernatorial campaign. In late 1996 in Virginia, former governor Douglas Wilder, the only African American to win a major statewide election in the South since Reconstruction, decried the all-white, all-male Democratic 1997 statewide ticket. "If you want to think of healing," Wilder wrote the party's gubernatorial candidate, as reported in the Virginia chapter, "it would be well to start 1997 with a Democratic slate of candidates which don't represent retrogression." The authors of the South Carolina chapter note: "Black Democrats have long observed that their white fellow Democrats, while more than happy to win election to political power with the votes of black citizens, have been more than a little reluctant to share that power once in office."

To fully illustrate these strains frequently requires descent into an array of governmental details that even in this book's state chapters would have required tedious digression. Still, at this point it is useful to offer a specific illustration of the tensions from a level of the political arena where the day-to-day conflicts occur. Such is provided in the complaints of black Democratic legislators in South Carolina, as reported by Lee Bandy in *The State* on March 6, 1994, in an article headlined "Black Caucus Tells Party to Listen Up: Minority Democrats Ready to Leave Fold, Say Support Lacking." Bandy wrote: "The chasm between black and white Democratic legislators has been growing since last year, when [Representative Lucille] Whipper [a black Democrat from Charleston] was soundly defeated in her bid for House speaker pro tem, a largely ceremonial post. Most white Democratic members, including [Democratic] House Speaker Bob Sheheen, supported Republican David Wilkins of Greenville. The vote was 86–36. 'That didn't give us much encouragement,' said Representative Jesse Hines of Lamar, a caucus member." (Incidentally, Wilkins became speaker in 1995 when the GOP took control of the house.)

Bandy listed several other grievances: failure of house Democratic leaders to appoint blacks to key conference committees, such as those on the budget and on governmental restructuring; the defeat of the Legislative Black Caucus's efforts to create more black-majority state house districts; and a lack of interest on the part of the leadership to push the black caucus's agenda, particularly as it related to welfare reform, crime, government jobs, and economic development. Citing the vote against Whipper, Representative Willie McMahand, a black Democrat from Pinewood, is quoted as follows in Bandy's article: "We vote seemingly along racial lines, not party lines. That's just the way the House operates. Very few white Democrats support blacks. Why? Racism. I don't see anything else."

The grievances spurred talk among the black caucus members about leaving the Democratic party. Representative Don Beatty of Spartanburg said he was so angry with the situation that he might join the GOP. "We've been Democrats and loyal Democrats and it doesn't seem to have gotten us any place." Two caucus members quoted in the article disagreed with the idea of a party bolt. Representative Gilda Cobb-Hunter of Orangeburg said: "That's not reality-based. The Republican Party might entertain our ideas to get us in there but drop them once we got there."[11] Senator Darrell Jackson of Columbia called for reason and calm, saying he wasn't prepared "to throw out the baby with the bath water."[12]

Similar situations could be recounted throughout Dixie.[13] These tensions are not new. The diverse black-white Democratic coalition that took hold in the South in the post–civil rights era has grappled with them for several decades and continues to do so.[14] In the southern elections of the 1990s, however, this coalition has not collapsed either at the voter or the leadership level.[15] The Republican advance has been impressive, as the details in the state chapters as well as the summary statistics show. But many of those GOP victories were won narrowly—such as the 1996 Republican Senate victories of Jeff Sessions in Alabama with 51.9 percent to Democrat Roger Bedford's 45.7 percent and of Tim Hutchinson in Arkansas with 52.7 percent victory to Democrat Winston Bryant's 47.3 percent. Two Democratic Senate victories that year were even closer: Max Cleland's 48.8 percent in Georgia over Republican Guy Millner's 47.6 percent and Mary Landrieu's 50.2 percent in Louisiana over Republican Woody Jenkins's 49.8 percent. In South Carolina in 1996 against a fifty-year political legend (Strom Thurmond was elected governor in 1946!), the Democratic biracial coalition produced 44.0 percent of the vote for a well-financed political newcomer. A moment's reflection on the details of the major two-party statewide contests of the 1990s as described in the state chapters should substantiate the continued endurance of the coalition as it underwent its severest test yet in the two-party era.

The Democratic biracial alliance even appears to have weathered the thorny black-majority congressional district controversy. Developments in 1996, 1997, and the first half of 1998 suggest that this redistricting controversy may have lapsed into a broad "compromise" resolution, although with so many players involved in this complex and far-flung conflict it is not possible to have a settlement through a single action. The hostility of a five-member U.S. Supreme Court majority to the creation of the twelve new southern black-majority districts, which was discussed in Chapter 1, resulted in six districts being redrawn with white majorities before the 1996 elections. Five of the six black incumbents ran for reelection in restructured districts that ranged between 35 percent and 45 percent black; they all won.[16]

Further, although North Carolina's two new black-majority districts were declared unconstitutional before the 1996 elections, a three-judge panel allowed the use of the existing lines in 1996. In 1997 the North Carolina legislature adopted a new plan that reduced the First District's black population from 57 percent to 50 percent and the Twelfth District's from 57 percent to 46 percent. The new districts were approved by the Justice Department and the supervising federal court,[17] but a successful additional challenge to the Twelfth District in early 1998 resulted in a further reduction in the district's black population to 36 percent (its black voting-age population was estimated at 33 percent). Eva Clayton in the First District was expected to win easy reelection in 1998. In the much-watched Twelfth District, Mel Watt was still the favorite in 1998, but he faced his first seriously contested reelection campaign.

In South Carolina, the Republican plaintiffs challenging Jim Clyburn's 62 percent black-majority Sixth District agreed to a settlement that leaves the district in place through 2000; in exchange the state acknowledged that its purpose in drawing the district was to create a black majority, an obvious point but one that apparently holds legal significance in such a suit. In June 1997 the Supreme Court upheld a lower court ruling declaring Virginia's Third District an unconstitutional racial gerrymander; the Virginia legislature redrew the lines in early 1998, lowering the black-majority percentage from 64 to 54. Finally, in August 1997, Alabama's 67 percent black-majority Seventh District became the last of the new districts to draw a court challenge, but the plaintiffs withdrew their suit six weeks before a scheduled May 1998 trial date.[18]

Thus, despite the challenges, South Carolina, Virginia, and Alabama still had black-majority districts with their African American incumbents prohibitive favorites for reelection. If one couples these three cases plus the North Carolina outlook with the 1996 U.S. House election victories of African Americans in Georgia, Texas, and Florida, the overall result appears to be a "compromise" that allows for a significant increase in southern black congressional representation[19] while leaving the opponents of black-majority districts, at least temporarily, with all the legal doctrinal victories.

At issue, of course, is a fundamental philosophical question regarding the nature of an appropriate representation scheme. Viewing the issue from the perspective of African Americans, the authors of the Florida chapter expressed the dilemma well: "Did African American voters benefit more from having three of their own representatives [elected to Congress] than from having influence in a greater number of districts?" In the heat of the battle, two other actors in the "racial gerrymandering" dispute—white Democrats and Republicans—don't appear to be troubled by the philosophical dilemma. Tom Slade, the Florida Republican leader, assessed recent reapportionment action in the Sunshine State this way: "Blacks and Republicans have joined together in an unholy alliance to do in the white Democrats, and we have succeeded. We have been spectacularly successful."[20] After the Supreme Court's 1996 ruling striking down North Carolina's black-majority districts, Gary Pearce, a white North Carolina Democratic strategist allied with Governor Jim Hunt, speculated, "The redistricting decision could save the Democratic party in the South." The reality surrounding the black-majority district controversy is far murkier than either of these two partisan assessments. If the compromise solution outlined above holds, this redistricting controversy may well fade away as other, newer challenges arise. The philosophical dilemma involved in the dispute, however, will persist, as all such difficult-to-answer questions must.[21]

Recognizing that the biracial southern Democratic coalition—despite its tensions—remains in place, what are its likely future prospects? How are the coalition's leaders changing to adjust to the new mature phase of two-party competition? And what of the Republicans? All signs point to a continuation of their advance down to the farthest reaches of the ballot;[22] after all, there are still arenas in the South—particularly local governments in the countryside—that have not been fully affected by the rising GOP tide. What problems will the GOP likely face during the next phase of its growth in Dixie? What direction can be discerned from the decisions of young southern politicians concerning their best route for seeking public office? Consideration of these questions, starting with the focus on the Democrats, will complete this portion of the concluding chapter devoted to intraregional partisan change.

The successful southern Democratic party of the mid-1990s is epitomized by leaders like Jim Hunt of North Carolina and Zell Miller of Georgia. They are moderate coalition-builders with good instincts for issues with broad popular appeal, such as Governor Miller's lottery-based Hope scholarship program in Georgia. Consider how strategist Pearce described his political patron, Governor Hunt: "He has charted a course in which Democrats can build a coalition of Republican-leaning, moderate-to-conservative business people and traditional, progressive Democratic constituencies—teachers, minorities. There is nothing magical and mysterious about it. It's how Clinton got elected in 1992. It is how he [Clinton] brought himself back in 1995."

These southern Democratic leaders stress fiscal responsibility, support public education, favor welfare reform, and promote efforts to fight crime. They shy away from the unpopular "tax-and-spend liberal" label associated with their party's losing presidential nominees of the 1980s—Walter Mondale and Michael Dukakis. They are quite comfortable with Bill Clinton, as he is with them. After all, he comes out of their political tradition and embodied it himself in the Arkansas context. Further, in winning reelection in 1996, Clinton's 46.2 percent of the southern vote was almost two percentage points higher than the regional Democratic party strength percentage of 44.3 that year (see Figure 1), and, of course, Clinton did not have a straight two-party race, losing some votes to Ross Perot's third-party effort. Thus, Democrats in Dixie in the first difficult post-1994 election had the advantage of a national candidate who was not a drag on their ticket the way Mondale and Dukakis had been. (More will be said about the general impact of the national arena on southern politics in the second part of this chapter.)

The successful moderate course adopted by Hunt, Miller, and others like them is likely to be followed by the next generation of statewide Democratic leaders. Mississippi, for example, offers an abundance of statewide elected officials who fit the mold, from the popular attorney general, Mike Moore, on down. "The mix that seems to work for Democrats in Tennessee," the Volunteer State authors write, "is one of cultural conservatism with a leftward tilt on pocketbook issues," and they mention west Tennessee Democratic congressman John Tanner as one successful Democrat who follows the approach. The Georgia chapter writers point out that Democratic success in close elections in the Peach State resulted because the party recast itself "as a moderately conservative middle-class party with strong support among African Americans."

Furthermore, white and black Democratic leaders are showing an impressive sophistication in dealing with each other, as the "compromise" on the black-majority district dispute suggests. Another area of biracial accommodation is developing as Democrats show interest in promoting balanced slates of statewide candidates. For example, for the 1998 elections in Georgia, where Governor

Miller in 1997 appointed an African American state legislator, Thurbert Baker, to be the state's first black attorney general, party leaders are pushing Baker for election in his own right as part of a slate balancing effort. Clearly, the southern Democratic leaders of both races, under assault by the GOP's growth in the 1990s, recognize their mutual need for each other if they are to remain a viable electoral force.[23]

Shifting attention to the South's Republican party, what are some of its strengths and weaknesses? As many state chapters demonstrate, the party has benefited significantly from its ability to present itself as the party of reform. The authors of the South Carolina chapter capture the notion well: "The story of the GOP's rise . . . is in part a tale of youth, strategic savvy, and organizational energy that enabled the Republicans to position themselves as the party of the future. By contrast, the complacency and organizational ineptitude of the Democrats prevented them from shaking an image as the party of the past and 'good ol' boy' corruption." The Alabama chapter writers pointed out that their state's Democratic statewide losers in 1994 were those who had been "tainted" by scandal or under an "ethical cloud." Untainted Alabama Democrats won that year. In Arkansas, Mike Huckabee and other GOP winners have effectively employed a "clean-up-the-system motif" to advance in a state where a criminal corruption conviction ended the career of the Democratic governor who followed Clinton. The GOP line, to quote the Arkansas chapter authors, is that "the political system constituted one huge cesspool in need of total draining," an image that received regular reinforcement as the Whitewater investigation unfolded.

The pace of the Republican advance of the 1990s, of course, differed from state to state, a point that cannot be overlooked as one reads the eleven separate state accounts in this book. In South Carolina, for example, a variety of elements came together in 1994, creating a momentum that encouraged more Democratic politicians to switch parties,[24] which fueled yet more forward movement. Alabama appears to have reached such a "critical mass" in 1996. Perhaps Georgia is on the verge of it in 1998.

Although this notion of momentum is a nebulous one, it can have an important impact on the choice of party by young politicians. In 1979, when I interviewed one of Alabama's first Republican leaders, U.S. representative Jack Edwards of Mobile, he emphasized the dispiriting nature of facing an entrenched, broad-based Democratic party: "One of our major problems is the perception that we cannot win statewide. And it is hard for me to argue with young people that . . . we can win and we need to pioneer and we need good people to run if we are ever going to win. Of course, all of that is true, but for a guy who really wants to be attorney general or governor, you have to look at the cold, hard facts, that we have not been winning statewide races." The breakthrough years of the 1990s have put an end to the drawback Congressman Edwards noted almost two decades ago. A few days after the 1994 elections an Atlanta Republican consultant, Whit Ayres, was quoted directly on this point: "What's happened is that young, aspiring white politicians will now see their route to positions of power in the Republican rather than the Democratic Party. That has substantial long-term implications for the balance of power in the South for many years to come."[25] The authors of the Georgia chapter make the point as well: "By the late 1990s, however, the balance of power had changed, as many ambitious young politicians saw the Republican party as their best chance for winning office."

One potential dark cloud in the GOP's future was introduced above, namely the divisions between the party's economic conservatives and its social and religious conservatives. Or as the authors of the North Carolina chapter colorfully depict the situation: "The GOP ranges from Brooks Brothers–attired bankers sipping a fine Merlot at the country club to Scripture-quoting fundamentalists who drink nothing stronger than sweet tea." The danger for the Republican party, of course, is that the latter forces will carry the party in an extreme direction, and Democrats are gleeful at the possibility. A Democratic Congressional Campaign Committee official expressed his party's hope for Dixie's GOP this way: "The silver lining in the South is the Republican Party continues to lurch to the right. And if it keeps on lurching, it's going to leave the bulk of voters who are moderate, mainstream voters uncomfortable with their agenda."[26]

The skilled politicians the GOP has and is attracting fully recognize the necessity of holding their contentious factions together, just as Democratic leaders do in regard to their factional difficulties. A Louisiana Republican who has been in the thick of that state's intra-GOP battles, former state senator Ben Bagert of New Orleans, explained the situation. "We need both the economic conservatives and the social conservatives. They aren't really that different. The economic conservatives are cultural conservatives and the cultural conservatives are economic conservatives. The difference is why they're there. They come from different starting points. . . . It's a question of emphasis. . . . Instead of having a civil war, we ought to go out and beat up on the Democrats." A short quote from a New York *Times* article describing the outlook of a South Carolina Republican religious conservative conveys the nature of the challenge GOP leaders like Bagert face: "In Greenwood County, one of the places where the old Republican order has been thrown out by Christian-right newcomers, Bonnie Grancelli, a leader in local anti-pornography campaigns, was recently elected the county's new Republican chairman. She credits her victory to a lack of conviction on the part of the old order. 'They are people who can go either way on some issues,' she said. 'But now we have people in place who are dogmatic on how they feel about some things. When I say dogmatic, I mean that when it is the word of God you are talking about, you don't compromise.' "[27]

Another obvious challenge the GOP faces as it advances in the South is the responsibility for governing. The Republican party has occupied the governorship in every southern state so far except Georgia.[28] Thus, southern voters are building an impression of the party as it exercises power, and that impression will be vital to the next phase of Dixie's partisan development. The Alabama chapter authors put the point well: "Recent GOP successes have, for the first time in more than a century, made Republicans responsible for operating state government. How well they perform this role in the eyes of Alabama's voters will undoubtedly affect their party's fortunes."

THE NATION AND THE SOUTH: TOWARD THE TWENTY-FIRST CENTURY

The striking advances in southern partisan growth in the 1990s have finally removed the barrier that has prevented the country from having a truly national party system since the Civil War era, a development that has important implications for the nation and the South. In fact, national forces are likely to influence the South's future partisan direction at least as much as the regional forces depicted so far in this concluding chapter. Thus, elucidation of the South's progression in the national scheme serves as a vital guide to the future.

It is sometimes said that the big changes in southern politics since the 1960s amount to a "realignment." If the term *realignment* is used to indicate that considerable change has occurred in the region's politics, there can be no argument as to its appropriateness.[29] But, if it is used in the more precise way some political scientists have employed it to help explain national party system change, then its application exclusively to a regional phenomenon is incomplete at best.

In an influential 1955 article, V. O. Key called attention to a type of election "in which the decisive results of the voting reveal a sharp alteration of the pre-existing cleavage within the electorate." These "critical elections" or realignments have been the subject of a voluminous literature. In *Dynamics of the Party System: Alignment and Realignment of Political Parties in the United States*, my own favorite treatment of the topic, James L. Sundquist observes that realigning eras contain at their core a shift in underlying partisan attachments among a large segment of the voters. In these eras many people either switch their allegiance or are mobilized out of their indifference to participate in the electoral process.[30]

Why do these changes occur? Sundquist provides a compelling answer. At the beginning of any realignment period, one finds a party system in which the two parties are divided along a set of issues and philosophy rooted in past battles. Then there arises a new issue or a cluster of issues different from the old issues that had divided the parties. In Sundquist's phrase, the new issue or cluster "cuts across" the existing line of cleavage. For example, the cleavage that divided the Whig party and the Democratic party in the 1830s and 1840s had little to do with slavery. Determined abolitionists forced their "crosscutting" issue to the center of national debate by the 1850s, dividing the parties in new ways and precipitating the first major realignment. In fact, the strain was so great on the Whig party that it disappeared and was replaced by the Republican party.

In examining U.S. political history since the formation of mass political parties in the 1820s, Sundquist identifies three major realignments. The first, the Civil War–era realignment just mentioned above, actually occurred in the mid-1850s, in the years leading up to the start of the bloody sectional conflict in 1861. The war itself embedded the new partisan attachments deep in the fabric of the nation's politics for several generations, and, of course, launched the South on its separate political path. In the North the Grand Old Party, the victorious party of national unity, became the dominant political institution, although the northern Democratic party survived being on the "wrong side" of the Civil War, as James MacGregor Burns put it, to remain remarkably competitive in the 1870s and 1880s.[31]

Then came a major reshuffling in the 1890s, culminating in the critical 1896 election when the Democrats and Populists under William Jennings Bryan failed to make common cause with their natural allies—laborers in the cities of the East—and were decisively beaten. Under the leadership of William McKinley and Marcus Hanna, the GOP "emerge[d] as a grand new party combining its old business, farm, veterans, and black support with widening labor backing; it was emerging also as a powerful governing instrument in Washington and in many of the state capitals."[32]

By the turn of the century, the South's separate path was well established. The party of Lincoln, emancipation, and Reconstruction failed to take root in the South outside of the mountain regions in the decades immediately after the Civil War. By 1900 an all-white Democratic party in the South had constructed a one-party system in the eleven states of the former Confederacy with the overriding purpose of maintaining white supremacy, a critical historical development recounted in the first pages of this book. As long as whites remained united in the all-white Democratic party, the argument went, blacks could be isolated and prevented from exercising the balance of power and possibly bargaining with two competing white political parties for an end to their second-class status. For the first six decades of the twentieth century, this odd political arrangement meant that the South would remain a region politically apart from the national mainstream. Thus, any national realignments could be expected to play out differently in the South than in the rest of the country, and they did.

Figures 15 to 18 illustrate the South's separate political path as well as the great post–Civil War national realignments. The figures chart the strength of the Democratic party in the country's four regions—the Northeast, Midwest, West, and South—from 1872 to 1996 using the same method introduced in Chapter 1 for the eleven southern states and the region as a whole from 1932 to 1996. The dotted line is the Democratic vote for president and the solid line represents a measure of Democratic party strength constructed by totaling the Democratic vote for governor, U.S. senator, and U.S. House members for all the states in each region.[33] A vast amount of American political history is encapsulated in the twists and turns of these illustrations.

By ignoring for the moment the most striking feature of the regional portraits, that is, the South's singular pattern, the depiction in Figures 15 to 17 of the three nonsouthern regions—collectively, the North—illustrates key national movements. First, the northern figures capture the critical nature of the 1896 election, showing, among other things, the noticeable drop in Democratic strength in the Northeast during the first decades of the new century. Because the illustrations are only for the Democratic side, the golden Republican era from 1896 through 1932 is depicted in reverse, that is, by showing the minority status of the Democrats in all regions except the South.[34]

The era of national Republican dominance culminates in the 1920s with the three consecutive victories of the GOP's standard-bearers in the decade's presidential elections: Warren G. Harding in 1920, Calvin Coolidge in 1924, and Herbert Hoover in 1928. At the start of the economic boom of the 1920s, President Harding summed up the GOP's confidence: "This is essentially a business country. We hear a vast deal about 'big business,' but the big business of America is nothing but the aggregate of the small businesses. That is why we need business sense in charge of American administration, and why the majority of America has for more than a half a century been a Republican majority."[35] With the onset of the Great Depression following the October 1929 stock market crash, the faith of the country in businessmen and Republicans was to undergo a dramatic reassessment.

As the nation sank into the worst economic depression in memory, Governor Franklin D. Roosevelt of New York was swept into the presidency in the 1932 election because he was not Herbert Hoover. Or, as Sundquist put it simply: "When unemployment stands at 24 percent, as it did in 1932, an incumbent president is not reelected." In the campaign FDR avoided spelling out a specific program, but he did indicate in his famous "Forgotten Man" speech that his approach would differ from the Republicans': "These unhappy times call for . . . plans that . . . build from the bottom up and not from the top down, that put their faith once more in the forgotten man at the bottom of the economic pyramid." In office, Roosevelt initiated an unprecedented series of activist governmental initiatives that attempted to bolster the economy and to channel billions of dollars of aid—primarily work relief—to the millions of people in need. Further, in 1935, landmark structural changes were enacted into law, such as the National Labor Relations Act, which propelled the growth of vast industrial unions within a few years, and the Social Security Act. Of the latter, FDR said upon signing the measure that it was a long-overdue partial response to "startling industrial changes" and "gives at least some protection to thirty million of our citizens who will reap direct benefits through unemployment compensation, through old-age pensions and through increased services for the protection of children and the prevention of ill health."[36]

The scope of the federal government's activities—the regulation of banking, financial markets, and utility companies, the promotion of public power, aid to agriculture, and rural electrification, to give a partial listing—was unprecedented, as the leaders of the Republican party pointed out at every turn. Sundquist captured the flavor of the opposition by quoting former President Hoover's increasingly harsh denunciations of the New Deal: " 'a muddle of uncoordinated reckless adventures in government,' 'the color of despotism . . . the color of Fascism . . . the color of Socialism,' 'flagrant flouting of the Constitution,' . . . 'the philosophy of collectivism and . . . greed for power,' . . . 'the gospel of class hatred preached from the White House.' " Roosevelt responded in kind, asserting, for example, at a thunderous Madison Square Garden rally on the eve of his smashing 1936 reelection victory: "Never before in all our history have [the forces of organized money] been so united against one candidate as they stand today. They are unanimous in their hate for me—and I welcome their hatred. I should like to have it said of my first Administration . . . that in it the forces of selfishness and of lust for power met their match. I should like to have it said . . . of my second Administration that in it these forces met their master."[37]

The tumultuous events of the New Deal era precipitated a realignment of

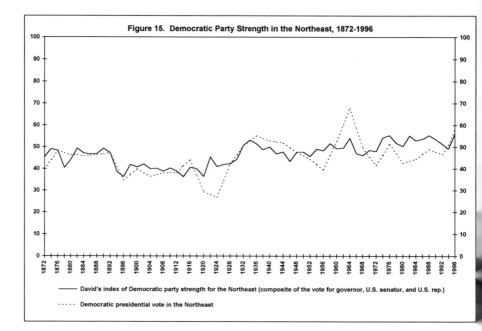

Figure 15. Democratic Party Strength in the Northeast, 1872-1996

—— David's index of Democratic party strength for the Northeast (composite of the vote for governor, U.S. senator, and U.S. rep.)

· · · · · Democratic presidential vote in the Northeast

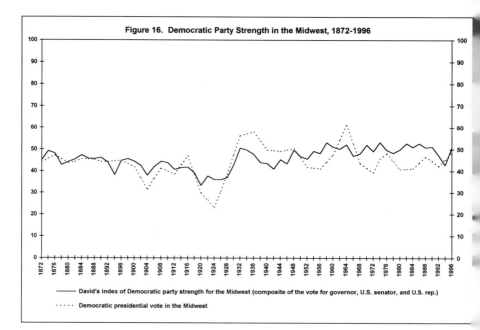

Figure 16. Democratic Party Strength in the Midwest, 1872-1996

—— David's index of Democratic party strength for the Midwest (composite of the vote for governor, U.S. senator, and U.S. rep.)

· · · · · Democratic presidential vote in the Midwest

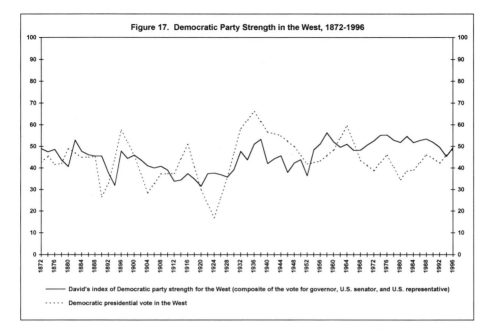

Figure 17. Democratic Party Strength in the West, 1872-1996

——— David's index of Democratic party strength for the West (composite of the vote for governor, U.S. senator, and U.S. representative)

· · · · · Democratic presidential vote in the West

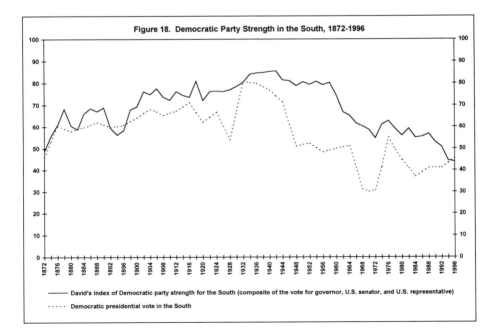

Figure 18. Democratic Party Strength in the South, 1872-1996

——— David's index of Democratic party strength for the South (composite of the vote for governor, U.S. senator, and U.S. representative)

· · · · · Democratic presidential vote in the South

American politics as powerful as the Civil War–era realignment. Roosevelt's leadership during the Depression crisis gave the party system a pronounced class division it had not had before the 1930s. Under FDR, the Democratic party came to be viewed as the champion of the working class. In 1940, one of the first of the early national public opinion polls captured the change. When asked which party they would like to see win the 1940 presidential election, 69 percent of lower-income respondents picked the Democrats while 64 percent of those in the upper-income category chose the Republicans.[38] The new cleavage in the party system manifested in the New Deal realignment revolved around the proper role of the federal government in the economic and social life of the country. The issues were clearly drawn. The Republicans held to the traditional view of a limited role for the federal government in the nation's economic and social life and favored reliance on the forces of an unfettered market to provide prosperity. Roosevelt led the Democrats to the embrace of an activist federal government aimed at helping "those who have less."[39]

Although FDR put the Democrats on the road to national majority status, the new path set in motion by the Depression and the New Deal was not a straight uphill one. Figures 15 to 17 show Democratic party strength in the North rising with Roosevelt's big victory in 1932 but dropping back even while the president is increasing his vote in 1936. The figures demonstrate that Democratic strength in the northern states does not take a sustained upward swing until after World War II. Although the figures mask considerable state-by-state variation, they do accurately portray this fascinating second-stage of the New Deal realignment that played out in the party system in the North well into the 1950s and early 1960s. Sundquist, who brilliantly and originally analyzed the phenomenon, labeled it "aftershocks of the New Deal earthquake—in the North." Those who were first attracted to Roosevelt in the early years of the Depression also supported his party at the state and local level at far higher levels than the previously hopeless northern Democratic minority had had any reason to expect. As FDR's popularity increased and the realignment continued through his 1936 landslide reelection, voters realized that the New Deal Democrats in Washington bore little resemblance to the Democratic parties in their states and localities, which were still anchored in the pre-1932 mold.[40]

After World War II there arose a new generation of Democratic politicians committed to the Roosevelt revolution and determined to build activist state parties along the lines blazed by the New Deal. These were men like Hubert H. Humphrey of Minnesota, Adlai Stevenson and Paul Douglas of Illinois, William Proxmire of Wisconsin, George McGovern of South Dakota, Edmund Muskie of Maine, Frank Church of Idaho, Alan Cranston of California. Sundquist calls them "programmatic liberals" and demonstrates how they were at the forefront of transforming the politics of the three regions of the country where Republicans once held safe majorities. To follow the New Deal transformation thoroughly—which is beyond the scope of this chapter—would require delving into the political histories of particular northern states and attempting to untangle various state party strength figures similar to those introduced in Chapter 1 of this book for the South. Overall, the programmatic liberals replaced the Democratic party's old image and leaders in the North, gave the party new life and electoral victories into the 1960s, and, in the process, brought politics in these three regions into general conformity with the national cleavages begun by FDR's New Deal at the presidential level.[41]

The New Deal realignment took a different course in the solidly Democratic South. Roosevelt remained popular in Dixie throughout his tenure, but, as Figure 18 shows, the partisan realignment he brought to the rest of the country did not disturb Dixie's one-party system, which was rooted in the older, overriding desire of southern whites to preserve white supremacy. Within the southern one-party system, pro–New Deal and anti–New Deal factions emerged, but both sides were firmly wedded to the Democratic party and what it stood for in racial terms. The New Deal did set in motion outside of the South, however, an important development that would lead to the national Democratic party's civil rights crisis after World War II. At the turn of the century, 90 percent of the nation's blacks lived in the South. An exodus of southern blacks to the cities of the North occurred in the first half of the twentieth century, resulting in 50 percent of the nation's African Americans living in the North by mid-century. And during the Depression, these working-class blacks of the North abandoned the party of Lincoln for Franklin Roosevelt and the Democratic party,[42] a change reflected symbolically by the seating at the 1936 Democratic National Convention of the first black delegates in the party's long history. At this juncture, the Democratic party thus became both the home of blacks in the North and the party of white supremacy in the South.

Although FDR managed through the end of his life to keep his distance from the impending crisis in the Democratic party over racial segregation in the South, his successor, Harry Truman, did not. In early 1947 President Truman established a civil rights commission to examine the plight of America's blacks. When the commission in October 1947 issued its "sweeping denunciation of all governmental and some private sanctions of race discrimination or segregation," Truman called the report, entitled *To Secure These Rights*, "an American charter of human freedom" and implemented many of its suggestions within his power, such as integrating the military. The next year, the 1948 Democratic

National Convention, as related in Chapter 1, adopted a strong civil rights platform amid stirring oratory from such northern liberals as Hubert Humphrey.
The southern reaction to these developments was swift and bitter. "There are
not enough laws on the books of the nation, nor can there be enough laws, to
break down segregation in the South," declared Governor Strom Thurmond of
South Carolina, who was nominated for president by the hastily formed States'
Rights party (nicknamed the Dixiecrats since, of course, nearly all of Dixie's
politicians of the one-party era were Democrats). There followed the familiar
story of the breakdown of the one-party South over the next fifteen years and
the rise of the two-party South, all key political events that served as this book's
starting point.

A glance at the last three decades of Figure 18 shows that Democratic
strength in the South lapsed into minority status by the 1994 and 1996 elections,
a complicated movement fully explored throughout this book. In sum, the last
years of Figure 18 picture a two-party system in the South that has now begun
to resemble the overall standard competitive party system pattern outside of the
South, as illustrated in the post–World War II portions of Figures 15 to 17.
Thus, by the 1990s the South and the rest of the nation had converged into a
nationwide system of two-party competition, one which exhibited remarkable
overall balance between the parties.[43]

The focus of this book, of course, has been on the dynamics of the southern
two-party system during the last decade of a three-decade-long process of dis-
mantling the one-party edifice. While the South was undergoing rapid change,
however, the national party system did not stand still. In fact, a series of "crosscutting" issues—to continue to employ Sundquist's useful framework—
disrupted the New Deal party system starting in the tumultuous decade of the
1960s. These disruptions were driven by bitter racial conflicts in the big cities
of the North, violent protests over U.S. involvement in the Vietnam war, and
a series of emotional social and cultural issues, including crime in the streets and
the accompanying calls for law and order, abortion, women's rights, gun control, and prayer in the schools. This new cluster of issues cut across the existing
New Deal line of partisan cleavage in the North and weakened the Democratic
party there by driving away a sizable number of the party's core supporters in
the white working class and lower-middle class,[44] thereby contributing mightily
to the Republican party's victory in five out of the six presidential elections
from Richard Nixon's first election in the chaotic political year of 1968 to
George Bush's election in 1988.

In my view, these disruptions—which temporarily eased somewhat in the
mid-1970s as a result of Watergate and the election of Jimmy Carter, the lone

successful Democrat during the era—constituted another realignment, which, for lack of a better term, I call the "Twenty-Five Years' Realignment." The period starts in 1964–1965, when the civil rights movement shifted attention to the North and U.S. involvement in the Vietnam war escalated. It ends in 1988–1989 with the 1988 presidential election—a "bloody shirt" campaign[45] capping off the era—and with the start in the following year of a sequence of events that would lead to the end of the Cold War and the Soviet empire.

In the 1988 election, Michael Dukakis, the Democratic standard-bearer, suffered in graphic fashion from the various accumulated Democratic party stigmas that made the Twenty-Five Years' Realignment a national partisan reshuffling favorable to the GOP. For example, as a result of the intraparty battles over Vietnam, the Democratic party, a party with impeccable Cold War credentials from Truman to Kennedy, became, to its electoral detriment, stigmatized as less steadfast in the worldwide struggle with the Soviet Union and too willing to cut the defense budget. Likewise, the "Social Issue," as the domestic disruptions associated with "racial strife, Vietnam, and crime and lawlessness" came to be labeled,[46] diminished the Democrats' electoral base. In an insightful and influential book on these disruptions, Thomas Byrne Edsall and Mary D. Edsall explain the situation this way:

> As the civil rights movement became national, as it became clearly associated with the Democratic party, and as it began to impinge on local neighborhoods and schools, it served to crack the Democratic loyalties of key white voters. Crucial numbers of voters—in the white urban and suburban neighborhoods of the North, and across the South—were, in addition, deeply angered and distressed by aspects of the expanding rights revolution. It has been among the white working and lower-middle classes that many of the social changes stemming from the introduction of new rights—civil rights for minorities, reproductive and workplace rights for women, constitutional protections for the criminally accused, immigration opportunities for those from developing countries, free-speech rights to pornographers, and the surfacing of highly visible homosexual communities—have been most deeply resisted.[47] Resentment of the civil rights movement among key white voters was reinforced and enlarged by cultural and economic conflicts resulting from the rights revolution.[48]

The Bush campaign strategists in 1988 fully understood how the national Democrats had been put on the defensive during this period, and they crafted a skillful bloody shirt campaign designed to capitalize on the disruptive, crosscutting issues of the Twenty-Five Years' Realignment. They aired television ads criticizing Governor Dukakis for "a Massachusetts prison furlough program in which a convicted murderer named Willie Horton, released for a weekend during Dukakis' tenure, fled and later committed rape"; they attacked him for opposing the death penalty; and they criticized him for vetoing a Massachusetts bill requiring the firing of schoolteachers who refused to lead students in the pledge of allegiance to the flag, legislation the liberal governor had objected to as unconstitutional under U.S. Supreme Court precedents. Also, Dukakis, who lacked experience in national security matters, was hammered in ads as a representative of a Democratic party all too eager to slash the defense budget. Two chroniclers of the election wrote that the negative TV ad campaign left viewers with "the inference that the Democratic nominee was not only unpatriotic and soft on crime but also soft or weak on national defense."[49]

The point of lingering on the 1988 campaign is not to pass judgment on the Bush tactics but to demonstrate how a Republican presidential candidate benefited from tying his Democratic opponent to the issue positions that over a twenty-five-year period disrupted and weakened the national majority party's electoral base. With the end of the Cold War and the decline in significance of national security issues, a part of the Democratic stigma faded. And in 1992 a "New Democrat," Bill Clinton, as related in Chapter 1, moved his national party away from an array of "liberal" domestic positions that were viewed as electoral losers. In a sense, Clinton conceded the reality of the recent realignment by conducting himself in his two presidential campaigns and in most of his presidency as a "me too" Democrat much as Thomas Dewey and the other "me too" Republicans had done when they made peace with the New Deal and adopted many of its tenets while pledging to administer the new social programs more efficiently.[50]

The value for southern politics of this exposition of the Twenty-Five Years' Realignment is that it offers a framework not only for understanding partisan change in the North but, more importantly, for visualizing how the northern changes were at first moving simultaneously on a separate (but related) track with the South's partisan path, that is, in the early years—the 1960s and into the 1970s. Gradually, as the southern one-party structure receded, the two regions began to move closer together politically. By the presidency of Ronald Reagan in the 1980s, the issues of this realignment were running fairly close together in the North and the South, as was suggested by Lee Atwater's 1981 comments on the GOP's "new Southern strategy," cited in Chapter 1. For the South in the 1960s, the most important political event was the passage of national legislation that finished off the region's system of racial segregation and brought to an end Dixie's dedication to a one-party monolith as a means of preserving racial segregation. For the North, the last half of the 1960s was a time when African Americans focused attention—particularly in the big cities—on the existence of widespread de facto discrimination, which led to considerable white-black friction there but was not an epoch-ending episode. The race riots of the late 1960s, for example, were primarily a northern phenomenon, and the accompanying white backlash outside the South worked to the detriment of the Democratic party there. Further, the other nonracial crosscutting issues that reshuffled the party system during the Twenty-Five Years' Realignment were more significant outside the South during the early years. After all, the nascent southern two-party system, as described in Chapter 1, was heavily preoccupied with sorting through the confused partisan environment left in the aftermath of the collapse of the Democratic state-level monopoly. By the end of the Carter interlude, the divisive national nonracial issues grew in significance as the southern two-party system developed as a sophisticated partisan vehicle that could embody both the nonracial and the racial cleavages of the latest realignment.

It is essential to remember, however, that in the first decade or so of the two-party South, the southern parties were also still in the process of accommodating the New Deal–era cleavages that had worked their way into the partisan fabric of northern states in the 1940s and 1950s through the aftershocks process described above. Their penetration into the South had to overcome the huge barrier of the one-party system. When the bar finally fell, energetic, ambitious southern Republican leaders—Sundquist's "programmatic conservatives"— labored to implant "the aftershocks of the New Deal earthquake" in the South. These were economic conservatives—Bill Brock of Tennessee is a good example—who were skeptical of the enlarged role the federal government had embraced in the nation's economic and social life since the 1930s. The penetration of the New Deal cleavages affected the Democratic side, too, as the South's transformed Democratic party slowly became the regional heir of FDR's New Deal philosophy of government. Southern black leaders embraced the legacy easily, but the moderate white southern Democratic leaders of the biracial coalition tended to stay closer to the center than their northern counterparts. Here is how Sundquist in 1983 summed up the New Deal realignment's delayed penetration into Dixie, which he correctly viewed even at that late date as incomplete: "Through a series of aftershocks the realignment of the 1930s will settle into place throughout the region, pitting state and local Democratic parties aligned with the national party, though less outspokenly activist and liberal, against Republican parties that mirror the conservatism of the national GOP."[51]

Thus, as the older New Deal cleavages worked their way into the southern partisan scheme, the newer cleavages of the Twenty-Five Years' Realignment were also flowing into Dixie's new party system. With these two complex crosscurrents at work simultaneously in the still young two-party South, it is understandable that the new politics of Dixie provided an analytical challenge for outsiders and the uninitiated alike.

The great value of the realignment framework offered here is that it allows one to understand how the South has gradually over these recent decades rejoined the national political mainstream. (Considering that the nation's four top elected officials as of mid-1998—President Bill Clinton, Vice President Al Gore, House Speaker Newt Gingrich, and Senate majority leader Trent Lott—were all from the South, northerners might be forgiven for concluding that the South had rejoined the national political mainstream a little too exuberantly!) With the arrival of the mature years of southern partisan competition in the 1990s, the country now has a genuinely national party system for the first time in nearly a century and a half. This does not mean that there is a total homogenization of politics in the fifty states and the four regions. There are commonalties, for example, in the politics of Maine, New York, Ohio, Iowa, and Oregon, although different traditions, based on a multiplicity of factors, also persist in those states. But today, politics in Virginia, the Carolinas, Georgia, and Florida, to pick five southern states, is far more similar to politics in those five northern states than at any time since the Civil War.

Nor does the nationalization of southern politics mean that differences between the regions have evaporated. For example, white southerners tend to be more conservative on social and cultural issues than white northerners, although on economic and role of government issues whites in the South and North divide about the same.[52] And even as the South has rapidly joined the national economic mainstream, the region retains certain distinctive cultural features.[53]

This nationalization of southern politics, in the advanced stage it has reached in the 1990s, was very much in evidence in the 1994 elections. The GOP sweep that year was national in scope, and, at the congressional level, the South's contribution to the victory was matched in other regions. Yet, as this book's state chapters demonstrated, 1994 also marked an unprecedented forward spurt of the ongoing settling in of two-party competition in Dixie, a process that was propelled at least partly by regional dynamics set in motion long before the events of 1994 unfolded at the national level. In the 1996 elections, the southern GOP gains came primarily from the regional momentum running in the Republicans' favor that year. As the region's two-party system stabilizes further in the years ahead, the regional forces that fueled the new competitive system's formation will dissipate since they will have completed their work with the result of tying southern politics even more closely to national political developments. Thus, we may reach a time in the not-too-distant future when the operating watchwords will be: As goes the nation, so goes the South.[54] What a turnaround that would represent for a region that operated in political isolation for so many decades!

While we await the South's impending full political reintegration into the Union, the region has already accomplished a remarkable feat in the 1990s: By installing a fully functioning, mature system of two-party competition, the South has advanced the cause of democracy for all its citizens. Too often we see the spread of democratic practices as something that only needs to happen in other nations. Yet our own democratic development—even in long established two-party states,[55] not to mention on the national level—is incomplete.

How far the South has come is best conveyed by quoting Key's 1949 assessment of the impact of the one-party system on the region's political life: "Consistent and unquestioning attachment, by overwhelming majorities, to the Democratic party . . . has meant that the politics within southern states—the election of governors, of state legislators, and the settlement of public issues generally—has had to be conducted without the benefit of political parties. As institutions, parties enjoy a general disrepute, yet most of the democratic world finds them indispensable as instruments of self-government, as means for the organization and expression of competing viewpoints on public policy. Nevertheless, over a tremendous area—the South—no such competing institutions exist."[56]

At another point Key wrote, "When all the exceptions are considered, when all the justifications are made, and when all the invidious comparisons are drawn, those of the South and those who love the South are left with the cold, hard fact that the South as a whole has developed no system or practice of political organization and leadership adequate to cope with its problems."[57] Further along these lines, Key wrote the following to his chief associate, Alexander Heard, in a July 4, 1947, letter during the research phase of the *Southern Politics* project:

> In those moments between going to bed and to sleep I've been speculating a little on our general strategy.
> One night I had the bright notion that maybe the thing to do was to set out our prejudices at the beginning (as a warning to one and all) and say that our purpose in talking cold turkey is to promote these ends. . . .
> We believe in a brawling, fighting, arguing, contentious democracy,

not because it promotes good government but because it insures popular government. . . .

Hence, we believe that popular government redounds to the good of all by keeping the top dogs on their toes, by encouraging the ablest woods colts to earn the position to which their inheritance entitles them, and by weeding out those of incompetence who presume to position.[58]

Fifty years later, no one can deny that Key's hope for a "brawling, fighting, arguing, contentious" democratic South has been realized in the current, competitive two-party system firmly in place throughout Dixie in the 1990s, a system that does provide the "means for the organization and expression of competing viewpoints on public policy" and that can—given intelligent and imaginative leaders—cope with the South's problems.

NOTES

Preface

1. Alexander P. Lamis and Nathan Goldman, "V. O. Key's *Southern Politics*: The Writing of a Classic," *Georgia Historical Quarterly*, LXXI (Summer 1987), 281.

2. V. O. Key, Jr., *A Primer of Statistics for Political Scientists* (New York, 1954), 125.

1. The Two-Party South: From the 1960s to the 1990s

1. Paul T. David, *Party Strength in the United States, 1872–1970* (Charlottesville, Va., 1972). David updated his party-strength figures for 1972 to 1976 in three *Journal of Politics* research notes. Before his death in 1994, David provided an endowment to the Inter-university Consortium for Political and Social Research to have the index updated and made available to researchers as part of the consortium's vast data holding. William Claggett of Florida State University, who is in charge of doing the updating for the consortium, kindly made the figures for 1976 to 1994 available to me with the permission of the consortium. Andrew Lucker, who received his Ph.D. in political science from Case Western Reserve University in 1998, did the 1996 calculations as well as the required updating of the 1994 figures. He also prepared all the fine figures displaying David's index, for which I am most appreciative. Incidentally, David actually offered three variations of his index; the one I use here he labeled Composite B.

All of a state's U.S. House elections are averaged to make up that office's one-third contribution to the biennial figure, all House races thus being equal to the statewide percentages for each of every state's two major statewide elections—for governor and U.S. senator. In order to have a figure for governor and senator every two years, David employs interpolation, averaging the preceding and following elections when there is no election for either of these offices. Because the crucial information from the following election when there is no election for governor or senator is not yet available, the figures for the most recent election are only tentative and have to be updated after the next election is held. Thus, the 1996 index figures used in this book will change somewhat after the 1998 elections.

2. In deriving the regional figure, the state figures are weighted roughly according to population. This is done by using the number of members of the U.S. House each state is allotted, a weight that, of course, changes every ten years when seats are reallocated by Congress to reflect population shifts revealed by the U.S. census. Furthermore, David's index can be calculated and plotted for Republican party strength, which would depict virtually the reverse of the pattern in Figure 1 and in the eleven state figures introduced below. My choice to limit these illustrations to the Democratic side is an arbitrary one, although it does have the benefit of highlighting the near total domination of the Democratic party in the earlier decades. Figure 13, used later in this chapter, portrays Republican growth directly. Incidentally, the South is defined as the eleven states of the former Confederacy.

3. George B. Tindall, *The Disruption of the Solid South* (New York, 1972), esp. Chapter 1, "Variations on a Theme by Hayes," 1–21. A fine entry point to the vast research on the Reconstruction era is Eric Foner, *Reconstruction: America's Unfinished Revolution, 1863–1877* (New York,

1988). And for an excellent general historical survey, see Dewey W. Grantham, *The South in Modern America: A Region at Odds* (New York, 1994). For more on the post-Reconstruction era, see C. Vann Woodward, *Origins of the New South, 1877–1913* (1951; rev. ed., Baton Rouge, 1971), J. Morgan Kousser, *The Shaping of Southern Politics: Suffrage Restriction and the Establishment of the One-Party South, 1880–1910* (New Haven, Conn., 1974), and Dewey W. Grantham, *The Life and Death of the Solid South: A Political History* (Lexington, Ky., 1988), 1–77.

4. The southern one-party system in all its complexity was brilliantly analyzed by V. O. Key, Jr., in his classic *Southern Politics in State and Nation* (New York, 1949). Key and his associates, chief among them Alexander Heard, who receives "with the assistance of" credit on the book's title page, dissected the region's odd political system just as it was beginning to unravel. For an account of how this famous research project was conducted, see Alexander P. Lamis and Nathan Goldman, "V. O. Key's *Southern Politics*: The Writing of a Classic," *Georgia Historical Quarterly*, LXXI (1987), 261–85.

5. Robert A. Garson, *The Democratic Party and the Politics of Sectionalism, 1941–1948* (Baton Rouge, 1974), 278.

6. On Kennedy's approach to civil rights, see Carl M. Brauer, *John F. Kennedy and the Second Reconstruction* (New York, 1977), and Richard Reeves, *President Kennedy: Profile of Power* (New York, 1993).

7. Bernard Cosman, *Five States for Goldwater: Continuity and Change in Southern Presidential Voting Patterns* (University, Ala., 1966). The five states were the southern states with the highest percentage of blacks (see Table 1). For more on these developments, see Chapters 2 and 3 and the various state chapters in Alexander P. Lamis, *The Two-Party South*, 2nd expanded ed. (New York, 1990), plus the many fine books cited in note 13 below.

8. Hastings Wyman, Jr., Review of Lamis's *The Two-Party South*, in *Election Politics: A Journal of Political Campaigns and Elections*, II (Summer 1985), 20–21. Wyman is publisher of the *Southern Political Report*, an invaluable Washington-based biweekly newsletter. The first edition of *The Two-Party South* was published in 1984. An expanded edition appeared in 1988, covering developments in the 1984 and 1986 elections. A final version of the book, the second expanded edition, was issued in 1990 as a paperback only and contained a postscript chapter on the 1988 elections and projections of future trends.

9. For an excellent treatment of the New Deal realignment, see James L. Sundquist, *Dynamics of the Party System: Alignment and Realignment of Political Parties in the United States*, rev. ed. (Washington, D.C., 1983), 198–297, 332–51. By the late 1940s and the 1950s, the "aftershocks" of the New Deal realignment had made the Democratic party the nation's majority party for the first time since the Civil War.

10. This paragraph draws almost completely from Lamis, *The Two-Party South*, 25–26.

11. Interview with Lee Atwater, conducted by Alexander P. Lamis and a newspaper reporter, July 8, 1981, and cited in Lamis, *The Two-Party South*, 26. For more on the controversial Atwater, who died in 1991 at the age of forty, see John Brady, *Bad Boy: The Life and Politics of Lee Atwater* (Reading, Mass., 1997).

12. Lamis, *The Two-Party South*, 37, 99.

13. This overview could cover only the most important elements of the first two decades of the two-party South; many of the more subtle features had to be omitted in a book focused on the 1990s. For more on the earlier period, see Lamis, *The Two-Party South*; Robert H. Swansbrough and David M. Brodsky, eds., *The South's New Politics: Realignment and Dealignment* (Columbia, S.C., 1988); Earl Black and Merle Black, *Politics and Society in the South* (Cambridge, Mass., 1987); Jack

Bass and Walter DeVries, *The Transformation of Southern Politics: Social Change and Political Consequence Since 1945* (New York, 1976); Numan V. Bartley and Hugh D. Graham, *Southern Politics and the Second Reconstruction* (Baltimore, 1975); and William C. Havard, ed., *The Changing Politics of the South* (Baton Rouge, 1972).

14. On May 28, 1997, at the age of ninety-four, Thurmond became the longest serving U.S. senator in American history. On December 5, 2002, less than a month before his current term expires, "Ole Strom," with the cooperation of higher authority, will become the Senate's first centenarian. For an account of his last campaign, see Kevin Sack, "Thurmond's Robust Legend Shields Him at 93," New York *Times,* October 24, 1996.

15. Hollings, who faced a tough reelection battle in 1998, was the only major southern Democratic politician who won his first statewide election during the one-party era—the governorship of South Carolina in 1958—to remain in office into the late 1990s.

16. For more on "Mountain Republicans," see Key, *Southern Politics,* 280–85, and Alexander Heard, *A Two-Party South?* (Chapel Hill, N.C., 1952).

17. The quotation comes from an interview I conducted on July 26, 1982, with Rob Christensen, then Washington correspondent of the Raleigh *News and Observer,* and cited in *The Two-Party South,* 138–39. Christensen is coauthor of the North Carolina chapter in this book.

18. Bartley and Graham, *Southern Politics and the Second Reconstruction,* 180; David S. Broder, *The Changing of the Guard: Power and Leadership in America* (New York, 1981), 368.

19. Ralph Eisenberg, "Virginia: The Emergence of Two-Party Politics," in Havard, ed., *Changing Politics of the South,* 75–76.

20. Cited in Lamis, *The Two-Party South,* 127, 129.

21. *Ibid.,* 259.

22. *Ibid.,* 77.

23. Donald S. Strong, "Alabama: Transition and Alienation," in Havard, ed., *Changing Politics of the South,* 457.

24. Cited in Lamis, *The Two-Party South,* 86.

25. *Ibid.,* 54.

26. In *The Two-Party South* I subtitled my Louisiana chapter "Sui Generis like Huey," explaining the label this way: "When Louisiana's most famous politician, Huey P. Long, was pressed once to explain his singular political style, he responded, 'Oh, hell, say that I'm *sui generis* [one of a kind] and let it go at that.' No more appropriate characterization can be found for his state's recent experience with two-party politics" (107). The observation still holds true in the 1990s.

27. Key, *Southern Politics,* 3. Key illuminated the debate over this marvelous Louisiana political giant with the following delightful sentences in his classic study: "Long dramatized himself as the champion of the people against the sinister interests and his production was by no means pure melodrama. For there are sinister interests and there are champions of the people, even though there may always be some good about the sinister and at least a trace of fraud in self-styled champions" (157).

28. Both quotations are cited in Lamis, *The Two-Party South,* 109, 111.

29. In updating David's index for Louisiana, Claggett employed the following special rules, to quote from the descriptive material he sent me along with the data: "To derive party percentages for gubernatorial and senatorial elections, I decided to use general election results if they existed. If not, I aggregated across the candidates in the first primary by party. . . . For congressional elections the first primary results were used exclusively."

30. James Bolner, ed., *Louisiana Politics: Festival in a Labyrinth* (Baton Rouge, 1982).

31. Key, *Southern Politics*, 259.

32. Cited in Lamis, *The Two-Party South*, 262.

33. *Ibid.*, 209.

34. David R. Colburn and Richard K. Scher, *Florida's Gubernatorial Politics in the Twentieth Century* (Tallahassee, Fla., 1980), 83.

35. Cited in Lamis, *The Two-Party South*, 183.

36. *Ibid.*, 185.

37. *Ibid.*, 293.

38. After the 1996 election, the GOP controlled 712 of the 1,782 legislative seats in the eleven states; by July 1998, the Republican total had risen to 740. In 1990 the party occupied only 495 of the 1,782 seats. The National Conference of State Legislatures in Denver provided the 1996 and 1998 figures; the partisan breakdowns reported here for 1990 and for the other years plotted in Figure 13 are from various volumes of *The Book of the States*, published by the Council of State Governments in Lexington, Ky.

39. Maureen Dowd, "From President to Politician: Bush Attacks the Democrats," New York *Times,* October 30, 1990.

40. David S. Broder and Ann Devroy, "Rebuilding, Regrouping and Rethinking Their Strategies for 1992," *Washington Post National Weekly Edition*, November 12–18, 1990; William E. Schmidt, "Shaken Gingrich Barely Avoids Going from Whip to Whipped in Georgia," New York *Times,* November 8, 1990.

41. On the national Democrats' woes in Dixie during the period, see Earl Black and Merle Black, *The Vital South: How Presidents Are Elected* (Cambridge, Mass., 1992). Starting with the 1984 contest, the organizers of the Citadel Symposium on Southern Politics, which is held in Charleston, South Carolina, in March of every even-numbered year, have edited books on each of the presidential elections in Dixie. The state chapters in the 1992 and 1996 volumes in the Citadel series are cited in this book's state chapters at the point in the various state narratives where presidential elections are considered. The two earlier volumes for the 1980s are, Robert P. Steed, Laurence W. Moreland, and Tod A. Baker, eds., *The 1984 Presidential Election in the South: Patterns of Southern Party Politics* (New York, 1986), and Laurence W. Moreland, Robert P. Steed, and Tod A. Baker, eds., *The 1988 Presidential Election in the South: Continuity Amidst Change in Southern Party Politics* (New York, 1991).

42. Thomas Byrne Edsall with Mary D. Edsall, *Chain Reaction: The Impact of Race, Rights, and Taxes on American Politics* (New York, 1991), 3–4, 6.

43. Robin Toner, "Centrist Democrats Set Agenda for '92," New York *Times*, May 8, 1991. For more on the Democratic Leadership Council, see Jon F. Hale, "The Making of the New Democrats," *Political Science Quarterly*, CX (1995), 207–32.

44. The four-page supplement was distributed by the Edsalls' New York publisher.

45. Thomas B. Edsall, "Black Leaders View Clinton Strategy With Mix of Pragmatism, Optimism," Washington *Post*, October 28, 1992. The article also quoted Jackson: "The DLC premise was that Reagan Democrats basically left the party because of racial anxieties and racial fears . . . Reagan's welfare queens and Bush's Willie Hortons. The fact is, that is not why they left. Under Carter we had 20 percent stagflation. When Reagan asked, 'Are you better off?,' the answer was unanimously no."

46. Robin Toner, "Poll Shows Price Bush Pays for Tough Economic Times," New York *Times*, January 10, 1992. This article begins: "Eight of 10 Americans say the economy is in bad shape and President Bush is paying a clear political price for their discontent."

47. Ellen Debenport, "Clinton Heats Up Tampa Crowd," St. Petersburg *Times*, October 28, 1992; Edward Walsh, "Clinton Barnstorms in South: Democratic Nominee Seeks to Recapture a Republican Bastion," Washington *Post*, October 28, 1992; Ed Anderson and Colleen McMillar, "Clinton, Gore Court N.O. Voters," New Orleans *Times-Picayune*, October 17, 1992.

48. Michael Kelly, "Encircling Arkansas, Bush Opens Harsh Attack on Clinton's Record," and "Excerpts from Bush's Speech on Clinton's Record," New York *Times*, September 23, 1992.

49. For more on this election in Dixie, see Robert P. Steed, Laurence W. Moreland, and Tod A. Baker, eds., *The 1992 Presidential Election in the South: Current Patterns of Southern Party and Electoral Politics* (Westport, Conn., 1994).

50. The bulk of the new seats went to the region's two megastates, Florida and Texas. Florida increased from nineteen seats to twenty-three; Texas went from twenty-seven to thirty. North Carolina, Georgia, and Virginia each received one, and Louisiana lost a seat.

51. After its creation in the early 1980s, the New Orleans black-majority district remained in the hands of a white Democratic incumbent, Lindy Boggs, until she retired in 1990 and was replaced by William J. Jefferson, an African American state legislator.

52. The old plantation counties with their rich black soil—"the black belts"—are still the places with the largest concentration of African Americans outside of the large urban areas.

53. In the 1990 census, Williamsburg had 23,681 African Americans out of a total population of 36,815, or 64.3 percent. For Colleton, the figures were 15,498 out of 34,372, or 45.1 percent.

54. Incidentally, these three states' black-majority districts, used here to illustrate the issue, did not initially become legal lightning rods; the first court challenges came in other states. After all, it was hard to argue against creating lone black-majority districts in states that, in 1990, were 30.1 percent black (South Carolina with 6 seats in Congress), 19.0 percent black (Virginia with 11 seats), and 25.6 percent black (Alabama with 7 seats). The later legal challenges to the black-majority districts in these three states are covered in Chapter 13.

55. In addition to the South Carolina, Virginia, and Alabama districts, two new black-majority districts were created in both North Carolina and Georgia, three in Florida, and one each in Texas and Louisiana.

56. The process is called *preclearance* and is required by Section 5 of the Voting Rights Act. On this particular point, see a new book on the topic, David Lublin, *The Paradox of Representation: Racial Gerrymandering and Minority Interests in Congress* (Princeton, N.J., 1997), 28, 30. Lublin asserts: "The Justice Department used its power under Section 5 to deny preclearance to force states to draw new majority-minority districts" (28).

57. Guy Gugliotta, "Black Democrats Are Remapping Their Path to Power: An Alliance with the GOP Aims at Boosting Minority Districts," *Washington Post National Weekly Edition*, May 18–24, 1992; Robert Pear, "Redistricting Expected to Bring Surge in Minority Lawmakers," New York *Times*, August 3, 1992.

58. The black-majority-district controversy also played out—and continues to play out—at the state legislative level, as touched on in several of this book's chapters.

59. Ronald Smothers, "2 Strangely Shaped Hybrid Creatures Highlight North Carolina's Primary," New York *Times*, May 3, 1992; Peter Applebome, "Georgia Redistrict Plan Rejected; Black-White Battle Seen as Likely," New York *Times*, January 22, 1991. Wits had a field day with the new districts. Georgia's Eleventh was nicknamed the "Sherman's-march-to-the-sea district" to correspond to North Carolina's "I-85 district." A Z-shaped district in north Louisiana, which was quickly struck down by a federal court, was dubbed the "Mark-of-Zorro district."

60. Ronald Smothers, "Fair Play or Racial Gerrymandering? Justices Study a 'Serpentine' Dis-

trict," New York *Times*, April 16, 1993; 509 U.S. 630 (1993); Linda Greenhouse, "Court Questions Districts Drawn to Aid Minorities," New York *Times*, June 29, 1993; 515 U.S. 900 (1995); Greenhouse, "Justices, in 5–4 Vote, Reject Districts Drawn with Race the 'Predominant Factor,' " New York *Times*, June 30, 1995; Greenhouse, "High Court Voids Race-Based Plan for Redistricting," New York *Times*, June 14, 1996. The North Carolina case was *Shaw v. Hunt* (517 U.S. 899) and the Texas case *Bush v. Vera* (116 S.Ct. 1941). For a discussion of the constitutional doctrines involved in the Shaw and Miller cases, see Richard K. Scher, Jon L. Mills, and John J. Hotaling, *Voting Rights and Democracy: The Law and Politics of Districting* (Chicago, 1997), 76–124; David K. Ryden, *Representation in Crisis: The Constitution, Interest Groups, and Political Parties* (Albany, N.Y., 1996), 62–65, and Anthony A. Peacock, ed., *Affirmative Action and Representation: Shaw v. Reno and the Future of Voting Rights* (Durham, N.C., 1997).

61. Rob Christensen, "Congressman Mel Watt Plans to Keep Cruising Interstate 85," Raleigh *News and Observer*, July 31, 1995; Kevin Sack, "A Redistricted Black Lawmaker Fires Back," New York *Times*, July 4, 1996.

62. Considerable dispute broke out concerning the impact of the new black-majority districts on the 1994 Democratic losses in the South. For an overview of the controversy, see Lublin, *Paradox of Representation*, 111–14, which cites an array of authorities on the matter. Lublin himself concludes that the national GOP tide accounts for most of the 1994 Republican gain (111), an assertion supported by Paul R. Abramson, John H. Aldrich, and David W. Rohde in *Change and Continuity in the 1992 Elections*, rev. ed. (Washington, D.C., 1995). They write that "some observers have speculated that [the creation of majority-minorty districts] played a substantial role in the Democrats' loss of the House majority because of the large number of seats gained by the Republicans in the South. In our view, even a cursory evaluation of the data shows that this interpretation is insupportable. The GOP gained sixteen seats in the South in 1994, and three of those were in states (Arkansas, Mississippi, and Tennessee) in which no new majority-minority seats were created after the 1990 census" (331–32).

For a slightly different view, see Charles S. Bullock III, "Affirmative Action Districts: In Whose Faces Will They Blow Up?," *Campaigns and Elections* (April 1995), 22–23. Bullock notes: "All districts held by Democrats in 1991 in which redistricting reduced the black percentage by more than 10 points have now fallen to Republicans. The GOP took four of these districts in 1992 and two more in 1994" (22). Joseph A. Aistrup reached a similar conclusion: "Finally, contributing to [GOP] top-down advancement efforts in 1994 was the 1990s redistricting. The bleaching of many of these districts led to the diminished capacity of the Democrats' black-white coalition to withstand the GOP assault in 1994." *Southern Strategy Revisited: Republican Top-Down Advancement in the South* (Lexington, Ky., 1996), 109.

In 1996, five of the twelve southern African American members of Congress who were elected in 1992 won reelection in redrawn white-majority districts, prompting argument that black-majority districts are not needed. The post-1996 state of the black-majority district controversy is covered fully in Chapter 13, and the underlying philosophical question raised by the districting issue is treated there as well.

63. A New York *Times*/CBS News Poll taken just before the November election revealed that those who thought things in the country would be worse in five years exceeded 40 percent for the first time since the "malaise" months toward the end of the Carter administration. Katharine Q. Seelye, "Voters Disgusted with Politicians as Election Nears," New York *Times*, November 3, 1994.

64. Richard L. Berke, "Lawmakers Face Most Close Races in Many Decades: Democrats Are in Peril," New York *Times*, October 21, 1994.

65. After the 1994 elections, there were 231 Republicans to 203 Democrats in the U.S. House; in the U.S. Senate, there were 53 Republicans and 47 Democrats; and the GOP held 31 governorships to 18 for the Democrats with one state chief executive an independent.

66. Michael Wines, "Clinton Sets Campaign Theme: Change Brings Fear," New York *Times*, September 23, 1994.

67. Gwen Ifill, "Clinton Finds a Middle Lane, and Liberals a Cold Shoulder," New York *Times*, January 27, 1994. Ifill goes on to say that Sen. Paul Wellstone of Minnesota, one of the most liberal members of the Senate—as well as other liberals interviewed for the article—scoffed at "the notion that there is any such thing as a new Democrat. 'It's completely nonsensical,' " Wellstone said.

68. For an engrossing account of the 1993–1994 effort to reform the U.S. health care system, see Haynes Johnson and David S. Broder, *The System: The American Way of Politics at the Breaking Point* (Boston, 1996).

69. This is also the view of a Republican pollster, Bill McInturff, who called the health care issue "enormously pivotal in this election" when he was interviewed by Robin Toner for her November 16, 1994, New York *Times* article, "Pollsters See a Silent Storm That Swept Away Democrats." In Toner's words, "McInturff said the perception that Mr. Clinton had proposed a 'big government [health care] plan' helped strip away his image as a 'new Democrat' among voters in the South and Mountain West."

70. The phrase comes from a passage in V. O. Key's *Southern Politics*: "Politics generally comes down, over the long run, to a conflict between those who have and those who have less" (307).

71. Katharine Q. Seelye, "With Fiery Words, Gingrich Builds His Kingdom," New York *Times*, October 27, 1994.

72. *Ibid.*

73. Gingrich made the comment at an Atlanta news conference on November 9, 1994, which was carried on C-Span; the transcription was done by the author from a videotape.

74. Edward Walsh, "North Carolina Reflects Voting Shift in South: GOP Takeover Nov. 8 Both Wide and Deep," Washington *Post*, November 26, 1994. The *New York Times*/CBS Poll cited above found 71 percent of its sample had not heard of the contract. Seelye, "Voters Disgusted with Politicians."

75. Eric Pianin, "For 'Switchers,' It's a Hit or Miss," *Washington Post National Weekly Edition*, September 16–22, 1996; Adam Clymer, "Under Fire, a GOP Convert Wins Party's Fierce Loyalty," New York *Times*, April 8, 1996. For more on party switchers, see Charles Prysby, "Party Switchers and the Party System," in Charles D. Hadley and Lewis Bowman, eds., *Party Activists in Southern Politics: Mirrors and Makers of Change* (Knoxville, 1998), 144–62.

76. For example, in his January 1996 State of the Union address, President Clinton evoked thunderous cheers from the Republican congressional ranks when he declared the "era of big government is over." For a recounting of the key events, see Alison Mitchell, "Stung by Defeats in '94, Clinton Regrouped and Co-opted G.O.P. Strategies," New York *Times*, November 7, 1996.

77. Mitchell, "Stung by Defeats"; R. W. Apple, Jr., "Gingrich Concedes Mistakes, but Sees G.O.P. Trend Intact," New York *Times*, June 25, 1996.

78. Blaine Harden, "Bob Dole's Garbled Message," *Washington Post National Weekly Edition*, November 11–17, 1996.

79. For a newspaper article that caught the trend early, see Richard L. Berke, "If Clinton Sees Votes in South, He's Not Just Whistling Dixie," New York *Times*, September 13, 1996. On the

election generally, see Laurence W. Moreland and Robert P. Steed, eds., *The 1996 Presidential Election in the South: Southern Party Systems in the 1990s* (Westport, Conn., 1997).

80. A barrage of Democratic TV ads in Florida warned senior citizens that the Republicans would slash Medicare, prompting this response from Senator Dole during a West Palm Beach appearance: "Instead of working with Republicans and with the Democrats to try to secure, preserve and strengthen Medicare, the President chose to engage in a campaign to scare American seniors. We call it Mediscare! Mediscare! Mediscare! All the ads you see in Florida, all the ads you see in Florida are negative Mediscare ads!" Katharine Q. Seelye, "In Blistering Attack, Dole Says Clinton Is Using Scare Tactics," New York *Times*, September 27, 1996. See also R. W. Apple, Jr., "Florida Victory No Sure Thing for the G.O.P.," New York *Times*, September 29, 1996, and Tom Fiedler, "Rewriting the Book on Florida: How President Bucked 20-Year Trend Toward GOP," Miami *Herald*, November 6, 1996.

81. David's index of Democratic strength, which had plunged in 1994 to 44.6 percent from the 1992 precipice of 50.1 percent, only went down slightly in 1996, to 44.3 percent, perhaps an indicator of a Democratic bottoming out. See Figure 1.

2. South Carolina: A Decade of Rapid Republican Ascent

1. Interview with Whit Ayres, conducted by Lee Bandy, September 16, 1996.

2. The early years of this story have been ably chronicled by several authors. See Alexander P. Lamis, *The Two-Party South,* 2nd expanded ed. (New York, 1990), 63–75; Jack Bass and Walter DeVries, *The Transformation of Southern Politics: Social Change and Political Consequences Since 1945* (New York, 1976), 248–83; Chester W. Bain, "South Carolina: Partisan Prelude," in William C. Havard, ed., *The Changing Politics of the South* (Baton Rouge, 1972), 588–636; William V. Moore, "Parties and Electoral Politics in South Carolina," in Luther F. Carter and David Mann, eds., *Government in the Palmetto State* (Columbia, S.C., 1983), Chap. 4; Cole Blease Graham, Jr., "Partisan Change in South Carolina," in Robert H. Swansbrough and David M. Brodsky, eds., *The South's New Politics: Realignment and Dealignment* (Columbia, S.C., 1988), 158–74; and Robert P. Steed, Laurence W. Moreland, and Tod A. Baker, "South Carolina's Party System," in Luther F. Carter and David Mann, eds., *Government in the Palmetto State: Toward the Twenty-First Century* (Columbia, S.C., 1992), Chap. 2.

3. Interview with Sam Tenenbaum, conducted by Lee Bandy, September 24, 1996.

4. Interview with Ayres.

5. Interview with Don Fowler, conducted by Lee Bandy, August 28, 1996; interview with Governor Carroll Campbell, conducted by Lee Bandy, July 22, 1996.

6. Interview with Campbell.

7. Lee Bandy, "Of Campbell's Past, Dole's Future," *The State* (Columbia, S.C.), July 28, 1996; Jerry Adams, "Campbell Thanks Rural Voters," *The State*, November 6, 1986.

8. Adams, "Campbell Thanks Rural Voters"; interview with Campbell.

9. Interview with Ayres; interview with Crawford Cook, conducted by Lee Bandy, July 16, 1996.

10. Interview with Ayres.

11. Interview with Warren Tompkins, conducted by Glen Broach, August 20, 1996.

12. See Robert Steed, "South Carolina," in Andrew M. Appleton and Daniel S. Ward, eds.,

State Party Profiles: A 50-State Guide to Development, Organization, and Resources (Washington, D.C., 1997), 287–95.

13. Because of the requirements of the 1965 Voting Rights Act, the South Carolina State Election Commission keeps records of voter participation by race for both primaries and general elections. The figures given here are from the commission's *Annual Reports* for 1986–1987 and 1990–1991.

14. Levona Page, "Mitchell Loss Not a Surprise," *The State,* November 7, 1990.

15. Interview with Senator Darrell Jackson, conducted by Glen Broach, August 25, 1996; interview with Cole Blease Graham, Jr., University of South Carolina, conducted by Glen Broach, August 30, 1996; Cindi Ross Scoppe, "Senate Expels Imprisoned Mitchell," *The State,* January 18, 1995.

16. Interview with Tenenbaum.

17. Page, "Mitchell Loss Not a Surprise"; interview with Rickey Hill, South Carolina State University, conducted by Glen Broach, August 13, 1996.

18. Clark Surratt, "SC Voters Send a Message," *The State,* November 8, 1990.

19. Clark Surratt, "Voters Give Campbell Big Win," *The State,* November 7, 1990.

20. Interview with Campbell.

21. For more on this election, see Laurence W. Moreland, "South Carolina: Republican Again," in Robert P. Steed, Laurence W. Moreland, and Tod A. Baker, eds., *The 1992 Presidential Election in the South: Current Patterns of Southern Party and Electoral Politics* (Westport, Conn., 1994), 83–100.

22. These figures are reported in the November 1992 issue of *The Carolina Report,* a public affairs newsletter edited by Glen T. Broach.

23. Lee Bandy, "Hollings Victorious in Mud-Caked Race," *The State,* November 4, 1992.

24. Michael Barone, Grant Ujifusa and Douglas Matthews, eds., *The Almanac of American Politics 1992* (New York, 1992), 1127.

25. Cindi Ross Scoppe, "S.C. Bucks National Change Trend," *The State,* November 4, 1992.

26. Interview with Fowler.

27. Cindi Ross Scoppe, "Beasley Switch Wounds Democrats," *The State,* September 12, 1991; interview with Governor David Beasley, conducted by Lee Bandy, November 18, 1996.

28. South Carolina Election Commission, *Annual Report 1994–1995,* p. 21.

29. V. O. Key, Jr., *Southern Politics in State and Nation* (New York, 1949), 135–42.

30. Lee Bandy, "Despite Light Touch, Theodore's a Heavyweight, Friends Say," *The State,* June 12, 1994; Lee Bandy, "Friends, Neighbors Saved Beasley," *The State,* November 10, 1994.

31. Lee Bandy, "Beasley Officially Kicks Off Run For Governor," *The State,* May 18, 1994.

32. Lee Bandy, "Theodore Promises a Better Tomorrow," *The State,* June 16, 1994.

33. Related by George Shissias, Richland County Republican chairman, during an interview conducted by Glen Broach, August 20, 1996.

34. Lee Bandy, "Adjutant General Joins GOP," *The State,* September 22, 1995.

35. Nina Brook, "Democrats' Strategy: Switch Now, Win Later," *The State,* August 10, 1995; Nina Brook, "GOP Lands Key Democrat," *The State,* August 9, 1995.

36. Earl Black and Merle Black, *Politics and Society in the South* (Cambridge, Mass., 1987). See Chap. 3, "The Rise of Middle-Class Society," esp. pp. 56–57.

37. Key, *Southern Politics,* 130–55; Bernard Cosman, *Five States for Goldwater* (University, Ala., 1966), 66–67; Donald Fowler, *Presidential Voting in South Carolina, 1948–1964* (Columbia, S.C.,

1966); Chester Bain, "South Carolina: Partisan Prelude," in William C. Havard, ed., *The Changing Politics of the South* (Baton Rouge, 1972), 588–636.

38. For a treatment of this phenomenon nationwide, see Thomas Byrne Edsall with Mary D. Edsall, *Chain Reaction: The Impact of Race, Rights and Taxes on American Politics* (New York, 1991).

39. Interview with Graham; Carol S. Botsch and Robert E. Botsch, "African Americans in South Carolina Politics," *Journal of Political Science*, XXIV (1996), 63–102.

40. John F. Persinos, "Has the Christian Right Taken Over the Republican Party?" *Campaigns and Elections* (September 1994), 22.

41. See Glen T. Broach, "The Political Attitudes of South Carolina Christian School Educators," *Journal of Political Science,* XXIII (1995), 141–55.

42. Interview with Shissias.

43. *Ibid.*

44. Robert P. Steed reported that South Carolina Democratic activists saw little improvement during the 1980s in their party's ability to perform such basic party functions as candidate recruitment, fundraising, and the effective use of modern campaign technology. The vast majority of Republican activists, on the other hand, gave their party high marks in performing these tasks. Steed, "South Carolina," in Appleton and Ward, eds., *State Party Profiles*, 292.

45. A survey of local party officials in South Carolina shows that Democratic officials are decidedly more liberal than Republicans both in ideological self-identification and on a wide range of social and economic issues. Robert P. Steed, Laurence W. Moreland, and Tod A. Baker, "Electoral and Party Development in South Carolina," *Journal of Political Science,* XXIV (1996), 33–62. See also by the same authors, "South Carolina: Toward a Two-Party System," in Charles D. Hadley and Lewis Bowman, eds., *Southern State Party Organizations and Activists* (Westport, Conn., 1995), 183–97.

46. *The State*, November 8, 1996.

47. For more on this election, see Laurence W. Moreland and Robert P. Steed, "South Carolina: Elephants Stroll Through the Palmettos," in Laurence W. Moreland and Robert P. Steed, eds., *The 1996 Presidential Election in the South: Southern Party Systems in the 1990s* (Westport, Conn., 1997), 111–28.

48. Interview with Jackson; Cindi Ross Scoppe, "Senate Redistrict Plan Keeps Democrats' Edge," *The State*, April 5, 1995.

49. These trends are identified from data published in the biennial reports of the South Carolina Election Commission.

50. Interview with Jackson.

51. *Ibid.*; interview with Hill.

52. Lee Bandy, " 'Blind Hogs,' Battle Flags and the GOP," *The State*, January 12, 1997; Lee Bandy, "Fairfield's Winds Favor Battle Flag," *The State*, February 15, 1997. Beasley's State of the State address was reprinted in *The State*, January 23, 1997.

53. Michael Sponhour, "SC Leaders Join Beasley on Flag Plan," *The State*, November 28, 1996.

54. See Murray Edelman, *Constructing the Political Spectacle* (Chicago, 1988).

55. Bandy, "Fairfield's Winds."

56. The flag issue is so divisive that for the most part both Republican and Democratic candidates avoided mention of it during the 1998 election campaign. An important exception was Beasley, who found himself in a close race for reelection against Democratic nominee Jim Hodges, a former legislator from Lancaster. Attempting to shore up his support in the "heritage community,"

the politically correct term for fervent supporters of the battle flag, Beasley renewed an earlier pledge to never again propose removing the flag from atop the statehouse. To support the governor, a group of Republican legislators who had opposed him on the issue signed a letter endorsing Beasley as the preferred candidate of flag adherents. Apart from this low-key effort by Beasley to mend Republican fences, the flag issue was rarely mentioned during the 1998 campaign.

3. North Carolina: Between Helms and Hunt No Majority Emerges

1. Ferrel Guillory, "N.C.'s 1950 Senate Race Echoed Again in 1990," Raleigh *News and Observer*, November 30, 1990.

2. For more on Helms's career, see Ernest Furgurson, *Hard Right: The Rise of Jesse Helms* (New York, 1986).

3. Interview with Gene Lanier, conducted by Rob Christensen, July 30, 1996; Voter News Service, North Carolina Exit Poll, November 1990 and 1996.

4. Rob Christensen, "Helms Targets Homosexual Donations to Gantt," *News and Observer*, October 24, 1990; Jane Ruffin and Bill Krueger, "Helms, Aides Deny Voter Intimidation, Suit Settled to Avoid Costly Court Fight," *News and Observer*, February 28, 1992.

5. Interview with Gary Pearce, conducted by Rob Christensen, June 14, 1996.

6. Jena Heath, "Get Out the Vote Effort in High Gear," *News and Observer*, November 4, 1996; interview with Thurston Quinn, conducted by Rob Christensen, July 30, 1996.

7. Interview with Carter Wrenn, conducted by Rob Christensen, November 6, 1996; Rob Christensen, "Helms, Gantt Reach for the Middle," *News and Observer*, September 22, 1996; interview with Alex Castellanos, conducted by Rob Christensen, July 20, 1996.

8. Christensen, "Helms, Gantt Reach for the Middle."

9. *Ibid.*

10. Interview with Jim Andrews, conducted by Rob Christensen, November 6, 1996; Voter News Service, North Carolina Exit Poll, November 1996 (see Table 9); interview with William Snider, conducted by Rob Christensen, November 6, 1996.

11. Bill Krueger, "Helms Breaks 20 Year Connection to Congressional Club," *News and Observer*, August 6, 1994; Bill Krueger, "Helms, Ex-Ally Feuding over Fund-Raising," *News and Observer*, October 3, 1994; Rob Christensen, "Wrenn Moves His Office to the Country," *News and Observer*, July 14, 1995.

12. Interview with Pearce. For more on the changing nature of the state's Democrats and Republicans, see Paul Luebke, *Tar Heel Politics: Myths and Realities* (Chapel Hill, N.C., 1990).

13. Interview with Wilton Duke, conducted by Rob Christensen, October 15, 1996; interview with Janice Faulkner, conducted by Rob Christensen, June 18, 1996. For more on these changes, see Earl Black and Merle Black, *Politics and Society in the South* (Cambridge, Mass., 1987), Chaps. 4–7 and 10, and Charles D. Hadley and Harold W. Stanley, "Blacks, the Biracial Coalition, and Political Change, " in Tod A. Baker, Charles D. Hadley, Robert P. Steed, and Laurence W. Moreland, eds., *Political Parties in the Southern States: Party Activists in Partisan Coalitions* (New York, 1990), 43–64.

14. Interview with Jack Hawke, conducted by Rob Christensen, June 18, 1996.

15. *Ibid.*

16. Joe Neff, "Funderburk Pleads No Contest," *News and Observer*, October 31, 1996; Jim

Rosen, "Income Comments Cause Flap," *News and Observer,* October 26, 1996; Joe Neff, "Labor Spending Dominated N.C.," *News and Observer,* October 19, 1996.

17. Rob Christensen, "Taking Off the Gloves," *News and Observer,* September 11, 1992.

18. Interview with Faulkner.

19. Interview with Pearce.

20. Interview with Chris Scott, conducted by Rob Christensen, June 28, 1996; interview with Hawke.

21. Marshall was recruited by the Democratic party to replace another good ol' boy politician, Rufus Edmisten. Edmisten, a former aide to U.S. Senator Sam Ervin, was an attorney general and gubernatorial candidate before being elected secretary of state in 1988. But he was forced to resign in 1996 because of allegations of mismanagement and putting a young woman friend on the state payroll. Edmisten was noted for hanging out at stock car races and giving lusty renditions of "Honkey Tonk Angel" at political events. "Can you not be a character any more and be in public life?" Edmisten asked as the newspapers and the state auditor were investigating him. "Can you not laugh and dance and sing and be in political life? Apparently not." Bill Krueger, "A Secretary with a Style All of His Own," *News and Observer,* October 22, 1995.

22. Rob Christensen, "The Snake Sure Is Ugly, but Is It Bad for North Carolina?" *News and Observer,* July 12, 1993.

23. *Shaw v. Reno,* 503 U.S. 630 (1993); *Shaw v. Hunt,* 517 U.S. 899 (1996); Juliana Gruenwald, "Minority Districts' Fate Uncertain Following Supreme Court Ruling," *Congressional Quarterly Weekly Report,* June 15, 1996, pp. 1705–06; David Rice, "State Senate Backs New Map of Districts," *Winston-Salem Journal,* March 28, 1997; "North Carolina's Map Heads To Justice, Judges for OK," *Congressional Quarterly Weekly Report,* April 5, 1997, p. 810; Alan Greenblatt, "Texas, North Carolina Maps Upheld by Federal Panels," *Congressional Quarterly Weekly Report,* September 20, 1997, p. 2250; David Rice, "Judges: Race Was Key," *Winston-Salem Journal,* April 15, 1998. See also Richard K. Scher, Jon L. Mills, and John J. Hotaling, "Voting Rights in the South After Shaw and Miller: The End of Racial Fairness?" in Robert P. Steed, Laurence W. Moreland, and Tod A. Baker, eds., *Southern Parties and Elections: Studies in Regional Political Change* (Tuscaloosa, Ala., 1997), 9–36.

24. Interview with Pearce; interview with Melvin Watt, conducted by Rob Christensen, July 20, 1995.

25. For more on the 1996 election in North Carolina, see Charles Prysby, "North Carolina: Republican Consolidation or Democratic Resurgence?" in Laurence W. Moreland and Robert P. Steed, eds., *The 1996 Presidential Election in the South: Southern Party Systems in the 1990s* (Westport, Conn., 1997), 165–81.

26. Institute for Research in Social Science, Carolina Poll (November 1996); Jack D. Fleer, *North Carolina Government and Politics* (Lincoln, Nebr., 1994), 152–58.

27. For a discussion of the turnout issue, see Fleer, *North Carolina Government and Politics,* 157; Paul R. Abramson, John H. Aldrich, and David W. Rohde, *Change and Continuity in the 1992 Elections,* rev. ed. (Washington, D.C., 1995), Chap. 4.

28. Mebane Rash Whitman, "The Evolution of Party Politics: The March of the GOP Continues in North Carolina," *North Carolina Insight* (September 1995), 81–97; Chandler Davidson and Bernard Grofman, eds., *Quiet Revolution in the South: The Impact of the Voting Rights Act, 1965–1990* (Princeton, 1994), Chap. 6; Institute for Research in Social Science, Chapel Hill, N.C., *North Carolina DataNet* (May 1994), 13–14.

29. William Snider, *Hunt and Helms* (Chapel Hill, N.C., 1985); interview with Ed Turlington,

conducted by Jack D. Fleer, July 30, 1996; Charles L. Prysby, "The North Carolina 1990 Senate Election," in Huey L. Perry, ed., *Race, Politics and Governance in the United States* (Gainesville, Fla., 1996), 29–46.

30. Prysby, "The North Carolina 1990 Senate Election," 38; Rob Christensen, "Jesse's People," *News and Observer*, October 6, 1996.

31. Carolina Poll, April 1996. See Robert Darcy, Janet M. Clark, Charles D. Hadley, "The Changing Roles of Women in Southern State Party Politics," in Baker *et al.*, eds., *Political Parties in the Southern States*, 88–102.

32. *North Carolina DataNet* (June 1996), 13; Gail Collins, "Wooing the Women," *New York Times Magazine*, July 28, 1996, p. 35; Steven Stark, "Gap Politics," *Atlantic Monthly* (July 1996), 71–80.

33. Voter News Service, North Carolina Exit Poll, November 1990, 1992, 1996; Jack D. Fleer, Roger C. Lowery, and Charles L. Prysby, "Political Change in North Carolina," in Robert H. Swansbrough and David M. Brodsky, eds., *The South's New Politics: Realignment and Dealignment* (Columbia, S.C., 1988), 102.

34. Interview with Sim DeLapp, conducted by Jack D. Fleer, July 16, 1996; *North Carolina DataNet* (January 1995), 6–7; Clyde Wilcox, *Onward Christian Soldiers? The Religious Right in American Politics* (Boulder, Colo., 1996); Tod A. Baker, "The Emergence of the Religious Right and the Development of the Two-Party System in the South," in Baker *et al.*, eds., *Political Parties in the Southern States*, 135–47.

35. Charles Prysby, "North Carolina: Conflicting Forces in a Confusing Year," in Robert P. Steed, Laurence W. Moreland, and Tod A. Baker, eds., *The 1992 Presidential Election in the South: Current Patterns of Southern Party and Electoral Politics* (Westport, Conn., 1994), 147–48; Voter News Service, North Carolina Exit Poll, November 1992, 1996; John F. Persinos, "Has the Christian Right Taken Over the Republican Party?" *Campaigns and Elections* (September 1994), 21–24; Wilcox, *Onward Christian Soldiers?* 76–77; interview with DeLapp; interview with James Holshouser, conducted by Jack D. Fleer, August 23, 1996.

36. *North Carolina DataNet* (March 1997), 4; North Carolina Board of Elections, election statistics for appropriate years.

37. Voter News Service, North Carolina Exit Poll, November 1990, 1992, 1996; *North Carolina DataNet* (October 1996), 4–5, (March 1997), 22.

38. *North Carolina DataNet* (May 1994), 8–9; Fleer, *North Carolina Government and Politics*, 163. The North Carolina experience duplicates a regional and national pattern of widespread incumbency reelection. See John F. Bibby, *Politics, Parties, and Elections in America*, 3rd ed. (Chicago, 1996), 287, 292, and 299–301.

39. Joseph A. Aistrup, *The Southern Strategy Revisited: Republican Top-Down Advancement in the South* (Lexington, Ky., 1996), Chaps. 5–10.

40. When Gardner became North Carolina's first twentieth-century Republican lieutenant governor, the Democratic majority in the state senate stripped him of the power to appoint committees and committee chairs and to assign bills. The senate Democrats found they liked a weak lieutenant governor and did not restore the powers to the office when Democrat Dennis Wicker was elected to the post in 1992.

41. Fleer, *North Carolina Government and Politics*, 165–8; Charles L. Prysby, "North Carolina," in Andrew Appleton and Daniel S. Ward, eds., *State Party Profiles* (Washington, D.C., 1997), 234–243; interview with Robert Wilkie, director, North Carolina Republican party, conducted by Jack

D. Fleer, August 21, 1996; interview with Libba Evans, chair, North Carolina Democratic party, conducted by Jack D. Fleer, August 19, 1996.

42. Helen Dewar, "North Carolina's Stark Clash: Faircloth, Democratic Lawyer Duel in Tight, Sharply Defined Race," Washington *Post*, July 11, 1998.

43. Interview with Hawke.

44. Interview with Pearce.

45. Interview with Hawke.

4. Georgia: Democratic Bastion No Longer

1. Interview with Johnny Isakson, conducted by Tom Baxter, September 27, 1996.

2. Deborah Scroggins and Jeanne Cummings, "Miller Actions Upgraded Pension," Atlanta *Constitution*, June 28, 1990.

3. V. O. Key, Jr., *Southern Politics in State and Nation* (New York, 1949), 112–17; A. L. May, "Young Gears Up for Statewide Race," Atlanta *Constitution*, February 5, 1990; Michael Binford, "Andrew Young for Governor," paper presented to the Voter Education Project conference, "From Protest to Politics: 25th Anniversary of the 1965 Voting Rights Act," Clark Atlanta University, November 16, 1990.

4. Interview with Zell Miller, conducted by Tom Baxter, September 30, 1996; A. L. May, " 'Barracuda' Has His Teeth in Miller's Bid for Governor," Atlanta *Constitution*, April 8, 1990; Jeanne Cummings, "Miller's Financial Clout Is Evident in His First TV Spots," Atlanta *Constitution*, April 21, 1990.

5. Interview with Miller; David Beiler, "White Knights, Dark Horses," *Campaigns and Elections*, VIII (September/October 1987), 42–53. The HOPE scholarship program was created to provide tuition scholarships to a state college or university for all B-average high school students whose parents' income was less than $66,000 per year. The student can keep the scholarship by maintaining a B average in college work.

6. Interview with Isakson; A . L. May, "Miller: Young Dodging Crime Issue," Atlanta *Constitution*, April 9, 1990; Tom Baxter and A. L. May, "Issues Outweigh Race More for Atlanta Blacks," Atlanta *Constitution*, July 13, 1990.

7. Jeanne Cummings, "Isakson Vows Not to Restrict Women's Right to Abortion," Atlanta *Constitution*, May 20, 1990.

8. A. L. May and Tom Baxter, "Miller Stuns Isakson as Debate Gets Personal," Atlanta *Constitution*, October 15, 1990.

9. Charles Walston, "In Contest for No. 2 Spot, Howard Tops $2 Million," Atlanta *Constitution*, October 29, 1990.

10. Tom Baxter, "Those Not in Running May Merit More Attention," Atlanta *Constitution*, July 1, 1991; Douglas Lavin, "Miller: Tighten Belts, Cut Vacant Jobs," Atlanta *Constitution*, January 9, 1991.

11. Interview with Miller.

12. Robert Watts, "Far-flung Eleventh," Atlanta *Constitution*, May 15, 1992.

13. Tom Baxter, "Strange Company," Atlanta *Constitution*, August 20, 1995; Kathey Alexander, "Blacks, GOP Pick Up Leverage in Redistricting," Atlanta *Constitution*, August 23, 1995; Tom Baxter, "Rethinking Reapportionment," Atlanta *Constitution*, January 26, 1992; Kevin Hill, "Does the Creation of Majority Black Districts Aid Republicans?" *Journal of Politics*, LVII (1995), 384–401.

14. Charles Walston, "Gingrich in a Cliffhanger Fight," Atlanta *Constitution*, July 22, 1992.

15. Tom Baxter, "McKinney and Bishop Use Different Strategies to Grab Primary Victories," Atlanta *Constitution*, August 12, 1992; Charles Walston and Steve Harvey, "State Sends Washington More Diverse Delegation" Atlanta *Constitution*, November 4, 1992.

16. Tom Baxter, "Georgia Just Might Make or Break 'em," Atlanta *Constitution*, August 19, 1992. For more on this election, see Brad Lockerbie and John A. Clark, "Georgia: A State in Transition," in Robert P. Steed, Laurence W. Moreland, and Tod A. Baker, eds., *The 1992 Presidential Election in the South: Current Patterns of Southern Party and Electoral Politics* (Westport, Conn., 1994), 39–50.

17. Mark Sherman, "Ex-Allies Turning Away from Fowler," Atlanta *Constitution*, October 3, 1992; Mark Sherman, "Fowler's Vote on Hill Case Is Defended," Atlanta *Constitution*, October 28, 1992; Mark Sherman, "Fowler Also Has a Big Fund-Raising Lead," Atlanta *Constitution*, October 15, 1992; Mark Sherman, "Senate Race Got Past Nasty," Atlanta *Constitution*, November 1, 1992.

18. Charles Walston, "Coverdell Launching TV, Radio Spots," Atlanta *Constitution*, September 30, 1992. The refrain of the jingle was: "Let's put Paul Coverdell in the Senate / and put Wyche Fowler out. / Wyche has proved we don't need him in it / and Georgia wants him out."

19. Mark Sherman, "Senate Race Heading into Home Stretch—Again," Atlanta *Constitution*, November 5, 1992; Mark Sherman, " 'Soft Money' Aided GOP in Runoff," Atlanta *Constitution*, December 2, 1992; Mark Sherman, "Outspent Overall, Coverdell Put More into Runoff Ads," Atlanta *Constitution*, December 10, 1992; Craig Teegardin, "Newcomers to Suburbia Bolster Republican Party," Atlanta *Constitution*, November 12, 1992.

20. Charles Walston, "6th District Race Captures the Eye of National Media," Atlanta *Constitution*, July 16, 1992; Walston, "Gingrich in Cliffhanger."

21. Mark Sherman, "Little Applause for Miller's Call to Change Flag," Atlanta *Constitution*, January 13, 1993; Tom Baxter, "Run This Up the Flagpole: What Is Zell Doing?" Atlanta *Constitution*, January 13, 1993.

22. Interview with Miller; interview with Howard.

23. Tom Baxter, "New Breed in Politics: Wealthy Businessmen," Atlanta *Constitution*, October 20, 1994; Mark Sherman and Ben Smith III, "Millner: 'Ordinary Guy' with 6 Baths, 16 Rooms," Atlanta *Constitution*, May 29, 1994.

24. Mark Sherman, "Candidates on Spending Spree," Atlanta *Constitution*, November 2, 1994.

25. Mark Sherman, "Personal Attacks Mark Governor's Race," Atlanta *Constitution*, October 12, 1994; Charles Walston, "New Millner Ad Tries to Link Governor with Federal Tax Increase, Clinton," Atlanta *Constitution*, September 28, 1994; Mark Sherman, "GOP Launches New Attack on 'Pork Barrel' Golf Course," Atlanta *Constitution*, September 28, 1994.

26. Mark Sherman, "Governor Likely to Make Finances a Campaign Issue," Atlanta *Constitution*, May 29, 1994; Ken Foskett, "Miller Goes South to Show Up a GOP Foe," Atlanta *Constitution*, May 5, 1994; Tom Baxter, "Governor Feisty in Old-Time Slug Fest," Atlanta *Constitution*, October 28, 1994.

27. Tom Baxter, "Student Aid a Good Bet for Miller," Atlanta *Constitution*, October 27, 1994.

28. Mark Sherman, "Zell Miller's Giant Scare," Atlanta *Constitution*, November 9, 1994.

29. Lucy Soto and Charles Walston, "Endangered Candidates? Johnson, Darden on List," Atlanta *Constitution*, November 1, 1994.

30. Mike Christensen, "No Perks for Switch, Deal Says," Atlanta *Constitution*, April 11, 1995.

31. 515 U.S. 900; Mark Sherman, "Redistricting Back in Hands of Federal Court," Atlanta *Constitution*, September 13, 1995.

32. Mark Sherman, "Map Has Legislators Reeling," Atlanta *Constitution*, December 14, 1995; Mark Sherman and Kathey Alexander, "Map Called a Disaster for Black Voters," Atlanta *Constitution*, December 14, 1995.

33. Scott Oliver, "The Sanford Bishop and Cynthia McKinney Campaigns," M.A. research paper, Georgia State University, 1997.

34. Marlin Manuel, "Coles Faces Tough Cookies in Bid to Unseat Gingrich," Atlanta *Constitution*, July 11, 1996; Marlin Manuel, "6th District Race May Top Election Tabs," Atlanta *Constitution*, December 6, 1996.

35. Mark Sherman, "A Cloud on Cleland's Ethics Record," Atlanta *Constitution*, September 15, 1996.

36. Tom Baxter, "What If They Held an Election and Nobody Came?" Atlanta *Constitution*, July 7, 1996.

37. Kathey Alexander, "Isakson Gambles by Pushing Abortion-Rights Stance in Ads," Atlanta *Constitution*, June 13, 1996.

38. Interview with Isakson.

39. See the Tennessee chapter for an account of Perdue's work in that state.

40. Kathey Alexander, "Millner Hasn't Won Over All His GOP Foes," Atlanta *Constitution*, September 15, 1996.

41. Rhonda Cook and Kathey Alexander, "Millner Airs Attack Ad About Freed Murderer," Atlanta *Constitution*, October 5, 1996; Siobhan Morrissey, "Traditions Die Hard at Exclusive Club," Atlanta *Constitution*, September 25, 1996; Federal Election Commission from www.fec.gov/1996/states/ga-02.htm.

42. For more on this election, see John A. Clark and Brad Lockerbie, "Georgia: Two-Party Political Reality!" in Laurence W. Moreland and Robert P. Steed, eds., *The 1996 Presidential Election in the South: Southern Party Systems in the 1990s* (Westport, Conn., 1997), 65–76.

43. Michael Binford, "Georgia: Political Realignment or Partisan Evolution," in Robert H. Swansbrough and David M. Brodsky, eds., *The South's New Politics: Realignment and Dealignment* (Columbia, S.C., 1988), 175–88; Tom Baxter, "It's Going to Be a Bumpy Ride," Atlanta *Constitution*, November 7, 1996. See also Arnold Fleischmann and Carol Pierannunzi, *Politics in Georgia* (Athens, Ga., 1997), and Brad Lockerbie and John A. Clark, "Georgia: Two-Party Political Reality?" in Charles D. Hadley and Lewis Bowman, eds., *Southern State Party Organizations and Activists* (Westport, Conn., 1995), 127–43.

44. Craig Teegardin, "Republicans' Sweep of South Tied to Suburban Boom," Atlanta *Constitution*, November 13, 1994.

45. *Demographics USA, 1996 County Edition* (New York, 1996); Eunice Moscoso, "Georgia to Keep Up Fast-Paced Growth," Atlanta *Constitution*, October 23, 1996; registered voter figures from Georgia Secretary of State's Office; David Pendred and Kathey Alexander, "Partisan Pains: Adjusting to a Two Party System Can Be Difficult," Atlanta *Constitution*, November 13, 1994.

46. Charmagne Helton, " Black Voter Turnout Gains," Atlanta *Constitution* July 11, 1996.

47. Based on official voter results, Georgia secretary of state's office.

48. David E. Sturrock, "Out of the Phone Booths: Republican Primaries in the Deep South," in Robert P. Steed, Laurence W. Moreland, and Tod A. Baker, eds., *Southern Parties and Elections: Studies in Regional Political Change* (Tuscaloosa, Ala., 1997), 95–108.

49. Interview with Paul Coverdell, conducted by David E. Sturrock, October 28, 1996.

50. Interview with Matt Metcalf, conducted by David E. Sturrock, October 29, 1996; interview with Alec Poitevint, conducted by David E. Sturrock, December 4, 1996. For more on recent

party organizational development, see John A. Clark, "Georgia," in Andrew M. Appleton and Daniel S. Ward, eds., *State Party Profiles: A 50-State Guide to Development, Organization, and Resources* (Washington, D.C., 1997), 66–72.

51. Charles Walston, "GOP Calls Win Proof of Power," Atlanta *Constitution*, November 26, 1996; interview with Whit Ayres, conducted by David E. Sturrock, October 15, 1996; interview with Poitevint.

52. See Alan Ehrenhalt, "Twilight of the Bubba Era," *Governing* (July 1995), for an account of how suburban and rural legislators interact.

53. Interview with Poitevint; David Pendred and Kathey Alexander, "Partisan Pains: Adjusting to a Two-Party System Can Be Difficult," Atlanta *Constitution*, November 13, 1994; *State of Georgia Official Directory of Federal, State and County Officers* (Atlanta, Secretary of State, 1995). In the Atlanta metropolitan area the following county commissions were majority Republican in 1995: Cherokee, Cobb, Coweta, Douglas, Fayette, Forsyth, Gwinnett, Henry, Rockdale and Spalding. Only Clayton, DeKalb, Fulton and Hall had Democratic majorities.

54. Interview with Tommy Irvin, conducted by David E. Sturrock, October 16, 1996; interview with Steve Anthony, conducted by David E. Sturrock, October 16, 1996; interviews with Coverdell and Ayres.

55. Interviews with Irvin and Coverdell.

56. Interview with Ayres.

57. Interview with Anthony.

58. Alexander P. Lamis, *The Two-Party South*, 2nd expanded ed. (New York, 1990), 99; interview with Tom Murphy, conducted by David E. Sturrock, October 25, 1996; interview with Ayres.

59. Interviews with Irvin and Anthony.

5. Virginia: Republicans Surge in the Competitive Dominion

1. V. O. Key, Jr., *Southern Politics in State and Nation* (New York, 1949), 19–35.

2. Interview with C. Richard Cranwell, conducted by Margaret Edds, September 5,1996.

3. For the letter to party activists in which Senator Robb explained his actions, see "The Text of Sen. Robb's Letter," Norfolk *Virginian-Pilot*, March 11, 1994.

4. Interview with Anne B. Kincaid, conducted by Margaret Edds, July 11,1996.

5. The trend line does not include the GOP's 1997 gubernatorial victory.

6. Interview with Mark R. Warner, conducted by Margaret Edds, July 22, 1996.

7. For data on these and subsequent elections, see Larry Sabato's *Virginia Votes* series, published annually by the University of Virginia's Weldon Cooper Center for Public Service.

8. Interview with M. Boyd Marcus, Jr., conducted by Margaret Edds, June 19, 1996.

9. Jeff Schapiro, Pamela Stallsmith, and Michael Hardy, "Equal-Say Agreement Is Reached," Richmond *Times-Dispatch*, January 16, 1998.

10. Interview with J. Randy Forbes, conducted by Margaret Edds, July 1996.

11. Dwayne Yancey, *When Hell Froze Over: The Untold Story of Doug Wilder: A Black Politician's Rise to Power in the South* (Dallas, 1988). For other books on Wilder, see Don Baker, *Wilder: Hold Fast to Dreams* (Cabin John, Md., 1989), and Margaret Edds, *Claiming the Dream: The Victorious Campaign of Douglas Wilder of Virginia* (Chapel Hill, N.C., 1990).

12. Edds, *Claiming the Dream*, 71.

13. *Ibid.*, 154, 192.

14. Interview with Marcus; interview with Jerrauld Jones, conducted by Margaret Edds, August 5, 1996.

15. Warren Fiske, "The Wilder Years," *Virginian-Pilot*, December 26, 1993. For an analysis of the Wilder term, see also Thomas R. Morris, "Virginia: L. Douglas Wilder, Governing and Campaigning," in Thad Beyle, ed., *Governors and Hard Times* (Washington, D.C., 1992), 189–204.

16. Interview with Jones.

17. *Ibid.*

18. The source asked to remain anonymous.

19. Interview with Mark Warner.

20. For a chronology of events, see John F. Harris, "Charles S. Robb: The Unmaking of a Politician," *Washington Post*, June 7, 1992.

21. For more on this election, see John J. McGlennon, "Virginia: A Different Story with the Same Ending," in Robert P. Steed, Laurence W. Moreland, and Tod A. Baker, eds., *The 1992 Presidential Election in the South: Current Patterns of Southern Party and Electoral Politics* (Westport, Conn., 1994), 181–93.

22. Interview with Michael E. Thomas, conducted by Margaret Edds, June 19, 1996.

23. *Ibid.*

24. *Ibid.*

25. The source asked to remain anonymous.

26. Rob Eure, "Wilder Criticizes Terry's Strategy in Campaign," *Virginian-Pilot*, September 29, 1993.

27. Interview with George Allen, conducted by Margaret Edds, August 10, 1996.

28. Interview with Gerald L. Baliles, conducted by Margaret Edds, September 1996.

29. Interview with Marcus.

30. Margaret Edds, "Goode Unveils TV Ad Linking Robb to 'Prostitutes,' 'Young Girls,' " *Virginian-Pilot*, May 28, 1994.

31. Warren Fiske and Margaret Edds, "GOP: North's the One," *Virginian-Pilot*, June 5, 1994.

32. Margaret Edds and Alec Klein, "Robb Counting on His Sense of Timing," *Virginian-Pilot*, November 5, 1994.

33. David Poole, Margaret Edds, and Greg Schneider, "Senate Campaign Turns Nasty, *Virginian-Pilot*, October 7, 1994; David M. Poole, "Robb Calls North Ad on Drug Dealer 'Blatant Lie,' " *Virginian-Pilot*, October 14, 1994.

34. Alec Klein, "Nancy Reagan Calls North a Liar," *Virginian-Pilot*, October 29, 1994; Warren Fiske, "Reagan: North Lying, Ex-President 'Steamed' by Candidate's Remarks," *Virginian-Pilot*, March 18, 1994.

35. *Moon v. Meadows* (U.S. District Court, Eastern District of Virginia, three-judge panel decision, February 7, 1997); Laura LaFay, "House Okays New 3rd District," *Virginian-Pilot*, February 3, 1998.

36. Margaret Edds, "Allen: Power To the People," *Virginian-Pilot*, January 14, 1994; interview with Allen.

37. Interview with Allen.

38. Interview with Douglas Wilder, conducted by Margaret Edds, July 1996.

39. David M. Poole, "Education and Environment Gain Allen's Support," *Virginian-Pilot*, December 21, 1996.

40. Democratic resilience at the state legislative level was demonstrated in special elections to

fill vacancies in 1996. Democrats held the open state senate seat vacated by Virgil Goode, who ran for Congress in 1996, and picked up one of two open GOP house seats in Northern Virginia.

41. David Poole, "Small Town Gets to Compare Warners," *Virginian-Pilot*, September 3, 1996.

42. David Poole, "John Warner Campaign Ad Used Altered Photograph of Foe," *Virginian-Pilot*, October 10, 1996.

43. Margaret Edds, "Could Bob Dole Really Lose Virginia?" *Virginian-Pilot*, August 11, 1996; Larry Sabato, "The 1996 Presidential and Congressional Contests: A Status Quo Election With Spice," manuscript draft, dated December 19, 1996, of a forthcoming volume in Sabato's *Virginia Votes* series, p. 48. For more on this election, see John J. McGlennon, "Virginia: Old Habits Die Hard," in Laurence W. Moreland and Robert P. Steed, eds., *The 1996 Presidential Election in the South: Southern Party Systems in the 1990s* (Westport, Conn., 1997), 209–20.

44. This discussion of voting behavior by Virginia regions relies on the classifications used by Larry Sabato in "1996 Presidential and Congressional Contests," in the *Virginia Votes* series.

45. That base was critical to Earley's winning a four-way primary race for the GOP nomination.

46. Larry Sabato, "The 1997 Virginia Election for Governor," manuscript draft, dated December 17, 1997, for a forthcoming volume in his *Virginia Votes* series, p. 3.

47. *Ibid.*, 27.

48. *Ibid.*, 8, 23, 31. Several years ago, Sabato, who has chronicled and analyzed state elections for over two decades in his *Virginia Votes* series, identified ten factors or "keys to the governor's mansion." The state of the economy is the first key, with the party controlling the governorship at the time of the election seen as benefiting in good times and disadvantaged in bad times. The other keys are: party unity, scandal, campaign organization and technology, campaign money, candidate personality and appeal, prior office experience of candidates, retrospective judgment on the previous governor, presidential popularity, and special issues or unforeseen circumstances. In 1997 Sabato saw Gilmore as controlling six of the ten keys (economy, party unity, organization and technology, money, judgment on previous governor, and special issues). Three others favored neither candidate, and Beyer held an advantage only in personality. Sabato, "The 1997 Virginia Election," 4.

49. Alexander P. Lamis, *The Two-Party South*, 2nd expanded ed. (New York, 1990), 145–62. See also John J. McGlennon, "Virginia's Changing Party Politics, 1976–1986," in Robert H. Swansbrough and David M. Brodsky, eds., *The South's New Politics: Realignment and Dealignment* (Columbia, S.C., 1988), 56–75, and John J. McGlennon, "Virginia: Experience with Democracy," in Charles D. Hadley and Lewis Bowman, eds., *Southern State Party Organizations and Activists* (Westport, Conn., 1995), 91–108.

50. David Poole, "Former Gov. Accuses Lt. Gov. Beyer of Stifling Racial Equality," *Virginian-Pilot*, December 12, 1996; Ledyard King, "Democrats Ask: What's the Best Way to Forge a Comeback?" *Virginian-Pilot*, December 7, 1997.

51. Frank B. Atkinson, *The Dynamic Dominion: Realignment and the Rise of Virginia's Republican Party Since 1945* (Fairfax, 1992), 430–36; Mark J. Rozell and Clyde Wilcox, *Second Coming: The New Christian Right in Virginia Politics* (Baltimore, 1996), 43–44.

52. Rozell and Wilcox, *Second Coming*, 186–7.

53. Sabato, *Virginia Votes, 1991–1994*, 52.

54. Rozell and Wilcox, *Second Coming*, 183.

55. Richmond *Times-Dispatch*, June 3, 1996.

56. See Rozell and Wilcox, *Second Coming*.

57. Commonwealth of Virginia, *1995 Report of the Attorney General* (Richmond, 1995), 165–68.

An adverse U.S. Supreme Court decision had required the party to seek Justice Department approval under the Voting Rights Act to charge the delegate fees necessary to fund its traditionally large conventions. *Morris v. Republican Party of Virginia*, 116 S.Ct. 1186 (1996).

6. Arkansas: Characters, Crises, and Change

1. The most extensive portrayal and analysis of Arkansas politics in both the traditional and contemporary periods is Diane D. Blair, *Arkansas Politics: Do the People Rule?* (Lincoln, Nebr., 1988).

2. Diane D. Blair, "The Big Three of Late Twentieth Century Politics: Dale Bumpers, Bill Clinton and David Pryor," *Arkansas Historical Quarterly,* LIV (1995), 53–79.

3. See Diane D. Blair, "Arkansas," in Robert P. Steed, Lawrence W. Moreland, and Tod A. Baker, eds., *The 1984 Presidential Election in the South: Patterns of Southern Party Politics* (New York, 1986); and Diane D. Blair, "Arkansas: Reluctant Republicans in Razorback Land," in Lawrence W. Moreland, Robert P. Steed, and Tod A. Baker, eds., *The 1988 Presidential Election in the South: Continuity Amidst Change in Southern Party Politics* (New York, 1991).

4. Interview with Ron Oliver, conducted by Jay Barth, August 15, 1996.

5. Interview with Sheila Bronfman, conducted by Jay Barth, August 15, 1996.

6. Richard F. Fenno, Jr., *Senators on the Campaign Trail* (Norman, Okla., 1996), 281, 282; interview with Bronfman.

7. Maria Henson, "GOP Opens Arms to Robinson," *Arkansas Democrat* (Little Rock), July 29, 1989; "What Robinson Said," *Arkansas Democrat*, July 29, 1989.

8. Interview with Skip Rutherford, conducted by Ernie Dumas, July 31, 1996.

9. Mark Shields, "Arkansas Miniseries," *Washington Post National Weekly Edition*, May 28–June 3, 1990. Even Shields might have found far-fetched the future strange-but-Arkansas-typical story that Jones and Nelson became partners with a then-obscure personage named James McDougal in an ill-fated project to sell vacation plots at Campobello Island off Nova Scotia.

10. Jim Nichols, "Robinson Short on Spunk, Tall in Eyes of His Believers," *Arkansas Gazette,* March 4, 1990.

11. The total GOP primary turnout was 86,977, compared with the nearly 500,000 votes cast in the Democratic primary.

12. While precision in pinpointing the crossover impact isn't possible, the raw turnout figures are suggestive. In Pulaski County 29,124 voters participated in the 1990 GOP primary; four years later, only 7,663 did so.

13. Interview with Rutherford.

14. Interview with Gloria Cabe, conducted by Ernie Dumas and Jay Barth, September 16, 1996.

15. The source requested anonymity for these remarks.

16. Interview with Cabe.

17. David Maraniss, *First in His Class: A Biography of Bill Clinton* (New York, 1995), 456. It is these charges that, during the 1992 presidential nomination campaign, were published in the tabloid *Star.* Soon thereafter, Gennifer Flowers, one of the women identified, came forward to tell her story about a long-term relationship with Clinton.

18. Interview with Richard Bearden, conducted by Jay Barth, August 20, 1996.

19. Larry Rhodes, "Broken Promise Would Be Forgiven, Lawmakers Say," *Arkansas Democrat,* August 16, 1992.

20. Diane D. Blair, "Arkansas: Ground Zero in the Presidential Race," in Robert P. Steed, Lawrence W. Moreland, and Tod A. Baker, eds., *The 1992 Presidential Election in the South: Current Patterns of Southern Party and Electoral Politics* (Westport, Conn., 1994), 105.

21. *Ibid.,* 112.

22. Interview with Bronfman.

23. Jane Fullerton, "59% in Poll Support Bumpers," *Arkansas Democrat*, October 10, 1991; "Time to Return Government to People, Huckabee Says," *Democrat* (Lonoke, Ark.), July 8, 1992; Joe Farmer, "Huckabee in Favor of Strict Solutions to Crime Problems," *Arkansas Democrat-Gazette* (Little Rock), August 6, 1992; "Senate Hopeful Sees America in Trouble," *News* (Jacksonville, Ark.), June 12, 1992.

24. Randy Lilleston, "Huckabee Keeps Spending In-House on Campaign Work," *Democrat-Gazette*, August 9, 1992; "Marilyn Quayle Explains Comments," *Democrat-Gazette*, October 1, 1992.

25. John Brummett, "A Long Way, Baby?" *Democrat-Gazette*, August 25, 1995; Noel Oman, "Twin Trouble for Party: No Lincoln, No Incumbents," *Democrat-Gazette*, January 10, 1996.

26. Joe Farmer, "McCuen Rejects Dickey's Challenge, Says 'I Don't Need to Debate,' " *Democrat-Gazette*, 13 October 1992.

27. Interview with Bronfman; interview with Cabe. For a fuller discussion of the Clinton presidency's impact on the state Democratic and Republican parties, see Diane D. Blair and W. Jay Barth, "Arkansas," in Daniel S. Ward and Andrew Appleton, eds., *State Party Profiles: A 50-State Guide to Development, Organization, and Resources* (Washington, D.C., 1996), 24–32.

28. Interview with John Yates, conducted by Jay Barth, September 13, 1996.

29. Rachel O'Neal, "Candidate for No. 2 Spot Wants Audit, Consolidation," *Democrat-Gazette*, May 22, 1993; interview with Nate Coulter, conducted by Jay Barth, September 19, 1996.

30. Interview with Yates; interview with Bearden.

31. Interview with Jerry Russell, conducted by Ernie Dumas, July 24, 1996.

32. Interviews with Coulter and Bronfman.

33. Dick Morris, "GOP Wins One in Arkansas," *Campaigns and Elections* (November 1993), 46–47.

34. For a discussion of the Nelson role in promoting the Whitewater—and related—stories, see Gene Lyons, *Fools for Scandal: How the Media Invented Whitewater* (New York, 1996).

35. *Arkansas Times,* November 5, 1992. For the political influence of the *Arkansas Gazette,* see Blair, *Arkansas Politics,* 271–72.

36. A total of 365,797 voters cast ballots in the Democratic primary; 47,353 participated in the GOP primary.

37. For details on these and other Nelson tactics, see John Brummett, "Nelson: A Lot of Explaining to Do," *Democrat-Gazette,* March 28, 1994.

38. Interview with Russell.

39. The source sought anonymity for these remarks.

40. Interview with Yates.

41. John Brummett, "That Old Bryant Magic," *Democrat-Gazette,* June 15, 1996; Elizabeth Caldwell, "Consumers, Business See Bryant Differently," *Democrat-Gazette,* February 11, 1996.

42. Rachel O'Neal, "A Bear But Not 'Wild,' McMath Runs Against Slickness for Senate," *Democrat-Gazette,* November 20, 1995; Rachel O'Neal, "Lawyer Bill Bristow, Homespun Farm Boy, Stumps for Senate Seat," *Democrat-Gazette,* November 27, 1995; John Brummett, "The Lu Hardin Project," *Democrat-Gazette,* October 7, 1995.

43. Max Brantley, "Huckabee Gets a Bipartisan Scolding," *Arkansas Times*, February 9, 1996.

44. Patricia Manson and Joe Stumpe, "Defendants Respectful of Verdict," *Democrat-Gazette*, May 29, 1996.

45. Rachel O'Neal, "Quitting Race Is 'Right Thing,' Huckabee Says," *Democrat-Gazette*, May 31, 1996; Rachel O'Neal, "Tucker Ousted," *Democrat-Gazette*, July 16, 1996.

46. Interview with Bearden; Noel Oman and Kevin Freking, "Leaders Recall Tortuous Monday," *Democrat-Gazette*, July 17, 1996.

47. John Brummett, "Crucial Senate Runoff," *Democrat-Gazette*, June 1, 1996; Kevin Freking and Dave Hughes, "Hutchinson Shocks GOP, Won't Seek Senate Seat," *Democrat-Gazette*, June 4, 1996; Rex Nelson, "GOP 'All-Star Cast' Pressures Hutchinson to Run for Senate," *Democrat-Gazette*, June 11, 1996; Kevin Freking, "Hutchinson Reverses: He'll Seek Pryor Seat," *Democrat-Gazette*, June 15, 1996.

48. Rachel O'Neal, "Analysts: Ads in Race Give Heat, Little Light," *Democrat-Gazette*, September 9, 1996.

49. Grant Tennille and Patricia Manson, "Mistakes May Free Murderer," *Democrat-Gazette*, October 1, 1996; Grant Tennille, "Judge: Bryant's Office 'Neglected Duty,' " *Democrat-Gazette*, October 2, 1996; Joe Stumpe, "Bryant, Hutchinson Stay Neck and Neck," *Democrat-Gazette*, November 1, 1996.

50. Rachel O'Neal, "Hutchinson Says Race Boils Down to Who Would Least Embarrass State," *Democrat-Gazette*, October 30, 1996; Noel Oman and Rachel O'Neal, "Fatal Crash Dampens Senate-Race Stumping," *Democrat-Gazette*, November 2, 1996; Rachel O'Neal, "Senate Bid Cost Rivals $3 Million," *Democrat-Gazette*, January 4, 1997; Doug Smith, "Senate Candidates Find the Loophole in Campaign Finance Laws," *Arkansas Times*, September 20, 1996.

51. For a treatment of how negative campaign advertisements suppress turnout, see Stephen Ansolabehere and Shanto Iyengar, *Going Negative: How Political Advertisements Shrink and Polarize the Electorate* (New York, 1995).

52. For example, as a first-termer, Dickey introduced legislation to withhold federal aid from states that did not enact laws to require public floggings for misdemeanors and mandatory live television coverage of all executions, though he said he did not want to televise death by lethal injections because there would not be enough twitching and thrashing by the strapped-down prisoner to slake the public's thirst for suffering by criminals. Ernie Dumas, "Is Dickey Nuts, or Just Stupid?" *Arkansas Times*, July 14, 1994.

53. Emmett George, "Dickey Left to Fight Shadows in Race, *Democrat-Gazette*, November 3, 1996.

54. Grant Tennille and Mark Minton, "Davis Quits 3rd District Race," *Democrat-Gazette*, September 5, 1996; Dave Hughes, "Henry Sent In to Give Hutchinson 'A Fight,' " *Democrat-Gazette*, September 15, 1996; Michael Whiteley, "Henry Contributions Outpace Hutchinson's," *Democrat-Gazette*, October 17, 1996; Doug Smith, "Woman on a White Horse," *Arkansas Times*, September 20, 1996; Michael Whiteley, "GOP Sure Thing Becomes a Race," *Democrat-Gazette*, November 3, 1996.

55. Kevin Freking, "Berry, Donaldson Square Off on TV," *Democrat-Gazette*, June 8, 1996; Kevin Freking, "Dupwe Battling Berry, Status Quo," *Democrat-Gazette*, November 3, 1996.

56. John Brummett, " 'Bud the Stud' Turns Comedian," *Democrat-Gazette*, October 10, 1996; Michael Haddigan, "A Race Turns Nasty," *Arkansas Times*, November 1, 1996.

57. Elizabeth Caldwell and Jake Sandlin, "Snyder Hotly Denies Suggestion He Leans Toward Communism," *Democrat-Gazette*, October 29, 1996.

58. John Brummett, "Rockefeller a Conspicuous No-Show," *Democrat-Gazette*, October 1, 1996; Joe Stumpe, "Rockefeller Woos Vote of Blacks," *Democrat-Gazette*, September 30, 1996.

59. John Brummett, "Setback for Huckabee," *Democrat-Gazette*, November 9, 1996. Incidentally, with only a couple of exceptions the Republican senators and representatives come from the traditional areas of GOP strength in the northwest corner of the state and the areas of sharp population growth in and around Little Rock.

60. Joe Stumpe, "Behind Ballot Tally Lies Puzzle for Parties," *Democrat-Gazette*, November 7, 1996; Ronald Smothers, "For Arkansas Democrats, the Times Turn Painful," New York *Times*, June 23, 1995; Richard L. Berke, "Some Images Stick. Some Don't. Why?" New York *Times*, September 15, 1996.

61. Rex Nelson, "Poll Shows Clinton Little Touched by Trial," *Democrat-Gazette*, June 7, 1996; Channel 7 Poll, conducted September 30-October 4, 1996, by Opinion Research Associates, Inc.

62. The text of Clinton's victory speech was found on the World Wide Web at http://library.-whitehouse.gov/.

63. John Brummett, "Meet Michael Dale Huckabee," *Democrat-Gazette*, July 4, 1996. Jay Barth, " 'Opportunity Ladders' in the Contemporary South: Differences in the Quality of the 'Products' Offered by the Two Parties," paper presented at the Annual Meeting of the Southern Political Science Association, November 3, 1993, Atlanta.

64. Interview with Bill Paschall, conducted by Jay Barth, August 22, 1996.

65. John Brummett, "That Huckabee-Hutchinson Hug," *Democrat-Gazette*, September 19, 1995.

66. For instance, network exit polls for the 1996 presidential election showed that a plurality of Arkansas voters between eighteen and twenty-nine supported Bob Dole. All other age groups supported Clinton, who gained a whopping 63 percent of Arkansas voters sixty years of age or older.

7. Tennessee: A Partisan Big Bang amid Quiet Accommodation

1. Michael Barone and Grant Ujifusa, *The Almanac of American Politics, 1996* (Washington, D.C., 1995), 1226.

2. The story of the Republican origins in the state is most famously laid out in V. O. Key, Jr., *Southern Politics in State and Nation* (New York, 1949), 75–81, and the emergence of the party in recent decades is well chronicled in Jack Bass and Walter DeVries, *The Transformation of Southern Politics: Social Change and Political Consequence Since 1945* (New York, 1976); see also J. Leiper Freeman, *Political Change in Tennessee, 1948–1978: Party Politics Trickles Down* (Knoxville, 1980). For more contemporary developments, see Alexander P. Lamis, *The Two-Party South,* 2nd expanded ed. (New York, 1990), 163–78. A quantitative analysis of the persistence and erosion of Civil War trends is found in Anne Hopkins, William Lyons and Steve Metcalf, "Tennessee," in Robert P. Steed, Laurence W. Moreland, and Tod A. Baker, eds., *The 1984 Presidential Election in the South: Patterns of Southern Party Politics* (New York, 1986).

3. Bass and DeVries, *Transformation of Southern Politics,* 300–302.

4. Philip Ashford, "McWherter Dwells on Race Theme," Memphis *Commercial Appeal*, July 25, 1986.

5. Terry Keeter and Philip Ashford, "Olive Branch Is Quickly Extended by McWherter to Eskind and Fulton," *Commercial Appeal*, August 9, 1986; Philip Ashford, "Blacks Hold Trump Card in McWherter's Race," *Commercial Appeal*, August 25, 1986; Philip Ashford, "McWherter, Party Embark on Unity Tour," *Commercial Appeal*, August 26, 1986.

6. Philip Ashford, "Conflict Issues Raised as Campaign Strategy," *Commercial Appeal*, October 22, 1986; Philip Ashford and Terry Keeter, "McWherter Triumphs," *Commercial Appeal*, November 5, 1986.

7. Interview with Keith Miles, former press secretary to Senator Sasser, conducted by Philip Ashford, January 7, 1998.

8. Philip Ashford, "Andersen: 'A New Generation to Carry On,' " *Commercial Appeal*, October 2, 1988.

9. For more on this election, see David M. Brodsky and Robert H. Swansbrough, "Tennessee: A House Divided," in Laurence W. Moreland, Robert P. Steed, and Tod A. Baker, eds., *The 1988 Presidential Election in the South: Continuity Amidst Change in Southern Party Politics* (Westport, Conn., 1991), 201–19.

10. Richard Locker, "Henry Sticks to Tax Theme as McWherter Speaks Softly," *Commercial Appeal*, November 4, 1990.

11. Bob Holladay, "The Other Governor—John Wilder: His Power, His Persistence (And His Surprising Passion)," *Nashville Scene*, June 22, 1995.

12. Richard Locker, "Democrats Fuming Over 'Bipartisan' Wilder," *Commercial Appeal*, November 8, 1996.

13. Interview with Randle Richardson, conducted by Richard Locker, December 17, 1996.

14. Richard Locker, "Henry Sees Income Tax as Top Issue in Attacking McWherter," *Commercial Appeal*, August 24, 1990.

15. Locker, "Henry Sticks to Tax Theme."

16. Richard Locker, "Lottery, Taxes Heat Up Tepid Governor's Race," *Commercial Appeal*, October 24, 1990.

17. Interview with Ted Welch, conducted by Richard Locker, December 13, 1996. Welch also noted that he had tried to persuade Fred Thompson to run for governor, but that Thompson had demurred, saying the timing wasn't right for him.

18. Richard Locker, "McWherter Rolls to Second Term," *Commercial Appeal*, November 7, 1990.

19. *Ibid.*

20. Interview with Eugene (Chip) Forrester, conducted by Philip Ashford, September 14, 1996.

21. Paula Wade, "Hawkins Campaign Slow Without Funds," *Commercial Appeal*, October 18, 1990.

22. Philip Ashford, "GOPigs Go to War," *Nashville Scene*, August 8, 1991, p. 5.

23. "Hopper Statements Anger Prominent Republicans," *Tennessee Journal*, September 9, 1991; interview with Richardson. Former governor Lamar Alexander and former senator Baker were among those who brought pressure on Hopper to resign. By the mid-1990s Hopper was serving as a southern regional political officer for the Republican National Committee (RNC), and in 1997 he became the RNC's political director. Interview with Tommy Hopper, conducted by Richard Locker, November 18, 1996.

24. For more on this election, see David M. Brodsky and Robert H. Swansbrough, "Tennessee: Favorite Son Brings Home the Bacon," in Robert P. Steed, Laurence W. Moreland, and Tod

A. Baker, eds., *The 1992 Presidential Election in the South: Current Patterns of Southern Party and Electoral Politics* (Westport, Conn., 1994), 157–68.

25. Terry Keeter, "Tanner to Stay Put; Says He Won't Seek Gore's Seat," *Commercial Appeal,* November 25, 1992; James W. Brosnan, "Tanner Has No Regrets He Refused 'Promotion,' " *Commercial Appeal,* March 14, 1993.

26. Richard Locker and Terry Keeter, "Thompson Gears Up for Quick Trip to Senate; Fellow GOP Newcomer Frist Crosses State, Thanks Backers," *Commercial Appeal,* November 10, 1994.

27. Interview with Tom Perdue, conducted by Richard Locker, December 17, 1996. See this book's Georgia chapter for more on Perdue's role in Peach State politics.

28. Paula Wade, Cornell Christion, and Sarah Derks, "Frist Ends Long Reign of Sasser," *Commercial Appeal,* November 9, 1994.

29. *Ibid.*

30. *Ibid.*

31. Cornell Christion, "Frist Pounds on Sasser at Rallies Across Shelby," *Commercial Appeal,* November 3, 1994.

32. Wade, Christion, and Derks, "Frist Ends Long Reign of Sasser."

33. James W. Brosnan, "Thompson Tops in Votes, Not Cash," *Commercial Appeal,* November 9, 1994.

34. Theda Skocpol, *Boomerang: Clinton's Health Security Effort and the Turn Against Government in U.S. Politics* (New York, 1996), 105; interview with David Cooley, Bredesen's campaign manager, conducted by Philip Ashford, September 14, 1996.

35. Richard Locker, "Thompson Tells Why Lobbyist Pay Rose with GOP Senate," *Commercial Appeal,* November 5, 1994.

36. Richard Locker, "Thompson Relishes Rhetoric, Glamor of Autumn Campaign Day," *Commercial Appeal,* October 30, 1994; Brosnan, "Thompson Tops in Votes, Not Cash."

37. Richard Locker, Rob Johnson and Jody Callahan, "Winner Thompson Will Soon Be 'Senior' Senator," *Commercial Appeal,* November 9, 1994.

38. Reed Branson, "Sundquist Shows Off Group of Democratic Supporters," *Commercial Appeal,* September 15, 1994; interview with John Summers, conducted by Philip Ashford, November 23, 1996. One of the authors of this chapter, Philip Ashford, played a role in Bredesen's administration as mayor of Nashville.

39. Richard Locker, "Governor's Race Cost Record, *Commercial Appeal,* February 3, 1995.

40. Reed Branson, "Sundquist, Bredesen Differ Only by Degrees," *Commercial Appeal,* October 30, 1994.

41. Nate Hobbs, "Sundquist Rips Bredesen's 'Attacks,' " *Commercial Appeal,* November 5, 1994; Reed Branson, "Governor's Race Seems to Focus on Personalities," *Commercial Appeal,* November 6, 1994; Richard Locker, "Tennessee High Court Unseals Kirby Pines Records," *Commercial Appeal,* June 11, 1996.

42. Reed Branson, "Northerner for Governor? Tennessee Opens Doors," *Commercial Appeal,* August 7, 1994.

43. Interview with Don Sundquist, conducted by Richard Locker, December 12, 1996.

44. Paula Wade, "Losers Save Face After Voters' Cold Shoulder," *Commercial Appeal,* November 10, 1994.

45. For more on this election, see Robert H. Swansbrough and David M. Brodsky, "Tennessee: Belle of the Presidential Ball," in Laurence W. Moreland and Robert P. Steed, eds., *The 1996 Presidential Election in the South: Southern Party Systems in the 1990s* (Westport, Conn., 1997), 183–95.

46. "Dole Making Gains on Clinton, State Poll Shows," Nashville *Tennessean,* October 9, 1996. The poll, which had 809 respondents, was conducted for the newspaper by Mason-Dixon Political/Media Research.

47. The county-by-county returns for Clinton in 1992 and 1996 yield a correlation coefficient of .95, indicating a very strong relationship.

48. Paula Wade, "Gordon to Seek Senate Seat Held by Thompson," *Commercial Appeal,* May 9, 1994; Richard Locker, "Spring for the Senate: Thompson Shows 'Feel for the People' on Final Tenn. Tour," *Commercial Appeal,* October 30, 1996; interview with Houston Gordon, conducted by Richard Locker, November 6, 1996; interview with Fred Thompson, conducted by Richard Locker, October 28, 1996.

49. Larry Daughtrey, "The Mud Is Knee-Deep This Season," *Tennessean,* October 27, 1996; Richard Locker, "To Wilder, It's All in 'Family,' " *Commercial Appeal,* September 29, 1996.

50. Interview with Jim Neeley, state AFL-CIO director, conducted by Philip Ashford, December 13, 1996.

51. Robert Swansborough and David Brodsky, "Tennessee: Weakening Party Loyalties and Growing Independence," in Swansborough and Brodsky, eds., *The South's New Politics: Realignment and Dealignment* (Columbia, S.C., 1988), 91–93; interview with Richard Lodge, conducted by Philip Ashford, September 30, 1996.

52. Interview with Richardson; interview with Sundquist.

53. Incidentally, Frist has been more useful than the average freshman senator, once resuscitating a tourist who had a heart attack during a tour of the Capitol and on another occasion saving a Republican donor at a fundraising event after the man started choking on some finger food.

54. "Poll Indicates Voters Like State GOP Brass," *Tennessean,* October 9, 1996. Thompson stood at 62 percent in the same poll while Frist received a 55 percent approval. The poll, which surveyed 809 respondents, was conducted for the *Tennessean* by Mason-Dixon Political/Media Research.

55. For an earlier assessment along these lines, see David M. Brodsky and Simeon J. Brodsky, "Tennessee: Democratic Party Resilience," in Charles D. Hadley and Lewis Bowman, eds., *Southern State Party Organizations and Activists* (Westport, Conn., 1995), 55–72.

8. Alabama: The GOP Rises in the Heart of Dixie

1. Tom Gordon, "Win Every Office, Party Chairman Tells GOP," Birmingham *News,* January 12, 1997; Tom Gordon, "Siegelman Wants Demo Party Fixed," Birmingham *News,* March 9, 1997.

2. Comments by Joe Turnham to Democratic Executive Committee, Montgomery, Alabama, March 1997, recorded by Tom Gordon; interview with Roger McConnell, conducted by Tom Gordon, January 10, 1997.

3. For a more complete description of the 1986 campaign, see Patrick R. Cotter and James Glen Stovall, "The 1986 Election in Alabama: The Beginning of the Post-Wallace Era," *PS: Political Science and Politics,* XX (1987), 655–63.

4. Tom Gordon, "Elections Prove a Mixed Bag for State's Hopeful Republicans," Birmingham *News,* November 16, 1986. In 1983 the GOP made modest gains in an unusual special court-ordered legislative election. The state Democratic executive committee chose the party's nominees rather than hold a primary, and the whole occasion became a power play by the party's

dominant groups—labor, the Alabama Education Association, the black Alabama Democratic Conference, and plaintiffs' lawyers. In a weekend party gathering in Birmingham, these groups booted out a number of duly elected legislators by not "renominating" them. Some of the rejects mounted successful independent campaigns to regain their seats while some other "handpicked" Democratic nominees lost to Republican challengers. "The handpicking," as the affair came to be known, gave Republicans fodder for future election cycles, which they employed with glee.

5. David White and Tom Lindley, "Lack of Controversy Helps Hunt as He Gambles for Second Term," Birmingham *News*, May 6, 1990. At each 1987–1990 reading of the governor's popularity, a majority of the public said that Guy Hunt was doing an "excellent" or "good" job. Patrick R. Cotter, James Glen Stovall, and Samuel H. Fisher III, *Disconnected: Public Opinion and Politics in Alabama* (Northport, Ala., 1994).

6. Tom Gordon and John Mangels, "Runoff a Battle for Conservative Votes," Birmingham *News*, June 10, 1990.

7. Justin Fox, "Paul Hubbert's Political Style," Birmingham *News*, September 9, 1991.

8. Dana Beyerle, "Siegelman Repeats Attacks," Tuscaloosa *News*, June 24, 1990.

9. Tom Gordon and John Mangels, "Hubbert Wins Right to Meet Hunt; Race Offers Clear Choice," Birmingham *News*, June 27, 1990.

10. Amy Herring, "Hunt Repays $650,000 in Four Years," Montgomery *Advertiser*, September 9, 1990; "Hunt-Hubbert Spar over Finances," Tuscaloosa *News*, September 12, 1990.

11. "Stories Were Wrong," Montgomery *Advertiser*, September 13, 1990; Ted Bryant, "Election Eased Hunt's Money Woes," Birmingham *Post-Herald*, October 15, 1990.

12. John Mangels, "Hunt Ties Hubbert to Left-Wing Demos," Birmingham *News*, October 13, 1990.

13. Justin Fox, "Teacher Testing: Word War Heats Up," Birmingham *News*, October 6, 1990; Justin Fox, "Hubbert Blasts Recent Hunt Ads as Show of Racism," Birmingham *News*, October 14, 1990; Dana Beyerle, "Hubbert Accepts Some Teachers Support Hunt," Tuscaloosa *News*, October 19, 1990.

14. Philip Rawls, "Hunt Says Education to Become Key Issue in Race with Hubbert," Montgomery *Advertiser*, June 28, 1990; Mangels, "Hunt Ties Hubbert to Left-Wing Demos."

15. Mangels, "Hunt Ties Hubbert to Left-Wing Demos."

16. The results of pre-election surveys showed that Hunt did best among more educated, higher-income, male, and white voters. Cotter, Stovall and Fisher, *Disconnected*, 100–102.

17. Michael Brumas, "Conservative? Liberal? Heflin Keeps 'em Guessing," Birmingham *News*, September 30, 1990.

18. Ronald Smothers, "After 115 years, a Black Will Represent Alabama," New York *Times*, May 23, 1992.

19. Elizabeth Hayes, "Alabama Moves to Right in Congress," Montgomery *Advertiser*, November 15, 1992.

20. *Congressional Quarterly Almanac,* 102nd Cong., 2nd Sess. No. 48, p. 24b (Leading Scorers: Party Unity).

21. For more on this election, see Patrick R. Cotter, "Alabama: No Winners or Losers," in Robert P. Steed, Laurence W. Moreland, and Tod A. Baker, eds., *The 1992 Presidential Election in the South: Current Patterns of Southern Party and Electoral Politics* (Westport, Conn., 1994), 25–38.

22. David White, "Hunt: These Outrageous Charges Are Absolutely False," Birmingham *News,* December 29, 1992; "Chronology of Hunt Indictment," Birmingham *News*, December 29, 1992. In June 1997, amidst much controversy, Hunt received a pardon—on the rare grounds of

innocence—from the state board of pardons and paroles, two of whose three members he had appointed.

23. In a 1954 campaign speech when he was successfully seeking a non-consecutive second term as governor, Folsom said: "Sure, I'll admit that I did some stealing while I was your governor. But the crowd I worked with, the only way you could get it [money to help the people] was to steal." Bob Ingram, "Folsom Rally at Coliseum Pulls Disappointing Crowd," Montgomery *Advertiser*, May 1, 1954.

24. Interview with Guy Hunt, conducted by Tom Gordon, October 15, 1996.

25. Associated Press, "Chamber Wants Battle Flag Hauled Down," Birmingham *News*, July 31, 1992; Associated Press, "Confederate Battle Flag Plan Unwrapped," Birmingham *News*, July 21, 1993.

26. Jon Rabiroff, "Folsom Says He's Sorry and Invokes Mercedes," Birmingham *News,* October 16, 1994.

27. Dana Beyerle, "Folsom Easily Beats Hubbert," Tuscaloosa *News*, June 8, 1994.

28. Campaigning in a yellow school bus in 1978 and running the most professional and effective television ad campaign the state had seen up to then, James promised a new beginning and said the state needed better management and not always more money. While he had some substantive accomplishments, such as adding more prison space, laying off state employees, promoting an investment plan for the state's offshore oil revenues, and appointing the first black justice to the state supreme court, he proved in other ways to be hardheaded, eccentric, and ineffective. His wife flew on the state airplane to religious gatherings, he supported Ronald Reagan's candidacy in 1980 (despite being a Democrat at the time), and toward the end of his term he pushed for a law to allow teacher- or student-led prayer in public schools. The law did not stand, but James was to return to the issue in the 1990s. Tom Gordon, "Old AU Tailback Will Run from Same Playbook," Birmingham *News*, April 17, 1994; Tom Gordon and Phil Pierce, "A Non-Politician in State's Political Town, James Fought System and Sometimes Won," Birmingham *News*, April 17, 1994.

29. John Milazzo, "Bedsole Beats Out Blount," Montgomery *Advertiser*, June 9, 1994.

30. Gordon, "Old AU Tailback."

31. Ted Bryant, "James Aims Ads at Folsom," Birmingham *Post-Herald*, October 19, 1994.

32. Rabiroff, "Folsom Says He's Sorry"; Bryant, "James Aims Ads at Folsom."

33. Chris Roberts and Robin DeMonia, "James, Folsom Swap Blasts on Tech Plus," Birmingham *News,* November 5, 1994.

34. Tom Gordon, "Political Earthquake for Alabama's GOP," Birmingham *News*, November 9, 1994.

35. Interview with Jere Beasley, conducted by Tom Gordon, March 20, 1997.

36. Robin DeMonia, "Sessions Ends Evans' Long Watchdog Reign," Birmingham *News*, November 9, 1994.

37. Tom Gordon, "Blacks and Republicans Benefited from Redistricting," Birmingham *News*, July 11, 1995.

38. Michael Brumas and the Associated Press, "Demos Lose Rep. Shelby and Control of Congress," Birmingham *News*, November 9, 1994; Michael Brumas, "Democratic Leaders Say Shelby Move Shows Ingratitude," Birmingham *News*, November 10, 1994.

39. Tom Gordon and Steve Visser, "GOP Herds 10 Jeffco Judges into Its Camp," Birmingham *News*, January 3, 1996.

40. Dana Beyerle, "Folsom Transfers $450,000 to Evans to Keep Office Afloat," Tuscaloosa *News*, October 11, 1994.

41. Janis L. Magin, "Bennett Wins Primary, Todd, Ford in Runoffs," Birmingham *News,* June 8, 1994; Robin DeMonia, "Baker, Ford Focus on Qualifications," Birmingham *News,* June 16, 1994.

42. David White, "Siegelman Becomes Clinton in Graddick Ad," Birmingham *News,* September 14, 1994; David White, "Siegelman's Lead Steady over Graddick at 19 Percent," Birmingham *News,* November 6, 1994.

43. Robin DeMonia, "Secretary of State Candidates: Same Goals, Ideas Differ," Birmingham *News,* October 27, 1994.

44. Tom Gordon, "Candidates Spent $25 Million in '94 Contested Races," Birmingham *News,* February 5, 1995.

45. For more on this election, see Patrick R. Cotter, "Alabama: The Elephants Trumpet," in Laurence W. Moreland and Robert P. Steed, eds., *The 1996 Presidential Election in the South: Southern Party Systems in the 1990s* (Westport, Conn., 1997), 51–64.

46. Tom Gordon, "Sessions Raises Issue of Party Pedigree," Birmingham *News,* June 9, 1996.

47. Michael Sznajderman and David White, "Bedford, Sessions Debating Issues, Personal Character," Birmingham *News,* June 27, 1996.

48. *Ibid.*

49. Michael Sznajderman, "Bedford Steered Funds to Waterline, Documents Claim," Birmingham *News,* October 9, 1996.

50. Michael Sznajderman, "State Congress Candidates Avoiding Party Apron Strings," Birmingham *News,* July 14, 1996; David Pace, "Record $22 Million Spent on State Congressional Races," *Birmingham News,* December 16, 1996.

51. Pre-election surveys indicate that Sessions ran strongest among younger, white, higher-status, and male voters. Tom Gordon, "Sessions Leads Bedford by 11 Points in Poll," Birmingham *News,* November 3, 1994.

52. Stan Bailey, "Ingram Campaign Helped Them Lose, Some Demos Feel," Birmingham *News,* November 20, 1996.

53. For more on party identification and the partisan balance in Alabama, see Patrick R. Cotter and James G. Stovall, "Party Identification and Political Change in Alabama: A Mid-1990s Update," *American Review of Politics,* XVII (1996), 193–211. This article's Figure 3, "Partisan Balance in Party Identification by Race," shows that after 1986 more whites identified with the Republican party than the Democratic party. The GOP advantage among whites fluctuated from 10 percentage points to slightly over 20 percentage points through 1996.

54. For more on the party image measures, see Cotter and Stovall, "Party Identification and Political Change in Alabama: A Mid-1990s Update" and Cotter, Stovall, and Fisher, *Disconnected.*

55. Incidentally, one effect of the increased competitiveness of Alabama politics is that turnout in the Democratic primary election has declined from more than 900,000 in the 1986 gubernatorial contest to about 300,000 in the 1996 U.S. Senate race. At the same time, turnout in Republican primaries has increased, although not yet quite to the level of the Democratic primary.

56. For more on the factors affecting partisan change in Alabama, see Patrick R. Cotter and Glen Stovall, "Party Identification and Political Change in Alabama," in Robert H. Swansbrough and David M. Brodsky, eds., *The South's New Politics: Realignment and Dealignment* (Columbia, S.C., 1988), 142–57; and Patrick R. Cotter, "Alabama: The Unsettled Electorate," in Maureen Moakley, ed., *Party Realignment and State Politics* (Columbus, Ohio, 1992), 91–105.

57. Interview with Marty Connors, conducted by Tom Gordon, October 15, 1996; interview with Victor Poole, conducted by Tom Gordon, October 10, 1996.

58. Interview with Pete Mathews, conducted by Tom Gordon, November 10, 1996.

59. Cotter and Stovall, "Party Identification and Political Change in Alabama: A Mid-1990s Update"; Rose Livingston, "Blacks Rejected Riley's Efforts," Birmingham *News,* November 8, 1996.

60. Robin DeMonia, "Demo Flier Uses Klan Picture to Boost Black Voter Turnout," Birmingham *News,* November 5, 1996; interview with Roger McConnell, conducted by Tom Gordon, March 30, 1997.

61. Interview with John Baker, conducted by Tom Gordon, October 15, 1996.

62. Tom Gordon, "Alabama Demos' Voter Guides to Focus on Candidates' Faith," Birmingham *News,* October 13, 1996.

63. Michael Sznajderman, "Advocates Delighted with James' Signing Ban on Late-Term Abortion," Birmingham *News,* May 23, 1997; David White, "State Welfare Reform Proposal Clears Senate," Birmingham *News,* March 26, 1997.

64. Jerry Underwood and Stan Bailey, "State High Court Cuts to $50,000 Award over BMW," Birmingham *News,* May 10, 1997.

65. David White, "Siegelman Opposes Civil Liability Changes; Limits on Damages Needed for Economy, James, Clark Retort," Birmingham *News,* February 13, 1997; David White, "House Snuffs Cigarette Tax: Children's First Fund Fails," Birmingham *News,* April 24, 1997.

66. Charles J. Dean, "High Court Gives State One Year to Fix Schools," Birmingham *News,* January 11, 1997; Robin DeMonia, "DHR Case Volume, Planning Criticized," Birmingham *News,* May 5, 1997; Charles J. Dean, "Tax Hike May Worsen School Inequities," Birmingham *News,* March 9, 1997.

67. Interview with Paul Hubbert, conducted by Tom Gordon, November 10, 1996; Interview with Mathews.

68. Interview with Al LaPierre, conducted by Tom Gordon, February 1, 1997.

9. Mississippi: From Pariah to Pacesetter?

1. Dale Krane and Stephen D. Shaffer, *Mississippi Government and Politics: Modernizers Versus Traditionalists* (Lincoln, Nebr., 1992), 103–105.

2. Bill Minor, "Eyes on Mississippi," Jackson *Clarion-Ledger,* September 15, 1991.

3. S. Gale Denley, "Neshoba Fair Leaves One Full of Memories," *Clarion-Ledger,* August 18, 1991; Mark Leggett, "Challengers Throw Barbs at Incumbents," *Northeast Mississippi Daily Journal,* (Tupelo) August 1, 1991; Philip Moulden, "Dowdy, Johnson Hammer Away at Mabus Record as Governor," Meridian *Star,* August 1, 1991.

4. Frank Fisher, "Mabus Blasts Rival Dowdy in Neshoba Fair Speech," *Northeast Mississippi Daily Journal,* August 2, 1991; Carole Lawes, "Mabus Goes on Attack Against Dowdy," *Clarion-Ledger,* August 2, 1991; Philip Moulden, "Mabus Fires Back at His Challengers from Fair Stump," Meridian *Star,* August 2, 1991.

5. Andy Kanengiser, "Espy Does Radio Ad for Mabus," *Clarion-Ledger,* July 30, 1991; Sarah C. Campbell, "Delta Group Picks Mabus over Dowdy," *Clarion-Ledger,* September 14, 1991.

6. Jay Eubank, "Republican Governor's Race Hotter," *Clarion-Ledger,* August 19, 1991, and "Ad Watch," *Clarion-Ledger,* September 15, 1991.

7. Jay Eubank, "Republican Takes Off His Gloves," *Clarion-Ledger,* August 8, 1991, and Jay

Eubank, "2 GOP Hopefuls Cry 'Change' as One Hits on Education Funding," *Clarion-Ledger*, September 1, 1991.

8. Jay Eubank, "GOP Gloats About Votes in Primary," *Clarion-Ledger*, September 20, 1991; Stephen D. Shaffer and David A. Breaux, "Mississippi: The 'True Believers' Challenge the Party of Everyone," in Charles D. Hadley and Lewis Bowman, eds., *Southern State Party Organizations and Activists* (Westport, Conn., 1995), 171.

9. Jay Eubank, "Pete Johnson Campaign Signs Up Jack Reed," *Clarion-Ledger*, September 20, 1991; J. Lee Howard, "Former Foe Endorses Johnson," *Clarion-Ledger*, September 22, 1991; Jay Eubank, "GOP Stalwart Carmichael Backs Fordice," *Clarion-Ledger*, October 3, 1991.

10. Jay Eubank, "Jobs Issue Works For, Against Top Candidates," *Clarion-Ledger*, October 27, 1991. The television ads were recorded by Stephen D. Shaffer.

11. Editorial, "Governor: Mabus Can Push Reform," *Clarion-Ledger*, November 3, 1991; Jay Eubank, "Next Governor? 24% Undecided," *Clarion-Ledger*, November 3, 1991.

12. Sid Salter, "Mississippi Learning: Democrats' Monopoly Busted in 1 Fell Swoop," *Clarion-Ledger*, November 10, 1991; Bill Minor, "Will Fordice Be Able to Put Mississippi in Gear and Make a Change?" *Clarion-Ledger*, November 10, 1991.

13. Wire Service Report, "Analysts: Democrats' Racial Policy Boosts GOP," *Clarion-Ledger*, November 10, 1991; Dennis Camire, "Cochran: No Proof of Racial Politics," *Clarion-Ledger*, November 8, 1991; Steve Walton, " 'I Don't Want to Link David Duke and Fordice,' " *Clarion-Ledger*, November 10, 1991.

14. Bill Minor, "Crafty Dye Does 180-Degree Turn on Initiative and Referendum," *Clarion-Ledger*, August 4, 1991.

15. Jay Eubank, "Ad Watch," *Clarion-Ledger*, September 15, 1991.

16. Sarah C. Campbell, "Briggs Challenges Dye to Come Out and Fight," *Clarion-Ledger*, September 24, 1991.

17. Mark Leggett, "Northeast Mississippi Voters Keep Most Incumbent Legislators," *Northeast Mississippi Daily Journal*, November 5, 1992; Bill Minor, "Democrats, Republicans Weigh Caucus Potential," *Northeast Mississippi Daily Journal*, November 12, 1992.

18. For more on this election, see Stephen D. Shaffer, "Mississippi: Friends and Neighbors Fight the 'Liberal' Label," in Robert P. Steed, Laurence W. Moreland, and Tod A. Baker, eds., *The 1992 Presidential Election in the South: Current Patterns of Southern Party and Electoral Politics* (Westport, Conn., 1994), 67–82.

19. *Ibid.*, 73–74.

20. Kitty Cunningham, "Contest for Espy's Seat Drawing Large Field," *Congressional Quarterly Weekly Report*, March 6, 1993, pp. 534–37; Kitty Cunningham, "Thompson the Favorite in Runoff with Dent," *Congressional Quarterly Weekly Report*, April 3, 1993, p. 859; James M. Glaser, *Race, Campaign Politics, and the Realignment in the South* (New Haven, Conn., 1996), 163; Cunningham, "Contest for Espy's Seat," 534–37.

21. Jennifer Babson, "Voters in the 1st District Create Double Runoff," *Congressional Quarterly Weekly Report*, June 11, 1994, p. 1545; Jennifer Babson, "State Legislators Win Runoffs to Try to Succeed Whitten," *Congressional Quarterly Weekly Report*, July 2, 1994, p. 1823, Jennifer Babson, "Stakes High in Whitten's District as GOP Makes Inroads," *Congressional Quarterly Weekly Report*, April 23, 1994, pp. 951–53.

22. Delarie A. Henderson, "African–American Public Opinion: A Comparative Analysis of the

1994 Mississippi Telephone Public Opinion Poll and the 1992 Pre-Election National Election Study Public Opinion Poll" (M.A. thesis, Mississippi State University, 1996).

23. Analysis by Stephen D. Shaffer and David A. Breaux using the 1994 Mississippi Poll, conducted by the Social Science Research Center at Mississippi State University.

24. Emily Wagster, "No Honeymoon in Fordice-Molpus Debate," *Clarion-Ledger*, April 14, 1995.

25. Emily Wagster and Mac Gordon, "Fordice, Molpus Come Out Swinging," *Clarion-Ledger*, August 4, 1995.

26. Mac Gordon, "Governor Imitates Molpus' Wife's Voice, Says TV Ad Untruthful," *Clarion-Ledger*, October 20, 1995; Mac Gordon, "Fordice, Molpus Squabble after Debate," *Clarion-Ledger*, October 25, 1995.

27. V. O. Key, Jr., *Southern Politics in State and Nation* (New York, 1949), 229–53.

28. Andy Kanengiser, "Molpus Ad Criticized as 'Race Baiting,' " *Clarion-Ledger*, November 4, 1995.

29. Mac Gordon, "Waller, Dye Make Donations to Fordice Campaign," *Clarion-Ledger*, November 6, 1995; interview with former state Republican chairman Clarke Reed, conducted by Stephen D. Shaffer, October 3, 1996; interview with Mike Retzer, conducted by Stephen D. Shaffer, October 4, 1996.

30. Jerry Mitchell, "GOP Reign in Senate Possible, Some Say," *Clarion-Ledger*, August 14, 1995.

31. Emily Wagster, "Opponent Blasts Briggs' Record on Juvenile Crime," *Clarion-Ledger*, July 20, 1995; Mac Gordon, "Musgrove Presses Briggs to Reveal '92 Timber Profit," *Clarion-Ledger*, October 19, 1995.

32. Matt Friedeman, "Lt. Gov. Eddie Briggs' Stance on Abortion Simply Not 'Conservative,' " *Clarion-Ledger*, September 27, 1995; Matt Friedeman, "A Vote on Straight GOP Ticket Might Go to a Democrat in 'Disguise,' " *Clarion-Ledger*, October 6, 1995; interview with Retzer.

33. For more on this election, see Stephen D. Shaffer and Randolph Burnside, "Mississippi: GOP Consolidates Its Gains," in Laurence W. Moreland and Robert P. Steed, eds., *The 1996 Presidential Election in the South: Southern Party Systems in the 1990s* (Westport, Conn., 1997), 95–109.

34. *Ibid.*, 102–103.

35. *Ibid.*, 101–104.

36. Reed Branson, "Will Incident Be Fordice's Symbol?" *Commercial Appeal*, January 23, 1997; Bobby Harrison, "Does Fordice Want Us to Know the Truth?" *Northeast Mississippi Daily Journal*, January 21, 1997.

37. Interview with Reed; interview with Retzer.

38. Document prepared by the Republican National Committee, "Elected Officials Who Have Switched to the Republican Party Since Bill Clinton Was Elected President," September 16, 1997; Associated Press, "Woods Switches," Starkville *Daily News*, June 28, 1996; interview with Alice Skelton, conducted by Stephen D. Shaffer, September 30, 1996.

39. Stephen D. Shaffer, Telemate Jackreece, and Nancy Bigelow, *Stability and Change in Mississippians' Political and Partisan Views: Insights from 14 Years of Opinion Polling* (Social Science Research Center, Mississippi State University, 1996).

40. Emily Wagster, "Dems Hope 'Magnificent Seven' Will Draw State Voters Back to Party," *Clarion-Ledger*, January 19, 1996.

41. McLemore is quoted *ibid.*

42. Andy Kanengiser, "Fordice Says Color Reason Nominees Rejected," *Clarion-Ledger*, May 10, 1996; Emily Wagster, "Fordice Rips Senate over Nominees," *Clarion-Ledger*, July 12, 1996.

43. Arnold Lindsay, "Jackson Has Its First Black Mayor," *Clarion-Ledger*, June 4, 1997; Emily Wagster, "Walker Routs Loviza, Regains Mayor's Office in Vicksburg," *Clarion-Ledger,* June 4, 1997.

44. Emily Wagster, "Legislators Override Fordice Veto," *Clarion-Ledger*, April 11, 1995. For more on this, see Stephen D. Shaffer and Monica Johnson, "A New Solid South? The Drama of Partisan Realignment in the Deep South State of Mississippi," *American Review of Politics*, XVII (1996), 171–91.

45. Emily Wagster, "Black Senators to Lead Record Number of Panels," *Clarion-Ledger*, January 6, 1996.

46. Interview with Skelton; Scott Hawkins, "Clark Stresses Pride as Mississippi Demo," Starkville *Daily News*, February 13, 1996.

47. Interview with Reed.

48. Interview with Eric Clark, conducted by Stephen D. Shaffer, October 1, 1996; Kevin M. Tate, "Dale Says Political Costs and Factions Dangerous to Democracy," Columbus *Commercial Dispatch*, April 18, 1996; interviews with Skelton and Retzer.

49. Interview with Clark; interview with Reed.

10. Louisiana: Still *Sui Generis* Like Huey

1. This analogy was used by Alexander P. Lamis in *The Two-Party South*, 2nd expanded ed. (New York, 1990), as the title of his Chapter 8, "Louisiana: Sui Generis like Huey."

2. *Statistical Abstract of the United States 1990*, p. 209; National Center for Education Statistics, U.S. Department of Education, 1993–94; Jason Block, "Louisiana: The Last Preserve of the Southern Democratic Party" (senior thesis, Department of Politics, Princeton University, Princeton, N.J., 1997), 24; Susan Howell and Robert Sims, "Abortion Attitudes and the Louisiana Governor's Election," in Malcolm Goggin, ed., *Understanding the New Politics of Abortion* (Newbury Park, Calif., 1993), 161.

3. For more on these points, see Earl Black and Merle Black, *Politics and Society in the South* (Cambridge, Mass., 1987); Chandler Davidson and Bernard Grofman, eds., *Quiet Revolution in the South: The Impact of the Voting Rights Act, 1965–1990* (Princeton, N.J., 1994); and Wayne Parent, "Race and Republican Resurgence in the South: Success in Black and White?" in John C. Kuzenski, Charles S. Bullock III, and Ronald Keith Gaddie, eds., *David Duke and Politics of Race in the South* (Nashville, 1995), 117–26.

4. Interview with U.S. Rep. Robert L. (Bob) Livingston, conducted by Edward F. Renwick, September 12, 1997.

5. Jack Wardlaw, "La. Republicans Struggle to Gain Foothold," New Orleans *Times-Picayune,* September 21, 1997.

6. Lamis, *The Two-Party South*, 113.

7. Interview with Quentin Dastugue, conducted by Edward F. Renwick, July 15, 1997.

8. Interview with Livingston; interview with William (Billy) Nungesser, conducted by Edward F. Renwick, July 17, 1997.

9. For more on the open primary's effect on Louisiana politics, see Wayne Parent, "Louisi-

ana," in Andrew M. Appleton and Daniel S. Ward, eds., *State Party Profiles: A 50-State Guide to Development, Organization, and Resources* (Washington, D.C., 1997), 126–32.

10. Interview with Livingston; interview with Dastugue.

11. Interview with Mike Foster, conducted by Jack Wardlaw, January 6, 1996.

12. As quoted in Lamis, *The Two-Party South*, 277.

13. Wayne Parent, "The Rise and Stall of Republican Ascendency in Louisiana Politics," in Robert H. Swansbrough and David M. Brodsky, eds., *The South's New Politics: Realignment and Dealignment* (Columbia, S.C., 1988), 213.

14. Bella Stumbo, "Cajun King's Crown Slips in Louisiana," Los Angeles *Times*, August 14, 1985; Peter Applebome, "Rogue or Reformer," New York *Times*, November 11, 1991.

15. Stumbo, "Cajun King's Crown Slips in Louisiana."

16. Tyler Bridges, "The Men Who Would Be Governor," *Times-Picayune*, November 3, 1991.

17. James Welch and Kim Chatelain, "Duke Always Controversial," *Times-Picayune,* February 5, 1989; Edward F. Renwick, "The 1991 Louisiana Gubernatorial Campaign: How an Incumbent Reform Governor with the Full Support of the Press and No Scandals in His Administration Couldn't Make a Runoff Against a Former Ku Klux Klan Leader Who Didn't Hold a Job, or a Former Governor Who Had Been Indicted by the Federal Government Surrounded by Charges of Scandal and Was Constantly Embroiled in Controversy" (Paper presented at 1992 annual meeting of the American Political Science Association, Chicago, September 36, 1992), 30.

18. Tyler Bridges, "Bagert Quits to Keep Duke Out of Runoff; Johnston a Virtual Shoo-In," *Times-Picayune*, October 5, 1990.

19. Statewide poll of 750 registered voters conducted August 17–26, 1990, for the *Times-Picayune* by Edward F. Renwick; statewide poll of 750 registered voters conducted July 31–August 5, 1990, for the *Times-Picayune* by Edward F. Renwick; Renwick, "The 1991 Louisiana Gubernatorial Campaign," 42.

20. Jack Wardlaw, "Duke Beats Duke for Senate," *Times-Picayune,* October 7, 1990; John Maginnis, "The Hazards of Duke," *New Republic,* November 5, 1991, p. 25. For a discussion of left and right populism in the South since World War II, see Wayne Parent and Peter A. Petrakis, "Populism Left and Right: Politics of the Rural South," in R. Douglas Hurt, ed., *The Rural South Since 1945* (Baton Rouge, 1998).

21. Interview with Nungesser.

22. Jack Wardlaw, "Has the Roemer Revolution Lost Its Momentum?" *Times-Picayune,* May 14, 1989.

23. Interview with Nungesser.

24. Interview with Dastugue; interview with Nungesser.

25. Interview with Nungesser.

26. Roberto Suro, "Simple Agenda in a Louisiana Election: Revenge," New York *Times*, November 2, 1991; Jack Wardlaw, "Little Man" Column, "Nobodies Buddy Doesn't Get It," *Times-Picayune*, October 23, 1991.

27. Carl Redmann and Marsha Shuler, "Analysts Say Roemer Failed to Build on His 1987 Victory," Baton Rouge *Advocate*, October 21, 1991.

28. Chris Adams and Chris Cooper, "Edwards/Duke Hot on Campaign Trail," *Times-Picayune*, November 10, 1991; James Gill, "Promises, Promises in the Runoff," *Times-Picayune,* October 27, 1991.

29. Editorial, "Edwards for Governor," *Times-Picayune*, November 10, 1991; statewide survey of 750 registered voters conducted November 5–10, 1991, by Edward F. Renwick for WWL-TV.

30. Renwick, "The 1991 Louisiana Gubernatorial Campaign," 64; Voter Research and Surveys Exit Poll, November 16, 1991; "A Portrait of Louisiana Voters," New York *Times*, November 18, 1991; Baton Rouge *Advocate* statewide poll of 900 registered voters conducted December 1–11, 1991, by Edward F. Renwick; Bill Walsh, "Anti-Duke Votes Help Edwards Win," *Times-Picayune*, November 17, 1991.

31. Renwick, "The 1991 Louisiana Gubernatorial Campaign," 70.

32. For more on this election, see Charles D. Hadley, "Louisiana: The Continuing Saga of Race, Religion, and Rebellion," in Robert P. Steed, Laurence W. Moreland, and Tod A. Baker, eds., *The 1992 Presidential Election in the South: Current Patterns of Southern Party and Electoral Politics* (Westport, Conn., 1994), 51–65.

33. Jack Wardlaw, "Duke Shadows Governor's Race," *Times-Picayune*, September 27, 1995.

34. Interview with Ed Murray, conducted by Edward F. Renwick, August 19, 1997.

35. Jack Wardlaw, "Landrieu Booed in Appearance on Southern Stage," *Times-Picayune*, October 20, 1995.

36. Jack Wardlaw, "Fields: Party Changes Ahead," *Times-Picayune*, December 5, 1995. After Foster's election, Fields said, "All my life, I've been supporting the Edwin Edwards and the Mary Landrieus of the world and it sure would have been nice to have had them with me."

37. Interview with Jon Johnson, conducted by Edward F. Renwick, August 14, 1997; interview with Murray. Murray articulated another complaint African Americans have against white Democratic leaders: "In Louisiana the speaker [of the house] is a [white] Democrat but a majority of the committee chairmen are Republicans. Only one chairman is a black, although there are nearly as many blacks in the House as there are Republicans." Murray put part of the blame for this situation on the open primary system.

38. Adam Nossiter, "Louisiana Primary Aids Democrat," New York *Times*, September 21, 1996.

39. Bill Walsh, "Ieyoub Dips into Coffers Often: Carpet, Artwork Purchases," *Times-Picayune*, August 29, 1996; Bruce Alpert, "Can Jenkins Break the GOP's Log Jam? GOP Seeks to Avoid Demo Sweep," *Times-Picayune*, September 13, 1996.

40. Jack Wardlaw, "Family Feud," *Times-Picayune*, September 10, 1996.

41. Ed Anderson, "Landrieu Booed in Appearance at Southern University," *Times-Picayune*, October 19, 1996.

42. Press release distributed by Archbishop Hannan: "No Catholic should vote for the President or Mary Landrieu. Mary Landrieu says she is pro-life and pro-choice. She is really pro-abortion."

43. Jack Wardlaw, "Difficult to Assess the Fallout from Hannan's Remarks," *Times-Picayune*, November 2, 1996.

44. For more on the importance of the abortion issue in this election, see Block, "Louisiana: The Last Preserve of the Democratic Party," 34, which contains an analysis of a poll conducted October 5–13, 1996, by Susan Howell, director of the University of New Orleans Survey Research Center.

45. Frank Donze, "Gambling Street Money Aided Landrieu," *Times-Picayune*, November 6, 1996; WWL-TV exit survey of 696 black voters, November 5, 1996.

46. For more on this election, see Charles D. Hadley and Jonathan O. Knuckey, "Louisiana: Laissez les Bon Temps Rouler!" in Laurence W. Moreland and Robert P. Steed, eds., *The 1996 Presidential Election in the South: Southern Party Systems in the 1990s* (Westport, Conn., 1997), 77–93.

47. Jack Wardlaw, "Intraparty Feuding by GOP at Federal and State Level," *Times-Picayune*, July 30, 1997.

48. Interview with Ray Teddlie, conducted by Edward F. Renwick, July 18, 1997.

49. Interview with Jim Brown, conducted by Jack Wardlaw, October 6, 1996; interview with Murray.

50. Interview with Fox McKeithen, conducted by Jack Wardlaw, October 8, 1996.

51. Interview with David Duke, conducted by Jack Wardlaw, October 9, 1996.

52. In December 1997 the U.S. Supreme Court unanimously ruled that Louisiana's open primary system must follow a federal law that requires congressional elections to be held nationwide on the same date in November. The current Louisiana system did not meet the test since four out of five congressional candidates win office in the September open primary and never get to the November runoff (Linda Greenhouse, "High Court Strikes Down Voting Rules in Louisiana," *New York Times*, December 3, 1997). When the Louisiana legislature failed to remedy the situation during the spring of 1998, a U.S. District Court judge ruled in May that the 1998 open primary for the U.S. Senate and U.S. House would have to take place on November 3; any needed runoffs were scheduled for December 5. The judge did not disturb the timing of the open primary for state and local elections; these elections can still take place prior to the national November general election date (Jack Wardlaw, "Open Primary Upheld, but Judge Blasts Legislature," *Times-Picayune*, May 12, 1998). The ruling, which also upheld the open primary law generally, apart from the timing of federal elections, was affirmed by a U.S. appeals court (Jack Wardlaw, "Congressional Elections Set for November: Court Upholds Nonpartisan La. Primary," *Times-Picayune*, July 17, 1998).

11. Texas: Republicans Gallop Ahead

1. David Barboza, "Republicans Strike Deep in the Heart of Texas," New York *Times*, November 29, 1996.

2. The long struggle between conservative and liberal factions for control of the Democratic party is summarized in Chandler Davidson, *Race and Class in Texas Politics* (Princeton, N.J., 1990), 155–97.

3. Hill defeated incumbent governor Dolph Briscoe in the May Democratic primary and focused more on planning his administration than on campaigning against the little known but wealthy Clements. Like "President" Thomas Dewey in 1948, he was surprised by a late surge of support for his underdog opponent.

4. For more on these trends, see Davidson, *Race and Class in Texas*, 237–39, 251–59. *Anglo* is used here, as it is commonly used in Texas political circles, to refer to all non-Hispanic whites.

5. *Ibid.*, 198–220.

6. For two other accounts of Texas electoral change, see Arnold Vedlitz, James A. Dyer, and David B. Hill, "The Changing Texas Voter," in Robert H. Swansbrough and David M. Brodsky, eds., *The South's New Politics: Realignment and Dealignment* (Columbia, S.C., 1988), 38–53, and Jeanie R. Stanley, "Party Realignment in Texas," in Maureen Moakley, ed., *Party Realignment and State Politics* (Columbus, Ohio, 1992), 74–90.

7. Sam Attlesey, "Slim Majority Want Remarks Reported," Dallas *Morning News*, May 26, 1990.

8. Wayne Slater, "Richards Message Personal, Jabs at Bush Alternate with Uplifting Notes," Dallas *Morning News*, July 19, 1988.

9. Celia Morris, *Storming the Statehouse: Running for Governor with Ann Richards and Dianne Feinstein* (New York, 1992), 72–76. Morris details Ann Richards's rationale for refusing to discuss past drug use.

10. Christy Hoppe and Anne Marie Kilday, "Gubernatorial Hopefuls Turn Up Heat," Dallas *Morning News*, March 6, 1990.

11. Morris, *Storming the Statehouse*, 97.

12. *Ibid.*, 109.

13. *Ibid.*, 111; David Whitman, "The Sharpie in Cowboy Duds," *U.S. News and World Report*, July 16, 1990, p. 41.

14. Wayne Slater and Joseph Garcia, "Williams Comment Despicable, Says Richards," Dallas *Morning News*, September 22, 1990; Frank Trejo, "Richards Liar, Says Williams," Dallas *Morning News*, October 12, 1990.

15. Sam Attlesey, "Candidates Spar on Final Weekend: Williams Defends '86 IRS Filing," Dallas *Morning News*.

16. Also on this election, see Sue Tolleson-Rinehart and Jeanie R. Stanley, *Claytie and the Lady: Ann Richards, Gender, and Politics in Texas* (Austin, 1994).

17. Michael Barone and Grant Ujifusa, with Richard E. Cohen, *The Almanac of American Politics* (Washington, D.C., 1995), 1264.

18. Interview with Ben T. Reyes, conducted by Richard Murray, November 17, 1995.

19. Interview with Bill White, conducted by Richard Murray, January 12, 1997.

20. There was more to Clinton's Houston visit. In over thirty years of watching and analyzing campaigns, one of this chapter's authors, Richard Murray, has never witnessed a more impressive performance under pressure than the one the future president gave on Monday afternoon and evening, January 27, 1992. Clinton flew into Houston in mid-afternoon and hurried to a reception for small givers and party activists at the Seafarers Union hall near downtown Houston. He worked the crowd expertly, then gave a strong stump speech before departing for the Warwick Hotel for a $250-per-person reception held in the main ballroom. The governor again worked through the audience of two hundred or so with remarkable ease and confidence for a candidate fighting for his political life. He finished up with a different version of the union hall talk, then retired to watch President Bush deliver what was to be his last State of the Union speech. Immediately following the President's address, Governor Clinton held a press conference attended by a contingent of the national press that was now following the candidate around to get more details about his sex life. The first questions he fielded were hardball personal life queries that he deflected as well as one could without giving specifics. Finally, the questioning turned to his evaluation of the President's speech, and Clinton dissected it with skill. After the press conference, he did a live hookup with Ted Koppel on *Nightline* and acquitted himself well when aggressively questioned by one of television's best interviewers. Then it was back upstairs to the Warwick's penthouse for the main event of his visit, a $1,000-per-person dinner. The governor table-hopped for twenty minutes before giving yet another version of his earlier speeches that incorporated his response to what President Bush had just said. Just before midnight he left to fly back to New Hampshire. The next morning's television news showed him live shaking hands with workers outside a factory.

21. Carolyn Barta, *Perot and His People: Disrupting the Balance of Political Power* (Fort Worth, 1993), 6.

22. Jerome M. Mileur, "The General Election Campaign: Strategy and Support," in William Crotty, ed., *America's Choice: The Election of 1992* (Guilford, Conn., 1993), 52.

23. For more on this election, see Frank B. Feigert and John R. Todd, "Texas: Friends, Neigh-

bors, and Native Sons," in Robert P. Steed, Laurence W. Moreland, and Tod A. Baker, eds., *The 1992 Presidential Election in the South: Current Patterns of Southern Party and Electoral Politics* (Westport, Conn., 1994), 169–79.

24. Ronnie Dugger, "The Fairness Question," *Texas Observer*, July 12, 1991; R. G. Ratcliffe, "Richards Taps Away from National Role," Houston *Chronicle*, September 8, 1991; R. G. Ratcliffe, "Few Fault Richards on Style, but Substance Is Another Matter," Houston *Chronicle*, May 1, 1994.

25. Just 746,641 persons voted in the runoff, down from the 1,027,909 votes cast in the March primary.

26. Associated Press, "Richards Calls Bush Jerk for Attacks on Administration," Dallas *Morning News*, August 17, 1994; Wayne Slater and Sam Attlesey, "Richards, Bush Step Up Attacks, Unveil Strategies," Dallas *Morning News*, October 23, 1994.

27. Bush widened his lead over Richards after Perot's endorsement, taking over 60 percent of the late-deciding voters, according to the Voter News Service exit poll.

28. William Pack, " 'Prince Charming' Joins Campaign," Houston *Post*, June 22, 1994.

29. The statewide low-visibility races in Texas, where voters typically know almost nothing about the candidates save their party, include the nine positions on the Texas supreme court, the nine positions on the Texas court of criminal appeals, and the three railroad commission posts. The other seven statewide positions—giving Texas an amazing 28 elected statewide offices—are governor, lieutenant governor, attorney general, treasurer, comptroller of public accounts, land commissioner, and agriculture commissioner.

30. Sam Attlesey, "Democrats Try to Throw Positive Spin on Recent Election," Dallas *Morning News*, November 20, 1994.

31. Sam Attlesey, "Parties Have Cause for Optimism, Each Other," Dallas *Morning News*, December 24, 1995.

32. Terrence Stutz, "Religious Groups Back Education Candidates," Dallas *Morning News*, October 27, 1996.

33. Clinton's job approval ratings in Harte-Hanks Texas polls taken in 1995 and 1996 showed that he consistently lagged about 10 points behind his national poll ratings with all the difference accounted for by lower ratings among Anglo voters in the state compared to the nation. This pattern persisted through the November 1996 balloting, when, according to Voter News Service exit polls, Clinton received 31 percent of the white vote in Texas compared to 36 percent in the South at large and over 45 percent in the nation.

34. Sam Attlesey, "Hispanic Ballots Seem a Key in Bryant-Morales Runoff," Dallas *Morning News*, April 8, 1996. Attlesey's article employed a regional analysis that showed Morales won heavily Hispanic counties by 100,000 votes and lost elsewhere by 80,000 votes.

35. For more on this election, see Frank B. Feigert and John R. Todd, "Texas: Suppose They Gave an Election and Nobody Came," in Laurence W. Moreland and Robert P. Steed, eds., *The 1996 Presidential Election in the South: Southern Party Systems in the 1990s* (Westport, Conn., 1997), 197–207.

36. Sam Attlesey, "Democrats Rally Behind Morales," Dallas *Morning News*, April 11, 1996.

37. Sam Attlesey, "Abortion Rights Opponents Getting Ready to Rumble," Dallas *Morning News*, July 14, 1996.

38. Sam Attlesey and Susan Feeney, "Gramm Donors Mass Before Campaign D-Day," Dallas *Morning News*, February 24, 1995.

39. Sam Attlesey, "Gramm, Morales Spar in Interviews," Dallas *Morning News*, September 30, 1996.

40. County and urban precinct analysis by the Center for Public Policy, University of Houston, February 1997.

41. The political significance was lessened by the bipartisan tradition of the modern Texas senate, which continued in 1997 under the leadership of the veteran presiding officer, Democratic lieutenant governor Bob Bullock.

42. The 70 percent figure is based on estimates provided to the authors by Democratic and Republican state party officials in January 1997.

43. Republicans have an advantage in statewide races by very high voter turnout in their suburban base areas. However, in district races for Congress and the legislature, much of that advantage is lost because seats are apportioned on the basis of population, not voter turnout, and Democrats generally do well in heavily populated but low turnout areas.

44. See Scott Keeter, "Public Opinion and the Election," in Gerald Pomper, ed., *The Election of 1996: Reports and Interpretations* (Chatham, N.J., 1997), 109–11.

45. Turnout dropped in all urban precinct groups, but was especially lower in working-class Anglo and Hispanic precincts that provide a large share of the Democratic vote base. Precinct analysis conducted by the Center for Public Policy, University of Houston, and reported in the Houston *Chronicle*, November 11, 1996.

46. V. O. Key, Jr., *Southern Politics in State and Nation* (New York, 1949), 254; On a wide variety of indicators Texas is much closer to national means than to those of the other ten former Confederate states. For example, 20.3 percent of the U.S. adult population have college or advanced degrees, compared to 20.4 percent in Texas but just 17.2 percent in the other ten southern states. Nationally, 79.8 percent of the population live in metropolitan areas, compared to 84.1 percent in Texas and 66.6 percent in the rest of the South. The national annual pay for employed persons was $26,959 compared to $25,959 in Texas and $23,383 in other southern states. Data from U.S. Bureau of the Census, *Statistical Abstract of the United States*, 116th ed. (Washington, D.C., 1996), 39, 161, 425.

47. Steve H. Murdock *et al.*, *The Texas Challenge: Population Change and the Future of Texas* (College Station, Tex., 1997).

48. Also hurting the Texas GOP among Hispanics was a highly publicized dispute in Del Rio in which two Anglo Republican candidates defeated two Hispanic incumbents in the heavily Mexican American area with the absentee votes of military personnel who had once served at a local air force base. John Harwood, "Parties Mull Agendas in High-Stakes Battle for Hispanic Votes," *Wall Street Journal*, April 22, 1997.

12. Florida: A Volatile National Microcosm

1. Students of southern politics describing Florida as a different state politically include V. O. Key, Jr., *Southern Politics in State and Nation* (New York, 1949), 83–86; Manning J. Dauer, "Florida: The Different State," in William C. Havard, ed., *The Changing Politics of the South* (Baton Rouge, 1972), 92–94; Alexander P. Lamis, *The Two-Party South*, 2nd expanded ed. (New York, 1990), 179; Robert J. Huckshorn, ed., *Government and Politics in Florida* (Gainesville, 1991), 1–6; and James M. Glaser, *Race, Campaign Politics, and the Realignment in the South* (New Haven, Conn., 1996), 14.

2. Susan A. MacManus, "An American Microcosm," in *The World and I*, XI (August 1996), 36–41, and Albert J. Nelson, *Democrats Under Siege in the Sunbelt Megastates: California, Florida, and Texas* (Westport, Conn., 1996), 1–2.

3. *Florida Statistical Abstract, 1996* (Gainesville, 1996), 22, 18; *1990 Census of Population, Social*

and Economic Characteristics, Florida (Washington, D.C., 1993), 25. Incidentally, the black proportion of the population in 1996 also increased nearly a percentage point from 13.6 percent in 1990.

4. *Florida Statistical Abstract, 1996*, 33. The impact of retirees on public policy is discussed in Walter Rosenbaum and James Button, "Is There a Gray Peril? Retirement Politics in Florida," *Gerontologist*, XXIX (1989), 300–306, as well as in Susan A. MacManus, *Young v. Old: Generational Combat in the 21st Century* (Boulder, Colo., 1996), 245–55, and Mireya Navarro, "Florida Is Cutting-Edge Lab for Big Generational Shifts," New York *Times*, August 7, 1996.

5. Survey Research Laboratory, Florida State University, *Florida Annual Policy Survey* for 1980 and 1995. In 1980, 56 percent of the respondents in the northern part of the state, 40 percent of the male respondents, and 43 percent of those 18 to 30 identified themselves as Democrats. In 1995 the percentages for the respective categories were 33 percent, 20 percent, and 17 percent. See also Paul Allen Beck, "Realignment Begins? The Republican Surge in Florida," *American Politics Quarterly*, X (1982), 421–38.

6. Manning Dauer, "Florida: The Different State," 79–80; Tom Fiedler, "Florida's States of Mind," Miami *Herald*, September 15, 1996. See also the following *Herald* articles by Fiedler: "Way Up North in Dixie; Florida, That Is," September 16, 1996; " 'Barbell' a Bastion of GOP Strength," September 17, 1996; "Holding on to the Land of Crackers," September 18, 1996; "Center of State Pivotal Point for Presidential Race," September 19, 1996.

7. Tom Fiedler, "Listening to That Inner Voice," Miami *Herald*, April 15, 1990.

8. Tom Fiedler, "Allies Desertion a Key to Gov. Martinez's Defeat," Miami *Herald*, November 11, 1990.

9. Tom Fiedler, "Tide Is Reversed in State Now, Republicans Find," Miami *Herald*, November 8, 1990.

10. Ellen McGarrahan, "Senate President Wins Agriculture Post," Miami *Herald*, November 7, 1990.

11. For more on this election, see William Hulbary, Anne E. Kelley, and Lewis Bowman, "Florida: A Muddled Election," in Robert P. Steed, Laurence W. Moreland, and Tod A. Baker, eds., *The 1992 Presidential Election in the South: Current Patterns of Southern Party and Electoral Politics* (Westport, Conn., 1994), 126–33.

12. "Lack of Cash, Support, Doesn't Keep Candidate from Contest," Miami *Herald*, November 1, 1990.

13. Paul Anderson, "Graham Beats Jinx by Winning 2nd Term," Miami *Herald*, November 3, 1992. For a discussion of Graham's style, see David Poppe, "Man in the Middle," *Florida Trend*, XXXIX (June 1996), 37–45.

14. Ellen Debenport, "Chiles Battles Slumping Support," St. Petersburg *Times*, August 29, 1993; Tom Fiedler, "Despite Polls, Governor Is Confident," Miami *Herald*, March 20, 1994.

15. Tom Fiedler, "Bush (Jeb, That Is) Vows Name Won't Tilt Campaign," Miami *Herald*, July 9, 1993.

16. Mark Silva and Bill Moss, "4 Rivals All Bash Bush," Miami *Herald*, September 7, 1994.

17. Tim Nickens, "Bush, Chiles Different in Personality, Politics," Miami *Herald*, September 13, 1994.

18. Interview with Kenneth (Buddy) MacKay, conducted by Tom Fiedler, September 20, 1994.

19. Tim Nickens and Mark Silva, "A Return to Willie Horton?" Miami *Herald*, October 26, 1994.

20. Tom Fiedler, Tim Nickens, and Terry Neal, "Chiles-Bush in Fierce Finale," Miami *Herald*,

November 2, 1994; Mary McGrory, "Chiles' Folksy Style Effective in Debate," Jacksonville *Times-Union*, November 7, 1994.

21. On the basis of exit polls, the Center for the American Woman and Politics (CAWP) listed the Chiles-Bush race as one in which women made a difference in the outcome: 55 percent of women voted for Chiles compared to 46 percent of male voters. "1994 Races Where Female and Male Voters Made Different Voting Choices," *CAWP News and Notes*, X (Winter 1994), 9.

22. Mark Silva, "His Last Race Is Governor's Toughest," Miami *Herald*, November 9, 1994.

23. Tom Fiedler, "When Chiles (in 1991) Won," Miami *Herald*, November 13, 1994.

24. Terry Neal, "A Nasty Tone in Race for Education Post," Miami *Herald*, November 5, 1994.

25. Steve Bousquet, "GOP Makes Inroads on Cabinet," Miami *Herald*, November 9, 1994.

26. John Koenig, "Home Free," *Florida Trend*, XXXVII (August 1994), 41–45.

27. Tom Fiedler, "It's Official: Hugh Rodham Running for U.S. Senate Seat," Miami *Herald*, March 2, 1994.

28. Tom Fiedler, "Clinton Serious About Winning Florida Vote," Miami *Herald*, September 24, 1995. See also Alison Mitchell, "Clinton Seeks Florida Votes with a Focus on Medicare," New York *Times*, September 6, 1996, and R. W. Apple, Jr., "A G.O.P. Sure Thing for Years, Florida Now Seems Up for Grabs," New York *Times*, September 26, 1996.

29. Tom Fiedler, "Dole Preaches to the Choir, Clinton Woos Swing Vote," Miami *Herald*, October 24, 1996, and "Rewriting the Book on Florida: How President Bucked 20-Year Trend Toward GOP," Miami *Herald*, November 6, 1996. For more on this election, see Kathryn Dunn Tenpas, William E. Hulbary, and Lewis Bowman, "Florida: An Election with Something for Everyone," in Laurence W. Moreland and Robert P. Steed, eds., *The 1996 Presidential Election in the South: Southern Party Systems in the 1990s* (Westport, Conn., 1997), 147–63.

30. Dauer, "Florida: The Different State," 119–31; and Manning J. Dauer, Michael A. Maggioto, and Steven G. Koven, "Florida," in Susan A. MacManus, ed., *Reapportionment and Representation in Florida: A Historical Collection* (Tampa, 1991), 171–78.

31. Susan A. MacManus and Ronald Keith Gaddie, "Reapportionment in Florida: The Stakes Keep Getting Higher," in MacManus, *Reapportionment and Representation in Florida*, 470–72.

32. Richard K. Scher, Jon L. Mills, and John J. Hotaling, *Voting Rights and Democracy: The Law and Politics of Districting* (Chicago, 1996), 236–38.

33. Interview with Peter Wallace, conducted by Joan Carver, August 22, 1996; interview with Tom Slade, conducted by Joan Carver, July 19, 1996.

34. Mark Silva, "Florida's Legislature," in Tom Fiedler and Margaret Kempel, eds., *The Miami Herald Almanac of Florida Politics, 1994* (Miami, 1993), 55. For an analysis of the impact of the reapportionment, see Susan A. MacManus and Lesa Chihak, "The 1992 State Legislative Reapportionment: An Overview of the Outcomes Under the New Plan," *Governing Florida*, IV (Fall-Winter 1993), 3–11.

35. Interview with Slade; interview with Kenneth (Buddy) MacKay, conducted by Joan Carver, August 7, 1996.

36. Tyler Bridges, "GOP Eyes a Legislative Prize," Miami *Herald*, July 28, 1996.

37. Tyler Bridges, "GOP Got Decisive Cash Jolt," Miami *Herald*, February 27, 1997.

38. Mark J. Lynn and James B. Allen, "The Rise of the Republican Party in Florida" (Paper presented at the annual meeting of the Southern Political Science Association, Tampa, November 1–4, 1995). See MacManus, ed., *Reapportionment and Representation in Florida,* for thirty-four articles covering various aspects of reapportionment and representation in Florida.

39. Michael Barone and Grant Ujifusa, *The Almanac of American Politics, 1992* (Washington, D.C., 1991) 289.

40. Scher, Mills, and Hotaling, *Voting Rights and Democracy*, 88–89, 223–24; interview with Corrine Brown, conducted by Joan Carver, August 15, 1996.

41. Tim Nickens, "Grinding Ambition Stalls Redistricting," Miami *Herald*, March 15, 1992; Randolph Pendleton, "3rd District Discarded," Jacksonville *Times-Union*, April 18, 1996, and "Districts Set, Qualifying Begins," Jacksonville *Times-Union*, June 17, 1996. The legal and political implications of redistricting are well described with Florida used as a case study in Scher, Mills, and Hotaling, *Voting Rights and Democracy*, particularly 215–43.

42. A study by L. Marvin Overby and Kenneth Cosgrove suggests that white incumbents who lost black constituents did become less sensitive to the concerns of African Americans. See their "Unintended Consequences? Racial Redistricting and the Representation of Minority Interests," *Journal of Politics*, LVIII (1996), 540–49.

43. David Roman, "The Roman Report: District Lineups Give Democrats Smiles," Jacksonville *Times-Union*, October 18, 1996. Tom Slade, the Republican chair, is quoted as saying that he did not recommend running candidates in districts where the party had no chance of winning. "When you don't have any chance at all to defeat a candidate, and if that candidate will bring out votes that will be negative to the remainder of your candidates, then I have always been an advocate of not challenging those races." His view did not prevail.

44. Interview with Scott Falmelen, conducted by Joan Carver, August 15, 1996.

45. Michael A. Fletcher, "New Tolerance in the South or Old Power of Incumbency?" Washington *Post*, November 23, 1996.

46. Mark Stern, "Florida's Elections," in Manning J. Dauer, ed., *Florida's Politics and Government*, 2nd ed. (Gainesville, 1984), 87–88; "How They Voted in the House in 1996," *National Journal*, December 14, 1996, pp. 2683–92. The *National Journal* calculates a liberal and conservative score for each member of Congress for three types of issues: economic, social, and foreign. From this a composite score is developed.

47. Biographies, including party affiliation, of the sheriffs of each of Florida's sixty-seven counties are provided annually in the *Sheriff's Star*. See Vol. XXIV (March-April 1980) and Vol. XL (January-February 1996).

48. Interview with Slade. See also David Roman, "Sticking with 'Fresh Start' Message Did It for Delaney," Jacksonville *Times-Union*, May 10, 1995.

49. John Daigle, "It's Mayor Delaney," Jacksonville *Times-Union*, May 10, 1995.

50. Jim Schoettler, "Glover Wins; Voters Pick First Black as Sheriff," Jacksonville *Times-Union*, April 12, 1995; Steve Patterson, "Glover Took Almost All Sections of City," Jacksonville *Times-Union*, April 13, 1995.

51. William E. Hulbary, Anne E. Kelley, and Lewis Bowman, "Florida: From Freebooting to Real Parties," in Charles D. Hadley and Lewis Bowman, eds., *Southern State Party Organizations and Activists* (Westport, Conn., 1995), 19; Key, *Southern Politics*, 82; Robert J. Huckshorn, "Political Parties and Campaign Finance," in Huckshorn, ed., *Government and Politics in Florida* (Gainesville, 1991), 66; interview with Slade. Anne E. Kelley provides an overview of Florida party organization in "Florida," in Andrew M. Appleton and Daniel S. Ward, eds., *State Party Profiles: A 50-State Guide to Development, Organization, and Resources* (Washington, D.C., 1997), 58–65.

52. Interview with Max Karrer, conducted by Joan Carver, July 30, 1996. See also Meg James, "Coalition 'Will Be Back Again and Again,' " Palm Beach *Post*, May 15, 1995, and staff report,

"Poll: Religious Right Comprises a Minority of Florida Voters," Tallahassee *Democrat*, July 29, 1994.

53. "Chiles Wins Struggle for Democratic Party Power," Jacksonville *Times-Union*, June 12, 1995.

54. Mark Hollis, "Are Florida's Democrats on the Way Out?" Gainesville *Sun*, December 8, 1995.

55. Karen Testa, "NAACP Takes Aim at Democrats: Logan Ouster Promotes 'War,' " Jacksonville *Times-Union*, January 24, 1998; Mireya Navarro, "Democrats' Vote Opens a Racial Rift in Florida," New York *Times*, February 8, 1998; B. Drummond Ayres, Jr., "Race Matters, a Lot, for Florida Democrats," New York *Times*, July 20, 1998. Representative Lesley Miller of Tampa, a leading black candidate for the post, was quoted as follows in the article: "I'll try to pull every facet of our party together. I'm a loyal Democrat." (Miller eventually was elected to the post.) The article also reported that Logan had established "a political action committee that he says will be financed with money from Republicans and dissident Democrats and will support Republican candidates running against House Democrats who opposed him in January."

56. Mireya Navarro, "Chastened by Loss, Jeb Bush Looks Unbeatable in Florida," New York *Times*, May 12, 1998; Steve Bousquet, "Democrats Seek Revival with Broward Chairman," Miami *Herald*, June 1, 1998.

57. Interview with Jon L. Mills, conducted by Joan Carver, August 16, 1996. For more on the DLC, see Howard Troxler, "Democrat Group Hunts for the Center," St. Petersburg *Times*, August 27, 1995, and Nicol C. Rae, *Southern Democrats* (New York, 1994), 111–27.

58. Hulbary, Kelley, and Bowman, "Florida: From Freebooting to Real Parties," 19. The authors argue that Florida's "demographic swirl enhanced the atomized, rootless character of Florida's population and inhibited development of a political culture stressing long-term commitment to the state and its people." In the first half of the 1990s the theme of the Florida Humanities Council was "Making Florida Home," with the goal of encouraging Florida residents to accept the idea that Florida, not the place from which they had migrated, was now their home. See also Stephen J. Whitfield, "Florida's Fudged Identity," *Florida Historical Quarterly*, LXXI (1993), 413–35.

59. Paul Allen Beck and Anneliese Reich, *The 1980 Florida Annual Policy Survey: Policy Preferences and Priorities of the Florida Public* (Tallahassee, 1980), 33; and Suzanne L. Parker, *Florida Annual Policy Survey, 1995* (Tallahassee, 1995), 3–21; Lance deHaven Smith, *The Florida Voter* (Tallahassee, 1995), 96–101.

60. Key, *Southern Politics*, 83.

61. In the annual survey by the Survey Research Laboratory at Florida State University, 34 percent of the voters identified themselves as independent in 1995. *Florida Annual Policy Survey, 1995*, 25.

62. Florida's experience with growth has posed a number of challenges for the state, challenges that have frequently gone unmet. Raymond A. Mohl and Gary R. Mormino point out that "few leaders seem ashamed that Florida ranks at the bottom of all fifty states in per capita support for higher education, or that the state's public schools are badly overcrowded and notoriously undersupported, or that Florida ranks high among the states in the number of prison inmates per capita." They go on to conclude that "getting beyond the tourist imagery, there are many shadows in the Florida sunshine." Mohl and Mormino, "The Big Change in the Sunshine State," in Michael Gannon, ed., *The New History of Florida* (Gainesville, 1996), 445. See also Lance deHaven Smith's discussion of growth management in *The Florida Voter*, 77–96.

63. For a discussion of issues facing Florida in the future, see Jonathan K. Hage, "The Three

Big Social Issues," *The World and I,* XI (August 1996), 30–35; James R. Hagy, "What's It Going To Be?" and "The Welfare State," in *Florida Trend,* XXXVI (December 1993), 40–50; and Susan MacManus, *Young v. Old,* 252. MacManus suggests that age is likely to be "to the next millennium what race has been to the last half of the twentieth century—a high profile, highly divisive problem for which it will be extremely difficult to devise solutions that work."

13. Southern Politics in the 1990s

1. Calling 1994 a turning point for the GOP in down-ticket contests, Hastings Wyman reported the following based on data provided him by David E. Sturrock: "Of 67 races for lesser statewide offices in Southern states this year [1994], Democrats ran candidates for all 67, Republicans contested 58. GOP candidates won 31 races, Democrats won 27 contested races and 9 uncontested races. Thus, the GOP won 46% of the lesser statewide offices on Southern ballots, compared to 12% in 1990 and 8% in 1986." *Southern Political Report,* No. 401 (December 6, 1994).

2. For more on this topic, see David E. Sturrock, "Out of the Phone Booths: Republican Primaries in the Deep South," in Robert P. Steed, Laurence W. Moreland, and Tod A. Baker, eds., *Southern Parties and Elections: Studies in Regional Political Change* (Tuscaloosa, Ala., 1997), 95–108.

3. White southerners claiming independent status increased from 18 percent in 1960 to 42 percent in 1992, before dropping to 32 percent in 1996. These regional party identification figures are from the National Election Studies, conducted by the Center for Political Studies at the University of Michigan. The 1960 figures are from Alexander P. Lamis, *The Two-Party South,* 2nd expanded ed. (New York, 1990), Table 3-4, p. 36. The 1990s figures are from Paul Allen Beck, "Changing American Party Coalitions" (paper presented at the Conference on the State of the Parties: 1996 and Beyond, held at the University of Akron, Ray C. Bliss Institute of Applied Politics, Akron, October 9–10, 1997).

4. Here are the 1990 figures for the other ten states (that is, per capita income as a percentage of the national average): Alabama, 80.4 percent; Arkansas, 75.9 percent; Florida, 99.1 percent; Georgia, 91.2 percent; Louisiana, 77.8 percent; Mississippi, 68.6 percent; North Carolina, 87.2 percent; Tennessee, 84.9 percent; Texas, 89.4 percent; and Virginia, 105.2 percent. The source for these percentages is the 1990 U.S. census.

5. Earl Black and Merle Black, *Politics and Society in the South* (Cambridge, Mass., 1987), 52, 53, 57.

6. For an informative account of this process in Alabama's St. Clair County, east of Birmingham, see Ronald Smothers, "G.O.P. Gains in South Spread to Local Level," New York *Times,* April 11, 1995. For a recent study of local party organization, see Robert P. Steed, John A. Clark, Lewis Bowman, and Charles D. Hadley, eds., *Party Organization and Activism in the American South* (Tuscaloosa, Ala., 1998).

7. John F. Persinos, "Has the Christian Right Taken Over the Republican Party?" *Campaigns and Elections* (September 1994), 21–24.

8. The national scope of the GOP cleavage was apparent in a May 26, 1996, New York *Times* article by Richard L. Berke headlined, "Rifts in G.O.P. Are Widening in Many States." The bulk of the article focused on the bitter infighting in the Minnesota Republican party between the religious right and GOP moderates. The article also discussed similar divisions in Kansas, Illinois, and Indiana. Virginia was the only southern state covered.

9. Persinos, "Has the Christian Right Taken Over?" 24. A good entry point to the vast litera-

ture on this topic is Clyde Wilcox, *Onward Christian Soldiers? The Religious Right in American Politics* (Boulder, Colo., 1996). See also Mark J. Rozell and Clyde Wilcox, eds., *God at the Grass Roots: The Christian Right in the 1994 Elections* (Lanham, Md., 1995), and Oran P. Smith, *The Rise of Baptist Republicanism* (New York, 1997).

10. In fact, so prominent is the Virginia case that a lengthy scholarly study of it was recently published: Mark J. Rozell and Clyde Wilcox, *Second Coming: The New Christian Right in Virginia Politics* (Baltimore, 1996).

11. In January 1998 Gilda Cobb-Hunter was elected minority leader of the South Carolina house, becoming the first African American to lead a legislative caucus in the state in this century. At the time of the vote, the house Democratic caucus consisted of 25 blacks and 24 whites. *The State* reported that "the vote came after weeks of quiet maneuvering designed to keep conservative white Democrats from bolting if the liberal Cobb-Hunter was elected." The article continued: "While Cobb-Hunter is widely respected as a forceful and articulate leader, many in the party worried that she is too liberal. Others also fretted that Democrats in majority-white districts would face GOP attacks for supporting a black party leader." Upon her election, Cobb-Hunter was quoted as follows: "This is America, and . . . one can advance based on one's capabilities. The Democratic Party does indeed put its money where its mouth is. We're not afraid to deal with issues of race." Michael Sponhour, "House Caucus Rallies Behind Cobb-Hunter," *The State*, January 21, 1998. In a profile article after her election, Cobb-Hunter said she aspires to be "the voice for the voiceless," adding: "We will not continue to write off white voters to the Republican Party. You have people in power who have a vested interest in making sure poor whites don't understand that they have more in common with people of color than they do with rich white people." Jay Taylor, "New Top Democrat Fights on Standing Up for Beliefs," *The State*, January 26, 1998. See also Michael Sponhour and Lee Bandy, "The Colors of a Caucus: Will White Conservatives Flee Their Party if Black Woman Leads House Democrats?" *The State*, January 10, 1998.

12. Senator Jackson's actions in maintaining black-white Democratic cohesion when drawing state senate districts is discussed in the South Carolina chapter; also see his comments in that chapter on the approach a black statewide candidate should take in order to win with the electorate.

13. A recent example came in early 1998 with the removal of an African American as leader of Florida's house Democrats. See Mireya Navarro, "Democrats' Vote Opens a Racial Rift in Florida," New York *Times*, February 8, 1998.

14. Our understanding of current black-white Democratic party relations in the South would be immeasurably enhanced if extensive state case studies of these biracial coalitions existed. They would make excellent doctoral dissertation topics.

15. In the October 14, 1997, issue of his *Southern Political Report* (No. 469), Hastings Wyman surveyed the state of black-white Democratic relations in the region and concluded: "Despite conflicts, both black and white Democrats are well aware of their mutual dependency and are anxious to accommodate one another most—but not all—of the time."

16. They were Cynthia McKinney and Sanford Bishop of Georgia; Eddie Bernice Johnson and Sheila Jackson Lee of Texas; and Corrine Brown of Florida. (Incidentally, Lee's Houston district was one of the five southern black-majority districts in existence prior to the early 1990s creation of the twelve new black-majority districts.) Cleo Fields of Louisiana did not seek reelection in 1996; he did run unsuccessfully for governor in 1995, as recounted in the Louisiana chapter. For more on these five congressional elections, see Michael A. Fletcher, "New Tolerance in the South or Old Power of Incumbency? Blacks Won in Five Redrawn Mostly White Districts," *Washington Post*, November 23, 1996.

17. Alan Greenblatt, "Texas, North Carolina Maps Upheld by Federal Panels," *Congressional Quarterly Weekly Report*, September 20, 1997, p. 2250.

18. Cindi Ross Scoppe, "6th District's Lines Stand: Settlement Leaves Clyburn Clear for '98— and Even 2000," *The State*, August 8, 1997; Tom Gordon, "Parties Drop Challenge to District Seven," Birmingham *News*, March 24, 1998. Incidentally, of the twelve new black-majority districts only the two in south Florida—Carrie Meek's Seventeenth District and Alcee Hastings's Twenty-Third District—had not been challenged as of mid-1998; a Florida legal challenge, which was successful, came only in Corrine Brown's Jacksonville-to-Orlando Third District. Also, in this tangled redistricting episode, Louisiana is once again *sui generis*. The Bayou State, which had the second highest southern percentage of blacks in its 1990 population, did not replace its invalidated second black-majority district by creating a new district in which blacks were a substantial minority, known as an "influence" district in the jargon of redistricting. Rather, Louisiana ended up with three districts that are each just under 30 percent black and two in the low 20s, which may help explain why Congressman Fields was the only southern black incumbent member of Congress not to seek reelection. The 63 percent black-majority New Orleans district and a 90 percent white New Orleans suburban district completed the state's seven-district picture.

19. In the 125-member southern congressional delegation of the 1990s, the 16 African Americans elected in 1996 made up 12.8 percent of the total. After the 1990 election and before the creation of the 12 new black-majority districts, there were only five African Americans in the then-116-member southern delegation, or 4.3 percent. (See Table 1 for the percentages of African Americans in the southern states.) Incidentally, those five black Democrats in 1990 constituted 6.5 percent of the southern Democratic delegation of 77 members. In 1996 the 16 African Americans amounted to 29.6 percent of the diminished southern Democratic congressional delegation of 54 members, a situation that vividly exhibits the party's biracial reality in its leaner 1990s guise.

20. He was specifically referring to the state legislative level, but the notion applies to congressional districts as well.

21. For more on the representation dilemma, see David Lublin, *The Paradox of Representation: Racial Gerrymandering and Minority Interests in Congress* (Princeton, N.J., 1997), and David K. Ryden, *Representation in Crisis: The Constitution, Interest Groups, and Political Parties* (Albany, N.Y., 1996). For a helpful short essay, see Mark E. Rush, "Gerrymandering: Out of the Political Thicket and into the Quagmire," *PS: Political Science & Politics* (December 1994), 682–85, which begins: "There is more to gerrymandering than debates about cartographical aesthetics. The issue goes directly to the heart of theories of democracy and representation and is replete with controversy, irony, and inconsistency."

22. For an earlier prediction along these lines, see Alexander P. Lamis, "The Future of Southern Politics: New Directions for Dixie," in Joe P. Dunn and Howard L. Preston, eds., *The Future South: A Historical Perspective for the Twenty-First Century* (Urbana, Ill., 1991), 323–24.

23. As part of this transformation, the southern Democratic party may even have moved closer to becoming a force that promotes the interests of "those who have less" of both races, although the evidence from the state chapters is inconclusive. (See note 11 above for a fascinating glimpse of the process at work in South Carolina in early 1998.) For more on this aspiration from a Huey Long Democrat's perspective, see Lamis, *The Two-Party South*, 231–32, 325–26. For example, surveying the situation on the eve of the 1990s, I made this prediction tinged with philosophical hope: "A weakened Southern black-white Democratic coalition, slowly drained of its more conservative elements, faced with increasing opposition at the lower ballot levels, and subjected to strong nationalizing tendencies will be forced to abandon its current centrist, straddling posture and become a party

with serious policy content and a meaningful program for its adherents. . . . If what I am predicting occurs, in essence, 'those who have less' of both races will finally have attained the vehicle that Professor Key predicted in 1949 would flow from a dissolution of the one-party South" (325–26).

24. When asked about the rash of Democrats abandoning his party, South Carolinian Don Fowler, then chairman of the Democratic National Committee, emphasized the positive side: "If you're that cavalier about what you believe, in terms of issues, you don't do the party you're leaving any damage because you aren't doing it any good by staying." He also noted that the switchers to the GOP "are doing it for reasons that relate to their own ambition." Katharine Q. Seelye, "Democrats Fleeing to G.O.P. Remake Political Landscape," New York Times, October 7, 1995.

25. Lamis, The Two-Party South, 83; Peter Applebome, "The Rising G.O.P. Tide Overwhelms the Democratic Levees in the South," New York Times, November 11, 1994.

26. Richard L. Berke, "Democrats Fear That the South Will Leave Them Out in the Cold," New York Times, May 21, 1994.

27. Jack Wardlaw, "La. Republicans Struggle to Gain Foothold," New Orleans Times-Picayune, September 21, 1997; B. Drummond Ayres, Jr., "Christian Right Splits G.O.P. in South," New York Times, June 7, 1993.

28. The GOP in the South has yet to hold both houses of a legislature and the governorship at the same time. In fact, in only one state—Florida—does the GOP currently control both houses of the state legislature, and there the governor is a Democrat. As of early 1998, the GOP also controlled the house in North Carolina and South Carolina and the senate in Texas. In both houses of the Virginia legislature, power-sharing arrangements were in place.

29. For more on this topic, see "Realignment and Southern Politics" in Lamis, The Two-Party South, 301–304, which draws from my "Realignment as a Synonym for Change: A Conceptual Assessment with Reference to Recent Southern and National Electoral Politics" (Paper delivered at the Annual Meeting of the American Political Science Association in Chicago, September 3–6, 1987).

30. V. O. Key, Jr., "A Theory of Critical Elections," Journal of Politics, XXI (1955), 4; James L. Sundquist, Dynamics of the Party System: Alignment and Realignment of Political Parties in the United States, rev. ed. (Washington, D.C., 1983). An excellent entry point to the literature is Byron E. Shafer, ed., The End of Realignment? Interpreting American Electoral Eras (Madison, Wis., 1991), which grew out of papers presented at the Harold G. Lasswell Symposium at the 1989 annual meeting of the American Political Science Association in Atlanta. In addition to the fine essays by Joel H. Silbey, Everett Carll Ladd, Byron E. Shafer, Samuel T. McSeveney, and Walter Dean Burnham, the volume contains an invaluable and exhaustive guide to the realignment literature by Harold F. Bass, pages 141–178. For an interesting recent article on the topic, see Peter F. Nardulli, "The Concept of a Critical Realignment, Electoral Behavior, and Political Change," American Political Science Review, LXXXIX (March 1995), 10–22.

31. James MacGregor Burns, The Workshop of Democracy (New York, 1985), 205.

32. Ibid., 233.

33. The first hundred years of Figures 15 to 18 are drawn from Paul T. David, Party Strength in the United States, 1872–1970 (Charlottesville, Va., 1972), 28–31. See Chapter 1 and note 1 of that chapter for details on the construction of the index and on how it was updated through 1996. Retaining David's regional divisions, I have included Kentucky and Oklahoma with the eleven states of the former Confederacy in Figure 18. Incidentally, the regional figures are weighted to account for population differences among the states.

34. One major deviation during the period resulted from the titanic Republican schism of

1912. The split between President William Howard Taft, the Republican nominee, and the former Republican president Theodore Roosevelt, the nominee of the Progressive (Bull Moose) party, allowed the Democratic presidential standard-bearer, Woodrow Wilson, a one-term progressive governor of New Jersey and a native southerner, to win the White House. It was only the Democratic party's third presidential victory since 1856.

35. Burns, *Workshop of Democracy*, 486

36. Sundquist, *Dynamics of the Party System*, 210; James MacGregor Burns, *The Crosswinds of Freedom* (New York, 1989), 75.

37. Sundquist, *Dynamics of the Party System*, 213; Burns, *Crosswinds of Freedom*, 86 (italics removed).

38. When major changes sweep over the party system, they never erase everything in their path. Sundquist illustrated the point with his marvelous "overlay" analogy, which deserves full quotation: "In every new alignment of the party system, then, there will be large, perhaps dominant, elements carried over from the old. Successive realignments can be best understood as new patterns drawn on transparent overlays. Each overlay defines a new line of party cleavage within the electorate (or redelineates an old line) and so distributes some elements of the voting population on either side of that line in new arrangements. But beneath the latest overlay can be discerned all the lines of cleavage of the past, some more distinct than others by virtue of their recency or the strength of the color in which they were originally drawn" (17). Sensitivity to this residue of history is useful when trying to sort out the full impact of a new realignment on the previous patterns. After the New Deal "earthquake" the most important "cleavage of the past" that stood out in bold relief was, of course, the continued persistence of the one-party Democratic South dedicated to the preservation of the post-Reconstruction racial status quo.

39. The pre-Rooseveltian Democratic party was quite different, as partly captured in this acidic 1931 commentary in the *Nation*: "[The Democratic party] differs from the G.O.P. only in that its desire to become the party of privilege has never been satisfied. . . . Essentially there is no difference between the two major parties except that the bankers and businessmen have found the Republicans more dependable." Quoted in Sundquist, *Dynamics of the Party System*, 205. Although the *Nation*'s characterization of the pre-1932 Democrats is an exaggeration, it does serve to emphasize the break wrought by FDR's New Deal activism. For more on the complexities of the Democratic party as it entered the new era, see Douglas B. Craig, *After Wilson: The Struggle for the Democratic Party, 1920–1934* (Chapel Hill, N.C., 1992). For example, Craig writes in his introduction: "While the party was engaged in bitter disputes over prohibition, urbanism, and Catholicism, it was also torn apart by a fierce struggle between conservatives and liberals for control of the party's economic and social policies. . . . To the existing ethnocultural catalog of splits between wets and dries, urbanites and rural dwellers, Catholics and Protestants, and immigrants and natives, this book adds a fifth division between liberals and conservatives" (2). Incidentally, the term "those who have less," as noted in Chapter 1, is borrowed from Key, *Southern Politics*, 307.

40. Sundquist, *Dynamics of the Party System*, Chap. 11. The author elaborated on the problem: "The Democrats who rode into positions of power on the crest of the Roosevelt tide lacked the appeal, the public respect, the motivation, and the competence that would have enabled them to quickly consolidate the support the party had temporarily gained in the early 1930s. The leadership was too old or too conservative to appeal to Roosevelt supporters, or more deeply committed to the party's patronage than to its program, or all of these. . . . The Democratic party in many states was still too Catholic to appeal to the Protestant majority, and it was too urban to appeal to the rural and small-town population" (262).

41. *Ibid.,* 267.

42. On this situation, Theodore H. White wrote: "Time was, forty years ago, when Negroes voted solidly Republican out of gratitude to Abraham Lincoln and emancipation. ('I remember,' once said Roy Wilkins, Executive Secretary of the National Association for the Advancement of Colored People, 'when I was young in Kansas City, the kids threw rocks at Negroes on our street who dared to vote Democratic.') But Franklin D. Roosevelt changed that. Under Roosevelt, government came to mean social security, relief, strong unions, unemployment compensation. ('Let Jesus lead me, and welfare feed me' was a Negro depression chant.) And, like a heaving-off of ancient habit, as the Negro moved north he moved on to the Democratic voting rolls." White, *The Making of the President 1960* (New York, 1961), 232.

43. For example, David's preliminary index of Democratic party strength for the nation in 1996 was 49.4 percent.

44. Thomas Byrne Edsall and Mary D. Edsall, *Chain Reaction: The Impact of Race, Rights, and Taxes on American Politics* (New York, 1991), 3–31.

45. The term refers to the post–Civil War era use of the deadly sectional conflict by northern Republicans and southern Democrats to remind the faithful of their underlying hatred for the other side.

46. The three issues in quotation marks are from Sundquist, *Dynamics of the Party System,* 376. In his chapter "Years of Disruption: Crosscutting Issues Nationwide" (376–411), Sundquist offers an excellent overview of the conflicts of the time. The term used to describe the domestic side of the turmoil—"Social Issue"—was coined by Richard M. Scammon and Ben J. Wattenberg in *The Real Majority: An Extraordinary Examination of the American Electorate* (New York, 1970).

47. For a fine narrative account of the origins of these cleavages, see James T. Patterson, *Grand Expectations: The United States, 1945–1974* (New York, 1996), Chap. 21. Patterson entitles this chapter of his excellent book "Rights, Polarization, and Backlash, 1966–1967."

48. Edsall and Edsall, *Chain Reaction,* 5. In a prescient 1970 book, *The Hidden Crisis in American Politics,* Samuel Lubell captured the essence of what was happening. Although his book also delineated the new nonracial cleavages, he concluded: "The New Deal coalition has not collapsed in one heap . . . but broke down at one enormously important point, that of racial conflict" (29). Years later, other researchers—using an array of statistical data—have substantiated Lubell's quick contemporary assessment. See, for example, Edward G. Carmines and James A. Stimson, *Race and the Transformation of American Politics* (Princeton, N.J., 1989).

49. Jack W. Germond and Jules Witcover, *Whose Broad Stripes and Bright Stars? The Trivial Pursuit of the Presidency, 1988* (New York, 1989), 10, 409. For a full, insightful discussion of the Willie Horton ad and what it epitomized in American politics, see Dan T. Carter, *From George Wallace to Newt Gingrich: Race in the Conservative Counterrevolution, 1963–1994* (Baton Rouge, 1996), 72–80. After highlighting the Horton episode, Carter went on to describe the 1988 Bush tactics as benefiting from two decades of Democratic vulnerability. Concluding a discussion of the Edsalls' analysis, Carter wrote: "Yet race seemed to be the glue that held it all together. . . . Unwilling to make their case on the basis of pocketbook issues and well aware that such racial and social issues split the major elements of the old New Deal, Democrats stumbled along, offering few alternatives to the rising GOP challenge." The author added a telling item a few sentences later: "As one indiscreet GOP campaign official said gleefully in the 1988 campaign, every time Michael Dukakis appeared on a platform with Jesse Jackson, the Republican votes started coming up like change on a cash register" (80).

50. Sundquist, *Dynamics of the Party System,* 334–36.

51. *Ibid.*, 297.

52. See Lamis, *The Two-Party South*, 242–48 (especially Table 16-5) and 311–13 (especially Table 19-4). These tables are based on data from the 1980s, but the same trends persist when similar calculations are done using surveys from the 1990s. For a recent article that finds racial prejudice "markedly higher" in the South, especially among white southern men, see James H. Kuklinski, Michael D. Cobb, and Martin Gilens, "Racial Attitudes and the 'New South,' " *Journal of Politics*, LIX (1997), 323–49.

53. Dewey W. Grantham provides a thoughtful discussion of this topic in "The Persistence of Southern Distinctiveness," the next-to-last chapter in his *The South in Modern America: A Region at Odds* (New York, 1995), 311–31. Also, see the many works of John Shelton Reed, starting with *The Enduring South: Subcultural Persistence in Mass Society* (Lexington, Mass., 1972), and the numerous relevant entries in Charles Reagan Wilson and William Ferris, eds., *Encyclopedia of Southern Culture* (Chapel Hill, N.C., 1989).

54. For an intriguing exposition of the long-term intertwining relationship of the South with the rest of the country, see Grantham's concluding chapter in his *The South in Modern America*, 332–42. In the final paragraph, he writes: "Thus, the interplay of the South, the North, and the nation represents a rich and instructive theme in modern American history" (342).

55. The strengths and weaknesses of the political system of one large northern state with a well-established two-party system—Ohio—were impressed upon me when I assembled a team of political scientists and journalists in the early 1990s to investigate all aspects of the state's politics. See Alexander P. Lamis, ed., *Ohio Politics* (Kent, Ohio, 1994).

56. Key, *Southern Politics*, 11.

57. *Ibid.*, 4.

58. Alexander P. Lamis and Nathan Goldman, "V. O. Key's *Southern Politics*: The Writing of a Classic," *Georgia Historical Quarterly*, LXXI (1987), 279.

CONTRIBUTORS

PHILIP ASHFORD is a Princeton, New Jersey, management consultant. He received a B.A. in political science from the University of Connecticut and an M.A. in political science from the University of Delaware. In addition, he earned an M.S. in journalism from Columbia University and an M.S. in management from the Massachusetts Institute of Technology. From 1991 to 1997, he served as special assistant for policy and research to Nashville mayor Phil Bredesen. Previously, he spent six years as a reporter in the Nashville bureau of the Memphis *Commercial Appeal* and also worked at the Baltimore *Sun* and the Associated Press.

SAM ATTLESEY is political writer and deputy chief of the Austin bureau of the Dallas *Morning News*. He holds a B.A. in political science from Baylor University and a B.A. in journalism from East Texas State University. He has covered local, state, and national politics since he began his newspaper career in 1973 at the Lubbock *Avalanche-Journal*. He joined the Dallas paper in 1975 and became its political writer in 1978. He is coauthor of *Political History of Texas*.

LEE BANDY is chief political writer for *The State* newspaper in Columbia, South Carolina. He holds a B.A. in radio and television speech from Bob Jones University. For thirty years, he served as Washington correspondent for *The State*. He is a former chairman of the Standing Committee of Congressional Correspondents and an associate member of Washington's Gridiron Club.

JAY BARTH is assistant professor of politics at Hendrix College. He holds a Ph.D. in political science from the University of North Carolina at Chapel Hill. His published works have covered partisan change in the South, voting behavior, and gubernatorial behavior.

TOM BAXTER is political editor of the Atlanta *Journal and Constitution*. A native of Montgomery, Alabama, he is a graduate of Washington University. Before joining the *Journal* as a reporter in 1974, he worked at newspapers in Montgomery; Columbia, Maryland; and Charleston, South Carolina. In Atlanta he was the first editor of the newspaper's Sunday Perspective section and later national editor of both newspapers.

MICHAEL B. BINFORD is associate professor of political science at Georgia State University, where he has taught for the last twenty years. He holds a Ph.D. from the University of North Carolina at Chapel Hill. His research and writing have focused on electoral politics and voting rights, southern politics, and Georgia elections.

DIANE D. BLAIR is professor of political science emeritus at the University of Arkansas, where she taught for thirty years. She holds a B.A. from Cornell University and an M.A. from the University of Arkansas. She is the author of *Arkansas Government and Politics: Do the People Rule?* and *Silent Hattie Speaks: The Personal Journal of Senator Hattie Caraway*, along with articles and book chapters on state politics, Arkansas politics, and women in politics. In 1993 she was named by President Clinton to the board of the Corporation for Public Broadcasting, which she currently chairs.

DAVID A. BREAUX is associate professor of political science at Mississippi State University. He holds a Ph.D. in political science from the University of Kentucky. He has published articles and book chapters on comparative state politics, political party organization, and Mississippi electoral politics.

GLEN T. BROACH is professor and chair of political science at Winthrop University. He holds a Ph.D. in political science from the University of Alabama. He has written extensively on South Carolina politics and is editor of the *Carolina Report*, a governmental affairs newsletter. Before joining Winthrop in 1984, he taught at East Tennessee State University and the University of South Alabama.

JOAN S. CARVER is dean of the College of Arts and Sciences and professor of political science at Jacksonville University. She received her Ph.D. in political science from the University of Florida. Her major areas of research and publication are elections and political parties, women in politics, urban government reform, and Florida politics.

ROB CHRISTENSEN is the chief political writer and columnist for the Raleigh *News and Observer*. Educated at the University of Tennessee, he has covered North Carolina politics and government for twenty-five years, both from Raleigh and Washington. He was a contributor to *Discovering North Carolina*.

PATRICK R. COTTER is associate professor of political science at the University of Alabama. He received his Ph.D. in political science from Ohio State University. A partner in Southern Opinion Research, a Tuscaloosa survey research firm, he has published many articles and book chapters on Alabama and southern politics.

ERNEST C. DUMAS is assistant professor of journalism at the University of Central Arkansas. He received B.J. and A.B. degrees from the University of Missouri. He was the chief state Capitol correspondent for the Arkansas *Gazette* for fourteen years and associate editor and editorial writer for the newspaper for thirteen years. He currently writes a weekly political column for the Arkansas *Times*.

MARGARET E. EDDS is an editorial writer for the Norfolk *Virginian-Pilot*. She holds a B.A. from Tennessee Wesleyan College. A former fellow of the Alicia Patterson Foundation, she has covered state politics and government in Virginia for two decades. She is the author of *Free At Last: What Really Happened When Civil Rights Came to Southern Politics* and *Claiming the Dream: The Victorious Campaign of Douglas Wilder of Virginia*.

TOM FIEDLER is political editor and columnist for the Miami *Herald*, a post he has occupied since 1984. He holds a B.S. in engineering from the U.S. Merchant Marine Academy and an M.S. in journalism from Boston University. He joined the Orlando *Sentinel* in 1971 and moved to the *Herald* two years later. His reporting assignments have included stints as a statehouse reporter in Tallahassee and as a Washington correspondent. He is the author of the *Almanac of Florida Politics*.

JACK D. FLEER is professor in the Department of Politics at Wake Forest University, where he served for twenty years as chairman of the department. He holds a Ph.D. in political science from the University of North Carolina at Chapel Hill. The author of *North Carolina Politics:*

An Introduction and *North Carolina Government and Politics,* he has also written articles and book chapters on various aspects of southern and North Carolina politics, including campaign finance, interest groups, and political parties.

TOM GORDON is a state reporter for the Birmingham *News,* a position he has held since 1982. He earned a B.A. at the University of Alabama and an M.J. at the University of Missouri. Before joining the *News,* he was a reporter and state editor for the Anniston *Star* from 1974 to 1981 and then worked as a freelance journalist in West Africa. He was the principal architect of *Wallace: A Portrait of Power,* his newspaper's recent special section and subsequent book on the late Alabama governor George C. Wallace.

ALEXANDER P. LAMIS is associate professor of political science at Case Western Reserve University. A native of Charleston, South Carolina, he holds a Ph.D. in political science from Vanderbilt University and a J.D. from the University of Maryland Law School. A specialist on elections and political parties, he is the author of *The Two-Party South* and articles and book chapters on southern politics. He is also the editor of *Ohio Politics,* his first book project involving journalists and political scientists. Before joining Case Western Reserve University in 1988, he taught at the University of North Florida and the University of Mississippi and worked as a research assistant at the Brookings Institution. He recently became a member of the Ohio bar.

RICHARD LOCKER is chief of the Nashville bureau of the Memphis *Commercial Appeal.* A graduate of the University of Tennessee with a B.S. in journalism, he covered county government and state politics for the Knoxville *Journal* from 1975 to 1979, then reported on business and state government for the Nashville *Banner* for three years before joining the *Commercial Appeal* in Memphis in 1982. He has worked out of the paper's statehouse bureau since 1983.

BILL MINOR is a Jackson, Mississippi, syndicated political columnist who has covered every aspect of Mississippi politics as a newspaperman since 1947. His fifty years of distinguished reporting was honored in 1997 when he became the first recipient of the University of Pennsylvania's John Chancellor Award for Excellence in Journalism. A graduate of Tulane University and a World War II combat veteran, he worked for thirty years as the Mississippi correspondent of the New Orleans *Times-Picayune*, covering the turbulent civil rights era. Later, for seven years, he published his own weekly newspaper in Jackson. His articles have appeared in a wide variety of national and regional publications. He also served for several decades as the Mississippi stringer for the New York *Times* and *Newsweek* magazine. His column, "Eyes on Mississippi," appears in forty state newspapers.

THOMAS R. MORRIS is president of Emory & Henry College as well as professor of political science at the college. He holds a Ph.D. in political science from the University of Virginia. He is the author of *The Virginia Supreme Court* and coauthor of *Virginia Government and Politics* and has written articles and book chapters on various aspects of state government. Before becoming president of Emory & Henry College, he taught political science for twenty-one years at the University of Richmond.

RICHARD MURRAY is professor of political science and director of the Center for Public Policy at the University of Houston, where he has taught since 1966. A native of Louisiana, he holds a Ph.D. in political science from the University of Minnesota. He is coauthor of *Texas Politics: An Introduction* and *Progrowth Politics: Change and Governance in Houston* and is the author of various articles and book chapters. He has conducted polls for the news media since 1978 and has consulted in more than two hundred political campaigns.

WAYNE PARENT is associate professor of political science at Louisiana State University. A Louisiana native, he received his Ph.D. from Indiana University. He is coeditor of *Blacks and the American Political System* and has written several articles and book chapters on electoral coalitions, black politics, southern politics, and Louisiana politics.

EDWARD F. RENWICK is associate professor of political science at Loyola University in New Orleans and director of Loyola's Institute of Politics, a position he has occupied since 1970. He holds a Ph.D. in political science from the University of Arizona. A pollster since 1971, he is the political analyst for the CBS television affiliate in New Orleans. His specialty is Louisiana politics.

STEPHEN D. SHAFFER is professor of political science at Mississippi State University. He holds a Ph.D. in political science from Ohio State University. He has directed the Mississippi Poll since 1981 and is coeditor of *Mississippi Government and Politics: Modernizers Versus Traditionalists.* A leader of the Mississippi team of the Southern Grassroots Party Activists project and a regular contributor to the Citadel's "Presidential Election in the South" book series, he has published extensively on Mississippi politics.

DAVID E. STURROCK is associate professor of political science at Southwest State University in Marshall, Minnesota. He holds a Ph.D. from the University of California at Riverside. In addition to his published work on southern politics, he has authored articles and chapters on the political life of California, Iowa, Minnesota, New York, and Ohio. He also has experience in practical politics as an activist, pollster, party official, and candidate.

JACK D. WARDLAW is chief of the Baton Rouge Capital Bureau of the New Orleans *Times-Picayune.* He received an M.S. in journalism from Northwestern University. He joined the New Orleans *States-Item* in 1961 and has covered Louisiana politics since 1965. He became Capital Bureau chief for the *States-Item* in 1979 and for the *Times-Picayune* in 1980.

INDEX